E·W·GODWIN

DINING ROOM

E · W · GODWIN
AESTHETIC·MOVEMENT
ARCHITECT·AND·DESIGNER

CATHERINE ARBUTHNOTT

FANNY BALDWIN

JOANNA BANHAM

RICHARD W. HAYES

JULIET KINCHIN

LIONEL LAMBOURNE

LINDA PARRY

AILEEN REID

SUSAN WEBER SOROS

CLIVE WAINWRIGHT

NANCY B. WILKINSON

·

SUSAN WEBER SOROS, EDITOR

Published for The Bard Graduate Center for Studies in the Decorative Arts, New York,
by Yale University Press, New Haven and London

This catalogue is published in conjunction with the exhibition
"E. W. Godwin: Aesthetic Movement Architect and Designer" held at
The Bard Graduate Center for Studies in the Decorative Arts from
November 17, 1999, to February 27, 2000.

Project director: Susan Weber Soros
Exhibition curator: Susan Weber Soros
Project assistant: Catherine Arbuthnott
Catalogue editors: Martina D'Alton, New York,
and Sally Salvesen, London
Designer: Michael Shroyer

Director of exhibitions: Nina Stritzler-Levine

Library of Congress Cataloging-in-Publication Data

Godwin, E. W. (Edward William), 1833–1886.
     E. W. Godwin : aesthetic movement architect and designer /
edited by Susan Weber Soros.
          p.   cm.
     Catalog of an exhibition held at the Bard Graduate Center in the
fall of 1999.
     ISBN 0-300-08008-5 (cloth : alk. paper).—ISBN 0-300-08009-3
(paper : alk. paper)
     1. Godwin, E. W. (Edward William), 1833–1886 Exhibitions.
2. Architecture, Modern—19th century—Great Britain Exhibitions.
3. Aesthetic movement (British art) Exhibitions.   4. Interior
decoration—Great Britain—History—19th century Exhibitions.
I. Soros, Susan Weber.   II. Bard Graduate Center for Studies in the
Decorative Arts.   III. Title.
NA997.G6A4   1999   99-24645
720' . 92—dc21   CIP

On the cover: E. W. Godwin. "Frank Miles's House and Studio," 44 Tite
Street, Chelsea, London: front elevation, section, and plans, 1878. This
design was rejected by the Metropolitan Board of Works, London.
Pencil and watercolor; 8⅝ x 19¼ in. (22 x 49 cm). Trustees of the
Victoria and Albert Museum, London, E.553-1963. *Checklist no. 88*

Endpapers: E. W. Godwin. "Butterfly" Brocade, ca. 1874. Made by
Warner, Sillett and Ramm. Jacquard woven silk; 34 1/16 x 21 9/16 in.
(86.5 x 55 cm). Trustees of the Victoria and Albert Museum, London,
T.152-1972. *Checklist no. 54*

Frontispiece: Proposed decoration for the fireplace wall in the dining
room at Dromore Castle, County Limerick, Ireland, ca. 1869. India
ink, pen, colored washes, and gouache; 7⅛ x 18½ in.
(18 x 47 cm). British Architectural Library Drawings Collection,
RIBA, London, Ran 7/B/1 (67).

"E. W. Godwin: Aesthetic Movement Architect and Designer"
has been funded in part through a generous grant provided by
The Graham Foundation for Advanced Studies in the Fine Arts.

•

Additional funding has been provided by Jan and Warren
Adelson, Edgar Astaire, Donna and Carroll Janis, James Joll,
Martin Levy, the Samuel I. Newhouse Foundation,
Murray Weber, and an anonymous donor.

Dedicated to Clive Wainwright (1942–1999)
—friend, scholar, and mentor.
S.W.S.

ABOUT THE AUTHORS

Catherine Arbuthnott—researcher and master's candidate, Birbeck College, London.

Fanny Baldwin—theater historian, London; Ph.D., Courtauld Institute, London; author of the dissertation, "Victorian Artists and Stage Design, 1870–1905" (1991).

Joanna Banham—former archivist, Arthur Sanderson and Sons, London; former curator, Leighton House; chairperson of the Wallpaper History Society in England; co-author of *Victorian Interior Design* (Cassell, 1991); and editor of the *Encyclopedia of Interior Design* (Fitzroy Dearborn, 1997).

Richard W. Hayes—architect, New York; Ph.D. candidate, Department of Art History and Archaeology, Columbia University, New York; Master of Architecture, Yale University School of Architecture, New Haven.

Juliet Kinchin—lecturer at the Glasgow School of Art and Glasgow University; contributor to *Charles Rennie Mackintosh* (Glasgow Museums / Abbeville Press, 1996).

Lionel Lambourne—former head of the Department of Prints and Drawings, Victoria and Albert Museum, London; author of many books, including *The Aesthetic Movement* (Phaidon Press, 1996).

Linda Parry—curator of textiles, Victoria and Albert Museum, London; author of several books, including *William Morris Textiles* (Weidenfeld and Nicolson, 1983); editor of *William Morris*, exhibition catalogue (Victoria and Albert Museum / Philip Wilson, 1996).

Aileen Reid—architectural historian; Ph.D., Courtauld Institute, London; author of the dissertation, "E. W. Godwin (1833–1886): Towards an Art-Architecture" (1999), and several articles, including "Dromore Castle, County Limerick: Archaeology and the Sister Arts of E. W. Godwin" (*Architectural History*, 1987).

Susan Weber Soros—founder and director of The Bard Graduate Center for Studies in the Decorative Arts; Ph.D., the Royal College of Art, London; author of the dissertation, "E. W. Godwin: Secular Funiture and Interior Design (1998), and of *The Secular Furniture of E. W. Godwin* (Yale University Press, 1999).

Clive Wainwright (1942-1999)—senior research fellow, Nineteenth Century Studies, Victoria and Albert Museum, London; lecturer in the Royal College of Art / Victoria and Albert Masters Programme in Design History; has written extensively on the decorative arts, including contributions to numerous design journals and exhibition catalogues; author of *The Romantic Interior: The British Collector at Home, 1750–1850* (Yale University Press, 1989); co-editor of *Pugin: A Gothic Passion* (Victoria and Albert Museum / Yale University Press, 1994).

Nancy Burch Wilkinson—associate professor of art at Oklahoma State University; Ph.D., University of California, Los Angeles; author of the dissertation, "E. W. Godwin.and Japonisme in England" (1987).

CONTENTS

·PREFACE·

CLIVE WAINWRIGHT

By the 1920s, E. W. Godwin, like other nineteenth-century British architects and designers, with the exception of William Morris, had fallen into complete obscurity, at least among architects and art historians. Nikolaus Pevsner, in his seminal book *Pioneers of the Modern Movement from William Morris to Walter Gropius* (1936), made no mention of Godwin, but he did not single him out for omission either. Figures as diverse as Owen Jones, Bruce Talbert, J. P. Seddon, and Edwin Lutyens were also absent, and A. W. N. Pugin merited only a single brief reference. Morris figured prominently in the text, as did Christopher Dresser, both fitting Pevsner's criteria as pioneer "Modern Movement" designers. Indeed Pevsner was so taken with Dresser's apparent modernity that he devoted an entire essay to him in *Architectural Review* in 1937.[1]

Pevsner was constantly reexamining the architecture and design of the nineteenth century, and soon he played an important part in the rediscovery of Godwin. The second edition of *Pioneers*, published in 1949 by The Museum of Modern Art in New York City, still does not include any mention of Godwin, but interestingly, Pevsner had not only mentioned Godwin but praised him in a 1948 article, "Design and Industry through the Ages," published in the *Journal of the Royal Society of Arts*. The article first criticized Morris for not being sympathetic to industrial design and then cited Godwin for his wallpaper designs.

Also in 1949 Dudley Harbron's groundbreaking biography of Godwin, *The Conscious Stone*, was published, draw-ing Godwin to the notice of a whole generation of young architectural and design historians, who were beginning to look anew at the nineteenth century. Pevsner encouraged this process and gave a platform for many of these scholars in the *Architectural Review*, where he was one of the editors at this time. Harbron's book prompted a spate of further texts, beginning with Montgomery Hyde's "Oscar Wilde and his Architect" in *Architectural Review* (March 1951). This

Fig. i. This photograph is the first twentieth-century publication of the ebonized sideboard designed by E. W. Godwin. The sideboard shown was made about 1867 and belonged to Evelyn Hartree, who inherited it from her father, architect Frederick Jameson, Godwin's friend and colleague. From Pevsner, "Furniture: A Godwin Sideboard" (1952): 273.

Fig. ii. Godwin's "Greek" chair and small ebonized table as they appeared in the brief publication accompanying the "Exhibition of Victorian and Edwardian Decorative Arts" in 1952. From Victoria and Albert Museum, *Victorian and Edwardian Decorative Arts* (1952), pl. 18.

article was not illustrated, and as Harbron's book only had eight illustrations, the public was yet unaware of the actual appearance of most of Godwin's work.

It was Pevsner himself who brilliantly developed the furniture aspects of Harbron's work, in an essay entitled "Art Furniture of the Eighteen-Seventies" in *Architectural Review* (January 1952). There were nine illustrations of Godwin furniture, mostly engravings, including the celebrated ebonized sideboard, but even these were not clear, because examples of the actual objects had not yet surfaced. As so often happens, the publication of the article led directly to an important discovery. A photograph of an ebonized sideboard was sent to *Architectural Review* by Mrs. Evelyn Hartree, a daughter of architect Frederick Jameson, who had been one of Godwin's assistants. In the April issue of the journal,[2] Pevsner published the photograph (fig. i) with a short note; this would seem to be the first publication of what was to become one of the best-known, most frequently illustrated pieces of all nineteenth-century furniture.

Pevsner had conceived his article in conjunction with the seminal "Exhibition of Victorian and Edwardian Decorative Arts," which opened at the Victoria and Albert Museum in October 1952. Pevsner's influence at the exhibition was everywhere apparent in its structure, and in his review in *Architectural Review* he stated that "the opposition to Victorian hamfistedness begins as early as William Morris and Edward Godwin."[3] Sections in the exhibition were devoted to a wide range of architects, including Burges, Jones, A. W. N. Pugin, and Voysey, with Godwin sharing a section with Jeckyll and being represented by five pieces of furniture and two wallpapers. The centerpiece of the Godwin display was the newly discovered sideboard, which was acquired in 1953 by the museum.[4] As far as the British public at large and the few foreign visitors were concerned, this exhibition was their introduction to Victorian and Edwardian design in a museum, and Godwin was firmly established within that context. Sadly, the catalogue was not illustrated, and the small accompanying picture book only had thirty-two illustrations,[5] which limited the exhibition's international impact. The only photograph devoted to Godwin showed his "Greek" chair and a small ebonized table (fig. ii). At the time of the exhibition the galleries of the museum ended with the death of George IV in 1830; it was not until the mid-1960s that they extended even to 1900. In addition the European and American museums in the 1950s and 1960s rarely displayed nineteenth-century applied arts.

When in 1960 Pevsner published the revised edition of his book—its title truncated to *Pioneers of Modern Design* (Penguin Books)—he devoted several pages to Godwin, although he only allotted him one illustration—the White House in Chelsea (fig. iii), which Godwin had designed for James McNeill Whistler. Since 1960 students of design and architecture have cut their teeth on this Penguin paperback,

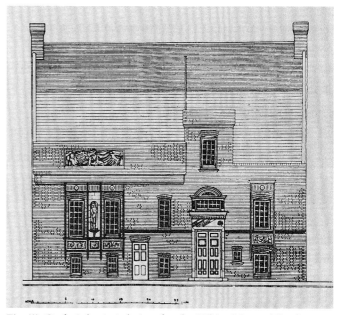

Fig. iii. Godwin's 1878 design for the White House, Tite Street, Chelsea, as it was shown in Pevsner's *Pioneers of Modern Design* of 1960 (this example from the 1975 edition, p. 64, fig. 18).

although Pevsner himself once told me that he intended one day to revise the text yet again. Godwin might have loomed even larger had Pevsner lived to fulfill his intention.

Since the 1950s interest in nineteenth-century architecture and design has grown apace, and several people have carried out research on Godwin. He has been discussed in various books on aspects of nineteenth-century design as well as in several articles. It is altogether surprising, however, that until now no substantial publication on this key figure has appeared, and we have only Elizabeth Aslin's all-too-brief book of 1986, which focuses solely on Godwin's furniture and interiors.[6] *E. W. Godwin: Aesthetic Movement Architect and Designer*, bringing together fully illustrated essays by a wide range of scholars, will go a long way to redressing this balance; it will serve to make the public and scholars aware of what an important and influential figure Godwin was. It also makes a case for further research, for a full-dress biography by a single author, not least because there is nothing like an exhibition to flush out new examples of an artist's work, as well as previously unknown commissions; these may be too late for inclusion in the show but will be available to subsequent biographers and other scholars.

An exhibition on Godwin follows very naturally from the two recent exhibitions on A. W. N. Pugin, one at the Victoria and Albert Museum in 1994 and the other at The Bard Graduate Center in 1995. Extensive publications accompanied both exhibitions.[7] As these two projects demonstrated, Pugin was a pioneer in what today is called "product design." Although he practiced in the traditional way as an architect, he also designed directly for manufacturers. Eighteenth-century architects, such as Adam, Kent, or Chambers, designed furniture, carpets, textiles, light fixtures, and silver for their buildings, commissioning craftsmen to make them to their specifications. This tradition stretched back to the Middle Ages, when the architects of cathedrals and palaces also designed the furnishings for these projects, and it would not be surprising to learn that Vitruvius and his contemporaries also paid close attention to the furnishings of their buildings.

Interestingly, even after Pugin took this new direction, few other architects followed his lead. Street, Burges, Shaw, Richardson, Lutyens, Mackintosh, and others, including to a large extent even Frank Lloyd Wright, continued to design applied arts only for their own buildings, not for general production and sale. It was in this group that C. F. A. Voysey placed Godwin, when in 1831 he wrote in the *Architectural Review* that "William Burgess [sic], E. W. Godwin, A. H. Mackmurdo, Bodley and others regarded nothing in or outside a home as too small to deserve their careful considerations. So we find Burgess designing water-taps and hair brushes; Godwin and Mackmurdo funiture; Bodley, like Pugin, fabrics and wallpapers."[8]

Godwin, however, who worked for individual wealthy clients, designing whole interiors as subtle and integrated as any by Adam, Lutyens, or Mackintosh, was also in the thick of commercial production. This, of course, is what caught Pevsner's attention in 1948. Godwin was involved not just in a very successful furniture-marketing venture with William Watt—its success proven by the many ebonized sideboards that have been discovered—but also in designing furnishings for his own buildings, as well as textiles and wallpapers for commercial production.

Pugin had set high standards for others to follow, designing across a wide range of media—furniture, textiles, wallpapers, metalwork, ceramics, stained glass, stage sets, typography, and bookbindings. Like Pugin, Godwin was multifaceted, his work also including designs for the theater. Godwin's activities in the area of product design tie him closely to the *modus operandi* of twentieth-century designers, making him a particularly compelling figure for a late-1990s audience. The Bard Graduate Center has recognized this by including Godwin in its continuing series of exhibitions, where he fits comfortably with the 1997 exhibition on twentieth-century Italian architect-designers and that of 1998 devoted to Finnish Modern design. The artists included in these exhibitions all worked in exactly the tradition pioneered and established by Pugin, Godwin, and Voysey.

·

Note: Sources are given in shortened form; for full citations see the bibliography.

1. Pevsner, "Christopher Dresser" (April 1937): 183–86.

2. Pevsner, "Furniture: A Godwin Sideboard" (April 1952): 273.

3. Pevsner, "Victorian and Edwardian Design" (December 1952): 402.

4. Victoria and Albert Museum, *Exhibition of Victorian and Edwardian Decorative Arts* (1952): 56, no. K1.

5. Victoria and Albert Museum, *Victorian and Edwardian Decorative Arts* (1952).

6. Aslin, *E. W. Godwin* (1986).

7. Atterbury and Wainwright, eds., *Pugin* (1994); Atterbury, ed., *A. W. N. Pugin* (1995).

8. Voysey, "1874 and After" (October 1931): 91.

Fig. iv. Design for a Town Hall, probably Kensington Vestry Hall, London, 1877. Pencil and watercolor, pen and ink; 10⅜ x 8 in. (26.5 x 20.3 cm). Trustees of the Victoria and Albert Museum, London, E.634-1963. *Checklist no. 80*

·INTRODUCTION·

SUSAN WEBER SOROS

E.W. Godwin was an architect, designer, interior decorator, antiquary, theatrical producer, and a prominent writer and critic. As one of Britain's leading design reformers of the nineteenth century, he was dedicated to beautifying the home while promoting a healthful domestic environment. Like few others he embodied the aesthetic conscience of Britain between 1865 and 1885. It is no wonder that Oscar Wilde referred to him as "one of the most artistic spirits of this century in England."[1]

Although his death in 1886 occasioned an outpouring of praise for what one commentator called "an architect who had no compeer in England and a designer of consummate skill,"[2] Godwin's critical reputation seems to have begun to recede almost immediately. By the beginning of the twentieth century, he had been totally eclipsed by a new generation of modern architects and designers. Ironically, it would be almost another fifty years before a later group of architectural critics and historians with modernist eyes began to appreciate the abstract and functional nature of some of his work.

The first biography of Godwin was published in 1949, and a number of articles continued the Godwin trail. In 1986, to mark the centennial of his death, the Victoria and Albert Museum mounted the first retrospective exhibition of Godwin's work, based on their collection. Godwin, however, was not considered sufficiently important as an architect-designer to merit an accompanying catalogue. In the ensuing years, a scattering of articles and one small book focusing on specific aspects of his career brought limited recognition to his achievements. Until now, however, a thorough study of his life and career has been lacking. This exhibition and its accompanying catalogue attempt to redress the paucity of scholarship and to secure Godwin's rightful place in the history of nineteenth-century architecture and design.

E.W. Godwin: Aesthetic Movement Architect and Designer examines the multifaceted life and career of this prodigious talent of the nineteenth century through a series of thirteen essays. A biographical overview, beginning with his childhood in Bristol, covers the many stages of his productive but often ill-fated life. Two of the major sources of his style—antiquarian interests and Japonisme—are next examined. As a scholar and reformer, Godwin was a pioneer in the appreciation of earlier design cultures and their creations, studying subjects as diverse as ancient sculpture, medieval manuscripts, and Japanese architecture. His ability to respond to these different traditions, together with his scholarly and erudite knowledge of the past, resulted in highly original combinations of design elements and principles. His wide-ranging architectural achievements, from early church restorations to the design of avant-garde house/ studios, are then studied. Another chapter details his career as an architectural journalist. Godwin wrote forcefully and consistently on the main design issues of his day, producing more than 410 articles and 8 books in 35 years. These are examined in terms of nineteenth-century developments and polemics. Godwin the interior designer is the subject of a further chapter. Pertinent background information is included on such topics as marketing, technology, and standards of health and hygiene in nineteenth-century Britain. The changing nature of the critical attention given to him during his lifetime and after his death is the focus of an essay on Godwin and Modernism. Subsequent chapters concentrate on particular products of his design: furniture, textiles, wallpaper, and ceramics. Godwin's contributions to the Victorian theater ranging from the design of costumes and scenery to his role as designer-manager are then highlighted. The final chapter, a postscript, analyzes Godwin's achievements through the career of his son, theatrical designer Edward Gordon Craig.

The thirteen chapters are illustrated with more than one-hundred and fifty selected exhibition items as well as dozens of comparative pictures, from period photographs to engravings. The exhibition objects represent the formation and flowering of Godwin's oeuvre, from his designs for architecture, interiors, furniture, wallpaper, and textiles to his original contributions to the Victorian theater. Each object is detailed in a separate checklist, where materials, measurements, probable dates, provenance, and publication history are given.

An illustrated chronology of Godwin's work and a full bibliography of primary and secondary sources serve as valuable resources for scholars. The chronology allows an assessment of Godwin's various activities at any one moment and reveals the changing nature of his fields of work. The bibliography is the first full bibliography on Godwin to be published. It includes hundreds of articles written and/or illustrated by him in the architectural press and brings together the many secondary sources that mentioned Godwin in his lifetime. This section will be particularly useful to future scholars and interested collectors who wish to pursue Godwin studies. More recent publications and background sources are also included.

Acknowledgments

This exhibition and its accompanying catalogue are the result of several years spent in the company of Edward William Godwin, pursuing his writings and ideas and studying his achievements in architecture and the decorative arts. It is an outgrowth of my doctoral dissertation, "E. W. Godwin: Secular Furniture and Interior Design," written at the Royal College of Art, London, under the supervision of Dr. Clive Wainwright, who helped with all aspects of this project, spending many hours discussing Victorian design with me and reading and commenting extensively on my contributions to this exhibition cata-

logue. He has also written the elegant preface, for which I am most grateful. Unfortunately, he did not live to see the completion of this volume, but I am gratified that he was able to review the final mechanical with me.

I would also like to offer personal thanks to those fellow Godwin enthusiasts who have been generous with their time and knowledge, contributing essays to this catalogue, and assisting in the selection of the items in the exhibition: Catherine Arbuthnott, Fanny Baldwin, Joanna Banham, Richard Hayes, Juliet Kinchin, Lionel Lambourne, Linda Parry, Aileen Reid, and Nancy Burch Wilkinson.

I would like to recognize the extraordinary talent and superhuman effort of my research assistant, Catherine Arbuthnott. During the past three years, she has attended to all the organizational and logistical details, guided me through the numerous archives and libraries in Great Britain, and assisted with the photography of Godwin material in Great Britain. This project would not have been possible without her dedication, passionate interest, and thoughtful insights. Thanks are also due to Leon Botstein, President of Bard College, Kenneth Ames and Pat Kirkham of The Bard Graduate Center, Laurie Schneider Adams, professor of art history, John Jay College of Criminal Justice, CUNY, The Graduate Center, all of whom read my chapters and offered advice and criticism. Peter Haiko of the Institut für Kunstgeschichte, Vienna, provided useful information and help through the archives of Vienna. At an important stage in the development of this catalogue, I received critical support from Barry Bergdoll, Colin Cunningham, and Terence Riley.

I am also grateful to the many dealers who have done much of the groundbreaking research on Godwin, opened their archives to me, and introduced me to many of the Godwin collectors: Martin Levy of H. Blairman and Sons, London; David Bonsall, London and Belper; Meg Caldwell, New York; William Clegg, The Country Seat, Henley-on-Thames; Jeremy Cooper, London; Peyton Skipwith and Andrew McIntosh Patrick of the Fine Art Society, London; Michael Whiteway of Haslam and Whiteway, London; Margot Johnson, New York; Scott Elliot, Kelmscott Gallery, Chicago; Paul Reeves of Paul Reeves, London and Cirencester; Tim Sullivan, New York; David Drummond, Theatre Bookshop, London; Reg Wingfield, Bradford-on-Avon; and the staff at the Moderne Gallery, Philadelphia. Special thanks to Annamarie Stapleton of the Fine Art Society, Helen Dunstan of Haslam and Whiteway, and Richard Bryers of Paul Reeves for endless research assistance.

All of the collectors of Godwin decorative arts gave me access to their collections. I am pleased to acknowledge the kindness of Mathew and Jane Argenti, Saretta Barnet,

Ivor Braka, Peter Brant, Charlotte Gere, Stuart Grimshaw, James Joll, Gary Kemp, Ng Lu Pat, Mary O'Connell, Jimmy Page, Andrew McIntosh Patrick, Lynda Resnick, Peter Rose and Albert Gallichan, Sheri Sandler, William Taubman, Mr. and Mrs. Valsecchi, Paul F. Walter, and David Warren.

I thank all of the owners of Godwin buildings and the keepers of Godwin-designed churches and town halls who allowed access and helped with this study of Godwin's work: Rev. P. W. Rowe, Almondsbury Church; Peter McKay, the Estate Office, and Sue Hoggs, Castle Ashby Conference Centre, Castle Ashby; Jamie MacGregor, Ashley House, Bristol; Mr. and Mrs. H. Pratt, Beauvale House; Canon John Ayres and John Goulstone, church of Saint Christopher, Ditteridge; Rev. Angela Berners-Wilson, Colerne Church; David Dingle, Council Works Department, Congleton Town Hall; Rev. Stewart Rayner, George Clifford, and Dorothy Freeman, Eggington Church; Rev. N. Boundry, Sheila Bisset, and Clare Coles, Highbury Chapel, Bristol; Mrs. N. Stewart, The Manse, Moor Green; Mrs. L. Vaughan, Frank Miles's House, London; Jennifer West, Mr. Bancroft, Mr. and Mrs. Spencer, Sheila Davis, Maggie Guillon, and Charles Knott, Moorgreen; John Dunkley and Roger J. B. Morris, Northampton Guildhall; Mr. B. Fawcett and Mr. P. Searle, 10-11 Rockleaze, Bristol; Rev. Anthony Charles Smith, Saint Botolph, Northfleet; Rev. Canon Malcolm Widdecombe and Mr. Riley, Saint Philip and Saint Jacob's Church, Bristol; Mrs. Kerswill, Stockland Church, Bristol; Sandra Cronin, Tower House, London; Rev. J. F. Smart, Walton Parish Church; and Rev. R. J. Thomas, Winterbourne Down Church.

I am especially pleased to acknowledge the help of Edward Anthony Craig (who died before publication), Helen Craig, and Tom Craig. As Godwin family members they provided interesting records, photographs, and recollections.

The Victoria and Albert Museum is the major lender to the exhibition, and I am grateful to Timothy Stevens, Assistant Director, Collections; Gwin Mills, Head of Major Projects; David Wright, Chief Registrar; and Catherine Kurtz, Registrar's Assistant. I would like to recognize the many other institutions and individuals who generously loaned work from their collections. A special note of thanks goes to the Prints and Drawings division of the Royal Institute of British Architects for making their rich holdings of Godwin's drawings available for the exhibition. I am also grateful to the other lenders: The Brant Foundation, Connecticut; Bristol Museums and Art Gallery, Bristol; The British Museum; Chelsea Library, Local Studies Collection; The Detroit Institute of Arts; English Heritage, London; Manchester City Art Galleries; The Metropolitan Museum of Art, New York; Musée d'Orsay, Paris; Museum für Kunst und Gewerbe, Hamburg; National Gallery of Victoria, Melbourne; Northampton Guildhall; Public Record Office, United Kingdom; The National Trust, Ellen Terry Memorial Museum, Smallhythe Place, Tenterden, Kent; National Museums and Galleries on Merseyside, Walker Art Gallery; Arthur Sanderson and Sons Limited; The Mitchell Wolfson Jr. Collection, The Wolfsonian-Florida International University, Miami Beach, Florida; and Gary Kemp, Brendan Mc Mahon, Catherine Mc Mahon, Dennis Mc Mahon, Ng Lu Pat, Paul Reeves, Sheri Sandler, Nancy Tierney, and William Taubman.

Many museums in Great Britain, the United States, and elsewhere generously granted access to their collections and shared their accumulated knowledge of Godwin. Bodelwyddan Castle Trust, Rhyll: Debby Davis. Brighton Museum and Art Gallery: Stella Bedoe. Bristol Museums and Art Gallery: Alan Justin and Karin Walton. The British Museum: Judy Rudoe. Camden Arts Centre: Martin Holman. Carisbrook Castle Museum: Rosemary Cooper. Carnegie Museum of Art, Pittsburgh: Sarah Nichols. Centre for Whistler Studies, Glasgow: Margaret MacDonald and Nigel Thorpe. The Detroit Institute of Arts: Alan P. Darr. Dorman Museum, Middlesbrough: Genette Harbron. English Heritage, London: John Thornycroft. Cecil Higgins Art Gallery, Bedford: Caroline Bacon. Hunterian Art Gallery, Glasgow: Martin Hopkinson. Judges' Lodgings Museum, Lancaster: Steven Sartin. Kensington Palace State Apartments, London: Nigel Arch and Jenny Lister. Kunstgewerbemuseum, Staatliche Museen zu Berlin: Barbara Mundt. Leighton House, London: Reena Suleiman. Lady Lever Art Gallery, National Museums and Galleries on Merseyside: Lucy Wood. Liverpool Museum: Robin Ennison. Lotherton Hall Gallery and Museum, Aberford: Adam White. The Metropolitan Museum of Art, New York: William Rieder (European Sculpture and Decorative Arts); Mechtild Baumeister (Sherman Fairchild Center for Objects Conservation). Minton Museum, Stoke-on-Trent: Joan Jones. Musée d'Orsay, Paris: Marc Bascou. Museum of Fine Arts, Boston: Jeffrey Munger. National Gallery of Victoria, Melbourne: Terence Lane. The National Trust, Smallhythe Place, Kent: Margaret Weare. Northampton Museums: Judith Hodgkinson (Keeper of Social History). Paxton House, Scotland: Martin Purslow. Royal Institute of British Architects, British Architectural Library: Charles Hinde, Jill Lever, and staff. Staatliches Museum für angewandte Kunst, Munich. Stoke-on-Trent Museum: Miranda Goodby (Ceramics Department). Usher Art Gallery, Lincolnshire: Richard Wood. Victoria and Albert Museum, London: Frances Collard, Sarah Medlam, Wendy

Monkhouse, Matthew Winterbottom, James Yorke, and Christopher Wilk (Furniture and Woodwork Department); Linda Parry and Debbie Sinfield (Department of Textiles); Cathy Haill (Theatre Archive); Susan Lambert, Michael Snodin, and Charles Newton (Prints and Drawings); Haydn Hansell (Picture Library); Jennifer Opie and Jill Creak (Department of Ceramics); and Eva White (Archive of Art and Design). Virginia Museum of Fine Arts, Richmond: David Park Curry. Walker Art Gallery, National Museums and Galleries on Merseyside: Andrew Renton. The Whitworth Art Gallery, Manchester: Christine Woods. Wightwick Manor, Wolverhampton: Monty Smith. The Mitchell Wolfson Jr. Collection, The Wolfsonian-Florida International University, Miami Beach, Florida: Wendy Kaplan.

In addition I am grateful to the staffs at the following institutions: Abbey House Museums, Leeds; Cleveland County Museums Service; Abingdon Museum, Northampton; Armley Mills Museum, Leeds; Hamburg Museum für Kunst und Gewerbe; Geffrye Museum, London; Manchester City Art Gallery; The Museum of Modern Art, New York; National Gallery, London; National Gallery of Victoria, Melbourne; National Portrait Gallery, London; The National Trust, Standen, West Sussex; Powerhouse Museum, Sydney; Stockwith Mill Museum, Lincolnshire; Rhode Island School of Design; and Bradford Museum.

Librarians and archivists at many institutions, collections, and agencies provided valuable assistance: Antiquarian Booksellers Association; Society of Antiquaries; The Arts Club, London; The Avery Architectural and Fine Arts Library, Columbia University, New York; Bedford Estate Archive, Woburn Abbey; Bodleian Library, Oxford; Bristol Architecture Centre; Bristol Central Library; Bristol Record Office; The British Museum (Manuscripts Collection); the British Newspaper Library, Colindale; Bury Metropolitan Archive; Compton Family Documents, Castle Ashby, Northampton; Chelsea Library (Local Studies Collection); Cheshire Record Office; Church House, London; City of London Record Office; Cleveland Archive and Record Office; Companies House; Libraries of the Courtauld Institute of Art; Council for the Care of Churches; Country Life Photographic Library; Derby Church House; Derbyshire Country Archive and Record Office; Edinburgh City Library (Art Library Section); Eton College Library; Family Records Centre, Islington; Thomas Ford and Partners, Chartered Architects and Surveyors; Free Library, Philadelphia; Glasgow University Library (Special Collections); Gloucester Record Office; Harpenden Library; the Greenall Group, Newcastle-on-Tyne; Guildhall Library, Corporation of London; Hertfordshire Record Office;

Hyde Collection, Four Oaks Farm, Somerville, New Jersey; Historic Royal Palaces Agency; Holborn Library, Camden (Local Studies Section); Hulton Getty Photo Archive, London; Irish Georgian Society; Jackson Solicitors; the Judges' Lodgings Museum, Lancaster; Keele University Library; Kilby Fox, Chartered Accountants; Kingston Library (Local Studies Section); Labyrinth Group (B. T. Batsford); Lambeth Palace Library; Lancashire Record Office; Library of Congress, Washington, D.C.; Limvaddy Library, County Londonderry (Local Studies Section); Limerick Central Library; Tennyson Research Centre, Lincolnshire Library Services; London and Continental Stations and Property Limited; London and Provincial Antique Dealers Association; London Metropolitan Archives; The McLaren Society; Melbourne Hall; Central Library, Middlesbrough Reference Library; National Health Service Estates; National Library of Ireland; National Monuments Record Centre and the Royal Commission on the Historical Monuments of England, Swindon and London; the New York Public Library; National Trust; Northampton Library (Local Studies Collection); Northamptonshire Record Office; Nottinghamshire County Library; Nottinghamshire Archive; Proctor and Palmer, Architects, Clevedon, Somerset; Public Record Office, Kew; Punch Archive; the R. W. A. School of Architecture Library, Bristol University; Redland Park United Reformed Church ("Highbury Chest"); Reece Winstone Archive, Bristol; Rockwell College, Cashel; The Royal Collection Trust (The Royal Archives); Royal Commission on Historical Manuscripts; Royal Holloway, University of London, Department of Victorian Studies; Royal Institute of British Architects, British Architectural Library; The Royal Library; Shakespeare Birthplace Trust; Society for the Protection of Ancient Buildings; South Tees Health Authority; Southwell Diocese Church House; Surrey Record Office, Kingston on Thames; the Tennyson Society; Ellen Terry Memorial Museum, Smallhythe Place, The National Trust; The Theatre Museum Archive, Covent Garden; Tiles and Architectural Ceramics Society; Tower Hamlets Library and Archive, London; Victoria and Albert Museum (Archive of Art and Design; Museum Archive and Registry; National Art Library); Victoria Reference Library; Victorian Society (Northern Office); Warner and Company Archive, London; Watson Library, The Metropolitan Museum of Art, New York; Weidenfeld and Nicolson Archive; Westminster Archives Centre, London; Whicheloe MacFarlane Architects (Bristol Society of Architects Archive); and Wolverhampton Central Library, Archive Section.

Finally, I am indebted to the staffs of various auction houses for information and photographs: Christie's, London and Glasgow; Sotheby's, London; Phillips, London and Edinburgh; Louis de Courcy Auctioneers, Limerick; William B. Fitt Auctioneers, Limerick; Clevedon Sales Rooms, Clevedon, Somerset; and Nestor and Conshannahan, Limerick.

An exhibition of this size requires excellent and extensive logistical planning. My most sincere thanks to the exhibition department at The Bard Graduate Center. Nina Stritzler-Levine, director of exhibitions, played an important role in the organization of the exhibition and its accompanying catalogue. Steve Waterman designed and coordinated the installation. Dana Bielicki, Nicole Linderman, and Jason Petty of the exhibition department assisted on many aspects of production. Thanks are also due to Heather Jane McCormick, Janis Mandrus, and Sandra Fell who organized the bibliography, proofread and checked the footnotes, and arranged for photographic permissions. My former assistant Kathryn Gettles-Atwa undertook the typing and proofreading of manuscripts and was meticulous in her efforts.

The entire Bard Graduate Center staff has helped to make this exhibition a success. Greta Earnest, chief librarian, and librarians Irina Kandarasheva and Stephanie Sueppel assisted in solving many research problems. Lorraine Bacalles, director of finance and administration, kept the financial aspects of the project in order. Tim Mulligan, director of communications, coordinated and cultivated the public relations campaign. Lisa Podos, director of public programs, developed the fine education programs that accompany this exhibition. Susan Wall, director of development, led the fundraising effort. Great appreciation goes to John Donovan, facilities manager of The Bard Graduate Center, and his staff for their support and assistance.

The superb photography in this catalogue was the work of several professionals: David Allison, Harland Walshaw, and the photography department of the Victoria and Albert Museum. It makes a remarkable contribution to this publication. Additional photography was provided by Danika Volkert of The Bard Graduate Center, and Simon Cuff assisted with photography in England.

I am fortunate to have worked with John Nicoll and Sally Salvesen at Yale University Press in London on the production of this catalogue. Thanks also to Martina D'Alton, the style editor of the catalogue, and Michael Shroyer, designer, for their extraordinary efforts. Glorieux Dougherty undertook the trying task of the catalogue index with great care. The final texts were skillfully prepared and typeset by Lora Ewing and Carol Liebowitz and were proofread by Roberta Fineman.

Finally, special thanks to the sponsors for their generous funding: The Graham Foundation for Advanced Studies in the Fine Arts, Jan and Warren Adelson, Edgar Astaire, Donna and Carroll Janis, James Joll, Martin Levy, the Samuel I. Newhouse Foundation, an anonymous donor, and my father, Murray Weber.

1. Wilde, "Truth of Masks" (1930): 238.

2. "Obituary of E. W. Godwin, *Art Journal* (November 1886): 352.

Editor's note: In the captions, height precedes width precedes depth; the checklist number, when given, indicates an object in the exhibition and refers the reader to the Checklist of the Exhibition. In the footnotes, a shortened form of citation is used—author's last name, abbreviated title, and date of publication—for sources listed in full in the Bibliography. Several archives are cited in abbreviated form, and a key to abbreviations will also be found in the Bibliography.

Fig. 1-1. Edward William Godwin, with sketchbook in hand, ca. 1880. Courtesy of Helen Craig.

CHAPTER 1

EDWARD·WILLIAM·GODWIN·(1833–1886) AESTHETIC·POLYMATH

LIONEL LAMBOURNE

A favorite Japanese puzzle—an elaborately inlaid box—can serve as a useful analogy for the career of Edward William Godwin (fig. 1-1). There is no apparent method of opening the box, but as oblique hidden panels are slid carefully from each side, intricate secret compartments are in turn revealed, until the center of the box is reached. In it a toy bird whistles derisively. Godwin's multifaceted life resembles this box. It contained many enthusiasms and contradictions. He was, by turns, archaeologist, architect, furniture designer, textile and wallpaper designer, journalist and editor, and, finally, an appalling businessman. Such diversity establishes him as one of the great Victorian polymaths. An all-around man of the theater, he loved to dress up, yet there is no record of him actually acting.[1] Although a charismatic figure, with a dangerous appeal for women, his private life remains shadowy, and to capture his elusive personality is not easy. His appointment diary lists many meetings with James McNeill Whistler and Oscar Wilde, but he was no Samuel Pepys, and the aphorisms generated on these occasions are lost. Far more revealing are his sketchbooks, which vividly record his myriad visual interests. Despite the difficulties, this essay will try to present the complex plot of Godwin's life, only finally resolved long after his death, and to introduce the cast of characters who played important roles in the Godwin drama.

Edward William Godwin was born at 12 Old Market Street, Bristol, on May 26, 1833. He was the youngest of five children. Two of his brothers, both called William, died in infancy.[2] Godwin's father, also William, was a currier, or leather merchant.[3] His mother, Ann, was Welsh, the daughter of Joseph Davies, a tiler, plasterer, and painter. The surviving papers of family members in the late eighteenth and early nineteenth centuries indicate that both sides of the family were propertied—comfortably off, but not particularly wealthy.[4] Various members held honorary offices in the parish of Saint Philip and Saint Jacob[5]; they were local parish worthies rather than figures of citywide importance, small businessmen, rather than professional men. That William Godwin encouraged both of his surviving sons to enter professions shows an aspiration for additional social cachet to match the family's newly acquired wealth as William Godwin's leather business prospered. When Joseph Davies died in 1827, William Godwin bought Davies's building and decorating business, which he ran at a distance, doing the accounts and collecting a share of the profits.[6] Some time after 1833 he was able to buy the Earl's Mead Estate on the outskirts of Bristol, with its garden backing onto the Frome River. Earl's Mead, to which the family moved, was the "principal house in the neighbourhood."[7] In its garden were "fragments and crumbling bits from old churches,"[8] which held a mysterious fascination for young Edward, who sketched Bristol's fine medieval architecture and grew up determined to be an architect.

Edward was educated at a private school run by John Exley in Highbury, Bristol. It was later described as having

Fig. 1-2. No. 7 Brunswick Square, Bristol, the office of architect William Armstrong. Photographed in 1998.

been filled with the young men of the upper middle classes.[9] John Exley "was a schoolmaster of the old school, who did not believe in sparing the rod and spoiling the child."[10] Godwin wrote of only one memory of his school-days: on the street opposite the school Butterfield's High-bury Chapel was being built while Godwin attended, and he said that this and the stones in his father's garden were his education in art.[11] If he had any formal training in draw-ing, no record of it seems to have survived, but Godwin also recalled later in life that as a child he copied the illustrations from J. R. Planché's history of costume, published serially in *Knight's Monthly Volume for all Readers*.[12] Godwin's passion-ate interest in costume, particularly theatrical costume, was

to run parallel with his architectural career, perhaps even overtaking it in the 1880s as he became more and more involved in theatrical productions.

William Godwin's social aspirations for his son were more than met: Edward's clients were to include royalty and members of the most exclusive social circles in the coun-try.[13] Financially, however, the picture is very different. Money troubles dogged Edward for most of his life, begin-ning, most probably, in 1846 when his father died, and God-win, aged thirteen, was still at school. The Earl's Mead Estate was sold, and he received a legacy of one hundred pounds on his coming of age, which went to pay debts.[14] His mother lived frugally, even poorly, on the income from her property at 71 Old Market Street in Bristol.[15] Godwin reported that it was felt that engineering paid better than architecture as a profession and was more suitable, therefore, for him to enter,[16] but in spite of this he was articled to the architect William Armstrong, who appears to have been in debt to the deceased William Godwin, an obligation that was discharged by taking the young Edward as a pupil.[17]

In 1876 Godwin vividly described a crowded and untidy architect's office, possibly the office of his pupilage at 7 Brunswick Square, Bristol (fig. 1-2):

There is a large room for the pupils and general assistants with the bare floor, the long desk against the windows, the high stools, and the general ware-house look supposed to be so eminently conducive to respectability of practice. In this room a high nest of drawers forms a sort of counter screen near the door to keep builders and casual callers at bay. Here, too, are dusty piles of the architectural periodicals, uncut, but with many of the photo-lithographs missing. On the mantelpiece is a plaster cast of a font, some small squared specimens of building stone, and three villainous-looking tiles. The colour boxes are always in the last stage of dried-up decay—the enamel gone, the colours hard and cracked. The windows are grimy with dirt, and there is a good deal of dust everywhere.[18]

Godwin also described the head assistant locking up the photolithographs and adapting one or two of these published designs to the requirements of each commission. "This practice," he wrote, "is by no means confined to our office. . . . So, then, as far as design and drawing are con-cerned, the pupil need expect but little help in this kind of office. . . . He will have to learn by observation, and not look to be directly taught."[19]

Later, as Armstrong's assistant, Godwin began to

design buildings for the practice. He recalled making his first design for a building, which Armstrong inspected, approved, and signed, taking the credit for the design.[20] This was not an unusual practice; Godwin was to call it "the secret manufacture of architecture" and remembered his very mixed feelings of both pride that his creation had been approved and resentment that he had not been allowed to claim the design as his own.[21] He added that he would gladly have given Armstrong an extra year's service for the privilege of adding his own initials to the corner of the drawing.

Overall, Godwin's time with Armstrong was not a happy experience. Perhaps as a result of such mediocre training, however, he developed an avid interest in the teaching of architecture. He wrote several articles and letters in the *British Architect* and the *Architect* for the benefit of those learning the profession[22]; he worked on committees for the development of a formal process of professional training and recognition for students[23]; and he acquired a reputation as "the student's friend."[24] George Freeth Roper, who had worked in Godwin's office, wrote of "the desire he always shows to *teach* you something."[25]

Godwin's pupilage ended in the early 1850s. In 1853 he received his first commission for a school in Easton, and in 1854 he was responsible for restoration work to the Church of Saint John the Baptist, Colerne (see fig. 6-5). Work came slowly, and in 1856 he joined his brother Joseph Lucas Godwin in Londonderry, Ireland, to take part in a competition for the design of a railway bridge. They did not win, but in the three years Godwin was in Ireland, he designed and built three Roman Catholic churches (see fig. 6-8)[26] and planned a series of small cottages—with attached pigsties—at least one of which was later built but has not been identified.[27] He also made a series of measured drawings of Celtic crosses and studied castles and abbeys.[28]

It may have been through his archaeological interests that Godwin met his first wife, Sarah Yonge. Sarah had subscribed in 1850 to Godwin's first publication: *The Architectural Antiquities of Bristol and its Neighbourhood* (see fig. 2-2).[29] In about 1853 Godwin dedicated an article he had written "To Miss Yonge with many affectionate remembrances of the archaeological studies with the author."[30] They were married on November 1, 1859, in the parish church of Henley-on-Thames where Sarah's father was vicar. In 1862 Godwin moved with his wife to 21 Portland Square in Bristol (fig. 1-3). The home they created there became famous for its startlingly original decoration, distinguished by Persian rugs laid on bare, polished boards, walls painted in plain colors, early eighteenth-century furniture, and, the most unusual feature, a few Japanese prints,

Fig. 1-3. No. 21 Portland Square, Bristol, which was home to E. W. Godwin and his wife Sarah from 1862 to 1865. Parts of the facade and rear elevation were reconstructed after bomb damage in World War II. Photographed in 1998.

possibly acquired in Bristol[31]—one of the great ports of England—or at Messrs Farmer and Rogers Oriental Warehouse in Regent Street, London, run by an energetic young manager named Arthur Lasenby Liberty. Items from the Japanese Court at the 1862 International Exhibition that was held in London were for sale at the warehouse.[32]

It may have been at Farmer and Rogers' shop in the early 1860s that Godwin first met his lifelong friend James McNeill Whistler, who shared with Godwin not only an enthusiasm for Japanese art but also a delight in controversy. Both men operated simultaneously as aesthetes, polemicists, and wits and were quick to respond to feminine beauty.[33] They shared a delight in a bohemian lifestyle, illuminated by

Fig. 1-4. E.W. Godwin. Sketch of James McNeill Whistler in a Turkish bath, 1877. Sketchbook. Pencil on paper; 5¾ x 3¼ in. (14.6 x 8.3 cm). Trustees of the Victoria and Albert Museum, London, E.244-1963: 74.

the art longings and thoughts of the yet busier brain; and of the many lovely things which he has left behind him, I know of none to compete in interest with those tiny memorandum books, containing as they do his first ideas of nearly everything he subsequently carried out, and of many a dream beside."[38] These words could with equal justice describe Godwin's own sketchbooks, one of which includes a charming portrait of Burges dated 1875 (fig. 1-5).[39]

Burges and Godwin both shared an erudite love of Gothic architecture, a whimsical sense of humor, and a passion for Japanese prints. Some of Burges's print collection survives in the Victoria and Albert Museum, pasted into a scrapbook.[40] To turn its pages is an exciting experience, enabling us to look over Burges and Godwin's shoulders and share vicariously the thrill of seeing for the first time the exotic patterns and bold designs of Japan. From one of these—a print by Ichiyusai Shigenobu (fig. 1-6), who was a pupil of Hokusai—Godwin sketched a number of Japanese *mon* (heraldic crests) into a sketchbook of 1870 (see fig. 10-6).[41] Godwin was to use these designs to create some brilliantly original textiles, tiles, and wallpapers, which helped to assimilate Japanese art into the mainstream of European design.

a vivid sketch in one of Godwin's sketchbooks showing Whistler in a Turkish bath (fig. 1-4).[34]

Another extrovert with a love of Japanese art was the ebullient Gothic Revival architect William Burges, who was immortalized by Dante Gabriel Rossetti in the limerick:

> There's a babyish party named Burges
> Who from infancy hardly emerges:
> If you had not been told
> He's disgracefully old,
> You'd offer a bull's eye to Burges.[35]

Burges and Godwin met some time after 1858 when Godwin was impressed by a Burges design for a fountain at Gloucester and introduced himself.[36] Throughout the 1860s and 1870s when Burges was beginning to work on his two great architectural masterpieces—Saint Fin Barre's Cathedral, Cork (1865–76) and Cardiff Castle (1865–81)—they met frequently in Bristol and London, and twice enjoyed a working holiday in Ireland.[37] They both shared a love of sketching, and Godwin described how "in his little pocketbooks . . . the cunning fingers were ever busy noting down

Fig. 1-5. E.W. Godwin. Sketch of William Burges, in Godwin's sketchbook, 1875. Pencil on paper; 3⅜ x 5⅞ in. (8.5 x 14.8 cm). Trustees of the Victoria and Albert Museum, London, E.236-1963: 59.

Fig. 1-6. This print by Ichiyusai Shigenobu was pasted into William Burges's scrapbook of about 1855. The designs are actors' *mon*, or heraldic crests. Trustees of the Victoria and Albert Museum, London, 8827.119: 58.

Godwin's relationship with Burges was occasionally prickly and combative. "We had our little tiffs," he wrote. "We even quarrelled more than once...," but this was still "a friendship which was more intimate and sincere than any friendship of my life."[42] Godwin does seem to have been a contentious individual. He managed to alienate James Hine, the great friend of his pupilage, over their professional relationship.[43] Another friend and partner, Henry Crisp, worked with Godwin from 1862 until 1871, when they parted company acrimoniously over some rather sharp practice on Godwin's part to do with a furniture commission.[44] He quarreled professionally with George Gilbert

Scott[45] and George Edmund Street, writing the most bitter and rancorous letter of his entire career in response to Street's proposed "restoration" of Bristol Cathedral.[46] The diary of a contemporary, George Price Boyce, makes a single reference to Godwin: he is described as engaged in a fierce political argument over dinner at the Arts Club with Street, Ford Madox Brown, Burges, and Algernon Swinburne.[47]

Godwin's relationships with clients were no less fraught: Pickering Phipps, the mayor of Northampton, who had become a friend in the 1860s, dismissed him as architect after an altercation in 1871; he quarreled with

Fig. 1-7. E. W. Godwin in Medieval dress, ca. 1861–65. Collection of the National Trust, Ellen Terry Memorial Museum, Smallhythe Place, Kent, SMA PH: 122. *Checklist no. 2*

Percy Waite, who had taken on Joseph Lucas Godwin's son Willy as a pupil and at one time had commissioned a house from Godwin; he wrote a sharp letter to his client Joseph Shuttleworth concerning the seats in a bay window; and several commissions ended with threats of litigation.[48] Maurice B. Adams, his collaborator on a book of designs for conservatories,[49] wrote in 1912 that Godwin's career was "largely a failure owing to his own personal short-comings,"[50] although this comment could apply as much to

Godwin's unconventional lifestyle as to his combative character.

In spite of Adams's remark, Godwin's professional career as an architect was distinguished by early success. During the late 1850s and early 1860s, he designed a carriage works for Messrs. Perry and Son (see fig. 6-24) and an "Early English" factory (see fig. 6-23); he won a competition to design a school attached to his old parish of Saint Philip and Saint Jacob (see fig. 6-4) and was engaged on restoration and rebuilding work on churches in Wiltshire, Devon, Cornwall, and Kent.[51] He also steeped himself in Ruskin's *Stones of Venice*, required reading for all aspiring Gothic Revival architects.

The year 1861 marked Godwin's first major, national success, when he won the competition for a design for Northampton Town Hall.[52] His design—in the approved Italian Gothic style (see figs. 6-15, 6-16)—brought congratulatory letters from John Ruskin[53] and propelled the twenty-eight-year-old provincial architect into the public eye, one of the rising stars of his generation.

The exterior of Northampton Town Hall (see fig. 6-1) is distinguished by polychrome stonework and vigorous sculpture, which ranges from eight impressive life-sized figures of English kings to relief panels showing local trades, such as shoemaking (see fig. 6-17). Other sculptural treatments on the facade possess a whimsical humor reminiscent of Godwin's friend Burges. There is a series of capitals depicting fables such as the Cock and the Jewels, and the Great Hall is a richly decorated medieval fantasy, at its most exciting when viewed from one of the small balconies near the roof, which is supported by elaborate iron ribs.[54]

Architecture was only one of Godwin's varied interests. He was musical and is said to have played the organ for his dying wife in 1865 and to have played Bach late into the night with Ellen Terry at Harpenden where they lived together in the early 1870s.[55] He also read widely, finding inspiration for decorative schemes in Chaucer's *Romaunt of the Rose* and in Spenser's *Faerie Queen*.[56] He studied the history of costume and began his lifelong involvement with the theater by writing a series of reviews entitled "Theatrical Jottings," signed simply "G," for Bristol's *Western Daily Press* from 1862 until 1864.

Theatrical criticism could be a risky occupation. On one occasion an actor whom he had criticized severely called and was shown to a room where Godwin, who loved dressing up (fig. 1-7), was attired in the costume of Henry V. Clad in hose, he could offer little resistance when the actor produced a horsewhip.[57] But work as a drama critic also had its compensations. On visits to London in the 1850s Godwin had admired the historical accuracy of the sets designed by the Grieve family for the famous Shakespearean productions of Charles Kean at the Princess's Theatre, London, from 1848 to 1859.[58] On one of these occasions Godwin may have seen and enjoyed the performance of a child actress named Ellen Terry, in her London debut as Puck in *A Midsummer Night's Dream* (fig. 1- 8).[59] This most magical of Shakespeare's comedies was to play an important part in the lives of both Godwin and Ellen Terry, who would become the most charismatic and loved woman on the

Fig. 1-8. Ellen Terry as Puck in *A Midsummer Night's Dream*, 1856. Photograph by Adolphe Beau. Trustees of the Victoria and Albert Museum, London.

Victorian stage. She brought something very special to her childhood roles, inspiring the Reverend Charles L. Dodgson, amateur photographer and, under the nom de plume Lewis Carroll, creator of *Alice in Wonderland*, to describe her as "a beautiful little creature, who played with remarkable ease and spirit."[60]

In March 1863 the Chute stock company visited the Theatre Royal, Bristol. Ellen Terry, now aged fifteen but already a seasoned performer, and her sister Kate were part of the company. Godwin invited the two actresses to assist with a play-reading at his home,[61] and the Terry sisters both became frequent visitors to the Godwin household, where they met William Burges and James Hine. In her memoirs Ellen Terry recalled how "the house, with its Persian rugs, beautiful furniture, its organ, which for the first time I learned to love, its sense of design in every detail, was a revelation to me, and the talk of its master and mistress made me *think*. I was fourteen years old at Bristol but I now felt that I had never really lived at all before. For the first time I began to appreciate beauty, to observe, to feel the splendour of things, to *aspire*!"[62]

The magic of Shakespeare's play was soon to transform Ellen Terry into Titania, for Chute decided to open the Theatre Royal, Bath, with *A Midsummer Night's Dream* in March 1863, with her playing the role. Godwin designed her costume for her, which she called "the first lovely dress that I ever wore."[63] They made it together at Godwin's home in Bristol, and Ellen Terry recalled that "He showed me how to damp it and 'wring' it while it was wet, tying up the material as the Orientals do in their 'tie and dye' process, so that when it was dry and untied, it was all crinkled and clinging."[64] Like the star-crossed lovers of Shakespeare's comedy, the paths of Godwin and Ellen Terry would converge again.

P. G. Wodehouse once remarked, apropos his fictional Blandings Castle, that if there was one thing universally recognized about the Victorians it was that they were not to be trusted with a pile of bricks and some mortar. The architectural profession, conscious of the problems caused by the incredible growth of building in nineteenth-century England, attempted to raise standards and to set official charges for fees and to support conservation. Godwin was part of this effort, representing the Bristol Society of Architects on committees and at general meetings of the Royal Institute of British Architects and the Architectural Association.[65]

The practice of holding architectural competitions was on the increase: there were hundreds of them for the building of lunatic asylums, cathedrals, law courts, libraries, cemeteries, schools, memorials, and, especially, town halls. The competition system was a mixed blessing. Godwin's career had been established by two successful competitive designs: for the town halls of Northampton in 1861 and Congleton in 1864 (see figs. 6-18, 6-19). His reputation was further enhanced by his success, with Henry Crisp, in winning all three prizes for designs for the Bristol Assize Courts (see fig. 6-21) in 1866, but these designs were rejected, and a new competition was held, at which they only won the second prize.[66] More often than not, the results of competitions were greeted with howls of outrage from bested competitors, results were sometimes set aside, and there was a predisposition on the part of town councils to ignore the professional architectural assessor's judgment or to award the work to local men. Godwin was awarded premiums for his competition designs for town or guild halls in East Retford (1865), Plymouth (1869), Leicester (1871), and Sunderland (1874). Of these, only Plymouth was built

(see fig. 6-20).[67] In spite of these disappointments, Godwin continued to compete, although in 1876 he denounced "sham competitions, these paltry pretences, these puerile make-believes."[68]

On the death of his first wife, Sarah, in 1865, Godwin moved to London, although he remained in partnership with the Bristol-based Henry Crisp. His professional career as an architect seemed secure when he received commissions for two castles in Ireland. His imaginative plans for Dromore Castle, County Limerick (see fig. 6-32), and Glenbeigh Towers, County Kerry (see fig. 6-35), included distinctive Irish features, such as stepped battlements and round towers.[69] He also designed the furniture and interior decoration for Dromore. Sadly, both buildings were affected by damp, and at Dromore Castle this prevented the artist Henry Stacy Marks from painting murals based on Spenser's *Faerie Queen*, which Godwin had specified for the first-floor dining room.[70] Later in life, Godwin facetiously advised young architects who were offered commissions in Ireland to refuse them, because "Ireland was sea-girt, and always damp, and . . . could not help it."[71] To these two commissions for titled clients was added a troublesome third: work at Castle Ashby for Lord Northampton, which included a grand gatehouse with two lodges at the South Avenue entrance (see figs. 6-37, 6-38), which Lord Northampton insisted be taken down partway through construction and rebuilt with the lodges farther apart.[72] In the 1870s Godwin was to receive commissions from a number of Lord Northampton's aristocratic relatives, including an unexecuted design for a tower for Ashridge House, home of Earl Brownlow, and a small country house called Beauvale, built for the Earl Cowper from 1871 to 1873 (see figs. 6-40, 6-41).

In London Godwin initially had offices at 27 Baker Street, then at 197 Albany Street, Regents Park, which he furnished with his first designs for pieces made of "ebonised deal with no mouldings, no ornamental work and no carving . . . such effect as I wanted gained by the mere grouping of solid and void and by more or less broken outline."[73] Beginning in 1867 the design of furniture became a central activity, both the celebrated "Anglo-Japanese" furniture and the less familiar "Anglo-Greek" and "Anglo-Egyptian" styles. These projects took up more and more of his time in the early 1870s and formed a major source of his income. The well-known firm of Collinson and Lock paid him a retainer of £450 per annum and a fee of three guineas per design.[74] In 1873 and 1874 Godwin designed a ceiling and chairs for Prince Esterhazy, a mantelpiece and an octagonal table for the house of Major Goodwin in Connecticut, a set of interiors with furniture for Middlesbrough ironmaster, William Randolph Innes Hopkins, and a set of furniture for

Fig. 1-9. George Frederic Watts. *Choosing: Portrait of Ellen Terry*, ca. 1864. Oil on panel; 18⁹⁄₁₆ x 13⅝ in. (48 x 35.2 cm) National Portrait Gallery, London.

Fig. 1-10. Ellen Terry wearing a kimono, ca. 1874. Photograph by Samuel Walker. Collection of the National Trust, Ellen Terry Memorial Museum, Smallhythe Place, Kent.

the Vienna International Exhibition. He also designed, until 1868, for the short-lived Art Furniture Company, and most importantly for the firm of William Watt, culminating in a published catalogue of designs in 1877 (see fig. 3-18) and a major display at the Paris Exposition Universelle of 1878, on which Whistler collaborated (see fig. 4-9).[75]

While Godwin's career was taking shape, Ellen Terry's had temporarily come to a virtual halt. On January 20, 1864, when only sixteen, Ellen Terry, wearing a brown silk gown designed by Holman Hunt as a wedding dress, had married a forty-six-year-old artist, George Frederic Watts. It was an ill-starred union for the young girl, who had to cope not only with a middle-aged husband but also with members of London's leading salon run by the seven formidable Pattle sisters (known collectively as "Pattledom"), the eldest of whom, Sara, had virtually adopted the otherworldly Watts. Another Pattle sister was the pioneering portrait photographer, Julia Margaret Cameron, who revelled in the opportunities to meet the "great and the good" at the Pattles' "open house" that was held every Sunday afternoon.[76] It was described irreverently by *Punch* cartoonist George du Maurier as "a nest of proeraphaelites [*sic*], where Hunt, Millais, Rossetti, Watts, Leighton etc., Tennyson, the Brownings and Thackeray etc., and *tutti quanti* receive dinners and incense, and cups of teas handed to them by these women almost kneeling."[77]

Watts was captivated by Ellen Terry's beauty and used her as model for several enchanting portraits, such as *Choosing* (fig. 1-9) and, more disturbingly, for a painting of Saint George.[78] But the "hot-house" atmosphere of Pattledom and the irritation of being constantly patronized by the Pattle sisters proved overwhelming for the young Ellen Terry. In June 1865, after a year of marriage, the couple separated, and Ellen returned to her family and the stage. In 1867 Godwin and Ellen met again and began a relationship which she later recalled as "my best times, my happiest times."[79] They eloped together on Saturday, October 10, 1868, after Ellen performed in "a comedietta" called *The Household Fairy*.[80]

Although they never actually married, for the next six years Godwin and Ellen Terry lived together near Harpenden, at first in a cottage facing Gustard Wood Common, called the Red House (see fig. 7-5),[81] and later at a house called Fallows Green (see figs. 6-30, 6-31),[82] designed by Godwin for his new family. The "medieval" facade of Fallows Green covered interiors that were startlingly Japanese.

There were two children: Edith Craig, known as Edy, was born in December 1869, and Edward Gordon Craig, in January 1872.[83] In Godwin's diaries during the six years of their relationship, he always refers to Ellen Terry as

Fig. 1-11. Edy, daughter of E. W. Godwin and Ellen Terry, ca. 1874. Collection of the National Trust, Ellen Terry Memorial Museum, Smallhythe Place, Kent.

"Mother," as, for example, in "I gave mother £1.1s.0d to take the children to the Japanese Conjuror at St. Albans."[84]

The couple saw few friends at Harpenden, with the exception of William Burges,[85] but they did, however, make one long, enjoyable visit (in August 1872) to Normandy and the great cathedrals of Lisieux, Nantes, and Bayeux.[86] At home Ellen welcomed the opportunity to stop worrying about her appearance, as two likenesses reveal—a comic caricature of her by Godwin with her hair in curlers, inscribed "Before,"[87] and a photograph of her, arms akimbo, dressed in a kimono (fig. 1-10). Another photograph shows Edy also clad in a kimono, which was said to have been given to her by Whistler (fig. 1-11).[88]

Fig. 1-12. E. W. Godwin. The entrance gate with pigeon loft at Fallows Green, Harpenden. Built 1871–73. Photographed in 1904 by Frederick Thurston. Courtesy of Eric Meadows.

The six years of rural life, from 1868 to 1875, may have been far removed from any contact with the stage, but during those years Godwin and Terry must surely have discussed issues related to the theater. Godwin wrote his series of thirty-two articles on Shakespeare, entitled *Architecture and Costume of Shakespere's* [*sic*] *Plays*, published from 1874 to 1875 in the *Architect*.

Life as always with Godwin was not without its financial difficulties. The year 1873 was especially trying, with the expense of building Fallows Green, which had more than twenty acres of ground, a stable, and a small folly of an entrance gateway complete with pigeon loft (fig. 1-12). The same year, Godwin went on holiday to the Continent, and his assistant wrote in the office diary that it was rumored that Godwin had "cut the country for good."[89] Certainly, he returned to find that the news of his financial

Fig. 1-13. Photograph of Beatrice Philip, ca. 1876, at age nineteen. The Glasgow University Library, Department of Special Collections.

problems had spread, his creditors were pressing for payment, and there were lawyers camping in his office.[90]

Seeing bailiffs in Fallows Green helped motivate Ellen Terry to return to the stage the day after her twenty-seventh birthday. On February 28, 1874, she played in Charles Reade's *Wandering Heir*, lured by the then vast salary of £40 per week.[91] Presumably, Godwin approved of Ellen's return to the stage; later in the year, when she received an offer

(which later fell through) from Charles Calvert, manager of the Prince's Theatre, Manchester, to appear as Rosalind and Juliet, Godwin made designs for her dresses, writing affectionately that they should be worn "*anyhow* but your how especially" (see fig. 2-21).[92]

Back in London in the spring of 1874, they took rooms in Taviton Street, Gordon Square. Money melted in the hands of the talented but improvident couple,[93] however, and all too soon the bailiffs were back and the house completely stripped of furniture. When the theatrical manager Mrs. Bancroft came to call, the floor was still covered with Japanese matting, but all that was left in one room was a cast of the Venus de Milo, almost the same size as the original.[94] Mrs. Bancroft planned a production of *The Merchant of Venice* at the Prince of Wales Theatre and wanted Ellen to play Portia. Godwin was appointed to advise on the designs of the sets and costumes. He helped to create a remarkable visualization of the glory of Venice, using as one of his sources a contemporary Venetian original, Cesare Vecellio's *Habiti Antichi, et Moderni di tutto il Mundo* (1589).[95]

Godwin added an aesthetic frisson of powerful effect to the high-minded archaeological reproductions produced by the Grieve family for Charles Kean. Sets, props, and most of all costumes were both accurate and sumptuous. Oscar Wilde, then an Oxford undergraduate, attended the first night and wrote a sonnet to Ellen Terry, describing her costume designed by Godwin:

> For in that gorgeous dress of beaten gold
> Which is more golden than the gold sun
> No woman Veronese looked upon
> Was half so fair as thou whom I behold. . . .[96]

Later, Godwin and Wilde were to form a friendship which lasted until Godwin's death.

Portia was Ellen's first great triumph in a Shakespearean role, while Godwin's designs were acclaimed for their originality.[97] But their dual success must have had a Pyrrhic quality for both actress and designer, since their seven-year liaison was nearing its end. Like many such events the break was embittered by a dispute over the custody of the children, as a surviving letter from Ellen Terry to a Mr. Wilson reveals:

> I must beg you not to act as mediator between Mr Godwin and myself. Our separation was a thing agreed upon by *both* of us many weeks before it actually took place. The first steps were taken by *him*. . . . Part of our compact was that we should always maintain a kindly, friendly relation to one another—He has since Tuesday last made this an IMPOSSIBILITY. He tried by unfair means to get my little girl from me (I *had offered* to let him have the boy) and now I distinctly refuse to hold any communication whatever with him.
>
> I do feel sorry that he is ill.
>
> If Mr Godwin's friends knew his temperament as I do and the effect of change of scene upon him,

they would advise him leaving London and *staying with friends* for a time at least. He should not go alone as he is apt to brood and imagine all kinds of ills which do not exist. You say in your letter— *I really fear for his reason*—When I knew him in his home life 13 years ago I had the same idea, and at the same time he had an utterly sorrowless life—a devoted help mate—success—friends— *everything*—. He never was happy—he never will be . . . .[98]

After the anguish of parting had subsided they resumed their friendship. Long after their separation Godwin continued to advise, both on the decoration of Ellen Terry's home and on her costumes and sets,[99] although clearly they agreed to differ on Godwin's access to his children. The bizarre story of Godwin's attempted removal of Edy has its counterpoint in a letter Godwin wrote to Edy, which Ellen kept from her daughter until 1887: "Well well child *think* and *think* what the word kindness means & perhaps you will make things round you always happy and smiling," Godwin wrote, adding rather mysteriously, "It is only because we *don't know* that any kind of suffering comes . . . learn then all drama . . . ask questions . . . *Tell Mama Everything* & sometimes blow a kiss to your PAPA."[100] Far from blowing a kiss, Edy learned to hate him. Her brother Edward almost certainly did not see his father again after the age of three.[101]

In 1874 Godwin had written an article on the employment of women in the architectural profession.[102] One of his pupils, according to Godwin's biographer Dudley Harbron,[103] was a young woman named Beatrice Philip (fig. 1-13), the daughter of the sculptor John Birnie Philip. Beatrice Philip designed jewelry and painted decorative panels for furniture.[104] She and Godwin formed an attachment, and on January 4, 1876, when she was eighteen and he forty-two, they were married. They enjoyed a honeymoon in Belgium and up the Rhine, and their son Edward, known as Teddy or Ted, was born on October 1, 1876.

Thus far, thus conventional, but we can gain some idea of their life together from the pages of Godwin's diary. Throughout their ten years of marriage he referred to Beatrice as "Wife" with very rare exceptions, such as the entry for May 11, 1881, which reads: "4 stalls Opera Comique. With Trixie to have her tooth out at Evans £1.1s.0d. . . . & home . . . on to R.I.B.A. to shake hands with G. E. Street the new President."[105]

From the diaries it is clear that Godwin and his wife led amicable yet fairly separate lives. He often records returning home unexpectedly to find her out, leading him

Fig. 1-14. Oscar Wilde, 1882. Albumen silver print by Napoleon Sarony. At the time of this photograph Wilde was age twenty-six and on a lecture tour of the United States. The Metropolitan Museum of Art, New York, The Elisha Whittelsey Fund, 1969.

to find solace and his evening meal at his club. Godwin was an inveterate joiner and frequenter of clubs. He had been a founding member of the Arts Club in 1863, and it was here, with Whistler, that he had toasted the birth of Edward Gordon Craig in 1872.[106] He then joined the Hogarth Club and was a member, with Burges, of the Verulam Club, and in the 1880s, of the New Athenaeum Club.[107] Godwin and Whistler were founding members of the Saint Stephen's Club, which became Wilde's first London club.[108]

A circle of close friends features frequently in Godwin's diaries as visitors to Godwin's own home, notably Whistler and Oscar Wilde (fig. 1-14); artist Frederick Sandys; writer Sheridan LeFanu; actors Johnston Forbes-Robertson, Herbert Beerbohm Tree, and Hermann Vezin;

and dramatist W. G. Wills, who gave evidence on behalf of Whistler in the Ruskin libel trial.

In the summer months Godwin and Beatrice frequently visited Sheerness and Broadstairs together by boat with their son Ted.[109] Trips to Paris for the Salon, or to Antwerp, Ypres, or other towns with noted Gothic architecture in Belgium and Northern France, were also fairly frequent. Godwin generally traveled with male friends, such as W. G. Wills, but he sometimes went with Beatrice.

We also glean from the diaries and ledgers an inkling of Godwin's erratic sources of income, made up of commissions such as those for designs for sets of tiles on the familiar themes of the seasons, months, and hours (see fig. 11–17), or for plans for such projects as a house at Gothenburg in Sweden in 1876 (a week's work, account still unpaid two months later). At this time, gentlemen neither advertised nor touted for work. The Gothenburg commission came through a middleman called Constable, who also took away designs by Godwin to show, and attempt to sell, to firms such as Waugh and Sons on the Tottenham Court Road.[110] Godwin also earned money through his journalism.[111] On Christmas Day in 1876, Godwin noted: "at home with wife and babs." This picture of domesticity is rather ruined by further entries for the day: he spent Christmas working on the Anglo-Japanese catalogue for William Watt and writing a letter asking for "your cheque for £30 for work already done."[112]

The following year, 1877, Godwin and Whistler saw each other almost daily as Godwin's diary notes. There were several reasons for this intimacy, notably Whistler's commission to Godwin to build him a London studio house on a double plot of land in Tite Street close to the River Thames at Chelsea. Whistler planned to start an "atelier" for students, with large and small studios and living accommodation.[113] An entry in Godwin's diary, dated July 22, 1877, suggests the atmosphere of such an atelier: "Called on Whistler, Pellegrini, Jopling, & others. Saw Whistler paint full length of Mrs J. in an hour & a half an almost aweful [sic] exhibition of nervous power and concentration. Whistler with me home to duck and green peas."[114] This is the first mention of Louise Jopling, a talented artist herself, who became a staunch friend of both Godwin and Whistler.

During the next year the frequent visits continued, and one result of them was Whistler's conversion, encouraged by Godwin, to designing and painting his own frames.[115] They also collaborated on the famous "Butterfly Cabinet," designed by Godwin as the central feature of William Watt's stand at the Paris Exposition Universelle in 1878. This cabinet was made in bright mahogany, and painted by Whistler in yellow and gold (see fig. 4-9).

The oft-told, sad story of the Whistler/Ruskin libel trial and Whistler's subsequent bankruptcy in May 1879 needs little rehearsal here, save to recall the scene on the Sunday in September, before Whistler left the house on Tite Street forever and went on a working visit to Venice. Godwin was one of the guests at Whistler's last reception at the house, and presumably at Godwin's suggestion Whistler climbed a ladder and wrote over the Portland stone door the Biblical inscription:

THE WHITE HOUSE, TITE STREET, CHELSEA
EXCEPT THE LORD BUILD THE HOUSE
THEY LABOUR IN VAIN THAT BUILD IT.
E. W. GODWIN, F.S.A., BUILT THIS ONE.[116]

On Whistler's return from Venice a year later, in November 1880, the friendship was renewed, and Godwin wrote a sympathetic review of the 1881 exhibition of Whistler's Venetian pastels.[117] It was held at the Fine Art Society, for which Godwin was to design a new facade (1881–82; see fig. 6-61).

In 1878 Godwin worked on another house and studio in Tite Street, Chelsea, calling the first design for it "the best thing I ever did" (see fig. 3-26).[118] The Metropolitan Board of Works rejected this version, however, and Godwin was forced to add some "Queen Anne" details to the spare, strikingly modern-looking facade. The client, George Francis (Frank) Miles, was a portrait painter who specialized in Aesthetic ladies. His close friendship with Wilde, with whom he shared two sets of rooms, ended tragically when Miles's clergyman father criticized Wilde's lifestyle. On November 7, 1881, Godwin noted in his diary: "To Club and Bond St. coming . . . from having hair cut met Willie Wilde who told me a long story about [Albert] Moore & the separation of [Frank] Miles & his brother Oscar how Miles requested Oscar to leave his ho[use] as his papa & mama objected to the writer of such poems as a companion for their son!!!"[119] Wilde left, and Frank Miles subsequently had a breakdown and was sent to a lunatic asylum near Bristol, four years before his death in 1891.

Since their first meeting, Godwin and Wilde had become close friends; many of Wilde's ideas on interior decoration and dress, which were advanced in his lecture tours, had been adapted from Godwin's own pronouncements. It was thus inevitable during the summer of 1884 that Godwin should advise on the decoration of the "house beautiful," the house in Chelsea, 16 (now 33) Tite Street, which was to be the home of Constance and Oscar Wilde (see fig. 7-48). There were the usual horrendous difficulties with builders and tradesmen, including a lawsuit, and it says

Fig. 1-15. James McNeill Whistler. *Arrangement in Black: La Dame au brodequin jaune (Lady Archibald Campbell)*, 1882–83. Oil on canvas; 86 x 43½ in. (218.4 x 110.5 cm). Philadelphia Museum of Art, W. P. Wilstach Collection.

much for the friendship between younger and older man that the challenging contract ended on good terms, for surely no interior decorator has ever received a more gracefully worded letter of thanks from a satisfied client than Wilde's to Godwin: "You have had a good deal of trouble over the house" he told him, "for which I thank you very much, and must insist on your honorarium being not ten but fifteen guineas at least," and he continued with a eulogistic note, "Each chair is a sonnet in ivory, and the table is a masterpiece in pearl."[120]

Such projects provided much of Godwin's erratic income. In the 1880s he worked on decorative and furniture schemes for Gwladys, Countess Lonsdale, the Countess of Shrewsbury, and the actor Hermann Vezin. Another source of income was Godwin's costume design. As his fame as a designer of costume spread, he was approached by several actors and actresses, including Lillie Langtry[121] and Ellen Terry, to provide them with historically accurate dress for a number of productions. Godwin designed dresses for Ellen Terry's role as Camma in Tennyson's *The Cup*, performed at the Lyceum in 1880. In the archives of the Ellen Terry Memorial Museum, Smallhythe Place, at Tenterden is a delightful little note with drawings by Godwin, made during a performance, showing the attitudes that are, and are not, archaeologically justified in an actress representing a Greek priestess. *The Cup* ran for 125 nights. On the hundredth performance Ellen Terry sent Tennyson a three-handled cup, pipkin shaped, standing on three legs, which she had had made in silver to Godwin's design.[122]

Godwin's knowledge of Greek costume also proved invaluable to his close friend, the dramatist W. G. Wills, whose play *Claudian* was produced by Wilson Barrett at the Princess's Theatre in December 1883, with sets and costumes by Godwin. These were extravagantly praised by Wilde, who described Godwin as "one of the most artistic spirits of this century in England."[123]

Godwin's interest in dress was also much in evidence in 1882 when he was greatly occupied with the foundation of the Costume Society. In 1884 he became an advisor on dress at Liberty's and persuaded the shop to open costume studios where any kind of dress, ancient or modern, could be made. His main preoccupation in the mid-1880s, however, was his work for the Pastoral Players, which began in 1884 with a production mounted not in the reassuring environment of a theater but in a Surrey wood. This was the inspired whim of a wealthy titled lady described by Wilde in a letter to Whistler as "the Moon Lady, the Grey Lady, the beautiful wraith with her beryl eyes, our Lady Archie."[124] Wilde was referring to Janey Sevilla Callander who married Lord Archibald Campbell in 1869. Lord Archibald's brother, the Duke of Argyll, was married to Princess Louise, for whom Godwin had designed a studio in 1878-79. In reality Lady Archie, as she was usually known, was far more than Wilde's beautiful wraith, being indeed one of the most important women in the Aesthetic movement.

The first meeting between Godwin and Lady Archie took place while she was sitting, or rather standing, in 1882–83 for her portrait for Whistler, the controversial *Arrangement in Black: La Dame au brodequin jaune* (fig. 1-15).[125] The sitter glances back provocatively over her shoulder while revealing her foot clad in an elegant yellow shoe, a color then associated with sexual daring.[126] An accomplished amateur actress, Lady Archie believed that what was essential to a production was "freedom of mood,"[127] and that this was more important than the archaeological tradition of stage design. She pioneered the production of pastoral plays in the open air, using amateurs who acted for love of the art, as well as professionals. On meeting Godwin, they discussed open-air plays. Godwin "set to work upon his notebook, and cutting up two copies of the complete edition of *As You Like It*, he pasted the pages in the note book, designing the dresses as he came to each character."[128]

In July 1884, with Godwin's help as designer, director, and producer, Lady Archie put on Shakespeare's *As You Like It* in the grounds of Dr. McGeagh's hydropathic establishment at Coombe Wood, Norbiton, Kingston-upon-Thames. Godwin borrowed the costume of a friar from the actor-manager Wilson Barrett,[129] so that he could appear on the scene at any time to direct events where necessary.[130] In the photograph of the cast (fig. 1-16), this is how he is dressed: he looks tired and rather ill.[131]

The event was a fashionable success, helped by the patronage of the Prince of Wales, who no doubt enjoyed the opportunities provided by Godwin's costumes for admiring the attractive legs of Orlando, played by Lady Archie, and Rosalind, played by the American actress Eleanor Calhoun. Godwin's friend Whistler also attended performances of the play and painted a charming small oil portrait of Lady Archie, *Note in Green and Brown: Orlando at Coombe*, which greatly resembles a drawing in one of Godwin's sketchbooks.[132]

As so often happens with the organization of semi-

professional events, unexpected problems abounded, ranging from demands for money to complaints from cross musicians concerning the abusive conductor: "Please beg Mr Batson to behave like a gentleman—tell him to leave off insulting the singers by caustic remarks . . . he walks without knocking into their *bedrooms* . . ."[133] One of the actresses conducted a comical amorous pursuit of one of the actors and then refused to work with him, while increasingly frantic letters from Godwin cajoled society ladies to turn up for rehearsal.[134] The whole story of the Pastoral Players was affectionately described by Max Beerbohm in an essay in the *Yellow Book* as "the very Derby Day of Aestheticism"[135] and could one day form a comedy as rich in characters and irony as the satirical *Mapp* and *Lucia* novels of the 1920s by E. F. Benson.

The next year, in July 1885, an even more ambitious

Fig. 1-16. Cast members of *As You Like It,* with E. W. Godwin (third from right) dressed as a friar, 1884. Trustees of the Victoria and Albert Museum, London. *Checklist no. 135*

production took place at Coombe: *The Faithfull Shep-herdesse* by John Fletcher. Godwin adapted and bowdlerised the script so as not to offend Victorian standards of taste and morals. The language of this play, Godwin wrote, though poetic, was unnecessarily strong.[136] This production was followed in 1886 by *Fair Rosamund*, adapted by Godwin from Tennyson's *Becket* and produced at Wimbledon. But in April Godwin began to suffer from an illness which led to his convalescence in the countryside, at the house of Lady Archie's recently widowed sister. His illness is a theme of many letters written to him by members of the Pastoral Players from 1884 to 1886. It appears he was often in a great deal of pain and that this was something more than the "Rheumatics" that he had noted once or twice before in his diaries. This illness prompted a sympathetic letter from Wilde, who noted: "the white furniture reminds us of you

daily, and we find that a rose leaf can be laid on the ivory table without scratching it—at least a white one can . . . My wife sends her best wishes for your health."[137]

Constance Wilde was to take part in Godwin's dramatic venture of May 1886, *Helena in Troas*, a play by John Todhunter based on Sophocles's tragedy. It was staged at Hengler's Circus which stood in Argyll Street on the site of the London Palladium (see fig. 12-46). Louise Jopling vividly described the rehearsals of the production in her memoirs:

E. W. Godwin—or "the wicked Earl" as some of his friends called him—was one of the most fascinating of men. He worshipped Greek art . . . Although I had known him slightly I did not become intimate with him until I joined the company of Mr

Fig. 1-17. Aubrey Beardsley. *The Fat Woman*. 1894. Watercolor on paper; 7 x 6⅜ in. (17.8 x 16.2 cm). The Tate Gallery, London.

Todhunter's *Helena In Troas*. . . . The play was in blank verse . . . and it was given as it would have been in Ancient Greece, bar the masks, and the speaking trumpets. . . . A stage was erected on one side of the circle, and for the pediment I was instructed to drape, and seat, half a dozen figures in the same attitudes as those on the frieze of the Parthenon [see fig. 2-22]. The poor things had to remain without moving during the whole time the play was in progress! They were attired in unbleached calico draperies, which simulated the white marble, just tinged with age, wonderfully well. . . . Godwin was a splendid producer: he spared no trouble, and, incidentally, no expense, to arrive at perfection. In looks he was like the portraits of Henry IV of France, but his soul must have been the reincarnation of a Greek sculptor.[138]

In 1884 Godwin at last managed to realize a long-planned project, a tower of apartments with studios at 46 Tite Street, completed in 1885, next door to the house he had built for Frank Miles. Godwin and Whistler both urged Mrs. Jopling to take one of the studios, but she

declined, although she remained a friend until Godwin's death. He wrote his last letter to her on August 23, 1886: "I have not put my hand to paper since I wrote to you . . . I am so very, very weary . . . The next move I make is to St Peter's Hospital, where I have bespoken a ward all to myself; then the next ward may be 6 x 4 x 2. I feel completely done with life."[139]

Godwin died on October 6, 1886, at 7 Great College Street, Westminster. He never rallied from lithotomy (removal of kidney stones) and in an age without antibiotics, he died of associated complications. With him at the end were Beatrice, who had been summoned home from Paris, Whistler, and Lady Archie. Early the next morning Whistler asked Louise Jopling to go and tell Ellen Terry the news of Godwin's death, before she read it in the newspapers. "When I told her," wrote Louise Jopling, "I shall never forget her cry: 'There was no one like him.'"[140]

Legends surround Godwin's funeral. One account describes Whistler, Beatrice Godwin, and Lady Archie having an impromptu sandwich lunch off the top of the coffin as they jolted along in a farm wagon.[141] According to another account, the cortege halted in Oxfordshire at

a beautiful old Elizabethan building, with a large racket court, in the centre of which the coffin was placed, and covered with a white dining cloth and decorated with a profusion of wild flowers. After lunch . . . A procession was formed, consisting of the brougham with the three ladies, the widow in a white fur-lined cloak with her wild gypsy-like hair flying round her uncovered head, the second lady in a yellow Ulster with a turquoise blue tam-o'-shanter, and the third in a French grey sailor blouse and hat. . . . and as mourners on each side of the cart were six farm-hands. On our arrival at the churchyard the parson galloped up . . . just returned from a day's cub-hunting. The coffin was shouldered by the rustics, and burial duly performed.[142]

The tributes were mixed, with a number of eulogistic obituaries from the theatre and art worlds. The architectural periodicals praised his brilliance but noted his eccentricity, his difficult personality.[143] One of them said that "like all men, he was not without his weaknesses. Edward Godwin assumed an air of superiority at times, but he found many who willingly recognised his right to it."[144] The consensus among the architects seems to have been that Godwin was a genius who had not lived up to his early promise. Then there were the tributes from his friends. Oscar Wilde, then in the unlikely role of editor of a magazine called *Woman's World*, asked Lady Archie for an appreciation of Godwin's life which appeared in November 1888 and sensitively restates Godwin's aesthetic credo: "to create beautiful things for the mere sake of their loveliness, this was his object, not wealth, not position, not fame even. . . . Poet of architects and architect of all the arts, he possessed that rare gift, a feeling for the very essence of beauty."[145]

The dramatists John Todhunter and W. G. Wills both wrote sonnets to the memory of their friend. Wills's lines struck an appropriate elegiac note concerning "The Prospero who conjured up the light / Of Antique Grecian days, with them deceased."[146] It was designed to be an epitaph on a memorial stone, but no stone was ever cut for Godwin. Years later, on November 30, 1907, Lady Archibald Campbell explained why, writing from Inverary Castle, Argyll, to Godwin's nephew Willy, who had emigrated to Canada. "The grave of your uncle Edward Godwin is at North Leigh," she wrote, "near Witney, Oxfordshire. He was a great friend of my sister Mrs Dawkins who lived at Wilcote. . . . My sister and I and my daughter from time to time lay on his mound flowers to his memory. . . . you will find no stone to mark his grave because he objected to grave stones. . . . the sexton does not know the name."[147] Today, the exact whereabouts of the grave are unknown.

Beatrice Godwin survived her husband by ten years. On August 11, 1888, at the age of thirty-one, she married Whistler at Saint Mary Abbot's, Kensington, to the delight of the *Pall Mall Gazette* which ran the headline: "The Butterfly chained at last!"[148] The couple moved to Cheyne Walk that autumn and later set up a home in Paris in the Rue du Bac.

Beatrice, who married two extraordinary men, herself possessed a remarkable personality. It was perhaps most vividly described by Louise Jopling who met her in 1886: "Mrs Godwin worked at times in a studio in Paris . . . she was very handsome, and looked very French. She had a delightful devil-may-care look in her eyes which was very fascinating."[149] It would seem to have been this aspect of her personality which later led Aubrey Beardsley to caricature her in a drawing entitled *The Fat Woman* (fig. 1–17)[150] and two caricatures in the *Bon Mots* series. Whatever form her appeal took, she brought to marriage with Whistler a vital ingredient missing in the acrimonious controversies of his life, although sadly the marriage was to last only eight years. In 1894 she became ill, they closed up their Paris home, and returned to London where cancer was diagnosed. From that time they lived a peripatetic existence flitting from hotel to hotel. In two rare lithographic portraits, *The Siesta* and *By the Balcony* (fig. 1–18), Whistler shows her

Fig. 1–18. James McNeill Whistler. *By the Balcony*, 1896. Lithograph; 11⁷⁄₁₆ x 8⅝ in. (29.2 x 21.9 cm). National Gallery of Art, Washington, D.C., Rosenwald Collection.

lying in bed at the Savoy Hotel. These likenesses capture his deep love for her and his consciousness of her illness, anticipating his desolating sense of loss after her death which took place in May 1896.

Ellen Terry lived until 1928, long enough to act in four films as a very old woman.[151] She never forgot her years with Godwin, the father of her children, who remained for her a potent symbol of romantic love.[152] After her death a copy of Todhunter's sonnet was found written in her hand which still stands as an appropriate memorial to an extraordinary man:

They tell me he had faults—I know of one:
Dying too soon, he left his best undone.[153]

Note: Most published sources are cited below in shortened form (author's last name, abbreviated title, date of publication); full references will be found in the bibliography. Frequently cited archives are abbreviated below; for a key to the abbreviations, also see the bibliography.

1. Godwin is known to have appeared in costume, however, in at least one production (see fig. 1-16), during which he sketched a blessing ("Our Omnibus Box" [1 September 1884]:158–59).

2. This information is from the Godwin family bible, which is in the possession of his descendants. His surviving brother and sister were Joseph Lucas Godwin and Ann (Annie) Godwin.

3. Godwin's grandfather, John Godwin, had also been a currier, according to the will of Jane Godwin (E. W. Godwin's grandmother) dated 25 April 1824 (Bristol Record Office).

4. Jane Godwin left her daughter, Ann Wait, £200; her eldest son, John, the leasehold of a cottage at Whitehall in Gloucester; and her other son, William (E. W. Godwin's father), the interest in a house in Captain Carey's Lane, Bristol.

5. Joseph Davies (Godwin's grandfather) was "Overseer of the Poor in the parish" in 1821, and William Godwin was churchwarden from 1823 (Parish Records of Saint Philip and Saint Jacob, Bristol Record Office).

6. Articles of Agreement, dated 29 December 1827 between William Godwin and William and Robert Smith and Henry Barber, Bristol Record Office, 5755 (49). The Smiths and Barber were expected to do the work of the business full time for their half share of the profits, whereas William Godwin contributed the premises (71 Old Market Street) and tools and was to act as cashier of the business.

7. Godwin, "Answers to Queries: Earl's Meadows," *Ulster Journal of Archaeology* 4 (1857). I am grateful to Aileen Reid for this information.

8. Godwin, "On Some Buildings I Have Designed" (29 November 1878): 210–12.

9. Freeman, *Bristol Worthies,* 2d series (1909): 29.

10. Ibid.

11. Godwin, "On Some Buildings I Have Designed" (29 November 1878): 210–12. See also chap. 6 in this volume.

12. Harbron, *Conscious Stone* (1949): 6. Godwin, "The Cyclopaedia of Costume" (16 October 1875): 208–9. Godwin expresses his "respect for and gratitude to" Planché for introducing him to the history of costume.

13. Escott, *Society in London* (1885): 84. Escott mentions "two or three small and exceedingly exclusive sets" in society, led by, among others, Lady Cowper, Lady Marion Alford, and Lady Northampton. Godwin's titled clients included Lords Northampton, Brownlow, Cowper, and Ferrers, Lady Alwyne Compton, Lady Marion Alford, Lady Shrewsbury, Gwladys Countess Lonsdale, and Princess Louise. The Prince of Wales was a staunch supporter of Godwin's theatrical productions.

14. Letter from Godwin to R. M. Bryant, dated 15 December 1871, V&A AAD, 4/22-1988: 197, letterbook, vol. 1.

15. Copy of a letter from Thomas Dix to Messrs Abbot & Leonard, dated 11 December 1871, V&A AAD, 4/22-1988, letterbook, vol. 1, p. 200: "It is understood that Mrs Godwin's circumstances were not very good and that at the last her income was almost if not quite insufficient to support her in a comfortable manner." Godwin describes his mother living on the rents from 71 Old Market Street and an unidentified house in "the Dings," an area of Bristol (ibid., p. 197).

16. Godwin, "On Some Buildings I Have Designed" (29 November 1878): 210–12.

17. "The premium paid Armstrong when I entered his office was I always understood by way of a receipt for a debt that Armstrong owed my father" (letter from Godwin to R. M. Bryant, dated 15 December 1871, V&A AAD, 4/22-1988: 197, letterbook, vol. 1).

18. Godwin, "Scraps for Students," part 4 (13 May 1876): 303.

19. Ibid.

20. Godwin, "Secret Manufacture of Architecture" (7 February 1873): 145–46.

21. Ibid.

22. Godwin, "Scraps for Students," parts 1–6 (15 April–27 May 1876); "A Few Words to Architectural Students" (1 February 1878): 51; "To Our Student Readers," parts 1–3 (30 July–27 August 1880); "To Art Students," 10 letters (2 May–11 June 1884). July 1884.

23. Godwin helped to establish students' classes run by the Bristol Society of Architects. The minute books of the Bristol Society of Architects include a letter from Godwin to S. B. Gabriel dated 2 March 1864, in which he discusses the best way of getting students through the new architectural examination set by the RIBA. In another series of letters he wrote of educational reform at the institute and the provision of art classes for students (V&A AAD, 4/22-1988: 163–68, letterbook, vol. 1).

24. Godwin, "To Our Student Readers," part 1 (30 July 1880): 48. Godwin quotes this phrase from a letter he has received from an assistant in a provincial architect's office who is looking for further training in London.

25. Letter from G. F. Roper to Col. R. W. Edis, dated 25 December 1872, V&A AAD, 4/402-1988.

26. These churches were Saint Baithen at Saint Johnstown, County Donegal, and Saint Columcille, Tory Island. The third Irish church, All Saints Church at Newtowncunningham, may date from after Godwin's departure from Ireland.

27. It is described as "the cabin of an Irish Patriot" ("Rambling Sketches," part 1 [25 February 1881]: 105, illus). The illustration is almost the same as that of another Irish cottage by Godwin, described as "Thatched cottage 'adapted to the usages' from a design by E. W. Godwin, F.S.A., carried out in Glenbegh [sic], Co. Kerry, 1870" ([Godwin], "Thatched Cottage" [27 May 1881]: 267, illus.).

28. For some of Godwin's drawings of Celtic crosses, see Godwin, "On the Architecture and Antiquities of the Western Part of the Province of Ulster," parts 1–5 (April–June 1872); for other unpublished sketches, see RIBA Mss, GoE box 4.

29. For a list of subscribers, see RIBA Mss, GoE/3/5/1. I am grateful to Aileen Reid for this information.

30. For the dedication, handwritten on the flyleaf of an offprint of an article by Godwin, see V&A AAD, 4/537-1988. For the article, see Godwin, "Notes on some examples of Church Architecture in Cornwall" (December 1853): 317–24. I am grateful to Aileen Reid for this information.

31. Ellen Terry remembered Godwin telling her "about his friends among the skippers of sailing ships, and how they brought him, from the Far East, many of the things in his house" (Edward Anthony Craig, *Gordon Craig* [1968]: 34).

32. See Adburgham, *Liberty's* (1975): 12–14. Also see chap. 3 in this volume.

33. A hint of Godwin's rather sharp wit is given in a letter to Godwin from the sculptor J. E. Boehm, dated 22 January 1884 (V&A TA, Godwin collection, box 7). Boehm, who was hiding from Godwin because his face had swelled up with gout, wrote "I should not for the world have liked to elicit your sarcasm & ready quotations." There are several examples of Godwin's appreciation of feminine beauty, for example, in his journals: in 1852, he notes the "pretty chambermaid at the Talbot" (V&A AAD, E.227-1963), an inn at which he was staying while on holiday in Cornwall; 21 February 1854, "introd. to Mrs & Miss Christie both beautiful" (V&A PD, E.226-1963); 15 April 1854, "Miss Butler an uncommonly pretty woman very nice mouth and teeth" (ibid.).

34. V&A PD, E.244-1963: 74, sketchbook dated 1877.

35. Dante Gabriel Rossetti, "Nonsense Verses," in William Michael Ros-

setti, *Rossetti Papers* (1903): 494 (quoted in Crook, *William Burges* [1981]: 91).

36. Burges' design for the Sabrina Fountain, Gloucester, was exhibited at the Architectural Exhibition of 1858, and Godwin saw the published version: "The thing that led me to call first on Burges was an illustration in *The Builder* (May 29th, 1858) I greatly admired; it was a design by him of a fountain for the city of Gloucester" (Godwin, "Friends in Council . . . Burges" [29 April 1881]: 213–14).

37. From the abstracts of William Burges's diaries, copies of which are in the V&A National Art Library. Burges visited Godwin in Bristol in 1863, 1864, and 1865; in Conway in 1865; and in Ross Bay, Ireland, in 1867.

38. Godwin, "Friends in Council . . . Burges" (29 April 1881): 213.

39. The sketch is dated 25 June 1875 (V&A PD, E.236-1963: 59).

40. Burges scrapbooks, V&A PD, 8827.119: p. 58.

41. "Powderings or Crests," V&A PD, E.280-1963: 9.

42. Godwin, "Friends in Council . . . Burges" (29 April 1881): 213–14.

43. See the series of letters concerning the work on the Plymouth Guildhall (e.g. V&A AAD, 4/22-1988, letterbook vol. 1, pp. 95, 190, 205, 207, 209, 211, 214, 215–16, 218–19) and replies from Alfred Norman on behalf of the partnership (V&A AAD, 4/256-1988 and 4/261-1988).

44. Only Crisp's side of the correspondence survives as six letters from Crisp to Godwin in a letterbook belonging to the architectural firm Proctor and Palmer, Clevedon, Somerset. These are water damaged and almost illegible, but were quoted extensively in Harbron, *Conscious Stone* (1949): 72–73.

45. Godwin, "Sir George Gilbert Scott" (5 April 1878): 155. Here Godwin writes, "We had our little fights about archaeological questions, art criticisms, and even competitions. Sometimes we hit one another perhaps a trifle hard."

46. Godwin, "Mr Street on the Bristol Cathedral" (9 August 1867), pp. 549–51.

47. Arthur E. Street, "George Price Boyce" (1980): 47, entry dated 24 April 1868.

48. For details of the quarrel with Phipps, see V&A AAD, 4/22-1963, letterbook vol. 1: 21 (27 June 1871) and 32–36 (19 July 1871). For Godwin and Waite, see ibid., p. 54, letter from E. W. Godwin to Percy Waite dated 1 August 1871; and ibid., pp. 50–53. For Godwin and Shuttleworth, see V&A AAD, 4/31-1988, letter to Joseph Shuttleworth dated September 27, 1882: "As a matter of style affecting the whole character of the interior I enter here my Architectural protest against the removal of the window seats . . . I cannot quite stultify myself, or appear to outrage the style I have adopted." Examples of commissions that ended with litigation include Glenbeigh Towers, Beauvale, and Oscar Wilde's house.

49. Messinger and Company, *Artistic Conservatories* (1880).

50. M. B. Adams, "Architects from George IV to George V" (27 July 1912): 643–45.

51. For another illustration of the "Early English" factory in Merchant Street, Bristol (built ca. 1856, demolished 1956), see "Warehouse, Bristol" (30 October 1858): 719. The carriage works (built 1858) at 104 Stokes Croft, Bristol (sometimes called Anderson's Warehouse after subsequent owners), is still standing but is empty and until recently was threatened by demolition. The parish school at Marybush Lane, Bristol, was altered by Godwin and Crisp in 1868–69 and for a number of years was thought to have been demolished, until its rediscovery by Aileen Reid in 1997; it is now an ambulance station. Godwin's church projects include: St. John the Baptist, Colerne, Wiltshire (1853–55); St. John, Littlehempston, Devon (1859–60); St. Paul de Lyon, Staverton, Devon (1858–60); St. Christopher, Ditteridge, Wiltshire (1859–61); St. Grada, Grade, Cornwall (1860–61); St. Wynwallow, Landewednack, Cornwall (1860); St. Botolph, Northfleet, Kent (1862). Also see chap. 6 in this volume.

52. For a good description of the Northampton Town Hall competition, see Harbron, *Conscious Stone* (1949): 26–29.

53. Godwin mentions, apropos Northampton Town Hall, that "Ruskin wrote him two or three very complimentary letters about it" (Godwin, "On Some Buildings I Have Designed" [29 November 1878]: 211).

54. Some parts of Godwin's decoration survive, such as the row of shields around the walls of the Great Hall. The redecoration by Roderick Gradidge and Christopher Boulter in 1992 re-created something of the atmosphere of the original decoration. See Hall, "Modern Gothic: Restoration of Northampton Guildhall" (4 February 1993): pp. 48–51.

55. Harbron, *Conscious Stone* (1949): 54. Ellen Terry also refers to the organ at Godwin's house at Portland Square in Bristol (Terry, *Ellen Terry's Memoirs* [1933]: 38). A new organ was bought for the studio at Fallows Green (Edward Anthony Craig, *Gordon Craig* [1968]: 41) and Godwin and Ellen Terry used to play Bach's "Prelude [*sic*] and Fugue" late into the night (ibid.).

56. For a decorative scheme inspired by Chaucer's *Romaunt of the Rose,* see V&A AAD, 4/16-1988. For a discussion of Spenserian inspiration at Dromore, see Reid, "Dromore Castle" (1987): 129, 131.

57. The source for this story is Harbron, *Conscious Stone* (1949): 35–36. Harbron drew heavily on the recollections of Bristol architect Sir George Oatley (1863–1950), who was Henry Crisp's partner from 1888 to 1896. This story almost certainly came from Crisp.

58. Godwin wrote to Charles Kean about the sets of Macbeth in 1858. Kean replied, "I am sure Mr Grieve will always be glad to see you . . ." (Ellen Terry Museum, letter dated 10 March 1858).

59. Harbron, *Conscious Stone* (1949): 36. Ellen Terry played Puck from 1856 to 1858, and again in 1861.

60. Dodgson may have written this in his diary after seeing Ellen Terry in her role as Mamillius at the Princess's Theatre on 16 June 1856 (Terry, *Ellen Terry's Memoirs* [1933]: 26).

61. Ibid., p. 38; Harbron, *Conscious Stone* (1949): 36.

62. Terry, *Ellen Terry's Memoirs* (1933): 38. Terry was actually fifteen, not fourteen, when she first visited Godwin's house.

63. Ibid.

64. Ibid.

65. For example: Godwin sat on the committee to consider whether to adopt the London system of measuring and valuing (minute book of the Bristol Society of Architects [see n. 23 above], 4 May 1864); he reported on a meeting of the Architectural Alliance at which were set standards for the scale of charges and for competitions (ibid., 1 June 1864); he proposed a standing committee for conservation of ancient monuments (ibid., 2 November 1864). Also see a letter from Godwin dated 9 February 1867 discussing a new form of contract proposed in London, which was to be debated by a subcommittee of the Bristol Society of Architects (V&A AAD, 4/176-1988).

66. For the Bristol Assize Courts Competition, see appendix 3 in Gomme, Jenner, and Little, *Bristol* (1979): 428–29. Also see chap. 6 in this volume.

67. James Hine and his partner Alfred Norman actually won the competition with Godwin as "consulting architect" (see chap. 6 in this volume).

68. Godwin, "Unjust Competitions" (9 December 1876): 336.

69. For an account of Dromore Castle, see Reid, "Dromore Castle" (1987): 113–42.

70. Regarding the condition of the walls, F.V. Hart, Godwin's assistant at Dromore, wrote to Godwin, "At every change of the weather my bed room walls run down with water & saturate everything in the room. . . ." (letter dated 17 December 1869, V&A AAD, 4/186-1988). The designs were eventually used in London on the ceiling of the main staircase of

the Midland Grand Hotel, now known as Saint Pancras Chambers.

71. Godwin, "On Some Buildings I Have Designed" (29 November 1878): 211.

72. Correspondence relating to this commission, Compton Family Documents, Castle Ashby, Northamptonshire. I am grateful to the marquess of Northampton for granting access to the archive and to the archivist, Peter MacKay.

73. Godwin, "My Chambers And What I Did To Them," part 1 (1 July 1876): 5. Also see chap. 7 in this volume.

74. Letter from Collinson and Lock to E. W. Godwin dated 29 July 1872, V&A AAD, 4/8-1988.

75. For a list of prices of furniture designs given to several different furniture companies, including the Art Furniture Co., see V&A AAD, 4/2-1988; for a list of designs sold by Godwin to the company and furniture bought by Godwin from the company in 1867–68, see V&A AAD, 4/9-1980: 81–2. For a fuller discussion of Godwin's furniture designs, see chap. 8 in this volume and Aslin, *E. W. Godwin* (1986).

76. For more information about "Pattledom," see Helmut Gernsheim, *Julia Margaret Cameron: Her Life and Photographic Work* (1948), 2d ed. (New York: Aperture, 1975).

77. Daphne Du Maurier, ed., *The Young George Du Maurier: A Selection of His Letters, 1860–67* (London: Peter Davies, 1951): 112.

78. For a discussion of G. F. Watts's portraits of Ellen Terry, see David Loshak, "G. F. Watts and Ellen Terry" (November 1963): 476–85. Ellen Terry remembered posing for Watts wearing armor, "and never realising that it was heavy until I fainted!" (Terry, *Ellen Terry's Memoirs* [1933]: 42).

79. Part of a letter of 1890 from Ellen Terry to a friend from her Harpenden days, see Terry, *Ellen Terry's Memoirs* [1933]: 96, n. 3.

80. Edward Anthony Craig, *Gordon Craig* (1968): 38.

81. This house is unidentified, but was called "the Red House" or "the Firs." Edward Craig, Godwin's grandson, remembered visiting the area with Ellen Terry when he was a child, and called the house "The Red Cottage" (ibid., pp. 18, 39). For Godwin's sketch of the house, and its floor plan, see V&A PD, 273-1963.

82. The house stood in Sun Lane, Harpenden; it is sometimes called "Pigeonwick" perhaps after the pigeon-loft gatehouse, which was demolished in 1926. The house itself survived until the early 1960s. Where it stood is a modern estate on two roads, one now called Fallows Green and the other, Pigeonwick.

83. During a tour of Scotland in the 1880s with Henry Irving, they visited Ailsa Craig, an island in the Clyde. Ellen gave her son "Craig" as a surname and gave "Ailsa" as a stage name to Edith. Her son changed his name to "Gordon Craig" by deed poll on 24 February 1893. For more information about Edith Craig (1869–1947) and Edward Gordon Craig (1872–1966) see chap. 13 in this volume.

84. E. W. Godwin diary 1873, entry for 12 November, V&A AAD, 4/1-1980.

85. Godwin refused to divulge his home address to acquaintances; for example, he wrote to Percy Waite, "I stay a good deal in the country, but to avoid the disturbance of letters, and callers, I keep the whereabouts of my small farm to myself, & *myself alone*" (letter dated 15 June 1871, V&A AAD, 4/22-1988: 13). For Burges's visits to Godwin and Ellen Terry in Harpenden, see Harbron, *Conscious Stone* (1949): 71–72. Harbron's source for this information is unknown.

86. Terry, *Ellen Terry's Memoirs* [1933]: 69.

87. E. G. Craig, *Ellen Terry* (1931): facing p. 28.

88. Ellen Terry wrote that Whistler "sent my little girl a tiny Japanese kimono when Liberty was hardly a name" (Terry, *Ellen Terry's Memoirs* [1933]: 101).

89. E. W. Godwin diary 1873, entry dated 24 April, V&A AAD, 4/1-1980. The source of the rumor had been Lady Cowper, and Godwin wrote to Earl Cowper's agent, Mr. F. Fox, on June 18, 1873 that it had "come to my ears that during my absence a report was circulated that I had absconded . . . this sort of report was enough to *create* financial difficulties & the annoyances I have experienced in consequence have been quite difficult for I am neither a man of property who can afford to laugh at everything nor physically capable of suffering without acute feelings from such causes" (Lothian Papers, DDLM 209/11/128).

90. Earl Cowper's solicitors, or messengers from them, were in the office throughout the last week of April and the first week of May 1873 (E. W. Godwin 1873 diary, V&A AAD, 4/1-1980).

91. Terry, *Ellen Terry's Memoirs* [1933]: 69.

92. Ibid., p. 95; undated letter, Ellen Terry Museum. Godwin wrote two letters to Ellen Terry in 1875 (now in the Ellen Terry Museum) about his designs for her Juliet costumes.

93. Godwin left his Taviton Street home in December 1874 having defaulted on the Michaelmas payment of the poor rate ("Poor Rate" books, parish of St. Giles and St. George, Bloomsbury, London, in the Holborn Library, Local Studies Section). I am grateful to Aileen Reid for this information.

94. Terry, *Ellen Terry's Memoirs* [1933]: 83–84.

95. For specific responsibilities in the Bancroft Production of *The Merchant of Venice*, see chap. 12 by Fanny Baldwin in this volume. For Godwin's sources for costume design, including Cesare Vecellio, see Godwin, "The Architecture and Costume of Shakespeare's plays: *The Merchant of Venice*" (3 April 1875): 196–97.

96. Terry, *Ellen Terry's Memoirs* [1933]: 140–41; Harbron, *Conscious Stone* (1949): 112.

97. Gordon Craig, writing under the pseudonym "John Semar," recalls Herbert Beerbohm Tree's admiration for Godwin's theatrical productions (Edward Anthony Craig, *Gordon Craig* [1968]: 242).

98. Ibid., pp. 47–48.

99. Smallhythe Place, Ellen Terry's home in Kent, now the Ellen Terry Memorial Museum, houses a number of pieces of furniture designed by Godwin after their separation, such as the Shakespeare Furniture set. The collection also includes a scrapbook of drawings and designs by Godwin for costumes for Ellen Terry, several of which are for productions of the 1880s. Ellen Terry eventually divorced Watts and married a handsome actor Charles Wardell (whose stage name was Charles Kelly) in 1877, but they separated in 1881 (Wardell, an alcoholic, died in 1885) and in 1907 Ellen Terry married American James Carew.

100. Undated letter from E. W. Godwin to Edith, Ellen Terry Museum. Edy later wrote on the letter that it had been written in 1877 and not given to her until 1887, but this cannot be correct because by 1877 Godwin and Ellen Terry were no longer living together and Godwin had remarried.

101. Edward Anthony Craig, *Gordon Craig* (1968): 47.

102. Godwin, "Industrial Education Bureau" (6 June 1874): 5. The article was reprinted as Godwin, "Lady Architects" (13 June 1874): 335; and again as "Mr. E. W. Godwin on Lady Architects" (12 June 1874): 378.

103. Harbron, *Conscious Stone* (1949): 98.

104. For more information on Beatrice, see Hunterian Art Gallery, *Beatrice Whistler* (1997).

105. Godwin diary 1881, entry for 11 May, V&A AAD, 4/6-1980.

106. For background on the club, see G. A. F. Rogers, *The Arts Club and Its Members* (London: Truslove and Hanson, 1920): 78. For Godwin and Whistler, see Edward Anthony Craig, *Gordon Craig* (1968): 32.

107. For frequent mention of the Hogarth Club, Charlotte Street, Fitzroy Square, see Godwin's diary 1874/1876, V&A AAD, 4/2-1980. For

description of the club in the "Merry Seventies" as "an artists' club, and a thoroughly bohemian one," see Harry Furniss, *My Bohemian Days* (London: Hurst and Blackett, 1919): 61. For the Verulam Club, see Crook, *William Burges* (1981): 355, n. 42. For Godwin at the New Athenaeum Club, see his letters of the 1880s, written on New Athenaeum Club note paper (V&A TA, Godwin collection, boxes 5 and 9,). Its address is variously given as Suffolk Street, Pall Mall, and 3 Pall Mall East.

108. For the Saint Stephen's Club, see Ellmann, *Oscar Wilde* (1988): 67.

109. For a sketch of a man and a child paddling in the sea at Sheerness, see V&A PD, E.258-1963.

110. For Waugh and Sons, see Godwin ledger, V&A AAD, 4/12-1980: 27–28; for J. W. Wilson, Gothenburg, and Mr Constable, see ibid., pp. 35–36; for Constable and Waugh and Sons, see ibid., pp. 39–40.

111. For Godwin's substantial earnings from the *Architect*, particularly in 1876, see Godwin ledger, V&A AAD, 4/12-1980: 31–32. For his late-1870s and early-1880s involvement with the *British Architect and Northern Engineer*, see V&A AAD, 4/12-1980: 47–48, 51–52. Although he was paid for his writing and for finding new subscribers and advertisers, he also made editorial suggestions (letters to Godwin from the Davidson brothers, editors Oliver and Thomas Raffles, V&A AAD, 4/285-330-1988).

112. E. W. Godwin diary 1874/1876, entry dated 25 December 1876, V&A AAD, 4/2-1980.

113. For Whistler's atelier, see Harbron, *Conscious Stone* (1949): 125.

114. Godwin diary 1877, entry dated 22 July, V&A AAD, 4/3-1980. Carlo Pellegrini was the cartoonist "Ape" of *Vanity Fair*. Godwin built a double house and studio at 60 Tite Street for Pellegrini and Archibald Stuart Wortley (see chap. 6 in this volume).

115. Harbron, *Conscious Stone* (1949): 113–14.

116. Ibid., p. 138.

117. [Godwin, Notes on Current Events] (4 February 1881): 62–63; also see Godwin, "With Whistler's Critics" (25 February 1881): 98–99.

118. Godwin, "Studios and Mouldings" (7 March 1879): 261.

119. Godwin diary 1881, entry dated 7 November, V&A AAD, 4/6-1980.

120. Hart-Davies, ed., *Letters of Oscar Wilde* (1962): 172; also quoted in Hyde, "Oscar Wilde" (March 1951): 176.

121. Letter from Lillie Langtry to E. W. Godwin dated 7 September 1885, V&A AAD, 4/174-1988.

122. The Tennyson Research Centre in Lincoln has a manuscript copy of *The Cup,* which was used in the 1881 production and includes a sketch of an ornate, single-stemmed cup probably by J. H. Allan, not at all like the description of it in Terry, *Ellen Terry's Memoirs* [1933]: 156.

123. O. Wilde, "Truth of Masks" (1891; reprint 1930).

124. Letter to Whistler dated June 1882, in Hart-Davies, ed., *Letters of Oscar Wilde* (1962): 121.

125. The account of their meeting comes from "a well-informed correspondent" ("Our Omnibus Box" [1 September 1884]: 158–59).

126. "Greenery-Yallery" and yellow sunflowers had become associated with Aestheticism in the 1870s and early 1880s. Yellow came to symbolize a certain artistic bohemianism, or freedom from convention. Into the nineties, *The Yellow Book* published dangerously risqué drawings by Aubrey Beardsley. Oscar Wilde's downfall (he was reported to have been arrested while reading "a yellow book") underlined the symbolism that yellow was sexually daring, certainly "arty" and possibly even dangerous.

127. Campbell, "Woodland Gods" (November 1888): 2.

128. "Our Omnibus Box" (1 September 1884): 158–59.

129. V&A TA, Godwin collection, box 1, letter from Wilson Barrett to Godwin dated 19 August 1884.

130. "Our Omnibus Box" (1 September 1884): 158–59.

131. Photograph, V&A TA, Godwin collection, box 9.

132. V&A PD, E.264-1963.

133. Letter from D'Arcy Ferris to Godwin, n.d., V&A TA, Godwin collection, box 7.

134. For the actor being "persecuted," see letter from Lady Archibald Campbell's sister, M. J. Santoris (?) to Godwin, n.d., V&A TA, Godwin collection, box 7. For Godwin's letters, see ibid., uncatalogued letters.

135. Beerbohm, "1880" (January 1895): 280.

136. "It was necessary to exclude much that belonged to the vocabulary of [Fletcher's] time—unnecessarily strong for ours" (Edward William Godwin, ed., *Faithfull Shepherdesse* [1885], preface). Godwin's adaptation was registered at Stationers' Hall.

137. Hyde, "Oscar Wilde" (1951): 176.

138. Jopling, *Twenty Years* (1925): 289 et seq.

139. Ibid., p. 292 et seq.

140. Ibid., p. 293.

141. Harbron, *Conscious Stone* (1949): 185.

142. Woodville, *Random Recollections* (1914): 139–40. The two other "ladies" were probably Lady Archie and her sister.

143. E.g., "A brilliant, if somewhat eccentric, character . . . yet his life . . . has been, for the most part, one of unfulfilled promise" ("The Late E. W. Godwin, F.S.A." *Building News* 51 [15 October 1886]: 589).

144. [Obituary] "The Week," *Architect* (London) 36 (15 October 1886), p. 217.

145. Campbell, "Woodland Gods" (November 1888): 2.

146. Wills, *W. G. Wills* (1898): 229.

147. Letter in the Ellen Terry Museum.

148. "The *Pall Mall Gazette* had an article in that afternoon's issue, headed "The Butterfly Chained at Last!" (Jopling, *Twenty Years* [1925]: 296–97). According to Jopling, the wedding was on Saturday 11 August 1888; her husband, George Rowe, obtained the special licence while Louise and Whistler interviewed the clergyman the Rev. the Hon. Mr Byng.

149. Ibid, p. 291.

150. Published in *Today* (12 May 1894). The original indian ink and wash drawing (ca. 1894) is in the Tate Gallery, London.

151. Terry, *Ellen Terry's Memoirs* [1933]: 299. Her films include *Her Greatest Performance* (1916), *The Pillars of Society* (1920), *The Bohemian Girl* (1921), and *Potter's Clay* (date unknown).

152. A page from Ellen Terry's notebook contains a photograph of Godwin, below which she wrote: " 'Tis better to have loved and lost than never to have loved at all." For a photograph of this, see Edward Anthony Craig, *Gordon Craig* (1968), facing page 33.

153. Ellen Terry Museum.

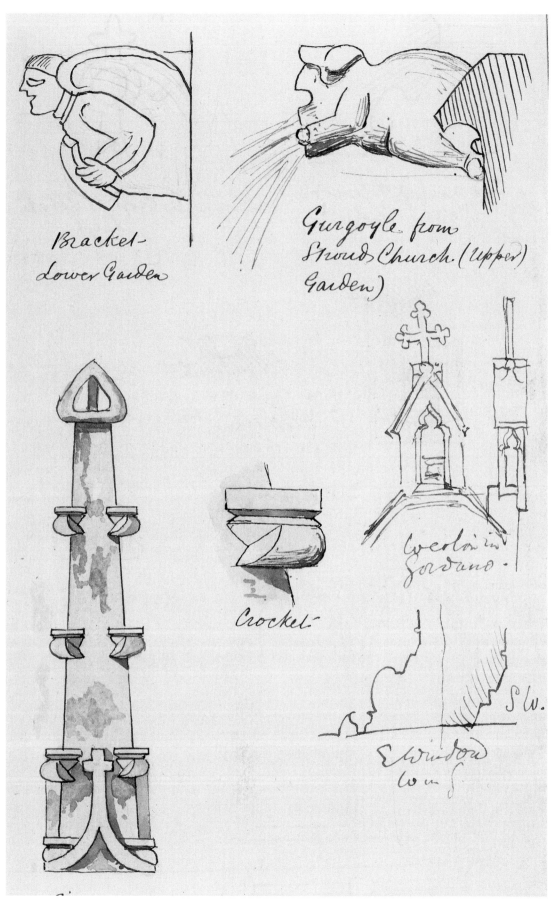

Fig. 2-1. E. W. Godwin. Antiquarian sketches, ca. 1849. Sketchbook. Pencil, pen and ink, sepia wash; 6¾ x 9¼ in. (17.3 x 23.5 cm) Trustees of the Victoria and Albert Museum, London, V&A PD E.267-1963: 2. *Checklist no. 3*

CHAPTER 2

E·W·GODWIN·AS·AN·ANTIQUARY

Catherine Arbuthnott

E. W. Godwin's best-known designs are those in which he appears to have escaped from the evolutionary dead end of the Gothic Revival. The White House, Frank Miles's studio, and the famous Godwin sideboard with its spare, stark functionalism seem to have no precedents. Yet in 1858 Godwin believed that a true, original Victorian style would emerge from the Gothic, not in opposition to it.[1] Godwin's antiquarian studies ranged far beyond the Gothic, taking him to Homeric and classical Greece, Celtic Ireland, eleventh-century Denmark, and Saxon, Jacobean, and even Restoration England. "Archaeology" permeated every aspect of his career. It was the foundation for much of his architectural, theatrical, and journalistic work, and also for his interior design practice, including furniture and textiles. The study of the past provided Godwin with design ideas, introduced him to friends and clients, gained him a formidable reputation as an "authority," and gave him some splendid opportunities for argument with his professional brethren. For Godwin it was more than a professional necessity, it was an enthusiasm and a delight.

Gothic Revival architecture, in its early phase, was a matter of decorative "quotations," such as crockets, castellations, and pointed-arch windows with elaborate tracery, which were instantly recognizable to laymen as "medieval," applied haphazardly to forms that were not. This romantic, picturesque approach gradually gave way to a more scholarly use of medieval forms in architecture. In the early and mid-nineteenth century, Thomas Rickman, John Britton,

Robert Willis, J. H. Parker, and William Whewell, among others, established a nomenclature, chronology, and classification for medieval buildings, which, although the details were still being argued decades later, provided a framework for the study and selection of architectural styles.[2]

Godwin was eager to establish his credentials as a successor to these men, who had raised this branch of knowledge to the "dignity of a science."[3] He stressed his own scientific methodology in his antiquarian writing. For example, in a series of articles he wrote for the *Architect* in 1875, entitled "Old English or Saxon Building," Godwin emphasized the scientific nature of his inquiry by appropriating the language of forensics: he listened to evidence and called witnesses; he examined and tested them; he summed up and finally arrived at a verdict.[4] For Godwin, however, antiquarian science was not an end in itself. It was merely the secure foundation for the exercise of the imagination. Toward the end of his life, he wrote that the study of the past was "a science that clothes and reanimates the dead, and gives colour to the pale, shadowy forms of forgotten folk. The purpose of the archaeologist is to bring before us those old times, to make history a reality."[5] This remark shows that Godwin's response to the past was as close to the emotionally charged historical romanticism of Ruskin as to the scholarship of the pioneering "scientific" antiquaries.

Godwin spent part of his childhood in a house called Earl's Mead on the outskirts of Bristol. Its garden was full of crumbling fragments of old buildings collected by his father William.[6] One of Godwin's early sketchbooks contains undated drawings—a bracket carved in the form of an angel, a gargoyle, and a fragment of a perpendicular window—which are labeled "Lower Garden" and "in Upper Garden" (fig. 2-1).[7] It seems likely that these objects were sketched by Godwin at Earl's Mead when he was a boy. Godwin's interest in other antiquarian studies, such as heraldry and costume, appears to have predated his architectural pupilage,[8] but his first serious forays into the study of the past are inextricably linked with his architectural training. Godwin learned to be an antiquary as part of the process of becoming an architect.

By the time Godwin began his architectural pupilage, in about 1848, it was becoming accepted that knowledge of medieval styles was an important part of an architect's training and would in all likelihood be a requirement of his practice. Several of the older generation of architects, George Gilbert Scott and George Edmund Street, for example, were already building in Gothic Revival styles firmly rooted in antiquarian scholarship rather than in mock-Gothic picturesque. There was a difference between best practice and usual practice: throughout Godwin's lifetime, architects and builders continued to produce buildings consisting of incongruous mixtures of medieval decoration stuck onto inappropriate forms, or of scraps from the many available illustrated architectural pattern books, cobbled together with what Godwin called "a most amusing disregard of conventionality, both of time and place."[9] However, for the men at the top of the profession—and Godwin aspired to be one of them—scholarly knowledge of the buildings of the past was a professional necessity. In Godwin's ledgers his membership fee for the Society of Antiquaries appears as a professional expense, along with drawing materials and the cost of entertaining clients.[10]

There were architects who considered antiquarian study a waste of time. Godwin's pupil master, the Bristol architect William Armstrong, appears to have been one of them. In 1878 Godwin characterized Armstrong as a "practical man."[11] He may have been remembering his own training when he remarked that practical men "look upon archaeology with disdain and talk of it as 'an amusement all very well for those who have nothing to do,' . . . believe me, this is no fanciful picture, but, on the contrary, one drawn from the very expressions that I have heard used."[12] Although Godwin did write of sketching and measuring expeditions with Armstrong,[13] it seems that as an antiquary he was largely self-taught, initially from architectural books and periodicals.

Recalling his own pupilage, Godwin published an open letter to architectural students in 1880, advising them on suitable reading matter for their studies.[14] In keeping with his imaginative, romantic approach to the past, he said that he had learned more about the ancient world, the Middle Ages, and the Renaissance from the Bible, Chaucer, and Shakespeare than from books on architecture. He went on, however, to recommend a selection of architectural books from which a pupil might learn the basic vocabulary and grammar of Gothic. These books were his own foundation as a "scientific" antiquary.

While in Armstrong's office, in his "first steady settling down to the study of Gothic," Godwin had read "Parker's 'Glossary,' Bloxham's [sic] capital little book, Rickman, Barr, and sundry serial works."[15] Matthew Bloxam's *Principles of Gothic Architecture,* which gave a selection of examples and then a chronological classification, was particularly useful. Godwin suggested in 1880 that "What Bloxham did for Gothic architecture might well be done for Chinese, Indian, Egyptian and other styles."[16] Godwin also recommended publications that had careful, accurate illustrations, such as *Architectural Parallels* (1848) by Edmund Sharpe, and a series by Henry Bowman and J. S. Crowther entitled *The Churches of the Middle Ages* (1845–53). Many of the standard books on Gothic architecture were available in the library of the Bristol Society of Architects, which Godwin joined soon after its foundation in 1850.[17]

At an early age, Godwin also began to put together a small library of his own. Half of his £100 legacy from his father, who died in 1846, "went to pay bills or a/cs at Booksellers incurred during [his] minority."[18] This was a large sum of money, only just under half of what an architectural clerk might earn in a year. Godwin's purchases in about 1849[19] include Thomas Rickman's *Attempt to discriminate the styles of architecture in England from the Conquest to the Reformation,* the book that had established the nomenclature of Early English, Decorated, and Perpendicular styles; A. C. Pugin's *Specimens of Gothic Architecture,* with text by E. J. Willson (four guineas for the two volumes); and the volumes on Gloucester Cathedral and Wells Cathedral from John Britton's *Historical and descriptive accounts . . . of English Cathedrals.*[20] Godwin noted the names of the engravers and the illustrators as well as the authors. More than twenty years after buying his copy of Pugin's *Specimens,* Godwin was still an admirer of the "careful architectural drawings, with their dimensions clearly indicated, and their details elaborately and scientifically displayed."[21] The engraver John Le Keux, who had collaborated with A. C. Pugin, was a particular favorite, appearing several times on the list.

Good, accurate drawings were important to Godwin. Although he sketched extensively in England, he never traveled widely in Europe or farther afield. He was one of the enthusiasts for Early French Gothic in the 1860s but did not visit France until he was in his late twenties. He returned from this trip with only one sketch, of shadow falling on a string course.[22] His most likely sources for illustrations of French buildings are W. E. Nesfield's book, *Specimens of Mediaeval Architecture*, and the then-unpublished measured drawings by fellow architect William Burges.[23] Godwin did not visit Belgium and Germany until he was in his forties. His brief enthusiasm for thirteenth-century Italian Gothic, fueled by Ruskin's *Stones of Venice*, had relied on George Edmund Street's careful illustrations in *Brick and Marble Architecture in the Middle Ages: Notes of a Tour in the North of Italy* (1855). Ruskin's book was illustrated with beautiful, almost impressionistic etchings rather than useful measured drawings. Godwin never visited Italy, nor did he go to Greece, although he was to write extensively on Greek antiquities. He did visit Denmark while researching architecture and costume for *Hamlet*, but for his articles on the painted decoration at Roda and Bjeresjøe churches he had to rely on the illustrations in N. M. Mandelgren's book, *Monuments scandinaves du moyen-âge*.[24]

Although Godwin studied other people's illustrations, he did not entirely trust their accuracy. He recognized the potential of photography early in his career and gave a lecture to the Royal Institute of British Architects in 1867 on the photographs exhibited that year by the Architectural Photographic Association.[25] Toward the end of his life, he used photographs for reliable visual evidence in the creation of historically accurate costumes for the play *Claudian*.[26] Although he argued that students would gain more of an understanding of a building by extensive sketching than by photography or the use of published illustrations, he seems to have considered photography and sketching to be complementary,[27] and in his open letter to students in 1880, in addition to his recommended list of architectural books, he advocated "the contemplation and enjoyment—the critical examination and comparison of photographs and other illustrations of the best art works of all times."[28]

From books, photographs, and illustrations Godwin learned to date and classify portions of buildings on stylistic grounds. An early notebook, of about 1850–51, contains his architectural descriptions of Sussex churches. It shows how he used his reference books while he was learning this skill.[29] He wrote the descriptions from tracings of published illustrations rather than from the churches themselves and backed up his work with measurements and quotations taken from "authorities": Parker, Bloxam, and Rickman.

Godwin's reliance on other people's facts, measurements, and illustrations was to lessen over the years as he accumulated a body of information from his own direct observation of buildings. His earliest dated sketch, of the east window in the north transept of West Kington Church, was made on May 12, 1849, when he was fifteen years old.[30] His earliest surviving sketchbook, of 1848–51, includes a "list of places to visit—1849."[31] An undated, handwritten list at the back of an offprint of an article by Godwin of 1853 is inscribed "Summary of Churches visited." There are 145 locations, including holy wells and crosses, in Bristol, Somerset, Gloucestershire, Wiltshire, Cornwall, Oxfordshire, Warwickshire, and Wales.[32]

Much of Godwin's early antiquarian work is undated, but it is possible to discern some development in his methods from the time of the notebook on Sussex churches. At some point between 1849 and 1851, he began to look in a limited way at original documents, taking some notes and measurements from James Nasmith's 1778 edition of William de Wyrcestre's *Itinerary*, which is an important source of information for Bristol's early ecclesiastical foundations.[33] Godwin began to add his own initials to his lists of authorities consulted. In March 1852, for example, he constructed "A Chronological table of the existing Wall bell-turrets of England." Of the eleven places on this list, Godwin had visited six. For the church of Leigh de la Mere (which was one of the buildings Godwin had felt he should visit in 1849), the authorities are listed as the Reverend J. L. Petit, the *Builder*, and himself.[34]

Godwin also learned that other people's facts should be checked. Among his papers are two sets of measured sketches of Saint James's Church in Bristol. One is marked: "St James (according to Dudley)" and the other is headed: "St James Ch. (according to J. H. & E.W.G.)" with some small differences in the measurements.[35] "J. H." was James Hine, a fellow pupil in Armstrong's office and Godwin's companion on a number of sketching expeditions, including an antiquarian holiday in Cornwall in 1852.[36]

Hine was three years older than Godwin, and it is a measure of Godwin's remarkable precocity as an antiquary that the two issued the prospectus of an illustrated series, *The Architectural Antiquities of Bristol and its Neighbourhood*, in March 1850 when Godwin was still only sixteen years old.[37] The series was intended to be published in six parts, although only the first was issued, in 1851.[38]

The text of the book is unattributed, but it is likely that Godwin contributed at least the section on Saint Mary Redcliffe, in which the architectural description and classification are limited by the space available. The historical information is very thin: "old chronicles of the city" are quoted but not identified. One manuscript source was used,[39] and the other information came from the *Chrono-*

Fig. 2-2. E. W. Godwin. "The Church of St Mary, Redcliffe: Doorway, North Porch." Engraving by William Corbett Burder. From Burder, Hine, and Godwin, *Architectural Antiquities of Bristol* (1851), pl. 3. Trustees of the Victoria and Albert Museum, London, NAL 33 E.82. *Checklist no. 4*

logical Outline of the History of Bristol (1824) by John Evans.[40] Godwin contributed two plates: one showing the north porch of Saint Mary Redcliffe (fig. 2-2), and the other, the porch's carved capitals. Among Godwin's papers are several inked preliminary drawings (fig. 2-3) which give measurements and show sections of the moldings of the capitals and details of carved figures and flowers.[41] These do not appear in the published plate, however, nor are they present in Godwin's fine wash drawing from which the plate was taken. Soon after this book was published, Godwin abandoned pretty drawings in favor of "scientific" clarity. There is only one other example of a published antiquarian paper by Godwin that is illustrated by drawings without their accompanying "scientific" details or sections of moldings, or plans, "A Notice of a singular and ancient coffin lid in St Philip's Church, Bristol," which was also written in 1851 and subsequently published in the *Archaeological Journal* in 1853,

the first of eight papers that Godwin contributed to that journal between 1853 and 1865.[42]

The year 1851 was pivotal in other ways as well. Following the publication of *The Architectural Antiquities of Bristol and its Neighbourhood*, Godwin joined the Archaeological Institute of Great Britain and Ireland, which held its annual conference in Bristol in July 1851.[43] Several distinguished antiquaries contributed papers, including E. A. Freeman and John Britton. Godwin himself read his short paper on the ancient coffin lid in Saint Philip's to the section of antiquaries at the conference.[44] A temporary museum was set up; among its exhibits were drawings of all of the objects in the Royal Irish Academy. Decades later, in 1878, Godwin was to suggest the use of "some combinations taken from some of the treasures of the Royal Irish Academy" in the decoration of Princess Louise's studio.[45] The objects in the R.I.A. also provided inspiration for some of the decorative designs at Dromore Castle in about 1868–69.[46] A group of Danish relics was shown at the Bristol Conference, presented by Jens Jakob Asmussen Worsaae, a Danish historian and archaeologist who lectured at the University of Copenhagen. In 1884 Godwin would consult Worsaae on the costumes of *Hamlet*.

The highlight of the conference, however, was a lecture and demonstration on Wells Cathedral, given by the Jacksonian Professor of Natural and Experimental Philosophy at Cambridge, Robert Willis, who was to have a profound effect on Godwin's development as an antiquary. Godwin may have heard Willis lecture before this occasion. There is a suggestive concentration of Oxford buildings in Godwin's sketchbook of 1848–51, which may coincide with the Oxford conference of the Archaeological Institute, held in 1850, at which Willis had read a paper.[47] Godwin was clearly familiar with Willis's work in developing a commonly understood architectural nomenclature when he used Willis's term "scoinson arch" to describe the inner arch of the east window of Colerne Church in a manuscript paper of October 1851.[48] That he had heard Willis lecture is also obvious from Godwin's obituary of the architect Sir George Gilbert Scott, in which Godwin refers to "the many who used to listen with bated breath to Willis's wonderful lectures at the annual outings of the Archaeological Institute . . ." and to "the professor's brilliant demonstrations."[49]

Willis's method was characterized by its emphasis on documentary sources of information. His first step before beginning to examine a building was to lay a foundation of historical facts. He would consult the existing written records: the fabric-rolls, estate records, and muniments. From these documents he produced a chronology of the building works. Once he had this information he would study the building itself. Willis's second characteristic was a reluctance to make dogmatic statements without proof. He would build evidence, piece by piece, until "at last he had succeeded in deciphering [the history of the building] beyond the possibility of mistake . . . ."[50] Thirdly, his study was unusually thorough, and he was praised in his obituary as a "demonstrator of the anatomy of ancient buildings . . . not content with the ordinary vague recognition of one portion as thirteenth century and another as fourteenth, and so on, he strove to discover the portions which each individual had directed, to trace the place where the work had been abandoned, and to detect by small peculiarities of design or workmanship the resumption of it by a different hand."[51] From Willis, Godwin acquired a methodology, a respect for original documentary sources, an increased concern for "scientific" accuracy in antiquarian study, and a penchant for anatomizing (rather than merely classing) buildings. "If a building is worth your study at all, it is worth dissecting," Godwin wrote in 1878. "Take your subject to pieces."[52]

During the 1850s Godwin gradually—and rather unevenly at first—adopted Willis's methods. In October 1851 he wrote a minutely detailed "Architectural Description and history of Saint Peter's Church Colerne Wilts."[53] In its favor, the paper demonstrates Godwin's close observation of the fabric of the church. Otherwise, it reveals Godwin to be rather cavalier with dates and careless to the extent of wrongly identifying the name of the dedicatee of the church—it should have been Saint John the Baptist. He is also dogmatic in his conclusions without presenting any of the underlying arguments. In a later paper based on this study, dated August 1855 in the text and published by the *Wiltshire Archaeological and Natural History Magazine* in 1857,[54] Godwin revised the essay, cutting it considerably and adding a section that shows him attempting to use Willis's methods. In the 1855 revision he mentioned that he had "not been able to look into the Acts of William de Colerne, Abbot of Malmsbury" but had consulted the Colerne muniments in the possession of New College. He also noted, however, that "in the absence of all documentary evidence relative to the history of this church, we are obliged to refer to the character of the architecture for the dates of the several portions."[55] He did this quite successfully, pointing out the junctions between later and earlier masonry, and where he could not prove his points, he was careful with his phrasing, using "it appears," "it is not improbable," and "it is more than probable" to signify the uncertainty.[56]

There are traces of Willis in several of Godwin's papers of the 1850s, but the full flowering of his influence

Fig. 2-3. E. W. Godwin. Measured sketches of Saint Mary Redcliffe, including the North Porch, ca. 1851. Pen and ink; 12¾ x 8 in. (32.5 x 20.4 cm). British Architectural Library Manuscripts Collection, RIBA, London, GoE/3/6/24 (G/BRI.7/1).

came in the early 1860s, when Godwin revived the moribund Bristol Society of Architects and began to organize excursions, with lectures and demonstrations, along Willisian lines. The first excursion, in August 1862, was to Wells Cathedral, on which Willis had lectured in 1851. There followed excursions to Queen Charlton and Chew Magna, Exeter, Llandaff, churches in Somerset, Salisbury and Gloucester cathedrals, Chepstow and Caldecott castles, and sites in Bristol itself. Godwin lectured on almost every occasion, and several of his papers, notably those on Wells, Exeter, and Gloucester cathedrals, show him duplicating Willis's practice and referring frequently to Willis's own remarks on those buildings.[57] In a paper on Bristol Cathedral, in which Godwin attempted to "dissect its various styles," he not only came to the conclusion that "archaeology is not fully satisfied unless we fairly estimate the traditional and documentary evidence,"[58] but also managed to upstage the professor by arguing that doubts raised by Willis in 1851 at the Bristol conference as to the extent of the Decorated-style rebuilding of the cathedral at the time of Edmund Knowle could have been cleared up by consulting William de Wyrcestre's *Itinerary*.

A great many architects sketched and measured: the process was part of training to be a Gothic revivalist and an architect. Many also published papers on antiquarian subjects. Godwin stands out from the majority of his contemporaries for several reasons. There was his enthusiasm for the study of the past which was captured by a writer for the *Western Daily Press* in a report on one of the Bristol Society of Architects' excursions, during which Godwin "led at a slapping pace . . . [and] dashed into his subject with such impetuosity" that he left most of his followers behind. The reporter caught up at the site of the Pithay gate, where he found "Mr Godwin, a lighted cigar in one hand and a silk umbrella in the other . . . describing with great spirit" surrounded by puzzled locals. After a long walk, "Mr Godwin had now been talking . . . for more than three hours— during which the lecturer's attention never flagged, and his umbrella seldom failed to point out some object of interest."[59]

This enthusiasm explains another way in which Godwin began to diverge from the norm among his contemporaries. He increasingly made forays into documentary, literary, and manuscript evidence for their own sake as well as to complement his studies of the fabric of buildings. In 1875, the year of Willis's death, Godwin published the series of articles entitled "Old English or Saxon Building."[60] These essays are characterized, like Willis's papers, by their reliance on documentary evidence, the thoroughness of the research, and the step-by-step methodology. Godwin claimed to have "personally examined . . . every page of more than two dozen manuscripts." Where he was unable to see original documents—such as the original ninth-century plan of the monastery of Saint Gall—he consulted as many copies as possible, passing comment on the "inaccuracies of omission and commission" on the part of the great French architect and antiquary Eugène Viollet-le-Duc and the architectural writer James Fergusson.[61] When he consulted facsimiles, not originals, he was careful to say so.

The subject of Saxon architecture was a difficult one, and Godwin, in his interpretation, was going against the grain of contemporary thinking. Fergusson had questioned whether "any such thing existed as true Saxon architecture," and J. H. Parker had argued that before the year 1000 the Saxons had constructed only in wood.[62] The "witnesses" were already well known; individually they had been dis-

missed as unreliable.[63] What Godwin did in his paper was to reexamine the whole question in a rigorous, thorough, and methodical way, eliminating as many of the potentially unreliable secondary sources as possible. The most striking characteristic of this research was the extent to which the documentation eclipsed the evidence provided by actual buildings. This was only partly an accident of survival. Godwin had gone further than Willis by not only looking at building rolls and such contemporary illustrations as there were, but also at literary sources. He was convinced that historical truth underlay poetic license.

Godwin's literary sources for Saxon building included two rather fanciful histories, two poems, and an account of the miracles of Saint Swithin. These, according to a reviewer in the *Examiner,* might on their own have been dismissed as "mere rhetoric" or "poet's manufacture."[64] Used in conjunction with the documentary, pictorial, and built evidence, however, this literary evidence began to look much more substantial and was crucial in establishing Godwin's theory that the Saxons did indeed build in stone, and that several features believed to be characteristic of Norman architecture were present in the earlier buildings. It was a triumph of methodology, and the same writer in the *Examiner* noted that the evidence had never before been examined with "so much method or fullness."[65]

Godwin's early antiquarian papers were mostly published in specialist archaeological and antiquarian journals, and they are, frankly, rather dull. The "Old English or Saxon Building" series, while fiercely erudite and self-consciously "scientific"—Godwin never did wear his learning lightly—have a dimension that the early papers lack. The foray into literature marks a fusion of Godwin's romantic enthusiasm for the past with his intellectual appreciation for the dry, accurate antiquarian science. This process had begun in 1871–72 with articles on "Geoffrey Chaucer as Clerk of the King's Works,"[66] "Spenser's Castles, &c" and "Kilcolman,"[67] and continued in 1874 and 1875 with a series of thirty-two articles entitled "The Architecture and Costume of Shakespere's [*sic*] Plays." By 1886 Godwin's literary enthusiasm had begun to overwhelm his "scientific" methodology. In that year he published "The Greek Home According to Homer,"[68] an essay that was fundamentally flawed by its overreliance on literary texts.

What the Victorians believed to be two epic poems written by a man called Homer are now considered to be late versions of long-surviving orally transmitted poems, composed anew in each retelling and subject to inevitable interpolations over the years between their first appearance and the time at which they were written down. The texts are a difficult and unreliable source to use as history. Godwin was well aware that "it is in . . . pieces of collateral evidence that so much value lies as it enables us to separate the real from the fanciful not uncommonly confronted when one source of information is too much insisted on,"[69] but the collateral evidence known to the Victorians—that of archaeology—was also flawed. Godwin's reading of the text of the Homeric poems made him extremely dubious about Heinrich Schliemann's excavation of the hill of Hissarlik in Turkey, the supposed site of Troy. In 1875, in spite of Schliemann, Godwin decided to "take Homer's colouring of things as tolerably literal, after allowing for poetical license,"[70] and he did not change his opinion even after Schliemann had lectured in 1877 at the Royal Institute of British Architects and explicitly stated that it was not possible to reconcile Homer's descriptions of Troy with what he had excavated.[71] In fact, neither Schliemann's archaeology nor the Homeric poems are reliable, but Godwin chose to give far greater weight to the literary evidence than to the archaeological, which is a reversal of the common hierarchy of evidence that insists on the primacy of physical remains. In "The Greek Home according to Homer," Godwin attempted to draw conclusions about the plan of Odysseus's house at Ithaca based almost solely on internal textual evidence in the *Odyssey* and the *Iliad*, accepting archaeological evidence only where it upheld his theory.[72]

By contrast, one of the earlier "literary" studies shows Godwin's hierarchy of evidence working properly. For his article on Edmund Spenser's castles, published in 1872,[73] Godwin had seen and sketched Kilcolman castle (see fig. 5-3),[74] and the information from Spenser's poems came lower on the scale of reliability than the evidence of Godwin's own eyes. Discrepancies were placed firmly at the door of the poetic imagination. In his work on Greek architectural antiquities, Godwin did not have the wide-ranging practical and primary knowledge of the subject that he demonstrates in his antiquarian studies of medieval buildings.

Enthusiasm for the past had carried Godwin into areas of antiquarian study that were not immediately relevant to his practice of architecture. He did believe, however, that "archaeology" was a useful, even necessary, adjunct to architecture—a sister science, perhaps. The nature of the relationship between the two was a problem with which he and all the other revivalist architects had to grapple. Godwin's lectures and articles are full of warnings against the misuse of archaeology in architectural design: "I have always maintained that we must have a little of it, only to help us recover certain principles of our art which have been lost, but, on the other hand, it is quite possible that we may have too much of it; that instead of its leading us to think for ourselves it may entice us into an almost boundless ocean of antiquarianism; instead of its bringing out our own powers of design it may make us mere collectors and transcribers of the designs of others."[75]

This anxiety lies behind Godwin's most striking divergence from Robert Willis's method of studying old buildings. Like Willis he studied, classified, and recorded buildings, but one writer noted that, in addition, Godwin had "struck out a somewhat new line for himself, for he has ventured to criticise the work of our forefathers with a courage, which, were it not based on sound judgment and wide knowledge, would be called presumption."[76] Willis was not an architect, whereas Godwin approached buildings from the point of view of a practitioner.

Godwin's lectures during the excursions of the Bristol Society of Architects are a mixture of Willisian "dissection," critical aesthetic commentary, and practical instruction. An excursion in 1864 to Gloucester Cathedral found him occupying the "unpleasant office . . . of fault finder to the Bristol Society of Architects" and employing some splendid invective such as "paralytic masonry" and "architecture in fits" to describe some portions of the building in a lecture entitled "Notes on Architectural Design Illustrated by Gloster [*sic*] Cathedral."[77] The title gave notice that the antiquarian excursion was to have a practical architectural purpose. Toward the end of his lecture, Godwin asked: "If the instruction and warning which the Cathedral of this town has offered us today be rejected. . . . If the architectural design as exemplified in Gloucester Cathedral is to be of no use to us what business have we here? . . . . our excursions had better cease."[78]

The purpose of a critical appraisal of an old building was to distill "principles" of architecture from which the architect could then develop his own designs. Godwin suggested that the principles to be learned from Gloucester Cathedral were those of simplicity of arrangement and of proportion and muscular development, by which he meant the relationship of the solids to the voids, "in a word, the power of the design."[79] There were parts that were to point a warning: in particular the overrichness of some of its ornamentation.

The idea of copying principles rather than forms or motifs was far from new. A. W. N. Pugin had suggested it, as had Scott, Street, Burges, and a number of other writers on the Gothic Revival.[80] In a sense it was the only possible theoretical solution to the problem of a revival that aimed for both archaeological accuracy and originality. For Godwin this was the legitimate use of antiquarian study. In 1871, writing on the Gothic Revival, Godwin stated that "No amount of mere *form* will give us a living architecture. We

Fig. 2-4. E. W. Godwin. Design for gatehouse, Dromore Castle, County Limerick, Ireland, ca. 1869–71. Pen and ink on tracing paper; 5⁹⁄₁₆ x 8½ in. (14.3 x 21.5 cm). British Architectural Library Manuscripts Collection, RIBA, London (G/IR.3/2/8).

must have the *raison d'être*, the principles of the construction of that form manifested."[81]

Theory and practice, inevitably, came adrift from time to time. Godwin did borrow "scraps" from buildings and incorporated them almost unchanged into designs. For example, a gatehouse design for Dromore (fig. 2-4) took the corbelling of its machicolations directly from Kilmacleurine Castle (fig. 2-5).[82] Godwin also borrowed the triangular ornaments on the facade of Northampton Town Hall (fig. 2-6) from Ruskin's illustrations of the archivolt on the Duomo of Murano (fig. 2-7)[83] and used similar motifs in his pulpit at Saint Christopher's Church in Ditteridge (fig. 2-8). A shop doorway sketched by Godwin at Saint Lô, Normandy, and published in the *Building News*[84] appears, slightly altered in proportion, as the front door of the parsonage at Moor Green, Nottinghamshire (see fig. 6-46).[85]

The temptation for Godwin to copy directly from old buildings was undoubtedly fueled by his habit of extensive sketching and measuring. He admired his friend William Burges for his powers of "adaptation and assimilation" and for his ability to be "an evolutionist or developist rather than a revivalist."[86] Burges had borrowed an idea from the thirteenth-century French architect Villard de Honnecourt, which was to eschew the careful, accurate antiquarian measured sketch in favor of creative sketching. There are scattered examples of this in Godwin's own sketchbooks, such as a design "after a church I saw at Rothersthorpe. July 25.68,"[87] or another, suggested by a building he had seen at

Fig. 2-5. E. W. Godwin. Kilmacleurine Castle, 1869. Pencil on paper; 6 x 3¾ in. (15.3 x 9.5 cm). British Architectural Library Manuscripts Collection, RIBA, London (G/IR.3/2/3/2).

Fig. 2-6. E. W. Godwin. Triangular ornaments on the facade of Northampton Town Hall, Northampton. Built 1861-64. Photographed in 1998.

Fig. 2-7. John Ruskin. Archivolt on the Duomo, Murano, Italy. From Ruskin, *Stones of Venice*, vol. 2 (1853), pl. 5.

Cadgwith in 1861,[88] or two designs for fountains (fig. 2-9), one "After Burges" and the other suggested by a fountain in a manuscript Godwin had seen in the British Museum.[89] This was an attempt to use the past creatively for design ideas and inspiration rather than merely as a source to copy.

Godwin warned against another danger of archaeology, stemming from overenthusiasm for the past. In 1872 he wrote, "To the delight an artist would naturally experience as each new treasure of embroidery, furniture, armour, jewellery, &c, dawned upon him, may be traced many of the

anachronisms in the best of our modern Gothic works."[90] He added dismissively that "there is a certain boyish romance about all this, no doubt . . . ," as if he had never himself indulged in this, or any, enthusiasm. Godwin was particularly prone to the anachronisms he attributed to overenthusiasm for the past. At Castle Ashby he designed a kitchen garden with vast pier walls topped by tiled coping (see fig. 6-39). After Dromore, his mind may have been running on Irish castles. One sketch (fig. 2-10) in a letter to Lady Alwyne Compton of September 20, 1867, shows a for-

Fig. 2-8. E. W. Godwin. Pulpit at Saint Christopher's Church, Ditteridge, Wiltshire, 1859. Photographed in 1998.

Fig. 2-9. E. W. Godwin. Designs for fountains, ca. 1860–77. Sketchbook. Red ink; 9 x 6 ¼ in. (22.9 x 15.9 cm). Trustees of the Victoria and Albert Museum, London, E.270-1963: 6.

tified, battlemented wall several feet thick. A flat-coped wall seemed to Godwin "a most objectionable thing as it is easy to scale."[91] Lady Alwyne remarked in her memorandum book that "the 'herbary' . . . was a device of Mr Godwin who delights in Mediaeval subtleties—The roofs to the walls are said to make too much shadow . . . he did not consult the gardener here, who disapproves of them."[92] In 1878 Godwin admitted to having fallen into the trap of anachronism, by creating designs that were archaeologically correct but functionally flawed. Neither Northampton Town Hall nor Dromore Castle were appropriate to the

age. An archway at Dromore, which might have been all right for the period of Edward I, "was decidedly too low for the time of Queen Victoria. A four-in-hand . . . could not go in there."[93]

By 1879, a year after he had written this critique of his own work at Dromore and Northampton, Godwin was well aware that he had broken out of the straitjacket of the revival and built something full of "art and originality," and "different to the conventional."[94] These buildings, to which he owes much of his fame today, were the studio houses in Tite Street, and especially those he designed for Frank Miles and James McNeill Whistler. Godwin's continual harping on the theme of learning "principles" rather than borrowing forms perhaps provides a clue to the sudden and surprising emergence of his acclaimed "proto-modern" studio designs. Gloucester cathedral and Frank Miles's house (see fig. 3-26) appear to belong to entirely different worlds, yet it is precisely those qualities Godwin most admired in Gloucester[95] that appear in the studio design: muscularity, balance, simplicity of arrangement, and the pleasing proportions of solids and voids. Another lesson of Gloucester had been that these qualities could be ruined by overelaborate decoration. In the facade of the first design for Frank Miles's studio, the decoration is restrained, and used sparingly.

In his lecture entitled "Studios and Mouldings," published in 1879, Godwin wrote about the influence of Greek antiquities on his design of Whistler's White House (see

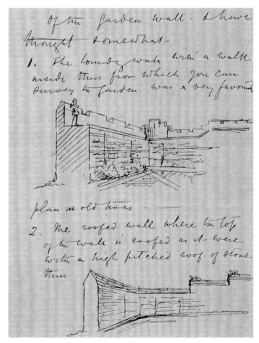

Fig. 2-10. Letter from E. W. Godwin to Lady Alwyne Compton, dated 20 September 1867, discussing the walls of the kitchen garden. Compton Family Documents, Castle Ashby. Courtesy the Marquess of Northampton.

Fig. 2-11. E. W. Godwin. "Jacobean Oak Sideboard," 1885. Drawn by Maurice B. Adams. From *Building News* 48 (15 May 1885): 785 (detail).

fig. 6-52): "when we talk about architecture as a fine art we mean refinement, finesse, gentleness; and these qualities we can always trace in Greek mouldings. At Whistler's house there is an entrance doorway in Portland stone, in which I have endeavoured to express these ideas."[96] Godwin explic itly linked the study and understanding of the principles of Greek work and thirteenth-century Gothic with the evo lution of an "architecture of the future."[97] He also implied that his studio designs were the first step in that evolution. There is a certain irony in the fact that the Metropolitan Board of Works, which rejected the first design for Frank Miles's studio house and forced Godwin to alter his design for the White House, was advised by the architect George Vulliamy, who had signed Godwin's acceptance papers wel coming him as a promising new member of the Archaeo logical Institute of Great Britain and Ireland nearly thirty years before, in 1851.[98]

Furniture design did not have to carry the weight of the ory that Godwin applied to architecture. There were no jeremiads about the perils of archaeology or anxieties about where the Gothic Revival was taking its adherents. Beyond a few mild remarks about stop chamfers, Oxford frames, and cabinets with shrinelike roofs having had their day,[99] God win had no qualms even about reproduction. His furniture designs run the full gamut, from strikingly original to out right and unrepentantly imitative. The "Shakspere" (sic) fur niture set included a sideboard with turned pendants below the canopy, which owed its general appearance to the seventeenth-century press cupboard. This was considered "original" enough to be the subject of a patent registra tion,[100] whereas the armchair in this set (see fig. 8-43) was a reproduction of a chair said to have belonged to Shake speare.[101] Another suite of furniture manufactured by

William Watt to Godwin's designs was "of English charac ter . . . to the close of the fifteenth century." It was exhib ited at the Royal School of Art Needlework, South Kensington, in 1884, and one writer noticed that it included several pieces of reproduction furniture, including a fire place from Haddon Hall.[102] By contrast, the "Jacobean Oak Sideboard" (fig. 2-11) published in the *Building News* in 1885 has Jacobean elements—such as the cup-and-cover mold ings on the legs, the acanthus brackets, and the pendants below the canopy—and precedents can be found for the open-rail doors in the upper portion, but the proportions

Fig. 2-12. E. W. Godwin. Woman seated on a klismos chair, from a Greek vase in the British Museum, ca. 1874–86. Pencil on paper; 9 x 5½ in. (22.8 x 14 cm). British Architectural Library Manuscripts Collection, RIBA, London (G/GR.2/26/6).

Fig. 2-13. E. W. Godwin. Design for tables with klismos-style legs, ca. 1872–79. Sketchbook. Pencil and watercolor; 5 ⅞ x 4 in. (15 x 10.3 cm). Trustees of the Victoria and Albert Museum, London, E.233-1963: 31.

and the central leg give the piece a strikingly unusual appearance.[103]

Godwin's use of the Greek klismos form—a type of chair with splayed curved legs and a curved back originating in ancient Greece—shows the same range, from copyism to creativity. He sketched an example of a klismos from a vase in the British Museum (fig. 2-12)[104] and made two designs which are near-reproductions: one appeared sketched into the courtyard of Godwin's design for Lillie Langtry's house, and the other is in an undated sketchbook (see fig. 8-37).[105] Two small tables designed by Godwin (fig. 2-13) have the exaggerated sabre leg that is a feature of the klismos, and the influence of the form can be seen in a design for a washstand in which the curve of the legs is continued up into the towel holders at the sides of the piece in much the same way that the curving stiles of the klismos continue past the seat to form the back rest (fig. 2-14).[106]

In decorative design Godwin seems to have been happy to plunder the past for design motifs and to use ideas without reference to the media in which or on which they were originally expressed. A carpet from Holbein, which Godwin had sketched from the *Handbook of Painting,*

Fig. 2-14. E. W. Godwin. Design for a washstand, 1876. Sketchbook. Pencil and watercolor; 5 ⅞ x 4 in. (15 x 10.3 cm). Trustees of the Victoria and Albert Museum, London, E.233-1963: 35.

Fig. 2-15. E. W. Godwin. Design for wall decoration, ca. 1870–86. Sketchbook. Pencil, ink, and watercolor; 6 ¾ x 4 ¾ in. (17.1 x 11.8 cm). Trustees of the Victoria and Albert Museum, London, E.285-1963: insert 1.

"scraps" and a compositional idea have been welded together into a coherent, harmonious, original design.

This fireplace also demonstrates the wide range of Godwin's knowledge. In 1878 he dispensed the following advice to architects: "Be archaeologists— . . . know all about the past; study Greek, Gothic, Renaissance, the Roman and later developments, study it in all its different phases and countries. . . Study all; take what good [you can] from every country and every age; but work in no particular style."[112] The ambition to "study all" inevitably compromised the depth of Godwin's antiquarian studies and collided with one of his characteristics as an antiquary, that is, the impulse to categorize, catalogue, and organize. This

Fig. 2-16. E. W. Godwin. Fireplace in the studio ingle, Frank Miles's House, 44 Tite Street, Chelsea, 1879. Cast iron. Made by Shillit and Shorland. Photographed in 1997.

became an idea for a wall decoration.[107] A Greek floral meander from an archaic Greek jug in the British Museum was used on a design for a toilet set made in about 1876 and reappeared as a diaper in a wall decoration (fig. 2-15).[108] In the same wall decoration, Godwin used a palmette motif from an archaic Greek three-handled jar, which reappeared in 1878 in cast iron on a Shillit and Shorland fireplace in Frank Miles's studio (fig. 2-16).[109] A design for a frieze of tiles (see fig. 11-15) was taken directly from a border in the Arundel Psalter, which also provided a series of diapers and decorative circular motifs that Godwin suggested could be used in the painted decoration of buildings.[110]

This archaeological kleptomania is mitigated by Godwin's strong sense of design. Frank Miles's fireplace is often assumed to be Japanese in inspiration (and is, in composition). The pattern on the left is archaic Greek, and the one on the right appears in a sketchbook as "Indian."[111] Two

Fig. 2-17. E. W. Godwin. Illustrations from *Dress and Its Relation to Health and Climate*. As reprinted in *Building News* 47 (25 July 1884): 120.

had shown itself during Godwin's pupilage, when he had compiled endless comprehensive lists of antiquarian information. In the 1850s, rather than merely reading Spenser, he had "read and re-read, indexed and annotated" the book in company with an old schoolfellow.[113] His instinct was to be comprehensive.

Depth and range are difficult to achieve together. Godwin's published oeuvre as an antiquary is mostly journalistic, and in this, he did achieve range. His articles on Shakespeare's plays alone required him to have a working knowledge of the architecture and costume of a large number of different periods in different countries. His surviving papers, however, also contain the bones of a number of failed, overambitious books: one on armor (which included every example of Greek armor depicted in the vase rooms of the British Museum); another on Irish Antiquities; another, which consisted of a "catalogue of all the illuminated MSS in the Brit. Mus. annotated and illustrated by me."[114]

There was also a book on his earliest antiquarian enthusiasm: historical dress. In 1875 he wrote, "Even with the elaborate Dictionnaire of M. Viollet-le-Duc before me, with Jacquemin's effective plates, with the splendid work of Hefner, I am inclined to think that *the* history of costume has yet to be written."[115] However, as a writer in the *Standard* pointed out in 1882, this work would require "not only a certain historical faculty, but a knowledge also of the outlines of history and of the details of dress in every country throughout the world."[116]

This was too great a task for one man, and Godwin's 1884 publication, *Dress and its Relation to Health and Climate* (fig. 2-17), although it was wide-ranging lacked sufficient depth to be *the* book. The *Standard* further declared costume to be a study "which, unlike most others, can be followed more advantageously by a Society than by a single individual."[117] In 1882 Godwin founded the Costume Society, which held its first meeting in his chambers in July. From the start its aim was publication, and at the initial gathering Godwin was asked to get estimates for lithographic printing of 2,000 copies of a sample illustration.[118]

There was no shortage of published illustrations of costume already available, but Godwin complained of the "incomplete and disjointed condition of things."[119] There were isolated drawings in publications such as *Archaeologia* and the *Archaeolgical Journal*, and in books on armor, on ecclesiastical costume and monumental effigies, and on classical and medieval dress. The many sources of information were too widely scattered to be helpful to the occasional users such as painters, sculptors, theatrical managers, or actors looking for information about how to create a historically accurate costume. One aim of the society, therefore, was to circumvent the confusion by gathering examples in one place and acting as an advisory body. For a small fee, an inquirer would "receive without unnecessary delay a coloured drawing showing him precisely what he wished to know."[120]

Another problem at the time was that the published works available were riddled with mistakes. In 1880 Godwin listed "some of the grosser errors" in the English edition of Lacroix's book on costume which was "we are sorry to say, in the hands of a large number of students."[121] In 1875 he had reviewed the first volume of J. R. Planché's *Cyclopaedia of Costume,* which was "marred by woodcuts which are bad as woodcuts, bad as drawings, and bad as illustration of the subject."[122] Planché had ignored "the three great, real, trustworthy sources for the illustration of costume, viz., sculpture, painting, and MS. drawings" and had used large numbers of woodcuts taken from copies.[123] The Costume Society's published drawings were all to be taken from original sources, and their fidelity to the originals was to be directly and personally verified by expert members of the society.

The research was intended to be useful. The *Standard* pointed out that "painters and designers of costumes for the stage are the two classes of artists who should derive most advantage from the labours of the new Association."[124] Godwin had previously attacked both groups. In his theatrical criticism he had devoted as much energy to denouncing historically inaccurate costume and mise-en-scène as to discussing the acting. In 1875 several painters exhibiting at the Royal Academy had come in for some vitriolic criticism on the subject of their depiction of dress, which Godwin considered to be "travestied . . . vulgarised . . . [and] ludicrous."[125] To be truly useful to painters, sculptors, actors, and managers, the Costume Society had to be both accurate and comprehensive.

It was an enormously ambitious project, even for a group that would eventually include some three hundred members and subscribers.[126] This was nothing less than an attempt to "further a complete and scientific knowledge of historic costume."[127] The list of members and subscribers of 1883 reads like a Who's Who of the British artistic, theatrical, and museum worlds, and included distinguished honorary foreign members and a number of institutions.

At the first general meeting of the society, Godwin had argued that "we should be careful to remember that we are a scientific society for the purpose of research and teaching, and not for the purpose of issuing pretty pictures."[128] There are hundreds of drawings of costume among Godwin's papers that testify to this aim, including the published plates, which are signed by the copyist and certified by another member.[129] Usually these signatures were those of Godwin, E. Maunde Thompson (Keeper of Manuscripts at the British Museum), and Burges's friend the Baron de Cosson, whose particular interest was armor.

The costumes are depicted in outline, without shading, and the lines are often much clearer and cleaner than those of the original sources. In a painting in the illuminated manuscript called Arundel 38, for example, a strip of ermine that conceals the fastenings at King Henry V's neck was painted over by the original illuminator whereas the Costume Society drawing shows the trimming—the correct mode of dress—and erases the visible error made in the original.[130] In the plates still at the proof stage, the concern for accuracy shows itself in corrections made to the drawings: the border of the mantle of a figure from the Tiberius C.vi manuscript has been annotated "to be made more accurate."[131] A drawing of Saint Sebastian, from Carlo Crivelli's *Madonna della Rondine* altarpiece in the National Gallery, is marked for slight alterations to be made to the buttons on the collar.[132] Most interesting of all is a drawing of two figures on tracing paper (fig. 2-18), which shows the Costume Society at work. It is covered with annotations by Godwin and the painters Henry Woods and Luke Fildes: "?what is here on the belt / an open buckle with tongue / can this ornament be made out? / pearls I think HW / Where do these taps and points come from? / Impossible to say. I believe they come through sleeve."[133] Most of the questions are in Godwin's handwriting.

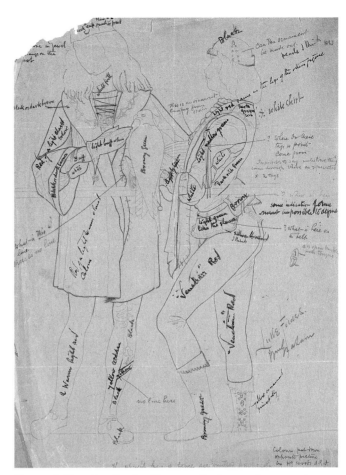

Fig. 2-18. Drawing for the Costume Society with annotations and corrections by E.W. Godwin, Luke Fildes, and Henry Woods, ca. 1882–84. Pencil and colored ink on paper. Trustees of the Victoria and Albert Museum, London, Archive of the Theatre Museum (Blythe House), Godwin collection, box 4.

The society published only one volume, *The Costume Society* (fig. 2-19), which was published in 1883, although plates were prepared for a second volume. The publication was flawed in several ways: it was almost exclusively medieval; there were too few depictions of female dress; and, as Baron de Cosson pointed out, the drawings were "to my mind too Archaeological and not sufficiently artistic."[134] The baron reminded Godwin that there were many subscribers who took part in the society simply "to *look* at the plates, rather than to make use of them."[135] There were too few subscribers and consequently too little money. The last dated meeting of the office holders of the society was held in July 1884. A meeting was called for August, but it seems that by then the society had collapsed.

It may have been in response to Godwin's work with the Costume Society that Arthur Lasenby Liberty decided to employ him as a consultant to Liberty's newly opened

Fig. 2-19. E. W. Godwin. Plate 3 from *The Costume Society*, part 1 (1883). Trustees of the Victoria and Albert Museum, London, 980 452. *Checklist no. 104*

over the door of Notre Dame de Corbeil. The decorated border at the neck was taken from a textile found in a tomb at Notre Dame in Paris. The girdle belt was from an example illustrated in Viollet le Duc's *Dictionnaire raisonné du moblier Français*. Although this sketch design survives among Godwin's collection of Costume Society drawings, it does not properly belong there among the accurate, perfectly transcribed copies of images of historical dress but relates more closely to Godwin's work as a theatrical designer and consultant.

If the Costume Society demonstrates the science of archaeology, Godwin's work for the theater demonstrates the art. In 1885 in an article in the *Dramatic Review*, Godwin wrote that the purpose of the archaeologist was "to make history a reality" but added that "the stage demands of the antiquary something more than this. Stage pictures of the past times should be treated . . . as life itself is treated by the dramatist. The archaeologist, in a word, must be *an artist*."[140]

In 1874 and 1875, Godwin published his most extensive work of theatrical archaeology: a series of articles in the *Architect* entitled "The Architecture and Costume of Shakespere's [*sic*] Plays" in which he attempted to "fix" the time of each play and discussed the appropriate historical sources for staging and costume. Above all, in this series of articles Godwin argued that productions should be designed rather than just researched: "the mere archaeologist is not all that is wanted. There must be joined to the antiquarian knowledge more or less of the architects' skill in composition or design; for although every detail of a scene may by itself be correct, it may so happen that in the aggregate the individual bits of even careful archaeological research may be dominated by the absurdity of the general construction."[141]

In his articles on Shakespeare's plays Godwin did not confine himself to discussing the static visual mise-en-scène, but also commented on matters that touched on the acting and directing. For instance he claimed that the manners of the period of *The Merchant of Venice* "were characterised by courtesy combined with a stately dignified action, and that what we call stiffness of manner was then regarded as quite correct," adding that "correctness of costume, and scenery, and properties, and furniture is all very well, but if, through it all, we see nineteenth-century action, modern style, . . . then the picture must be discordant, and the dramatic representation woefully incomplete."[142]

Archaeology, then, was merely a foundation for theatrical art, and the aim of the art was what Godwin called "the illusion I long to witness."[143] By this he meant a production with costume, scenery, and properties all historically accurate and in harmony with each other, and the actors'

costume department. The text of the department's advertising material might have come straight from Godwin's book, *Dress and Its Relation to Health and Climate*, stating that "the craft of dressmaking should be established upon some hygienic, intelligible and progressive basis."[136] In addition the department was set up "for the study and execution of costumes embracing all periods, together with such modifications of really beautiful examples as may be adapted to the conventionalities of modern life without rendering them eccentric or bizarre."[137] One of these costumes, which appears in Liberty's 1893 catalogue as "Norman 12th Century,"[138] is based on a design by Godwin (fig. 2-20).[139] This is taken from a statue Godwin had sketched at Chartres, with additions from other sources. The bodice came from a statue of Queen Clothilde, which was situated gestures, bearing, speech, and stage business so natural and unstagy in the historical context that the illusion of reality was perfect. Occasionally he could glimpse isolated parts of this illusion in the contemporary theater. Of a production of *Macbeth* at Sadler's Wells theater, he wrote: "The costumes here and there were strangely true; one waiting woman might have walked out of the pages of Cleopatra C.viii, or Claudius B.iv."[144] What Godwin wanted to see in the theater was history, living and breathing.

What Godwin lacked, however, was control of the production. Much of his design work for the theater consisted of costumes for individual actors and actresses, where a single point of archaeological accuracy was all he could hope to achieve. The harmony of the whole was beyond his control. In these circumstances there was no concern to make the costumes "so natural as to be unobtrusive,"[145] even though he had insisted on this point in his Shakespeare articles. In 1875, for instance, he designed a costume for Ellen Terry to wear as Juliet. In a letter to her describing the design, he wrote, "I have made the thing as swell as possible *too* swell perhaps for history's sake."[146] Godwin's careful listing and quoting of sources in his Shakespeare articles leaves the impression that his costumes were largely reproductions of the illustrations in these sources, but his detailed description of Juliet's clothing for the ball scene shows him creating a costume. The headdress, for instance, was to consist of a gold band with white daisies at intervals, over a caul made of pearls and gold cord (fig. 2-21).[147] The band of daisies was an idea taken from an illuminated manuscript in the British Museum.[148] In the original, however, the band was a ribbon with small red roses at intervals. The caul is a more elaborate version of one depicted in a different illumination in the same manuscript.[149] The two originals had been altered and combined by Godwin to form a new design.

Godwin's ambition to create the illusion of living history on the stage was hampered by his relative powerlessness as a consultant archaeologist. The programs for John Coleman's production of *Henry V* at the Queen's Theatre in 1876 credited Godwin with the "superintendence" of the archaeology of the play, but in a letter to Coleman dated September 2, Godwin listed a number of mistakes made by Coleman which "outrage not merely history but common sense."[150] These had not been corrected by the first performance, and Burges's subsequent cannonade in the *Architect* criticizing the archaeological errors in the piece,[151] which is usually considered a tongue-in-cheek dig at Godwin,[152] was most likely set up by Burges and Godwin together in order to give Godwin a chance publicly to disclaim responsibility for most of the mistakes. Godwin's letter to Coleman

Fig. 2-20. E. W. Godwin. Annotated costume sketches, based in part on a twelfth-century statue at Chartres, France, ca. 1884. Pencil and watercolor on paper; 7⅝ x 4⅜ in. (19.3 x 11 cm). Trustees of the Victoria and Albert Museum, London, S.191-1998. *Checklist no. 106*

demonstrates how little he was able to exert any authority as a mere "superintendent" of the archaeology. He even felt he had to apologize for sending a list of suggested changes,

Fig. 2-21. E. W. Godwin. Design for Ellen Terry's "Juliet" headdress, 1875. Pencil and watercolor on paper. Trustees of the Victoria and Albert Museum, London, Archive of the Theatre Museum (Blythe House), Godwin collection, box 3.

writing: "I wish to avoid as much as possible even the show of interference."[153]

That this changed in the 1880s was due partly to Godwin's increasing reputation as a theatrical "authority." In 1885 Godwin recounted how, many years earlier, he had to threaten the leading actress in an unnamed production, telling her that "my name is published as responsible for the historical accuracy of the representation, and if there is anything on the stage opposed to my designs, I shall not hesitate to say so in print."[154] Godwin's situation in 1885 was quite different: "Now-a-days . . . I do not threaten to write to the papers. My work is known fairly well by this time."[155] Even so, Godwin often did have recourse to the press. It was a brave actor or actress who asked him for advice and then ignored it. An anonymous review in the British Architect

probably written by Godwin discusses the costumes of Romeo and Juliet worn by Mr. R. B. Mantel and Miss Wallis. The reviewer praises the former, who had worn his Godwin-designed costume, and pokes fun at the latter, who had not worn hers.[156] Godwin was equally capable of praising or condemning the theatrical managers who controlled the visual ensemble of productions, and this ability tended to reinforce his archaeological suggestions. The general climate was also changing: the 1880s and 1890s were the apogee of "archaeological realism" in the theater, with contributions from Lord Leighton, Professor Warr, Henry Irving at the Lyceum, and Wilson Barrett at the Princess's Theatre.[157] Barrett and Godwin collaborated in 1883 on the archaeological tour-de-force, Claudian. Unlike Coleman, who had made a fiasco of Godwin's "superintendence" of Henry V, Barrett allowed Godwin to have considerable control over the archaeology of the production.

Godwin wrote an account of his researches for Claudian in the form of an open letter to Barrett, which was published in the British Architect and in pamphlet form.[158] His main problem was his reliance on secondary sources. Although Barrett was to fund Godwin's trip to Denmark to research the costumes for a production of Hamlet in 1884, a journey to Istanbul was clearly out of the question. "I wanted to go to Byzantium for Claudian," Godwin said rather wistfully to an interviewer from a contemporary journal, "but that is rather far."[159]

Godwin's methodology with his theatrical research mirrors that of his architectural research. He aimed to find good copies of contemporary illustrations if he was unable to see the originals.[160] The most important source of information for costume was found in the reliefs on the pedestal of the obelisk of Theodosius in the Hippodrome at Constantinople. For these he consulted A. Stuart Murray, a friend at the British Museum, who recommended the illustrations of the pedestal in Seroux d'Agincourt's Histoire de l'Art. Murray wrote, "you will find the engravings much behind what you would like: but I can't think of any better & have seen much worse. Photographs would not be easily got."[161] A handwritten list of "Authorities"[162] documents Godwin's attempts to overcome the problem of relying on secondary sources and to test his witnesses. He did find a photograph of the obelisk of Theodosius. He duplicated certain work, using several sources for comparison purposes, such as O. Gebhardt's edition of the Codex Rossanensis for examples of borders, which he compared with borders in the Codex Alexandrium. The British Museum contained Godwin's most important primary sources of information. In his pamphlet on Claudian, Godwin acknowledged that he had had to use published illus-

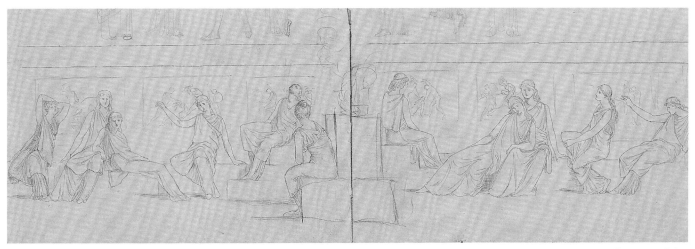

Fig. 2-22. Artist unknown. Drawing of the chorus in *Helena in Troas*, 1886. Pencil on paper; 7 x 20 in. (17.8 x 57 cm). Collection of the National Trust, Ellen Terry Memorial Museum, Smallhythe Place, Kent.

trations but added, "where possible to me I have gone to the objects preserved in our museum cases belonging to the period: e.g., swords, spears, shields, axes, personal ornaments of gold, silver, bronze, precious stones, cameos, &c."[163]

After the production, a caricaturist rather unfairly satirized the eminent archaeologist and the interfering and ignorant manager, who attempted to alter the "S.P.Q.R." of the Roman banners to an alphabetical "P.Q.R.S."[164] In fact Barrett seems only to have discarded two of Godwin's archaeological creations—a litter (see fig. 12-24) and a red and purple tunic with appliquéd decoration that Barrett refused to wear, "fearing it to be much too garish."[165] Godwin had adapted the tunic from that of "a little Roman bronze warrior in the British Museum."[166]

In his book *Resistible Theatres*, John Stokes argued that in the face of the power of theatrical managers to ignore the suggestions of their archaeological advisors, Godwin was "obliged to invent a new role for himself, and indeed for the modern theatre: that of 'producer,' a man endowed with final artistic control over a whole production, and complete power over the other participants."[167] In the last three years of his life, Godwin succeeded in expanding his role as archaeological superintendent into direction, production, and management. This was a logical step: Godwin's stated aim in 1875 in his Shakespeare articles had been to combine the archaeologically accurate costume and scenery with the correct historical stage action.[168]

In his collaborations with Wilson Barrett, Godwin had been able to make directorial suggestions, but ultimate authority still lay with Barrett. In the summer of 1884 Godwin took control of the production, direction, and management of a successful open-air production of the forest scenes of *As You Like It*, performed by Lady Archibald Campbell's Pastoral Players in Coombe Wood near Kingston-upon-Thames. Godwin and the Pastoral Players went on to perform adaptations of John Fletcher's *Faithfull Shepherdesse* in 1885, and Tennyson's *Fair Rosamund* in 1886, the same year that Godwin produced, directed, and managed John Todhunter's *Helena in Troas*. Finally, he was in a position to mold whole productions, with only financial considerations to hamper the creation of the perfect illusion.

In these productions, Godwin's archaeology immediately expanded from the static visual ensemble on stage into stage movement and music. The women of the chorus of *Helena in Troas* were rehearsed until they could move gracefully and arrange themselves into moving, harmonious pictures. A series of line drawings show the attitudes into which the chorus sank while resting: they are visually striking, and some are recognizable poses from Greek sculpture (fig. 2-22).[169] A surviving photograph taken during a performance of *The Faithfull Shepherdesse* shows the cast paying homage to a statue of Pan (fig. 2-23).[170] Godwin had researched the dances, taking notes from a Roman prose fantasy, *The Golden Ass*, by Lucius Apuleius. As for music, in 1875 Godwin had argued that "there can be no possible excuse if the characteristic music of the age is omitted when the text or stage business suggests its introduction."[171] He wrote to a Mr. Lawson in March 1884 asking him to help with *As You Like It*. "What we want is not only the songs and music . . . but hunting horn business played in the real distance & coming nearer. . . . A German Doctor of music has offered, but before he was accepted I suggested you as being the true Archaeological musician of the day."[172]

Fig. 2-23. A scene from *The Faithfull Shepherdesse* as it was performed in Coombe Wood, Surrey, 1885. Trustees of the Victoria and Albert Museum, London, Archive of the Theatre Museum (Blythe House), S.165-1998. *Checklist no. 145*

Archaeologically speaking, *Helena in Troas* was the most ambitious of Godwin's productions of the 1880s because in it he attempted not only to create a historically correct picture upon the stage but also to draw the whole audience into the illusion by re-creating an entire Greek theater inside Hengler's Circus in London (see fig. 9-23). In the program Godwin wrote, "My intention has been to give to the story stage surroundings like those which I suppose a play on such a subject may have received at Athens or Corinth in the days of Sophocles."[173] In effect, Godwin added another layer to the audience's perception of the historical truth of what they saw by placing them inside that truth, in the position of the historical spectators of the drama.

A reviewer in the *Morning Post* wrote of the stage at Hengler's Circus that "Mr E. W. Godwin had to rely . . . rather upon 'inward consciousness', aided by scholarly tradition, than upon the testimony of vision, there being no existing example to furnish matter for architectural illustration,"[174] but this was not true. The Odeum of Regilla in Athens, the theater of Herodes Atticus at Dramyssus, and the great theater at Epidaurus had all been excavated by

1886. Most importantly, by 1865 the theater of Dionysus had been uncovered on the Athenian Acropolis, and drawings had been published in Germany,[175] though not in Britain. Godwin must have been aware of this discovery: Thomas Henry Dyer's *Ancient Athens*,[176] which was one of Godwin's sources for his Greek theater, incorporated information from the excavation. One of Godwin's correspondents wrote that the whole subject of Greek theaters needed to be reviewed in the light of the new information from Athens,[177] which tended to cast doubt on Godwin's other major source of published information, J. W. Donaldson's *Theatre of the Greeks*.[178] Godwin followed Dyer more closely than Donaldson; for example, his stage was between four and five feet high, as Dyer recommended, rather than twelve feet, as suggested by Donaldson.[179]

As for the costumes, Godwin wrote to Cecil Smith of the British Museum, asking for information about the theatrical masks worn in Classical Greek theater and about a voice amplifier that he believed must have been used to allow Classical actors to be heard.[180] At this point in the planning of the production, Godwin seems to have been intending to stage the play in Greek theatrical costume.

Greek actors wore exaggerated, bulky, padded costumes with masks and stiltlike shoes. To costume his own actors in this way would have been correct, but obtrusive, unnatural, and stagy. Some time after March 1886, Godwin stopped looking for authentic Greek theatrical costume and began instead to design dress correct to the daily life of the time of the play's production, with additional notes taken from the Homeric poems.[181] The costumes and masks of the Classical theater were abandoned, and in their place Godwin began to create a hybrid: Classical Greek with Homeric accents, close to the spirit of the play, which was itself a hybrid, but not to the history of the Classical theater, nor to Homer, nor to the time of Troy.

Oscar Wilde wrote of Godwin's production: "The performance was not intended to be an absolute reproduction of the Greek stage in the fifth century before Christ: it was simply the presentation in Greek form of a poem conceived in the Greek spirit; and the secret of its beauty was the perfect correspondence of form and matter, the delicate equilibrium of spirit and sense."[182] Godwin had created his "perfect illusion I long to witness"; it was not historical, although it had its roots in history. The purpose of archaeology was no longer to fix a play in real time,

matching its individual elements of costume, scenery, and behavior to that time, but to discover and realize on stage the "spirit" of an age and to harmonize all the elements with that spirit. The science of archaeology, in other words, had become merely a springboard for the imagination.

This is akin to what Godwin aimed to achieve with his architecture. His theory that the architect should study the principles rather than copy the forms of old buildings often fell down in practice. Nevertheless, the coherent thread that runs through his career is of design being inspired by but transcending the scientific study of the past. The "spirit" of an age was not ultimately recoverable through facts, but through the imagination, and if that spirit was often expressed in Godwin's designs in the idiom of archaeology, it was also original.

A year before his death Godwin wrote, "the Archaeologist or Antiquary . . . is something more than a frequenter of museums and a patron of pigeon-holes. His method or mental attitude is of special significance; and you can no more make him off hand than you can make an artist: indeed he must have some of the artist's qualities, or, at least, be able to truly imagine in his mind's eye the features of the past and interpret its records and memorials."[183]

Note: Most published sources are cited below in shortened form (author's last name, abbreviated title, date of publication); full references will be found in the bibliography. Frequently cited archives are abbreviated; for a key to the abbreviations, also see the bibliography.

I would like to thank Fanny Baldwin and Aileen Reid for information about Godwin's theatrical and architectural activities; and Susan Weber Soros, Aileen Reid, Robert Arbuthnott, and Owen Wheatley for reading and commenting on the draft of this essay.

1. Godwin, "Taunton Tower" (21 August 1858): 572.

2. See Pevsner, *Some Architectural Writers* (1972).

3. Godwin, "Archaeology on the Stage," part 1 (8 February 1885): 19.

4. Godwin, "Old English or Saxon Building," parts 1–4 (14–28 August 1875).

5. Godwin, "Archaeology on the Stage," part 1 (8 February 1885): 19.

6. Godwin, "On Some Buildings I have Designed" (29 November 1878): 210.

7. V & A PD, E.267-1963, insert.

8. For a description of his early interest in the history of costume, see Godwin, "Cyclopaedia of Costume" (16 October 1875): 208.

9. "Mr E. W. Godwin on Architecture And Somerset Churches" [ca. 1864], lecture by Godwin to the Bristol Society of Architects, V & A AAD, 4/560-1988: cuttings book [cutting probably from *The Western Daily Press*].

10. See, for example, V & A AAD, 4/10-1980, p. 75, ledger.

11. Godwin, "On Some Buildings I have Designed" (29 November 1878): 210.

12. "I remember when I was a pupil at Bristol, that two of my contemporaries . . . were always sorely troubled when summoned by the master to accompany him in a measuring expedition" (Godwin, "British Architect Art Club" [19 January 1883]: 32. Godwin may have been a little unfair in his characterization of Armstrong: the prospectus of Godwin and Hine's *Architectural Antiquities of Bristol and Its Neighbourhood* was issued from Armstrong's office in Bristol. Armstong subscribed to the publication, and Godwin also acknowledged Armstrong's help in an article on the Priory of the Dominicans. (I am grateful to Aileen Reid for this information. CA)

13. "Mr E. W. Godwin on Architecture And Somerset Churches" in V & A AAD, 4/560-1988.

14. Godwin, "To Our Student Readers," part 2 (13 August 1880): 70.

15. Ibid. The books Godwin lists are: Parker, *Glossary of Terms used in . . . Architecture* (1836); Bloxham, *Principles of Gothic Architecture* (1829); Thomas

Rickman, *Attempt to discriminate the styles of architecture in England* (1817 and 1848); and Barr, *Anglican Church Architecture* (1842).

16. [Godwin], Notes on Current Events, "Mr Stone . . ." (9 April 1880): 169.

17. Bristol Society of Architects, "First Annual Report, for the year ending May 1851," Bristol Society of Architects Archives. *The Civil Engineer and Architect's Journal* was not exclusively practical, but its title does betray its priorities.

18. Letter from Godwin to R. M. Bryant, dated 15 December 1871, V & A AAD, 4/21-1988: 197–98.

19. For a list of these purchases, see V & A PD, E.225-1963: 10.

20. Rickman, *Attempt to discriminate the styles of architecture in England* (1817 and 1848); A. C. Pugin, *Specimens of Gothic Architecture* (1821–23); Britton, *Historical and descriptive accounts . . . of English Cathedrals*, vol. 4 (1836); ibid., vol. 5.

21. Godwin, "Gothic Revival" (2 December 1871): 271.

22. Godwin, "On Some Buildings I Have Designed" (29 November 1878): 211.

23. Nesfield, *Specimens of Mediaeval Architecture* (1862). Godwin knew and approved of the book as he awarded it as a prize for Architectural Drawing to a student member of the Bristol Society of Architects in 1864 (minute book entry dated 4 May 1864, Bristol Society of Architects). Burges's sketches were eventually published in 1870 ([Burges], *Architectural Drawings*), but his visits to France and Italy had taken place in the 1850s and 1860s. Godwin would have seen the unpublished drawings before 1870.

24. Godwin, "Painted Decoration" (3 August 1866): 507; Mandelgren, *Monuments scandinaves* (1862). Burges owned a copy of the book.

25. Godwin, "Photographs of the Architectural Photographic Association," part 1 (22 February 1867): 147–48; part 2 (1 March 1867): 164–66.

26. V & A TA, Godwin collection, box 1. Godwin used a photograph of the reliefs on the pedestal of the obelisk of Theodosius in the Hippodrome at Constantinople. This photograph is an item on the list of "authorities" for *Claudian,* handwritten inside Godwin's copy of his privately printed pamphlet, Godwin, "A Few Notes on . . . *Claudian*" (1883).

27. Godwin wrote, "There was once a little cross church in Somersetshire of great interest to us. We sketched it, and measured it, and photographed it till one fine day passing by we found it had been 'restored'" [Godwin], Notes On Current Events ([21 May 1880]: 241). G. E. Street was the culprit who had "restored" it, but the church is unidentified. Compare Burges on photography—"Measure much, sketch little, and, above all, keep your fingers out of chemicals"—quoted in Crook, *William Burges* (1981): 67.

28. Godwin, "To Our Student Readers" part 2 (13 August 1880): 70.

29. RIBA Mss, GoE 6/5/1 (G/Sax/1).

30. V & A PD, E.267-1963, inserted page at the front of the sketchbook.

31. V & A PD, E.225-1963, n.p.

32. V & A AAD, 4/538-1988.

33. V & A PD, E.225-1963, pp. 105, 107. Godwin had not seen the original manuscript, in Corpus Christi College, Cambridge, until some time after 1857, at which time he wrongly assumed the original to be in the British Museum (see Godwin, "Antiquarian Notes and Queries" [April 1857]: 157–58). Wyrcestre (ca. 1415–ca. 1491) was a Bristol burgess, who surveyed the town, measuring it in paces, and published his notes and measurements. [William de Wyrcestre], *Itineraria Simonis Simeonis et Willelmi de Worcestre Quibus accedit Tractatus de Metro, in quo traduntur regulae, a scriptoribus medii aevi in versibus Leoninis observatae MSS . . .* , ed. J. Nasmith (Cambridge, 1778).

34. RIBA Mss, GoE/7/3/1. Rev. John Louis Petit (1801–1868) was an architectural writer and artist, as well as clergyman.

35. RIBA Mss, GoE/3/6/25 (G/Bri.5.i-ii).

36. V & A PD, E.227-1963. This sketchbook contains Godwin's journal of the holiday in Cornwall with James Hine.

37. RIBA Mss, GoE/3/5/1 (G/Bri.1).

38. Godwin and Hine were joined in this venture by W. C. Burder, who engraved the plates and provided two of the drawings.

39. Godwin identifies this manuscript only as "Ms. Hobson." (I have been unable to locate it.)

40. John Evans, *Chronological Outline of the History of Bristol* (Bristol, 1824).

41. RIBA Mss, GoE/3/6/24 (G/Bri.7.i).

42. Godwin, "Ancient Coffin Slab" (December 1853): 182–83. For the other seven articles published in the *Archaeological Journal* see the Bibliography. Godwin also wrote several articles for the *Wiltshire Archaeological and Natural History Magazine.*

43. "Proceedings of Meetings at the Archaeological Institute" (1851): 322–40.

44. Godwin, "Ancient Coffin Slab" (December 1853): 182–83.

45. Draft letter from Godwin to Princess Louise, n.d., V & A AAD, 4/190-1988.

46. See Reid, "Dromore Castle" (1987): 135.

47. For Godwin's sketches of Oxford buildings, see V & A PD, E.225-1963. Robert Willis's lecture is reported in "Proceedings of Meetings at the Archaeological Institute," (1850): 315.

48. Godwin, "Architectural Description and history of Saint Peter's Church Colerne Wilts," RIBA Mss, GoE/4/4/4, p. xi, footnote (G/Wil.2/4).

49. Godwin, "Sir George Gilbert Scott" (5 April 1878): 155.

50. "Professor Willis" (6 March 1875): 134–35.

51. Ibid.

52. Godwin, "A Few Words to Architectural Students" (1 February 1878): 51.

53. Godwin, "Architectural Description and history of Saint Peter's Church Colerne Wilts," RIBA Mss, GoE/4/4/4.

54. Godwin, "An Account of the Church of St. John the Baptist, Colerne" (1857): 358–66.

55. Ibid.

56. Ibid.

57. The excursions of the society and the lectures of Godwin and others were extensively reported in the *Western Daily Press,* a Bristol newspaper. Cuttings from the paper are pasted into the minute book of the Bristol Society of Architects.

58. Godwin, "Bristol Cathedral" (March 1863): 38–63. This paper was first read in October 1862 at a meeting of the Bristol Society of Architects.

59. "An Antiquarian Tramp through Old Bristo" *Western Daily Press* (10 September 1864): 4.

60. Godwin, "Old English or Saxon Building," parts 1–4 (14–18 August 1875).

61. James Fergusson (1801–1886) was an R.I.B.A. gold medallist (1871) and the author of *A History of Architecture in all Countries from the Earliest Times to the Present Day* (1865–67).

62. "Saxon Architecture" (4 September 1875): 996.

63. For example, Parker (quoted in ibid.) had reproduced a page of the manuscript Claud. B.4. in his *Domestic Architecture in England* and had noted that "there is considerable doubt whether the representations in Anglo-Saxon Mss. can be relied on; also whether they are intended to represent stone buildings or wooden structures with metal ornaments."

64. Ibid.

65. Ibid.

66. Godwin, "Geoffrey Chaucer as Clerk of the King's Works," part 1 (4 November 1871): 221–22; part 2 (11 November 1871): 233–34.

67. Godwin, "Spenser's Castles," part 1 (27 January 1872): 41–42; part 2 (3 February 1872): 54–55; Godwin, "Kilcolman" (17 August 1872): 91–92 and illus.

68. Godwin, "Greek Home According to Homer" (June 1886): 914–22. For Godwin's handwritten draft of this article, see RIBA Mss, GoE/5/1/1-3.

69. Letter from Godwin to J. H. Pollen, n.d., V & A AAD, 4/447-1988.

70. Godwin, "Architecture and Costume of Shakespere's [*sic*] Plays: The Greek Plays" (8 May 1875): 271.

71. For a report of an extraordinary meeting for the purpose of presenting Schliemann with a diploma of election as an honorary member, see "Societies: Royal Institute of British Architects," *British Architect* 7 (4 May 1877): 272.

72. Schliemann's colleague Wilhelm Dörpfeld gave an account of the excavations of 1883–84 on the Acropolis of Tiryns that also tended to cast doubt on Homer, but Godwin dismissed Tiryns as "thoroughly Eastern," being unable to match the ground plan of the complex there with anything he had found in the *Iliad* or *Odyssey* (Godwin, "Greek Home According to Homer" [June 1886]: 922). Godwin's notes on Tiryns are in RIBA Mss, GoE/5/2 (G/GR.2/18/1). His scepticism about Schliemann is also obvious in one of his sketches of Greek armor, which is annotated: "one of a row of figs on fragment of Pottery found by Dr Schliemann at Mycenae Don't believe in it. EWG. July/83."

73. Godwin, "Spenser's Castles," part 1 (27 January 1872): 41–42; part 2 (3 February 1872): 54–55.

74. Godwin, "Kilcolman" (17 August 1872): 91–92 and illus. Several of Godwin's sketches of Kilcolman Castle are in RIBA Mss, GoE/6/1.

75. "Mr E. W. Godwin on Architecture And Somerset Churches," V & A, AAD 4/560-1988.

76. "Professor Willis" (6 March 1875): 134–35.

77. E. W. Godwin, "Notes on Architectural Design Illustrated by Gloster [*sic*] Cathedral," undated cutting from the *Western Daily Press*, minute book of the Bristol Society of Architects for 1864.

78. Ibid.

79. Ibid.

80. See Pevsner, *Some Architectural Writers* (1972).

81. Godwin, "Gothic Revival" (2 December 1871): 272.

82. For Godwin's design for the gatehouse, see RIBA Mss, GoE/4/6 (G/Ir.3/2/8); for Godwin's sketch of Kilmacleurine Castle, see RIBA Mss, GoE/4/6 (G/Ir.3/2/3/2).

83. M. W. Brooks, *John Ruskin* (1987): 207. For the illustration of the archivolt on the Duomo of Murano, see Ruskin, *Stones of Venice,* vol. 2 (1853), pl. 5.

84. [Godwin], "Mr E. W. Godwin's Measured Sketches" (29 May 1874): 584 and illus. [595].

85. I am grateful to Aileen Reid for this information.

86. Godwin, "Home of an English Architect," part 1 (June 1886): 172.

87. V & A PD, E.268-1963.

88. V & A PD, E.270-1963, p. 17.

89. V & A PD, E.270-1963, p. 6, "After MS.Reg.15.E.iv."

90. Godwin, "Modern Architects and Their Works" part 6 (11 October 1872): 291.

91. Letter from E. W. Godwin to Lady Alwyne Compton, dated 20 September 1867 (Compton Family Documents, Castle Ashby).

92. Lady Alwyne Compton's memorandum book: 85 (Compton Family Documents, Castle Ashby).

93. Godwin, "On Some Buildings I Have Designed" (29 November 1878): 211.

94. Godwin, "Studios and Mouldings" (7 March 1879): 261.

95. Godwin, "Notes on Architectural Design Illustrated by Gloster [*sic*] Cathedral" (see n. 77 above).

96. Godwin, "Studios and Mouldings" (7 March 1879): 261.

97. Ibid.

98. Godwin's acceptance papers for the Archaeological Institute of Great Britain and Ireland, dated 12 May 1851, RIBA Mss, GoE/7/7/1.

99. [Godwin], "Furniture" (15 June 1872): 1–2.

100. Public Record Office, Board of Trade Records BT 43/58, registered design no. 372557.

101. A number of more or less spurious examples of "Shakespeare" furniture were known in the nineteenth century. Until 1893 four oak chairs and part of a fifth from Shakespeare's birthplace were in the possession of the Hornby family in Stratford on Avon. Another supposed Shakespeare chair had been removed to Poland in 1790 by Princess Isabel Czartoryska, and another was exhibited at the Philadelphia Centennial Exhibition of 1876 and subsequently bought by George Godwin, the editor of the *Builder*. (I am grateful to Ann Donnelly, curator of the Shakespeare Birthplace Trust, for this information.)

102. Notes on Current Events, "The exhibition of furniture . . ." (22 February 1884): 86.

103. [Godwin], "Jacobean Oak Sideboard" (15 May 1885): 766 and illus. [785].

104. RIBA Mss, GoE/5/2 (G.Gr/2/26/5).

105. For Godwin's 1882 designs for Langtry's house, see V & A AAD, 4/170-1988. For the undated sketchbook, see V & A PD, E.229-1963, p. 109.

106. For the two small tables, see V & A PD, E.233-1963, p. 31. For the washstand, see V & A PD, E.233-1963, p. 35.

107. For Godwin's design for the wall decoration, see V & A PD, E.241-1963, p. 163; for Godwin's sketch of the carpet from the *Burgomaster Meyer's Votive Picture,* by Holbein, see V & A PD, E.229-1963, p. 61. The illustration Godwin used came from the *Handbook of Painting: The German, Flemish, and Dutch Schools. . . .* , part 1 (1860): 192.

108. For Godwin's sketch of the jug, see V & A PD, E.473-1963, verso. The jug is an East Greek *oinochoe,* of ca. 600-550 B.C., in the British Museum (Blacas Collection, GR.1867.5-8.925). For Godwin's design for the toilet set, see V & A PD, E.233-1963, p. 27.

109. The jug is in the British Museum (GR.1870.10-8.121 [A831]).

110. For Godwin's design for a frieze of tiles, see V & A PD, E.377-1963. For the sketches made by Godwin in 1866 from the Arundel Psalter, see V & A PD, E.285-1963, p. 9. For Godwin's suggestions for diapers and "powderings," see Godwin, "Painted Decoration," part 10 (19 July 1867): 491, and part 11 (18 October 1867): 716.

111. V & A PD, E.241-1963: 23.

112. Godwin, "On Some Buildings I have Designed" (29 November 1878): 211.

113. Godwin, "To Our Student Readers," part 2 (13 August 1880): 70.

114. For the book and sketches on armor, see RIBA Mss, GoE/5/2 (G/Gr.2/19-20). The book on Irish antiquities was to be illustrated with a vast number of sketches, some of which were published in the *British Architect* (1880–81), with the editor commenting that it was a "store . . . we are not likely to be able to exhaust" (Notes on Current Events, "Three Irish Crosses" [26 November 1880]: 228). Godwin's draft manuscript, notes, and some of the sketches are in RIBA GoE/4/6/1-9. For the catalogue, see letter from Godwin to W. C. Angus, dated 13 August 1884, V & A TA, Godwin collection box 3.

115. Godwin, "Cyclopaedia of Costume" (16 October 1875): 208; Viollet-le-Duc, *Dictionnaire raisonné* (1858–75); Hefner-Alteneck, *Trachten des christlichen Mittelalters,* 3 vols. (1840–54).

116. "Persons of taste . . ." (28 September 1882): 5.

117. Ibid.

118. Minutes of the Costume Society (27 July 1882), V & A TA, Godwin collection, box 3.

119. Minutes of the Costume Society (28 October 1882), V & A TA, Godwin collection, box 3.

120. "Persons of taste . . ." (28 September 1882): 5.

121. [Godwin], "Notes On Current Events" (16 April 1880): 183; also, Godwin, "Theatrical Jottings: Shakspere [*sic*] at the Imperial" (19 March 1880): 134; Paul Lacroix, *Manners Customs and Dress during the Middle Ages and during the Renaissance period* (London: Chapman and Hall, 1874).

122. Godwin, "Cyclopaedia of Costume" (16 October 1875): 208; Planché, *Cyclopaedia of costume* (1875 and 1879).

123. Godwin, "Cyclopaedia of Costume" (16 October 1875): 208.

124. "Persons of taste . . ." (28 September 1882): 5.

125. Godwin, "Notes on the Costume in the Pictures at the Royal Academy" (29 May 1875): 314–15.

126. The society at first had some difficulty, however, in attracting subscribers. See V & A PD, E.263-1963, pp. 27–30.

127. Minutes of the Costume Society (28 October 1882), V & A TA, Godwin collection, box 3.

128. Ibid.

129. These are in V & A TA, Godwin collection, boxes 3 and 4.

130. Arundel 38 is the manuscript of Thomas Hoccleve's poem "De Regimine Principium" written ca. 1411–12. The only illumination in it is on p. 37 and represents Hoccleve (or possibly Chaucer) presenting a poem to King Henry V. For the Costume Society drawing, see V & A TA, Godwin collection, box 4.

131. V & A TA, Godwin collection, box 3.

132. Ibid. Crivelli's altarpiece, *Madonna della Rondine* (ca. 1490), was formerly in the Church of the Franciscans at Matelica and is now in the National Gallery, London (no. 724).

133. V & A TA, Godwin collection, box 4.

134. Letter from the Baron de Cosson to Godwin, dated 15 July 1883, V & A TA, Godwin collection, box 3.

135. Ibid.

136. Adburgham, *Liberty's* (1975): 52.

137. Ibid.

138. Liberty's, *Fancy Dress* (1893), no. 7 (Liberty Archives 788/44/3).

139. V & A TA, Godwin collection, box 3.

140. Godwin, "Archaeology on the Stage" part 1 (8 February 1885): 19.

141. Godwin, "Architecture and Costume of Shakespere's [*sic*] Plays: Richard III" (13 February 1875): 88.

142. Ibid.: "The Merchant of Venice" (3 April 1875): 197.

143. Godwin, "Theatrical Jottings, No. XIII" (15 October 1880): 176. Godwin is praising the acting—though not the costume—of Madame Modjeska in *Mary Stuart*, Lewis Wingfield's adaptation of Schiller's play.

144. Godwin, "Theatrical Jottings, No. V: Shakspere [*sic*] at Sadler's Wells" (26 March 1880): 145.

145. Godwin, "Architecture and Costume of . . . 'Twelfth Night'" (April 24 1875): 241.

146. Letter from E. W. Godwin to Ellen Terry, n.d., but a companion letter referring to the same costume is dated 24 July 1875 (Terry Museum).

147. Page dated 8 July 1875, V & A TA, Godwin collection, box 3.

148. British Library, Mss. 15.D.ii, p. 122.

149. Ibid., p. 181.

150. Draft letter and memo from E. W. Godwin to John Coleman, dated 2 September 1876, V & A TA, Godwin collection, box 7.

151. Burges, "'Henry V' at the Queen's Theatre" (23 September 1876): 188; Burges, "Archaeology on the Stage," part 1 (14 October 1876): 224–25; part 2 (21 October 1876): 238–40.

152. For example, Harbron, *Conscious Stone* (1949): 111–12; Stokes, *Resistible Theatres* (1972): 40.

153. Draft letter and memo dated 2 September 1876, V & A TA, Godwin collection, box 7.

154. Godwin, "Archaeology on the Stage," part 6 (10 October 1885): 92–93.

155. Ibid.

156. [Godwin], Notes on Current Events, "Mr R. B. Mantel . . ." (1 July 1881): 330.

157. See chap. 12 in this volume.

158. Godwin, "A Few Notes on . . . 'Claudian'" (7 December 1883): 267–70. The pamphlet was privately printed in 1883. There is a copy in the British Library and another, annotated with a handwritten list of "Authorities," in V & A TA, Godwin collection, box 1.

159. "'Hamlet' at the Princess's: An Interview with Mr E. W. Godwin" (October 16, 1884): 312.

160. For the costumes of *Claudian* he used illustrations of the consular diptychs which he had found in Antonio Francese Gori, *Thesaurian Veterium Diptichorum* (Florence, 1759); for images of the disc of Theodosius I he used Antonio Delgado, *Memoria Histórico* (Madrid, 1849). Godwin consulted both books at the British Library on 24 September 1883 and kept his library slips (V & A AAD, 4/24-25-1988). He annotated the Delgado slip: "Very Beautiful large outline plates of the silver disc of Theodosius."

161. Letter from A. S. Murray to Godwin, dated 14 September 1883, V & A TA, Godwin collection, box 1. For Louis-Georges Seroux d'Agincourt's *Histoire de l'Art,* Murray recommended the German edition (n.d.) edited by Mast, pl. 10. (I have not been able to find a copy of this edition.)

162. Handwritten list of "Authorities" for *Claudian,* V & A TA, Godwin collection, box 1.

163. Godwin, "A Few Notes on . . . 'Claudian'" (7 December 1883): 267–70.

164. Unidentified undated cutting possibly from *Punch* (V & A TA, God-

win collection, box 1).

165. Godwin, "A Few Notes on . . . 'Claudian'" (7 December 1883): 267–70. Instead Barrett wore a simple, off-white tunic with a loosely draped white cloak and plain metal wrist bands. Barrett was photographed in this costume (Theatre Museum, Production Box, "Claudian").

166. The "little bronze warrior" was referred to by Godwin in "A Few Notes on . . . 'Claudian'" (7 December 1883): 267–70.

167. Stokes, *Resistible Theatres* (1972): 40.

168. Godwin, "Architecture and Costume of . . . Merchant of Venice" (3 April 1875): 197.

169. These drawings, tentatively ascribed to Edward Gordon Craig, are in the Ellen Terry Memorial Museum.

170. V & A TA, Godwin collection, box 5.

171. Godwin, "Architecture and Costume of . . . Merchant of Venice" (3 April 1875): 197.

172. Letter from Godwin to Mr Lawson, dated 18 April 1884, V & A TA, Godwin collection, box 6.

173. Printed leaflet advertising the performances of *Helena in Troas* 1886, V & A TA, Godwin collection, box 8, p. 3.

174. "Helena in Troas" (18 May 1886): 5.

175. Souder, "E. W. Godwin and the Visual Theatre" (1976): 109. (There is a copy in the Theatre Museum, Covent Garden, London. I am indebted to Alvin Souder's thesis for much of the information in this section on Godwin's production of *Helena in Troas*.)

176. Thomas Henry Dyer, *Ancient Athens* (London: Bell and Daldy, 1873).

177. Letter from a correspondent from the Fitzwilliam Museum, Cambridge [illegible signature] to Godwin, dated 20 October 1885, V & A TA, Godwin collection, box 6.

178. J. W. Donaldson, *The Theatre of the Greeks: A Treatise on the History and Exhibition of Greek Drama,* 7th ed. (London: G. Bell and Sons, 1860).

179. Souder, "E. W. Godwin and the Visual Theatre," p. 112.

180. "I have looked through all the authorities I know upon the Greek Stage arrangements and cannot find any trace of the voice strengthener of which you speak" (letter from Cecil Smith to Godwin, dated 2 March 1886, V & A TA, Godwin collection, box 6).

181. Godwin's notes from the Homeric poems, sketched costume designs, and color notes are in an exercise book, V & A TA, Godwin collection, box 8.

182. W. C. K. Wilde, "Helena in Troas" (22 May 1886): 161–62.

183. Godwin, "Archaeology on the Stage," part 7 (24 October 1885): 113.

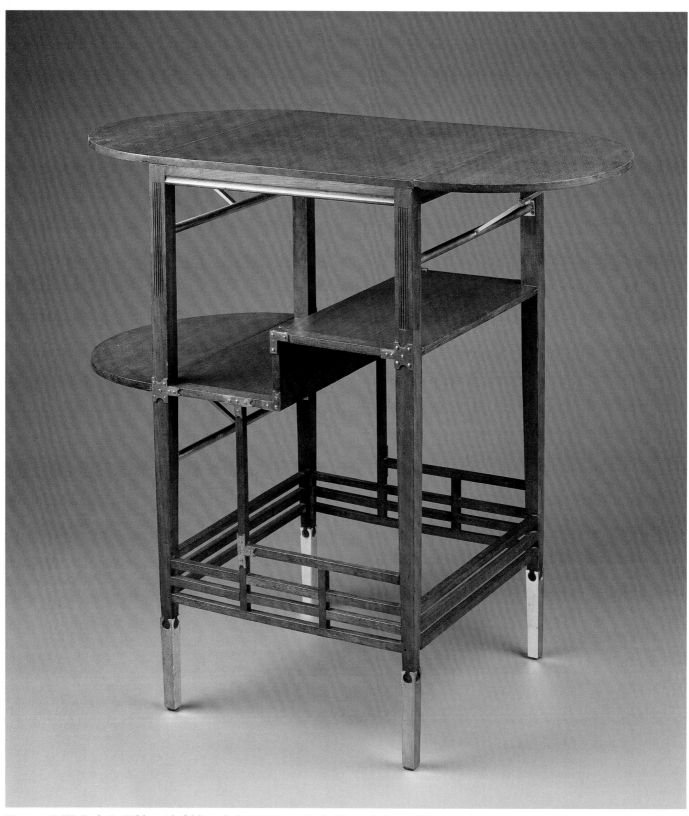

Fig. 3-1. E. W. Godwin. Table with folding shelves, ca. 1872. Probably made by Collinson and Lock. Walnut with gilt brass fittings; 29⁷⁄₁₆ x 16 x 32⅛ in. (74.7 x 40.6 x 81.5 cm). The Metropolitan Museum of Art, New York, Purchase, Rogers Fund; Margaret A. Darrin Gift; Gift of Ogden Mills, by exchange; Gift of Bernard Baruch, by exchange; Anne Eden Woodward Foundation and Friends of European Sculpture and Decorative Arts Gifts, 1991 (1991.87). *Checklist no. 71*

CHAPTER 3

E·W·GODWIN·AND·JAPONISME IN·ENGLAND

NANCY B. WILKINSON

In 1876 Edward William Godwin wrote in the *Architect* that "No. 218 Regent Street is from front to back and top to bottom a warehouse literally crammed with objects of Oriental manufacture."[1] He was referring to East India House, a grand name that belied the small space the shop occupied on Regent Street in London. To artists and architects such as Godwin, who had owned and studied Japanese objects for fifteen years, watching them become increasingly fashionable, it was known simply as the Japanese Warehouse. Its owner was the young Arthur Lasenby Liberty.

Godwin's article further described the reception given the arrival of a new shipment of Japanese fans at the shop: "There was quite a crowd when we arrived. A distinguished traveller had button-holed the obliging proprietor in one corner; a well known baronet, waiting to do the same, was trifling with some feather dusting brushes; two architects of well known names were posing an attendant in another corner with awkward questions; [and] three distinguished painters with their wives blocked up the staircase."[2] On a more ominous note, he wrote that "The fans of ten years ago are for the most part lovely in delicate colour and exquisite in drawing, but the great majority of the fans of today . . . are impregnated with the crudeness of the European's sense of colour, and are immeasurably beneath the older examples."[3]

By this time Japanese influence in English art and design had reached a high-water mark. Between 1870 and 1875 Godwin, James McNeill Whistler, and other artists had created some of their finest Japanese-inspired work (fig. 3-1). Although Godwin began to question the quality of the Japanese objects then being created for the Western trade, he continued to use Japanese artistic principles in his furniture, wallpaper, and interior design and his greatest architectural creations—his London studio houses, impossible without a grounding in Japanese art—were still to come in the late 1870s. After 1880 fascination with Japan passed from the artists and architects to the general public, where it was popularized by fantasies such as Gilbert and Sullivan's *Mikado*. Among the next generation of architects and designers—those of the Glasgow School and the Arts and Crafts movement—many would study not Japan, but Godwin.

The impact of Japanese culture on Western art and design in the second half of the nineteenth century, or the Japonisme movement as it was known, progressed from a "taste for things Japanese" through a serious study of art and architecture to the assimilation of Japanese design principles into Western products. Unlike France, where Japanese colored wood-block prints strongly affected developments in painting and the visual arts, in Britain it was primarily in the decorative arts that Japanese design had its most direct influence.

Historically, Japan's first contact with the West came in 1542 when Portuguese traders sailed to the islands. This began the "foreign century" in Japan, as the Portuguese

Fig. 3-2. "The International Exhibition: The Japanese Court." From the *Illustrated London News* (20 September 1862): 320. Trustees of the Victoria and Albert Museum, London.

were quickly followed by Spanish and Dutch traders and Christian missionaries. The next century saw a civil war in Japan in which the foreigners' role, especially in converting small sections of the population to Christianity, was more an irritant than a cause of conflict. In 1615 a powerful prince, or *daimyo*, succeeded in unifying Japan, adding a new dynasty, the Tokugawa, to a long succession of military rulers. The ruling Tokugawa general, known as a *shogun*, established the new city of Edo (later Tokyo) as the capital of Japan and began to consolidate power by weakening rival elements in society. In 1639 he banned Christianity and all foreign contact, with the exception of the Dutch, who were interested in trade and not religious conversion. He allowed them to maintain a small trading post or factory on the man-made island of Deshima in the bay of Nagasaki, a site remote from Edo. From there the Dutch exported a small but continuous stream of Japanese products to the West. Particularly influential in the Netherlands was an increased

volume of Japanese porcelain exported for a period in the second-half of the seventeenth century.

The first major collection of Japanese art to reach Europe was imported about 1830 by a German physician and scholar, Philipp Franz von Siebold, who had been allowed to travel to Edo from Nagasaki, where he lived from 1823 to 1829. Von Siebold acquired ceramics, lacquer ware, paintings, and a varied group of important woodblock prints.[4] He established a museum in Leiden in 1837 and published an extensive, multivolume study of Japan (1832–54).[5]

In the two hundred years following the establishment of the Tokugawa dynasty, Japanese culture developed in relative isolation. The military government remained in power but gradually lost ground economically to a growing middle class. Western interaction with Asia accelerated, and the British challenged the supremacy of the Dutch East India Company, based at Batavia in Java, with the establishment of the British East India Company factory in Hong Kong in 1725. By the mid-nineteenth century, British pressure in China to open markets to Western trade led to bitter conflicts between the two nations known as the Opium Wars. France, Russia, the United States, and other countries were anxiously pursuing trade with Asia, and Japan was not able to maintain its isolation in the face of such expanding economic realities.

In 1853 Commodore Matthew Perry led a force of American ships into a Japanese harbor with the purpose of opening Japan to foreign trade. Soon, Japanese objects and works of art began to make their way to Western cities. The first "sighting" has traditionally been identified as the collection of wood-block prints by Katsushika Hokusai, the *Manga*, which became known in about 1856 in Paris.[6] In England, William Burges catalogued his own small collection of Japanese prints in October 1858.[7]

During the 1860s members of the British diplomatic missions to Japan recorded frenetic trading activities by small businessmen wherever Westerners landed. Laurence Oliphant, Lord Elgin's secretary, who accompanied him to Japan to sign a formal trade treaty in 1858, published an account of his trip in 1859 in which he described several bazaars with "avenues of brilliant novelties" in Yokohama, Nagasaki, and Shimoda, the site of the American consulate, noting they were "established for the benefit of foreigners."[8] Large-scale trade was also accelerating. At one point the British government had to warn against illegal trade before the official treaty date of July 1, 1859. During the second half of 1858, nineteen of the forty ships that traded at Nagasaki were British.[9]

The first British consul to Japan, Sir Rutherford Alcock, who served from 1859 to 1864, was a medical doctor by profession but had already been a British consul to China for fifteen years. Fascinated with Japan, Alcock published a two-volume account of his stay there, which was widely read in both Britain and America.[10] Like Oliphant he praised the Japanese for their industry, cleanliness, and morality, and maintained an optimistic outlook toward Anglo-Japanese relations.

Early in his tenure Alcock was officially requested by his government to put together a display of Japanese works of art and industry for the International Exhibition to be held in London in 1862. On his own, with little help from commercial traders or the Japanese government, whose "most earnest desire was to preserve as far as possible the long-cherished isolation of the country from foreign influences and interests,"[11] Alcock assembled and displayed a large number of Japanese works, marking the first time a significant collection had been seen in the West.[12] The

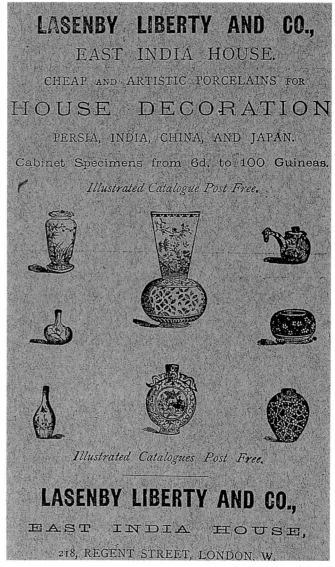

Fig. 3-3. An advertisement for Liberty and Company, ca. 1875. From John Hungerford Pollen, *Ancient and Modern Furniture and Woodwork* (London: Chapman and Hall, 1875).

Japanese Court (fig. 3-2), as it was known, can be seen as the beginning of the Japonisme movement in Britain. More than one thousand exquisitely crafted objects of wood, lacquer, straw, paper, metal, textile, and ceramic, as well as two hundred wood-block prints, were exhibited.[13] Among the enthusiastic visitors were many of England's most innovative architects and designers, such as William Burges and Christopher Dresser, both of whom wrote articles about the collection.[14] Godwin, living in Bristol in 1862, made a trip to London in July as a delegate to the national meeting of the Architectural Alliance.[15] Although there is nothing to confirm it, it would be surprising if he did not visit the Japanese Court at the International Exhibition, which ran from May to September.

Fig. 3-4. Aimé Humbert. "Commerce de Curiosités: Boutique d'Objets d'art et d'industrie à Yokohama." From Humbert, *Le Japon illustré*, vol. 2 (1870): 371.

By the time of the next large international show, the Exposition Universelle in Paris in 1867, events in Japan had changed dramatically. Semi-autonomous *daimyo* were aggressively building trade partnerships with the West in defiance of the "antiforeign" laws of the shogun's government. One in particular, the *daimyo* of the southern province of Satsuma, had traded at the Ryukyu Islands with the British firm of Jardine, Matheson since the late 1840s and in 1865 bought a warship through the firm.[16] It was also the *daimyo* of Satsuma who put together the largest display of Japanese goods, primarily from his own province, for the Paris Exposition of 1867. He insisted on registering his display separately from the smaller one of the official government of the shogun. Although Godwin had been on an advisory board regarding British architecture for the exposition, his documents do not indicate that he actually went to Paris in 1867. Many of his colleagues did, however, and because the Japanese works were sold in Paris, some found their way to England.[17]

In 1868 the Tokugawa period of Japanese history came to an end with the overthrow of the military government and the restoration of the imperial family to power after seven centuries. The new emperor, Mutsuhito, who reigned as Emperor Meiji, championed pro-Western forces in Japan, especially those anxious to build international trade, and quickly led his country into the community of world powers. Japan became an enthusiastic participant in succeeding international trade fairs, such as the 1873 exhibition in Vienna, the Philadelphia Centennial in 1876, and the Exposition Universelle in Paris in 1878. At all of these, the Meiji government built authentic Japanese

buildings, bringing prefabricated structures and construction workers from Japan. Objects in the exhibitions were later sold in the West; one of the Japanese buildings in Vienna, for example, was brought to London and erected in Alexandra Park, where interested designers, such as Godwin, could study it in detail. By the mid-1870s, the Japanese were producing items specifically for a Western clientele, often adapting existing Western designs, a trend Godwin lamented in his 1876 review of the Japanese Warehouse. Conversely, British companies increasingly copied Japanese designs for everyday objects.

This was not true in the early days of the English Japonisme movement, when the first Japanese objects, mostly those collected by Alcock, were received with surprise and admiration. When the 1862 International Exhibition closed and the Japanese objects were sold, the bulk went to Farmer and Rogers' Great Shawl and Cloak Emporium on Regent Street, where they were displayed in an annex next door, called the Oriental Warehouse. One of the young men hired to manage the shop was Arthur Lasenby Liberty, who would later open East India House (fig. 3-3), today known as Liberty and Company. When the Oriental Warehouse opened in 1862, it was "the first house of business . . . in England for the sale of the art productions of Japan," and it soon became a magnet for "such noted masters as . . . Albert Moore, E. W. Godwin, Burges, Nesfield, Rossetti, and an array of others of equal repute."[18]

Most collectors still acquired objects out of context, without documentation. After the initial travel accounts that appeared in the early 1860s, little was published about Japan to help collectors place their kimonos, lacquer trays, and other items into an understandable cultural context. Because Japan had been essentially closed to foreign contact for two centuries, its literature, philosophy, religion, and social structure were almost unknown in the West. This changed, but relatively slowly over the succeeding decades. During the early phase of Japonisme in England, in the 1860s and 1870s, what artists learned about Japan and its art came through a study of the actual objects, as well as prints, paintings, and photographs. The opening of Japan coincided with the development of photography, which made possible a flood of visual information. Aimé Humbert's *Le Japon illustré* (1870), for example, which presented hundreds of lithographs primarily copied from photographs (fig. 3-4), was very influential in Godwin's artistic development.

Small shops such as Liberty's, however, remained the primary source of imported Japanese objects until after 1870 when general department stores began to carry Asian works. Two other London shops that sold to artists and architects in the 1860s were William Hewett's and William Wareham's. Hewett specialized in Chinese goods and became an important source for Godwin. Wareham also sold Japanese and Chinese works to Godwin but was listed simply as a dealer in "works of art and curiosities."[19]

Like-minded aficionados, who frequented these shops and visited international exhibitions, shared information and insights on Japan. A coterie of enthusiasts developed in London, including Godwin, two of his closest friends—archi-tect William Burges and American artist James McNeill Whistler—as well as architect-designers William Eden Nesfield, Thomas Jeckyll, and Christopher Dresser.[20] Burges was an early collector of Japanese prints and Godwin probably first saw some of these in about 1858 amid the clutter of exotic objects that filled Burges's studio.[21] Burges's use of Japanese elements in his own work was rare. They appeared as unrelated additions to his otherwise medieval revival designs such as an elaborate elephant inkstand that had a Japanese netsuke attached to the lid. This was illustrated by Godwin in an 1886 article for *Art Journal*.[22] Burges's importance for the English Japonisme movement was his early and open enthusiasm for Japanese objects. His interest stimulated colleagues to begin the process of integrating Japanese design principles into their work.

Whistler was the first to do this successfully. His 1863 painting, *La Princesse du pays de la porcelaine*, reflects an understanding of Japanese pictorial space, composition, and color not previously seen in a Western painting.[23] Whistler continued to explore Japanese design in the 1860s, with paintings clustered around two periods, 1863–64 and 1868–69. In the early 1870s he moved away from recognizable Japanese details to abstractions known as "Nocturnes," which retained Japanese aesthetic and design principles.

The first use of Japanese design in English architecture is only as surface decoration in Nesfield's Cloverley Hall, Shropshire, in 1865.[24] Nesfield borrowed circular

Fig. 3-5. E. W. Godwin. Proposed decoration for the fireplace wall in the dining room at Dromore Castle, County Limerick, Ireland, ca. 1869. India ink, pen, colored washes, and gouache; 7⅛ x 18½ in. (18 x 47 cm). British Architectural Library, Drawings Collection, RIBA, London, Ran 7/B/1 (67).

Fig. 3-6. E. W. Godwin. Design for Japanese-inspired wall decoration at Dromore Castle, County Limerick, Ireland, ca. 1869. Watercolor and pencil; 5 5/16 x 7 1/2 in. (13.5 x 19 cm). Trustees of the Victoria and Albert Museum, London, E.491-1963. *Checklist no. 20*

Japanese family crest designs, or *mon*, which he called "pies," to decorate interior wood or stucco wall friezes and doorways.[25] Nesfield, his partner Richard Norman Shaw, and their associate, the sculptor James Forsyth, used "pie" motifs in several buildings during the late 1860s but dropped these obvious decorative details in their later works.

Japanese *mon* motifs were integrated more successfully in the work of architect and furniture designer Thomas Jeckyll. Between 1866 and 1870 he created cast-iron fire screens with bold Japanese designs using geometric patterns as well as *mon*. He later designed the interior spaces and woodwork of the "Peacock Room" for Frederick Leyland (more famous for Whistler's wall paintings) and a large cast-iron pavilion in the shape of a Japanese Buddhist temple for the 1876 Philadelphia Centennial in America.[26]

Among the designers, Christopher Dresser was most involved intellectually with Japan and its culture. Alcock noted, "Dr. Dresser was . . . a close student of the various objects in the Japanese Court of the Exhibition of 1862."[27] He traveled in Japan for several months in 1876–77 and in 1882 published an illustrated book on the subject.[28] Beginning in the 1860s Dresser's works of decorative art, glass, silver, and ceramic objects reflected his deep understanding and appreciation for the Japanese aesthetic.

Whistler and Godwin collected Japanese and Chinese prints, crafts, and blue-and-white china until 1880, when their interests shifted in other directions. In fact Godwin is known to have assembled an "impressive collection" of "blue china," or Chinese blue-and-white porcelain, as early as 1862, which places him among the earliest in England to

have done so.[29] Living in the busy port city of Bristol during the 1850s and 1860s gave Godwin a rare opportunity to acquire Asian art directly from ships' captains returning from the Far East. When Godwin moved his practice to London, he continued to collect, decorating the small house he shared with actress Ellen Terry with "India matting" (used for floors and the lower section or dado of some wall surfaces), "a Turkey carpet," "Japan Pictures," Chinese porcelain, screens and fabrics, and Japanese ceramics, cabinets, trays, dresses, and two bronze elephants.[30]

It was around 1869 that Godwin first began to integrate Japanese elements in his interior design for clients, in both wall decoration and furniture. At Dromore Castle, an otherwise medieval-style building he created for the Earl of Limerick in County Limerick, Ireland, he introduced a palette that was clearly Japanese in origin. In 1869, with construction well underway, he revised the original color scheme, which had called for monumental rooms with tones of dark reds, golds, and browns. The colors were lightened to sage greens, peaches, and soft blues, as seen in a watercolor sketch of the dining room fireplace wall (fig. 3-5).[31] Panels of flat color alternate with figures and oval vases sprouting flowering branches. There is a Japanesque simplicity about the branches and the spatial proportions of the design. Another watercolor sketch, not with the architectural drawings, is even more direct in its suggestion of source (fig. 3-6). It shows a kimono-clad woman set against a wall with trellis wallpaper and earthenware vases with Japanesque flowering branches exactly like the ones intended for Dromore. The painting, like the Dromore walls, is composed of a solid area of soft sage green on the lower half, while the dominant color of the kimono is a russet peach. Godwin explored a bold Japanesque scheme in the small watercolor, then took out the most obvious Japanese elements for his plans at Dromore, leaving the spacing, color, and some decorative details.

The damp Irish climate at Dromore precluded realization of Godwin's color scheme, and it was abandoned. He used the soft colors he devised for the project, however, in other interior decoration throughout his career, usually specifying exact formulas to be followed in mixing paints and often performing this task himself. He was very discerning in his choice of color. In one case, a notation he made described "colours from partially faded pineapple."[32] Godwin also lamented the inability of commercial firms to reproduce the subtle colors of his wallpaper designs: "[I showed] on the drawing the colours I wished to see reproduced, carefully copied from Japanese work. [The manufacturer printed] a green, blue, and red of his own, and which, I need hardly say, were very harsh translations of my Japanese tones."[33]

Of Godwin's more than fifty extant designs for wallpaper, the majority date from the 1870s and are drawn from Japanese models. Some of these are known from the black-and-white reproductions in trade journals of the day, while a few colored drawings remain among Godwin's papers.[34] In one (see fig. 10-1) bamboo leaves, tendrils, and stems are rendered in delicate tones of peach, gold, blue, and green against a warm, neutral background in a color scheme typical of Japanese color prints.[35]

Asian sources also appear in many of Godwin's designs for furniture. Although he is best known for his Anglo-Japanese designs, such as the celebrated black sideboard (see fig. 4-1), he also explored Chinese antecedents. Chinese hardwood furniture played an important role in the development of his furniture designs. Its influence is all the more compelling because, unlike the Chinese, the Japanese did not use furniture forms such as tables, chairs, or beds.

Although Godwin's opportunity to study Chinese domestic hardwood furniture in England between 1865 and 1870 was limited by the scarcity of examples in the muse-

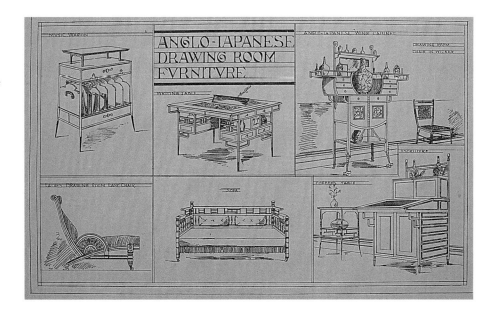

Fig. 3-7. E. W. Godwin. "Anglo Japanese Drawing Room Furniture." From William Watt, *Art Furniture* (1877), pl. 8. The Mitchell Wolfson Jr. Collection, The Wolfsonian–Florida International University, Miami Beach, Florida, TD 1990.40.62.

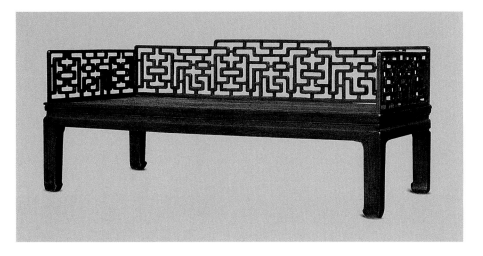

Fig. 3-8. Chinese *kang* with lattice rails, Qing dynasty. Huali wood; 82⅝ x 31½ in. (210 x 80 cm). Private collection.

Fig. 3-9. E. W. Godwin. Settee, ca. 1869. Made by William Watt. Mahogany, upholstered back and seat, brass castors; 35 x 66⅛ x 22⅞ in. (89 x 168 x 58.1 cm). Private collection. Courtesy of the Fine Art Society, Plc. *Checklist no. 24*

ums, there were pieces for sale in shops in London. When Godwin moved to London in 1865, he set up his office at 23 Baker Street, a short distance from the Baker Street Bazaar that housed William Hewett's Chinese Warehouse, where Chinese and other Asian goods were offered. Hewett, who began in 1840 as a grocer and tea dealer at a location near the docks, had become an importer of Chi-

nese goods by 1850. In 1863 he opened a branch store on fashionable Baker Street and over the years purchased from almost every auction and sale of Chinese or Japanese goods.

An examination of some of Godwin's furniture designs published by William Watt in the *Art Furniture* catalogue of 1877, such as plate 8 (fig. 3-7), reveals unmistakable borrowings from the elegant, restrained hardwood furniture used in Chinese homes since the Ming dynasty. Chinese derivation is most obvious in the sofa, the form of which refers to a Chinese couch known as a *kang* that is low and deep enough to allow two men to sit on it cross-legged. Godwin could have seen an example at William Hewett's Chinese Warehouse. Among the pieces Hewett purchased in 1851 at the Christie's auction of the Chinese collection of Nathan Dunn was one described in the catalogue as "a model of a Mandarin's couch, called Kang, richly carved of *muh-wang*-wood."[36] The seat of a Chinese *kang* is often surrounded on three sides by a latticed wood railing (fig. 3-8).[37] The lattice design in the center of the back railing in Godwin's sofa and in the side panels of his settee (fig. 3-9) are typically Chinese.

A similar rail design is seen in Godwin's two-tiered table, also seen in Watt's plate 8, which exhibits another Chinese element, a yokelike apron panel, or spandrel, under the top surface. Seen frequently in Chinese tables and chairs, such panels can be plain or ornate, but generally retain the yoke contour, as in the Ming Chinese rosewood desk (fig. 3-10), whose slender proportions and straight lines are close to many of Godwin's best works, including the black sideboard (see fig. 4-1). An interesting feature of this desk is that it is made in three separate parts—two drawer sections and a horizontal panel. In some cases, the horizontal section, which can also hold drawers, is raised on stiles to provide rectangular sections of open or negative space.

Open spaces are used by Godwin in his writing table or desk (shown in fig. 3-7) and other pieces as early as the 1867 sideboard. There are open brackets under the desk tops

or drawer sections of the writing table and the escritoire, those on the escritoire being double or repeated. Open brackets, such as these, often in multiples, are another feature found in many Chinese tables, desks, and chairs. They contribute to the pleasing, symmetrical arrangements of solids and voids. In addition, Godwin has carefully observed and copied the slender, straight rails of the Chinese prototype that meet at right angles, the outer corners rounded with restraint.

Rounded rails, which can be seen in the open mid-section of his black sideboard and in many other Godwin designs, became one of the elements associated with his Anglo-Japanese style. They are a pronounced feature of the so-called Monkey Cabinet made for his own use about 1876 and currently in the Victoria and Albert Museum (fig. 3-11). Godwin left a detailed watercolor of this piece in one of his sketchbooks.[38] The cabinet has authentic Japanese carved wood panels, and netsuke in the form of monkeys for drawer pulls. The use of actual Japanese objects in this new style of furniture may help to explain its ultimate labeling as Anglo-Japanese.

In addition to actual specimens from Asia, printed sources also played a pivotal role in the development of Godwin's Anglo-Japanese style. Sketches from Aimé Humbert's *Le Japon illustré* (1870) and Hokusai's *Manga* can be found in Godwin's sketchbooks and published writings. Humbert, who had spent some time in Japan, from 1863 to 1864, as minister plenipotentiary of the Swiss Republic, had traveled extensively outside the foreign settlements and recorded many aspects of Japanese life in photographs

Fig. 3-10. Desk. Chinese, 18th century. Huali wood; 33½ x 61⅝ x 25¾ in. (85 x 156.5 x 65.5 cm). Trustees of the Victoria and Albert Museum, London, FE3-1971.

Fig. 3-11. E. W. Godwin. Cabinet known as the "Monkey Cabinet," ca. 1876. Probably made by William Watt. Walnut with carved boxwood insets and ivory handles; 75½ x 78 x 19½ in. (190.5 x 198 x 49.5 cm). Trustees of the Victoria and Albert Museum, London, Circ. 34-1958.

"taken for the most part under our eye."[39] Most of the more than three hundred lithographic images in his book came from photographs, although some were drawn from Japanese paintings and prints. There were many examples of architecture, both exterior and interior views. Godwin filled two sketchbooks with drawings, mostly of isolated architectural or design motifs, taken directly from Humbert's illustrations.[40]

Several of these motifs made their way into Godwin's production. One of the most direct examples is Godwin's "Peacock" wallpaper (fig. 3-12), registered by Jeffrey and Company in 1873.[41] The bird motif in Godwin's sketchbook (fig. 3-13) is taken from a street scene in Humbert's book,[42] identified by Godwin as "A Library at Yedo," in which the circular motif appears on the walls of the Japanese building. It is the well-known crane crest, the crane being a revered symbol of longevity in Japan. Round crests, known as *mon,* were used to designate Japanese families or clans and were found on buildings, banners, and clothes. Many of Godwin's Japanese-inspired wallpaper designs came almost directly from Japanese *mon.* On another page in the same sketchbook (see fig. 10-7), he copied *mon* in carefully arranged rows, including the crane *mon.*[43] He combined the somewhat stylized Japanese crane with a watercolor sketch of a more animated crowned crane (see fig. 10-7) "taken from the life," which he had drawn on a visit to the London zoo in 1868,[44] to create a more dynamic design, now referred to as a peacock.

Another plate in *Le Japon illustré* (see fig. 3-4) inspired Godwin to sketch a *tansu,* or chest with shelves (fig. 3-14). The bottom of the *tansu* is obscured in the Humbert plate, and Godwin added a traditional Western base in his sketch. He was particularly interested in the asymmetrically divided shelves, which he highlighted in red. This arrangement is correctly associated with Japanese design, having been found in built-in wall shelves in Japanese homes for centuries,[45] but it was also used in Chinese and Korean furniture forms. Nevertheless, the *tansu* Godwin sketched was probably Japanese, its design by now traditional.

Godwin used the broken irregular shelves from his sketch in the design for a small table. There are two extant examples of this table (see fig. 3-1), one of which was made for the Godwin-Terry home in about 1871.[46] Besides the shelf design, which was first used by Godwin in this table, he also borrowed the metal pieces used to decorate the shelves' edges from Humbert's illustration. As on the actual Japanese model, they are placed in the center and at the corners of the shelves. Another feature of this table can also be traced to Humbert's book. Godwin sketched a tall, narrow table with what appears to be a curved leaf or flap on one

Fig. 3-12. E. W. Godwin. Design for "Peacock" wallpaper, ca. 1872. Watercolor and pencil on tracing paper; 13¾ x 10½ in. (35 x 26.8 cm). Trustees of the Victoria and Albert Museum, London E.513-1963. *Checklist no. 66.*

Fig. 3-13. E. W. Godwin. Japanese crane crest from the library at Yedo, ca. 1870. Sketchbook. Pencil, pen and ink, colored washes; 9 x 6½ in. (22.9 x 16.5 cm). Derived from a plate in Aimé Humbert, *Le Japon illustré* (vol. 2 [1870]: 5). Trustees of the Victoria and Albert Museum, London, E.280-1963: 1.

Fig. 3-14. E. W. Godwin. Sketches of furniture, ca. 1870. Sketchbook. Pencil, pen and ink, colored washes; 9 x 6½ in. (22.9 x 16.5 cm). Derived in part from illustrations in Aimé Humbert, *Le Japon illustré* (1870). Trustees of the Victoria and Albert Museum, London, E.280-1963: 5.

side (fig. 3-14). Its exact source is not clear, but a similar table, used as a prop stand by an itinerant Japanese story-teller, is illustrated in Humbert.[47] Godwin combined the features from these two sources—the broken shelves, metal plaques, side leaf, and tall, narrow table proportions—in a number of his later furniture designs and interior decoration schemes.

Godwin also sketched from Humbert the corner of a gong or bell (fig. 3-14, center right), which would eventually evolve into a produced design. Bells and gongs are found in Buddhist temples throughout Asia, although their origin is probably Chinese. Godwin's gong is in a free-standing wood frame (fig. 3-15), approximately 2½ feet high. The frame, although simplified, retains the shape of the sketch, and the top bar curves like a Japanese *torii* and is tipped with decorative metal pieces.

The *torii*, a freestanding gateway to Shinto shrines, is a purely Japanese architectural feature. Upright posts lean slightly inward and are separated by two beams, of which

the top beam curves upward with ends projecting beyond the posts. Humbert illustrated many *torii* in his book, and Godwin sketched at least one of these.[48] Beginning at this time Godwin used the *torii* design in numerous furniture pieces, such as the hanging cabinet (fig. 3-16),[49] or a later piece from about 1879, an Anglo-Japanese wall cabinet with shelves (fig. 3-17).[50] The open, curved rectilinear railings recall Chinese sources. The upturned lintels of the *torii* are retained, but this element is understated and well integrated into the overall design.

Fig. 3-15. E. W. Godwin. Gong and stand, ca. 1875. Probably made by William Watt. Oak and iron frame, bronze gong, wood striking stick; 32½ x 17¾ x 17⅛ in. (81.8 x 45.2 x 43.4 cm). National Museums and Galleries on Merseyside, Walker Art Gallery, 1994.17. *Checklist no. 1*

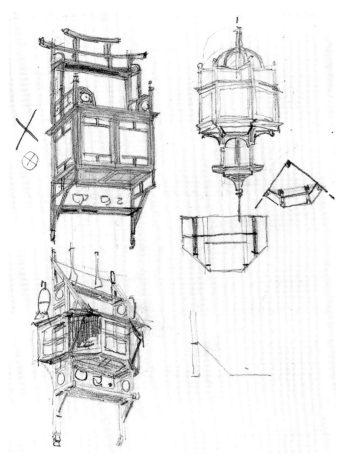

Fig. 3-16. E. W. Godwin. Designs for Anglo-Japanese hanging cabinets, 1872. Sketchbook. Pencil and colored washes; 5⅝ x 3⅝ in. (14.3 x 9.3 cm). Trustees of the Victoria and Albert Museum, London, E.229-1963: 73.

Fig. 3-17. E. W. Godwin. Design for an Anglo-Japanese hanging cabinet, 1872–79. Sketchbook. Pencil and colored washes. Trustees of the Victoria and Albert, Museum, London, E.233-1963: 113a.

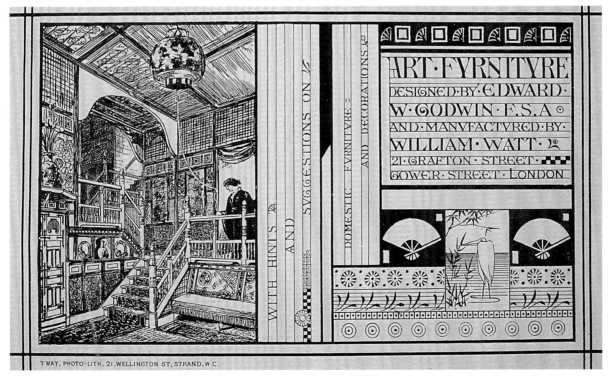

Fig. 3-18. E. W. Godwin. Frontispiece and title page (plate 1). From William Watt, *Art Furniture* (1877). The Mitchell Wolfson Jr. Collection, The Wolfsonian–Florida International University, Miami Beach, Florida, TD 1990.40.62. *Checklist no. 72*

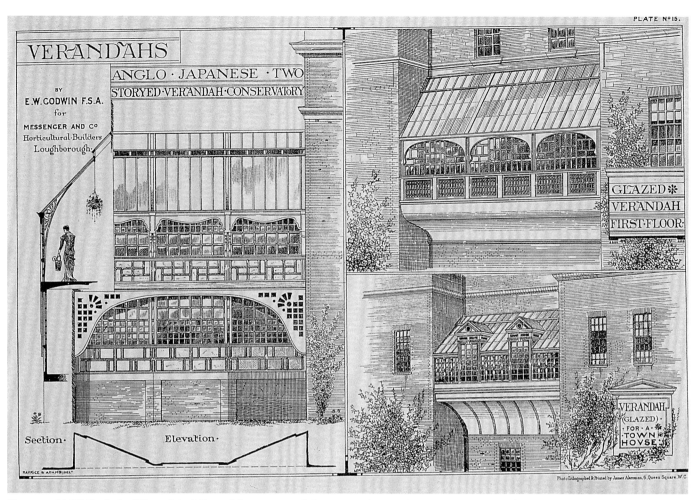

Fig. 3-19. E. W. Godwin. "Verandahs." From Messenger and Company, *Artistic Conservatories* (1880): pl. 15.

Fig. 3-20. Aimé Humbert, "Galerie au premier étage d'une hôtellerie japonaise." From Humbert, *Le Japon illustré*, vol. 1 (1870): 214.

Fig. 3-21. E. W. Godwin. Anglo-Japanese designs, ca. 1872–73. Pen and ink, with watercolor; 7⅞ x 11⅝ in.(20 x 29.5 cm). Trustees of the Victoria and Albert Museum, London E.482-1963. *Checklist no. 69*

Godwin's frontispiece for Watt's 1877 *Art Furniture* catalogue (fig. 3-18) is the most Japanese of his interior designs. A color sketch, with its blue-greens, golds, and peaches, reveals a much softer interior than suggested by the black-and-white print.[51] The wide, curved lintel above the staircase on the left is an architectural feature that derives from Humbert's illustration of the court of the Gankiro of Yokohama.[52] Godwin sketched this scene carefully, using highlights to emphasize the railings and curved lintel.[53] He later used this lintel to create alcoves or inglenooks in interior spaces, including Whistler's White House and a studio designed for Princess Louise, Queen Victoria's daughter, in Kensington Palace Gardens.[54] Similar inglenooks, often with fireplaces and bench seating, became popular in the next several decades, both in Britain and America. As late as 1880 Godwin referred back to his sketch for elements incorporated in his "Anglo-Japanese Verandah," in *Artistic Conservatories,* a design book published by the greenhouse manufacturers Messenger and Company (fig. 3-19).[55]

An inverted heart-shaped cut-out design is seen on the far left panel in the frontispiece to *Art Furniture.* Godwin found this pattern in a Humbert plate of a Japanese hotel balcony (fig. 3-20), from which he sketched a section of the balcony railing, emphasizing the rails and cut-out

patterns and titling his drawing "Balcony, Kanasawa Hotel."[56] He used the heart-shaped or "cloud" pattern occasionally in his furniture, usually for sides or backs of hanging cabinets. A detailed watercolor dating about 1876 shows such a piece (fig. 3-21), as well as a curved lintel creating an alcove, in a room full of furniture labeled by the artist "Anglo-Japanese Designs."[57] The heart-shaped cut-out was used later in furniture made by Liberty's and became practically a trademark for Heal and Son, a well-known manufacturing firm in the 1890s.

In February 1875, Godwin published two illustrated articles in the *Building News* entitled "Japanese Wood Construction." He consulted several sources, including his copy of Humbert, which he mentions in the text, but he primarily used "a Japanese book [of prints;] for all I know it may be quite a common collection of prints, or it may be out of print and rare . . . . The book consists of fifty-six pages of illustrations, of which one-half or thereabouts are devoted to timber architecture."[58]

Elizabeth Aslin has identified this book as volume five of Hokusai's *Manga* (1816), which Godwin probably owned.[59] The two pages of illustrations that accompanied Godwin's articles show details taken directly from the book, including five different *torii* gates, various railing

Fig. 3-22. E. W. Godwin. Details of Japanese architecture. From Godwin, "Japanese Wood Construction" (19 February 1875): 214.

designs, hipped and gabled roofs, brackets under eaves, and lattice-filled bell-shaped windows (fig. 3-22). Two details of cloud-pattern cut-outs are shown, both on wooden panels, one a temple door and the other, the side section of a lantern. They are very similar to the cloud-pattern on the left wall of the *Art Furniture* frontispiece.

Bell-shaped windows with lattice or "trellis-work" figured in a tall, elegant cabinet of satinwood and mahogany made by Godwin in about 1877 (fig. 3-23). The two openings that are inserted in the front doors compare very closely to one of the drawings Godwin based on Hokusai.[60] In this cabinet design, however, the Japanese element seems out of place, at odds with the upper panels that were painted with figures representing the four seasons, which were designed by Godwin in a Pre-Raphaelite style.[61]

Godwin's long study of Japanese artistic principles

contributed to startling innovations in his architecture of the late 1870s. His first design for the White House, James McNeill Whistler's studio house in Chelsea (fig. 3-24 and see fig. 6-52), borrowed from Japanese architecture (fig. 3-25) in the use of separately roofed units, which were part of the *shoin* style of domestic dwellings, and the inclusion of hipped and gabled roofs common in Buddhist temples since the sixth century. The front elevation was unlike anything Godwin had previously designed, with varied rectangles of door and windows asymmetrically placed against a plain wall. A large window on one side dominated the facade, actually cutting through the roof line, a dramatic feature that went beyond its Japanese origin.

The London Metropolitan Board of Works, who had to approve any architectural designs to be built on city land, rejected Godwin's original design as "ugly and unsightly."[62] The house as it was built was less stark and had a more conventional roof and smaller windows (see fig. 6-53), leaving behind obvious Japanese details but retaining principles of geometric spacing and balance and including decorative sculptural details of a more palatable Western style on the facade. Subtle colors were to enliven the front, with white walls, a soft green roof and doors, and yellow-beige door frames and entablature.

The interior detailing of the White House incorporated a number of Japanese elements: a curved lintel that created a small alcove or inglenook around the drawing room fireplace; Japanese-style railings on staircases; dado or lower wall surfaces textured to emulate matting; and built-in cabinets in the Anglo-Japanese style. (For further discussion of this interior, see chap. 7.)

Even more dramatic than Whistler's house was the design for Frank Miles's house at 44 Tite Street (see chap. 6). The front elevation of the original (unbuilt) plan of 1878 remains one of the most remarkable designs of the nineteenth century (fig. 3-26). The irregular arrangement of rectangles, the off-center placement of the dominant vertical windows, the projecting balcony, and the two horizontal windows just beneath the roof all have antecedents in Japanese architecture (fig. 3-27). The vertical–horizontal emphasis was continued by the extension of the balcony to the right, the projecting entablature over the door, and the careful placement of pipes and windows. The result was an asymmetrical design of projecting and receding rectangles that allowed no curves. The size and location of doors and windows related to their interior use, although the resulting exterior presented a carefully considered balance of shapes.

This plan also called for the stark facade to be softened by color and sculptural reliefs. Green slate would cover the

Fig. 3-23. E. W. Godwin. Cabinet known as the "Four Seasons Cabinet," ca. 1877. Probably made by William Watt. Satinwood with painted and gilt panels, ivory handles, and brass fittings; 70 x 50½ x 16 in. (177.8 x 128.3 x 40.6 cm). Trustees of the Victoria and Albert Museum, London, W15-1972.

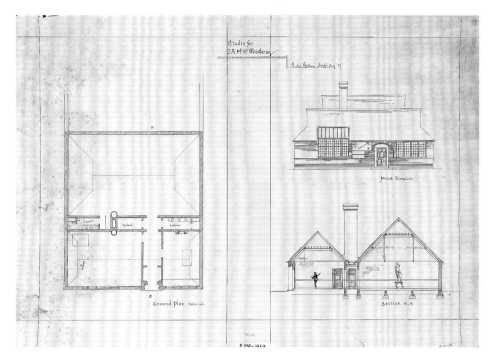

Fig. 3-25. Main Building, Katsura Imperial
Villa, Japan: side and front elevations. Built
1620-63. From Werner Blaser, *Japanese
Temples and Tea-Houses* (Basle: Werner Blaser,
1956): 78.

roof, the walls were to be of alternating red and yellow brickwork, and the frieze decoration was to be of warm terracotta red. Green foliage would cascade from the balcony as indicated in Godwin's sketch. Miles was an amateur horticulturalist who collected exotic flowers and plants.

Unfortunately, Godwin's dramatic design was not accepted by the Metropolitan Board of Works, and the design that was finally passed by the board had lost much of its revolutionary character (see fig. 6-56). Godwin added a bay window, a curved Dutch chimney, some fashionable "Queen Anne" decorative details, and, as he put it, "the thing was pronounced charming. This is very sad."[63]

Godwin oversaw every aspect of the interior decoration of Frank Miles's house. He used Japanese motifs more directly than he had on the facade: alcoves and inglenooks with rounded lintels and Japanese woodwork patterns throughout. A letter from Miles to Godwin of December 15, 1878, notes, "I will go in for *one* door done with the Japanese work if it does not exceed £5.10. . . . I have no doubt they are beautiful and will be very effective. You must

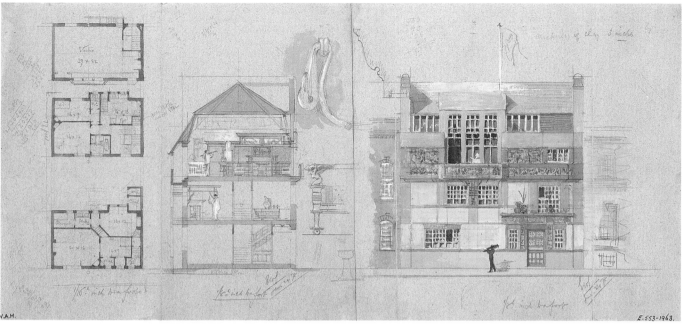

Fig. 3-26. E. W. Godwin. Frank Miles's House and Studio, 44 Tite Street, Chelsea, London: front elevation, section, and plans, 1878. Pencil and watercolor; 8⅝ x 19¼ in. (22 x 49 cm). This design was rejected by the Metropolitan Board of Works, London. Trustees of the Victoria and Albert Museum, London, E.553-1963. *Checklist no. 88.*

decide which door to put them in."[64] Godwin's color selections could have served as a primer for the Aesthetic movement: "Drawing Room: wood cinnamon, walls and ceilings toned golden yellow (north light). Your bedroom: wood blue, walls grey blue-green, ceiling white."[65]

Godwin's unprecedented original design for Frank Miles's house had resulted from years of thinking about and working with Japanese art. In the early 1870s he had explored the use of specific Japanese devices and forms in his architecture but tended to eliminate them in his final plans, partly at the request of his patrons. He retained the basic geometry of Japanese design, however, and blended this with his own powerful sense of proportion. It would be another twenty years before a design similar to Frank Miles's house would appear—in the early Prairie Houses of Frank Lloyd Wright—and another forty years after that until even closer descendants were to emerge in the works of Le Corbusier.

Fig. 3-27. Shôgetsu-tei. "Tea-houses of Pines in the Moonlight," Sambo-in, Daigo-ji, Kyoto, Japan. Built 1818–29. From Werner Blaser, *Japanese Temples and Tea-Houses* (Basle: Werner Blaser, 1956): 58.

Note: Most published sources are cited below in shortened form (author's last name, abbreviated title, date of publication); full references will be found in the bibliography. Frequently cited archives are abbreviated below; for a key to the abbreviations, also see the bibliography.

1. Godwin, "A Japanese Warehouse" (23 December 1876): 363.

2. Ibid.

3. Ibid.

4. Watanabe, *High Victorian Japonisme* (1991): 69–70.

5. Van Siebold, *Nippon* (1832–54). Also see Weisberg and Weisberg, *Japonisme* (1990): 7–12, nos. 8, 9, 13.

6. Hokusai's *Manga*, or "random sketches," was a collection of 15 volumes of black-and-white prints, published in book form in Japan between 1814 and 1878. See Hillier, *Hokusai* (1978): 50–54.

7. Burges' small collection of Japanese prints is today in the Victoria and Albert Museum (V&A PD, 8827). It has an inventory sheet signed and dated by him 18 October 1858.

8. Oliphant, *Narrative of the Earl of Elgin's Mission to China and Japan,* vol. 2 (1859): 76–77.

9. Fox, *Britain and Japan* (1969): 49–52.

10. Alcock, *Capital of the Tycoon* (1863).

11. Alcock, *Art and Art Industries in Japan* (1878): 1–2.

12. Before 1862 a few Japanese objects had been shown in London as part of the Chinese display at the Great Exhibition of 1851. In 1854 there was a small public showing of Japanese works of applied art at the Old Watercolour Society's headquarters in London. Both of these displays were miniscule compared to the comprehensive exhibit in the 1862 Japanese Court. For a more complete discussion, see Wilkinson, "Edward William Godwin and Japonisme" (1987): 63–66.

13. See Alcock, *Catalogue of Works of Industry and Art* (1862).

14. Burges, "International Exhibition," part 1 (June 1862): 665; part 2 (July 1862): 10–11; idem, "Japanese Court" (September 1862): 243–54; Dresser, "Japanese Ornamentation" (2 May 1863): 308–9; idem, "Ornamental Art of Japan" (23 May 1863): 364–66; idem, "Japanese Ornament" (13 June 1863): 423–24.

15. Harbron, *Conscious Stone* (1949): 34–35.

16. Fox, *Britain and Japan* (1969): 46–47.

17. *List of the Objects Obtained during the Paris Exhibition of 1867* (1868): v.

18. Baldry, "Growth of an Influence" (February 1900): 46–47.

19. Kelly's Directories, *Post Office Directory of London, 1868*, p. 1314.

20. Dresser described himself as an architect on the birth certificate of his daughter Nellie in 1840, but there is no evidence that he designed buildings. See Durant, *Christopher Dresser* (1993): 20.

21. See n. 7; Godwin and Burges met after 1858 (see chap. 1 in this volume).

22. Godwin, "Home of an English Architect," part 1 (June 1886): 171–72.

23. For an illustration see Young, MacDonald, and Spencer, *Paintings of James McNeill Whistler* (1980): pl. 35, cat. no. 49.

24. For an illustration of Cloverley Hall see Eastlake, *Gothic Revival* (1872), opp. p. 340.

25. William Eden Nesfield, original plans for Kinmel Park, Denbighshire, dated 3 February 1874, V&A PD, D. 1499-1907, no. 336. On this drawing Nesfield wrote, "No. two pies in soffit to be carved by Forsyth in deal. . . . No. two large pies in frieze ditto."

26. For more information about Jeckyll, see Linda Merrill, *The Peacock Room: A Cultural Biography* (New Haven and London: Yale University Press with the Freer Gallery of Art and the Smithsonian Institution, 1998).

27. Rutherford Alcock, *Art and Art Industries in Japan* (London: Virtue, 1878): 48–49.

28. Dresser, *Japan, Its Architecture* (1882).

29. Edward A. Craig, *Gordon Craig* (1968): 34.

30. Godwin sketchbooks, V&A PD E. 230-1963, pp. 4, 13, 22; V&A PD, E. 273-1963: 21; Godwin ledger (1858–69), V&A AAD, 4/9-1980, n.p. The ledger entry is a long list of Oriental objects with prices paid. Most entries indicate the shop from which the item was purchased. The shops listed are Wareham's, Hewett's, and Farmer and Rogers'.

31. RIBA Drawings, Ran 7/B/1(67). This drawing was published in black and white (Godwin, "Dromore Castle" [20 August 1870]: 106 and illus.). The other sketches, RIBA Drawings, Ran 7/B/1(68) and RIBA Drawings, Ran 7/B/1(69), show an even airier quality, with more use of blue.

32. V&A PD, E. 233-1963, p. 37.

33. Godwin, "My Chambers," part 2 (8 July 1876): 19.

34. Godwin, wallpaper designs, V&A PD, E. 513, 515-1963 and E. 241-1963.

35. E.g., the prints of Suzuki Harunobu (1725–1770) and Kitagawa Utamaru (1753–1806).

36. Christie and Manson, *Catalogue of the Celebrated Assemblage which formed "The Chinese Collection," 10–14 December 1851,* auction cat. (London, 1851), lot 52.

37. See, e.g., George Norbert Kates, *Chinese Household Furniture* (New York: Dover, 1968): pl. 70.

38. V&A PD, E. 233-1963, p. 75.

39. Humbert, *Le Japon illustré*, vol. 1 (1870): ii.

40. V&A PD, E. 280-1963 and E. 283-1963.

41. Public Record Office, BT 43/100, no. 270551, and register BT44/9, dated 18 February 1873.

42. Humbert, *Le Japon illustré*, vol. 2 (1870): 5. It might also be noted that the cross pattern sketched on the same page as the *mon* from the "Library at Yedo" found its way into the background of the final design of the "Peacock" wallpaper.

43. V&A PD, E. 280-1963, p. 9.

44. Godwin wrote in the sketchbook with the crowned crane, "All the sketches in this book are drawn by me from the life" (V&A PD, E. 272-1963, p. 1). Another sketchbook with birds has the notation, "The Zoo July 31, '68," the same date as one of the drawings on the page with the crowned crane (V&A PD, E. 268-1963, opp. p. 19).

45. Staggered shelves or interconnected shelves of different heights were a characteristic feature of the *shoin* style of domestic architecture in Japan dating from the Ashikaga Period (1336–1573). The earliest extant example is in a tea room, completed in 1486, at the Silver Pavilion complex (Jishōji) in Kyoto. *Shoin* means "writing hall" and refers to the main reception room in the house or castle. The divided shelves (*chigaidana*) occupy a section of the back wall. Christopher Dresser illustrated a *chigaidana* in his book (Dresser, *Japan* [1882]: 269, fig. 106). He explained, "While there is no furniture in a Japanese room, there is generally a little arrangement of fixed shelves in a corner, on which objects may be placed" (ibid.).

46. This table is now in the Ellen Terry Museum. The approximate date of 1871 has been assigned by the author based on the close stylistic relationship of the table with the sketches from Humbert, published in 1870. It should be noted that Godwin often returned to the sketches in later years for details; however, the resulting pieces were usually more removed from the original sources than this table.

47. Humbert, *Le Japon illustré*, vol. 2 (1870): 210.

48. Ibid., vol. 1, p. 133; Godwin's drawing is in V&A PD, E. 283-1963, p. 1.

49. Elizabeth Aslin dates this sketch "about 1877" (Aslin, *E. W. Godwin* [1986]: 78, pl. 58), but it is in a sketchbook that has designs dated 1872 and 1873, some made for the Collinson and Lock display at the International Exhibition in Vienna in 1873 (V&A PD, E. 229-1963, pp. 39, 47).

50. A drawing on the page next to this sketch is labeled "Sent to Frank Miles, Ap. 24, '79" (Godwin, V&A PD, E. 233-1963, p. 114).

51. V&A PD, E. 233-1963: 69.

52. Humbert, *Le Japon illustré*, vol. 2 (1870): 369.

53. V&A PD, E. 280-1963, p. 2.

54. "Section. Studio House for James McNeill Whistler, Nov. 1877," V&A PD, E. 542-1963; sketches in a letter from Godwin to Princess Louise, "Aug. 31, 1878," V&A AAD, 4/189-1988.

55. Messenger and Company, *Artistic Conservatories* (1880), pl. 15.

56. Humbert, *Le Japon illustré*, vol. 1 (1870): 214; Godwin's sketch, V&A PD, E. 283-1963, p. 5.

57. V&A PD, E. 482-1963.

58. Godwin, "Japanese Wood Construction," part 5 (12 February 1875): 173.

59. Aslin, *E. W. Godwin* (1986): 24.

60. Godwin, "Japanese Wood Construction," part 6 (19 February 1875): after 201.

61. It is believed that the paintings were executed by Godwin's second wife, Beatrice, an artist who may have studied architecture briefly with Godwin and later studied painting with Whistler (Aslin, *E. W. Godwin* [1986]: 24, no. 10). Also see chap. 1 in this volume.

62. Girouard, "Chelsea's Bohemian Studio-Houses" (23 November 1972): 1371.

63. Godwin, "Studios and Mouldings" (7 March 1879): 261.

64. Letter from Frank Miles to Godwin, 15 December 1878, V&A AAD, 4/158-1980.

65. Letter from Godwin to Frank Miles, 22 May 1979, V&A AAD, 4/159, 160-1980.

Fig. 4-1. E. W. Godwin. Sideboard, ca. 1877. Made by William Watt. Ebonized mahogany with brass pulls and hinges, glass panels; 72½ x 100½ x 19¾ in. (184.2 x 255.3 x 50.2 cm); Private collection. *Checklist no. 57*

CHAPTER 4

E·W·GODWIN·AND·MODERNISM

JULIET KINCHIN

Godwin was well aware of the mechanisms by which critical reputations are constructed. As a prominent figure in the London art scene and above all as a journalist and obituarist, he was in a position to speed his contemporaries toward recognition or anonymity. The last articles he wrote were reflections on his close friend William Burges, who had died in 1881, and Godwin, preoccupied with his own delicate health, must have mused over how he himself would be remembered.[1] "If a painter of easel pictures dies," he once observed, "you can gather his life's work together into one place, and at loan exhibitions from time to time, even centuries after his death, they can command new, diverse and large audiences."[2] By contrast he pointed to the difficulties of trying to summarize the varied achievements of a designer or architect. Their grander urban projects might attract acclaim, but what of the scattered, apparently inconsequential, and often anonymous examples of their creative energy, a power "that was satisfied in creating, and is nameless, or shamefully carries credit to another's name"?[3] Godwin would surely have sympathized with the organizers of his own retrospective exhibition and with all those researchers who in recent years have been faced with the problems of disentangling who did what and discerning the interrelationship between Godwin's multifarious activities. The nature and extent of his creative collaborations with friends and family can never be unraveled conclusively, and his input is similarly difficult to extricate from the complex machinery of commerce, manufacture, and the media. Oscar Wilde perhaps came closest by describing him, in disembodied terms, as an "artistic spirit."[4]

Godwin himself had a vested interest in campaigning on questions of authorship and copyright, just as museums, dealers, and collectors of his work do now. These are also questions that are at the heart of any discussion of Godwin in relation to Modernism, since traditionally any "canon" has relied upon isolating the individual designer, delimiting his oeuvre, and establishing links to the work of other great designers and artists. If Godwin is difficult to pin down, so too is any comprehensive definition of "Modernism," a fluid, dynamic term that has developed throughout this century in a constant dialectic with contemporary culture and history. It has been used to cover many different, often conflicting types of practice and theory.[5]

Even so, since around 1960 Godwin has been assigned a place on the margins of the development of the Modern movement.[6] After a probationary period in the wilderness of decadent Aestheticism, he became linked with evolutionary views of Modernism because some of his works appeared to embody the potential abstraction of visual language, a premonition of standardized, reproducible forms, and an identification with values of simplicity, health, economy, and utility. As a precursor, Godwin was posthumously enlisted in the grand search for "absolutes" and a generalized tendency toward nonrepresentational work, valid on its own terms, rather than tied to historically specific conditions and localized place. Godwin's work is not widely known; usually only a tiny number of works are cited—specifically, his Anglo-Japanese furniture (fig. 4-1) and the famous White House designed for Whistler in Chelsea. These free-floating icons are frequently presented as milestones in a journey toward twentieth-century design. Critical reputations were mediated through exhibitions and the marketplace, and it is this reading of Godwin as a pioneer that still lends itself to representation in museum displays and to the commodification of his furniture as "cult objects."

Challenges to Modernist visual culture in recent decades, however, have also colored the perception of its history, fracturing any faith in a single-strand view of the past. "Modernism" is now seen to embrace a number of alternative traditions. A more flexible approach to the significance and contextualization of Godwin's symbolist tendencies, for example, or his radicalized domesticity and creative involvement in the shifting formations of the London art world, can offer a more sympathetic, inclusive view of his role within Modernism. In his own time Godwin was both an avant-garde artist and critic, and an observer and designer of modern life. Examining him in this light suggests an approach to thinking about Godwin's experience and his expression of what was modern in *his* time, rather than viewing him as some kind of historical expedient in a longer narrative.

From "Wicked Earl" to "Pioneer of Modern Design"

As recently as 1994, Godwin was singled out as the "unrivalled forefather" of the Modern movement.[7] The first source in which one might expect to find validation for such a bold claim is Nikolaus Pevsner's seminal text, *Pioneers of Modern Design: From William Morris to Walter Gropius*. Yet Godwin is notable by his absence from both the first 1936 edition (entitled *Pioneers of the Modern Movement*) and the second, expanded version of 1948 produced in collaboration with the Museum of Modern Art in New York. Only in the 1960 edition were an illustration of a design for Whistler's White House and a couple of references to Godwin squeezed in. So in the Pevsnerian scheme of things, Godwin was never one of the major players like a Morris, Mackintosh, or Gropius. Why then the delayed acceptance into the official canon, and on what grounds was he ultimately included?

When Pevsner was formulating *Pioneers* in the 1930s, "the architecture of reason and functionalism was in full swing in many countries."[8] Judging by the inaccurate and lackluster entry in the *Dictionary of National Biography*, Godwin's critical reputation was at an all-time low, with

little of his work clearly identified or recorded.[9] Although his influence resonated in architectural and theatrical circles for a time just after his premature death in 1886, Godwin's name appears to have plummeted rapidly from the public gaze. By 1890, when Whistler caused a public fracas in defense of Godwin's reputation, Godwin was so little known that the newspapers had difficulty explaining to their readers who he was, beyond referring to him as some deceased friend of the artist.[10] After an initial lull, however, the 1895 trial of Oscar Wilde, another of Godwin's friends and a vocal supporter, effectively tied Godwin's critical fortunes to the most decadent forms of Aestheticism, a linkage reinforced by his inclusion in the notorious *Yellow Book* published that same year.[11] The backlash to the excesses of Aestheticism was not long coming in intellectual circles. The painter and critic Roger Fry, for example, was of a generation that had come of age amid its most commercialized manifestations. Writing in 1919, he shuddered at the memory of the 1880s, not so much on account of the sham Chippendale and the sham old oak, but "a still worse horror—a genuine modern style which as yet has no name, a period of black polished furniture with spidery lines."[12] He continued presciently, "We have at this moment no inkling of the kind of lies they (our successors) will invent about the eighties to amuse themselves."

The colorful and complex nature of Godwin's private life was always going to make objective evaluation of his work difficult. The whiff of scandal and Bohemia continued to seep out in anecdotal snippets among the memoirs and biographical studies of those Godwin had known. Generally, he makes a shadowy appearance as a brilliant and charming womanizer, nicknamed "the wicked Earl."[13] In this respect Godwin's famous illegitimate son, the philandering and flamboyantly theatrical Edward Gordon Craig, was seen as carrying on a family tradition. But while to the up-and-coming generation of High Modernists of the 1920s and 1930s, the decadence and elitism with which Godwin was associated were distasteful, a wider audience was thirsting for salacious detail.[14] Godwin's first biographer, George Dudley Harbron, predicted that "the psychological interest inherent in his person may lead to reconsideration of Godwin earlier than will the character of his work. The majority of readers are more curious about persons than concerned for the things they created."[15] Harbron's book, *The Conscious Stone: The Life of Edward William Godwin* (1949), went some way toward setting the record straight and identifying the range of Godwin's achievements, but it did not have the authority of a monograph such as Thomas Howarth's *Charles Rennie Mackintosh and the Modern Movement*, which was published around the

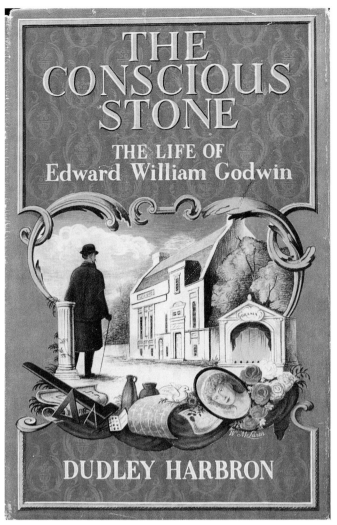

Fig. 4-2. W. McLaren. Dust jacket. From Dudley Harbron, *The Conscious Stone: The Life of Edward William Godwin* (1949). The cover romanticizes key elements of Godwin's life: art, architecture, and design, represented by Whistler's White House, a scrolling architectural plan, drafting tools, and wallpaper; the proscenium arch of a theater, and a portrait of Ellen Terry.

same time. The colorful and cheerfully romantic design of Harbron's dust jacket was eloquent (fig. 4-2).[16] Meanwhile Godwin the proto-Modernist, the rational bringer of light, simplicity, and health, was on the verge of being disengaged well and truly from Godwin the Wicked Earl and the slimy gloom of latter-day Aestheticism.

Building on Harbron's research, Pevsner's 1952 article, "Art Furniture of the Eighteen-Seventies," flushed one of Godwin's sideboards from obscurity.[17] The piece was included in a groundbreaking exhibition of Victorian and Edwardian decorative arts that was held at the Victoria and Albert Museum in 1952. There, Godwin's furniture and textiles appeared alongside the work of established design reformers such as William Morris, Bruce Talbert, and Christopher Dresser.[18] At this point one could say Godwin's public rehabilitation as a serious designer was under way. Among those stimulated by the exhibition was the Scandinavian scholar Alf Bøe, whose 1957 study of Victorian design theories was to make a case for tracing the origins of twentieth-century functionalism to Godwin and Christopher Dresser rather than to William Morris.[19] The following year an article by Edgar Kaufmann, Jr., an extremely influential figure in promoting European Modernist design in the 1950s through exhibitions and publications at the Museum of Modern Art in New York, also picked up on Godwin as a significant figure in the nineteenth-century genesis of the International Style.[20] And in 1960 Godwin finally made it into Pevsner's *Pioneers of Modern Design*, the standard history of the period in the English-speaking world. By this time the ideological foundations of the Modern movement were already being brought into question, but the seductively simple thrust of the *Pioneers* argument was to survive revision for many years to come.

Pevsner packaged Godwin to suit his evolutionary narrative, emphasizing certain aspects of Godwin's contribution and suppressing or diminishing others. In his earlier article on art furniture, for example, Pevsner saw a premonition of 1890s Art Nouveau in the details of Godwin's designs for Anglo-Japanese drawing-room furniture: "these precariously projecting shelves, these thin curved brackets, these spidery tapering legs" (fig. 4-3).[21] We know from other contexts that he viewed Art Nouveau as a throwback, the work of "fantasts and freaks," a "blind alley."[22] Pevsner's article, however, went on to draw attention to the "functionalist side of Godwin" exemplified in a wardrobe's simple outline and rectilinear units, which were "so rational that few would hesitate to date it in the early years of the twentieth century."[23] We may ask why Godwin's furniture for more "masculine" contexts, such as the dining room and library, or for the less visible areas of the home (servants' quarters and bedrooms), should be judged as more radical *per se* than his "feminine" side, the more curvilinear, delicate, and decorative idiom brought out by the drawing room? The latter was just one aspect of Godwin's style which did not fit Pevsner's pioneer polemic and the kind of macho-Modernist aesthetic it celebrated, but arguably it was these very ambiguities and tensions that made Godwin's work so rich.[24] The only reference Pevsner ever made to Godwin's theater work was a passing mention of his interest in the staging of Greek plays.[25] Godwin's more voluminous Shakespearian scholarship and productions could have been related just as strongly to his furniture designs, but it suited

Fig. 4-3. E. W. Godwin. Design for a drawing room. From William Watt, *Art Furniture* (1877), pl. 7. The Mitchell Wolfson Jr. Collection, The Wolfsonian–Florida International University, Miami Beach, Florida, TD1990.40.62

Pevsner to dwell on the Greek ideal, which was closer to the aesthetic of the Modern movement.

Similar judgments infuse the 1960 edition of *Pioneers of Modern Design*. Godwin is described as the inventor of some "fantastic decoration," which is enough to link him immediately with the Art Nouveau designer Emile Gallé, who used "fantastic colours," and with the "fantastical rantings" of Antoni Gaudí and Antonio Sant'Elia.[26] This vein of unreal fantasy and "the suspiciously sophisticated and refined" qualities of Art Nouveau were contrasted with the sobriety and sanity of the Arts and Crafts movement.[27] The praise for Whistler's White House is undercut in the same way: it is described in positive terms as "original, challenging," but its "witty" quality and the "highly capricious" fenestration reveal it as transitional.[28] "Capricious" had echoes of the willful Gaudí, while wit and playfulness were for Pevsner the antithesis of the seriousness and discipline that were to characterize the Modern movement. The torch of progress is passed from the White House to Arthur H. Mackmurdo's Enfield home of about 1883, the latter being identified as "much more orderly."[29] Pevsner goes on to describe the plain walls, lightness, and sparse furnishings of

Godwin's 1862 Bristol home and of the White House as projecting us into the early years of the twentieth century, "no longer in the days of Ruskin and Morris,"[30] then immediately qualifies this by classing Whistler (and by implication Godwin) as antimodern, an Impressionist, "and therefore an object of passionate hatred to those who worked for a new outlook on life and art."[31] For Pevsner Impressionism was identified with "superficiality and concern with personal rather than communal interests," and it signified a "refusal to distinguish the changing and the lasting, the absolute and accidental."[32] It represented art for art's sake versus a renewed faith in the social purpose of art.[33]

The paradox inherent in any linear history written backward from the present was neatly summed up by a bemused correspondent in the *Building News* of 1872: "We hardly know whether E. W. G. is centuries before or centuries behind his time."[34] As soon as we try to extend Pevsner's trajectory of progress forward from the 1930s, breaking the time lock in which the orthodox history of the Modern movement seems sealed, his value judgments are suddenly inverted. Far from leading to a cul-de-sac, many of the qualities he relegated there—wit, eclecticism,

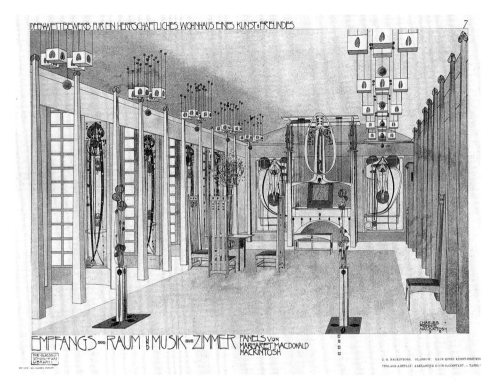

Fig. 4-4. Charles Rennie Mackintosh and Margaret Macdonald. Design for a Music Room in the house for an art lover (*Haus eines kunst freundes*), 1901. Lithograph; 20⅞ x 15½ in. (52.9 x 39.4 cm). The Glasgow School of Art Library.

rejection of universal values—have come back into their own. Like the other pioneers, Godwin is presented as grappling with a range of conflicts or contradictions, between historicism and the challenge of new materials and mass production; between retrogressive decorative impulses and tectonic values of form and structure; between "useless" and socially useful design. These polarized dualities are seen to pull Godwin in opposing directions, whereas a fuller picture of his theory and practice suggests that, for him, such qualities were part of a continuum and not necessarily mutually exclusive.

Pevsner did not single-handedly invent the critical tradition within which he located Godwin but was picking up selectively on debates that had been elaborated within design reform circles since the mid-nineteenth century—debates in which Godwin himself had participated. The themes of economy, utility, and simplicity recur frequently in Godwin's writing. But an institutionalized hierarchy of artistic genres existed in the late nineteenth century, which meant that even in Godwin's lifetime his radical contribution to "sub" genres such as theater and dress was rarely discussed, despite his attempts to raise the visibility of such art forms. Similarly, although the Modern movement purported to promote the unity of the arts, it was theorized by critics and early historians of its development, including Pevsner, around the paradigm of architecture, which has undoubtedly skewed our sense of Godwin as a Modernist.

While retaining an emphasis on practicality and usefulness, Godwin had joined the steady drift away from the moral overtones of the Gothic Revival and its "stern recog-

nition of truthfulness in design."[35] The Arts and Crafts movement of the 1880s and 1890s, however, continued to develop a rhetoric that emphasized a socially moral dimension to Godwin's equation of health, rationality, and economy. This overriding sense of moral purpose, which held such an appeal for Pevsner, had come through strongly in the analysis of one of Godwin's sideboards in 1892 by Aymer Vallance, who argued that it offered a form of rectilinear resistance to the "swollen monstrosities [which seem] sadly significant of the decadence of these latter days of ours."[36] Vallance further suggested that the "aggressive affectation of any past style" encouraged the outbreak of dirt and disorder, injurious to art and bodily health alike.[37]

Although Godwin never had a large architectural practice and his few pupils were a fairly undistinguished lot, there is plenty of circumstantial evidence to suggest that scholars such as Pevsner and Bøe were right to connect aspects of Godwin's work with the next generation of architect-designers, such as Charles Rennie Mackintosh, George Walton, Arthur Heygate Mackmurdo, and Charles Ashbee. Godwin's lectures, papers, and published articles had an impact on the younger members of the profession, as did the competitions he set and judged in the *British Architect* Art Club from 1879 to 1884.[38] C. F. A. Voysey, for example, while distancing himself from Morris, saw Godwin as one of the architect-designers who had set his generation free from a formulaic and inappropriate use of past styles.[39] Godwin's *Art Furniture* catalogue for William Watt was being studied at the Glasgow School of Art, courtesy of the South Kensington loan scheme, at a time when Mack-

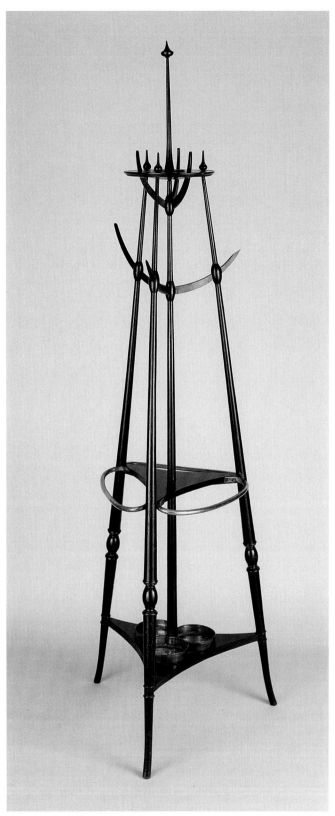

Fig. 4-5. George Walton. Coatstand for the Buchanan Street Tearoom, Glasgow, ca. 1897. Ebonized wood; 72 x 16⅛ x 14⅛ in. (183 x 41 x 36 cm). Glasgow Museums and Art Galleries.

intosh (fig. 4-4) and Walton (fig. 4-5) were enrolled as young students.[40] When designing studio houses in Chelsea, both Ashbee (fig. 4-6) and later Mackintosh looked inevitably to Godwin's example.[41]

It was the architect and critic Hermann Muthesius who provided an important link between this generation of British architect-designers and the quest for a modern industrial design culture in early twentieth-century Germany. Like Pevsner, Muthesius formed a partial view of Godwin that was driven by a clear political and ideological agenda and colored by a reaction against the more expressionist tendencies in *Jugendstil* (the German form of Art Nouveau). Above all it was Godwin's furniture designs in the Watt catalogue that struck Muthesius as "responsive to rational progress," showing "a great advance" in their lightness and elegance, and foreshadowing "the idea of the modern interpretation which was soon to follow."[42]

Godwin was a designer in the modern sense of the word, arguing that design resided in the drawing and concept rather than the craft with which an object was executed, and he worked within the parameters of industrial production. In 1886 the *British Architect* had described his Anglo-Japanese designs as "more suited to a proper use of wood in design than any other modern furniture we have seen."[43] The potential for the reproduction of his wallpaper and furniture designs had been confirmed by their proliferation internationally, from America to Europe and Australia. As far as Muthesius could see, the type of "English" furniture he had come across in German and French shops well into the 1890s was so like the designs in the Watt catalogue that they were possibly copied from Godwin.

In 1914 Muthesius was to argue vehemently for the adoption of standardized forms compatible with mass production. But Godwin himself almost certainly would have taken the position of Henri van de Velde, Muthesius's opponent in the Deutsche Werkbund, who had argued that a style imposed from above would stultify the creativity of the individual artist. Godwin believed in a functional, structural approach to design and the concept of fitness for purpose, but he was equally an unflagging advocate of individualism. He had witnessed how the strict rules and orthodoxy of the Gothic Revival had enslaved architects; any "new style" had to be a servant.[44] Style could never be fixed or universal. It was always to be refracted through the individual's perceptions and the particular context of the times. This emphasis on individual expressivity could be construed as prefiguring Modernist *art,* but was antithetical to theories of Modernism in design. Godwin deliberately set out to avoid monotonous regularity, and his individualism was expressed in ways that contemporary critics often praised as being picturesque or quaint designs.[45] For Muthesius and Pevsner, however, such tendencies were viewed as outbreaks of willful disorder. It also does not sound as though Godwin would have been happy with a soulless machine aesthetic, despite his apparent acceptance of mechanized production as a fact of life which an artist could learn to exploit. "There is a charm about the old we all more or less feel—a charm never, or very, very rarely, found in modern," he wrote; this was not simply a question of age, but the presence of "natural feeling and artistic spirit as opposed to the essentially unartistic, mechanical modern spirit."[46] As far as Godwin was concerned, a young artist could never know too much of history.[47] Nevertheless Muthesius's feeling that English Arts and Crafts design was "excessively primitive" chimed with the urban sophistication of Godwin, who disliked what he called the "Farmyard School" in all its manifestations; "modern life is artificial enough without the addition of that worst of artificialities—the assumption of a rural simplicity."[48] Godwin wished nothing to do with "cottage interiors, farm-yards, agricultural labourers and the like."[49] Nothing struck him as more pretentious than pretending to live in the country when in a city.[50]

In the changing intellectual climate of the 1960s, the values of the Modern movement were brought into question, and there was a corresponding rise of interest in Victorian studies. The strains on progressivist views of developments in the nineteenth century were signaled by scholars such as Elizabeth Aslin who openly challenged any view of the Aesthetic movement that presupposed the superiority of twentieth-century work.[51] In the 1970s Godwin came into his own as a "Pioneer of a Free Manner," the title of an essay in a collection attempting to revalue the "wayward integrity" of Edwardian architecture outside of the mainstream of development toward the interwar Modern movement.[52] These essays highlighted the complex and confused nature of tendencies in the late nineteenth century and posited a range of progressive options rather than Pevsner's single-strand interpretation. Godwin's architecture was shown to connect in Britain not only to the Arts and Crafts, but also to an Edwardian Free Style, characterized by eclecticism, and the "rogue architecture" of the neo-Baroque Grand Manner.[53] This mulitiple legacy was exemplified by the architecture of James MacLaren, a talented admirer of Godwin.[54]

In the history of fine and decorative arts, Symbolism and Art Nouveau, so vilified by Pevsner, began to receive more attention as part of an alternative tradition within the Modern movement, to which Godwin related more convincingly than pure functionalism. In this context Godwin

Fig. 4-6. C. R. Ashbee. 72-74 Cheyne Walk, Chelsea, London, 1894-98. From *Neubauten in London* (Berlin, 1900): pl. 16.

was a particularly strong role model for Glasgow Style designers, such as Walton and Mackintosh, whose Aesthetic and Symbolist qualities have come to the fore in recent studies.[55] Godwin's influence resonated in the ethereal, poetic, and theatrical qualities of the interiors they created, their delicate use of color, and the slender attenuated forms of the ebonized furniture they designed. Godwin urged students, when asked what style they followed, to reply, "It is my own,"[56] just as Mackintosh was to exhort his fellow art-workers to "go alone."[57]

Avant-Garde Artist and Critic

It is as an "artist" in the broadest sense of the word that Godwin is to be considered. His contribution to Modernism is generally discussed in relation to his architecture and furniture, but arguably he interacted with the world of avant-garde art in a more sustained and sophisticated way than any other designer or architect at that time. In other words his Modernism was not only revealed in the design of products, but in his whole mindset, the way he lived, and his public image, as mediated through the press. On moving to London from Bristol, he reinvented himself—one of his great achievements—as a kind of free-ranging "artistic spirit" whose role was incidentally that of architect, designer, theater director, critic, and teacher.

Part of this stance as "brilliant, if somewhat eccentric" was to provide a polemical critique of conventional attitudes and organizations from within the Bohemian margins of the art world, both through his journalism and his practice.[58] His "distinct personality" dominated "the little world of art."[59] A regular habitué of the club, theater, gallery, and studio circuit, Godwin collaborated with a number of artists, including his wife Beatrice, and wrote about their work in ways that also broadened debates within the related spheres of architecture and design. As a designer he created an innovative range of environments in which artists lived, worked, exhibited, and sold their works. In particular he worked in tandem with Whistler, with whose reputation his own became enmeshed. He was to prove one of the most perceptive and consistently supportive commentators on Whistler's work, which in turn reinforced his own cachet as an artist fighting Philistine incomprehension and reactionary constraint. All this was very different from the self-presentation of a fellow designer such as Christopher Dresser, doctor of philosophy and "workman," or that of a fashionable academician such as the architect Richard Norman Shaw, although these were individuals to whom Godwin was close stylistically.[60]

Godwin deliberately played upon the Romantic myth of the artist as a loner, an outsider rising above mundane concerns and endowed with spiritual insight beyond that of the common herd, a concept that was to feed directly into canonical Modernism. When he chose to, Godwin could talk as convincingly as the next architect about a building's sewage system, how it related to a local context and historical conditions, its construction and cost, and so on, but by stressing its art he signaled resistance to the quantification of architecture as a mere product of function, or as a purely material commodity. Godwin's rather superior and aloof manner reflected his view of himself as an aristocrat of the art world, rather than "on a dead level with mere craftsmen."[61] An art vocation became a means of flouting the strictures of social class and respectable behavior to which both he and Whistler would have had to conform had they succumbed to early pressure to become engineers. Their first duty was to their art rather than any political ideology or external code of morality and religion. In Godwin's home the ritual smoke of a perfumed censer curled around the ideal form of Venus de Milo, not a religious icon. He frequently resorted to language that implied idealism and aspiration to a transcendental realm of thought, feeling, and

pure emotion.[62] The stated aim of his art was to choreograph and beautify modern living in ways that cultivated the senses: "If there is any respect left among us for the human body, it must surely be among the very highest utilities to minister to its keenest sensibilities."[63] Like Whistler he often resorted to musical analogies to express compositional and atmospheric qualities.[64] In a letter to a client in 1873 he wrote, "I look upon all my work as Art Work. A building is to me as a picture to a painter or a poem to a poet."[65] Such a statement invites evaluation of his work in the abstract, formalist terms of Modernist art criticism.

While he despised pretentious "twaddle about art,"[66] quick-witted, barbed, and intense conversation was a hallmark of the cultured Bohemian. Art was a way of being, a form of sociability, sitting around in smoke-filled clubs, Turkish baths, backstage in theaters, or in the studios of friends at all times of day and night. The sexual radicalism, the drinking, smoking, and drug-taking within Godwin's circle, were a modern type of behavior familiar to us now, but certainly beyond the pale for respectable society in the late nineteenth century. True artists were above conventionally defined moral codes and social responsibilities. The irregular timekeeping, the lack of visible productivity, and the apparent self-indulgence were a form of coded resistance to the Protestant work ethic at the heart of capitalism and to the commodification of time and art. Godwin's lifestyle was an artwork in itself, which, to be genuine, had to be on some level the "natural" and authentic expression of his individual artistic spirit. In this competitive environment it was the accreditation of "artist" that empowered Godwin to distance himself from the anonymous jobbing designer whose work was "daily rolled out between the two heavy cylinders of his brain with as much intelligence and delight as go to the production of sheet iron or milled lead."[67] As an "original," Godwin had to demonstrate constantly his capacity to distinguish true from false, real from sham, whether manifested in paintings, theater props, oriental ceramics, antique furniture, dress, or manners.[68] In the plurality of contexts in which he could work and act, and in the diversity of "authorities" which he could draw into his style, the only connecting force was the stamp of his individual "signature."

This preoccupation with authenticity was seen by Georg Simmel, a Berlin academic at the turn of the century, as a hallmark of modernity. Simmel saw the deepest problems of modern life as deriving from "the claim of the individual to preserve the autonomy and individuality of his existence in the face of overwhelming social forces."[69] It was a constant struggle for an independent artist to maintain his visibility within the regulatory systems of capitalism.

The London art market was booming, and in the fluid conditions of the late nineteenth century, various groups were jockeying for position within an increasingly codified hierarchy of skills and professions, threatening to limit the artist to ever more one-sided accomplishment. Godwin actively resisted such compartmentalization, canvasing to extend the interest of architects to related areas such as interiors, furniture, and garden design, and to theater or exhibition work. "Hitherto we have rarely allowed ourselves to step beyond the limits of one art, but for the future we hope to take a wider range," he wrote in the *British Architect*; "we shall embrace in our survey the broader ground of painting and sculpture, taking note the while of that art which involves all others, namely the art of the stage. . . . To reconcile the decorative and constructive, to work for greater harmony and unity in the surroundings of modern life will be one of our aims."[70]

One can see this mission statement as part of a broader trend within Modernism to reunify cultural production. There were precedents for the involvement of architects in interior and furniture design, but less so for the type of ambitious intervention Godwin envisaged in the world of the theater. Inevitably, there was a backlash from those whose patch he was colonizing: "let us take off our hats to *Godwin*, the renowned; *Godwin*, the architect and archaeologist; *Godwin* the manager and stage manager; *Godwin* the scene painter and inventor of the Pastoral Player; *Godwin* the Great Man Milliner!" jibed a disgruntled theater manager.[71] From a furniture manufacturer came searing criticism of those "singular beings with hobbies . . . architects who do not practice architecture, but devote themselves to furniture, pottery, landscape, sewerage, etc, etc.," which was followed by a demolition of designs by Godwin and his assistant, George Freeth Roper.[72]

Godwin was a successful and tireless advocate for the supremacy of the artist as innovator and arbiter of style. Like Whistler he took a combative stance in relation to the Establishment in its various forms and to the Philistines in general. In many ways the controversy sparked by the White House and the debates engendered by the famous Whistler versus Ruskin trial of the same year were similar, and the two were linked in public perceptions. Both incidents now appear as a symbolic watershed in the break with High Victorian values and the emergence of modern attitudes to art and design. Godwin's particular bogey was the Metropolitan Board of Works with whom he had a series of run-ins on matters of environmental health and architectural conservation as well as over his own designs for Tite Street.[73] The board pronounced the first austere White House elevation "like a deadhouse."[74] Nor could they tol-

erate the still more radical design for Frank Miles's house across the road. In Godwin's view the latter was the best thing he had ever done, but it did not comply with the stultified perception that architecture should consist of "cornices and parapets, and all the detail involved in a complete study of the Building Act."[75] Godwin was indignant. "Who were they who sat in judgement on the designs of those who had worked and laboured at their art for years?" he protested. "What judgement could successful farriers and cheesemongers of yesterday give, who had never drawn a line, and never seen a drawing until they were elected on this ill-constituted board?"[76]

Godwin considered his architecture, like all other expressions of his creative power, a distillation of constant unseen thought and observation filtered through his individually honed sensibility. In this respect the gauntness of the proposed Tite Street elevations which caused the brouhaha, was the product of a lifetime's brainwork, just as were Whistler's Nocturnes.[77] The time-consuming exercise of "the highest mental power"[78] often resulted in a deceptively simple outcome which could not be assessed simply in terms of the materials and physical labor involved, nor according to the scale of the project. As Godwin pointed out in the *Art Furniture* catalogue, even something as small as a coffee table did not come about by any "happy go lucky process." He recognized that "art" had become a marketable commodity and indeed worked with a range of art manufacturers, but he did not wish to sell out to them completely. At times he clearly resented operating in a world ruled by money, in which there was not time for quiet thought and in which art and architecture could apparently be bought by the square yard.[79]

Through the press Godwin battled to preserve the autonomy of the artist from interference by the patron or owner. In the cause célèbre of the Peacock Room in 1876, Godwin supported Whistler's art over the needs of shipping magnate F. R. Leyland, the client, just as Whistler supported Godwin over the visual vandalism of the White House, first by the Metropolitan Board of Works and then by the critic Harry Quilter who bought the property in 1879.[80] Godwin and Whistler shared an almost obsessive desire to control the context in which their art was displayed, and they collaborated on the installation of each other's work, as at the 1878 Paris Exposition Universelle. But such control was temporary. New tenants, such as Quilter, might alter Godwin's design, and, once an exhibition was over, whether of paintings by Whistler or furniture by Godwin, the decorative ensemble of the installation, an artwork in itself, was consigned to oblivion by "the restlessness of modern fashion, forever changing."[81] Godwin described how once Whistler's

Fig. 4-7. George Du Maurier. "The Mutual Admirationists." From *Punch* (22 May 1880): 234.

"notes, harmonies, nocturnes" had departed to their several purchasers from the exhibition at Messrs Dowdeswell in Bond Street, the gallery scheme, also designed by Whistler, would be swept away. "That these exquisitely lovely arrangements of colour should live as memories only," he wrote, "gives to the very nomenclature our painter has adopted a touch of pathos. The room in Piccadilly and the rooms at the Fine Art Society have gone, as Whistlerian compositions, quite as effectually as the vibrations of the last quartette."[82]

The movable artworks, cut loose from their creators and functioning within a larger world, also risked vandalism. On one hand, Godwin willingly engaged with modernized forms of mass production and distribution, while on the other, he fought a losing battle for control of the authorship and meaning of his reproducible designs. As an archaeologist he realized the importance of syntactical interrelationships in the study of material culture, and as a skilled collector he was practiced in recontextualizing existing objects into new envelopes of atmosphere and meaning. He was all too aware, therefore, of how the context in

which his furniture and wallpapers were seen and used could affect their meaning. He once remarked on the phenomenon of an actress being ridiculed on stage for her Aesthetic costume but passing unnoticed in the same style of dress out on the street (fig. 4-7).[83]

Publishing protests against caricatures and distortions was one way of trying to assert the rights of the individual artist; another was to make sure that the original designs were visibly credited through the media. To an extent Godwin could see imitation as a form of flattery, but not when the integrity of his original design was travestied in the process. In Godwin's view the "art" of such a design resided not in the workmanship and materials so much as the synthesis of lines, proportions, and color in the composition. He protested to his readers in 1877 that bootleg copies of his coffee table met him almost everywhere he went—"in private houses, in show-rooms, in pictures, and in books, very prominently in the frontispiece of Miss Garrett's 'Suggestions for House Decoration.'"[84] Despite this public reprimand, however, a year later he was having to take Mrs. Lucy Orrinsmith and her friends to task for not having the grace to acknowledge him as the source of their "original ideas" and illustrations.[85] Meanwhile, in the United States, Clarence Cook was using Godwin furniture designs unattributed to illustrate a series of articles for *Scribner's Monthly*, subsequently reprinted in book form in 1878 as *The House Beautiful* (fig. 4-8).[86]

If the Bohemian image emphasized Godwin's personal and artistic freedom, like Whistler he was still dependent on the various institutions of the art world and made a living by working in conjunction with the galleries and journals, as well as with dealers, retailers, and manufacturers. On closer inspection it becomes clear that he was involved both socially and professionally with many of those he criticized in the press. Although self-ostracized from conventional middle-class society, Godwin was able to deal with an increasingly large and anonymous public through his journalism and through working for a range of commercial firms. He was liberated from having to deal with individual clients or committees face to face and could communicate on a surprisingly intimate level with those who would sooner shake hands with a snake if they met him in person.[87] Through his columns and articles his readers accompanied him around the city and beyond, eavesdropping on his sparring matches with colleagues and the authorities, sharing his private musings, and, most extraordinary of all, in a series of articles on his office and home, being led from attic to basement into spaces to which even the most intimate friend would not normally gain access.[88] These were not interiors discussed in the abstract, nor were they described as the home of an unnamed "friend" or public figure. The articles opened the recesses of Godwin's home to the public gaze, challenging conventional notions of public-private and the self-contained privacy of the domestic ideal.

From the point of view of the firms for whom he worked, such as William Watt, Jeffrey and Company, and Liberty's, the exposure was ideal. They benefitted vicariously from Godwin's journalistic exploits and the glamour of his bohemian lifestyle (a source of gossip among the artistically informed, even if not discussed openly in the press). At the same time they were not identified so closely with him that they had to take moral responsibility for his actions. A touch of risqué artiness made for good publicity. Critics were by no means all complimentary, for example, about Godwin and Whistler's "Harmony in Yellow and Gold," also known as the Butterfly Suite, at the Paris Exposition Universelle of 1878 (fig. 4-9), but as Lewis Day pointed out, regardless of whether the famed cabinet that was the centerpiece of this suite was worth doing, "it cannot fail to be talked about."[89] By maintaining his critical

distance in the press, however, Godwin avoided appearing to be a mere puppet of commercial concerns such as Liberty's or Watt's.

The authority and wit with which Godwin wrote made him visible at the time and gave him considerable power to publicize his work. Arguably it was his influence as a theater critic for various publications that gave him the opportunities to innovate in that sphere. In the appropriate magazine, a successful media launch targeted a huge potential audience. It was through skimming back issues of the *Building News* that Jonathan Carr discovered Godwin, whom he hired as architect for his famous Bedford Park development.[90] The high profile of Godwin's Anglo-Japanese furniture, both in his own time and in the construction of his posthumous reputation, owed much to the long shelf-life of William Watt's *Art Furniture* catalogue, first published in 1877 and reprinted within a year. Prints of individual plates, which had appeared in the architectural press, copies of the actual catalogue, and the examples of various furnishings it had spawned were all widely available and easily recognizable. Following the death of Watt in 1885, Watt's "representatives" gave some of the designs further airing in the *Building News*.[91] For aspiring young designers the catalogue was further validated as a model for study through inclusion in the loan scheme to British Schools of Art and Design operated from South Kensington.[92] While the publications of the British design reformers Charles Locke Eastlake and Bruce Talbert seem to have had a greater circulation in the United States than the Watt catalogue, Godwin's printed designs were clearly known to an American audience.[93] Subsequently it was the Watt catalogue that drew the attention of both Muthesius and Pevsner to Godwin, and in 1978 it was reprinted as one of

Fig. 4-8. "Coffee-Table with Chair." From Clarence Cook, *House Beautiful* (1878): 70–72.

Fig. 4-9. The William Watt stand at the Paris Exposition Universelle, 1878. The installation was designed by E. W. Godwin and James McNeill Whistler and featured Godwin's Butterfly Suite. Trustees of the Victoria and Albert Museum, London.

"the 48 most important books of the Aesthetic and the Arts and Crafts Movements."[94]

Godwin's critical reputation and the wider diffusion of his work were closely bound to his use of the burgeoning art press.[95] This in itself was characteristic of his modernity. At a fundamental level the rise of the media was altering social relationships between designers, manufac-

turers, retailers, and clients. Inevitably, Modernism was mediated through the printed word, the engraver's line, and the photographer's art, and the leading individuals or groups within the contemporary visual arts were all to recognize the importance of such vehicles in representing and promoting their work.

Godwin had not been alone in combining the roles of critic and practitioner. A. W. N. Pugin, Owen Jones, William Morris, Christopher Dresser, and Bruce Talbert all heightened their visibility by committing their views and designs to print. But Godwin's range as a critic was arguably wider, his use of the press and printed media more sophisticated. As a teacher he responded to letters and designs submitted by young architects in a way more like a modern correspondence course than the traditional face-to-face instruction of an assistant in the office.[96] As a critic he created an image that was avant-garde and controversial, which paradoxically ended up strengthening his symbiotic relationship with those he attacked.

Observer and Designer of Modern Life

At least one commentator judged that Godwin's career was derailed by the move to London in 1865 with its fatal distractions.[97] But arguably it was precisely through his engagement with the great metropolis and the ways in which his sensibility, lifestyle, and practice were transformed that Godwin qualifies as a true "modern." From the comparative stability of his practice as a provincial, Reformed-Gothic architect, married to a vicar's daughter and living in the most respectable part of Bristol, Godwin's life, after his move to the big city, increasingly embraced movement and change, the dynamism characteristic of modernity.

To survey the twenty years or so Godwin spent in London gives a sense of the experimental and continually reflexive way in which he explored different approaches to working and living, all the time refining his ideas about his art, its role, and its audience. Ultimately it was the theater that seemed the most challenging and effective outlet for his creative energy. While he evidently revelled in the intensified psychic and sensory stimulation and in the new freedoms and the social and economic opportunities that the buoyant metropolis afforded, he also had to negotiate its less palatable side: the desensitization, filth, and chaos of the urban environment; the emphasis on novelty and the apparently relentless proliferation of trashy fashions; the commodification of time and art.

It was the end of an era of fixed places. London was an international center, which immediately connected Godwin with new audiences and developments elsewhere. Furniture, wallpapers, and textiles made to his design migrated around Britain and to Europe, Australia, America; his designs were featured in international exhibitions and on the printed page. Even in Bristol, one of Britain's larger ports, Godwin had developed the habit of frequenting the docks, observing the arrival of exotic imports, but in London, he had access to a still greater range of commodities, old and new, which fueled his collecting instinct and his curiosity about the material culture of different periods and places. Godwin described the spectacle of crowds gathering at Liberty's, for example, to watch the unpacking of the latest chests from the Orient.[98] The metropolis gave him the freedom to move and engage with experience at will. Cloaked in the anonymity it afforded, he became a tour guide to his readers: "I shall ask you to go to the theatre and the circus, to attend ecclesiastical functions, to go into all sorts of studios, to accompany me to sanitary exhibitions, to workshops and to picture galleries. Today we will go to the Grosvenor Gallery."[99] His roving eye introduced them to objects and ideas from Ireland to Liverpool, from Rye to Japan to Yarmouth, Copenhagen, Glasgow, Lisieux, Paris, Northampton, and Vienna. He also traveled within Britain and Ireland to supervise architectural commissions and to the Continent for work and pleasure—holidaying in Normandy, installing and reviewing exhibitions in Vienna and Paris, researching Shakespeare's *Hamlet* in Copenhagen. While exhorting architectural students to travel and to think internationally, however, he resisted the expansion of information and sources without knowledge and had a healthy respect for cultural differences; "let us spare the nations of the earth the infliction of our architectural fads and our archaeological art."[100] Increasingly Godwin's style represented a dialectical interplay between the local and the global, drawing from a diversity of options, and destabilizing the notions of moral certitude and national identity which had been implicit in the Gothic Revival of his early career. Such a liberally cosmopolitan approach was rooted in Britain's economic supremacy, and it contrasted with the jingoistic emphasis on "Englishness" which was soon to reappear as that imperial influence came under threat.

Artistically, financially, and emotionally, Godwin embarked on a life of risk-taking in London. This culture of risk was part of the capitalist dynamic of the markets and structures within which he worked. His diaries and office ledgers document his constant juggling of finances, his court appearances, and his battles with demanding clients. Godwin had sufficient faith in himself to gamble his material possessions and professional reputation on a series of speculative ventures. When Ellen Terry eloped with him, it was presumably a gamble to break the deadlock over her divorce, and although it failed in that sense, it was a break-

through in terms of the liberating collaboration which resulted. Godwin's subsequent career is littered with projects abandoned at various stages of completion. Such failures were important, however, both in his own creative development and in preparing the way for others. Participating in the Art Furniture Company, speculating on a development of studio flats, sinking money into a play, and planning a national theater, all show him to be exploring his potentialities in a proactive way.

Godwin's emotional life was also subject to fluctuation and experimentation. Modern living engendered new forms of social relations, new manners. Above all, he emphasized the need to avoid the "sham" in both his art and his love life. In 1875, for example, he described a new style blending Gothic and classic as "a union that should be more than a barren love-in-a-cottage sort of sentimentality."[101] One may connect this imagery to his personal life, to the breakdown at the time of his rural idyll in Harpenden with Ellen Terry. Terry, whom he called "Mother" in his diaries, was replaced by Beatrice Phillips, who was referred to as "Wife," and a succession of shorter-term liaisons from which he was constantly disengaging himself.[102] Friendships blew similarly hot and cold, and many could not stay the pace.[103] Nevertheless all the key relationships seemed to thrive when given a certain distance, and were bound by mutual respect rather than any conventional notion of morality and social responsibilities. His professional involvement with Ellen Terry continued after their affair had ended, and his open marriage with Beatrice Phillips seems to have extended to include his friend Whistler.

While Ellen Terry and Beatrice Godwin were shabbily treated in many ways, they had considerable social and artistic independence, compared to most middle-class women at the time. Their behavior was at odds with the conventional definition of the private interior space of the middle-class home as feminine territory, the antithesis of the public, external world of work peopled by men. Many of Godwin's public haunts were open to them—the shops, the galleries, the studios, and the theater—though not the clubs. Once back on the stage, Ellen Terry was frequently absent on tour, while Godwin often worked at home. Although Beatrice may have been left behind on many occasions, she herself was frequently absent from the home as Godwin would quite often note in his diary, writing, for example, "Home. Wife out. No light on. Nothing, so out again."[104]

At a fundamental level Godwin confirmed his attack on social norms by redesigning domestic spaces and home furnishings and challenging the conventional gendering of responsibilities in matters of design. Women were perfectly

Fig. 4-10. E. W. Godwin. Designs for lean-to conservatories. From Messenger and Company, *Artistic Conservatories* (1880): pl. 3. *Checklist no. 96*

capable of becoming architects,[105] and men could participate in the arrangement of the home or particular interiors, rather than leaving them solely to women.[106] In designing to reflect such shifts, Godwin inverted the conventional coding whereby dark and heavy signified masculine, and light, refined, and delicate was feminine: "Men do not drink deep nor quarrel at table as of old . . . . Seeing that all this is so, that the feasts we now have are unencumbered except with fairy-like articles, that our manners are either so brightly effervescent or so steadily sober as to render us almost unconscious of support; the style of furniture of our dining-rooms should also be light."[107] Indeed Godwin's whole style seems to celebrate lightness, delicacy, charm, and refinement.[108]

Godwin's studio houses, including the White House, served as vehicles for opening up the dust-infested gloom of the domestic interior, and for combining the production and consumption of art into a single environment. In this sense they challenged the conventional categorization of public and private, home and work. What most artists needed was light. In fact Carlo Pellegrini (the cartoonist "Ape" of V*anity Fair*) told Godwin "I wish to have nothing but light—walls and roof and everything."[109] Godwin's designs for conservatories further blurred the boundaries between inside and out. The preface to *Artistic Conservatories* (1880; fig. 4-10) proclaimed that "art seems about to be released from her prison, within the four walls of the house" and further pronounced that "the window has had more to do than any other feature, in bringing about the downfall of the Gothic style for domestic purposes."[110] For Godwin the transformed domestic environment was not to become a retreat into medieval fantasy or claustrophobic, neurotic introspection. He was highly critical of the morbidly hypersensitive for whom "the mildest baby food

causes absolute pain . . . . Some of our modern houses already look weird as if with foreboding of ghosts and haunted chambers."[111] This appears to be where Godwin parts company with the introversion of the next generation of more morbid Art Nouveau artists and designers. Rather than sealing the urban house off from external reality, Godwin wanted the light and air to flood in, which he rationalized as being both labor-saving and hygienic.[112] Having watched his first wife die and having suffered from a delicate constitution himself, he considered matters of hygiene to be of special importance. His emphasis on the perpetual motion of light, air, and people, and the increasing transparency and spatial penetration of his architecture through windows and conservatories were to become symptomatic of Modernism. Writing in the 1930s, the cultural theorist Walter Benjamin observed the effect of transparency in the new architecture of glass and steel, which for Benjamin marked the turning point of an epoch.[113]

Godwin's lifestyle was certainly full of discontinuities and instability. As the rent checks bounced and the bailiffs arrived, he moved from one office or home to another, continuing the process of constantly re-creating his environment. Even when not hounded by economic necessity, he would constantly fiddle with the composition of his home in the light of his shifting perceptions. But in a world of such unsettled habits, moving from one place to another, there was a need for stability, and Godwin set out to shape the environment of the home into "quiet, simple, unobtrusive" beauty as a way of dealing with "these high-pressure, nervous times."[114] His asymmetric compositions stilled all contradictions in a harmonious but often fragile balance of elements caught or "frozen" in transition. The practicalities of modern living meant traveling light, avoiding an accumulation of possessions. As it was for Walter Benjamin,

Godwin's modern house was the enemy of secrets and possessions. This was expressed in the paring down of room contents and the lightweight design of the furniture. Godwin described how the scantling of his sideboard had been reduced to a minimum in order to facilitate cleaning it and moving it when change was required. In fact the first version was so delicate that it fell to pieces. The light tones of his favored colorings and the teetering fragility of his Anglo-Japanese furniture hinted at the disintegration and dematerialization of experience, the shape-shifting of forms. The most radical of Godwin's sideboard designs was arguably the one which had no existence independent of the interior: the novel arrangement of serving from a shelf around the walls in Oscar Wilde's dining room. Such minimal arrangements created space in which the inhabitants, "the actors," could freely move.[115] Far from being pure exercises in abstraction, formal compositions of color, line, and form, his buildings were "only a background for figures."[116]

In particular his designs for clothing and the theater incorporated movement as a dimension of the composition. His costume designs only "worked" with a moving body and the dynamic this set up with the surroundings. Godwin's furniture and dress designs were for clothing modern *life*, not moldering skeletons. In this sense, day-to-day living was like a theatrical performance, one that could most easily be created and controlled within the artist's own home. This resonates with the way in which Adolf Loos was to talk about "staging" experience in 1898: "the artist, the architect, first senses the effect he intends to realize . . . . He senses the effect that he wishes to exert upon the spectator."[117] Ellen Terry was still very much on-stage when Mrs. Bancroft came to call.[118] But in real life extraneous, jarring components had a habit of intruding on this aesthetic creation.

It was through working as an art director-producer in the theater that Godwin could most effectively implement and control his vision. From the notion of composing a pictorial sequence of almost static tableaux framed by the stage, his theatrical productions began to explore the use of movement and changing light to choreograph the script. It was the whole performance—the combination of text, scenery and costumes, acting and direction—that constituted his art object, an object which could never be reconstituted exactly, an object which was only completed over time before disintegrating forever. It could neither be framed and hung in a gallery nor used and admired in the home. An evanescent theatrical performance did not add to the clutter and complexity of the physical world but could continue to resonate unseen in the imaginations of the

audience. For Godwin it was the theater that could most effectively demonstrate "the modern spirit of Renaissance" and meet the need for spectacle in modern life, which could no longer be satisfied by palatial building.[119]

In this reading of Godwin, the ephemeral qualities, the willful, "fantastic" elements from which the theorists of the Modern movement wished to distance themselves, are seen to encapsulate his modernity. At the same time it is Godwin's work in the theater that most clearly demonstrates the ideological gulf between him and the puritan, iconoclastic, socialist flavor of interwar Modernism. It was the area of design in which his archaeological approach was most visible and taken to radical extremes. The likes of Walter Gropius and Pevsner would surely also have looked back on the colossal expenditure of £2,675 for a nine-night production of *The Faithfull Shepherdesse*, a mere evanescent play for an elite audience, as supremely profligate.[120] Such extravagance undermined the view of Godwin as preoccupied with "economy" and "utility." The Modernist aesthetic prioritized the fixed and monumental, devaluing the ephemeral and eclectic, the contingent, decorative, and "feminine." Yet once all these devalued aspects are taken out of the art historical closet and inform our evaluation of Godwin's strengths, surely his status as a Pevsnerian pioneer begins to collapse.

Cult Objects

When wondering what "lies" future generations would invent about the "genuine modern style" with which Godwin was associated, Roger Fry added as an afterthought that "when the time comes the legend will have taken shape, and that, from that moment on, the objects of the time will have the property of emanation."[121] Certainly the idea of Godwin as a pioneer of modern design seems fairly resistant to the challenges and reworkings of Modernism in general, which have come from within the disciplines of design, art, and architectural history. In a strange way the Pevsnerian emphasis on functional design and the achievements of a small group of pioneers has been mapped neatly onto a resurgence of interest in "design classics" and the cult of "designer" values in general since the 1980s. The orthodox construction of Godwin as a Modernist designer picks up on the rhetoric of design as an autonomous activity and the designer as somehow divorced from the contexts of commerce and social usage, emphasizing the aesthetic qualities of almost fetishistic products. Architect-designed furniture, whether new, reproduction, or old, commands increasingly high prices, echoing the way "art" manufacturers used the names of famous architects and artists to glamorize their products over a century ago.

Fig. 4-11. Godwin's sideboard in the home of Wilfred Meynell. From *Art Journal* (April 1892): 112.

In recent decades public interest in Godwin, though scant, has been driven largely by a network of London dealers specializing in nineteenth-century design. Their enthusiasm and researches have surfaced in a series of small exhibitions and publications, occasionally in collaboration with museum curators and academics. Symptomatic of this development was the acquisition by the Hunterian Art Gallery in Glasgow of the famous Butterfly Cabinet (see fig. 8-45) designed for William Watt's display at the Paris Exposition Universelle of 1878. It resurfaced dramatically on the market in 1973, breaking the record price for a piece of nineteenth-century furniture when sold at Christie's for £8,400 ($21,000), despite being denounced in *Country Life* as a "deplorable cabinet . . . a fairly awful example of High Victorian insensibility . . . a tedious object."[122] Godwin's work is now represented in a growing number of museum collections internationally. Inevitably, however, both museums and dealers are drawn to the tangible, surviving aspects of Godwin's output, which have retained a commodity value. It would be difficult, if not impossible, to recover, let alone sell or display, one of his interiors or a theatrical performance.

Some pieces of Godwin furniture translate more readily to a museum context than others. As is evident from the photograph of Watt's exhibit at the Paris exhibition (see fig. 4-9), Godwin took extreme care over the presentation of his designs. The display demonstrated how the proportions, decoration, color, and texture of the overmantel would all tie into the larger conception of a room, with the top of the structure pinned in beneath the ceiling cornice. The way in which the panel decoration carried through onto the wall was described as "ingenious and suggestive."[123] Finishing touches to this "Harmony in Yellow and Gold" were provided by accents of color and texture in the oriental china, courtesy of Liberty's. Being a fixed, dominating feature and, therefore, part of the internal architecture, Godwin's fireplace served as a deliberate dramatic foil to the plainer, lighter furniture in the foreground. To an extent all museum objects are decontextualized, and the cabinet in its new setting in Glasgow now appears to be marooned against high, plain, off-white walls. In this instance Godwin and Whistler's "poem" has undoubtedly been destroyed.

The numerous variations of the famous Anglo-Japanese sideboard (see fig. 4-1) fare better in a museum context, and in some ways it is not easy to sense what has been omitted. The basic design has a self-contained strength and identity, a sculptural quality, which has eased its transformation into a "design classic." Displayed and photographed against white or plain walls and frequently stripped of vessels, the pieces can be more readily viewed as pure distillations of Godwin's thought. The controlled, taut geometry and its planar appeal are through the eye and mind rather than the hand. Yet from the illustration in Watt's catalogue (see fig. 4-3), or the 1892 photograph taken in the dining room of the critic Wilfred Meynell (fig. 4-11), one can see that Godwin evidently intended the severe rectilinearity of the furniture to be offset by and linked to the wall divisions. Like its vernacular antecedent, the humble cottage dresser, the sideboard was essentially a display item, a background for vessels, without which it was incomplete.[124] But in museums the famous sideboards are cut loose from the moorings of use, and the net effect is to highlight the structural, rational aspects of the design just as the polemic of Muthesius and Pevsner had done.

Godwin's ebonized sideboard accorded particularly well with the hi-tech Braun and Porsche aesthetic of the 1980s. It fitted all the defining characteristics of a "cult object": "businesslike, professional, serious, masculine even."[125] Such an object was mass produced, or at least its shape and finish suggested that it was produced by machine, giving the impression of at least the *existence* of limitless numbers of identical objects, and "hinting at an ideal universal form that is independent of its creator."[126]

In 1984 a version of the sideboard went on display in New York's Museum of Modern Art, and the design assumed such cachet that the same year it even entered crime fiction as the subject (and title) of John Malcolm's "second Tim Simpson adventure" (fig. 4-12).[127] Standing in front of the Godwin sideboard in the Victoria and Albert Museum, Malcolm's hero, an art investment advisor, explains to his client, "There are quite a few museums, not to mention a few collectors who are after one of these. It's not, as you can see, the workmanship or the craftsmanship particularly that you're buying, it's the design. No actually it's Art. This piece qualifies as a work of art rather than a piece of furniture, mainly because it's a milestone in the history of design. You can see that it's not far from this, made in the eighteen sixties or seventies, to the Modern Movement. A chunk of design history. Much the same applies to Mackintosh furniture. . . ."[128] He further proclaims its rarity "good for investment."[129]

Here we see a nexus between an orthodox, but dated, view of Modernism, museum collecting, and commercial interests, all apparently intent on hyping Godwin's pioneer status. But at the same time reservations about this escalation were being expressed by some real dealers and curators. The entry on Godwin in the *Penguin Dictionary of Design and Designers* (1984) concluded that his importance as a design reformer "has probably been exaggerated in recent years."[130] The author of this entry was Simon Jervis, the Victoria and Albert Museum curator responsible at the time for the Godwin sideboard that is featured in Malcolm's novel.

Nevertheless, in museum collections around the world, Godwin is indeed set to enter the twenty-first century more firmly ensconced than ever as a proto-Modernist on account of his furniture. In 1994 the sideboard series was described as "perhaps the most influential furniture design executed in Britain during the nineteenth century" and "the earliest Modern Movement icon."[131] Die Neue Sammlung in Munich will enshrine their version of the Godwin sideboard (see fig. 8-28) in a building for the new millenium opening in the year 2000, which will show the roots of European decorative art in the twentieth century. The museum catalogue describes Godwin's furniture as "the forebear of furniture art of the 20th century."[132] There is even a proposal to move Godwin into hyperreality, into a Platonic realm of *Pioneer* icons, with a reconstruction of the White House, not where it once stood, but on the University of Glasgow campus, opposite the re-created home of Charles Rennie Mackintosh (fig. 4-13).[133] Just as museums decontextualize objects, so such a project would lose the

references in scale, texture, and materials that Godwin was making to the artisanal housing and local character of Chelsea.

Following on from Philip Webb's Red House of 1859–60, which was built for William Morris and considered avant-garde in its day, the White House does indeed seem to usher in the whiteness and lightness of Modernism. It seems a short step from Godwin's concept forward to the white houses of Mackintosh, Baillie Scott, and Voysey, and from there to the white cubes of the Modernists and le Corbusier's paean in 1925: "If the house is all white, the outline of things stands out from it without any possibility of mistake; their volumes show clearly; their colour is distinct. The white of whitewash is absolute, everything stands out from it and is recorded absolutely, black on white; it is honest and dependable . . . . Whitewash is extremely moral."[134]

To package Godwin in this way with hindsight is seductively simple. On the most basic and compelling level, our eyes tell us that there *has* to be a connection between the unpretentious formal purity of the White House or of a Godwin sideboard and the design classics that follow. His

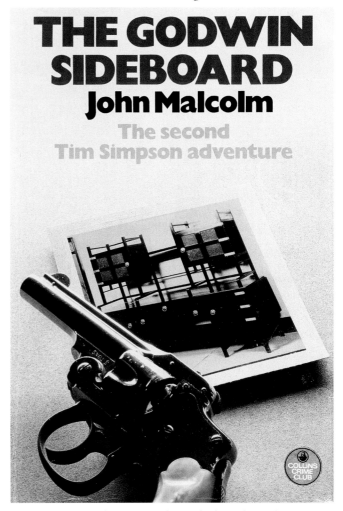

Fig. 4-12. Dust jacket. From John Malcolm, *The Godwin Sideboard* (London: Collins, 1984).

Fig. 4-13. Proposed reconstruction on the University of Glasgow campus of Godwin's original design for the White House, 1996. Courtesy of MBM Architects, Glasgow

designs and words still seem to "speak" to us across the years, in a language with which we are familiar, but the story we are reading is only partial and diminishes Godwin's innovations and contribution overall. His participation in the stirrings of Modernism was genuine, but both more subtle and far-reaching than we have generally been led to believe.

Note: Most published sources are cited below in shortened form (author's last name, abbreviated title, date of publication); full references will be found in the bibliography. Frequently cited archives are abbreviated below; for a key to the abbreviations, also see the bibliography.

1. Godwin, "Home of an English Architect," part 1 (June 1886): 170–73; part 2 (October 1886); 301–305. See also Godwin, "Friends in Council No. 15: William Burges" (29 April 1881): 213–15.

2. Godwin, "Painter and A Sculptor" (15 January 1876): 30.

3. Ibid.

4. Oscar Wilde, "The Truth of Masks," in Richard Ellmann, ed., *The Artist as Critic: Critical Writings of Oscar Wilde* (Chicago: University of Chicago Press, 1982): 418.

5. The critical history of Modernism itself is reflected in the way different facets of Godwin's art have been emphasized or suppressed over the years. Although Modernism has been manifested in all the arts, it has been theorized differently in each sphere of artistic activity. The so-called Modern movement in architecture and design, for example, had a different ideological slant to that of Modernist or avant-garde art, which creates additional problems in trying to assess the contribution of a figure as multitalented as Godwin. Any attempt to mesh Godwin and Modernism neatly together will always be provisional.

6. It was in 1960 that Godwin was first included in Pevsner's *Pioneers of Modern Design.*

7. Reeves, "Anglo-Japanese Buffet by E. W. Godwin" (1994): 36–37.

8. Pevsner, *Pioneers* (1960): 17.

9. See Oxford University Press, *Concise Dictionary of National Biography* (1939): 505. Godwin's principal achievements seemed to be that he had "assisted" Burges and Edis, had "restored" Dromore and Castle Ashby, and had designed some unspecified theatrical costumes and scenery; the only publications cited were *Temple Bar Illustrated* (1877) and an "adaptation" of *The Faithfull Shepherdesse* (1885).

10. Whistler struck Augustus Moore, editor of the *Hawk*, a newspaper, with his cane during the intermission at a Drury Lane theater premier. Moore had published an exposé of a swindle accusing Godwin of hav-

ing extracted money under false pretences for a bogus charity to fund his Greek Theatre. This incident put Godwin on a par with Manet, the other friend on whose behalf Whistler got violent.

11. Beerbohm, "1880," *Yellow Book* (1895), cited in Harbron, *Conscious Stone* (1945): xiii. This shortlived literary and art periodical was closely associated with the "Aesthetes" and "Decadents" of the 1890s, notably Aubrey Beardsley, who was one of the editors.

12. Fry, "Ottoman and the Whatnot" (June 1919): 529.

13. Jopling, *Twenty Years* (1925): 289. This appellation probably refers to Godwin's lifelong interest in the Saxon figure of Godwin Earl of Wessex. His first child, Edith, was called after the earl's daughter Eadgyth. Dudley Harbron notes that Godwin's interest in Saxon architecture "was not unmixed with an interest in the life of Godwin, Earl of Wessex" (Harbron, *Conscious Stone* [1945]: 57).

14. "High" Modernism in this instance refers to the development of full-blooded Modern-movement thinking in the late 1920s and 1930s, as opposed to the "early" or "proto" Modernism of the period immediately before and during the First World War.

15. Harbron, "Edward Godwin" (1945): 49.

16. The key components of Godwin's life are succinctly evoked and prioritized on the Harbron bookjacket. The figure of Godwin in the foreground directs his own and the readers' gaze toward Whistler's White House (mysteriously transposed among trees and blue skies). Isolated, enveloped in narcissistic communion with his masterwork, Godwin studiously ignores the miniaturized, lurid maw of a classical theater off to the right, and Ellen Terry's portrait tumbling out of the vignette amid a bunch of roses, a scroll of wallpaper, and his drawing tools.

17. Pevsner, "Art Furniture of the Eighteen-Seventies" (January 1952): 43–50. The sideboard was illustrated three months later (Pevsner, "Furniture: A Godwin Sideboard" [April 1952]: 273); it was subsequently purchased by the Victoria and Albert Museum, London.

18. See Victoria and Albert Museum, *Exhibition of Victorian and Edwardian Decorative Arts* (1952). Shirley Bury, one of the V & A curators, recalls finding one of the sideboards in use as a rabbit hutch. Another of the exhibition curators, Elizabeth Aslin, subsequently secured the "Monkey

Cabinet" as a purchase from the estate of Godwin's son, Edward, but it was many years before the museum was prepared to register the ten tea chests of designs and documentation which were also deposited.

19. Bøe connected the functionalist aspect of Godwin's Anglo-Japanese furniture to "a great number of pieces produced by still later people like Mackmurdo, C. F. A. Voysey, C. R. Ashbee, and others—not to mention the houses built by the later Scottish architect C. R. Mackintosh. They carry on the tradition from Whistler's White House built for him in Chelsea in 1877 by E.W. Godwin" (Bøe, *From Gothic Revival to Functional Form* [1957]: 148).

20. Kaufmann, "Edward Godwin and Christopher Dresser" (October 1958): 162–65. An edition of Alf Bøe's book had been published in New York the previous year. Subsequently, Godwin's position in the canon was legitimized by the long-term loan of a sideboard to The Museum of Modern Art, New York, from March 1984 to November 1992, and in 1996 the museum acquired a rosewood, octagonal table designed by Godwin.

21. Pevsner, "Art Furniture of the Eighteen-Seventies" (January 1952): 47.

22. "There was no question that Wright, Garnier, Loos, Behrens, Gropius were the initiators of the style of the century and that Gaudí and Sant'Elia were freaks and their inventions fantastical rantings. Now we are surrounded once again by freaks and fantasts" (Pevsner, *Pioneers* [1960]: 17); "the blind alley of Art Nouveau" (ibid., p. 89).

23. Pevsner, "Art Furniture of the Eighteen-Seventies" (January 1952): 47.

24. In the move away from historical revivalism, eclecticism became a sign of weakness. Godwin's direct contemporary, Colonel Robert William Edis, is presented in Pevsner's 1952 article as lacking a strong character; he had "no mission," and there was "no system" behind his influential book *The Decoration and Furniture of Town Houses*. Godwin's *Art Furniture* catalogue for William Watt, on the other hand, is described as "all very much in the same style, and Godwin calls it on one page Anglo-Japanese." In fact, Godwin used the terms "Old English" or "Jacobean" just as many times in the catalogue which also included Gothic church furnishings (plate 19) and a "Queen Anne" cabinet (plate 12). In omitting to mention that Edis was both a friend and collaborator Pevsner teased the two still farther apart. They had collaborated on a competition design for the Berlin Houses of Parliament. Edis appears in Godwin's diaries as a dining companion (for example, 1 and 2 February 1879), and Edis featured a Godwin chair in the frontispiece to *The Decoration and Furniture of Town Houses* (1881).

25. Pevsner, "Art Furniture of the Eighteen-Seventies" (1952): 47.

26. Pevsner, *Pioneers* (1960): 17, 102.

27. Ibid., p. 110.

28. Ibid., p. 64.

29. Ibid., p. 156. This view was echoed by Dennis Farr in 1973 who described the White House as "almost proto Art-Nouveau in its wilful asymmetry" (Farr, *English Art* [1978]: 141).

30. Pevsner, *Pioneers* (1960): 151.

31. Ibid.

32. Ibid., pp. 151–52.

33. Ibid.

34. Quoted in Harbron, *Conscious Stone* (1949): 80.

35. Messenger and Company, *Artistic Conservatories* (1880): 5.

36. Vallance, "Furnishing and Decoration of the House," part 4 (1892): 113.

37. Ibid.

38. See Service, "James MacLaren and the Godwin Legacy" (August 1973): 111–18.

39. Voysey, "Report of dinner" (November 1927): 53.

40. Register of loans from South Kensington [Victoria and Albert Museum], 1886, in the Glasgow School of Art Archives. The catalogue was loaned from 23 September to 11 November, 1886.

41. Ashbee's Chelsea houses (1893–1912) were concentrated in a stretch of Cheyne Walk more or less around the corner from Tite Street. The witty, "pictorial" composition of the elevations, the austere interiors, and the compact planning were particularly close to Godwin's. Mackintosh lived in Chelsea in the early 1920s, during which time he designed a studio complex in Glebe Place. His designs from the same period for an Artist's Town House and a theater for Margaret Morris also seem to make reference to Godwin.

42. H. Muthesius, *English House* (1904–5; reprint 1979): 157.

43. Obituary, "Edward W. Godwin," *British Arthitect* (15 October 1886): 347.

44. Messenger and Company, *Artistic Conservatories* (1880): 6.

45. See, for example, *American Architect and Building News* 20 (30 October 1886): 202.

46. Godwin, "Some Notes of a Month in Normandy," part 2 (11 September 1874): 308.

47. Godwin, "Frozen Music" (5 February 1876): 76.

48. Godwin, "Notes on the Costume in the Pictures at the Royal Academy" (29 May 1875): 314.

49. Godwin, "In the Studios of Some 'Outsiders'," part 1 (11 March 1876): 156. Ironically, Godwin designed a series of "cottage furniture" for Collinson and Lock and for William Watt (see chap. 8 in this volume.)

50. Godwin, "Curiosities of Architecture" (17 July 1875): 31.

51. Aslin, *Aesthetic Movement* (1969): 13. Nevertheless the book's concluding sentence still identified the Aesthetic movement as part of a transition from the eclectic historicism of the early nineteenth century to the disciplined and purposeful style of the Modern movement.

52. Service, ed., *Edwardian Architecture* (1975).

53. "Rogue architects" was a term coined by the architect and historian H. S. Goodhart Rendell. See Nikolaus Pevsner, "Conclusion: Goodhart-Rendell's Roll-Call," in ibid., pp. 472–84.

54. Service, "James MacLaren and the Godwin Legacy" (August 1973): 111–18.

55. See, for example, David Brett, *C. R. Mackintosh: The Poetics of Workmanship* (London: Reaktion Books, 1992); Timothy Neat, *Part Seen, Part Imagined: Meaning and Symbolism in the Work of Charles Rennie Mackintosh and Margaret Macdonald* (Edinburgh: Canongate, 1994); Karen Moon, *George Walton* (Wendlebury: White Cockade Publishing, 1992).

56. Godwin, "On Some Buildings I Have Designed" (29 November 1878): 211.

57. Charles Rennie Mackintosh, "G. Seemliness" (1902), in *Charles Rennie Mackintosh: The Architectural Papers*, ed. Pamela Robertson (Wendlebury, Oxon: White Cockade/Hunterian Art Gallery, 1990): 222–23. Godwin's career certainly appeared to confirm Mackintosh's view that "The Architect must become an art worker, and be content to forgo the questionable distinction & pleasure of being respected as the head (and perhaps the founder) of a large and successful buisness [*sic*]."

58. [Obituary], *Art Journal* (November 1886): 352; [obituary], *Building News* (October 1886): 589.

59. [Obituary], "The Week" *Architect* (15 October 1886): 217.

60. See Halén, *Christopher Dresser* (1990). Shaw used Godwin furniture in his home at Ellerdale Road in Hampstead, London.

61. [Obituary], "Edward W. Godwin" *British Architect* (22 October 1886): 348.

62. Godwin, "Frozen Music" (5 February 1876): 76–77. Perfection was impossible, "it is only in the *endeavour* to reach this ideal—in the act of moving ever and ever onwards—that a living Art is possible" (Godwin, " 'Daily News' Versus Art" [20 November 1875]: 282).

63. Godwin, " 'Daily News' Versus Art" (20 November 1875): 282.

64. Godwin, "Frozen Music" (5 February 1876): 76–77.

65. V&A AAD, 4/23-1988: 16–7, quoted in Aslin, *E. W. Godwin* (1986): 8.

66. Godwin, " 'Daily News' Versus Art" (20 November 1875): 281.

67. Godwin, "Present Aspect of Decorative Painting" (11 September 1875): 140.

68. The worst offences in Godwin's eyes were the artificially imitative behavior of fashion victims, "spurious make-believes" in the theater (Godwin, "Theatrical Jottings," part 2 [18 June 1875]: 684); "unnatural and stagey" dress, or the medievalist paintings of Frank Dicksee who had "outstaged the stage" (Godwin, "Notes on the Costume" [29 May 1875]: 314); or "stagey posing" in architecture (Godwin, "Curiosities of Architecture" [17 July 1875]: 30).

69. G. Simmel, "The Metropolis and Mental Life" (1902), reprinted in *Art in Theory, 1900–1990*, ed. C. Harrison and P. Wood (Oxford: Blackwell, 1992): 131.

70. Godwin, "To Our Readers" (4 January 1878): 1.

71. Coleman, "Fool's Revenge" (7 August 1886): 12.

72. "Architects and Furniture" (7 January 1874): 72–73. The letter continued "the proudest boast of their producers seems to reside in the fact that they are *intensely 'geometrical'* . . . Its candid angular lines stare grimly out at you, shouting 'We are SIMPLE, We are STONEY, We are STRONG! . . . We are *Architectural*! . . . bow down and worship us!' " A familiar tactic in the trade papers was to criticize Godwin's designs according to his printed pronouncements on issues such as practical convenience, economy, or truth to construction and materials. Roper was an architect and designer who worked for Gillow and Company among others in the 1870s. His work is often confused with that of Godwin (see "Our Lithographic Illustrations," *Building News* 26 [9 January 1874]: 49, which shows a buffet by Roper).

73. "Nothing could be more unfortunate for the Metropolitan Board of Works than the destruction of Temple Bar . . . . Everyone interested in making modern London a city worthy to be ranked with the modern cities of Europe looks frowningly, and even the *Daily News* has opened fire on what it calls a *group of mere nominees*—nominees whose immense power has been neglected or misused" ([Godwin], Notes on Current Events [11 January 1878]: 20).

74. "Architectural Association: The Designing of Studios" (8 March 1879): 146.

75. Ibid.

76. "Societies: London Architectural Association" (7 March 1879): 106.

77. In the Whistler v. Ruskin trial, when asked if the labor of two days, taken to paint *The Falling Rocket*, justified a price of 200 guineas, Whistler responded, "I ask it for the knowledge of a lifetime" (James M. Whistler, *The Gentle Art of Making Enemies* [London: William Heinemann Ltd., 1890]: 5).

78. [Obituary], *American Architect* (30 October 1886): 202. As early as 1863 Godwin had been complaining about the "absence of thought in all the so-called decorations of the present day"; the scramble to get rich meant that designers had no time to think, and their clients or audience no time to understand. (Godwin, *Handbook of Floral Decoration* [1865]: 11).

79. See, for example, Godwin, "Present Aspect of Decorative Painting" (11 September 1875): 140–41.

80. Whistler took up the cudgels once more when he returned from Venice, living "next door to himself" in Tite Street. In a letter drafted to the *Pall Mall Gazette*, Quilter was accused of "living in the White House of his betters—degrading it and defacing it, and leaving the mark of his abomination upon it. Thus is the Great ever linked to the little . . . . So are the clowns remembered with their masters" (Whistler Collection, Glasgow, GUL P14).

81. Godwin, "To Art Students, Letter No. 9" (11 July 1884): 13.

82. Ibid.

83. Godwin, "Theatrical Notes" (29 July 1881): 379.

84. Letter to William Watt dated 1 January 1877, printed in Watt, *Art Furniture* (1877): iii.

85. [Godwin], "We learn from an American newspaper . . ." (8 February 1878): 64. At issue was a book: Lucy Orrinsmith, *The Drawing-Room, its Decorations and Furniture* (London: Batsford, 1877).

86. The Godwin furniture was displayed in the New York showrooms of Daniel Cottier who started by importing Godwin furniture but subsequently had copies made in New York because the imports were arriving damaged.

87. Maud Holt tried to persuade her fiancé, Herbert Beerbohm Tree, not to join Godwin's Costume Society in 1882, describing Godwin as "such a man as she would no more shake hands with than with a snake" (quoted in Max Beerbohm Tree, comp., *Herbert Beerbohm Tree, some memories of him* . . . [London: Hutchinson, 1920]: 19). For the full text of the letter from Maud Holt to Tree, see Hesketh Pearson, *Beerbohm Tree: His Life and Laughter* (London: Columbus Books, 1988): 37–38.

88. Godwin, "My Chambers and What I Did to Them," part 1 (1 July 1876): 4–5; part 2 (8 July 1876): 18–19; idem, "My House 'in' London," part 1 (15 July 1876): 33–34; part 2 (22 July 1876): 45–46; part 3 (29 July 1876): 58–59; part 4 (5 August 1876): 72–73; part 5 (12 August 1876): 86; part 6 (19 August 1876): 100–101; idem, "From the House-Top" (26 August 1876): 112–13.

89. Day, "Notes on English Decorative Art in Paris," part 3 (12 July 1878): 16.

90. In an 1877 letter to the editor of the *Building News* ("Bedford Park Estate" [2 February 1877]: 134), Carr described how he selected Godwin on the basis of designs for a parsonage which had been published in that magazine in 1874 ("A Parsonage" [6 March 1874]: 256, 263, 266–67). When Godwin's preparatory designs for the Bedford Park development were published in the December 1876 and January 1877 issues of the *Building News* they were instantly criticized by William Woodward in the magazine as was the single design of his successors, Coe and Robinson. Media attention of this kind could be a double edged sword; it appears that the adverse criticism caused Carr to drop Godwin from the project in favor of Norman Shaw.

91. "Working Drawings of Inexpensive Furniture" (18 December 1885): 1011 and illus. 1008–9; these designs were "executed by the representatives of the late Mr. Wm. Watt." Similarly the design for a cabinet shown in the *Building News* was described as having been made formerly by the late Mr. William Watt and now by his "representatives" at his old address in Grafton Street ("Cabinet for Objects de Virtu" [5 March 1886]: 376 and illus. 390). The "art cabinet" illustrated in the following issue was described as now made by "Messrs. Watt. And Co." ("An Art Cabinet" [19 March 1886]: 456 and illus. 471).

92. By the time Fra Newbery moved to Glasgow to take up the post of headmaster in the Glasgow School of Art in 1885, he had already developed an admiration for both Whistler and Godwin while in London, and in 1886 he requested the loan of the Watt catalogue for his students. The loan reinforced already strong connections with Aesthetic circles in London and was still in the school at the time of Godwin's death which perhaps drew attention to the designs.

93. "Most of our readers know the quaint and pretty devices he produced so easily" (*American Architect* 20 [30 October 1886]: 202. See also *American Architect* 21 (18 November 1876): 372.

94. See Watt, *Art Furniture* (1877; reprinted 1878).

95. He published his first book at the age of seventeen and throughout his career was "a clear writer and thinker on many Art subjects, and most archaeological questions" ([obituary], "Art Notes and Reviews," *Art Journal* [November 1886]: 352). Ruskin's copious writings had established the idea of a mass audience for art, inspiring a generation of critics, among them Godwin. This adds another facet to the discussion of Ruskin as a formative influence, which is well documented in respect of Godwin's early architectural career and self-evident in his Town Hall designs. See M.W. Brooks, *John Ruskin and Victorian Architecture* (1987): 178–212.

96. George Freeth Roper (1872), letter to R.W. Edis, V&A AAD, 4/402-1988: "I think, however, a *true* Architect works for the advancement of his art, and when he publishes his designs he does so with the knowledge and hope that they may have influence on future work from other hands—I know Mr Godwin works in this spirit, from the [illegible] he always shows to teach you something."

97. "His removal to London did not help him as an artist. Here he found too many distractions" ([obituary], "The Week," *The Architect* [15 October 1886]: 217). Similarly William White commented in the *Building News* (23 April 1875), p. 472: "the most accomplished living architect in England is expending his tried powers over the trappings of a play."

98. Godwin, "Afternoon Strolls. A Japanese Warehouse" (23 December 1876). His significant role in the early stages of the nineteenth-century rediscovery of Japan and the development of a so-called Anglo-Japanese style is well documented elsewhere: see for example, Watanabe, *High Victorian Japonisme* (1991); N. B. Wilkinson, "Edward William Godwin and Japonisme" (1987); and chap. 3 in this volume. One writer remarked of wallpapers Godwin designed for Jeffrey & Co. that "Mr Godwin has gone beyond most people's notions of the boundaries of civilisation and has added Japan" ("Wallpapers" [October 1872]: 291).

99. Godwin, "To Art Students, Letter No. 1" (2 May 1884): 215.

100. Godwin, "Scraps for Students," part 3 (6 May 1876): 285.

101. Godwin, "The Ex-Classic Style Called 'Queen Anne'" (16 April 1875): 442.

102. "Mother," "wife," and "Mrs. Godwin" were the terms he used most commonly in his diaries. See, for example, the diary entry for 12 November 1873, V&A AAD, 4/1-1980: "Edy and Mother to St Albans to see Japanese conjurors"; and, by contrast, see also the entry for 2 September 1877, V&A AAD, 4/3-1980, "To Whistler with Wife," as well as chap. 1 in this volume. For brief liaisons, see Harbron, "Edward Godwin" (1945): 48. Harbron quotes the late T. P. O'Connor, who said, "He was a singularly attractive man to ladies, and had many adventures."

103. "His temperament was hardly calculated to attract close friendship, but he was extremely pleasant and genial company" (Obituary, "Edward W. Godwin" *British Architect* [15 October 1886]: 348).

104. Diary entry dated 14 October 1881, V&A AAD, 4/6-1980.

105. See, for example, Godwin, "Industrial Education Bureau" (6 June 1874): 5; idem, "Mr. E.W. Godwin on Lady Architects," (12 June 1874): 378; idem, "Lady Architects," (13 June 1874): 335.

106. Godwin, "My Chambers," part 1 (1 July 1876): 45. Godwin pointed out that usually "the wife takes the drawing-room as a matter of course under her especial protection, leaving the dining-room possibly, and the hall certainly, in the charge of her lord."

107. Godwin, "My House 'In' London," part 3 (29 July 1876): 58.

108. His main criticism of Burges was that his designs were "too masculine" and solid. Godwin, "Friends in Council: No. 15 William Burges" (29 April 1881): 214.

109. "Societies: London Architectural Association" (7 March 1879): 106.

110. Messenger and Company, *Artistic Conservatories* (1880): 5–6.

111. Godwin, "Correspondence: The Walker Exhibition" (22 January 1876): 58.

112. Watt, *Art Furniture* (1877): iv. The introduction emphasized the need for good light and plenty of fresh air in house design; "the open air is like the open sea. The sea is always fresh because it is in perpetual motion." See also chap. 1 in this volume.

113. Walter Benjamin, "Die Wiederkehr des Flaneurs," in *Gesammelte Schriften*, eds. R. Tiedemann and H. Schweppenhauser (1972): vol. 3, p. 168.

114. Godwin, "Furniture" (15 June 1872): 1–2, quoted in Aslin, *E.W. Godwin* (1986): 7.

115. Godwin, "My House 'In' London," part 4 (5 August 1876): 73. Godwin wrote, "I have thus plenty of free walking space."

116. [Obituary], "The Week," *The Architect* (15 October 1886): 217.

117. See Beatriz Colomina, "The Split Wall: Domestic Voyeurism," in *Sexuality and Space*, ed. B. Colomina (1992): 73–128.

118. Terry was clearly aware of the impact her dress and home environment made on visitors, and recalled how the formidable Mrs. Bancroft "came into a room which had been almost stripped of furniture. The floor was covered with Japanese matting, and at one end was a cast of the Venus de Milo, almost the same colossal size as the original. Mrs. Bancroft's wonderful grey eyes examined it curiously. The room, the statue, and I myself must all have seemed very strange to her. I wore a dress of some deep yellow woollen material which my little daughter used to call the 'frog dress' . . . ." (Terry, *Story of My Life* [1908]: 101).

119. Godwin, "Theatrical Jottings," part 2 (18 June 1875): 868; idem, "Scraps for Students," part 3 (6 May 1876): 284.

120. Accounts of the Pastoral Players, 1884–85, V&A TA, Godwin collection, box 4.

121. Fry, "Ottoman and the Whatnot" (June 1919): 529.

122. Davis, "Talking about Salerooms" (November 1973): 1543.

123. Day, "Notes on English Decorative Art in Paris," part 3 (12 July 1878): 15–16.

124. Crisp, "Art as applied to furniture" (6 January 1865): 7.

125. Sudjic, *Cult Objects* (1985): 16.

126. Ibid.

127. John Malcolm is the pseudonym of John Andrews (born 1936), himself an antique dealer and author of *The Price Guide to Antique Furniture* (1979) and *The Victorian and Edwardian Furniture Price Guide and Reason for Values* (1992), both published by the Antique Collector's Club, Woodbridge, England.

128. Malcolm, *Godwin Sideboard* (1984): 16.

129. Ibid.

130. Jervis, *Penguin Dictionary of Design and Designers* (1984): 204.

131. Reeves, "Anglo-Japanese Buffet by E.W. Godwin" (1994): 36–37.

132. The catalogue further calls it " . . . fundamentally different from the contemporary historicizing furniture in its basic severe forms, in its combination of simplicity and aesthetic refinement" (Neue Sammlung, *Century of Design* [1996]: 44).

133. It would house the university's Centre for Whistler Studies.

134. Le Corbusier, *The Decorative Art of Today* (1925), reprint, trans. J. Dunnett (London: The Architectural Press, 1987): 191–92.

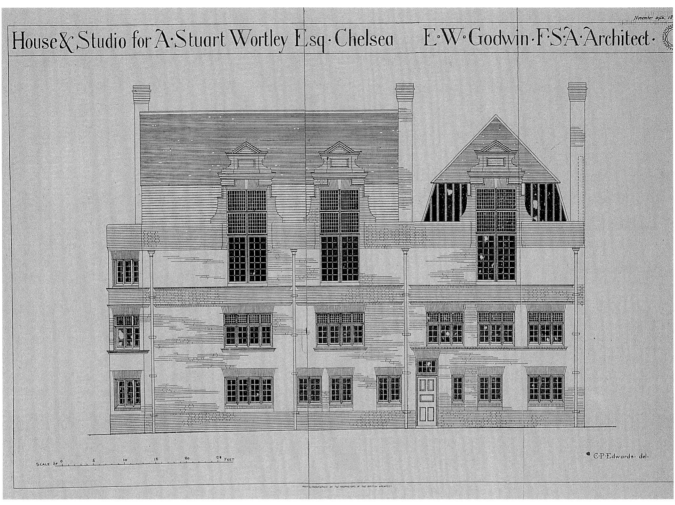

Fig. 5-1. E.W. Godwin. "House and Studio for A. Stuart Wortley, Esq., at Chelsea." From *British Architect* 10 (29 November 1878): 210.

CHAPTER 5

AN·AESTHETIC·EDUCATION: THE·ARCHITECTURE CRITICISM·OF·E.W. GODWIN

RICHARD W. HAYES

The accomplished architect will be the best seeker.—E.W. Godwin[1]

In June 1872 members of the Royal Institute of British Architects (R.I.B.A.) met in London for a week of meetings, which they termed a "General Conference." It was the second such gathering in the relatively brief history of the organization.[2] One of the topics of concern to the members was what they saw as a growing tide of criticism lodged against both individual architects and the profession as a whole. Throughout the course of the previous year, for example, the historian James Fergusson published several criticisms of architect George Edmund Street's designs for the new law courts, culminating in a strongly worded article in *Macmillan's Magazine* in January 1872.[3] In April 1872 the *Quarterly Review*, a magazine largely devoted to literary criticism, published a lengthy article titled, "The State of English Architecture." The essay opened with another punishing critique of the design of the law courts and moved on to a vitriolic censure of the profession as a whole.[4] The *Architect*, one of the three architectural periodicals of the time, characterized the article, not unjustly, as "reckless" and "profane"; it pointed to its "pitiless logic" and "personal offensiveness of manner."[5]

A number of the architects who gathered at the R.I.B.A. that June felt that they were open to attack both from fellow architects and from those outside the profession. T. Roger Smith, a member of the Institute Council,

claimed in the *Building News* that architecture "has been a good deal dragged through the mire of late, and to some extent by its own professors."[6] In his address to those gathered at the opening meeting of the general conference, the president of the R.I.B.A., Thomas H. Wyatt, sounded a similar note; he assailed "the violent personal attacks and criticisms now so often made."[7] He called for a greater commitment to unity and esprit de corps among architects in order to withstand public criticism. The *Building News* transcribed his speech, duly including in parentheses the frequent cheers of "Hear, Hear" from the assembled architects. In a vote of thanks to Wyatt, Robert Kerr, an architect, professor of the arts of construction at King's College, and member of the institute council, asked all who attended the conference "to present a bold and united stand to the public."[8]

Edward William Godwin, architect, critic, furniture designer, historian of costume, and supporter of reform in many fields, had a very different view of the situation. By 1872 Godwin had become a prolific contributor of articles to leading architectural periodicals. Although he strongly supported Street's designs,[9] his response to the recent criticisms of the architectural profession was markedly different from the R.I.B.A.'s reaction. A week after the general conference ended, he published an article in the *Building*

News with the sarcastic title "The 'British Architects' " stating in his opening paragraph that the architectural profession in his country "has no corps and therefore no esprit."[10] For Godwin, "the pleasant idea of brotherly association" was "but presumption." He questioned the right of the institute to speak with authority, despite its royal charter, for the majority of architects practicing in Britain. Reviewing the speeches made by the various officials of the institute, he said that "the president and his supporters flatter themselves." On the question of the seemliness of criticizing architects' work, he asked, "If a modern design is the genuine work of the man who fathered it, what has he to fear from adverse critics?" In contrast to the cheers at the institute in response to calls for unanimity, Godwin asked for a stronger individualism among architects. Deriding "the very shyness of criticism in the President's address," he advised architects to welcome criticism and to practice it themselves.[11]

Indeed, Godwin's line of approach was taken up two weeks later by an editorial in the *Building News*. Titled "Professional Tenderness," the unsigned editorial also upped the ante markedly. Its pointedness is still sharp enough to cut. "It may be taken almost as axiomatic that the architects of the present day are eminently thin-skinned," was the opening sentence.[12] Defending the right of "a professional critic" to write commentary with bite to it and not be regarded as "cantankerous" and "disagreeable," the editorial portrayed "the elders of the profession" as "men who are afraid of criticism." It mocked their "nervous tenderness and shrinking sensitiveness," and invited the bracing sting of criticism as a means to reform and improve the state of architecture in England:

> The cure for this unwholesome sensitiveness, we
> believe, lies in criticism, plenty of it, deep, broad,
> and technical, general, and specific. It is because
> architects have been so long exempt from hearing
> opinions of their work that they have become so
> tender about it.[13]

The editorial suggests the hand of Godwin in its combination of irreverence to the professional organization, respect for the achievements of a few individuals (John Ruskin and architects G. E. Street and G. G. Scott), and above all concern for the loss of artistic values among architects.[14] "Meanwhile, where is architecture?" the article asked. The editorial served in fact as an introduction to a six-part series of articles by Godwin in which he assessed the work of a few of the leading architects of his day.[15] Hoping that the architects thus reviewed "may soon grow

more hardy," the column set out an intention to "examine in detail a few modern buildings, extenuating nothing, nor putting aught in malice." A warning label was nonetheless affixed: "It is quite possible that we may tread on a few tender places, but we admit . . . that we shall care nothing about that."[16]

In the six articles that followed, titled "Modern Architects and Their Work," Godwin lived up to this prediction. He looked at the work of a few of the different combatants in the "Battle of the Styles." He wrote scornfully of architects associated with the R.I.B.A. such as Wyatt and, in particular, Professor Kerr. In one instance, Godwin wrote that he included Kerr in his survey, "not because of his work, but because his loquaciousness makes him prominent."[17] Kerr's designs demonstrate what Godwin called "the obliging shoppiness [sic] of modern architects, and how ready they are to wash their hands with invisible soap in imperceptible water"; Godwin advised these architects "to talk somewhat less and to learn more of art."[18]

Read from a safe remove, the articles and the spectacle of members of the architectural establishment pricked by the writer's sharp pen may seem to be merely amusing.[19] Gradually, however, it becomes apparent that Godwin is not just releasing destructive daggers of malice; his emphasis on the necessity of criticism has a larger and more constructive reach. Writing as an architect himself, Godwin stated that a vital component of an architect's creative work is the critical scrutiny he brings to his own work as well as to past works of architecture. What Godwin called "the sensual and mental condition of an architect" should be "acute, critical, and strong."[20] He advised architects to "believe in yourself and your work." The strength that came from this belief can allow for persistent self-criticism. Viewed in this light, criticism is part of an architect's practice and not something to be avoided.

"The truth is, we are not critical, we are overgrown with antiquarian rust," Godwin wrote in his analysis of a group of the lesser talents of the Gothic Revival, which he called "the Academy Gothic."[21] Independence of artistic character was one of Godwin's central principles. Subjecting the work of the past to a searching, critical analysis is the way for architects to avoid uninspired, unfelt, academic revivalism, what Godwin called "dictation." To be critical toward the past is part of being a modern. To be critical toward one's own work is part of being an artist. Godwin wrote:

> We have grown too rich and too mighty for the ser-
> vice which art rigidly demands of all who profess to
> follow her. We are advocates, not artists, and the bent

of our minds is to do anything rather than devote ourselves to architectural study. Thus it comes that we shirk all critical inquiry.[22]

Godwin himself did not shirk critical inquiry; indeed, it was one of the ruling passions of his life. It was what kept him devoting long hours to study in the British Museum, it was why he wrote in such a prolific fashion throughout his career, it was what he wanted to teach young architects. He fixed his critical eye not just on his fellow architects but on decoration and dress, costume and stage design, painting and sculpture, Irish castles, Saxon buildings, French chateaux, Greek moldings, and Gothic surfaces. In this series of articles on architects, he put his own work under the lens of his analysis and included his own career among those modern architects he took to task.

In the fourth of the six articles, published in the *Building News* of August 30, 1872, Godwin contrasted his work with that of architect William Burges. By this time, Godwin and Burges had been close friends for many years, so close that they have been described as "the Castor and Pollux" of English architecture of the 1860s.[23] Godwin had achieved enough of a reputation to allow him to engage his audience in this knowing way. Referring to himself in the third person, he pointed to "the Spartan-like severity" in many of his designs, a severity that suggested a "Corinthian column without its acanthus."[24] His designs often looked "as if they had been designed with the scissors instead of the pencil, for distant observation rather than for close examination."[25] He offered suggestions for self-improvement, showing other architects the type of self-criticism that he believed should be part of their habit of thought. His critical method was a closely attentive visual analysis. In a lecture delivered at the Manchester Architectural Association six years later, Godwin continued to advise architects to look at their own work "as if it were that of an outsider, upon which they were to publish some criticism."[26]

In the context of the six-part series in the *Building News*, Godwin's critique of his own work may seem to display the principle of fair play. Writing from his status as a fellow-practitioner, he earned the right to criticize the work of others by being hard on his own designs. But it was also a shrewd way of positioning himself in the public eye as he denigrated competitors.[27] At the conclusion of the article on his and Burges's work, Godwin wondered aloud, disingenuously enough, whether he was violating some standard of good taste by this personal reference. He wrote, "Let it be so. There is so much good taste visible everywhere, so much modesty, so much consistency, that I shall not mind the impeachment for the sake of the change."[28]

This episode in Godwin's career is a good introduction to many of the most important aspects of his role as an architectural critic. It shows the distance he maintained from the architectural establishment of his time, his reformist intentions, and individualist impulses. It also reveals how Godwin defined an architectural career as an artistic project in which self-scrutiny is important. He made his points with audacity, irreverence, and a sharp tongue.[29] Nikolaus Pevsner characterized one of Godwin's most important designs—his facade for Whistler's house and studio in Chelsea—as "original, challenging, witty,"[30] and these words fit Godwin's writings equally well. Yet Godwin's status as Young Turk and reformer is complemented by what may seem to be an old-fashioned belief in culture, learning, and high artistic achievement as transcendent values. Self-culture of the architect is one of his most important themes: his writings reveal his own strenuous efforts at self-instruction as he invites younger architects to learn from his experiences. As often instructive as he was biting, at his best he used his architectural criticism as a means to educate.

E. W. Godwin was one of the most prolific architectural critics of his time. In spite of his notable presence in the pages of English architectural periodicals from the late 1860s through the mid-1880s, Godwin, with his diverse activities and interests, is difficult to place in architectural history. His achievements are even harder to assess. A review of his writings, however, is a way to connect his many interests and to propose a reading of his life as a unified project. Like such modern architects as Adolf Loos, Le Corbusier, and Robert Venturi, Godwin combined the life of a practicing architect with a writing career of lively interest. He viewed writing and drawing as means for architects to increase their powers of observation, to refine sensibility, and to sharpen intelligence.

Godwin wrote prolifically throughout his life. The sheer volume and enthusiasm that characterize his writings show how he valued this part of his career. He was productive and industrious—he was, after all, a Victorian—and much of the eminence he achieved in his life rested in large part on his role as critic of architecture, art, and theater. His obituary in the *British Architect*, for example, noted that it was "chiefly as an architectural art critic and consulting architect that Godwin was best known to outsiders in the profession."[31] As a critic, Godwin fashioned a distinctive and confident voice. He took clearly and sometimes forcefully articulated positions on many of the most topical subjects of the architectural culture of his era.

His characteristic mark was to bring artistic criteria to bear on these topics. Godwin held, as with a clenched fist,

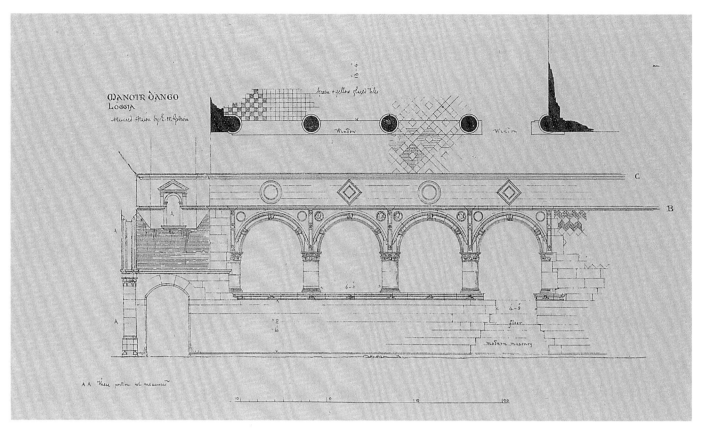

Fig. 5-2. E. W. Godwin. The loggia of the Manoir d'Ango. From *Building News* 26 (10 April 1874): 392.

to his commitment to architecture as an art. Visual acuity, critical scrutiny, and compositional ability—such as "the right proportioning of solid and void"[32]—are the hallmarks of the architect's art. Intensely visual, he could sum up the salient qualities of a design in a few words, and many of his judgments continue to persuade and to instruct.

Godwin's devotion to art "was the passion of his life,"[33] and his architectural criticism was a way to impart this passion to an audience. Godwin was often combative in conveying his thoughts. Defending "the fine art of architecture" meant "to carry on a war *à l'outrance*."[34] He advised students "to arm yourselves against ugliness and sham."[35] Toward the end of his life, he wrote that the so-called Battle of the Styles "was an entirely wholesome fight, for it brought to the front a good deal of earnestness, and increased the power of observation and criticism."[36]

Discussing his friendship with architect G. G. Scott, Godwin confessed, "we had our little fights about archaeological questions, art criticisms, and even competitions. Sometimes we hit one another perhaps a trifle hard."[37] William Butterfield once felt the blow of one of Godwin's hits, in a series of letters he and Godwin wrote to the *Times* in 1884 over proposals to restore Westminster Hall. In response to Godwin's criticism, Butterfield protested: "Mr. Godwin comes down upon me with some heavy words.

A good case only requires to be quietly stated."[38] Quiet statement was not Godwin's style as a critic, and he saw that in an age of growing mass media the quiet would not be heard.

Godwin originally wrote theater reviews for a local newspaper called the *Western Daily Press* during his early years in Bristol.[39] He reviewed under the heading "Jottings," a word he later used to describe his writings on architecture.[40] In some key ways, his architectural criticism is a continuation of his theater criticism. He knew how to get and hold the reader's attention. With an eye for the telling detail, he could also, at his best, enliven his criticism with a sense of the dramatic moment.

After establishing himself in London in the 1860s, Godwin contributed articles on a freelance basis to the *Building News* and the *Architect*, which were weekly periodicals. Through the reputation he developed, he secured a position as a regular contributor to the *British Architect and Northern Engineer* in 1877. He continued in this capacity until 1885, a year before his death. He also published articles in the *Globe and Traveller*, the *Art Journal*, and *Fraser's Magazine*. During the 1870s, Godwin no longer had the large public commissions that characterized the early years of his architectural practice, and he supported himself in part by his writings.

During these years Godwin entered into contemporary debates on historical styles and the emerging Queen Anne revival. These discussions became opportunities for him to clarify the direction he believed architecture should take. In a number of articles from these years, he articulated the principle of a "judicious eclecticism" combined with an acceptance of the realities of modern life.[41]

In an article in the *Building News*, for example, dated April 16, 1875, entitled "The Ex-Classic Style Called 'Queen Anne'," Godwin called for "a living style" of architecture that would be "big enough to embrace town-halls and law courts, chapels and cathedrals, as well as suburban villas," and strong enough "to influence the whole character of modern manufacture."[42] He did not think that reviving the vernacular style of the Queen Anne era could fulfill these needs. Instead, Godwin proposed that a relevant architecture would have to embrace the utilitarian and vernacular realities of the modern world and not merely revive a past vernacular architectural language. His tone was nonetheless one of resignation as he described "the vernacular, the builder's work, naked of ornament, void of style and answering to only one name—Utility."[43] He proposed a literary trope, in which he portrayed classical architecture as a beautiful maiden in need of a husband. Utility would play the role of husband, creating a union of "simple, unaffected Brutality and perfected Beauty."[44]

Not altogether happy about the prospect of this union, he went on to uphold sixteenth-century French architecture built during the reign of Francis I. He described these buildings as "thoroughly healthy and strong in idea and in mass as they are refined and tender in detail."[45] He published sketches of a building near Dieppe known as the Manoir d'Ango (fig. 5-2) which showed "the power of design then prevailing."[46] Mingling classical and Gothic elements in an expressive interplay, the Manoir d'Ango seemed to Godwin to have spoken a living vernacular architectural language for its time. Whether nineteenth-century England could achieve such a vital architectural vernacular was the question Godwin posed. Godwin found in such a building a touchstone comparable to Le Corbusier's later enthusiasm for "the simple beauty" of the small church of Santa Maria in Cosmedin, which Le Corbusier described in his polemical tract *Vers une architecture* (1923).[47]

As Godwin's sketches of the Manoir d'Ango show, he looked to past precedents for essential lessons in composition, modulation of profile, the handling of masses, and artistic expression. This is also true of the studies of Irish castles he published in the *British Architect* in 1879 (fig. 5-3), which are powerful studies in figure/ground relationships as well as inquiries into construction techniques.[48]

Fig. 5-3. E. W. Godwin. "Examples of Ancient Irish Architecture: No. 2 Kilcolman Castle." From *British Architect* 11 (21 February 1879).

About a year after his article on the Queen Anne revival, Godwin seemed to have become more enthusiastic about the possibility of finding architectural expression in utility. In an article in the *Architect* of June 24, 1876, he reviewed the deliberations of an architectural conference on Greek art and proposed that a relevant architecture for the nineteenth century would have to engage the realities of contemporary life. He attenuated the need for historical precedent as he wrote,

Let us take what modern civilization gives us: accept with thanks its sash windows, its plate glass, its iron construction, its many roomed habitations, and the rest, then using all with refinement, there will be evolved out of the commonplace of today, just as all modes hitherto have been evolved, a mode of building that shall be worthy to take its place in the sequence of historical styles.[49]

Themes such as utility and the realities of modern life may seem at odds with Godwin's antiquarian interests or with the subtleties of interior decoration, two subjects on which he wrote extensively in the 1870s. Nonetheless, a review of a few of his articles on these subjects shows an unanticipated unity of purpose in Godwin's interests.

In a seven-part series, titled "My House 'In' London," published in the *British Architect* in 1876, Godwin described how he furnished and decorated the terraced house he leased in Bloomsbury, London.[50] In the course of the series Godwin revealed many of the principles behind his decorative design.[51] An acute sensitivity to the subtle interrelationships between setting, mood, and meaning characterize this series as it does his writings on Shakespeare. The "realism" of his efforts at archaeological accuracy in the theater persists in his concern with function and utility in his domestic designs.

The "My House" series takes a new direction in the criticism of interiors. Works such as Charles Locke Eastlake's *Hints on Household Taste* (1868) and Viollet-Le-Duc's novel-like *Histoire d'une maison* (originally published in Paris in 1873) may have influenced Godwin, who is to some extent writing a counter argument to *The Gentleman's House* (1864) by Robert Kerr.[52] But Godwin's approach was something new, emphasizing individual, personal experience.[53] He took the reader through each room of his house, explaining the reasons for all of the design decisions he made. Beginning with a description of the neighborhood and facade, he brought the reader inside, through the hall and ground floor, into the dining room, up to the drawing room, and then to the bedrooms on the upper floor. In "Tops and Bottoms," the sixth of the seven articles, he discussed the nursery in the attic and the kitchen in the basement. Finally, from the roof he surveyed the view of London and thereby criticized a recently constructed tower of flats in Queen Anne's Gate.[54] Godwin suggested that floor-to-ceiling heights in residences need not be more than nine feet, making such high buildings unnecessary.

Throughout this guided tour, Godwin discussed how he set about correcting what he thought were the decorating and furnishing mistakes found in most middle-class interiors. His house served as laboratory for his design experiments, and with a strong, individual narrative voice,

he was at once specific and practical as well as phenomenological. As if illustrating the line, "Poetically man dwells," by the lyric poet Friedrich Hölderlin, Godwin showed the readers of a London weekly his synthesis of poetry and dwelling as he described how he set about creating an artistically heightened setting for himself and his family.[55]

Autobiographical in many ways, the series is also Godwin's most clear and enjoyable statement of the power of architecture and setting to influence mood and emotion. For example, he called the nursery "the first school in this life, and the eyes of its little inmates are among the first leading channels of unconscious instruction or experience."[56] He used the word "sensitive" to describe one paint color he sought, and explained: "I say sensitive, for a room has a character that may influence for good or bad the many who enter it, especially the very young. The influence of things seen is greater on some people than the influence of things heard."[57] The belief in the morally suasive power of architecture in John Ruskin and A. W. N. Pugin is here translated to the domestic realm. In his discussion of how his interior design will affect his children, Godwin followed a trajectory that characterizes his career as an architecture critic. After showing how design principles derive from personal experience, experience which includes practical necessities and artistic intentions, and in which critical reflection is vital, he moves to embrace the question of influencing and educating the young. Educational objectives were part of his research into Shakespeare and continued to play a role in the last phase of his career as architecture critic, when he became a regular contributor to the *British Architect and Northern Engineer*. In this position, Godwin wrote a number of columns offering advice to students.

His first article, "A Few Words to Architecture Students," appeared in the issue of February 1, 1878. In April 1878 Godwin's purview expanded to include running the *British Architect* Art Club. It was based on the Designing Club started earlier at the *Building News* under editor Maurice B. Adams. The idea was to encourage subscribers to take an interest in the magazine by holding competitions for awards in response to design problems set by the editor.[58] Godwin helped in selecting the topics, and he assessed the entries, often in a severe and exacting way. Many of the topics reflected Godwin's interests, such as one for an artist's house and studio or another for "an easy chair—economy, lightness, and strength to be combined with ease."[59] Commenting on the submissions, Godwin often remarked on how the entries were drawn; many of his judgments were abrupt. The number of students participating in the club declined in the mid-1880s, and the series ended in September 1885.[60]

Fig. 5-4. E. W. Godwin. Masthead for the *British Architect*. From the issue dated 28 November 1879.

Godwin also designed a new masthead for the journal, which was first published in the issue dated January 3, 1879. The design is a rather unexpected and original assemblage of Aesthetic motifs (fig. 5-4). It is similar to the frontispiece in *Art Furniture*, the catalogue Godwin designed for William Watt, published in 1877 (see fig. 3-18). A brief note introducing the new masthead described it in revealing terms: "we have in the lines and colouring of our new heading the clearness and decision, the *black and white* of Truth—in the foliage over the initial, the expression of elegance and grace—and in the laughing kingfisher perched below may be symbolised our flight over the world and our pleasantry."[61] A surprising, maybe inappropriate design for a journal whose full subtitle embraced, at least initially, "Summary of Mining News," the masthead was dropped after the December 1885 issue.

Along with the new masthead came the strong imprint of Godwin's personality. During the late 1870s and early 1880s the journal published many of Godwin's own designs, often in full-page or double-page lithographic prints. The issue dated November 29, 1878, for example, included Godwin's elevation drawing of Archibald Stuart-Wortley's house and studio spread out across two pages (see fig. 5-1). This was followed in the issue of December 6, 1878, by full-page elevations of the houses and studios for James McNeill Whistler and Frank Miles. These are graphically bold images, with simple, elegant borders and lavish blank white spaces.

Like the graphics, the content of a number of the articles reflected changes. At times, the journal seemed devoted to defending Godwin's personal interests, publishing his complaints against the Metropolitan Board of Works and his response to criticisms of his design of the White House.

The readers were kept informed of what Godwin was doing in the theater. During these years, Godwin wrote thoughtful obituaries of G. G. Scott, G. E. Street, and William Burges. He also wrote lengthy reviews of exhibitions at the Grosvenor and Dudley Galleries, and the Royal Academy. Burne-Jones and Whistler were prominently discussed, maybe more so than architects. The Whistler v. Ruskin libel trial was eagerly awaited, with anticipatory comments included in the pages before the proceedings.[62] The decision received a front-page editorial along with a transcript of the testimony at the trial, and the issue dated July 4, 1879, included a poem by Oscar Wilde, titled "Ave Maria Plena Gratia." The comings and goings of such aesthetic figures as Frank Miles and Lillie Langtry were duly noted in the "Current Events" column.

Although Godwin emphasized the unity of the arts in his writings, this was not a declaration of artistic autonomy. On the contrary, by introducing into the pages of commercial trade periodicals such subjects as costume and setting in Shakespeare, Godwin showed how architecture is part of the fabric of human culture. Similarly, writing in the May 2, 1884, issue of the *British Architect*, he advised students to attend plays, in order to sharpen their sensibilities, to improve their understanding of life, and so become better architects. This educational imperative was basic to Godwin's writing career, and his articles addressed to students are some of his most memorable writing. The *American Architect and Building News* acknowledged this in its obituary of Godwin, noting that he wrote "most instructively" for students and suggesting that his "admirable criticisms and suggestions" be collected for students to consult.[63]

Like many of his articles, his writings for students were serialized. He wrote a six-part series with the unfortunate title "Scraps for Students" that was published in April and May 1876 in the *Architect*.[64] For the *British Architect*, he wrote a three-part series, "To Our Student Readers," in 1880,[65] followed by ten "Letters to Art Students" in 1884.[66] His final signed article in the *British Architect* was an attempt to revive the Art Club, which Godwin used as an opportunity to offer numerous points of advice to students.

Throughout all of these articles, Godwin sounded a few themes. He directed his attention to the growth and development of what he called "the artist-mind."[67] He sought to foster an open, receptive temperament and to encourage critical inquiry. Above all, the student "must first learn to look, then to criticise,"[68] he wrote. Basing his advice on his own experiences he described how important lessons can be learned at the theater or the art gallery, by visiting buildings in a partially ruined condition or by sketching something as unexpected as a dead bird.[69] In July 1880 Godwin showed how the diligent, attentive student can profit from all his experiences:

> Nor let it be supposed that amusements are only good for recreation; the wise art student never forgets his art wherever he may be. In his country walks or street rambles his eyes are ever open to note the just proportion or the exquisite harmony, and his brain is ready to work out the reason thereof. At the theatre, on the lawn, or in the billiard room endless combinations of more or less beautiful form are perpetually presented to him.[70]

While this passage bears comparison to Charles Baudelaire's "Painter of Modern Life" and the conclusion to Walter Pater's *Renaissance* in its themes of visuality and the flux of modern life,[71] Godwin's advice was usually detailed, specific, and practical.

In "Scraps for Students," for example, he took the student through the early phases of a typical career, from pupil and apprentice to the early days of an independent practice. Just as he led the reader through all the rooms in his London home, Godwin guided the student through the various stages of becoming an architect. The article is divided into sections on topics such as outdoor sketching, where to spend the summer holiday, what books to read, how to use one's free time when home from the office, what to expect of clients. Godwin argued that as well as acquiring narrowly professional skills, the student should develop habits of critical analysis, thoughtful study, and sensitivity to the physical world.

For Godwin drawing was one of the most important means to this end, and he wrote consistently on drawing as a vital tool for learning. "Careful drawing is an exercise the young architect cannot have too much of," he wrote in 1880.[72] Godwin shared Ruskin's belief in the central importance of drawing in an architect's education. His remarks on drawing also bear similarities to articles Burges published in the 1860s and 1870s on outdoor sketching and measuring.[73] Godwin emphasized drawing as a critical and analytic tool. "Separate, distinguish, analyse," he advised student readers in 1885, "and you will not be surprised to find that in your drawing, as in your writing, a critical judgment will be developed."[74] He set out the core of his thoughts on drawing as an instrument of understanding in the following passage from "A Few Words to Architectural Students":

> If a building is worth your study at all, it is worth dissecting. Do not content yourself with plan and elevation, section and detail, such as were the fashion in Pugin's day, no matter how well measured or beautifully drawn. Take your subject to pieces, find out all about it, probe it and feel it if you cannot see it, in a word lay it *bare* and one such study, even if you were to lose all your drawings of it would be of more value to you than a library full of sketches shaded up with lovely gradations of album-like dexterity.[75]

During the final years of his life, Godwin shifted his earlier efforts at criticizing the profession onto educating students. In his ten letters to art students, published from May through July 1884 in the *British Architect*, Godwin made a point of addressing art students, explaining in the first letter, "I do so because I wish it to be clearly understood between us that Art is one body."[76] To be a good architect, the student should master the entire anatomy of this body, which in his view is composed of painting, sculpture, dress, and the theater as well as architecture. Godwin directed student readers "to go to the theater and the circus, to attend ecclesiastical functions, to go into all sorts of studios, to accompany me to sanitary exhibitions, to workshops, and to picture galleries."[77] Although Godwin's intention was to lead the students where they may "observe and profit," there is the sense in a few of the letters that he has left architecture behind.

Along with his role as judge of the Art Club, Godwin conducted in the pages of the *British Architect* what amounted to an extramural series of seminars. In their educational imperative, Godwin's letters to art students, written from an intensely personal point of view, can be compared to the series of letters Ruskin was publishing these same years under the title *Fors Clavigera*.[78] In many ways Godwin addressed the student in architects of all ages. In what was to be his last article in the *British Architect*, Godwin delineated a self-portrait as he advised students how to draw. He described how in youth, students work

> *for the love of our art*—that is still, I am inclined to think, the highest incentive. We liked to labour all day long for art's sake; in the summer strolling, joyous and hopeful, from village to village and town to town sketching, measuring, analysing everything that came our way which we thought good . . . I take up an early notebook at random, and there, sandwiched among sketches of old buildings and suggestions for new, I find an altar cloth, fragments of a nunnery by Butterfield, and a school by Street,

both then in progress; furniture ancient and modern, boats, rocks at the Lizard, iron girders, some few portraits, lazy children who have unconsciously served as models . . . [I]n those days we thought we had something to say and we said it. Not at first were we recognised by any honorarium. A little excusable vanity awoke at seeing our words in print.[79]

Making a transition from drawing to writing at the end of the passage, Godwin here revealed how they complemented one another in his life as an architect. Addressing students, Godwin returned to himself, not just the student he was when young, but the student he chose to be his entire life.

•

Note: Most published sources are cited below in shortened form (author's last name, abbreviated title, date of publication); full references will be found in the bibliography. Frequently cited archives are abbreviated below; for a key to the abbreviations, also see the bibliography.

1. Godwin, "To Art Students" (20 June 1884): 297.

2. The Institute for British Architects was founded in 1834 and received its royal charter in 1866 becoming the Royal Institute of British Architects (R.I.B.A.). The first general conference took place in 1871.

3. Fergusson, "New Law Courts" (January 1872): 250–56. The *Building News* published a review of Fergusson's article, saying, "In point of reasoning, it strikes us as hardly worthy of its author" ("Damnatory Art-Criticism," *Building News* [5 January 1872]: 1). The R.I.B.A. had awarded Fergusson its gold medal the previous year.

4. "State of English Architecture," *Quarterly Review* 132 (April 1872): 295–335. The occasion for the article was a review of five books on architecture, including George Edmund Street, *The New Courts of Justice: Notes in Reply to Criticisms* (London, 1872); and idem, *Some Account of Gothic Architecture in Spain* (London: J. Murray, 1869).

5. "The New Voice in the 'Quarterly,'" *Architect* 8 (26 October 1872): 227. The journal had earlier said of the article, "A jaundiced eye and a splenetic temper seem to have dictated every sentence," *Architect* 7 (27 April 1872): 209.

6. T. Roger Smith, "Coming Conference," *Building News* (7 June 1872): 465–66. Smith also noted that "the great question of internecine strife among rival artists ought to be opened unflinchingly, and the members of the profession ought to say and say boldly what they hold to be fair and what unprofessional in the way of pamphlets and newspaper letters."

7. T. H. Wyatt, "General Conference of Architects: Open Meeting, Monday, June 10," *Building News* (14 June 1872): 475. Wyatt stated, "I believe that the violent and personal language now so freely indulged in by the literary and professional critic does not carry conviction with it, and though exciting or amusing at the moment, is not to the taste of those whose opinion or influence is of real value."

8. Ibid.

9. Godwin refuted Fergusson's criticisms of Street (Godwin, "New Law Courts" [28 July 1871]: 73).

10. Godwin, "The 'British Architects'" (21 June 1872): 505. One reader wrote in to criticize Godwin's "sarcastic remarks on esprit de corps" ("Secret Deliberations," *Building News* 22 [28 June 1872]: 531).

11. Godwin, "The 'British Architects'" (21 June 1872): 505.

12. [Godwin] "Professional Tenderness" (28 June 1872): 515.

13. Ibid.

14. In the cuttings file, V&A AAD, 4/563, the editorial bears a penciled-in "EWG." Furthermore, its text repeats verbatim comments Godwin made five years earlier in a paper presented to the Architectural Exhibition Society, which was published in the *Building News* in 1867. "I cannot understand," Godwin wrote, "why architects should be treated more tenderly than the professors of other arts," and he called for "unsparing criticism" in order to create "a system of strong personalities" (Godwin, "The Architectural Exhibition" [17 May 1867]: 335).

15. Godwin, "Modern Architects and Their Works," part 1 (5 July 1872): 13; part 2 (12 July 1872): 35; part 3 (26 July 1872): 67; part 4 (30 August 1872): 167; part 5 (6 September 1872): 187; part 6 (11 October 1872): 291–92. The articles are similar to an earlier, twelve-part series ("Art Cliques") that Godwin published in the *Building News* from 15 September 1865 to 23 March 1866.

16. "Professional Tenderness" (28 June 1872): 515.

17. Godwin, "Modern Architects and Their Works," part 1 (5 July 1872): 13. Sir John Summerson has described Robert Kerr as a man "of acute intelligence and exceptional eloquence who was constantly being asked to address his professional colleagues on professional affairs and was fully reported whenever he did" ("The Evaluation of Victorian Architecture: The Problem of Failure," in *Victorian Architecture: Four Studies in Evaluation* by John Summerson [New York: Columbia University Press, 1970]: 7).

18. Godwin, "Modern Architects and Their Works," part 1 (5 July 1872): 13.

19. One reader, identified only as "Leicester," wrote, "Mr. Godwin has his revenge in holding up his contemporaries and rivals to popular ridicule" (*Building News* [13 September 1872]: 211).

20. Godwin, "Modern Architects and Their Works," part 3 (26 July 1872): 67.

21. Ibid.

22. Ibid.

23. Mark Girouard described how "in the 1860's Godwin and Burges were the Castor and Pollux of architecture" and noted that by 1873 their careers started to diverge (Girouard, *Victorian Country House* [1971]: 147–48).

24. Godwin, "Modern Architects and Their Works," part 4 (30 August 1872): 167.

25. Ibid. Godwin also wrote that he "dwells so long and so hypercritically on proportion and mass that he has no time for detail."

26. Godwin, "On Some Buildings I Have Designed" (29 November 1878): 211.

27. Elizabeth Aslin pointed out that "Godwin was something of a personal publicist" (Aslin, "E. W. Godwin and the Japanese Taste" [December 1962]: 782).

28. Godwin, "Modern Architects and Their Works," part 4 (30 August 1872): 167.

29. One reader of the *Building News* commented in 1872, "The initials 'E. W. G.' are familiar to all readers of T*he Building News*, and, in his time, the author has done good service to the profession. He has written on many subjects to advantage, and criticised most architects (himself included) and their works, with a vigour, a power, and an audacity unrivalled" ([13 September 1872]: 210).

30. Pevsner, *Pioneers of Modern Design* (1978): 64.

31. [Obiturary], "Edward W. Godwin," *British Architect* (15 October 1886): 348. The *Art Journal* published a brief notice of Godwin's death, in which it stated, "Mr. Godwin has for long been known as a clear writer and thinker on many Art subjects, and most archaeological questions" (Obituary, *Art Journal* 48 [November 1886]: 352).

32. Godwin, "Modern Architects and Their Works," part 3 (26 July 1872): 67.

33. M. W. Brooks, *John Ruskin and Victorian Architecture* (1987): 210.

34. Godwin, "Modern Architects and Their Works," part 3 (26 July 1872): 67.

35. Ibid.

36. Godwin, "British Architect Special Correspondence" (18 December 1885): 262.

37. Godwin, "Sir George Gilbert Scott" (5 April 1878): 155.

38. The correspondence was reprinted, presumably at Godwin's request, in the *British Architect* ("The Restoration of Westminster Hall" [19 December 1884]: 302–3). Publishing his own correspondence was one of Godwin's tactics of publicity. When the first of Godwin's two letters on Westminster Hall was published in the *Times* (London), Godwin's client Oscar Wilde sent him a letter from Leeds: "Dear Godwino, Your letter to the *Times* is excellent" (O. Wilde, *Letters of Oscar Wilde* [1962]: 165).

39. Harbron, *Conscious Stone* (1949): 35.

40. For example, in the 24 October 1873 issue of the *Building News*, he reviewed the work of Richard Norman Shaw and promised his readers "a few jottings" on the Queen Anne style (Godwin, "The Works of Mr. R. Norman Shaw, A.R.A." [24 October 1873]: 450).

41. Godwin wrote that a "judicious eclecticism" is what "I have pleaded [for] these many years" (Godwin, "Friends in Council" [30 December 1881]: 655).

42. Godwin, "Ex-Classic Style Called 'Queen Anne'" (16 April 1875): 442.

43. Ibid., p. 441.

44. Ibid.

45. Ibid.

46. Ibid. Godwin's measured drawings of the Manoir d'Ango were pub-lished in the *Building News* (27 February, 3 April, and 10 April 1874). These were followed later in the year by Godwin's series, "Some Notes of a Month in Normandy."

47. In "Lesson of Rome," Le Corbusier described how "this quite tiny church of S. Maria, a church for poor people, set in the midst of noisy and luxurious Rome, proclaims the noble pomp of mathematics, the unassailable power of proportion, the sovereign eloquence of relationship. The design is merely that of the ordinary basilica, that is to say the form of architecture in which barns and hangers are built" (Le Corbusier, *Towards a New Architecture*, trans. Frederick Etchells [New York: Holt, Rinehart and Winston, 1960], 149).

48. The drawings were published in Godwin, "Examples of Ancient Irish Architecture, *British Architect* 11 (31 January 1879); ibid. (21 February 1879); ibid. (7 March 1879); and ibid. (14 March 1879).

49. Godwin, "Greek Art at the Conference" (24 June 1876): 396.

50. The series was preceded by two articles on his bachelor's chambers (Godwin, "My Chambers and What I Did to Them," part 1 [1 July 1876]: 4–5; part 2 [8 July 1876]: 18–19).

51. For a discussion of Godwin's principles of interior design, see chap. 7 in this volume.

52. Godwin had an especial dislike of Kerr's book and attacked Kerr's illustration of a "Gothic House," writing, "To say that it is a parody or burlesque of Gothic would be untrue; it has not the cleverness of the one nor the fun of the other. It is, without the faintest exaggeration, nothing but a coarse rechauffé of scraps of Gothic, picked up, as it seems, by accident; and yet Mr. Kerr has the consummate assurance to say (A.D. 1871) that it shows modern Gothic 'at its best.' I venture to say, without any qualification whatever, that it shows it at its worst." (Godwin, "Modern Architects and Their Works," part 3 [26 July 1872]: 67).

53. Godwin wrote, "I have had a long experience in chambers and I hope that I have profited by it" (Godwin, "My Chambers," part 1 [1 July 1876]: 4–5).

54. Godwin referred to the building as "Mr. Hankey's stack of yellow bricks at Queen Anne's Gate" (Godwin, "My House 'In' London," part 7, "From the House-Top" [26 August 1876]: 112).

55. In *The English House*, originally published in 1904, Hermann Muthesius saw a vital tie between artistic culture and the private, single-family house in England. He described how a house owner becomes something of an artist when building a new house, confronted with the need to make decisions on a variety of issues in which artistic aspects are involved. "For the house-owner is now something of an artist himself, as we all were in our natural state," Muthesius observes. The private house is "the very basis of artistic education" (H. Muthesius, *English House* [1979]: 9). Written thirty years before Muthesius's book, Godwin's description of the intermingled practical and aesthetic intentions involved in the decoration of his house is a good precedent for Muthesius's thesis.

56. Godwin, "My House 'In' London," part 6, "Tops and Bottoms" (19 August 1876): 100.

57. Ibid., part 4, "The Drawing Room" (5 August 1876): 72. He went on to state, "With myself, I know that the memory of the eye's experience is far and away beyond that of the ear."

58. In introducing the club, the editors noted, "There is no restriction as to age, sex or profession" ("'British Architect' Art Club" [13 February 1880]: 77). Godwin supported women's entry into the architectural profession; see e.g., Godwin, "Lady Architects" (13 June 1874): 335.

59. [Godwin], Notes on Current Events, *British Architect* (13 August 1880): 73.

60. Two letters expressing regret that the series ended were printed in the issue dated 18 September 1885.

61. Notes on Current Events, *British Architect* (4 January 1878): 8. Ed. note:

emphasis retained from original.

62. "Whistler v. Ruskin," *British Architect* (29 November 1878): 207.

63. Obituary [E.W. Godwin], *American Architect* (30 October 1886): 202.

64. Godwin, "Scraps for Students," part 1 (15 April 1876): 237–38; part 2 (22 April 1876): 252–53; part 3 (6 May 1876): 284–85; part 4 (13 May 1876): 303–5; part 5 (20 May 1876): 320; part 6 (27 May 1876): 338–39.

65. Godwin, "To Our Student Readers," part 1 (30 July 1880): 48–49; part 2 (13 August 1880): 70; part 3 (27 August 1880): 95.

66. Godwin, "To Art Students," part 1 (2 May 1884): 215; part 2 (9 May 1884): 225; part 3 (16 May 1884): 238; part 4 (30 May 1884): 262; part 5 (6 June 1884): 273; part 6 (13 June 1884): 285; part 7 (20 June 1884): 297; part 8 (27 June 1884): 309–10; part 9 (4 July 1884): 1–2; part 10 (11 July 1884): 13.

67. Godwin, "To Art Students," part 9 (4 July 1884): 1.

68. Godwin, "Scraps for Students," part 3 (6 May 1876): 285. Godwin writes, "When I ask you to criticise, I mean that before selecting a building for study, you should weigh well the nature of its merits, and probe the depths of its failures or demerits."

69. Godwin advised students to draw "*everything that is beautiful or that fully answers its purpose* [original italics]. If you come across a dead bird draw every detail of its wing or head or leg as carefully as you would delineate every feature in a thirteenth century door, or seventeenth century staircase" (Godwin, "To Our Student Readers," part 3 [27 August 1880]: 95).

70. Ibid., part 1 (30 July 1880): 49.

71. Charles Baudelaire, *The Painter of Modern Life and Other Essays,* trans. Jonathan Mayne (London: Phaidon Press, 1995); Walter Pater, *The Renaissance: Studies in Art and Poetry* (originally published in 1873 as *Studies in the History of the Renaissance*), reprint (London: Macmillan and Co., 1913).

72. Godwin, "To Our Student Readers," part 3 (27 August 1880): 95.

73. W. Burges, "Measured Drawings Versus Sketches," *Building News* 12 (11 August 1865): 95.

74. Godwin, "British Architect Special Correspondence" (18 December 1885): 262. Godwin's emphasis on the critical intelligence of his student readers is what separates his writings from other handbooks, such as George Wightwick, *Hints to Young Architects* (London: John Weale, 1846).

75. Godwin, "A Few Words to Architectural Students" (1 February 1878): 1.

76. Godwin, "To Art Students," part 1 (2 May 1884): 215.

77. Ibid.

78. John Ruskin, *Fors Clavigera: Letters to the Workmen and Labourers of Great Britain,* in *The Works of John Ruskin,* vols. 30–32, ed. E.T. Cook and Alexander Wedderburn (New York: Longmans, Green and Co.: 1904). Godwin owned copies of letters 1 to 5 and 9 to 11 (V&A AAD, 4/548-1988).

79. Godwin, "British Architect Special Correspondence" (18 December 1885): 262.

Fig. 6-1. E. W. Godwin. Northampton Guildhall (formerly Northampton Town Hall), 1861–64. Photographed in 1998. *Checklist no. 9*

CHAPTER 6

THE·ARCHITECTURAL CAREER·OF·E. W. GODWIN

AILEEN REID

A brilliant, if somewhat eccentric character, who might, under happier conditions of life, have become the first architect of his age . . . ; his life . . . has been, for the most part, one of unfulfilled promise . . . . In later years Mr Godwin confined himself in designing almost exclusively to art furniture; but more recently he drifted off into the arrangement of scenery and the devising of costumes for theatres and amateur performances.[1]

This somewhat bleak assessment of E. W. Godwin's career comes from an obituary in the *Building News,* a journal that had loyally promoted his work for more than twenty years. Elsewhere, another obituarist omitted entirely to mention that Godwin was an architect.[2] This tendency to deprecate Godwin's achievements as an architect has persisted over time, partly as a consequence of the escalation in value of pieces of furniture designed by him, but it is misleading because, taken as a whole, Godwin's career was dominated by his architectural work (e.g. fig. 6-1).[3]

Although Godwin never mentions William Armstrong's name in print, there seems no reason to doubt Dudley Harbron's assertion that Godwin, at the age of fifteen or sixteen, was articled to Armstrong in 1848 or 1849.[4] Godwin later wrote that Armstrong, whom he identified only as "master," "knew nothing whatever about architecture—a thing by no means of rare occurrence; but he did know something of engineering."[5] This last seems to be supported by Godwin's contention that Armstrong was "a great friend of Brunel"[6] and by Armstrong's participation in the 1829 Clifton Suspension Bridge competition.[7] It also presumably referred to Armstrong's employment from 1836 until his death in 1858 as one of Bristol's three city surveyors, whose responsibilities included ensuring that new buildings in the city had adequate drains.[8]

Armstrong's surviving Bristol buildings include Brunswick Chapel in Brunswick Square and many houses in Cotham, Kingsdown, and Montpelier.[9] They are all in a slightly dull, restrained, classical mode. The disappointment that Godwin, fired up by his study of the Middle Ages, must have felt in this environment was echoed by many Victorian architects recalling their pupilages.[10] But Godwin had far more serious criticisms about his apprenticeship than the dullness of his master's designs. He claimed in 1878 that "he had no master's teaching . . . he was thrown upon his own resources."[11] Although one should be wary of the memoirs of successful architects keen to reconstruct themselves as self-made artist-geniuses, tales of inadequate pupilage, often invoking the cursed name of Pecksniff,[12] Dickens's unscrupulous "Architect and Land Surveyor" in *Martin Chuzzlewit,* are sufficiently common in the mid- and late nineteenth century for it to be clear that lack of training was a genuine problem.

In "The Secret Manufacture of Architecture," pub-

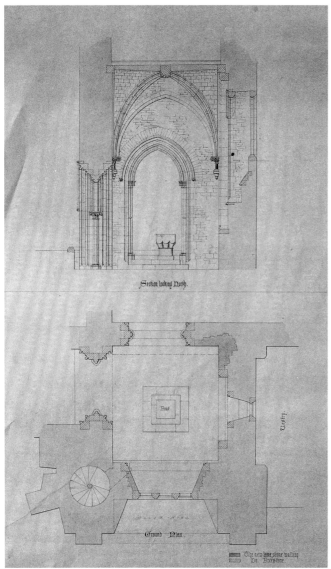

Fig. 6-2. E. W. Godwin and James Hine. Proposed restoration of the tower of Saint Philip and Saint Jacob's church, Bristol: section and plan, 1854. Pen and ink and colored wash; 21 x 14 in. (53.3 x 35.6 cm). Bristol Record Office, P/St P & J/PL/ 1 (d) i.

lished in 1873, Godwin made a more serious allegation against Armstrong: "When my venerable master signed my first design, not seen by him before the minute he fathered it, . . . there was a sense . . . that I was being deprived of something, and I would have given him gladly an extra year's service to have placed only my initials in the corner of my drawings."[13]

This account suggests that some buildings attributed to Armstrong were, in fact, by Godwin, but the evidence from surviving buildings and drawings is inconclusive.[14] One project credited to Armstrong on which Godwin

almost certainly worked was the restoration in 1850 of the north range of the Dominican friary in Bristol, and its conversion, rather implausibly, to a Quaker school.[15] Drawings by Godwin survive of the building, and he presented a paper on it to the Archaeological Institute's meeting at Bristol in 1851.[16]

The opportunities for formal learning outside the office were probably limited. The Bristol Society of Architects, of which Godwin was a student member in 1850–51, was then concerned more with protecting architects' social status as professionals than with questions of architectural training and design.[17] (Godwin himself revitalized the society in 1862–64.) There is no evidence that Godwin attended drawing classes, which is all the more remarkable given his evident accomplishment as an architectural draftsman. Godwin's archaeological studies—his measuring and sketching of old buildings—was probably as much a function of his architectural self-education as of a discrete antiquarian interest; the relationship between the two activities became increasingly osmotic in the 1850s and 1860s. For the rest of his life, he was to continue to sketch and make notes, both as an integral part of the process of architectural design and as an end in itself.

The Practice of Art-Architecture

In Godwin's 1878 account of his architectural career,[18] he makes no mention of his seven-year partnership with Henry Crisp, nor of any of the other architects, assistants, or pupils who collaborated with him in differing capacities from the early 1850s to the early 1880s. Yet these collaborations were in some ways crucial to Godwin in constructing himself as a "genius-designer"[19] and becoming, in the parlance of the late nineteenth century, an art-architect.

The notion of art-architecture had been mooted as early as the 1840s by both C. R. Cockerell and Robert Kerr. Cockerell advocated employing "the Art Architect to design, and the practical architect to carry out and superintend."[20] Kerr, elaborating on this in his *Newleafe Discourses* (1846), recommended an "improved division of labour . . . whereby the real Architect might be relieved from the inspection of sewers and cesspools and wells, and the shoring up of old houses, and the rating of dilapidations . . . and entrusted with the design of much of the decoration which is at present confided to the painter, upholsterer, cabinetmaker."[21] Godwin's entire architectural career can be seen as an attempt to achieve just such a division of labor, with himself in the role of Cockerell's "Art Architect."

Godwin, as far as can be ascertained, only entered into one official partnership—with Henry Crisp, from 1864 to 1871. However, his longest collaboration, lasting, albeit spo-

Fig. 6-3. James Hine and E. W. Godwin.
Western College, Plymouth (Member
Relation, Plymouth Co-operative Society),
1859–61. Photographed in 1998.

radically, for nearly twenty years, was with James Hine, a Plymouth architect who became the city's leading Gothic revivalist.[22] Hine had also been a pupil of Armstrong and co-wrote with Godwin *The Architectural Antiquities of Bristol and its Neighbourhood*, published in 1851.

Godwin and Hine produced a scheme for the restoration of Saint Philip and Saint Jacob, Bristol, in 1854. The drawings for this commission (fig. 6-2) appear to be by Godwin alone, and the handwriting of the description which accompanies them is also Godwin's, not Hine's.[23] It is difficult to know what part Hine played in the project, which was ultimately abandoned for lack of funds,[24] but from later examples of their collaboration it appears that Godwin was to be the designer, or "art-architect," and Hine the executive—or "practical"—architect.

From 1858 to 1860 Godwin supplied Hine with seven designs—"Italian Villa with tower; R.C. Schools, Jersey; College, Plymouth; Birmingham House; conservatory

dome; perspective of Western College; design for tower, Christ Church, Plymouth"[25]—at prices from 10/6 to 2 guineas. Of these only Western College seems to have been built. In the same ledger Godwin records, "Western College lowest tender £4000 . . . £50,"—meaning that the Western College project had matured into a commission, and he was to receive half of the architect's usual commission of 2½ per cent for the production of the designs.[26]

Western College, Plymouth, is regarded as one of James Hine's major early commissions in Plymouth.[27] Godwin is not mentioned as the designer in any of the contemporary press reports,[28] and when he reported on the contemporary architectural scene in Plymouth for the *Building News* in 1865,[29] he did not claim Western College as his work. Godwin was paid half the commission fee, however, and the unusual design of the tracery (fig. 6-3) is almost identical to his designs for Saint Paul de Leon, Staverton, Devon (see fig. 6-6),[30] dated only six weeks before his ledger entry for his Western College drawings. This evidence strongly suggests that Godwin played a major part in Hine's Western College project.

This pattern of collaboration, with Godwin fulfilling the art-architect's role and another architect acting in a supervisory capacity, repeated itself many times. The name of James Adams Clark appears on several drawings of buildings credited to Godwin—Saint Philip and Saint Jacob's schools (1860)[31] and Nos. 10 and 11 Rockleaze (1860–62)[32]—but it seems unlikely from the nature of other buildings that Clark designed in Bristol that he was actively involved in the design of these.[33] In 1863 he worked with Godwin on extensions to Highbury Chapel in Bristol (see figs. 6-13, 6-14), but in this case he acted solely as quantity surveyor.[34]

More significant for Godwin's establishment of himself as an art-architect was his partnership with Henry Crisp, which began in January 1864 and ended in 1871.[35] Crisp was older than Godwin and in many ways his exact opposite. He was an old-style provincial architect, trained in the office of the Bristol architect Thomas Foster,[36] and his practice included activities such as rent collection, valuations, and quantity surveying,[37] which Godwin felt were not commensurate with the architect's role as either professional or artist. A scrupulous businessman, Crisp had a reputation for making accurate estimates.[38] His status as a designer is hard to quantify: the designs he executed on his own account usually seem to be either reticent to the point of dullness or flamboyant to the point of roguishness[39]; he never achieved Godwin's expressive refinement.

Several years into the partnership Godwin wrote to one of his clients that "my partner's special department is to superintend the execution of my designs and to transact all business between contractors and ourselves,"[40] and a letter written by Godwin to Crisp after their partnership had been dissolved suggests that this division of labor was enshrined in their contract agreement.[41] The true picture appears to have been more complex than that, particularly after Godwin moved to London in 1865 and opened an office there. Certain projects, such as Cherry Orchard Farm[42] and the new wards in this Bristol Royal Infirmary,[43] are likely to have been Crisp's alone, both the design and superintendence. There were also projects, such as Rheinfelden in Northampton (1868–69; see fig. 6-27), which Godwin both designed and supervised.[44] With these exceptions, however, the partnership appears to have operated much as Godwin indicated, with Crisp doing most of the administration and supervision of Godwin's designs. This arrangement worked satisfactorily until Crisp became aware that Godwin had undertaken work which he had not

included in the partnership accounts, specifically fees Godwin had accepted from Lord Limerick for the design of furniture for Dromore Castle, County Limerick.[45] The underlying reason for Godwin excluding this from the accounts was presumably that it involved no supervision, which he clearly saw as Crisp's role in the business.

A further complication to the partnership was Godwin's continued collaboration with James Hine. In 1869 a major competition to build a new guildhall at Plymouth (see fig. 6-20) was won by Hine and Alfred Norman, with Godwin as "consulting architect." According to the contract drawn up by the three parties before they entered the competition,[46] Godwin supplied the design and Hine and Norman carried it out with almost no assistance from Godwin after the designs were submitted: the acme of art-architectural practice.

This type of single-project agreement clearly suited Godwin better than a full-scale partnership in which his behavior suggested that he considered his contribution as a designer to be worth more than that of a supervising architect. During his partnership with Crisp, and subsequently, he entered into at least three more agreements with other architects. Significantly, they were not with provincial "drains and dilapidations" men but with his peers in London—William Burges, J. P. Seddon, and R. W. Edis, who were all highly successful architects.

Godwin's collaboration with Burges was not unexpected. When Godwin wrote Burges's obituary in 1881 he described how he had met him "more than twenty years since" and that their friendship had been "more intimate and sincere than any friendship of my life."[47] They first met after Godwin had admired Burges's design for the Sabrina fountain in Gloucester, published in the *Builder* in May 1858, and when he called on Burges in his rooms in Buckingham Street, off the Strand: "he was hospitable, poured wine into a silver goblet of his own design, and placed bread on the table. With few words on either side we ate and drank . . . ."[48] They were especially close during the 1860s, when Burges became a corresponding member of, and sometime visitor to, the Bristol Society of Architects, in which Godwin was a leading light. Together they went to Ireland when Burges was supervising his Saint Fin Barre's cathedral in Cork and Godwin was working on Dromore Castle, County Limerick.[49]

But for all that they were close, their collaboration on architectural projects seems to have been very limited. In 1866 Godwin assisted Burges, possibly for a payment of £100,[50] with his entry for the Law Courts competition, spending a week "discussing and scribbling" at Burges's father's house in Blackheath, southeast London.[51] There was talk of them collaborating on the building of a theater,[52] and they also had planned, in the mid-1860s, a jointly written book on the "right and the wrong use of certain constructional forms,"[53] which did not materialize.[54] There seems to have been a cooling in their friendship in the later 1870s,[55] however, and by 1877 Godwin claimed that "I rarely if ever see Mr Burges."[56]

That, in any collaboration between two architects, one had to take the art-architect's role and the other the executive, was explicitly stated in Godwin's arrangement with R. W. Edis. In his draft agreement with Edis, Godwin stipulated, "That I am not required to make any working drawings but only to advise by rough sketches and consult on details, overlook these and other drawings generally and roughly altering same as requisite for working it out . . . . That in all Public works or exhibited drawings my name, if I so require, shall appear as consulting architect . . . That any work carried into execution my fee . . . be at the rate of £1.1.0 for every £100 expended in the carrying out of such work."[57] Edis's role was also explicitly outlined: "That all future works on which I [Godwin] may be personally engaged shall be designed by me as private work and that if any such work be carried into execution that you should superintend the same, make the working drawings, arrange with the tradesmen and be recognized as the superintending architect . . . That for your superintendence and work as described in the last clause stating you shall receive £2 [this was altered by Edis to 2½ percent in his amendments to the draft[58]] in every £100 expended in carrying out the said works."[59] Edis added a clause, stating "That this agreement shall in no wise constitute a partnership . . . and shall in no wise subject either to any professional or other liabilities of the other."[60] In the end their collaboration appears to have petered out after only two competition entries—perhaps because they were unsuccessful.[61]

A similar draft agreement was made between Godwin and Seddon around the same time for the purposes of entering the Saint Ann's Heath Lunatic Asylum competition for Thomas Holloway.[62] This did not specify the division of labor so precisely as the agreement with Edis, but such a division may be inferred from the fact that in a later collaboration between Godwin and Seddon, for a "People's Palace" on the Thames near Waterloo Bridge, an abortive speculative venture, "the elevation of the riverside facade . . . was the actual handiwork of Mr Godwin."[63]

Although the idea of dividing architectural practice in this way was periodically promoted in the architectural press,[64] such a division of labor as Godwin had with Crisp, Edis, and Seddon was exceptional. Inevitably, as the "art" part of architectural practice became more important, the more difficult it became to find an architect partner prepared to be seen as the "superintendent" solely. Godwin came to rely increasingly on his assistants, from drawing pupils to clerks to improvers,[65] for the day-to-day running of his office.

Church Projects

Although Godwin's architectural career is usually assessed in terms of domestic and civic buildings, until he won the competition for Northampton Town Hall early in 1861, the bulk of his income came from church work. His first independent commission, which came in 1853, was for a small Anglican church school. Although the records are scanty, it appears to have been the Trinity Branch School in Easton, part of the vast outparish of Godwin's family parish church of Saint Philip and Saint Jacob, which is presumably how he secured the commission.[66] Godwin later proudly proclaimed that the school was built for less than the estimate.[67] No photographs or elevations survive, but the Building Grant plan suggests it was a single-story structure, with one schoolroom and a porch, probably with simple lancet windows and a steeply pitched roof.[68]

Godwin also designed church schools in the 1860s for Saint Philip and Saint Jacob in Bristol (fig. 6-4),[69] and

Fig. 6-4. E. W. Godwin. Preliminary design for Saint Philip and Saint Jacob's Schools, Bristol, ca. 1860. Watercolor on paper; 21⅜ x 16¾ in. (54.3 x 42.5 cm). Scott Elliott, Kelmscott Gallery, Chicago.

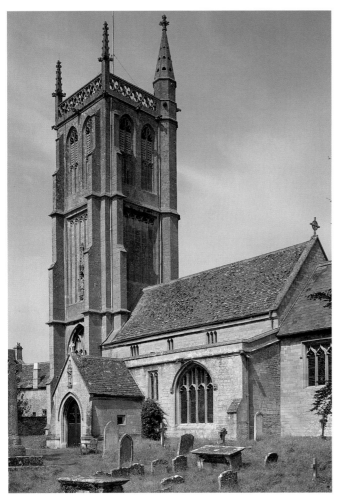

Fig. 6-5. Saint John the Baptist, Colerne, Wiltshire, altered by
E. W. Godwin, 1854–55. Photographed in 1998.

for All Saints, Winterbourne Down, just outside Bristol.[70] Both projects reveal Godwin's ability to design effective, low-cost buildings.[71] They are both in a vernacular Gothic, almost astylar in their plainness, with rubble walling and a careful disposition of single and triple square-headed stone-mullioned windows beneath relieving arches; at Winterbourne Down some of these are semicircular, with herringbone stone in the lunettes.[72]

By the time Godwin's architectural career was under way, restorations had overtaken the building of new churches in all but the fastest expanding urban areas,[73] and most of his work for the Anglican Church consisted of restorations and refittings of existing churches. His first restoration,[74] of Saint John the Baptist, Colerne, Wiltshire (fig. 6-5), illustrates the practical value to young architects of their antiquarian researches. He had visited the church, which was a few miles east of Bristol, several times in the

early 1850s and had written descriptions of it, including one that was published.[75] In addition, its incumbent, Reverend Gilbert Heathcote, was a fellow member of the Wiltshire Archaeological and Natural History Society, and Godwin and Heathcote were busy excavating a Roman villa near Colerne together.[76]

For the project, Godwin inserted a new Geometrical-style window, removing its Perpendicular predecessor at the east end, with stained glass by Joseph Bell of Bristol. He replaced the box pews of the chancel (but not the nave) with open seats. A new stone pulpit and wooden reading desk to Godwin's designs were made. The stone screen between the north aisle and chapel was "partially exposed," a new roof was put over the south aisle, and the large four-light window in the south aisle was furnished with new tracery and filled with stained glass by Bell. The central window of the clerestory—whose two-light tracery was partially discernible—was restored, and the two large three-light dormers were replaced by three-light decorated windows in keeping with the central clerestory window.[77]

In 1858 Godwin surveyed the church of Saint Paul de Leon, Staverton, Devon,[78] and furnished designs for the south-aisle windows for Vicar Henry Fox Atherley, who was Heathcote's brother-in-law. There is no visual record of the church before 1858, but what Godwin designed cannot possibly reflect what was there previously. The windows (fig. 6-6) have sharp and fanciful plate tracery that lacks medieval precedent but is clearly not Perpendicular. One source must be John Ruskin's "Nature of Gothic," a chapter in *The Stones of Venice*, in which the author writes, "—respecting the nature of tracery . . . it began in the use of penetrations through stonework of windows or walls, cut into forms which looked like stars when seen from within, and like leaves when seen from without."[79] Ruskin illustrates this with geometrical shapes and adds that "the best traceries are nothing more than close clusters of such forms."[80] Godwin's simple geometric tracery designs follow this dictum; they are also very close to the tracery of Western College in Plymouth (see fig. 6-3).

In March 1859 Godwin was again commissioned to supply window designs for the thirteenth/fifteenth-century Devon church of Saint John, Littlehempston, a parish near to Staverton.[81] He took a different approach, with results less startling than at Staverton, perhaps because the incumbent, Fitz-Henry Hele, was an enthusiastic antiquary from an old and wealthy Devon family[82] and presumably had ideas of his own and the means with which to realize them. Godwin's contribution is difficult to establish.[83] In March 1859 he drew the old windows and made designs for a new one, and a year later he made designs for the south-aisle

Fig. 6-6. E. W. Godwin. Tracery of one of the South Aisle windows at Saint Paul de Leon, Staverton, Devon, 1858–60. Photographed in 1998.

Fig. 6-7. E. W. Godwin. Windows on the south side of the church of Saint John, Littlehempston, Devon, 1859–60. Photographed in 1998.

windows of the nave. A view of the church as it was in 1832[84] shows the original south-aisle windows were all the same and of Devon Decorated type (still in use in the fifteenth century) with distinctive star tracery with which Godwin must already have been familiar as there is an example in the chancel at Staverton.[85] The new windows (fig. 6-7) are of an earlier Decorated type and are all different from one another. Two make use of a star motif, each in a different way.

A few months after he supplied his first designs to

Fig. 6-8. E. W. Godwin. Saint Baithen, St. Johnstown, County Donegal, Ireland, 1857–60. Photographed ca. 1970, before additions were made to the west end. Conway Library, Courtauld Institute of Art, London, 471/33(29a).

Hele, Godwin began work back in Wiltshire on Saint Christopher, Ditteridge, the neighboring parish to Colerne.[86] Most of his work concerned refitting the interior with a new pulpit (see fig. 2-8), new stained glass, and so on. The church is very different from the one at Colerne. It has a simple, aisleless nave and narrow chancel, and its Norman origins are much more obvious than Colerne's.[87] The rector, W. N. Heathcote, was a cousin of Gilbert Heathcote of Colerne. Much of the work at Ditteridge was minor: Godwin removed a plaster ceiling to reveal the roof timbers, which may have been extensively repaired, opened a small, blocked Norman window, and repaired other windows of varying forms and dates. Otherwise he redesigned the east window in a Geometrical style, though a bit less fanciful than at Staverton, with twin lancets beneath large cinquefoil, again furnished with stained glass. All in all, however, Ditteridge was a conservative restoration, and apart from the east window, Godwin used the furnishings as the outlet for his creative energies. The pulpit in particular shows his continuing enthusiasm for Ruskin. The bands of triangular carvings were derived from similar carving in the apse of the Cathedral at Murano, which had been illustrated and described by Ruskin in his *Stones of Venice* (see fig. 2-7).[88]

New Churches

In Godwin's designs for new churches it is obvious that he is not a church architect in the sense that William Butterfield or G. E. Street were. Whereas Butterfield was a high churchman to the extent that he is said to have felt he had

let himself down by taking as his first commission the design for a nonconformist church,[89] and most of his clients shared quite closely his high church beliefs,[90] Godwin's religious affiliation is far less certain. Although he was a churchgoer in his earlier life and married his first wife in church, his second wedding was in a register office, and the nature of his relationship with Ellen Terry clearly precluded conventional religious observance.

This may account for the broad range of his church work. His clients or potential clients included the Roman Catholic Church in Ireland and the Congregationalists, the Unitarians, and even the Greek Orthodox Church, as well as the Church of England. His first such commissions were for three small Roman Catholic churches in County Donegal, Ireland. That Godwin, an English Protestant, secured these commissions is significant. The Catholic church in Ireland had by the late 1850s assumed a notably nationalist character under the leadership of Paul Cardinal Cullen, who "imposed a spirit of religious absolutism that justified sectarianism in all its forms."[91] As a result by the late 1850s it was unusual for non-Catholics to be employed to design Catholic churches.[92]

Cullen's absolutism penetrated more slowly to the dioceses of Derry and Raphoe, however, where Godwin was working, and there was still considerable Catholic/Protestant accord in these areas, but the key to Godwin's success in Ireland seems to have been Father James Stephens, an antiquary whom Godwin may have met while sketching and measuring sites in Ireland. Stephens's own

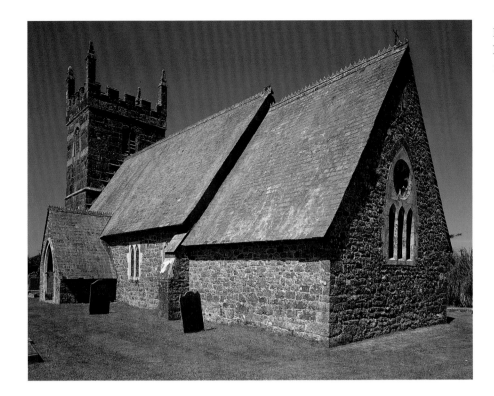

Fig. 6-9. Saint Grada, Grade, Cornwall. Restored and rebuilt by E. W. Godwin, 1860-63. Photographed in 1998.

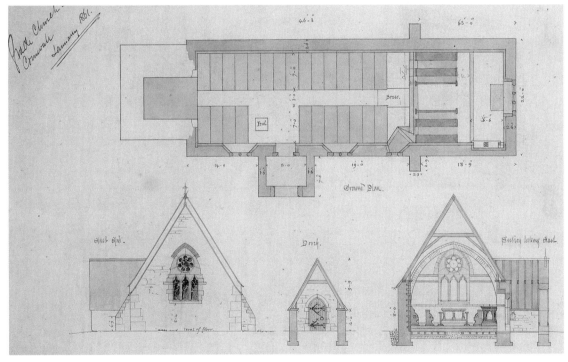

Fig. 6-10. E. W. Godwin, Saint Grada Church, Grade, Cornwall: ground plan, elevation of east end, transverse section through porch, and section looking east, 1861. India ink, red pen, and colored washes; 13 x 20 in. (33 x 50.8 cm). British Architectural Library Drawings Collection, RIBA, London, Ran 7/A/4 (2). *Checklist no. 5*

antiquarian researches resulted in a book in 1872 in which he mentions Godwin and his studies.[93]

Stephens was the parish priest of Saint Johnstown, a largely rural parish, and it was for him that Godwin designed the church of Saint Baithen (fig. 6-8) in 1857. This was the first and largest of Godwin's early Irish churches. In later life Godwin expressed dissatisfaction with his design, stating that it looked to him as if it were made of cast iron,[94] perhaps a reference to the unusually etiolated tracery. It is highly eclectic, especially the west window, which combines

uncusped circles, an Early English feature, with carved spandrels of a much later type—possibly an early example of Ruskin's influence.[95] What is perhaps most striking about the church, given Godwin's antiquarian knowledge, is how little concession it makes to the vernacular. Irish medieval churches were characterized by what Godwin described as "primitive simplicity of plan," drawing an analogy with the Cornish churches he knew well. According to Godwin, "The absence of constructive chancels, attached towers, porches etc" and a "paucity of fenestra-

135

Fig. 6-11. E. W. Godwin. Designs for stained glass for the East Window, Saint Grada, Grade, Cornwall, 1860-62. India ink, red pen, and colored washes; 20 x 12 13/16 in. (50.8 x 32.5 cm). British Architectural Library Drawings Collection, RIBA, London, Ran 7/A/4 (5). *Checklist no. 7*

tion"[96] were part of this simplicity. Saint Baithen is a cruciform church, albeit with short transepts, attached south porch and north sacristy, and a decidedly separate chancel, over the arch of which is a double bellcote. The roof pitches are exaggeratedly steep, showing a lack of concession to local traditions. Whatever Godwin's later opinion of the church, he was clearly pleased with it at the time, as he succeeded in having it published in the *Builder*, the first time his work had appeared in the architectural press.[97]

The other two churches—All Saints, Newtowncunningham, and Saint Columcille, Tory Island—were probably begun in 1857 or 1858 and were opened in 1860/61.[98] They cost a great deal less than Saint Baithen and are much

simpler in design. The church at Newtowncunningham is a low, steep-roofed building. It has no separate chancel—a small semipolygonal apse is the only emphasis on the east end. It had, when built, two south porches.[99] The tracery is much more primitive than at Saint Johnstown, somewhere between Y- and plate-tracery, with simple uncusped circles in the heads of most of the windows, and simple cusped daggers in the heads of the west windows.

Saint Columcille, West Town, Tory Island, has the same steeply pitched roof, and the tracery is a simplified version of that at Saint Baithen. When built, it had a small screen providing at least an internal division between nave and chancel. There was a three-light east window with stained

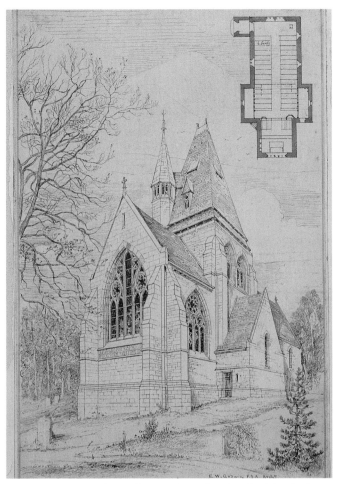

Fig. 6-12. E. W. Godwin. Competition drawing for Nottingham Church Cemetery Chapel, Mansfield Road, Nottingham, 1877. Pen and sepia wash; 12 3/16 x 7 3/4 in. (30.9 x 19.7 cm). British Architectural Library Drawings Collection, RIBA, London, Ran 7/E/8 (10). *Checklist no. 78*

Fig. 6-13. William Butterfield. Highbury Chapel, Cotham, Bristol (built 1842–43), showing apse and cloister by E. W. Godwin, 1862–64. Subsequently altered by Frank Wills in 1893. Photographed in 1998.

glass with the Crucifixion and figures of the Virgin and Child and Saint Patrick.[100]

Apart from the Nottingham cemetery chapel, which Godwin was to build nearly twenty year later (see below), these were the only complete churches of his architectural career, although his "restoration" of Saint Grada, Grade, Cornwall (fig. 6-9), in 1860, involved an almost complete rebuilding. The old Perpendicular church of Saint Grada was already in poor condition by the time the Reverend F. C. Jackson became the incumbent in 1853.[101] Godwin wrote in 1861, "[it was] in such a condition it is little wonder I found it impossible to repair. . . . The building is now unfit for service, and soon nothing will remain to tell where the old church stood, save the tower, the font, and the entrance doorway."[102]

Godwin built a new nave, with south porch, and a separate, lower chancel, all with steep-pitched roofs, and no transepts (fig. 6-10). The windows are simple Decorated single and double lancets with trefoil heads, and there is

a plate-traceried Geometrical east window with octofoil, above triple trefoil-headed lancets, filled with stained glass to Godwin's design (fig. 6-11). The only concession to the old church is the retention of the tower and the old foundations, and to vernacular forms is the rubble wall treatment using local stone.[103]

His one other realized Anglican church project came in 1877 when he won the competition for a small cemetery chapel in the Mansfield Road Cemetery, Nottingham (fig. 6-12).[104] Godwin achieved a certain individuality in the tracery, especially of the east window, which consists of two pairs of Decorated quatrefoils and sexfoils over two pairs of lancets, arranged on either side of a narrow central lancet which rises the full height of the window.[105]

Throughout his career Godwin worked for, or aspired to work for, the nonconformist churches. His one realized nonconformist church project was the enlargement of William Butterfield's Highbury Chapel in Bristol (fig. 6-13), which was opposite Exley's school. The original building

Fig. 6-14. William Butterfield. Highbury Chapel, Cotham, Bristol (built 1842–43), showing the tower built by E. W. Godwin, 1862–64. Photographed in 1998.

appears to have been a decision of the building committee. Surviving reports from the unsuccessful architects also make a point of stating that their designs are in keeping with Butterfield's.[109]

Initially Godwin proposed a short tower, with steeply pitched pyramidal roof, a freestone corner polygonal turret stair, and a crenellated parapet. Enthusiasm for the project among the congregation was such, however, that funds were made available for a much higher tower of 75 feet (fig. 6-14), which had clearly more to do with architectural effect than increased accommodation. Other apparently high-church features Godwin designed were a polygonal apsidal ending, at the east end, and a cloisterlike link from the east end to the new schoolroom/lecture hall to the east.[110]

All these were broadly in keeping with the late Gothic style of Butterfield's windows, although the disposition and variety of windows in the tower, and the mix of free-stone and rubble wall treatments, serve to indicate that this is a building of the 1860s not the 1840s. Godwin also designed a polygonal oak pulpit on a Caen-stone base, an oak screen across the apsidal ending, concealing the organ, and a stained-glass memorial window, made by Joseph Bell of Bristol, at the west end.[111]

Several other church projects came to nothing. Godwin's most substantial attempted works for the Anglican church came in 1862–63: Saint Fin Barre's Cathedral in Cork, the competition for which was won by his friend William Burges; and a major enlargement of Saint Mary, Cheltenham. The Saint Fin Barre design, of which only a perspective survives,[112] is resolutely French, but typically Godwin; even the plate tracery is delicate. The Cheltenham design,[113] submitted to the competition for this project, is Godwin's most robustly early French design, with a semicircular apse and ambulatory, much sculpture, a three-bay west front along the lines of Burges's Crimea Memorial Church competition designs of 1856–61, and a great wheel window to the west, like Burges's winning Saint Fin Barre design. Altogether it is the closest Godwin ever came to the massiveness of Burges.

The remainder of Godwin's church work reveals a startling diversity of responses to a wide range of denominational requirements. Some of the dozen or so churches border on the exotic while he also seems to have had an interest in central planning, as in a mausoleum based on a Greek Cross plan[114] and an idiosyncratic design for a "modern cathedral" with a circular nave.[115] This preoccupation was perhaps stimulated by the ongoing project, beginning in the 1860s, to complete Wren's Saint Paul's Cathedral, specifically to decorate the interior, which in turn drew attention to Wren's earlier plans for a Greek Cross design

had been under construction in 1842–43, when Godwin was a pupil at the school, and Godwin later cited it as having been the inspiration for his having become an architect.[106] By 1862 Highbury Chapel was suffering from an acute shortage of accommodation, partly because of the urbanization of the surrounding area and partly because of the popularity of the ministry of Reverend David Thomas.[107] Initially, plans were requested from four architects, and Godwin and Hine's were chosen.[108] Hine's name may have been included on Godwin's submission principally as an assurance of professional probity, because he appears to have taken no further part in the project.

Godwin's design was striking for a number of reasons, not least for the prominent tower that he proposed to build southeast of the chapel. He carefully followed Butterfield's design, incorporating the most easterly of Butterfield's windows in the south transept immediately to the east of the tower. This respect for the original design, however, for the cathedral, including the celebrated Great Model. Wren's influence may certainly be detected in Godwin's competition design for the Brompton Oratory of 1878,[116] although the site precluded any central planning. Godwin's design takes into account the competition rule that designs be in "Italian Renaissance style," and it is lifted, in part, from Sansovino's Library in Venice (1537). It is, therefore, much less fully blown Italian Baroque than Herbert Gribble's winning design, which owes a great deal to Vignola's Il Gesú, in Rome (1568). The competition designs including Godwin's, look forward to the great Baroque revival at the end of the century, but Godwin's tower, with its awkward, elongated termination, reveals his discomfiture with the manner.

Central planning also features in the most exotic of Godwin's abortive commissions, the design for a Greek Church in Notting Hill, West London, in 1873.[117] The Greek community in London had increased considerably following the War of Greek independence (1870–71), and Godwin appears to have formed a friendship with one of their number, Stavros Dilberoglue.[118] Godwin clearly relished the challenge of designing something unusual, but he seems uncharacteristically hesitant about his archaeological facts in his letter to Dilberoglue accompanying some sketch designs. He suggests a number of models ranging geographically from Moscow to Armenia, from Athens to Ravenna.[119] The continuing influence of Ruskin's *Stones of Venice* may be inferred from Godwin's preference for San Marco, Venice, as the ideal model, although he discounts it on grounds of cost, and his choice of Santa Fosca, Torcello, as the model for a more affordable design. The church was built a few years later by John Oldrid Scott, whose design was more obviously Byzantine than Godwin's, although its use of materials is similar.[120]

Civic and Commercial Projects

In the thirty-three-year span of E. W. Godwin's architectural career, no other building type, with the possible exception of the railway station, evolved as rapidly or saw such a wide proliferation as the town hall.[121] Nearly half of the fifty-four architectural competitions that Godwin entered were for town halls and, although only three of these competition designs were built, it is clear that the building type had a particular appeal for him.[122]

Godwin's career was established in 1861, when, at the age of twenty seven, he won the competition to design Northampton Town Hall (fig. 6-15 and see fig. 6-1). The professional assessor, William Tite, an architect who had worked largely in the classical style, had originally awarded first place to a classical design with the motto "Circum-

spice," by Louis De Ville, but the council overturned the decision and awarded the prize to Godwin's Gothic design, "Non Nobis Domine."[123]

By the 1860s, the town hall's symbolic role far outweighed its functional role,[124] and town hall buildings might consist only of a large assembly hall; a council chamber; an office or two for town clerk, mayor, and borough surveyor; and a committee room. A large part of the budget might be expended on displays of decoration, especially on the facade and in the public parts of the building, such as the assembly room.

The dual role of Northampton Town Hall is evident in Godwin's plans of the first floor and elevations (fig. 6-16). Aside from the upper parts of the Council Chamber, Great Hall, and courts, the other rooms are simply labeled "office," to be used at the council's discretion as and when it acquired further powers that could be exercised from these rooms.[125] Godwin's plan was to a large extent determined by the site, which is long and narrow, with the frontage on Saint Giles Square. At ground and first-floor level a spine corridor runs from a vaulted vestibule at the front to the reading room at the back, with the Great Hall to the right and Sessions Court to the left, both of which rise through two stories. The Council Chamber is at the front center of the first floor, with a mayor's balcony and with committee rooms ranging either side along the frontage.

Godwin later stated that the building was "entirely founded upon the *Stones of Venice*" which he had read on his return from Ireland in 1858.[126] By this he did not mean that he used Venetian buildings as his model: the style of Northampton Town Hall is broadly French, though with some Italian Gothic detail. But then Benjamin Woodward's Oxford University Museum of 1854–60, a building that caused great excitement at the time, was also seen as the quintessence of Ruskinism and is also highly eclectic in its sources.[127] Godwin's Northampton Town Hall, like Woodward's museum, has a symmetrical main front with central tower. Architecturally, the most obviously Ruskinian aspect of Northampton is the structural polychromy, with bands of alternating Harlestone and Ancaster stone and in the Great Hall, of different colors of brick. Northampton is also Ruskinian in its decoration. One of the attractions of Ruskin for architects was his statement, "The fact is, there are only two fine arts possible to the human race, sculpture and painting. What we call architecture is only the association of these in noble masses, or the placing of them in fit places."[128] This allowed architects a greater degree of latitude than Pugin's notion that decoration be applied only to emphasize a building's structure. Godwin developed this idea in a lecture he gave on a num-

Fig. 6-15. E. W. Godwin. Northampton Town Hall, 1861–64. Photographed ca. 1865. Courtesy, Northamptonshire Libraries and Information Service.

ber of occasions, including in Northampton in 1862, on the "Sister Arts and their relation to Architecture," in which he stressed the interdependence of the arts of painting, architecture, and sculpture.[129]

At Northampton the sculpture program included a series of eight large figures of kings and queens at first-floor level along the front facade. In the seven tympana of the ground-floor windows, there are reliefs depicting scenes of national and local history. Carved shields depicting local trades are at eye level on the ground-floor facade, and six additional reliefs of historical scenes are in the vestibule tympana. Most of the figures and reliefs were by Richard Boulton of Worcester, who raised the status of architectural carver almost to that of a profession; the two reliefs on the north wall of the vestibule were by Thomas Nicholls, who worked extensively with Godwin's friend William Burges.[130]

The most Ruskinian aspect of the carvings, however,

is in the many interior and exterior capitals. These were the work of Edwin White, a carver who had worked with Godwin on church projects at Grade and Ditteridge. A central tenet of Ruskin's creed was to allow the workman free rein, as only thus would good, "true" work be produced.[131] Godwin enjoyed this kind of working relationship with White, although how much free rein he was allowed is uncertain. Godwin had to be firm with the council about his choice of White, arguing, "having been really educated by him having done a number of things for him in the West of England, and having moreover, studied Ruskin . . . if you have been ten years in the profession, and have a carver who has been working all the time with you, he has got to understand what you want by a simple sketch."[132]

Entirely Ruskinian is the extraordinary variety in White's capitals; there is a charmingly bathetic contrast between those of the ground floor, which depict local industries among the foliage of the capitals (fig. 6-17), and those

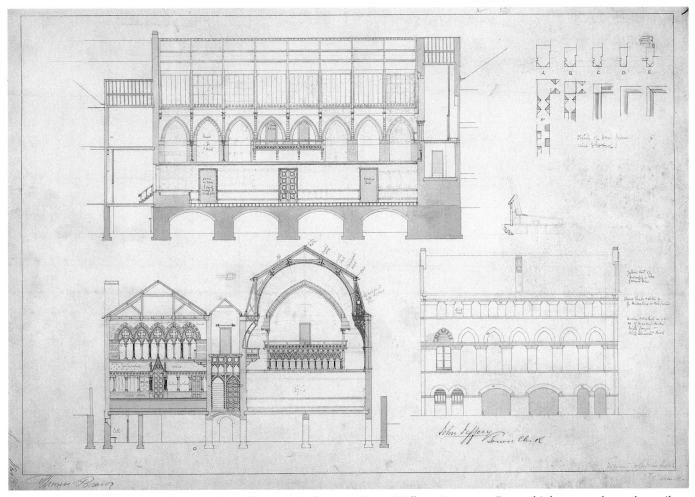

Fig. 6-16. E. W. Godwin. Great Hall and Court Room, Northampton Town Hall: sections, 1861. Pen and ink, watercolor and pencil; 19⁵⁄₁₆ x 27¹⁵⁄₁₆ in (49.1 x 71 cm). Trustees of the Victoria and Albert Museum, London E.592-1963. *Checklist no. 11*

Fig. 6-17. Capital depicting "Shoemaking" carved by Edwin White. Northampton Town Hall, vestibule, 1861–64. Photographed in 1998.

of the first-floor windows, where characters from Aesop's fables disport themselves among the leaves. The foliage of these capitals and of the shallow triangular reliefs in the vestibule walls, which are also by White, are each different and apparently "from nature." These vestibule reliefs, like White's carvings on the pulpit at Ditteridge (see fig. 2-8), have the general shape and disposition of the Murano reliefs illustrated in *The Stones of Venice* (see fig. 2-7).[133] The

Northampton examples are highly conventionalized, however, and perhaps more in keeping with the Design Reform genre of Owen Jones and Christopher Dresser than with Ruskin. Other triangular reliefs by White, in the main entrance hall, are copied more or less exactly from Ruskin's Murano illustrations.

In August 1863 Godwin also persuaded the council to spend almost £1,000 on painted decoration.[134] This con-

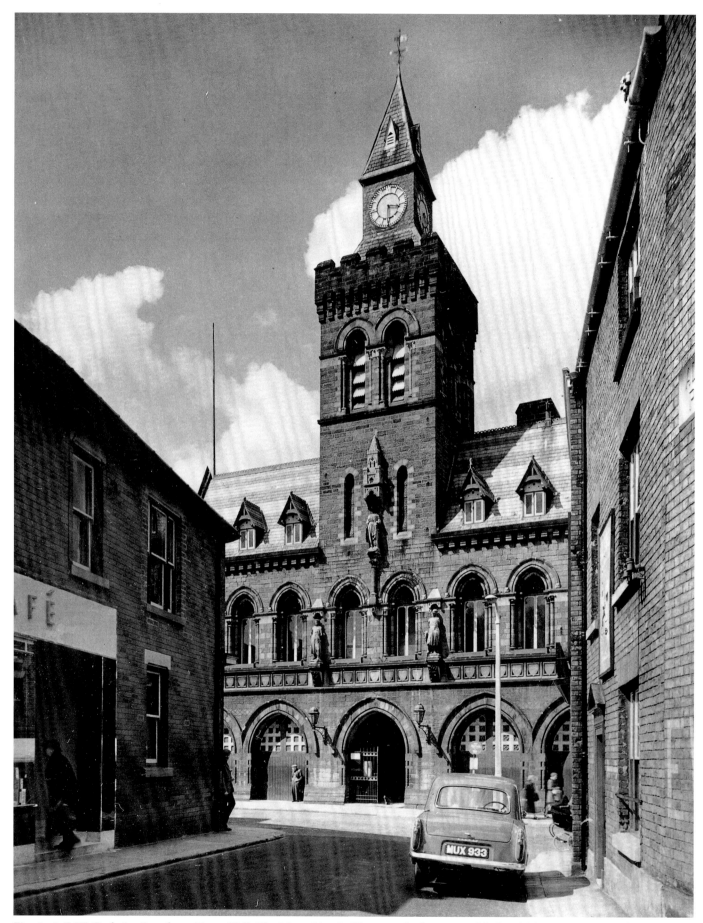

Fig. 6-18. E. W. Godwin. Congleton Town Hall, Cheshire, 1864–67. Photographed ca. 1950s. National Monuments Record.

Fig. 6-19. E. W. Godwin. Competition drawing for Congleton Town Hall, Cheshire: longitudinal section of hall, section through tower, and other sections, ca. 1864. India ink, red pen, colored washes, gold; 18 13/16 x 25 3/16 in. (47.8 x 64 cm). British Architectural Library Drawings Collection, RIBA, London, Ran 7/A/9 (7). *Checklist no. 17*

sisted largely of fictive stonework and hangings like those designed by William Burges for his rooms at Buckingham Street in London in 1861,[135] although Godwin's use of the fictive stonework may have come first (see chap. 9). This painting was executed by Green and King of London, who also made the council chamber furniture to Godwin's designs (see chap. 8). R. T. Bayne (of Heaton, Butler and Bayne, who made the roundels of stained glass in the great hall windows) executed wall paintings "in the medieval outline manner"[136] of the figures of Winter and Summer, from Spenser's *Faerie Queen*, above the fireplaces at either end of the council chamber. At either end of the Great Hall he executed large semicircular paintings, in a similar style, of Moses, symbolizing the law-giving function of the building, and of Alfred the Great, another reference to Northampton's ancient origins.[137]

Northampton was a turning point for Godwin, effec-

tively his first major mature commission. His involvement in all aspects of its design must have highlighted the scope that civic clients, with potentially large budgets, offered to art-architects such as himself, in their quest to realize municipal pride in built form. Godwin's next town hall design, for Congleton in Cheshire (figs. 6-18, 6-19), was built on a much tighter budget, but nonetheless strove to fulfill the twin aims of embodying civic pride and realizing his ambitions for "total design."

Congleton, like Northampton, was an ancient borough and market town. By 1860 its early-nineteenth-century town hall was in poor repair, and a competition for a new town hall was advertised in 1864.[138] The council selected a number of designs in a variety of styles[139] and asked Alfred Waterhouse to adjudicate, the first of many competitions he was to assess.[140] With a notable lack of partisanship he narrowed the choice to Godwin's Gothic

Fig. 6-20. James Hine and Alfred Norman: E. W. Godwin, consulting architect. Plymouth Guildhall, Devon, 1869–74. 19th-century photograph. Devon Library Service.

design and an Italianate design by John Burrell of Longton, Staffordshire,[141] with Godwin the ultimate winner.

Godwin's plan approximates a pared-down version of Northampton. A single-bay vestibule leads to a central spine corridor, which leads in turn to the center of the narrow end of an assembly hall that rises through three levels. Because the site was canted about 10 degrees, the hall joins the corridor at a slight angle, a problem that was ingeniously overcome by incorporating small structures in the angles of the walls, such as a "Gothic ticket office."

To the left of the vestibule was a market hall that extended the full depth of the site. On either side of the corridor, before the hall, were "ladies and gentlemen's retiring rooms." The two ground-floor bays on the right-hand front were also for the market, although on Godwin's competition design they appear as shop fronts[142]—perhaps to avoid the lower level of the facade being dominated by livestock—and in fact they were soon converted to shops. The staircase, which rose around a square to the middle of the right of the corridor, was more spacious than that at the much larger Northampton, and the two half-landings had structurally innovative domes on triple squinches.

At first-floor level a narrow spine corridor, running front-to-back above the ground-floor corridor, gives access at the end to the gallery of the Assembly Hall. To the left, off the corridor, opposite the top of the stairs is the Court. To the front were the judge and magistrate's room (which was soon appropriated as the Mayor's Parlour) and the Reading Room. The jury's Retiring Room occupied the awkward space between hall and court.

The Congleton facade is altogether less rigidly symmetrical than Northampton, although a central main tower is also a principal feature. Because the tower is the same height as at Northampton (110 feet) which is a much larger building, it is even more prominent. But whereas at Northampton there are seven bays at ground and first-floor levels, and no dormers, at Congleton the five open ground-floor bays are surmounted by eight lancets at first-floor level and six dormers at roof level.[143]

Congleton was designed at the height of Godwin's relatively brief flirtation with the early French taste, and the style is more resolutely French than at Northampton, where the architect had indulged what he later called a "fit about plate tracery."[144] The first-floor lancets are of a type Godwin had no doubt seen on a recent French holiday that took him to Paris, Amiens, and Chartres.[145]

At Congleton the impact of Ruskin is less obvious than at Northampton, perhaps because of the tighter budget—£5,400 at Congleton and more than £12,000 at Northampton. It was, as Godwin later said, "a very small business."[146] There is structural polychromy, but the contrast between the gray granite of the main facade and the brown-red stringing is subtle, as is the interior scheme where the granite is mixed with a creamy-gray sandstone. As Godwin later said "The Stones of Venice had been dropped."[147] Carving at Congleton included three figures on the facade, probably by Richard Boulton[148]—Queen Victoria, Henry Lacy (a local medieval worthy), and Edward I—musical figures at either end of the minstrels' gallery in the Great Hall, reliefs with a musical theme in the

· TEN HUNDRED AND SIXTY SIX ·
A.D. 1871.

Fig. 6-21. E. W. Godwin. Bristol Assize Courts: elevation after a competition drawing of 1866, 1871. India ink, sepia pen, and wash, mounted on blue card; 13 x 16⅞ in (33 x 42.9 cm). British Architectural Library Drawings Collection, RIBA, London, Ran 7/A/11 (1). *Checklist no. 18.*

spandrels of the minstrels' gallery, larger reliefs in the spandrels of the three windows at the end of the Great Hall, and dragon-type beasts carved in the tympana of the stair windows. It does not appear that Godwin used "his man" White as he had at Northampton, and most of the capitals are of a standard early-French type in keeping with the building, with little indication that the sculptor has been asked to respond to nature's inspiration.

Some of these items probably inflated the bill of extras, and Godwin got into an unpleasant stand-off with the corporation over his commission on the extras and issued a writ. The corporation backed down and paid him, but it brought an onslaught of abuse from the councillors. George Kent derided the building's "most beastly character" and described Godwin's extras as a "downright robbery on the ratepayer."[149] Councillor James Dakin added, "There has been bad Generalship. We have been nobly taken advantage of." Altogether the building cost £8,000.

Congleton is a prime example of what has been called Godwin's "theatrical facadism."[150] But whereas at Northampton there was at least some attempt to give the rear parts and rear elevation to Dychurch Lane some architectural character, Congleton barely makes it into three dimensions: originally the council intended the stone facing to be applied only to the main elevation, with the main gables in the plain-Jane red brick of which the rest of the exterior is built.[151] The rear parts of the building are spare to the point of minimalism, although John Betjeman's description of it as a "second-rate dance hall" is perhaps unjust.[152]

As the town hall as a building type grew more and

Fig. 6-22. E. W. Godwin. Preliminary design possibly for the Leicester Municipal Buildings competition, 1871. Pen and ink, pencil and watercolor; 12⅞ x 10⅞ in. (32.7 x 27.7 cm). The Board of Trustees of the Victoria and Albert Museum, London, E.633-1963. *Checklist no. 79*

more complex, and a much wider variety of administrative functions had to be accommodated for the same amount of money, Godwin's success in competitions declined. The days of the town hall as symbol were numbered. An exception to this trend was the Plymouth Guildhall competition of 1869. Plymouth was a sizable metropolis, with twice the population of Northampton, and also twice the budget for its new town hall. The Plymouth design (fig. 6-20) very explicitly reflects this shift to a functionally more complex town hall type because it has two ranges, the south range being the ceremonial part, with police courts and law courts laid out on either side of a vast hall, and the north range being the administrative part with council chamber and a complex array of offices.[153] In the south range there was a much higher degree of display, both in terms of decorations, with twelve carved reliefs by Richard Boulton,[154] seven soaring applied gables to the center of the range, marking the Great Hall, and a 160-foot tower.

The circumstances surrounding the Plymouth design were rather special because of the terms of Godwin's contract with James Hine and Alfred Norman. Although the building as a concept—elevations and perspective, to be specific—was Godwin's, he appears not to have been closely involved in the planning. It seems likely, however, that he did conceive this expression of the two basic functions, ceremonial/judicial and administrative. Otherwise, his involvement with Plymouth, once the premium had been awarded, seems to have consisted largely of accepting payment from time to time for his third share of the commission. He declined, when asked,[155] to produce more drawings to assist the progress of the building, and ill feeling understandably grew between Godwin and the hard-pressed Norman and Hine. His friendship with Hine appears to have ended as a result.[156]

Part of Godwin's frustration with the competition system must have stemmed from the fact that he won several further premiums in town-hall and other municipal competitions, including more than one first premium, but did not see any of the designs built.[157] The best known of these was for the Bristol Assize Courts competition in 1865–67, which was so badly organized that it took three competitions before a result was declared. It was widely considered that Godwin and Crisp's winning design for the second competition, judged by Alfred Waterhouse, should have won, and there was a great deal of correspondence about the matter in the architectural, local, and national press.[158] The design that won the first premium—with the motto "1066"—is probably Godwin's finest unbuilt municipal design (fig. 6-21). Others, such as that submitted under the motto "Manners Makyth Man" for the Winchester Guildhall competition of 1870,[159] reveal his ability to design for an island site that precluded the "facadism" evident at Congleton. But what is apparent from this, and even more so from his design for the much larger Leicester Town Hall competition of 1871 (fig. 6-22), is the reluctance of committees to select designs that were expensive to build, both because of structural complexity, such as complicated interlocking roofs and towers, and because of costly carved decoration.

After 1876, when Godwin's architectural career was

Fig. 6-23. E. W. Godwin. Smith's factory, Merchant Street, Bristol, 1856. Photographed ca. 1858. Reece Winstone Archive, Bristol.

beginning to decline, there was a sharp increase in the competitions he entered: in 1877 they numbered ten. The types of competitions ranged from major civic buildings to odd, minor projects such as for a boathouse at Putney, south London, or a lodge/teahouse. The commission on such small projects, had he won them, would only have been about £50.

The year 1876 holds further significance: he began his association with a new architectural periodical, the *British Architect*, which published a great many of Godwin's competition entries over the next decade. The *Building News* and the *Architect* had also published a substantial number in the previous decade, but after 1876, given that he did not win any competitions, yet increased the number he entered, the publication of his designs, both as a form of advertisement and as a design end in itself, must be seen as a major motivation for entering competitions.

Godwin's activities in the industrial sphere were very limited, as might be expected, given his appetite for the architecture of display. He designed two factories, one

Fig. 6-24. E. W. Godwin. Perry and Sons Carriageworks, 104 Stokes Croft, Bristol, 1858–59. 19th-century photograph. Reece Winstone Archive, Bristol.

before and one after his stay in Ireland in 1856–58, which are interesting for their very different interpretations of a medieval style applied to an industrial structure. In 1856 he designed a factory in Merchant Street in central Bristol for the horsehair merchant James Smith (fig. 6-23). It was admired in the *Builder* for showing "how easily Gothic architecture may be applied to structure[s] of this class."[160] In fact it is an early case of Congleton-type facadism, the gabled street elevation of three stories being enlivened with plate-traceried windows with central colonnettes. The premises were a very basic unornamented, almost shedlike attachment at the back.[161]

In 1858–59, after returning from Ireland, Godwin designed a carriageworks at 104 Stokes Croft for Perry and Sons (fig. 6-24).[162] The influence of *The Stones of Venice* is again evident in the polychrome stonework, but the effect is very subtle. Coursed rubble walls are dressed with two types of cut-stone voussoirs to the five ground-floor drop arches, which were originally open to the ground-floor showroom, while cut-stone and rubble alternate on the ten arches of the windows lighting the first- and second-floor showrooms.[163] The effect is massive, dignified, and appropriate. Like Saint Philip and Saint Jacob's Schools (see fig. 6-4), the project shows Godwin was not at a loss,

even as early as 1858, when designing buildings where the element of display resides in the structure, rather than the decoration.

But such clients, who wanted a lot of building for their money, were not appealing to the young Godwin. And the corporations who had promised to be generous and sympathetic clients to an art-architect intoxicated on *The Stones of Venice*, had turned out to be penny-pinching Philistines requiring functional buildings more notable for careful planning than Sister Arts display. Godwin turned increasingly away from them and began to rely instead on clients to whom he could relate on equal terms, gentleman to gentleman, professional to professional, and, ultimately, artist to artist.

Domestic Projects

Godwin's enduring reputation as an architect rests on the series of artists' houses and studios he designed in the late 1870s and early 1880s in Tite Street, Chelsea, especially his first design for Frank Miles's house (see fig. 3-26) and Whistler's White House (see fig. 6-52), and on his work in the early days at Bedford Park, Chiswick.[164] His four country-house projects have also received attention,[165] but his designs for smaller houses have been relatively neglected,

Fig. 6-25. E. W. Godwin. Nos. 10-11 Rockleaze, Sneyd Park, Bristol, 1860–62. Photographed in 1998.

even though two of them are as striking, in their way, as Frank Miles's house.

Godwin claimed in his 1878 lecture "On Some Buildings I Have Designed"[166] that he had designed "some small villas" when he had been in Ireland in 1856–58, but it has not been possible so far to identify these. His first identifiable houses are the extraordinary semidetached pair, 10 and 11 Rockleaze, Sneyd Park, Bristol (1860–62; fig. 6-25), designed for H. I. Brown, a solicitor and speculative builder.[167]

What is most obviously unusual about the pair is their resolute asymmetry. Unlike other asymmetrical semidetached pairs in Bristol at this time, where the asymmetry was achieved by one half having a gable, the other not, Godwin's design plays down the duality of the building to such a degree that it is not immediately obvious that this is not one house, an effect that would have been even greater in his original conception where only the right-hand house was to have a porch.[168] The left-hand house, No. 11, has a triple window at ground-floor level and a single corner window, with three single windows above, two of them grouped closely as a pair. In the right-hand house, No. 10, instead of the triple window, a canted bay rises through two stories with single windows at ground and first-floor level, neither pushed into the corner, as in No. 11.

This asymmetry is all the more conscious, if not contrived, because in plan and rear elevation, the houses are almost entirely symmetrical. Given the date, Ruskin is obviously the major influence. The asymmetry of the front elevation is an essay in "Changefulness," as described by Ruskin in "The Nature of Gothic," in which Ruskin warned against the monotony of symmetry.[169] It is doubtful, however, that Ruskin would have approved of the symmetry of the plan coupled with the asymmetry of the front elevation—the "change" or asymmetry was supposed to arise out of "practical necessities" and not be adopted for its own sake.

"Changefulness" is also expressed in the details and materials. The walls are in uncoursed rubble with brick dressings, a combination that appears to have been an innovation of Godwin's.[170] It both pays homage to the local vernacular—the rubble—and achieves a Ruskinian structural polychromy. The sizes of the stones are carefully chosen, those of the battered plinth being larger, to create an impression of strength. The string courses are variously of brick and dressed stone, which serve both to lend variety to the facade and to counteract any tendency to incoherence. Carved decoration is restricted to the capitals of porches and the columns of the window mullions of No. 11.

Godwin did not refer to Rockleaze in his 1878 lec-

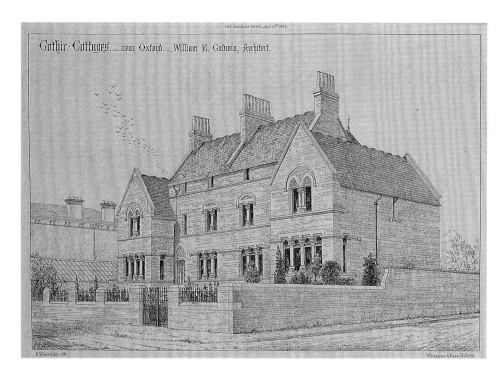

Gothic Cottages. _near Oxford._ William E. Godwin, Architect.

E. Wimbridge, lith.   Whiteman & Bass, Holborn.

Fig. 6-26. E. W. Godwin. Saint Martin's Villas, 43–44 Billing Road, Northampton, 1863–64. Illustrated as "Gothic Cottages Near Oxford." From the *Building News* 12 (21 July 1865): [517].

ture[171]: perhaps it was just a bit too "savage" for a man who had only just produced that essay in fastidious refinement, Whistler's White House, in Chelsea. He did, however, mention another pair of semidetached villas he built in 1863–64 at Northampton. Saint Martin's Villas, 43 and 44 Billing Road (fig. 6-26), provide a notable contrast to Rockleaze, showing how variously Ruskin's precepts could be applied to architecture.

Saint Martin's Villas were built by Pickering Phipps, who had been the Mayor of Northampton when Godwin won the Northampton Town Hall competition.[172] In the plan and elevation there is no artificially engineered asymmetry. It is basically an H-plan with a three-story central block, and two-story gabled cross-ranges, the whole raised over a half-basement. The windows are distributed symmetrically, and there is no attempt at "Changefulness" as at Rockleaze. The materials are also more sober and conventional, being local red brick with stone dressings, similar to the rear elevation of the Town Hall. There is rigid horizontal control through string courses of the dressed stone, some of it molded, and two single courses of dark-gray brick. Only the windows at the rear have a hint of a point, although the entrance doors and first-floor windows to the projecting bays at the front have pointed lunettes with relief carving, and the first-floor windows to the main block have drop-head lunettes with dragon carvings, very similar to those on the staircase at Congleton. The carvings in the lunettes over each front door give the villas their name: a depiction of Saint Martin and the beggar is on No. 43 and

Saint Martin distributing alms, on No. 44. Stained-glass panels of the type used at Congleton were introduced in the heads of the ground-floor windows.[173]

Altogether grander than Saint Martin's Villas was Rheinfelden (fig. 6-27), the house Godwin designed in 1868–69 for Phipps opposite the villas, on the south side of Billing Road. Rheinfelden displays an overtly picturesque medieval romanticism that is lacking in Rockleaze and Saint Martin's Villas but reflects the more personal approach to the Middle Ages that Godwin was by then exploring at Dromore Castle and Glenbeigh Towers. Rheinfelden is built of the same local brick as Saint Martin's Villas, stone is restricted to the string courses and copings, and there is no carving. The plan was described at the time as "somewhat unusually and ingeniously contrived."[174] The four-story main block contained kitchen and dining room at ground-floor level, drawing room and breakfast room on the first floor, and three bedrooms on the second and third floors, the latter housed in a steeply sloping red-tiled roof with hipped dormers.

An attached three-story block contained service rooms on the ground floor, and three bedrooms and a billiard room above, on different levels from the main block. Communication between the floors was by two spiral staircases, expressed externally in circular towers, each with steep conical cap. The billiard room had a corbelled-out balcony giving the gentlemen the not-very-romantic vista of the coal house.

The relentless upward thrust of the design is enhanced

Fig. 6-27. E. W. Godwin.
Rheinfelden, Billing Road,
Northampton, 1868–69.
Photographed ca. 1900. Courtesy,
Northamptonshire Libraries and
Information Service.

by the tall central chimneys and iron finials. It is resolutely Gothic and looks forward to the evolved Reform Gothic of Burges's Tower House, Melbury Road (1875–81; fig. 6-28). In the windows, however, there are already hints of Godwin's rejection of the overtly medieval. The lower sashes are plain plate glass, but the upper are divided by glazing bars, an inventive variation he was to develop at Beauvale. The stained glass, which is in "pale tints,"[175] has evolved from Saint Martin's Villas. At the same time, Godwin designed a cottage for Phipps for his estate at Collingtree, a pic-

turesque thatched affair,[176] perhaps influenced by the east lodge at Castle Ashby, where he was working for the Marquess of Northampton, but Phipps and Godwin had a falling out in 1871 over Godwin's stable designs, possibly for Rheinfelden.[177]

Also in 1868, Godwin used this romantic-but-minimal Gothic in two houses with shops at ground-floor level, built for the Reverend R. W. Gotch at 74 and 76 Stokes Croft, Bristol (fig. 6-29).[178] They too feature plain red-brick walls, towering chimneys, steep-pitched red-tiled

Fig. 6-28. William Burges. Tower House, Melbury Road, London, 1875–81. From *Art Journal* (June 1886): 170.

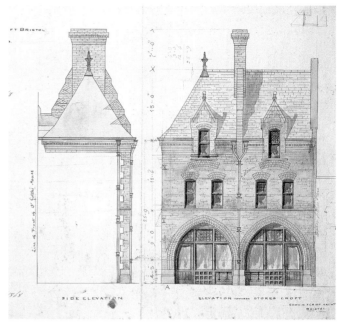

Fig. 6-29. E. W. Godwin. "Two Houses in Stokes Croft, Bristol," 1868. Ink and watercolor on paper; 14⅝ x 20¼ in. (37.1 x 51.4 cm). Scott Elliott, Kelmscott Gallery, Chicago.

Fig. 6-30. Johnston Forbes-Robertson. *Fallows Green, Harpenden, Hertfordshire,* ca. 1873. Oil on board; 5 x 6¾ in. (12.7 x 17.2 cm). Collection of the National Trust, Ellen Terry Memorial Museum, Smallhythe Place, Kent, SMA P. 138. *Checklist no. 39*

Fig. 6-31. Johnston Forbes-Robertson. *Fallows Green, Harpenden, Hertfordshire,* ca. 1873. Oil on board; 4½ x 6½ in. (11.4 x 16.5 cm). Collection of the National Trust, Ellen Terry Memorial Museum, Smallhythe Place, Kent, SMA P. 139. *Checklist no. 40*

roofs, and simple segmental-arch–headed windows, similar to Rheinfelden, with corbelled-out eaves that recall Rockleaze. The only stone is the coping to the gablets.

The evolution of the Rheinfelden type continued at Godwin's own house, Fallows Green, near Harpenden, Hertfordshire (figs. 6-30, 6-31),[179] which he designed in 1870–71. Here the grouping is looser, with lower ranges surrounding the main three-story block, and the treatment is the local vernacular rather than Reform Gothic, with timber-framing to the sides of the porch and the end-gables of the red-tiled gambrel roof.

This grouping was broadly what he was to use, on a much greater scale, at Beauvale (see fig. 6-40). A canted bay, with tile-hanging, rises through three stories off-center on the main block. An extraordinary entrance gateway (see fig. 1-12), timber-framed with brick nogging, with a red-tiled gambrel roof, the longer pitches dipping lower than those at the sides and tipping up at the edges, is a rare instance of his Japanese interests manifesting themselves in architectural form.

These smaller houses are a telling expression of Godwin's architectural priorities. Although such features as carving and stained glass are used in moderation where possible, the essential display is achieved through architectural form. But commissions for domestic architecture on a grander scale, and with a grander budget, were clearly desirable. The first opportunity of this type came in 1866 from the third Earl of Limerick, an Irish peer who had a home in Bristol. Godwin had known him since at least 1864, when Godwin designed a memorial at Almondsbury Church, Gloucestershire, to Limerick's father-in-law, and subsequently Limerick became president of the Bristol Society of Architects at Godwin's instigation.[180] He shared Godwin's antiquarian enthusiasms, and they made a number of sketching trips together.[181]

Limerick was that bogeyman of Irish history—an absentee Protestant landlord. When he succeeded to the title in 1866, his substantial property included 2,000 acres at Pallaskenry, west of Limerick city. The absence of a house on the estate eloquently pointed up the earl's absenteeism. Fenian violence, a reality at the time, rumbled on in Limerick in 1866, erupting in 1867 with attacks on person and property.[182] Building a house on the estate would be a symbol of Lord Limerick's "commitment" to his Irish estates.

But Dromore Castle (fig. 6-32), as Godwin designed it for the earl, was much more than a house. It was a castle, complete with machicolations, slit windows, and battlements. All this worked at a number of levels. As the description of the plans in March 1867 pointed out: "The corridors are kept to the outer side of the building, and all

Fig. 6-32. E. W. Godwin. Dromore Castle, County Limerick, Ireland, 1866–73. Photographed from the southwest in the 1940s. Courtesy of Brendan Mc Mahon.

the entrances are well guarded, so that in the event of the country being disturbed the inmates of Dromore Castle might . . . feel secure."[183] It was also an exercise in architectural saber-rattling, a warning to the Fenians about the power of the Union.

The house consists of four main blocks arranged around the north and part of the west side of a courtyard (fig. 6-33). The first of these is of three stories under a pitched roof, with a stone-vaulted entrance hall beneath a two-story chapel. This block adjoins a low wing containing ground-floor kitchen, large dining room, and anteroom on the first floor, major bedrooms and dressing rooms on the second floor, and servants' rooms, housed in the steeply pitched roof, on the third floor. The main five-story block at the northeastern corner is taken up with the principal rooms—servants' hall at the basement level, leading up, successively through drawing room, countess's bedroom

Fig. 6-33. E. W. Godwin. "Dromore Castle, Ireland." Perspective from the northeast drawn by Axel Haig for the *Building News* 14 (29 March 1867): 222, 224-25.

and earl's dressing room, night nurseries, and, reached by a turnpike stair, a billiard room at the top. To the right of the entrance a Great Hall ranged along the west flank of the courtyard to the chaplain's house at the southwest corner; a bakery was in a small isolated block at the southeast corner.

The precise form of the house is most notable.[184] It is an explicitly Irish castle, derived from Godwin's considerable knowledge of Irish medieval buildings, which had been acquired during his stay in Ireland in 1856–58, and on subsequent visits to his brother in Derry. Stepped battlements,

round tower, and the chaplain's house derived partly from Kilcolman Castle (see fig. 5-3); these features shouted out Irishness. And this was the point. Lord Limerick, as a member of the Irish peerage, needed to demonstrate his Irishness as an essential part of establishing the legitimacy of his power.

Inside, the Irish theme continues, but in a much less insistent way, as in the Celtic stenciled patterns to the paneled ceilings of the principal rooms (fig. 6-34), and the Celtic flavor of the capitals in the drawing room. But it is all rather low-key. The Earl did not have to press home the

Fig. 6-34. E. W. Godwin. Designs for ceiling decoration for the drawing room and music room, and detail of molding, Dromore Castle, County Limerick, Ireland, 1868 or 1871. India ink, colored washes, gouache; 19 1/16 x 23 1/4 in. (48.5 x 59 cm). British Architectural Library Drawings Collection, RIBA, London Ran 7/B/1 (82). *Checklist no. 27*

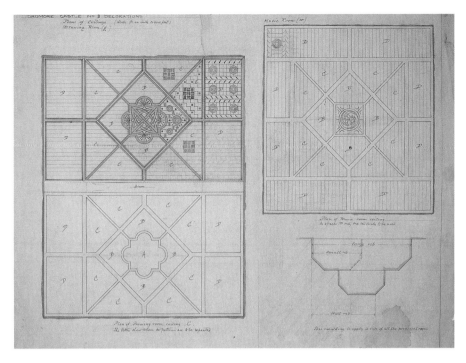

point of his Irishness to those who were invited inside Dromore. Mostly the interior is a testament to the earl's and Godwin's eclectic artistic tastes, with furniture and decorations variously medieval and Japanese (see fig. 7-12).

In 1867, shortly after Godwin began work on Dromore, he designed another Irish house for another absentee English landlord, the Hon. Rowland Winn.[185] Glenbeigh Towers, County Kerry (fig. 6-35), was a smaller and less militaristic building than Dromore. It was of the piled-up type of Rheinfelden, with a five-story main block, containing the principal rooms, adjoining a lower, three-story block with twin gables at right-angles, containing dining room, china stores, and so forth, and a single-story kitchen cross-block. A large entrance courtyard ran the width of the main blocks and led to a stableyard. A semi-octagonal bay rose through the five stories of the main block to a polygonal cap. An Irish square tower was mooted but apparently never built.[186]

The Irishness and the military character of Glenbeigh are altogether more muted than Dromore—the only piece of sabre-rattling was a bastion at the far corner of the main courtyard. An extraordinary circular room was designed but never built[187] as a type of conservatory that suggests security and leisure and has no obvious precedents, Irish or otherwise. Perhaps Winn, surrounded by 15,000 of his own acres, in relatively peaceable Kerry, did not feel the same need to pacify or cajole the locals.

Construction did not run smoothly at Glenbeigh. Henry Crisp, who supervised the building from Bristol, wrote nearly 300 letters to Solomon Turner, the long-

suffering clerk of works, and to Winn, who proved to be a difficult and indecisive client.[188] The problem of damp that had defeated Godwin at Dromore he attempted to solve at Glenbeigh by using the local red sandstone with a brick lining instead of limestone. This was no more successful than at Dromore, and eventually, Winn took Godwin and Crisp to court,[189] and the firm had to pay him compensation for calling in another architect, James Franklin Fuller, to fix the problem.[190]

The structural problems at Glenbeigh and Dromore, coupled with Godwin's high-handed way of dealing with clients, effectively put an end to his professional relationships with Lord Limerick and Rowland Winn. Such wealthy aristocratic clients, who shared his literary and artistic tastes, provided opportunities for realizing Godwin's ambitions both to unite the Sister Arts of architecture, painted decoration, and sculpture and to establish a role for himself as an art-architect, relegating the executive side to a partner such as Crisp. He was unlikely to find such an opportunity with many other types of commission.

Another wealthy aristocratic client was the third marquess of Northampton. Between 1867 and 1870 the marquess employed Godwin to design gate lodges and a kitchen garden at his Northamptonshire seat, Castle Ashby.

Castle Ashby presented a problem to a Victorian Gothic Revivalist like Godwin in that the main house, begun around 1574, was too late to be considered anything other than "debased"; later parts, notably the south front, then thought to be by Inigo Jones, were too obviously classical to be taken as any kind of model. In a letter of June

Fig. 6-35. E.W. Godwin. Glenbeigh Towers, County Kerry, Ireland, 1867–70. Photographed before 1914, from the northwest. Lawrence Collection, National Library of Ireland, Dublin, W.L. 2813. *Checklist no. 32*

1867 to Lord Alwyne Compton, Lord Northampton's brother, Godwin outlined his priorities in designing the entrances:

 1st To adhere to local traditions of construction dictated by the building materials of the country

 2nd To be in harmony with the style of the Architecture in which the older and greater portion of Castle Ashby is built, and

 3rd To secure such a character in plan and general form as would suggest the dignity of the old mansion to which they would be related.[191]

He went on to consider three types of lodge building—gate tower, gatehouse, and "modern lodge"—opting for a gatehouse as "the form which most thoroughly meet[s] the conditions with which I started . . . the *covered*

gateway with its vault or groin would suggest the age and dignity of the house far more than would any arrangement of gate piers. A greater opportunity would be afforded of securing picturesqueness in the one lodge and of breadth and mass in the other than could be secured by the adoption of the later method."[192]

In attempting to create a design that would be harmonious with the main house, Godwin allowed himself a fair degree of license. The picturesque lodge, known as the Railway Lodge (fig. 6-36), was the first one he built. The three-story gatehouse is attached to a two-story lodge, from which rises a circular stair turret topped with conical cap reminiscent of Rheinfelden. The massive off-set buttresses to the gatehouse and the carved lunette over the entrance door could not, by any stretch of the imagination, be described as Elizabethan.

The "breadth and mass" Godwin referred to was to be achieved at the South Avenue lodges (fig. 6-37), built in 1868. This pair are less of a medieval fantasy: two-storied with plain-chamfered stone mullion windows, and small ball finials to the gables and gablets. The most overtly "Elizabethan" feature is the South Avenue entrance gateway (fig. 6-38), about which the *Architect* stated, "For the design . . . his lordship is in some degree responsible. We feel that Mr Godwin, untrammelled, would hardly have left his usual path for the sake of harmonizing with Renaissance work so far off as to be invisible."[193] Godwin had written slightingly about "revived Elizabethan,"[194] and despite the "classical" details and features, the gate's form is broadly that of the gatehouse at Glenbeigh (see fig. 6-35). Lord Northampton, an exacting client, had the South Avenue lodges demolished and rebuilt farther apart to a slightly different design by Godwin, because he did not like the general effect. Nor was he satisfied with the style of the entrance gateway: "He thinks Mr Godwin's 'Elizabethan' rather too mediaeval."[195]

Nonetheless, Godwin was retained for a variety of interior and garden-building designs for which he was much more relaxed about adopting an Italian style, when required. He designed an Italian library, which was not built (see fig. 9-20),[196] and an enormous rectangular, apse-ended, kitchen garden with herbery, which was built. The high walls of the kitchen garden, with terracotta-tile coping that was definitely in the medieval-fantasy mode, were thought by the gardener to keep out too much light (fig. 6-39).[197]

Godwin contrived to remain on reasonably good terms with Lord Northampton and Lady Alwyne, and the contact proved very useful. The third marquess's niece, Lady Katrine, was married late in 1870 to the seventh Earl Cowper, K.G., and in 1871 Godwin was commissioned to design a house for the newlyweds on Lord Cowper's Nottinghamshire estate.

Fig. 6-36. E. W. Godwin. Railway Lodge, Castle Ashby, Northamptonshire: front elevation, 1867. India ink and colored washes; 21¾ x 15 in. (55.3 x 38.2 cm). British Architectural Library Drawings Collection, RIBA, London, Ran 7/C/3 (14). *Checklist no. 33*

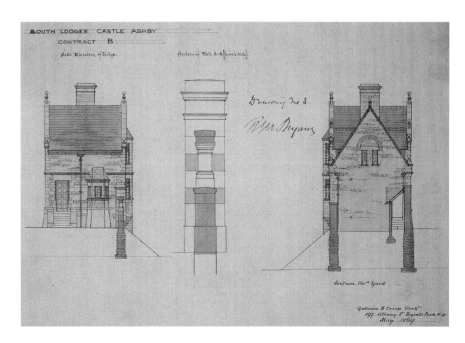

Fig. 6-37. E. W. Godwin. South Lodge, Castle Ashby, Northamptonshire: side elevation and sections, 1869. India ink, red pen, and colored washes; 10 x 14 in. (25.5 x 35.5 cm). British Architectural Library Drawings Collection, RIBA, London, Ran 7/C/3 (52).

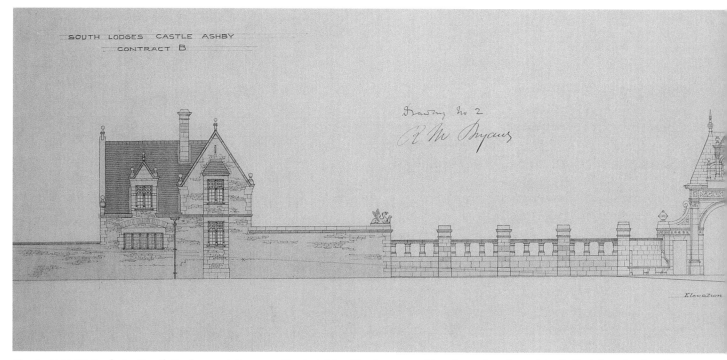

Fig. 6-38. E. W. Godwin. South Lodges and Gateway, Castle Ashby, Northamptonshire: front elevation, 1869. India ink and colored washes; 10¹⁄₁₆ x 38¼ in. (25.6 x 97.2 cm); British Architectural Library Drawings Collection, RIBA, London, Ran 7/C/3 (51). *Checklist no. 34*

Beauvale House (fig. 6-40), Godwin's largest surviving domestic building, evolved from his work at Fallows Green. The house was an ideal commission in many ways for Godwin. Lord Cowper already had several houses and spent much of his time at his seat, at Panshanger, Hertfordshire, or in his London house, so Beauvale was principally for amusement. The location was in the middle of High Park Wood, near Eastwood, and the precise site was chosen, according to Lady Cowper, when Lord Cowper upset the dogcart in the wood.[198] The siting of a house in the middle of a wood was a fashionable conceit popularized by Richard Norman Shaw's Leyswood and Cragside, and it also justified the "piled-up" configuration Godwin used for the building, and the high tower.

The plan was, broadly speaking, a simplified form of W. E. Nesfield's Cloverly, although without the complex changes of level. Beauvale is a sort of "Z-plan" with low service wing and stable yard attached to the main block by a short range containing the housekeeper's room. The visual effect of building up to the tower via single, two-, and three-story interconnected blocks is enhanced by the interplay of his favorite, steeply pitched, "Romantic Gothic" roofs, including Godwin's preferred gambrel roof.

Except for the tall chimneys, the pointed-arch front door (an emblem of "knightly" strength that Godwin could not resist), and the relentless upward mobility of the design (fig. 6-41), there is little that is overtly Gothic about Beau-

Fig. 6-39. E. W. Godwin. Gateway and wall of the kitchen garden, Castle Ashby, Northamptonshire, 1868-69. Photographed in 1998.

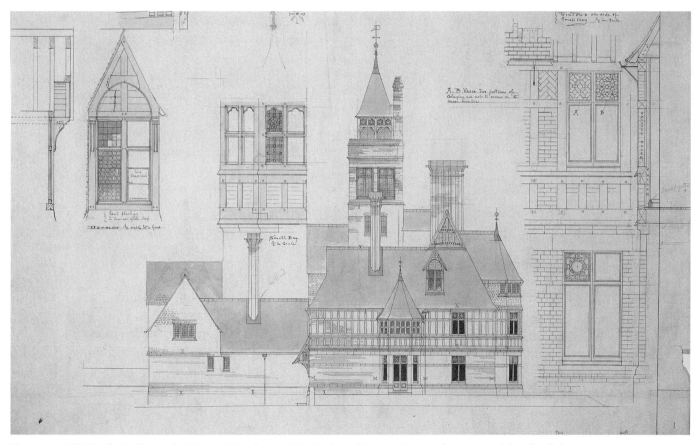

Fig. 6-40. E. W. Godwin. Beauvale House, Newthorpe, Nottinghamshire: southwest elevation and details of glazing patterns, ca 1872–73. India ink, colored washes and pencil details; 16 x 22 in. (40.7 x 55.8 cm). British Architectural Library Drawings Collection, RIBA, London, Ran 7/D/8 (8). *Checklist no. 43*

Fig. 6-41. E. W. Godwin. "Beauvale, Nottinghamshire." Drawing by E. F .C. Clarke for the *Building News* 27 (3 July 1874): 30–31.

Fig. 6-42. E. W. Godwin. Incised decoration on the southeast front of Beauvale House, Newthorpe, Nottinghamshire, ca. 1872–73. Photographed in 1998.

vale. Elements are fashionably Old English[199]—the timber-framing and tile-hanging—but they are handled in a personal, simplified, almost abstract way, and these and such features as the sgraffito decoration on the east front (fig. 6-42) anticipate Godwin's artists' houses.

The building of Beauvale was problematic: there are repeated claims from the clerk of works, who was a Cow-

per employee, that Godwin would not take seriously his complaints about the quality of the material[200]; Lord Cowper took offense when Godwin decided to paint the interior woodwork, instead of varnishing it as he had originally specified[201]; and the original completion date was missed by many months. The contractor blamed this on Godwin,[202] who mysteriously disappeared, amid rumors that he had "cut the country."[203] There was speculation at Beauvale that Godwin had financial difficulties although in fact he appears to have been away on his "Month in Normandy," but Lord Cowper's solicitor became involved, much to Godwin's irritation.[204]

These problems prompted an exchange between Cowper's agent, F. F. Fox, and his lawyer, L. R. Valpy. Fox wrote to Valpy on July 2, 1873, "I am sorry that this has happened as Mr Godwin, with some faults in practical points, is the only architect of . . . taste and ability that we have ever employed. . . . Mr Godwin supplied much that we want. He has artistic ability and is clever in designing and we flatter ourselves that we can carry out his designs in good style, without much reference to him, and that we can often improve upon his arrangements in practical points."[205] Valpy replied darkly, "I may say that personally I should much prefer to secure architectural designs from P. Webb than Mr Godwin. I will not enter into particulars . . . ,"[206] by which he meant, presumably, that Philip Webb could be relied upon not to commit any indiscretions with married actresses.

Between 1872 and 1875 Godwin supplied several designs for cottages for Lord Cowper's estate, most of which are variations on a theme: semidetached pairs (fig. 6-43), with a projecting, central, gabled two-story bay; the doors

Fig. 6-43. E. W. Godwin. "Moorgreen Cottages for Earl Cowper." From *British Architect* 15 (25 February 1881): 105.

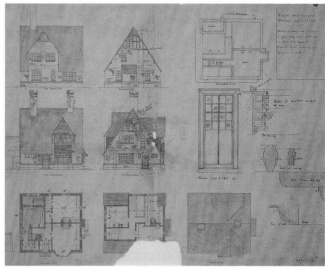

Fig. 6-44. E. W. Godwin. Minister's House, Moor Green, Nottinghamshire: plans, elevations, and details, ca. 1873. India ink and colored washes, pencil details on tracing paper; 17½ x 24 in. (44.5 x 61 cm). British Architectural Library Drawings Collection, RIBA, London, Ran 7/E/2 (1). *Checklist no. 47*

are in the return walls of each side of this, so that it is not immediately apparent that this is not a single house, echoes of Rockleaze. Fox had looked into the question of cottages very carefully, and he was able to make suggestions for the improvements in "practical matters"—such as not having one bedroom open off another.[207] Even in their amended form, the cottages are not models of convenience, with perilously steep staircases and bedrooms often higher than they are wide, a consequence of the picturesque roofs.

More significant was the house at Moor Green, which Lord Cowper had built to Godwin's designs for the Con-gregationalist Minister (figs. 6-44, 6-45); this was a paternalistic gesture, because many of Cowper's tenants were dissenters.[208] The house shares certain general features with both Beauvale Lodge and the cottages but is more like an expanded version of the latter—presumably because Lord Cowper wanted to keep the cost down to £550, around one third of what Rheinfelden had cost. It is basically a single two-story block, with a red-tiled roof that sweeps to the height of the top of the front door and the ground-floor windows. A two-story canted bay on the front elevation rises to a plain tile-hung gable of the cottage type. There is

Fig. 6-45. E. W. Godwin. Minister's House, Moor Green, Nottinghamshire, 1873. Photographed from the west in 1998.

Fig. 6-46. E. W. Godwin. Entrance doorway, the Minister's House, Moor Green, Nottinghamshire, 1873. Photographed in 1998.

a modest amount of decorative timber framing on the side gables; the right gable has decorative louvers to ventilate the loft space. A curious feature is the ogee-headed stone doorway (fig. 6-46), derived from doorways Godwin had drawn in Saint Lô and at the Château d'Ango in Normandy,[209] the same month he had made his Minister's House design.[210] Other features here, and at Beauvale, are more Old French than Old English in origin. The same could not be said of the staircase, which instead of balusters, has a delicate un-chamfered framework, Japanese in character.

When the Moor Green design was published a year later in the *Building News*,[211] it caught the eye of Jonathan Carr, then contemplating the development of an estate at Turnham Green in west London. Much has been made of Bedford Park, as the estate came to be known, and Carr's conscious appeal to a certain type of educated middle class with cultural interests.[212] Initially, however, Carr's aim was merely "to supply for the middle classes that which the Shaftesbury-park Estate has partially done for the labouring classes—namely, houses well planned, conveniently ar-

ranged, and constructed with regard for both stability and comfort and architectural character."[213]

Godwin was involved only in the early part of the project. Carr, although he was trying to attract a clientele that would have scorned the usual type of speculative building, with every house identical, was evidently looking for designs from Godwin that could be reproduced many times over, specifically a semidetached pair and a detached corner house. Godwin's first design for a semidetached pair included the tile-hanging and tiled roofs of the Minister's House at Moor Green, and some timber-framing on the side gables,[214] which was not adopted in the design that was built (fig. 6-47). Timber framing may have been considered too specifically rural and Old English. The original design also included kitchen and service rooms on a half-basement level, which was omitted in the final design,[215] creating difficulties for Godwin with the planning.

When Godwin's plans for the detached corner house (figs. 6-48, 6-49) were published in the *Building News* in December 1876,[216] William Ravenscroft of Reading and William Woodward of London sent detailed letters of criticism.[217] Ravenscroft, who claimed to be an admirer of Godwin's ability "to group the several features of his buildings," felt Godwin had achieved this "at the utter sacrifice of convenience of arrangement." He itemized fourteen faults in the planning, singling out for special criticism the steep, winding stairs, the smallness of the scullery and passageways in general, the smallness of the dining room rela-

Fig. 6-47. E. W. Godwin. Semidetached houses, Nos. 3 and 5 The Avenue, Bedford Park, Chiswick, London, 1876. Photographed in 1998.

Fig. 6-48. E. W. Godwin. No. 1 The Avenue, Bedford Park, Chiswick, London, 1875–77. From the *Building News* 31 (22 December 1876): 621 (detail).

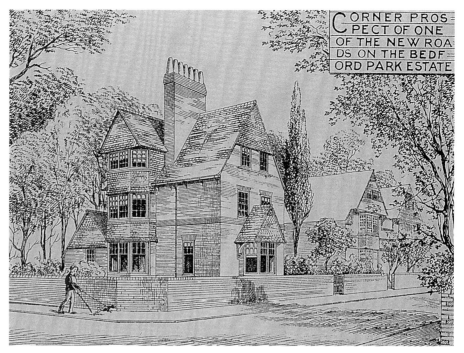

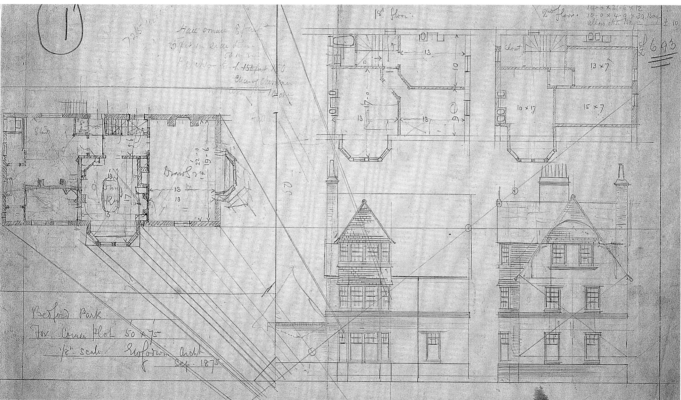

Fig. 6-49. E. W. Godwin. Design for a detached corner house, Bedford Park, Chiswick, London: plans and elevations, 1875. Pencil, pen and ink; 11 x 17½ in. (27.9 x 44.4 cm). Trustees of the Victoria and Albert Museum, London, E.577-1963. *Checklist no. 48*

tive to the drawing room, and the lack of a fireplace in some of the bedrooms.

    Woodward, who was surveyor to the Crown Estate Paving Commissioners, found little to admire except for the picturesque grouping of the houses and the garden fences. He reiterated many of Ravenscroft's points in more color-

ful language, stating, "The staircase to this house is the most extraordinary production it has been my lot to witness," and he noted with horror the inclusion of the lavatory within the bathroom: "No person can use the w.c. while the bath is in use: unavoidable smells will attend the bather." He also noted that none of the second-floor bedrooms was "square-

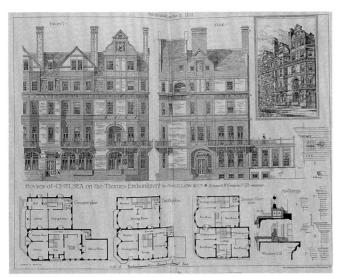

Fig. 6-50. E. W. Godwin. Nos. 4-6 Chelsea Embankment, London, 1877–78. From the *Building News* 34 (15 March 1878): 264.

ceiled," as had been the case at the Moor Green cottages, and that, as a consequence, "it must be a stipulation that only dwarf servants are engaged."[218]

When the *Building News* published Godwin's designs for the semidetached pairs,[219] Woodward wrote again, in a similar tone. Although he thought the plans for these were better, he found many similar faults to the detached house and declared that "the inspection of the kitchen to this house nearly resulted in producing upon me an apoplectic fit from laughter."[220]

Godwin did not deign to reply, although Carr did, admitting some of the criticisms and promising to correct some of the faults in subsequent versions of the designs.[221] The cramped hallway, for example, was altered in the semidetached designs; the entrance from a doorway parallel to the front windows opened into a porch, as at No. 16 The Avenue. But Godwin's association with Carr was at an end. Although adaptations of Godwin's corner-house design continued to be built, much of the subsequent building at Bedford Park followed Norman Shaw's designs,[222] and, later, those of E. J. May and M. B. Adams.

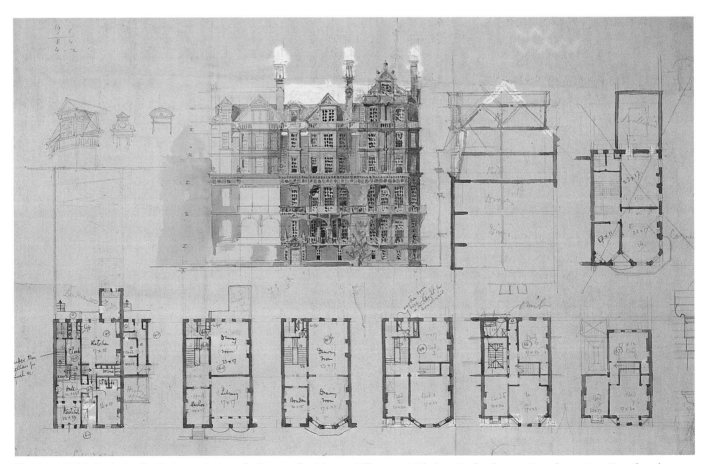

Fig. 6-51. E. W. Godwin. Preliminary designs for houses for Messrs. Gillow, 4-6 Chelsea Embankment, London, 1877. Pencil and colored wash, Chinese white; 13¾ x 19⁹⁄₁₆ in. (35 x 48.5 cm). British Architectural Library Drawings Collection, RIBA, London, Ran 7/G/1 (1). *Checklist no. 87*

Fig. 6-52. E. W. Godwin. The White House, 35 Tite Street, Chelsea, London: front elevation, 1877. This design was rejected by the Metropolitan Board of Works. Watercolor, pen and ink, and Chinese white; 15¼ x 21⅞ in. (38.6 x 55.5 cm). Trustees of the Victoria and Albert Museum, London, E.540-1963. *Checklist no. 83*

Godwin may not have been overly concerned with the breakdown of his relationship with Carr because 1877 saw the beginning of the "last flowering" of his architectural talent, the artists' houses in Tite Street, Chelsea. His first work at the site overlooking the Thames on the corner of Tite Street was not an artist's house, however, but a speculative venture for the furnishers Gillow and Company. The three houses Godwin designed at 4, 5, and 6 Chelsea Embankment (figs. 6-50, 6-51)[223] provide, along with his first designs for Whistler's house and Frank Miles's house, a telling example of the range that the term "Queen Anne Revival" could encompass. Where Bedford Park was all tile-hanging and plain gables, Chelsea Embankment is much grander and decidedly urban in character, with shaped gables. Where Bedford Park had off-the-shelf interior fittings, Chelsea Embankment had mantelpieces and woodwork designed by Godwin with sober, classical moldings in his latest "Greek" manner[224] and carved-brick panels on the exterior in the Aesthetic fashion.[225] The recessed canted

bays, a Godwin touch, were intended to afford the wealthy occupants privacy from the "double-barrelled gaze"[226] of their neighbors.

Godwin's other Tite Street projects were all individual commissions, which partly accounts for the fact that they are architecturally more daring. The tale of his Tite Street designs and the short shrift he was given by the Metropolitan Board of Works, who were the lessors of the site and therefore entitled to reject designs, has been told in detail.[227] The commissions of these house/studios should have been everything that Bedford Park and Chelsea Embankment could never have been. The clients were all artists who shared Godwin's artistic tastes, and, with the exception of Whistler, whose financial fragility was exposed all too soon by the Ruskin trial, they all had reasonably deep pockets.

The intervention of the Board of Works could not entirely ruin the best of the designs: those for Whistler's White House and Frank Miles's House. Initially, Whistler

Fig. 6-53. E. W. Godwin. Revised design for the White House, 35 Tite Street, Chelsea, London, ca. 1877-78. Design accepted by the Metropolitan Board of Works. Pen and ink; 13 x 19¾ in. (33.1 x 50.3 cm). Trustees of the Victoria and Albert Museum, London, E.544-1963. *Checklist. no. 85*

had wanted only a single-story studio for himself,[228] but Godwin persuaded Whistler to lease a double plot from the Board of Works in October 1877 and to build a house with two studios, one to be an atelier for the Whistler acolytes.[229] The front elevation of Godwin's first design (fig. 6-52)[230] was plain to the point of reticence. It had a green-tiled mansard roof (the roof of the back of the studios, whose windows were on the rear, northeast-facing elevation) and plain sash windows at varying levels reflecting, to some extent, the varying levels of the rooms within (see fig. 7-31). It was constructed of white brick with small amounts of stone dressing,[231] the woodwork painted a pale blue-gray. These "constructive colours" were chosen by Whistler.[232] The house was built to a height of about 12 feet before Whistler submitted his application to the Board of Works,[233] who were horrified, saying that it looked like a "dead-house."[234] Eventually they granted the lease, on the condition that

various forms of ornament were applied to the facade (fig. 6-53).

Even the forward-looking *Building News*, which had been an indulgently uncritical supporter of Godwin's work, was nonplussed: "The White House . . . is of an extraordinary character. . . . Architecturally, we cannot place it in any of the usual categories; there is decided evidence in the mouldings to the pediment of doorway of refined taste, and a semi-Greek feeling breathes in the delicately-cut members and incised window-heads which enrich the plain white brick and stone surface of an extremely severe and monumental type of building; though for anything beyond this, either artistically or architecturally, we cannot speak in praise."[235]

Whistler did not enjoy his house for long. By September 1879 he was bankrupt from his libel action against Ruskin, and the house was sold at auction to the critic

Harry Quilter who, among other alterations, raised the front facade to two stories, obscuring much of the green-tiled roof and destroying the rhythm of Godwin's design (fig. 6-54).[236]

Around the same time Godwin had similar bad luck with his design for Frank Miles's studio house in Tite Street. Miles was a successful society portraitist and friend of Oscar Wilde. The opportunities for dramatic articulation in the facade were greater than with Whistler's house because Miles's faced northeast, so the vast studio windows could be a feature of the street facade. Godwin believed his first design for Miles's house (see fig. 3-26) was "the best thing I ever did."[237] The street facade is higher than that of the White House, rising through three stories. The third, double-height studio story was contained within a mansard roof, with one large double-height window within a straight-topped gable; there were further studio windows in the lower part of the mansard roof. There is more decora-

tion than in Whistler's house, with carved-brick panels to the faces of the two balconies—one above the front door, the other canted out on plain sloping brick corbels in front of the studio windows. The materials were more conventional than Whistler's, with stock brick for the main walling and red brick for the dressings and upper part of the building; there was red tiling on the lower parts of the mansard, flanking the smaller studio windows, and green slates above. The Board of Works were not appeased, however, pronouncing it "worse than Whistler's."[238] Godwin revised the design twice (figs. 6-55, 6-56), introducing "some reminiscences of a visit to Holland"[239]—shaped gables over studio window and door—and removing stark, more artistic features, such as the corbels and the unusual carved-brick balconies, and the board was satisfied (fig. 6-57).

Godwin did not make the mistake three times. He designed several other studio houses, including, shortly before he designed Miles's house, a double studio for

Fig. 6-54. The White House, 35 Tite Street, Chelsea, London, after further alterations were made by Harry Quilter, the building's second owner, ca. 1879. Photographed ca. 1950s. The Royal Borough of Kensington and Chelsea Libraries and Arts Service, L/3206.

Fig. 6-55. E. W. Godwin. Frank Miles's House, 44 Tite Street, Chelsea, London, 1878. Design rejected by the Metropolitan Board of Works. Pen and ink, pencil and watercolor; 15¼ x 11⅜ in. (38.7 x 28.9 cm). Trustees of the Victoria and Albert Museum, London E.556-1963.
Checklist no. 89

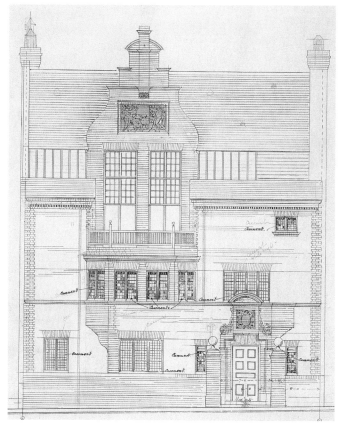

Fig. 6-56. E. W. Godwin. Revised design for Frank Miles's house, 44 Tite Street, Chelsea, London: front elevation, 1878. Design accepted by the Metropolitan Board of Works. Pen and ink, pencil, and watercolor; 20⅛ x 14⅝ in. (51.2 x 37.3 cm). Trustees of the Victoria and Albert Museum, London E.554-1963. *Checklist no. 90*

Archibald Stuart Wortley and the caricaturist Carlo Pellegrini at 60 Tite Street in 1878, which he subsequently altered for the Hon. Slingsby Bethell in 1879. In 1879–83, he built another house, at 29 Tite Street (fig. 6-58), for Stuart Wortley.[240] The Board of Works was mollified by the more conventional appearance of these houses, as was the *Building News*, which wrote that 60 Tite Street had "nothing in it in common with Mr Whistler's house. . . . It is a plain Old English type of house, with mullioned casements, and 17th century detail."[241]

In the late 1870s and early 1880s Godwin was involved with a number of projects that illustrate the considerable overlap between aristocratic, artistic, and theatrical circles in the metropolitan milieu. While some of Godwin's aristocratic patrons of the 1860s and early 1870s, such as Lord Limerick, had had artistic interests, most of the work Godwin had done for them—Beauvale for Lord Cowper, Castle Ashby for Lord Northampton, Dromore for Lord Limerick—had served to point up their status as lords of the manor. However, in Princess Louise, Marchioness of

Lorne, one of Queen Victoria's daughters, Godwin found a very modern type of patron—royalty aspiring to the condition of the artist. Princess Louise was "a passable and tolerable statuary,"[242] a pupil of J. E. Boehm, sculptor-in-ordinary to the queen (and an acquaintance of Godwin's),[243] and she wanted a simple studio-room—living quarters were not required as she had accommodation in Kensington Palace.

Godwin built her a studio 25 feet square and 17 feet high, with anteroom, hall, and three entrances (figs. 6-59, 6-60; see fig. 7-41). There was a mansard roof with three-light, small-paned studio windows.[244] The cost was kept down to around £650 by using the palace garden walls for the south, part of the west, and the east walls. Godwin added a shaped gable to this eastern wall, both a fashionable Queen Anne touch and an allusion to the late seventeenth-century architecture of Kensington Palace. It seems that Princess Louise did not find her studio entirely satisfactory as she had a new one built alongside in 1889.[245]

But the princess was not Godwin's only grand client

Fig. 6-57. E. W. Godwin. Frank Miles's house, 44 Tite Street, Chelsea, London, 1878–79. Photographed in 1972.

Fig. 6-58. E. W. Godwin. Studio house for Archibald Stuart Wortley, 29 Tite Street, 1879–83. Photographed in 1926.

in the later part of his career: he worked for Theresa, Countess of Shrewsbury, designing a house for her in Lennox Gardens, South Kensington,[246] which was not built, and altering her new house in Lowndes Square.[247] For Gwladys, Countess of Lonsdale, he also designed a house in Lennox Gardens that came to nothing.[248] At the same time he was designing a house, for a site somewhere in Kensington, for the actress Lillie Langtry.[249] What is interesting is that these clients were all female—only a few years after the first Married Woman's Property Act[250]—two of whom were aristocrats, and one of whom belonged to a profession that until recently had been considered only a step above prostitution. And yet Godwin is designing for them broadly similar houses in fashionable parts of London. It is interesting to note that the house he designed for Lillie Langtry contained a double-height studio-room: the form had evolved from its practical origins to become a fashionable conceit.[251]

This social blurring is also apparent in Godwin's

designs for the Fine Art Society and McLean's Gallery in 1882–84. This is commercial work, but could hardly be more different from his commercial work for Smith, the horsehair manufacturer, and Perry, the carriage-maker, in Bristol in the late 1850s. The story of Godwin's work at the Fine Art Society has been well described elsewhere.[252] The Fine Art Society was one of a new breed of art dealers set up in the late 1870s, the best known of which was the Grosvenor Gallery. They sought to distance themselves from the taint of trade and to align themselves rather with the art establishment, by staging exhibitions and pursuing other activities that were not strictly commercial but which raised the social tone of the enterprise. Godwin's new shopfront for the Fine Art Society, commissioned in 1881, can be seen in this light (fig. 6-61).[253] When the secretary of the society, Marcus B. Huish, wrote to Godwin in July 1881, he asked him to "alter our front and make it rather less of a shop front."[254] What Godwin did was to open up the front at two levels (fig. 6-62)—the ground-floor shopfront

Fig. 6-59. E. W. Godwin. Princess Louise's studio, Kensington Palace, London, 1878–79. Photographed ca. 1940, after alterations had been made to the windows. English Heritage, no. K1978. *Checklist no. 95*

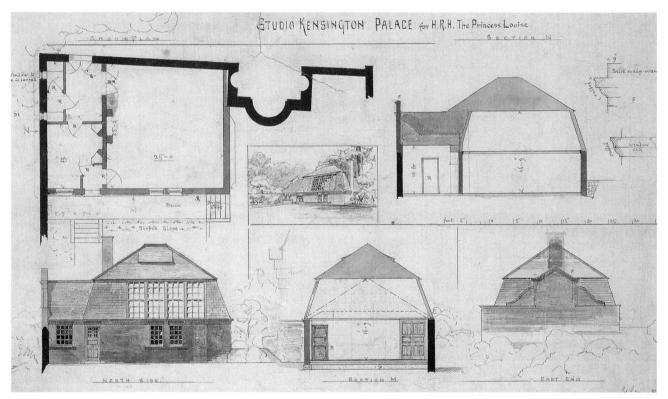

Fig. 6-60. E. W. Godwin. Studio for Princess Louise, Kensington Palace, London, 1878. Sepia and red pen, India ink, colored washes, and gouache; 12½ x 19½ in. (31.8 x 49.6 cm). British Architectural Library Drawings Collection, RIBA, London, Ran 7/F/2 (1). *Checklist no. 94*

and the upper gallery level. These divisions had to be carefully managed, as they were partly determined by the existing cornices and sills.[255] He set the ground-floor doorway back seven feet from the line of the front, and set display cases to either side of the door and perpendicular to it, thereby increasing the window-display space and creating a lobby that was both within the building yet open to the street; this blurring of inner and outer space applied also to the first-floor balcony.

The style of these additions is hard to classify, a difficulty that would have pleased Godwin. It has been described as "japoniste"[256] and "Free Renaissance."[257] The small-paned windows used in the wooden screens that form the entrance doorway on the ground floor and the wall

Fig. 6-61. E. W. Godwin. Facade of the Fine Art Society, 148 New Bond Street, London. Drawing by Thomas Raffles Davison for the *British Architect* 16 (16 December 1881): 632.

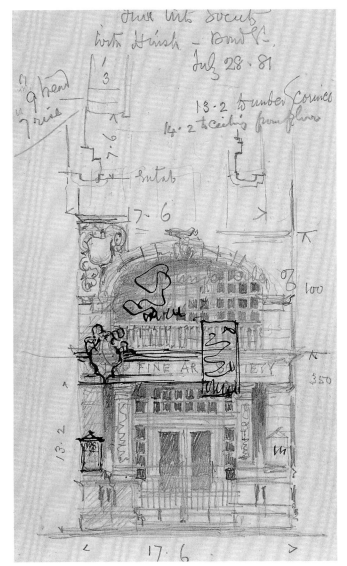

Fig. 6-62. E. W. Godwin. Sketch of a new facade for the Fine Art Society, 148 New Bond Street, London, 1881. Sketchbook. Pencil, pen and ink; 3 ¼ x 5 ¼ in. (8.3 x 13.3 cm). Trustees of the Victoria and Albert Museum, London, E.254-1963: 42. *Checklist no. 100*

between balcony and gallery on the first floor recall the divisions he had used in the Tite Street studios and Princess Louise's studio, but, although he had found parallels for such forms in Japanese woodwork, he had been toying with this type of division since his Gothic and Old English days in the 1860s. The drop arch to the balcony is a free adaptation of the loggia of the Manior d'Ango in Normandy, a drawing of which he published in 1874 (see fig. 5-2)[258] and which he had adapted in a number of other designs.[259]

But the stripped, classical, almost astylar, manner of the columns in antis to the ground floor is quite different, and this was a manner Godwin was to develop much further in an unexecuted design for another showroom, McLean's

Fine Art Gallery at 7 Haymarket, in 1884 (fig. 6-63).[260] This is the apotheosis of aesthetic architecture: the front breaks back and forth in subtle planes that serve no function beyond formal game-playing, the decoration is a mix of "japoniste" and Greek, plants spill from balconies at two levels. The client had apparently expressed an abhorrence of Queen Anne, because Godwin wrote to assure him: "No fear of Queen Anne. My affections are much more Greek."[261]

Back in Tite Street, Godwin used the small-paned windows once more in one of his final works, a tower of apartments with studios, at 46 Tite Street, from 1881 (fig. 6-64). Godwin had been trying to build on various sites in

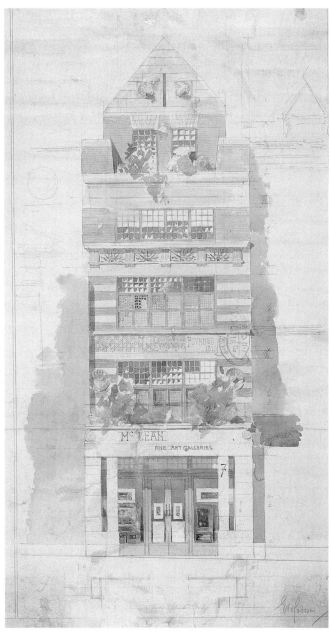

Fig. 6-63. E. W. Godwin. Unexecuted design for the facade of McLean's Fine Art Gallery, 7 Haymarket, London, 1884. Pencil and watercolor and Chinese white; 19⅝ x 11⅞ in. (50 x 30.2 cm). Trustees of the Victoria and Albert Museum, London E.629-1963. *Checklist no. 101*

Tite Street, as a speculative venture, since 1878. Whistler and Bram Stoker, the author of *Dracula*, were the potential tenants. Tower House was finally finished in 1885, and Whistler did, indeed, occupy one of the flats from 1888 to 1890, after Godwn's death.[262] It is a striking design: four vast studio windows, divided into tiny panes piled up on one side, balanced by a greater number of smaller windows on the other, culminating in bay windows and a cupola on top (fig. 6-65).

Godwin was involved in several speculative ventures in the 1870s and 1880s, which came to nothing but show Godwin's interest in forms of communal living. His earliest, in 1873, was a co-operative home for Mrs. E. M. King.[263] This project was published with an article outlining Mrs. King's progressive ideas.[264] Later, in 1879–80,

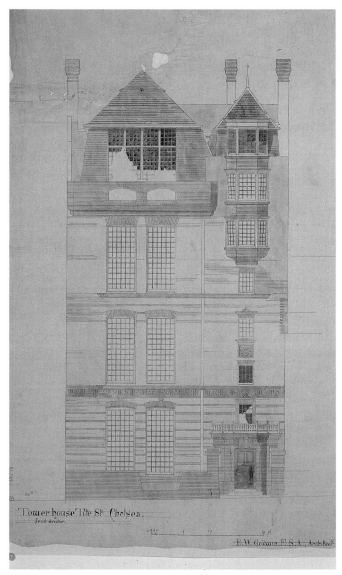

Fig. 6-64. E. W. Godwin. Tower House, 46 Tite Street, Chelsea, London: front elevation, ca. 1883. Pen and colored washes on tracing paper; 25½ x 16¾ in. (64.8 x 42.5 cm). British Architectural Library Drawings Collection, RIBA, London Ran 7/G/6 (7). *Checklist no. 99*

Fig. 6-65. E. W. Godwin. Tower House, 46 Tite Street, Chelsea, London, 1883–85. 20th-century photograph.

Godwin designed two blocks containing flats and a club for the Savoy Palace site by Waterloo Bridge, one of these in conjunction with J. P. Seddon,[265] and was working on a similar project in Brighton not long before his death.[266] More conventional would have been the houses he hoped to build in Holland Park,[267] near his friend William Burges's house in Melbury Road. Godwin's reputation for financial unreliability may have ensured that none of these ventures came to fruition.

Godwin's last significant domestic project took him back to Northampton, scene of his first great triumph. The client, Joseph Shuttleworth, was a successful tea merchant, and Godwin built a house for him called Elmleigh at Dallington, just outside Northampton (fig. 6-66). Godwin's design[268] of 1882–84 is surprisingly low-key after the shock tactics of the Tite Street houses. Late Gothic, if anything, in

style, with a Tudor, two-centered arch on the entrance porch and built of local Duston rubble, it resembles an inflated version of his South Avenue lodges at Castle Ashby.[269] Although artfully composed, in the piled-up manner of Beauvale, and with a modified Z-plan, it was a somber note on which to end his career. Even the semi-circular bay in the drawing-room, which appears to look forward to C. F. A. Voysey, is said to have been forced on him by his client,[270] who considered the house a "poem in stone."[271]

Godwin's architectural career is usually characterized by its "might-have-been" quality. Certainly there is an elegiac quality to many of his obituaries, a sense that personal shortcomings, bad luck, and poor health contrived to deprive him of the worldly success enjoyed by architects such as Scott and Waterhouse who made substantial fortunes

Fig. 6-66. E. W. Godwin. Elmleigh, Dallington Park, Northampton, 1882–84. From "A House at Northampton," *British Architect* 24 (2 October 1885): 145 (detail).

from their careers, or even his friend Burges who enjoyed a successful career without much of the taint of compromise, of artistry sacrificed to commerce. Worldly success was not something Godwin derived from his career, as the application for a pension for his widow demonstrates.[272]

Yet Godwin's name was to be bandied about as an influential one for decades to come. Certainly his prodigious output of architectural journalism and his success in seeing his work published in the *Building News*, the *Architect*, and the *British Architect* ensured him an audience far wider than the number of executed buildings would suggest was possible, or even justified. Perhaps this is the key to any assessment of Godwin as an architect. From the later 1870s he devoted as much time to architectural journalism, theater work, furniture and decorative design, and prepar-

ing illustrations of his buildings for publication, as he did to work on actual architectural commissions.

It is equally significant that the architectural commission from which he made the largest single sum of money was Plymouth Guildhall, a work for which he had provided only the initial competition designs.[273] Morris, Webb, and others identified with the Arts and Crafts movement can be seen as espousing an approach to architectural design, whereby the building's design evolved from the craft of its construction. Godwin, for all that he used some of the features usually identified as "Arts and Crafts," belongs at the opposite extreme. For Godwin, the design and the building were both imperfect realizations of the "design idea," that idea being the true work of art. While the building itself might be seen as a more complete or perfect realization of the idea than the drawing, the drawing, or even a description of it, has a value as a work of art and indeed as architecture.

The last ten years of Godwin's life can be seen as a desperate battle to achieve total artistic control. In the end the theater was the field on which he struggled, but he had been fighting the same fight as an architect since the early 1860s. At that time it manifested itself as a desire to reunite the sister arts of painting, sculpture, and architecture,[274] with Godwin expressing an increasingly hardened view that the overall control should be in the hands of the proponent of the "mother of the arts," the architect.[275] Until the early 1870s the pursuit was clouded by a number of factors. Firstly, there was the seductive appeal of Ruskin's prose, which had played a major part in Godwin's and many of his contemporaries' ideas about the sister arts, but which brought with it Ruskin's ideas about the crucial role of the workman, as well as an attitude to buildings that was essentially realist.[276] Then there was the search for a new style, a style of the nineteenth century.[277] As long as an architect was involved in this collective endeavor, as long as he was identified with the Gothic camp fighting a perpetual war of attrition against the classicists, that artistic control was always going to be compromised.

In the 1870s there was a gradual realization that the new style was not going to be found either in "developing" or by divining some inherent set of principles in Gothic architecture—a slow dawning that the wood of Gothic principles would always be obscured by the trees of Gothic forms. Those like Godwin, who had identified themselves with the Gothic camp, might talk bravely about having won the "Battle of the Styles,"[278] but they knew the war—to see a new style born out of the Gothic—was lost. A tacit acknowledgment of this was Godwin's giving up altogether the idea that the goal was to find a new style collectively representative of the age. As the 1870s progressed Godwin retreated from this grand, collectivist aim to a more personal one, a striving after a pure expression of his individual artistic vision. Hand in hand with this came a new faith in abstract notions of beauty. Beauty and individuality for Godwin supplanted truth as the defining quality in good architecture: he advised students in 1878 to reply, when asked what style they were working in, "it is my own."[279] This growing belief in a canon of taste can be seen most starkly in Godwin's architectural journalism where the recurring criticism is ugliness, not untruth.[280]

What compromised architecture as a profession for Godwin was the extent to which it was controlled by monetary exchange. Godwin had been inspired by the diatribe of anticapitalism in Ruskin, and it sounds like a tolling bell throughout Godwin's writings in the ongoing litany against money-grubbing architects.[281] This also underpins his disillusionment with the Royal Institute of British Architects, for which, in the 1860s, he had had great respect.[282] He saw the R.I.B.A. as concerned more with safeguarding what were at heart business interests, sacrificing all other considerations, whether architecture as art or the architect as the presiding genius, in the interests of client-cultivation and increased cash-flow.[283]

It is this resentment of the client and, at heart, the capitalist underpinning of the client/architect relationship that hampered Godwin throughout his career. Time and time again he antagonized clients, writing high-handed letters, overspending his budget, charging hefty expenses, while claiming to adhere to the institute's scale of charges, neglecting matters that he felt were the province of the builder or the "practical man," such as the cost or the quality of the materials, failing to ensure the completion date was met, resigning in pique when his wishes were overruled, and making changes without consulting the client. Various of these problems occurred in minor projects such as Saint Philip, Stepney, and Rheinfelden as well as major works at Dromore, Glenbeigh, and Beauvale.

Thus it was only logical that Godwin's last years were taken up with breaking this unholy hegemony by dispensing with the client entirely—by assuming his role. His approach to architecture in the last few years of his life is a precise equivalent to his involvement in theater production. He did not give up seeking conventionally organized commissions entirely in his final years, as his diaries reveal. There was talk with Whistler of another house, and with Lillie Langtry, of another project. Then there was Shuttleworth's house in Northampton. There were minor works, some of which were realized, others not. And there were competitions. But the great bulk of Godwin's time and energies were devoted to Tower House,[284] to the Metropolitan Mansions[285] on the Savoy site by the Thames, and to projects for new theaters in various sites, mainly in the West End of London.[286] What all these have in common is that Godwin would have been his own client. In most cases it would have been as a joint venture, and the extent of his financial exposure in the theater ventures remains obscure, but even as a joint client he was on a quite different footing from the usual client/architect relationship.

None of these plans came to anything. The correspondence suggests that he could not raise the finance. Whether it was the unsoundness of the businesses that Godwin planned or his own insecure financial position that put investors off is unclear. But the point is that he devoted an enormous amount of energy to these abortive architectural projects. If his brethren in the architectural press felt he had dissipated his energies and his health solely on theatrical production work, they were wrong. In the end what theater production came close to providing for Godwin was a means of translating his artistic vision most directly from the ideal to the real. It, too, ultimately failed. The exigencies of the market, of supply and demand, thwarted this as the tyranny of the client had his architecture.

.

Note: Most published sources are cited below in shortened form (author's last name, abbreviated title, date of publication); full references will be found in the bibliography. Frequently cited archives are abbreviated below; for a key to the abbreviations, also see the bibliography.

1. Obituary, "The Late E. W. Godwin" *Building News* (15 October 1886): 589.

2. "A facile sketcher, a good draughtsman, with a quick eye for harmonious groupings and proportions; a clear writer, an antiquary, well versed in the architecture, furniture, and costumes of all periods, a well-informed Shakespearian scholar, an excellent lecturer; and . . . a setter of plays unsurpassed" (Obituary, "The Late E. W. Godwin" *Pictorial World* [4 November 1886]: 461).

3. This essay is intended principally as a work of record, an attempt to rehabilitate the many unknown projects, rather than reinterpret a few "iconic" buildings. This has seemed the most useful approach in a necessarily limited format, given that the only comprehensive study of Godwin's work—Harbron, *Conscious Stone* (1949)—is hard to find and unreliable.

4. Harbron, *Conscious Stone* (1949): 8. Armstrong's name occasionally appears in Godwin's surviving sketchbooks, and it was from Armstrong's office in Brunswick Square, Bristol, that Godwin, James Hine, and William Corbett Burder issued their prospectus (copy in RIBA Mss, GoE 3/5/1) for *The Architectural Antiquities of Bristol and its Neighbourhood* in March 1850. He also refers to him in a letter to the builder R. M. Bryant in December 1871 (V&A AAD, letterbook 4/22-1988: 197–98).

   Godwin indicated that he only began his study, notetaking, and drawing of medieval churches in the Bristol area on his days off from his pupilage (Godwin, "On Some Buildings I Have Designed" [29 November 1878]: 210), and the earliest surviving sketchbook is dated 1848 (V&A PD, E.225-1963). He further suggested, on two separate occasions, that he had assumed full responsibility for most architectural design in Armstrong's office "since I was eighteen years old" (Godwin, "Secret Manufacture of Architecture" [7 February 1873]: 145–46) and "before he had been three years at work" (Godwin, "On Some Buildings I Have Designed" [29 November 1878]: 210), which again suggests that he was fifteen or sixteen years old.

5. Godwin, "On Some Buildings I Have Designed" (29 November 1878): 210.

6. Ibid.

7. Gomme, Jenner, and Little, *Bristol* (1979): 430.

8. Bristol Record Office, Building Grant Plans. Many of the plans in these volumes are signed by Armstrong. Drainage plans for new buildings had to be submitted after Bristol adopted the Public Health Act in 1851.

9. Gomme, Jenner, and Little, *Bristol* (1979): 228, 242, 257, 430.

10. George Gilbert Scott's experience of apprenticeship seems to have been remarkably similar to Godwin's in this respect: "A somewhat romantic youth, assigned to follow the noble art of architecture for the love he had formed for it from the ancient churches of his neighbourhood, condemned to indulge his taste by building houses at Hackney in the debased style of 1827!" (George Gilbert Scott, *Personal and Professional Recollections by the late Sir George Gilbert Scott*, ed. by his son G. Gilbert Scott [London, S. Low Marston, Searle, and Rivington, 1879]: 55–56).

11. Godwin, "On Some Buildings I Have Designed" (29 November 1878): 210.

12. Godwin, "Scraps for Students," part 3 (6 May 1876): 285; ibid., part 4 (13 May 1876); 304; see also George Wightwick, "Life of an Architect," *Bentley's Miscellany* (1853–54, 1857–58), quoted in Saint, *The Image of the Architect* (New Haven and London: Yale University Press, 1983): 54.

13. Godwin, "Secret Manufacture of Architecture" (7 February 1873): 145–46.

14. The only surviving Armstrong drawings are for work done before Godwin's pupilage: dated 1835, they are for a restoration of the nave and new galleries in Saint Philip and Saint Jacob's church in the Bristol Record Office (P/St P&J/Pl/l). They show that Armstrong was capable of designing, or at least drawing, Gothic buildings. A restoration of Saint Philip and Saint Jacob of 1850 (when Godwin was a pupil) has been listed among Armstrong's works (Gomme, Jenner, and Little, *Bristol* [1979]: 430), but there are no drawings for this in the Bristol Record Office. Other notes dated 1853, along with an undated color drawing among Godwin's papers, seem to relate to a pair of flat-fronted terraced houses, presumably commissioned from Armstrong (V&A PD, E.226-1963). The notes refer to "Mr Wilkins, Kenilworth Terrace" and the Bristol Record Office has a plan (Building Grant Plans [1853], p. 87) and section of the basement of a pair of houses for Mr. Wilkins, Kenilworth Terrace, which presumably are the same.

15. Not listed by Gomme, Jenner, and Little, *Bristol* (1979), but illustrated and described in the *Builder* (23 February 1850): 91. According to the text, "The architect was Mr W. Armstrong." In a further implausible change of use, Quaker Friars, as it is known, is now a register office.

16. Godwin, "Notes, Historical and Architectural, of the Priory of Dominicans, Bristol" (1853): 142–49. Godwin acknowledged the kindness of "Mr Wm Armstrong" in supplying him with measurements and enabling him to give a plan of the building before its alterations, but this does not necessarily indicate that it was Armstrong's work, if what Godwin wrote about Armstrong's attitude to his drawings is true (see Godwin, "Secret Manufacture of Architecture" [7 February 1873]: 145–46).

17. L. Wright, "An Account of the Bristol Society of Architects" (1950): 10–14.

18. Godwin, "On Some Buildings I Have Designed" (29 November 1878): 210–12.

19. The "genius-designer"—the layman's mythical notion of the architect against which Andrew Saint warns: "architects' offices neither are nor were studios, producing masterpieces by individuals for the general public . . . No architect produces his work in a vacuum, no building even by Webb or Voysey was dictated from first to last by its designer" (Saint, *Richard Norman Shaw* [1976]: 189–90).

20. Quoted in Saint, *Image of the Architect* (1983): 61.

21. Ibid., p. 62.

22. James Hine was related to the better-known Nottingham architects Thomas Chambers Hine and his son George Thomas Hine; T. C. Hine was one of several Hines whose names appear in the list of subscribers in *The Architectural Antiquities of Bristol*. James Hine was the son of a prominent Congregationalist minister, Thomas Collins Hine *Western Daily Mercury* [1 July 1860]). For James Hine's career, see Obituary [James Hine], *The Builder* 106 (1914): 277; Cherry and Pevsner, *Buildings of England: Devon* (1989), passim.

23. Bristol Record Office, P/St. P & J/PL/1 (d) i and ii.

24. The vestry minutes suggest they could not or would not raise the money for the project; John Norton supplied an alternative restoration design in October 1865 (Bristol Record Office P/St P & J/PL/1 [e] i, ii and iii); this was not carried through either.

25. V&A AAD, Ledger 4/9-1980: 1–2.

26. Ibid.

27. Cherry and Pevsner, *Buildings of England: Devon* (1989): 104, 658.

28. E.g., *Western Daily Mercury* (1 July 1860); ibid. (7 Sept 1860); ibid. (21 June 1861).

29. [Godwin], "Plymouth" (18 August 1865): 574–75.

30. V&A AAD, Ledger 4/9-1980: 3–4.

31. Saint Philip and Saint Jacob Church School Minutes, Bristol Record Office, P/St. P & J/S/1, plans for Saint Philip and Saint Jacob's Schools 22938 (19) 5001; RIBA Report by G. E. Street to Rev. Arthur B. Day on "proposed New Schools in the Parish of St Philip and Jacob" (RIBA Mss, GoE/1/5/1; see also V&A AAD, Ledger 4/9-1980: 24, 27, 28).

32. Contract drawings, private collection, Bristol; V&A, AAD Ledger 4/9-1980: 17–18.

33. Gomme, Jenner, and Little, *Bristol* (1979): pp. 281–82. For more information on J. A. Clark, see ibid., p. 431.

34. V&A AAD, Ledger 4/9-1980: 49–50; letters and memoranda relating to the extension of Highbury Chapel (Redland Park Church, Bristol, box known as "The Highbury Chest").

35. Harbron, *Conscious Stone* (1949): 72–73, 84.

36. RIBA nomination papers (23 January 1889), F v9 p. 87.

37. See Henry Crisp's letterbooks, Proctor and Palmer.

38. Obituary [Henry Crisp] *Western Daily Press* (9 June 1896).

39. Compare the new wards for the Bristol Royal Infirmary (now the University of Bristol Department of Rheumatology), of 1868, which are convincingly "in keeping" with the eighteenth-century infirmary buildings, with the violent structural polychromy of the Bristol Wagon Works of 1870–71, in Victoria Street, Bristol (demolished, but illustrated in *Bristol As It Was, 1963–1975*, compiled by John Winstone [Bristol, 1990], figs. 85 and 86) and contract drawing owned by Scott Elliot, Kelmscott Gallery, Chicago.

40. Incomplete undated letter, probably very early 1868, apparently to Lady Alwyne Compton, as Godwin discusses an unrealized project for an "Italian library" for Lady Alwyne (Compton Family Archive, Castle Ashby, Northamptonshire).

41. "There is a clause in our deed which says you are to do all the *superintendence* for the firm. I do my share of the firm's work in making the designs," letter of 20 February 1872, V&A AAD, letterbook 4/22-1988: 210.

42. Drawings and correspondence, Proctor and Palmer.

43. Ibid.

44. There are no letters in Crisp's letterbooks relating to this project; although Godwin's correspondence of this date does not survive, there are letters to the client, Pickering Phipps, from Godwin in 1871 (V&A AAD, letterbook 4/22-1988).

45. Harbron, *Conscious Stone* (1949): 72–73, 84; Crisp letterbook 2, Proctor and Palmer.

46. "Agreement between James Hine (for Norman and self) and E. W. Godwin," dated 6 April 1869, V&A AAD, 4/253-1988.

47. Godwin, "Friends in council . . . Burges" (29 April 1881): 213.

48. Ibid.

49. See Crook, *William Burges* (1981), passim.

50. Various letters from Henry Crisp to Godwin about amounts of money not declared during their partnership (Crisp letterbook 2, Proctor and Palmer).

51. Godwin, "Friends in council . . . Burges" (29 April 1881): 214.

52. Ibid., p. 215.

53. Godwin, "*British Architect* special correspondence" (18 December 1885): 262.

54. Godwin apparently reused part of this in Godwin, "Odds and ends about construction" (14 October 1876): 225–26; ibid. (28 October 1876): 248–49.

55. Burges's name appears progressively less in Godwin's diaries of 1873–83, V&A AAD, 4/1-8-1980.

56. Godwin, "Architectural poaching" (13 July 1877): 17.

57. Letter to R. W. Edis dated 16 April 1872, V&A AAD, 4/385-1988.

58. Memo on proposed terms of consultation, ibid.

59. Letter to R. W. Edis dated 16 April 1872, ibid.

60. Memo on proposed terms of consultation, ibid.

61. In the Berlin Parliament competition of 1872, they were jointly credited (*Architect* [13 July 1872]: 24); in the Battersea London Board school competition, only Edis's name appears, but Godwin's own copy of the illustration from *Building News* (19 December 1873) is annotated "Consulting architect E. W. Godwin" in Godwin's handwriting (V&A AAD, 4/563-1988).

62. Memorandum of agreement, 12 April 1872, V&A AAD, 4/384-1988.

63. "Design for a Proposed People's Palace . . . " (12 February 1887): 250. It appears that Godwin and Seddon did not make it clear to the adjudicators that any of their three entries in the St. Ann's competition—Economy (Seddon), Mens and Quadrant (Godwin)—were joint, but in a letter to *Building News* ([21 February 1873]: 231) apropos the controversy over the true authorship of Alexander Ross's entry for the Edinburgh Cathedral competition, Seddon states that "Mr E. W. Godwin and I conjointly sent in a design for Mr Holloway's Asylum."

64. E.g., apropos the Edinburgh Cathedral competition, "we are gradually learning that the *art* of architecture *is* an important part, and that we must have our labour and materials directed and applied in proper form, which can only be accomplished by the union of the artist with the practical man" ("W. H. L." [W. H. Lynn of Belfast?], *Building News* 24 [14 February 1873]: 201).

65. The pupils, improvers, and occasional assistants included William Sale Hannaford, Frank Morrish Harvey, Frederick Jameson, George Freeth Roper, E. F. C. Clarke, George William Webb, John Oliver Harris, and Frank S. Granger; the clerks included his nephews Fred and Willy Godwin.

66. In one of Godwin's notebooks there are site plans for a school variously labeled "Plan of ground at Easton for school" and "T.B.S.," dated May 1853 and April 1854, respectively (V&A PD, E. 226-1963). There is

also a plan of "Trinity Branch School, Easton/Twinnell Road," dated September 1853, in the Bristol Record Office (Building Grant Plans, i, p. 231). In an uncatalogued and unidentified cutting from a Bristol newspaper annotated in Godwin's handwriting "My 1st work. Oct 22 '53," the incumbent is described as Rev. David Cooper, who had since 1850 been the vicar of Holy Trinity, St. Philip's, the church in the outparish (V&A TA, Godwin collection, box 9). That part of the outparish was subsequently constituted as the separate parish of Saint Gabriel in 1867, and plans in the Bristol Record Office of the church school of Saint Gabriel by Joseph Neale, who also designed Saint Gabriel's church, include on the site plan "old school" which appears to be Godwin's 1853 Trinity Branch School. Saint Gabriel's church and school were demolished in 1975 and, presumably, Trinity Branch School with them.

67. Godwin, "On Some Buildings I Have Designed" (29 November 1878): 210.

68. Plans and elevations of several small schools of this type survive among the school-building grant plans in the Bristol Record Office.

69. Godwin and J. A. Clark evidently entered jointly (see G. E. Street's comments on competition designs, RIBA Mss, GoE/1/5/1), but Godwin appears from the minutes to have dealt with the project, while Clark acted only as quantity surveyor (Saint Philip and Saint Jacob's School committee minutes, Bristol Record Office, P/P & J/S/1; uncatalogued drawings, Proctor and Palmer; RIBA Drawings, Ran 7/A/3). Saint Philip and Saint Jacob's School survives in Marybush Lane, Bristol, although the windows were altered and the interior entirely rebuilt in the 1950s; it is now the headquarters of the Avon Ambulance Service.

70. Crisp letterbook 1, pp. 117, 122, 127, 131, 276, 284, 297, Proctor and Palmer.

71. Godwin and Crisp had to alter their design to reduce its cost to £400 (ibid., p. 284).

72. The school was substantially rebuilt in the 1960s when it was converted into a house.

73. For an assessment of Victorian restoration practice, see Chris Miele, "Their 'Interest and Habit': Professionalism and the Restoration of Medieval Churches, 1837–77," in The Victorian Church, ed. Brooks and Saint (1995): 151–72.

74. The Saint Philip and Saint Jacob's tower restoration was never carried out.

75. Godwin, "An Account of St John the Baptist, Colerne" (1857): 358–66.

76. Godwin, "Account of a Roman Villa Discovered at Colerne, in the County of Wilts" (1856): 328–32.

77. For Godwin's detailed journal of the work, see V&A PD, E.226-1963.

78. Account of "Revd H. F. Atherley, Staverton Vic[arage], Devon, nr Totness [sic]," V&A AAD, ledger 4/9-1980: 3. This was probably Godwin's first work after returning from Ireland, as Atherley's account is the first item, apart from the drawings he supplied to Hine, in what was presumably a new ledger.

79. John Ruskin, "The Nature of Gothic," in Stones of Venice, vol. 2 (1907): 219.

80. Ibid., fig. 16.

81. V&A AAD, ledger 4/9-1980: 5–6.

82. Worthy, Devonshire Parishes, vol. 2 (1889): 55–84.

83. The drawings of the windows (listed in the catalogue of the RIBA Drawings Collection) are missing, as are parish records for the period (listed in the catalogue of the Devon Record Office, Exeter). Although Godwin supplied drawings to Rev. Hele, he does not appear to have supervised the work, as he charged only for the drawings. The restoration has been dated to 1863 (Worthy, Devonshire Parishes, vol. 2 [1889]: 80; Cherry and Pevsner, Buildings of England: Devon [1989]: 538, where

Thomas Lidstone is given as the restorer). Christopher Brooks has postulated that Lidstone, who was from the Dartmouth family of builder-architects (Colvin), may have followed Godwin's designs (personal communication, 1993); some Godwin drawings, which remain in the possession of the parish, support this notion.

84. Spreat, Picturesque Sketches of the Churches of Devon (1832): pl. 40.

85. Cherry and Pevsner, Buildings of England: Devon (1989): 538–39, 758–59.

86. V&A AAD, ledger 4/9-1980: 15–16.

87. Godwin, "An account of Ditchridge [sic] church, Wilts" (1858): 146–48. "Ditchridge" is the archaic spelling of Ditteridge.

88. Ruskin, Stones of Venice, vol. 2 (1907): chap. 3, pls. 24, 25, and 26.

89. Ayres, Highbury Story (1963): 39–40.

90. See Paul Thompson, William Butterfield (London: Routledge and Kegan Paul, 1971).

91. Desmond Bowen, Paul Cardinal Cullen and the Shaping of Modern Irish Catholicism (Dublin: Gill and Macmillan, 1983): 293.

92. Jeanne Sheehy, "Irish church-building: Popery, Puginism and the Protestant ascendancy," in The Victorian Church, ed. Brooks and Saint (1995): 133–50; another exception was W. J. Barre.

93. James Stephens, Illustrated Handbook of the Scenery and Antiquities of South-West Donegal (Dublin: McGlashan and Gill, 1872). Stephens suggests that Godwin had intended to publish a book on the antiquities of Donegal; Godwin did finally publish a series of articles in which he acknowledged Stephens's help (Godwin, "On the Architecture and Antiquities . . . of Ulster" [1 June 1872]: 281).

94. Godwin, "On Some Buildings I Have Designed" (29 November 1878): 210–11.

95. Richardson, Gothic Revival Architecture in Ireland (1983): 492–93.

96. Godwin, "On the Architecture and Antiquities . . . of Ulster" (18 May 1872): 249.

97. "St Johnston, County Donegal, Ireland" (9 May 1857): 258–59.

98. For All Saints, Saint Columcille, and the St. Johnstown structures, see Dublin Builder 3, (15 July 1861): 578. For Saint Baithen's foundation stone (placed on 4 April 1857), and dedication of 9 December 1860, see ibid. (1 December 1861): 692. For reference to the "new" church at Newtowncunningham, see Dublin Builder 2 (1 June 1860): 282. For reference to the cost of new church at Saint Johnstown ("to date" £2,000), see ibid. (1 December 1860): 357. For reference to Tory Island church as having been built 1857–61 at a cost £392, see Rowan, Buildings of Ireland: Northwest Ulster (1979): 501.

99. A new south chapel was added in 1971 in a discordant neo-Gothick style, replacing the easterly south porch (Rowan, Buildings of Ireland: Northwest Ulster [1979]: 438); the westerly south porch has also been removed and replaced with a window broadly in keeping with the existing window. Rowan (p. 438) mistakenly writes that the 1971 addition replaced the apse. Godwin may have rebuilt rather than entirely replaced the existing church of 1810: this might explain the chamfered quoins which one can hardly imagine Godwin designing at this date.

100. Dublin Builder 3 (15 July 1861): 578; there is no indication that Godwin was involved in the design of the stained glass.

101. Godwin, "Notes on Some Examples of Church Architecture in Cornwall" (1853): 317–24.

102. Godwin, "Notes on Some of the Churches in . . . Cornwall" (1861): 230–52, 224–41.

103. For Godwin's work at Grade, see RIBA Drawings, Ran 7/A/4; Lambeth Palace Library, ICBS file no 5752; V&A AAD, ledger 4/9-1980: 25–26.

104. Estimate for erecting . . . a mortuary chapel, November 1877, Nottinghamshire Archive, CC/VI/C/5. The archive also contains designs for the chapel.

105. It is illustrated in "Nottingham Church Cemetery Competition" (23 November 1877): 254.

106. Godwin, "On Some Buildings I Have Designed" (29 November 1878): 210.

107. Ayres, *Highbury Story* (1963): 38–55; extensive uncatalogued records of the church's building and extension are kept in a box known as "The Highbury Chest," at Redland Park Church, Bristol.

108. Godwin was perhaps approached because he was known to Henry Overton Wills of the tobacco company, who was a prominent member of the congregation. Wills's family and that of Samuel B. Day, the late vicar of Saint Philip and Saint Jacob, were closely related by marriage, as was Wills's family and William Butterfield's.

109. Box labeled "The Highbury Chest," Redland Park Church, Bristol.

110. Ibid.

111. Ibid. The window was destroyed during the Second World War, and the pulpit, around 1970; Godwin's works have been heavily altered by later additions.

112. RIBA Drawings, Ran 7/A/7; also illustrated in Richardson, *Gothic Revival Architecture in Ireland* (1983).

113. Five competition drawings, RIBA Drawings, Ran 7A/8 1-5.

114. Ibid., Ran 7/K/11.

115. Ibid., Ran 7/A/1.

116. Ibid., Ran 7/F/3.

117. Ibid., Ran 7/D/12; two designs are reproduced in "New Greek Church in London" (17 January 1879): 26.

118. He addresses Dilberoglue as "Dear Stavros" or "My dear Dilberoglue" in his letters in RIBA Mss, GoE 2/5/1.

119. "Design for a Greek church Notting Hill to accommodate from 1,000 to 1,200 and to cost £12,000," letter from Godwin to Stavros Dilberoglue dated 30 March 1873, RIBA Mss, GoE 2/5/1. His sources appear to have been Ruskin, *Stones of Venice*, and André Couchaud, *Choix d'églises byzantines en Grèce* (Paris, 1842).

120. Curl, *Victorian Churches* (1995): 113; Howell and Sutton, eds., *Victorian Churches* (1989): 76; Dilberoglue appears to have consulted J. O. Scott's father, G. G. Scott, as early as 1873, much to Godwin's indignation (V&A AAD, letterbook 4/23-1988: 27–29).

121. For town hall building see Cunningham, *Victorian and Edwardian Town Halls* (1981): 264–84. Between 1853 and 1886, 409 "town halls," including other public-building types, were constructed in the United Kingdom; I have not counted town halls listed as "proposed" or "restored." When Godwin compiled a list around 1878 of all the competitions he had entered, he too grouped diverse types of municipal administrative service buildings together (V&A AAD, letterbook 4/12-1980: 29–31). Overall at least 1,449 competitions were held in Britain between 1853 and 1886 (R. H. Harper, *Victorian Architectural Competitions* [1983]: 363–95). The actual total is probably higher; the *Builder*, from which Harper's statistics are derived, missed many minor competitions. Harper lists 44 competitions in the *Builder* in 1857 (ibid., p. 369) while an apparently contemporary source gives the total that year as 69 (Frank Jenkins, *Architect and Patron: A Survey of Professional Relations and Practice in England from the Sixteenth Century to the Present Day* [London: Oxford University Press, 1961], p. 219).

122. V&A AAD, ledger 4/12-1980: 21–31.

123. "Report of Council Meeting," *Northampton Mercury* (20 April 1861).

124. See Cunningham, *Victorian and Edwardian Town Halls* (1981).

125. Plans of first floor, V&A PD, E.581 and E.585-1963; see also *Building News* 7 (8 November 1861): 892.

126. Godwin, "On Some Buildings I have Designed" (29 November 1878): 211. For the influence of Ruskin's ideas on Northampton Town Hall, see M. W. Brooks, *John Ruskin and Victorian Architecture* (1987): 201–9.

127. See Frederick O'Dwyer, *Deane and Woodward* (Cork: Cork University Press, 1997).

128. Ruskin, "Preface to the Second Edition," *Seven Lamps of Architecture* (1855).

129. Godwin, "Sister Arts and Their Relation to Architecture" copy in RIBA Mss, GoE/7/8/2.

130. Unidentified Bristol newspaper cutting (1864), in a scrapbook, V&A AAD, 4/558-1988.

131. See John Ruskin, "The Nature of Gothic," in *Stones of Venice*, vol. 2 (1907): 149–228.

132. Godwin, "On Some Buildings I Have Designed" (29 November 1878): 210–11.

133. Ruskin, *Stones of Venice*, vol. 2 (1907), chap. 3, pls. 24, 25, 26.

134. See report of the Town Hall Building Committee, 10 August 1863, in the Minute Book of the Council of Northampton (1861–72), Northamptonshire Record Office.

135. Crook, *William Burges* (1981): pl. 166.

136. See *Descriptive Guide to the New Town Hall* (1881): 22–24; for a description of the interior decoration, see also draft of Godwin's competition report, V&A AAD, 4/251-1988.

137. Ibid.

138. Special meeting of the borough council, 11 June 1861, in the Borough of Congleton Order Book (1846–61), Cheshire Record Office. Information about the corporation's decision-making is sketchy because a fire in the town clerk's office in 1877 destroyed many council records.

139. "Competitions: Macclesfield Town Hall" (19 March 1864): 211. The competition is called "Macclesfield," perhaps because the information came from the Macclesfield newspaper, but it is clearly Congleton. Macclesfield already had a town hall and never had a competition to replace it; Waterhouse did assess the Congleton competition.

140. Cunningham and Waterhouse, *Alfred Waterhouse* (1992): 282; Annual Statements of Accounts (1836–67), LBC "B" Box 8, Cheshire Record Office. The account for 1864 includes "Alfred Waterhouse, for reporting on design, £21.0.0."

141. "Competitions: Macclesfield Town Hall" (19 March 1864): 211.

142. Congleton Town Hall competition drawings, RIBA Drawings, Ran 7/A/9 (2).

143. A drawing of Northampton, made in the 1860s, apparently from Godwin's office, has dormers on the roof; this drawing was sold by Phillip's, London, on 1 November 1993. An illustration in the *Building News* also shows the roof with tiny dormers, which must have been intended for decoration rather than use (*Building News* 7 [8 November 1861]: 901).

144. Godwin, "On Some Buildings I Have Designed" (29 November 1878): 210.

145. Ibid., p. 211.

146. Ibid.

147. Ibid.

148. See "Sculpture, New Town-Hall, Northampton" (10 November 1865): 788.

149. Special meeting of the corporation, 2 January 1867, in the corporation and treasurer's committee meeting Minute Book (1865–67), LBC 47/13, Cheshire Record Office.

150. Cunningham, *Victorian and Edwardian Town Halls* (1981): 99.

151. Meeting of the corporation, 11 October 1865, in the corporation and treasurer's committee meeting Minute Book (1865–67), LBC 47/13, Cheshire Record Office.

152. From the *Spectator,* quoted in T. A. T. Robinson, "Congleton Town Hall" (typescript, Cheshire Record Office, n.d.).

153. Hine and Norman in their report to the Guildhall committee stated that the reason for having two ranges was to keep the Law Courts/Public hall separate from the public offices to "avoid confusion" and to express their "separate functions" (minutes of the Guildhall Committee, 28 February 1870, P5/G2, Plymouth and West Devon Record Office, Plymouth).

154. Harry Hems has erroneously been identified as the carver (Cherry and Pevsner, *Buildings of England: Devon* [1989]: 657). The council paid Boulton to carve two of the panels at £25 apiece; they then tried to persuade him to do the rest for £20 apiece, but he declined and was paid £25 each for the remaining ten panels (Minutes of the Guildhall Committee, 21 April, 24 April, and 22 June 1874, P5/G2, Plymouth and West Devon Record Office, Plymouth).

155. "I fear I cannot undertake to supply ½ inch details. My Agreement was to advise generally and furnish the general design and detail" (letter from E. W. Godwin to ?Alfred Norman, 28 March 1871, V&A AAD, 4/256-1988).

156. There is an aggrieved letter from Alfred Norman, on behalf of himself and James Hine, dated 16 July 1874, apparently addressing a dispute with Godwin, who appears to have been trying to secure part of the commission on the extras (V&A AAD, 4/261-1988).

157. In addition to a list of entries to competitions and results ("Competitions," V&A AAD, ledger 4/12-1980: 29–31), his office diaries for 1873, 1874, 1876, 1877, 1879–83 also record work on many competitions (V&A AAD, 4/1 and 4/8-1980).

158. The whole fiasco is described in Gomme, Jenner, and Little, *Bristol* (1979): 428–29.

159. Winchester Guildhall competition drawings, RIBA Drawings, Ran 7/D/6.

160. "Warehouse, Bristol," *Builder* 16 (30 October 1858): 719; the publication of the design in 1858 presumably accounts for the mistaken dating of the building elsewhere.

161. There is a plan dated 12 June 1856 in the Building Grant Plans, Bristol Record Office.

162. V&A AAD, ledger 4/9-1980: 9–10; he apparently did not supervize the building as he received only 2½ percent on the contract of £1,000.

163. For a description of the premises see "Perry & Co., Carriage Manufacturers," in *The Ports of the Bristol Channel* (1893): 194; Godwin apparently designed only the showroom block, as the building does not appear in the Building Grant Plans, Bristol Record Office, suggesting the showroom block was added to existing workshops.

164. See Girouard, *Sweetness and Light* (1984).

165. For Beauvale, see Girouard, *Victorian Country House* (1979): 329–35; for Dromore, see Reid, "Dromore Castle" (1987): 113–42; for Castle Ashby, see M. Hall, "Chinese Puzzle" (25 July 1991): 78–81.

166. Godwin, "On Some Buildings I Have Designed" (29 November 1878): 210.

167. By 1860 most of Rockleaze had been developed by a speculative builder, William Baker, with very large semidetached houses, some with full-height bows and round-arched windows and the walls of coursed rubble, but in a stodgy sub-classical style (Gomme, Jenner, and Little, *Bristol* [1979]: 279); see also Building Grant Plans, Bristol Record Office.

168. Godwin produced three sets of designs for 10–11 Rockleaze between February 1860 and June 1861 (V&A AAD, ledger 4/9-1980: 17–18). The contract drawings of the original design are in a private collection, Bristol.

169. John Ruskin, "The Nature of Gothic," in *Stones of Venice,* vol. 2 (1907): 170–79.

170. See Stefan Muthesius, *The English Terraced House* (New Haven and London: Yale University Press, 1982): 203.

171. Godwin, "On Some Buildings I Have Designed" (29 November 1878): 78.

172. Phipps was a brewer by trade; in the 1880s he developed a large area of eastern Northampton, known today as Phippsville (Gertude Hollis, *St. Matthew's, Northampton: The Oxford Movement in an English Parish* [London and Oxford: A. R. Moubray and Co., 1932]: 13).

173. Godwin produced sketch designs for St. Martin's Villas in the summer of 1863 and working drawings and specifications in October. The houses were complete by the summer of 1864 (V&A AAD, 4/9-1980: 47–48).

174. "House at Northampton" (7 January 1871): 10.

175. Ibid.

176. Godwin, "Cottage for P. Phipps Esq Collingtree, Northants." (4 February 1881): 66.

177. Letters to G. Rands (Phipps's cousin) dated 27 June and 19 July 1871, V&A AAD, 4/22-1988: 21, 32–36.

178. Contract drawings for 74 and 76 Stokes Croft, formerly in the possession of Proctor and Palmer, now owned by Scott Elliot, Kelmscott Gallery, Chicago (see fig. 6-29).

179. Designs for Fallows Green are in RIBA Drawings, Ran 7/L/5 and 7/L/6; those catalogued as Fallow's Green are of another house or may be an earlier design for Fallow's Green. Sketch drawings of the house, garden, and furnishings in Godwin sketchbooks, V&A PD, E.230, E.231, E.233, E.234, and E.273-1963.

180. Bristol Society of Architects Minute books, 20 December 1865, held by the architectural firm Whicheloe MacFarlane, Bristol.

181. "Roman pavements near Mells, Somerset. Visited with Lord Limerick," n.d. and "Nunney Castle, Somerset. Dec 26 1865. Visited with Lord Limerick," sketchbook, V&A PD, E.274-1963. These are fair copies of drawings of various dates; Limerick was still Viscount Glentworth in December 1865.

182. Charles Townsehend, *Political Violence in Ireland: Government and Repression since 1848* (Oxford: Oxford University Press, 1983): 35.

183. Godwin, "Dromore Castle" (29 March 1867): 222.

184. Reid, "Dromore Castle" (1987): 113–42.

185. V&A AAD, ledger 4/9-1980: 79–80.

186. Photographs ca. 1910 in National Library of Ireland, Lawrence Collection—2812 W. L.; RIBA Drawings, Ran 7/C/5 (2) and 7/C/5 (3).

187. Ibid.

188. Godwin and Crisp letterbook 2, *passim.*, Proctor and Palmer.

189. Ibid.

190. J. F. Fuller, *Omniana: The Autobiography of an Irish Octogenarian* (London: Smith, Elder and Co., 1916): 203–4; I am grateful to Jeanne Sheehy for having drawn this book to my attention.

191. Letter from Godwin to Lord Alwyne Compton, dated 3 June 1867, Compton Family Documents, Castle Ashby, Northamptonshire.

192. Ibid.

193. "Gateway to the South Avenue at Castle Ashby" (21 October 1871): 202; Godwin seems to have experimented with the later Gothic, almost Hispanic style, in an attempt to meet the requirement for an "Elizabethan" mode (see RIBA Drawings, Ran 7/C, 13 [3] and [49]).

194. Godwin, "Modern Architects and their Works," part 3 (12 July 1872): 35.

195. Lady Alwyne Compton's memorandum book, 27 February 1871, pp. 85–87, Compton Family Documents, Castle Ashby, Northamptonshire.

196. Several uncatalogued letters, accounts, and drawings, ibid.

197. Ibid.

198. [Katrine Cowper], Earl Cowper KG: A Memoir by his Wife (privately printed, 1913): 204.

199. Cowper might have seen the recently completed stables at the Rectory, Little Gaddesden, Herts, designed by Godwin in a half-timbered style. The stables were paid for by Lord Brownlow, Cowper's cousin, to whom he was close (ibid., passim).

200. Letters to and from Cowper's agent, F. F. Fox, clerk of works Samuel Taylor, and E. W. Godwin, dated 3 May 1872 to 17 July 1872, Nottinghamshire Archives, DDLM 209/11/78, 80, 91, 107–115.

201. Letters to Lord Cowper dated 26 March 1873 and 1 April 1873, V&A AAD, letterbook 2, 4/23-1988: 15–17.

202. Letter to F. F. Fox from L. R. Valpy dated 16 July 1873, Nottinghamshire Archives, DDLM/209/11/131.

203. Diary entry for 24 April 1873, V&A AAD, 4/1-1980.

204. Letter from E. W. Godwin to F. F. Fox dated June 18 1873, Nottinghamshire Archives, DDLM/209/11/128. At the beginning of the letter Godwin mentions that he has just returned from Normandy. His travel notes were published as Godwin, "Some Notes of a Month in Normandy," part 1 (28 August 1874): 251–52; part 2 (11 September 1874): 307–8; part 3 (2 October 1874); 395–96; part 4 (13 November 1874): 572–73.

205. Letter from F. F. Fox to L. R. Valpy dated 2 July 1873, Nottinghamshire Archives, DDLM 209/11/129 a-f.

206. Letter from L. R. Valpy to F. F. Fox dated 10 July 1873, Nottinghamshire Archives, DDLM 209/11/131; Valpy had commissioned Philip Webb to design his offices at 19 Lincoln's Inn Fields.

207. Letter from F. F. Fox to E. W. Godwin, n.d. [April/May 1872], Nottinghamshire Archives, DDLM 209/11/76.

208. [Katrine Cowper], Earl Cowper KG: A Memoir by his Wife (privately printed, 1913): 227.

209. For St. Lô, see Godwin, "Mr. E. W. Godwin's Measured Sketches . . . St. Lô" (14 August 1874): 194. For the Château d'Ango illustration (signed and dated April 1873), see Godwin, "Manor-House of Ango" (3 April 1874): 364.

210. Sheet of working drawings dated 7 April 1873, Nottinghamshire Archives, DDLM 50/2/6.

211. "A Parsonage for [£]550" (6 March 1874): 256, illus. 263, 266–67.

212. For social aspects of Bedford Park, see Margaret Jones Bolsterli, The Early Community at Bedford Park: "Corporate Happiness" in the First Garden Suburb (London and Henley: Routledge and Kegan Paul, 1977).

213. "Bedford-Park Estate, Turnham-Green" (22 December 1876): 621.

214. "Small double house for Bedford Park Estate," V&A PD, E.578-1963.

215. "Bedford Park Estate, Turnham Green" (12 January 1877): 36 and illus. [43].

216. "Bedford-Park Estate, Turnham-Green" (22 December 1876): 621 and illus.

217. Ravenscroft, "Villas, Bedford Park Estate" (29 December 1876): 679 (letter); Woodward, "Villas, Bedford Park Estate" (5 January 1877): 26–27 (letter).

218. Woodward, "Villas Bedford Park Estate" (5 January 1877): 26–27 (letter).

219. "Bedford Park Estate, Turnham Green" (12 January 1877): 36 and illus. [43].

220. Woodward, "Bedford Park Estate . . . Comical Construction" (19 January 1877): 77 (letter).

221. "Bedford Park Estate" (2 February 1877): 134 (letter).

222. For more information on the building at Bedford Park, see Greeves, Bedford Park (1975); T. and A. Harper Smith, A Middle Class Townlet (London: T. and A. Harper Smith, 1992). For Norman Shaw's work at Bedford Park, see Saint, Richard Norman Shaw (1976): 210.

223. For illustrations, see "Houses on the Thames Embankment at Chelsea" (15 February 1878): 76, 86; (15 March 1878): 122; (12 April 1878): 170; "New Houses at Chelsea" (15 March 1878): 264 and illus. [266-67].

224. "New Houses at Chelsea" (15 March 1878): 264.

225. For illustrations, see "Figure by C. W. Morgan" (10 January 1879): 16 and illus.; "Carved Brick Panels" (9 May 1879): n.p.

226. "What a pity . . . ," British Architect 11 (18 April 1879): 162.

227. See Girouard, "Chelsea's Bohemian Studio Houses" (23 November 1972): 1370–74. See also Walkley, Artists' Houses in London (1994): 78–92, 152–54.

228. Drawing dated August 1877, V&A PD E.538-1963; see also Godwin's office diary 1877, V&A AAD, 4/3-1980.

229. "London Architectual Association" (7 March 1879): 106.

230. Godwin's first expanded design for the White House, V&A PD, E.540-1963.

231. "White bricks" mean very pale stocks, not bricks glazed white; the house was whitewashed from an early date.

232. Godwin, "Some Facts about 'The White House'" (26 September 1879): 119.

233. Girouard, "Chelsea's Bohemian Studio Houses" (23 November 1972): 1371.

234. Godwin, "Studios and Mouldings" (7 March 1879): 261–62.

235. "Chelsea Embankment" (11 April 1879): 374.

236. Girouard, "Chelsea's Bohemian Studio Houses" (23 November 1972): 1371.

237. The design is V&A PD, E.556-1963; see also Godwin, "Studios and Mouldings" (7 March 1879): 261.

238. Godwin, "Studios and Mouldings" (7 March 1879): 261–62.

239. Ibid.

240. See Walkley, Artists' Houses in London (1994).

241. "Chelsea Embankment" (11 April 1879): 373.

242. Escott, Society in London (1886): 9.

243. According to Godwin, Princess Louise was told by a friend, possibly Boehm, to "go to Mr Godwin" about a studio (Godwin, "Studios and Mouldings" [7 March 1879]: 261–62). Godwin's office diary contains the entry, dated 13 January 1880, "Called on Boehm. Sent him full a/c of Princess Louise studio," V&A AAD, 4/5-1980.

244. Contract drawings for a studio for H.R.H. The Princess Louise, signed E. W. Godwin, dated 1878, RIBA Drawings, Ran 7/F/2; drawing for Studio Kensington Palace, signed E. W. Godwin, stamped "Office of

Works 13 Aug 1878,"Work 19/106, Public Record Office, Kew; contract, specifications, and correspondence regarding Princess Louise's studio, RIBA Mss, GoE/1/10.

245. Drawings for "Kensington Palace, proposed temporary studio," dated 15 January 1889, Work 34/734, Public Records Office, Kew; this studio was demolished in 1925 (Work 19/856, ibid.). I am grateful to Catherine Arbuthnott for copies of these papers: Godwin's studio apparently survived until after the princess's death in 1939.

246. Correspondence regarding a site in Lennox Gardens and fee for Godwin's designs dated March–July 1882, V&A AAD, 4/191, 199-1988.

247. Drawings for "Alterations to 37 Lowndes Square," RIBA Drawings, Ran 7/J/4; account of the Countess of Shrewsbury, April–July 1882, V&A AAD, ledger 4/12-1980; correspondence regarding alterations to 37 Lowndes Square dated July 1882–January 1883, V&A AAD, 4/194 to 235-1988.

248. Lady Lonsdale and Lady Shrewsbury apparently sent in tenders for two adjoining sites in Lennox Gardens which were not accepted (correspondence regarding Lennox Gardens, dated March–July 1882, V&A AAD, 4/191, 199-1988; see also Godwin's office diary, March–May 1882, passim, V&A AAD, 4/7-1980). The two houses may possibly be identified with two designs in RIBA Drawings, Ran 7/L/9 and 7/L/10.

249. Godwin's office diary from 1882, V&A AAD, 4/7-1980; and correspondence regarding projected house, V&A AAD, 4/163 to 164, 171-1988.

250. This legislation, which allowed women to retain their own property on marriage, was highly significant to a woman such as Langtry who earned her own money and was separated from her husband.

251. V&A PD, E.255-1963.

252. See O'Callaghan, "Fine Art Society and E. W. Godwin" (1976): 5–9; also see Hilarie Faberman, "'Best Shop in London,' The Fine Art Society and the Victorian Art Scene," in The Grosvenor Gallery, ed. Casteras and Denney (1996): 147–58.

253. Contract drawings for Fine Arts [sic] Society, 148 New Bond Street, RIBA Drawings, Ran 7/H/4; correspondence regarding Fine Art Society entrance, July 1881 to January 1882, RIBA Mss, GOE/2/4. Godwin may have received the commission through Whistler, who had exhibited there, or through Archibald Stuart Wortley, who was a director of the society.

254. Letter from M. B. Huish to E. W. Godwin, 28 July 1881, RIBA Mss, GoE/2/4.

255. Detail of moldings and section of front, RIBA Drawings, Ran 7/H/4 (2).

256. Faberman, "'Best Shop in London'" (see above, n. 252).

257. Wilkinson, "Edward William Godwin and Japonisme" (1987): 337.

258. Godwin, "Manoir d'Ango loggia" (10 April 1874): 392.

259. See, for example, designs for various buildings, RIBA Drawings, Ran 7/M/4, 7/M/21, 7/M/22.

260. Design for McLean Fine Art, 7 Haymarket, V&A PD, E.629-1963.

261. Letter to McLean, dated 5 June 1884, V&A AAD, 4/90-1988.

262. Walkley, Artists' Houses in London (1994).

263. Godwin diary, 20 January and 6 February 1874, V&A AAD, 4/2-1980; letter to George Freeth Roper dated 24 January 1874, V&A AAD, letterbook 4/23-1988. This letter makes clear that Godwin was to receive shares in the company formed to build and run the cooperative home, in lieu of a fee. Like many "paternalistic" housing ventures it was to be run on a commercial basis.

264. E. M. King, "Co-operative Housekeeping" (24 April 1874): 459–60; see also "Mrs E. M. King and the English Response," in Lynn F. Pearson, The Architectural and Social History of Co-operative Living (London: MacMil-

lan, 1988): 23–44.

265. For an illustration of one of these, see "Design for a Proposed People's Palace" (12 February 1887): 250. Designs for others are in RIBA Drawings, Ran 7/H/1 and 7/H/2.

266. This was the Housing Estate, Wish Farm, West Brighton, RIBA Drawings, Ran 7/J/7; RIBA Mss, GoE/1/1.

267. Drawings dated 1882 in RIBA Drawings, Ran 7/J/2.

268. RIBA Drawings, Ran 7/J/3.

269. For an illustration, see "A House at Northampton" (2 October 1885): 145 and illus.

270. Harbron, Conscious Stone (1949): 157.

271. Letter from Joseph Shuttleworth to Beatrice Godwin, 20 November 1886, V&A AAD, 4/96-1988.

272. Pall Mall Gazette (25 August 1887).

273. He made more money out of Northampton Town Hall and Dromore Castle, but this included a substantial commission on furniture and decoration.

274. For Godwin's views on the "sister arts," see Godwin, "[Notes on] Painted Decoration(s)," part 1 (20 April 1866): 247; part 4 (22 June 1886): 405; part 8 (16 November 1886): 757; idem, "Plymouth" (18 August 1865): 574; and idem, "Wall painting" (24 February 1872): 87.

275. For Godwin's views on the role of the architect as chief arbiter, see Godwin, "[Notes on] Painted Decoration(s)," part 6 (10 August 1866); 527; part 12 (3 January 1868): 6; idem, "Decorations of St Paul's Cathedral" (23 July 1870): 44: and idem, "Honour to whom honour is due" (28 February 1873): 235.

276. On Ruskin and architecture, see Robert Macleod, Style and Society: Architectural Ideology in Britain, 1835–1914 (London: RIBA Publications, 1971); Kristine Ottesen Garrigan, Ruskin on Architecture: His Thought and Influence (Madison, Wisc. and London: University of Wisconsin Press, 1973); M. W. Brooks, John Ruskin (1987); Mark Swenarton, Artisans and Architects: The Ruskinian Tradition in Architectural Thought (London: MacMillan, 1989).

277. On the style question, see John Summerson, "The evaluation of Victorian architecture: the problem of failure," in Victorian Architecture: Four Studies in Evaluation (New York and London: Columbia University Press, 1970): 1–18; Macleod, Style and Society (n. 276 above), and J. Mordaunt Crook, The Dilemma of Style: Architectural Ideas from the Picturesque to the Post-Modern (London: John Murray, 1989).

278. "It is the policy of the losing party . . . to work in the dark against the Gothic school" (Godwin, "The Times and the New Law Courts" [30 September 1871]: 164).

279. For Godwin's views on the need for individuality, see Godwin, "On Some Buildings I Have Designed" (29 November 1878): 210–12.

280. "We do not fight against the spirit of ugliness for any other object than to set up the standard of Beauty where the dragon of a foul 'Decoration' has left its trail upon the earth. . . ." (Godwin, "British Architect Special Correspondence" [18 December 1885]: 263).

281. For Godwin's views on money-grubbing architects, see Godwin, "Architectural Exhibition, 1867" (17 May 1867): 336–37.

282. For Godwin's early favorable views on the RIBA, see Godwin, "Destroyed Monasteries of Bristol" (23 February 1863); and idem, "Leicester and its Clock Tower Competition" (20 December 1867): 877.

283. For Godwin's loss of faith in the RIBA, see [Godwin], "Professional Charges and Surveyors" (11 May 1872): 241; idem, "The 'British Architects'" (21 June 1872); [idem], "Professional Tenderness" (28 June 1872): 515; idem, "To Our Student Readers," part 2 (13 August 1880): 70.

284. Drawings for Tower House, Tite Street, 1881–83, RIBA Drawings,

Ran 7/G/6; correspondence and other papers re Tower House, V&A AAD, 4/131, 134 to 155-1988; Godwin office diaries, 1881–83, passim., V&A AAD, 4/6-1980; Metropolitan Board of Works Minutes, 1878–83, MBW 1199/71 to 1230/102, London Metropolitan Archives; Godwin, "Tenders: The Tower House" (2 August 1884): 179; idem, "Tower House . . . " (22 May 1885): 252.

285. Design for Lancaster Club and Residences and Savoy Palace, 1879, 1880, RIBA Drawings, Ran 7/H/1 and 7/H/2; Godwin office diaries, 1881–82, passim.,V&A AAD, 4/5- and 4/6-1980; various notes by Godwin re Metropolitan Mansions, February to October 1880, RIBA Mss, GOE/2/6; uncatalogued material re Savoy Palace site, and the British Panorama Company,V&A TA, Godwin collection, box 6;"Metropolitan Residences," *British Architect* 13 (2 January 1880): 8 and illus.;"Design for a Proposed People's Palace" (12 February 1887): 250 and illus.

286. Godwin ledger, accounts of J. Hamilton Synge, 1880–81, and C. Ford Webb, August 1882,V&A AAD, ledger 4/12-1980; correspondence re theater-building projects in Manchester and London, V&A AAD, 4/276- to 4/284-1988; Godwin office diaries, 1876, 1880–83, passim., V&A AAD, 4/2- and 4/5 to 4/8-1980; various theater designs, including Northumberland Avenue, for Charles Wyndham, 1882 (Playhouse Theatre site), RIBA Drawings, Ran 7/H/3; Theater, near Fountain Court, Strand, in association with C. Ford Webb and Charles Wilmot, 1882, RIBA Drawings, Ran 7/J/1; theater in Panton Street, 1876 (in 1881 the Comedy Theatre was built on this site to designs of Thomas Verity), RIBA Drawings, Ran 7/E/1; Metropolitan Board of Works Building Act Committees, Sub-committee on Theatres and Music Halls, Minutes, 1 March 1882 to 3 February 1883, London Metropolitan Archives, MBW 796/1; drawings, memoranda, letters, and notes by Godwin on various theater projects, including Hyderabad, Manchester, and in London at Northumberland Avenue, Strand, Panton Street, and Knightsbridge, 1876–84,V&A TA, Godwin collection, box 6 (I am grateful to Catherine Arbuthnott for copies of her notes on and for photographs of this uncatalogued Theatre Archive material).

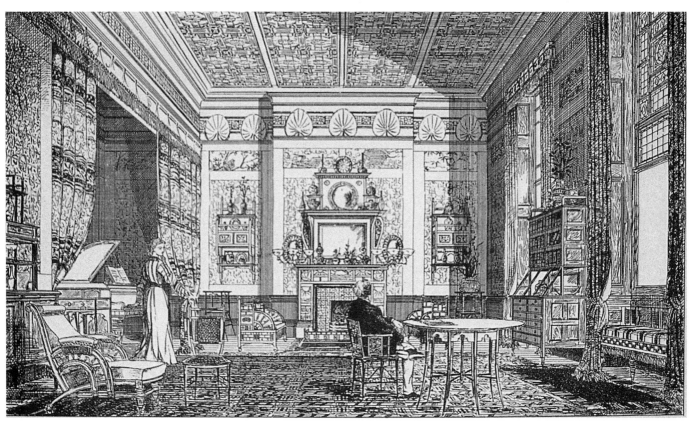

Fig. 7-1. E. W. Godwin. Interior. From William Watt, *Art Furniture* (1877), pl. 14. The Mitchell Wolfson Jr. Collection, The Wolfsonian-Florida International University, Miami Beach, Florida, TD1990.40.62.

CHAPTER 7

E·W·GODWIN·AND·INTERIOR·DESIGN

SUSAN WEBER SOROS

Domestic interior decoration played a significant role in Godwin's career. He was responsible for many highly original interior designs, ranging from an elaborate Gothic Revival scheme of decoration for an Irish castle to a severe, minimally furnished, Japanese-inspired interior for an artist's house-studio in London. A prominent figure in the reform movement in British design, Godwin pioneered the use of plain, distempered walls, bare wood floors covered with Oriental carpets or Indian matting, lightweight ebonized furniture, and simple window treatments. He was among the first to incorporate Japanese and Chinese accessories in a spacious setting. In the 1870s and 1880s Godwin's elegant decorating schemes played a leading role in shaping Aesthetic taste in Great Britain, America, and Australia.

The importance Godwin attached to his interior design work is evident from a letter to Lord Cowper of April 1, 1873, in which he wrote that "in each house I have built I have had the pleasure of regarding it as my own work entirely; down, or rather up to its coloured decoration by pictured wall, paper or paint. . . . In common with a few (I am sorry to say a very few) others in my profession, I look upon all my work as Art Work."[1] As a follower of John Ruskin, Godwin made the idea of a unified scheme of decoration, in which all the elements were considered worthy of the architect's attention, central to his interior design work. No detail was too small for him to select or to design.

With the exception of patches of stenciled decoration at Grey Towers, Godwin's "Art Work" schemes have all van-

ished. However, it is possible to reconstruct some of them through documentary evidence, including letters, estimates, specifications, drawings, and contemporary photographs. In addition, the memoirs of some of the artistic personalities for whom Godwin designed interiors, or who visited Godwin-designed interiors, often provide descriptions of these elegant environments. A prolific writer, Godwin also expressed his views on interior design through the pages of the architectural journals to which he contributed regularly from the 1860s through the 1880s.

For those unable to afford Godwin as an interior designer, his furniture, wallpapers, and accessories could be purchased from the showrooms of some of the large art furnishing firms—Collinson and Lock, Gillow and Company, Waugh and Company, and William Watt—that stocked his work. Entire schemes of Godwin decoration were displayed at the many furniture exhibitions and fairs of the era. Moreover, his designs were available to the general public through William Watt's catalogue, *Art Furniture from Designs by E. W. Godwin F.S.A., and Others, with Hints and Suggestions on Domestic Furniture and Decoration*, which was published in 1877 and again in 1878 (see fig. 3-18). Interior schemes were accompanied by instructional notes to assist middle-class consumers in incorporating artistic articles of decoration in a tasteful and unified interior. Watt's plate 14 (fig. 7-1) even illustrated an elaborate drawing room decorated with ebonized Anglo-Japanese furniture, patterned walls and ceiling, stained-glass windows, Oriental carpet, and striped draperies. The text advised that "the furniture and decoration throughout have been the result of a study of Japanese form adapted to modern English wants."[2]

Early Schemes of Decoration—Bristol and London

Adaptation of Japanese form to the requirements of modern life was already evident in Godwin's first interior design scheme, created for his own home at 21 Portland Square, Bristol, where he lived from 1862 to 1865 (see fig. 1-3). Godwin stripped bare the Regency house, painted the walls with plain colors, and arranged a few Japanese color prints asymmetrically. The bare wood floors were covered with Oriental rugs, and the rooms contained a few choice pieces of eighteenth-century furniture.[3] Godwin's collection of Chinese blue-and-white china completed the otherwise simple scheme.[4] Ellen Terry, who first visited the Godwin house in 1862, recalled years later to her grandson Edward Anthony Craig how excited she had been "at seeing . . . an impressive collection of blue china."[5]

Such an austere style of decoration was extremely original for its time. It signaled the beginning of the revolt against the overdecorated interior, what has been called "the great cleaning up."[6] Godwin disliked the overstuffed upholstery, heavy draperies, and cluttered rooms typical of middle-class interiors of the era. He considered such abundant furnishings dangerous to mental health and the moral psyche, writing that "we should guard against an excess of the appliances of physical luxury."[7] To Godwin the domestic comfort of the Victorian interior was to be viewed suspiciously as productive of a condition of piggish laziness."[8] True domestic comfort was to be achieved only when "the common objects of everyday life . . . [were] quiet, simple and unobtrusive in their beauty."[9]

Godwin's radical views on interior design were partly the result of his exposure to Japanese domestic design. He studied Japanese color prints, which were imported to London in the late 1850s and early 1860s, illustrations of Japanese subjects found in contemporary accounts, and photographs of Japan. The interiors reproduced were simple, neutral-colored spaces with sliding walls, tatami mats on the floor, a scattering of low, compact furniture (fig. 7-2), and a few, carefully selected and arranged works of art. Godwin applied and adapted this understated approach to decoration in his Portland Square rooms in Bristol.

Another formative influence may have been the understated furniture and decoration of Georgian England. Distempered walls painted in soft colors, a few beautifully crafted pieces of mahogany or satinwood furniture, and bare wood floors covered with Oriental rugs were also characteristic features of the Georgian upper-class and upper-middle-class interior recorded in many eighteenth-century period paintings.[10] This taste for Georgian furniture and interior decoration was shared by the Pre-Raphaelite painter Dante Gabriel Rossetti. In 1862 his house at 16 Cheyne Walk in Chelsea was decorated with art objects and antique furniture that included eighteenth-century specimens he admired for their simple lines and fine craftsmanship.[11]

Godwin's interest in Georgian furniture continued throughout his lifetime. In a series of articles on the decoration of his London chambers in 1876, Godwin wrote that he had "grown a trifle weary of modern designs" and thus had redecorated his London dining room with Georgian mahogany furniture and repapered the dado with an eighteenth-century–style wallpaper in a fruit pattern on a blue background. Godwin's pursuit of Georgian furniture was also fueled by economic necessity. In the same article, he wrote of the low cost of Georgian furniture, "so much below the least expensive of the specially made goods of the present day."[12]

Whatever the source of inspiration—Japanese color prints or Georgian furniture and decoration—Godwin's home in Portland Square, with its stark interior and Oriental accessories, made a vivid impression on visitors. Actress Ellen Terry later wrote, "This house, with its Persian rugs, beautiful furniture, its organ, which for the first time

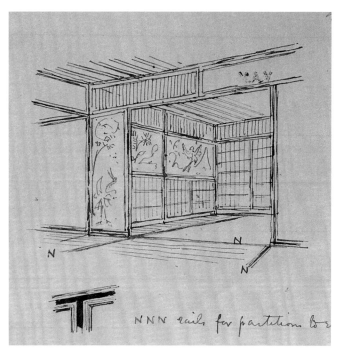

Fig. 7-2. E. W. Godwin. Sketch of a Japanese interior after an illustration in Aimé Humbert's *Le Japon illustré* (1870). Sketchbook. Pencil, pen and ink on paper; 9 x 6⅝ in. (22.9 x 16.8 cm). Trustees of the Victoria and Albert Museum, London, E.283-1963: 3.

Fig. 7-3. Drawing room in the home of
James McNeill Whistler, 7 Lindsey Row,
Chelsea, London. Photographed ca. 1865.
From Pennell and Pennell, *Whistler Journal*
(1921), facing p. 152.

I learned to love, its sense of design in every detail, was a
revelation to me . . . . For the first time I began to appreciate beauty, to observe, to feel the splendor of things, to
aspire!"[13]

Godwin's Oriental rugs were unusual for the time.
Although Oriental carpets began to be imported into England in large numbers by the 1840s and 1850s,[14] the most
popular form of floor covering was wall-to-wall carpeting
in bold patterns and vivid colors or rugs made by English
firms in imitation of Oriental examples. Godwin preferred
authentic Oriental carpets on bare wood floors, for he felt
that the floor should be "the quietest, most unobtrusive part
of the room."[15] He particularly admired the beautiful patterns and faded colors of second-hand rugs, commenting
that "it would have been next to impossible to have found
any Eastern fabric, especially a Turkey carpet, that would
not have been far too rich and bright, when *new*, for the
general tone, or scheme of colour adopted for the walls."[16]
William Morris had also begun purchasing Oriental rugs in
the 1860s and covered the floors of the Red House with
imported examples.[17] Charles Locke Eastlake also popularized their use in his *Hints on Household Taste* (1868), in which
he advised his readers to "chose the humblest type of
Turkey carpet or the cheapest hearthrug from Scinde and
be sure they will afford you more lasting eye-pleasure than
any English imitation."[18] By the 1870s the Oriental rug was
a prized work of art and an important ingredient in a fashionable interior.

What is certainly the most unusual aspect of Godwin's
interior design aesthetic, however, was his treatment of
walls. Strongly colored, boldly patterned wallpapers were
the most common form of wall decoration at this time.

Godwin, however, endorsed plain-colored walls or simple
wallpapers. He wrote of this preference in a series of articles on the decoration of his home in London: "My painting and papering—the 'decorations' as they are called—
have been carried out with a leaning, perhaps in excess,
towards lightness, and a simplicity almost amounting to
severity."[19]

Godwin's writings also provide evidence for his taste
in colors. In contrast to the popular enthusiasm for tertiary
colors that came as a reaction to the strong colors so prevalent in mid-nineteenth-century Victorian interiors, Godwin
preferred pure colors. He wrote of his preference for "certain yellows of a tone akin to old satin wood . . . light red
or Venetian red brightened by white and pure, or nearly
pure, white itself." He admitted, however, that he often had
"to assume a gloomier style" for his professional work, "for
the apostles of the tertiary creed, the devotees of madder,
brown, and terra verte."[20]

Although unusual, bare, painted walls in the 1860s
were not unique to Godwin. American expatriate painter
James McNeill Whistler also used this wall treatment in the
early 1860s in his rooms at 7 Lindsey Row, Chelsea (fig.
7-3). Whether Whistler knew of Godwin's Portland Square
scheme is not certain. The first recorded meeting of the two
men took place in 1863, a year after Godwin's decoration
of 21 Portland Square. Whatever the sequence of events,
Whistler's interior shared other design features with Godwin's Bristol house: bare wood floors covered with Oriental rugs; Chinese blue-and-white porcelain and Japanese
colored prints; eighteenth-century furniture; and a general
spacious and uncluttered quality.

Whistler and Godwin have both been credited with

Fig. 7-4. Drawing room in the home of Edward Linley Sambourne, 18 Stafford Terrace, London. Photographed ca. 1980. Courtesy of The Victorian Society.

starting a vogue for Oriental accessories in Great Britain and America that would turn into a mania in the 1870s and 1880s. Both men continued to design interiors with similar decorating schemes throughout their lifetimes, and they collaborated on a number of design projects, including the Butterfly Suite for the Paris Exposition Universelle of 1878 (see figs. 4-9 and 8-45). In the same year, Whistler would commission Godwin to build a studio house on Tite Street (see fig. 6-52).

London Chambers

In addition to plain painted walls, Godwin experimented with wallpapers in his chambers at 197 Albany Street in London in 1867.[21] Many of these papers were from Morris, Marshall, Faulkner and Company[22] and were also used in the interior of Rheinfelden, a house Godwin designed for Pickering Phipps in Northampton the same year.[23]

Godwin's green and white drawing room was decorated with a combination of patterned and floral Morris, Marshall, Faulkner and Company papers.[24] The walls were divided into three sections: the dado was papered with a small green diaper pattern (Morris "Diaper"); the main section was covered with a paper depicting branches of fruit (Morris "Fruit"); and the upper section, as well as the woodwork, was painted a creamy white. This division of the wall into separate areas was a novel approach, but a year later it was promoted by Eastlake as an alternative to the monotony of a single pattern extending from the skirting to the ceiling.[25] It would remain in fashion throughout the nineteenth century and into the first decade of the twentieth century.[26]

In 1872 Godwin repapered and repainted his flat. By then wallpaper manufacturers such as Jeffrey and Company had commissioned artists and architects, including William Burges, Owen Jones, and Godwin himself, to design two or three corresponding wallpapers for the same room. Some of these schemes were reproduced in *Art Furniture* (see fig. 10-7).[27]

Although Godwin designed many tripartite wallpaper schemes for the commercial market, he was never totally satisfied with them. He wrote of the general tendency of decorators "to indulge their customers not merely with two but with three papers—for dado, wall, and frieze—and the result is that we are so very much over-papered and over-patterned."[28] In his own dining room he simplified the wall scheme in 1872 by eliminating the wallpaper on the main section of the wall and replacing it with a creamy white distemper, to match the color of the ceiling. Japanese painted hangings were placed against the white walls. He also repapered the dado with a blue diagonal "H"-pattern wallpaper of his own design.

Another decorating device, possibly invented by Godwin, went hand in hand with the horizontal division of the walls into separate fields. He installed a shelf or ledge of wood around the upper part of the walls of the room. This shelf, which was used in each of the main rooms of Godwin's London flat, was "3½ inches broad and half an inch thick; the top of it had a moulding projecting altogether about 2 inches, with a groove on the top, so that it formed a ledge for brass dishes, plates &c."[29] It also served as a barrier between the main papered section of the wall and the top section. Artists Edward Linley Sambourne and James

McNeill Whistler would incorporate such a shelf in their drawing rooms in London in the mid-1870s. Both men collected porcelain and used this shelf in their drawing rooms to display some of the pieces from their collections (fig. 7-4).[30]

To balance the tripartite division of the decorative wall treatments, the floors in Albany Street were left bare. Godwin stained and varnished the floorboards and covered them with a combination of small floor coverings that included: "three Persian rugs, a large skin, and two pieces of Eastern matting."[31] He suggested that a wood border at least three feet deep be kept clear of floor coverings, favoring this treatment because of it was more hygienic and had an exotic appeal. To Godwin "fluff and dust . . . two of the great enemies of life" could be avoided if the carpets were "sufficiently small and free to be easily removed for beating."[32] This concern with health matters ensured that Godwin's treatment of floors would always remain minimal.

The drawing room was sparsely furnished. A sofa and several easy chairs were upholstered in a chintz floral pattern on a parchment-colored ground, which was also used for the curtains. A tall, Godwin-designed bookcase, a piano, two spindle-legged tables, four Japanese cane armchairs, two porcelain garden seats, and a few tall vases filled with plants completed the furnishings. The fenders and fire-irons were made of brass. A large circular mirror flanked by a pair of sconces hung over the mantel, and a series of smaller circular mirrors were on the walls.[33] This decorative use of mirrors, especially convex ones, became fashionable in France in the 1750s, reaching England by the last decade of the eighteenth century, and in the opening years of the nineteenth century, convex mirrors were considered the only acceptable type. The fashion was revived in the 1860s, and convex mirrors appeared throughout Godwin's home, including his green-and-yellow dining room.

In the dining room the dado was papered with the same green Morris "Diaper" that was used in the drawing room. The main section of the wall was covered with the Morris firm's "Trellis" wallpaper of roses and birds on a light-colored ground, and the woodwork was painted a dark green. The floor was stained and varnished, then covered with a faded secondhand Turkey carpet of square shape. The curtains were damask, adapted from a fifteenth-century–style design by A. W. N. Pugin and hung on small brass rings over a one-inch brass rod.[34] Godwin designed ebonized furniture for this room, including his classic sideboard (see fig. 4-1). Some ten years later he wrote of this design project:

When I came to the furniture I found that hardly anything could be bought ready made that was at all suitable to the requirements of the case. I therefore set to work and designed a lot of furniture, and, with a desire for economy, directed it to be made of deal, and to be ebonised. There were to be no mouldings, no ornamental metalwork, no carving. Such effect as I wanted I endeavoured to gain, as in economical building, by the mere grouping of solid and void and by a more or less broken outline. The scantling or substance of the framing and other parts of the furniture was reduced to as low a denomination as was compatible with soundness of construction. . . . All the furniture for the dining-room I designed specially, but I found deal to be a mistake, and had very soon to get rid of it, and have a new lot made of mahogany, also ebonised and decorated with a few gold lines in the panels.[35]

Godwin picked up the golden highlights of the furniture in the room's accessories, which included a large brass tray, yellow Chinese jars, yellowish green plates, and an embroidered yellow Chinese fabric.

In contrast to the elaborately decorated dining room, the bedroom was simply furnished with a plain brass bedstead, a double wardrobe, a washstand, a dressing table with mirror glass, a hanging bookcase, and some Sussex chairs. A large mirror glass flanked by sconces hung over the mantelpiece. The walls were covered with "a somewhat formal flower pattern on a white ground" and the dado with a "conventional meandering Italian paper in yellow."[36] The woodwork was painted a pale golden brown, and the floor was mostly bare except for a small rug at the side of the bed and two Eastern mats.

The Red House

Godwin's next recorded interior, dating from 1868–69, was the small two-story red brick house at Gustard Wood Common in Wheathampstead, Hertfordshire, where he lived with actress Ellen Terry and which he called the "Red House," the same name William Morris had given to a house Philip Webb built for him in 1860. A front elevation and plans for Godwin's red brick house survive in his sketchbooks, providing some idea of its appearance and furnishings (fig. 7-5).[37]

The first floor had five rooms. Room A, which seems to have been the sitting room, had a round table in front of the window, two chairs on either side of the mantelpiece, and a double-sided settee in the center of the room. A desk with a chair and an occasional table or chair were apparently the only other pieces of furniture. Curtains hung on

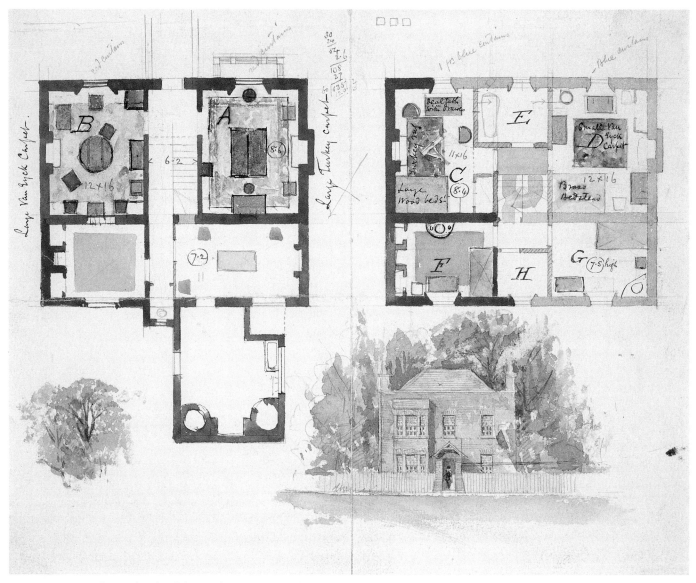

Fig. 7-5. E. W. Godwin. Sketch of the Red House, Gustard Wood Common, Wheathampstead, Hertfordshire, with floor plans showing the placement of furniture and carpets, ca. 1868. Watercolor, pencil, pen and ink; 10⅞ x 11⅛ in. (22.7 x 28.2 cm). Trustees of the Victoria and Albert Museum, London, E.273-1963. *Checklist no. 36*

the windows and a "Large Turkey Carpet" covered the floor. Room B, probably the dining room, had a large table in the middle of the room, a number of casually arranged chairs, and a storage cabinet. Red curtains hung on the windows and a "Large Van Eyck Carpet"[38] covered the bare wood floor. Ellen Terry recalled that: "the walls were painted pale yellow and the woodwork white; the furniture, designed by Edward, was slender and black."[39]

Godwin's choice of ebonized furniture was part of the general trend to blacken furniture that had begun in the first half of the nineteenth century with collectors who wanted to furnish their Romantic interiors with ebony furniture, which they believed to be of Tudor origin. This trend continued through the 1880s with the art fur-

niture movement. In 1868 the *Building News* commented on the manner of ebonizing furniture "by soaking a soft wood, such as poplar or lime, in a strong dye."[40] Ebonized furniture was also popularized by the availability of ebonized Regency furniture and the even earlier black-painted Sheraton fancy chairs in the London antique shops Godwin frequented.[41] Another stimulus was contemporary ebonized French furniture, particularly by cabinet makers such as Henri-Auguste Fourdinois.[42] These consciously historizing pieces, meant to evoke the great French tradition of *ébénisterie*, were exhibited at international exhibitions in London and Paris.

Oriental lacquer furniture also contributed to the promotion of ebonized furniture. Lacquer pieces were represented in Japanese prints, and actual black lacquer wares and woodwork were on view at the Japanese Court of the 1862 International Exhibition in London.[43] They were also available in the London shops that sold Oriental accessories in the 1860s and 1870s.

Despite the demand for ebonized furniture, Godwin recognized the shortcomings of overwhelming a room with black furniture. He wrote that if a room were to "look cheerful or even comfortable" the ebonizing must be restricted to a few pieces and these enlivened with "inlay of gold or ivory, or both."[44] To further relieve what he called the "funereal" look of ebonized furniture in these early interiors, Godwin decorated the first-story rooms of his house with a selection of Oriental accessories. Notes in his sketchbooks mention the purchase of "Japan Pictures" and "80 yds India matting 2 ft wide."[45] This matting may have covered some of the floors or the dado of one of the main rooms. The idea may have come from his friend Whistler, who already used it in his Chelsea home in 1866, where it harmonized with the color schemes of his rooms.

Godwin listed a great many other Oriental items in a ledger from 1868, including Japanese cabinets, a Chinese alabaster screen, Japanese blue plates, a blue Chinese table cover, and curtains for bookcases.[46] Godwin made these purchases from William Hewett and Company, William Wareham, and Farmer and Rogers's Oriental Warehouse, the major retailers of imported Chinese and Japanese objects and furnishings in London at this time.[47] In fact, there were so many Oriental accessories in the major rooms of this house that when a daughter was born to Ellen Terry and Godwin on December 9, 1869, Ellen Terry stated that "she looked as Japanese as everything which surrounded her" (see fig. 1-11).[48]

The second floor of the Red House had four austerely decorated bedrooms. Bedroom C had a large wood bedstead, a deal table with drawers, and two semicircular chairs. Blue curtains hung on the windows and a Turkey rug covered the floor. Bedroom D had a double brass bedstead with blue curtains and a "small Van Eyck Carpet." Bedroom F had a single bed, a washstand, a chair, a cabinet of some kind, and a square floor covering. Bedroom G had a single bed, a cabinet, an angled washstand, and a chair. No floor covering was indicated.

These minimally furnished bedrooms, which would become the standard formula for all Godwin's bedroom designs, gave primary consideration to issues of health and hygiene. Small carpets on otherwise bare wood floors allowed the floors to be easily scrubbed. They could be regularly removed and beaten. Brass bedsteads were also easy to clean, and they did not harbor insects. Other furniture, usu-

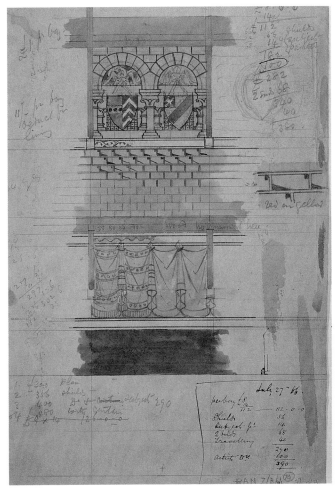

Fig. 7-6. E. W. Godwin. The Great Hall, Dromore Castle, County Limerick, Ireland: wall elevation, ca. 1867. Pencil and colored washes; 11 x 7⅞ in. (28 x 20 cm). British Architectural Library, Drawings Collection, RIBA, London, Ran 7/B/1 (79).

ally of a light-colored wood such as plain deal, would be limited to the barest of necessities so that the room would remain light, open, and spacious. To some of his critics these bedroom designs were "bare and cheerless."[49]

Dromore Castle

Godwin spent more than half of his working life as a Gothic Revival architect. This Gothic design tradition provided much of the inspiration for his numerous public and ecclesiastical commissions, as well as for his domestic house projects during the 1850s and 1860s. While living in the Red House, surrounded by a collection of Oriental objects, he designed Dromore Castle, a Gothic castle in County Limerick, Ireland (1867-73), for the third earl of Limerick

Fig. 7-7. E. W. Godwin. Design for curtain fabric for Dromore Castle, County Limerick, Ireland, ca. 1869–70. Pencil and colored washes; 7 x 10 in. (17.7 x 25.4 cm). British Architectural Library Drawings Collection, RIBA, London, Ran 7/B/1 (90). *Checklist no. 28*

(see fig. 6-32). Although Japanese design weighed heavily on Godwin's design sensibilities at this time, and thus a few Japanese design elements appeared at Dromore, the overall scheme of the interior leaned toward on medieval decoration in keeping with the castle's heavily fortified exterior. Godwin was involved with every detail, designing the furniture, fabrics, carpets, floor tiles, metalwork, stained glass, and painted wall decoration.

Many scholars tend to overstate the Japanese influence in Godwin's Dromore decoration; there were actually a great many other sources at work. Godwin was a consummate antiquary who studied Irish castles, English medieval churches, and illuminated manuscripts in the British Museum, London, and the Royal Irish Academy, Dublin, in addition to Japanese colored prints and woodcuts. Natural forms also appealed to Godwin, and his sketchbooks are full of sketches of plants, animals, and birds. These diverse sources were integrated into a unified design at Dromore.

One of the first drawings for the decoration of Dromore shows the Great Hall with a painted wall of curtains and shields in dark reds, browns, and golds (fig. 7-6).[50] The primary color scheme and choice of motifs, derived from medieval wall decoration, are reminiscent of Godwin's

Fig. 7-8. Isoda Koryu-sai. *Scenes on Six Tama Rivers: The Tama River at Ide*, eighteenth century. Woodblock; 30 x 9 in. (76.5 x 23 cm). National Museum, Tokyo.

1862 decorating scheme for the Council Chamber of Northampton Town Hall (see fig. 8-7). Another drawing, this one of a section of the staircase, shows two knights in medieval costume with horses approaching the castle.[51]

This same inspiration from medieval sources carries over to Godwin's designs for fabrics. Bold patterns of interlocking squares or diagonal stripes (fig. 7-7), golden disks, crossed or hatched lines, shields, and heraldic figures of lions and birds, which were found on the Limerick family coat of arms, provided the basic motifs. Inscriptions in the drawings for fabrics indicate that they were meant to be made in two major color schemes: red and black or the non-medieval combination of peach and gold,[52] an unusual choice for a castle that Godwin himself said was "founded on the Gothic of the latter part of the thirteenth or the beginning of the fourteenth century."[53] This combination of colors may be an indication of Japanese influence in the Dromore scheme, for it was a very common color palette in the Japanese color prints Godwin and his fellow Japonistes owned and studied in the 1860s (fig. 7-8). It is also an indication of the eclectic nature of Godwin's designs as he worked between two design traditions: the medieval and the Japanese. In the carpets, a similar Japanese-inspired color scheme was proposed, with peach and gold colors in a pattern of squares overlaid with disks and parallel lines (fig. 7-9).[54] This approach was continued in the ceiling decoration where Celtic interlacings and medieval disks in a peach and gold scheme were used.[55]

The proposed decoration of the dining room, suggested in a watercolor of the fireplace wall (see fig. 3-5),[56] reveals a mixture of Japanese and medieval sources again at work. The room was to be executed in peach and pale green, indicative of Japanese influence. The lower walls were to be painted pale sea green, above which a large painted frieze of figures represented the eight virtues of Temperance, Truth, Humility, Patience, Chastity, Charity, Liberality, and Industry and derived from Spenser's "Faerie Queene." These large-scale figures were to alternate with ovoid blue-and-white vases holding japanesque blossoming branches. The frieze was also to be punctuated by large ogival-shaped stained-glass windows with circular medallions filled with heraldic symbols that were clearly medieval in inspiration. The overriding architectural elements of ogival arches, sloped fireplace, plate-traceried windows, and painted wall decoration also point to medieval architectural traditions. A band of zig-zag lines and concentric circles derived from Irish manuscripts would separate the frieze from the lower part of the wall.[57] The actual frieze was begun by the painter Henry Stacy Marks, but was never completed because of problems created by the damp in the

Fig. 7-9. E. W. Godwin. Design for textiles for Dromore Castle, County Limerick, Ireland, ca. 1869–70. Pencil and colored washes on paper; 8½ x 6¹¹⁄₁₆ in. (21.5 x 17 cm). British Architectural Library Drawings Collection, RIBA, London, Ran 7/B/1 (91). *Checklist no. 29*

walls. Unlike the painted decoration, the stained-glass decoration was executed.

Another drawing of the dining room shows that the medieval flavor of the space extended to the furniture. The drawing represents a wall dominated by a massive sideboard executed in oak (see fig. 8-17).[58] Although this sideboard has the rectilinear outline of Godwin's Anglo-Japanese furniture, popularized in the 1870s, there are so many Gothic elements that the piece seems more medieval than Japanese in inspiration.[59] Medieval elements include the use of wainscot oak, the gabled canopy of the central portion with coat of arms, the tall floriated finials, and circular escutcheon with round pull handles of the type used in medieval furniture. A peacock sits on the pinnacle of the central gable. This has traditionally been attributed to Japanese influence in Godwin's work, but peacocks were also used in medieval times as a symbol of the resurrection. Although this motif would become a favorite of the Aes-

Fig. 7-10. E. W. Godwin. The drawing room fireplace, Dromore Castle. Photographed ca. 1940. Courtesy of Brendan Mc Mahon.

derived from medieval disks used to decorate fabrics in the fourteenth and fifteenth centuries. Viollet-le-Duc illustrated a canopy with the same pattern of disks taken from a medieval manuscript of the fifteenth century in his *Dictionnaire Raisonné*, which Godwin is known to have owned and even reviewed on its publication in England.[63]

The decoration of the drawing room was to be in a blue-and-green color scheme. A prominent frieze, composed of the figures of the four elements and the four winds alternating with flowering branches, was to encircle the room,[64] and a Japanese-inspired sun motif was to be painted above the fireplace. Although this wall decoration was never completed, the flat ceiling was painted with interlaced patterns based on Celtic ornament (see fig. 6-34). Heraldic shields decorated the mantelpiece (fig. 7-10), and plate-traceried windows were again set in pointed arches (fig. 7-11). Depictions of the twelve months of the year, derived from Spenser, filled the twelve roundels of stained glass that adorned the windows and encircled the room. Blue-and-white china ornamented the fireplace, part of the earl's large collection of Oriental porcelain, which was also displayed in the dining room.

A large suite of ebonized mahogany furniture de-

Fig. 7-11. E. W. Godwin. Design for wall decoration for the drawing room, Dromore Castle, County Limerick, ca. 1867. India ink, colored washes, pencil; 23¼ x 19³⁄₁₆ in. (59.1 x 48.7 cm). British Architectural Library Drawings Collection, RIBA, London, Ran 7/B/1 (80). *Checklist no. 21*

thetic movement, Godwin had already incorporated it into the pinnacle of the fireplaces in the Council Chamber of Northampton Town Hall in 1861 (see checklist, no. 10).

Other medievally inspired furnishings at Dromore included a set of sixteen oiled wainscot-oak chairs and two matching carvers with lion's head armrests, echoing the lion figure in the Limerick coat of arms (see fig. 8-15).[60] A pair of large refectory-style tables with baluster legs and planked tops occupied the middle of the dining room.[61] The chairs were upholstered "with cushions & backs of fine horsehair covered with common tanned uncoloured leather with stamped pattern in gold."[62] This gold-stamped pattern, traditionally ascribed to Japanese sources, is actually

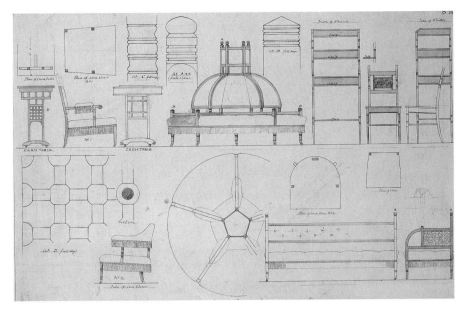

Fig. 7-12. E. W. Godwin. Designs for furniture for Dromore Castle, County Limerick, ca. 1869. Indian ink and brown wash; 12⅞ x 19¹¹⁄₁₆ in. (32.8 x 50 cm). British Architectural Library Drawings Collection, RIBA, London Ran 7/B/1 (53). *Checklist no. 23*

Fig. 7-13. E. W. Godwin. Design for a chess table for Dromore Castle, County Limerick, ca. 1869. Indian ink and colored washes; 13 x 19½ in. (33 x 49.5 cm). British Architectural Library Drawings Collection, RIBA, London, Ran 7/B/1 (55). *Checklist no. 22*

signed by Godwin filled the room (fig. 7-12). This suite included a chess table (fig. 7-13) with ebony and boxwood squares and Turkish lattice-type end panels, six "light chairs with plaited fine straw backs," a sofa with latticed panels at the ends, two armchairs with rounded backs, and a circular settee with receptacle for flowers in the center.[65] The sofa was a popular Godwin design that was put into general production by William Watt. Godwin himself owned one of these sofas, which is now in the Bristol Museums and Art Gallery.[66] Another surviving example (see fig. 3-9) may actually have belonged to the Dromore suite.

The upholstered pieces, including the sofa, were covered with "yellow satin in colour like that known in China as Imperial yellow."[67] The combination of "mahogany ebonized by penetrating stain and dry polished" and the yellow satin must have been an eye-catching, exotic display. Some of the Dromore furniture was made by the short-lived Art Furniture Company and by Reuben Burkitt of Wolverhampton, but the majority of the drawing room seating pieces were manufactured by William Watt.

Other plans of decoration for Dromore included a white and pale red scheme in the sitting room and blue-gray and pale yellow for one of the bedrooms on the first floor. Although Japanese color prints have been identified as the overriding influence in Godwin's selection of pale color schemes for the castle,[68] Godwin's study of thirteenth-century wall painting also provided prototypes for a pale color palette. In his "Sister Arts" lecture of 1864, Godwin spoke of the benefit of using faded colors in wall decoration and textiles. "In our interiors she [painting] would lead us to subdue the color of the walls and curtains, to note well those constant allusions to green . . . in the liberate rolls . . . . She would tell us . . . that green harmonizes with dark woods, and that purple is friendly inclined towards maple and the lighter woods. She might, perhaps, warn us . . . to guard against gold, white and the three primary

Fig. 7-14. E. W. Godwin. Dressing table, 1870. Made by Reuben Burkitt and Company, Wolverhampton. Pine with mirror glass and pewter fittings; 73⅝ x 59 x 18⅞ in. (187 x 150 x 48 cm). Musée d'Orsay, Paris, OAO 1280.

colors, and to use them like nature, with such wise economy that their great glory may be seen and known."[69]

Pale-colored oak and pine furniture was intended for the less formal rooms. A pair of pine dressing tables with large pivoting mirrors (fig. 7-14) is typical of the inventive yet austere furniture Godwin designed for the bedrooms.[70] With their stylized crenellated galleries at the top, paneled doors, and square escutcheons with round pull handles, these dressing tables resemble the other medievally inspired furniture Godwin designed for this extensive and important commission.

Fallows Green

From 1871 to 1873 Godwin worked on the design of a house for himself and Ellen Terry in Sun Lane, Harpenden, Herts. (see figs. 6-30 and 6-31). They named the three-story house, with a studio on the top floor, "Fallows Green."

Godwin designed it in "Old English" style, with a series of chimneystacks, a gabled, tiled roof, and timber framing. Surviving drawings (figs. 7-15, 7-16) reveal a vernacular Gothic-style interior with paneled doors; a mantelpiece with a circular hearth, inset convex mirror, and corbeled cornice; and a series of leaded-glass windows with circular medallion insets in the staircase.[71] Additional information comes from drawings and annotations in Godwin's sketchbooks for the years 1872 to 1874. Particularly informative are a rough drawing of a modest tiled fireplace annotated "Fallows Green fireplace" (fig. 7-17)[72] and a list of objects, some annotated "Harpenden," which were moved to his house in London at 20 Taviton Street, Gordon Square, in 1874.[73] At that time, Godwin transported a chest of drawers, brass fenders and fire irons, a clock, a brown sheepskin rug, a red chair, two black hanging bookcases filled with books, and an old library table from Fallows Green to Taviton Street.

What is particularly significant about this list is the inclusion of the hanging bookcases, one of which may be

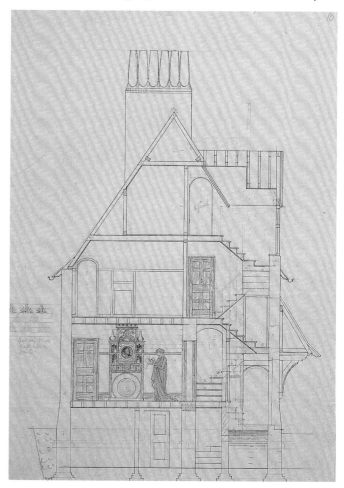

Fig. 7-15. E. W. Godwin. Fallows Green, Harpenden, Herts.: section, ca. 1869. India ink, colored washes and pencil details; 14 x 10 in. (35.5 x 25.5 cm). British Architectural Library Drawings Collection, RIBA, London, Ran 7/L/5 (10).

Fig. 7-16. E. W. Godwin. Fallows Green, Harpenden, Herts.: design for windows, ca. 1869. India ink, colored washes, and pencil details; 14 x 10 in. (35.5 x 25.5 cm). British Architectural Library Drawings Collection, RIBA, London, Ran 7/L/5 (14).

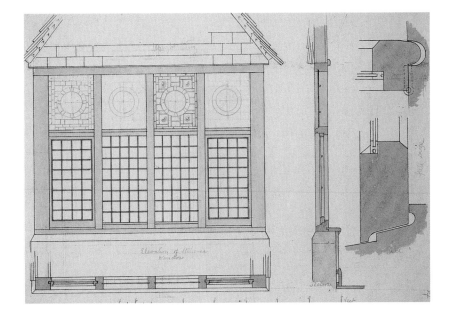

the ebonized hanging bookcase with stenciled gilt *mon*, originally in Godwin's possession and now in the Bristol Museums and Art Gallery.[74] Numerous examples are also in private collections (see fig. 8-27). Its inclusion among his possessions indicates Godwin's continuing taste for ebonized furniture, a taste that had first become evident in the furnishings of his London chambers in Albany Street in 1867.

Furthermore, a note in one of Godwin's sketchbooks provides us with some clues about the wallpapers used at Fallows Green. It mentions "6 pieces Blue Pomegranate. Dining room. Light Trellis-Staircase."[75] These were again probably from the firm of Morris, Marshall, Faulkner and Company, which was producing wallcoverings with these names in the 1860s.[76]

Taviton Street

Godwin's interior at 20 Taviton Street, Gordon Square, London, is the best documented of his own houses. His sketchbooks abound with notes and rough sketches for this interior. In addition, he penned a series of six articles published in 1876 in the *Architect*, entitled "My House 'In' London," that provide us with detailed descriptions of his rooms in this house.[77]

The interiors were sparsely decorated, for Godwin believed that "abundance of light, air, and cleanliness" were the primary objectives in a decorative scheme.[78] This concern with hygienic considerations was part of a general sanitary health movement prevalent in Victorian England that linked the environment to the transmission of disease. Standards of cleanliness for the urban home were outlined in publications and in educational classes aimed at the architect and even the housewife.[79]

Godwin's hall had bare wood floors that were oiled

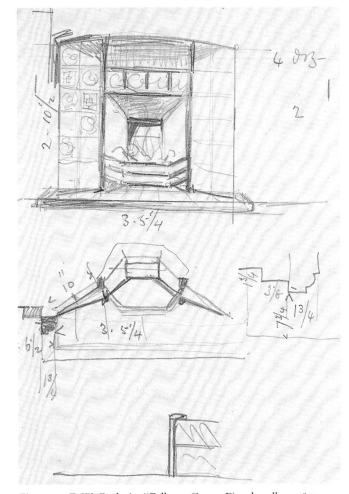

Fig. 7-17. E. W. Godwin. "Fallows Green Fireplace," ca. 1871–72. Sketchbook. Pencil; 5 ⅝ x 3 ¼ in. (14.4 x 8.2 cm). Trustees of the Victoria and Albert Museum, London, E.234-1963: 72.

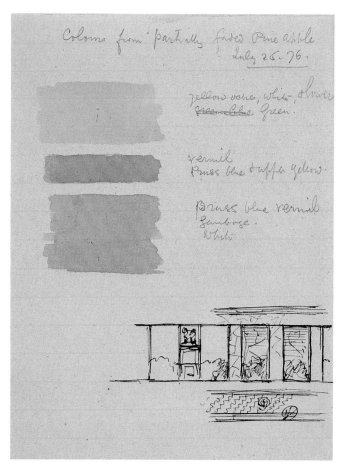

Fig. 7-18. E. W. Godwin. Color samples for a wall decoration, dated July 26, 1876. Sketchbook. India ink, colored washes, and pencil details; 6¼ x 4 in. (15.8 x 10.2 cm). Trustees of the Victoria and Albert Museum, London, E.233-1963: 37.

and waxed. A thick square rug lay in the middle of the outer hall. Another rug of Eastern origin was in the inner hall before the dining room. There were two mats at the front door entry. The main section or filling of the wall was distempered a vellum color. This method of painting was done with "pigments tempered with gum, or size, mixed with pipe-clay, whitening or some similar substance and used with a water medium." Distempering produced a clean surface that was cheaper than wallpaper and could be easily cleaned when the walls became dirty. The mixing of the colors, however, required some expertise because they tended to lighten in tone after drying.[80] A molded wooden chair rail separated dado from filling. A decorative frieze of stenciled umber- and vellum-colored diagonal lines demarcated dado from filling. The woodwork was painted a light red color. The staircase had a polished oak handrail, light red painted balusters, and treads inlaid with patterned lead. A white marble mantelpiece with a Sienna vein was in the

hallway. Godwin's red scheme of decoration for the hallway reflected his interest in the classical world, particularly the wall paintings at Pompeii. To this red scheme Godwin added a mirror glass with side brackets and a molded shelf for the display of blue-and-white china. Brass accents took the form of fender, fire irons, and grate for the fireplace, a brass chandelier, and a selection of brass trays. A double pair of Tunis curtains separated the inner and outer sections of the hall. Two side tables, two stands for flowering plants, and two wicker armchairs completed the decoration.[81]

As he had in the 1860s Godwin based the decoration of the drawing room on pure colors, an arrangement of well-designed furniture, and a few carefully selected accessories. He described the effect he wished to achieve as "ultra-refined" with "delicate tones of colour which form the background to the few but unquestionable gems in this exquisitely sensitive room."[82]

A drawing in Godwin's sketchbooks annotated "Colours from partially faded Pineapple" shows the distinctive yellow and green color scheme (fig. 7-18).[83] In contrast with the "cold and light" decoration of the typical drawing room with "satin paper and a general tone of bluish white," Godwin devised a scheme that was both warm and pleasant.[84] The woodwork, including the dado, was painted a dark yellow with white, blue, and vermillion accents blended into its yellow ocher base. Painted birds, among them peacocks, eagles, and pheasants, set against thick foliage and a blue sky, graced the walls. The pilasters separating the bird panels were painted a pale gray-green and hung with sconces with candle arms. The floor was covered with Indian matting over which rugs were placed. The curtains were of a straw-colored silk with amber and pale green embroidery.

The furniture included two low-backed sofas placed on either side of the mantel and three easy chairs, which Godwin advises us had "movable seats, so that there is no difficulty whatever in keeping the crevices free from dust." Three small coffee tables, one long cabinet, and an overmantel were made of "honduras mahogany, inlaid with ivory and panelled with cedar wood, carved in low relief." Godwin also informs us that he had a piano specially designed for this room, as well as brass fenders and fire dogs which "slope in curved section upwards and inwards."[85]

At the back of the drawing room, against the walls, Godwin placed sofas, which he called "lounges," and a few basket chairs. Lightweight easels of different woods displayed drawings and paintings in the center of the room. Large vases of flowers and plants stood in front of the windows. There was ample walking space in the room, avoiding the prevalent shortcoming of most drawing rooms of the middle classes, who "fill up their drawing-room with furniture and knicknacks until a short-sighted person is placed in constant peril."[86]

Godwin wanted his dining room to be "cheerful and bright" unlike the usually gloomy dining room with crimson-and-gold patterned wallpaper with matching curtains, heavy Turkey carpets, and dark massive pieces of furniture. Instead he chose a yellow and blue color scheme, with woodwork and dado painted a deep blue, and the Adam-style plastered ceiling and the cove left white. The lower part of the wall was painted yellow, reddish brown, and ivory white. The upper part of the wall was painted with figures representing the labors of the months, in relation to food and drink in the medieval tradition. These were set against a yellow background. Plain yellow Indian matting covered the floor, and an Indian carpet was laid over it in the center of the room. Two smaller carpets were placed in front of the hearth and at the sideboard, the two main pieces of cabinetwork which dominated the room.[87]

All the dining-room furniture, with the exception of the overmantel, was executed in Spanish mahogany with brass inlays. The overmantel was painted blue to harmonize with the blue woodwork of the room and had a central panel of silvered glass. It was flanked by a pair of low bookcases. The dining table was square and could be extended with leaves. It was usually covered with a cloth to the floor, concealing its plain legs. The dining chairs, which were circular in shape with open arms, cane seats, and movable leather cushions, were probably the Old Jacobean or English model illustrated in William Watt's catalogue (see fig. 8-18). The leather seat cushions, popular at this time, were also extremely practical because they could be easily cleaned and did not retain food and tobacco smells. Two large vases, one holding a fern, the other a palm, stood in the large windows. Although incorporating plants in the Victorian drawing room was common, potted ivy in particular, Godwin's placing of palms in Oriental vases in front of the windows prefigured a prominent feature of Aesthetic interiors[88] and matched the desire for increased sunlight in the home.

An appreciation of sunlight also led Godwin to simpler and lighter curtain treatments. He disliked the custom of "looping their window curtains instead of letting them hang straight."[89] Thus, the curtains for the doors and windows of Godwin's dining room, made of plain, brownish yellow linen, embroidered with bands of blue and yellow needlework, hung straight down in modest folds from thin brass rods of three-quarter-inch diameter.[90] Such simple window treatments would become one of the hallmarks of the Aesthetic interior.

Consistent with his other interior design commis-

sions, the bedrooms were the most austerely decorated of all of Godwin's rooms. He believed that bedrooms should be minimally furnished, reflecting their primary function as a place for repose and sleep. He rejected the more common nineteenth-century understanding of a bedroom "as a private sitting-room with a bed in it."[91] His more austere interpretation called for pale yellow color schemes, light-colored furniture, and brass bedsteads. The woodwork was distempered a whitish yellow and the walls a dark golden yellow to give the room a sunny appearance. Plain, painted walls, according to Godwin, did not "distract the tired or sick brain" and were the cheapest way to redecorate a bedroom, especially in times of sickness. The windows were covered with brown blinds and linen curtains of a brownish yellow "just full enough to hold slight folds when drawn out." In addition to linen for curtains, cretonne and chintz were also acceptable to Godwin, since they could be washed. With the exception of three small scatter rugs, placed on either side of the bed and before the hearth, and two small pieces of matting, situated before the washstand and the dressing table, the bare wood floors were left largely uncovered so that they could be easily scrubbed.

Godwin specified plain wood, preferably deal, birch, or ash, for the bedroom wardrobe and chest of drawers. The dressing table stand and washstand were not meant to be oiled or varnished so that they could be easily scrubbed, while the wardrobe and chest of drawers, which were not subject to the same wear, should be oiled or polished. The case pieces were raised between eight and nine inches from the floor and mounted on castors for easy cleaning and flexibility of arrangement.

Seating furniture consisted of a cane couch and two cane chairs. In contrast most bedrooms were filled with overupholstered sofas and easy chairs, which Godwin saw as assuming "an almost tyrannical position." Accessories were limited to a toilet set of light red earthenware glazed white inside, and blue-and-white vases filled with dried flowers for the mantelpiece, above which a single picture was hung.

The same austere style of decorating applied to the nursery on the top floor. Godwin rallied against the idea of it being a "show-room"[92] and encouraged the adoption of plain, hygienic furnishings. Cribs and cots should be of unadorned natural wicker; elaborate trimmings and fabrics would catch dust and all the other impurities in the polluted London air. Nursery cabinetwork was designed with a lower shelf at least nine inches from the floor and was mounted on castors.

In spite of this minimalist approach, Godwin recognized the importance of bright colors and pleasant furniture and accessories in the nursery to stimulate a child's intellect. He called this room "the first school in this life, and the eyes of its little inmates are among the first leading channels of unconscious instruction or experience."[93] Safety in the nursery was also an important issue, and Godwin suggested plain white deal furniture with rounded corners and squared-off legs to prevent injury. To engage a young mind, colored plates taken from Walter Crane's children's books or illustrations from other books for youngsters might be framed on the walls, inserted in the panels of the furniture, or reproduced in tiles around the mantelpiece. Godwin even suggested rotating the framed pictures to keep a child's interest. The art of Japan might even penetrate the nursery, with a few fans placed along the walls.

Collinson and Lock: The McLaren Commission

Godwin's interiors and the accompanying furnishings that he designed in the early 1870s for two large commissions

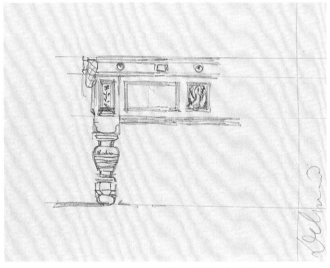

Fig. 7-19. E. W. Godwin. Design for a billiard table, ca. 1873. Sketchbook. Pencil on paper; 3¼ x 5⅝ in. (8.2 x 14.4 cm). Trustees of the Victoria and Albert Museum, London, E.234-1963: 18.

for the London firm of Collinson and Lock are far more elaborate than his own spaces, reflecting the showier taste of his commercial clients. The first commission was for the interior of 69 Addison Road, Kensington, London, for John Wingate McLaren in 1873.[94] Godwin's diaries and ledgers for that year reveal that he designed at least seven pieces of furniture, including an easy armchair,[95] a lady's chair, a music cabinet, a low cabinet for the drawing-room, a drawing room table, a mantelpiece, and a billiard table.[96] Although none of this furniture has come to light, notes describing the billiard room, including decoration of the ceiling and windows, are found in Godwin's sketchbooks, where a drawing of the billiard table indicates heavy cup-and-cover legs, adorned with decorative side panels with floral and Japanese sparrow motifs (fig. 7-19).[97] The attention given to the decoration of the billiard room was not unusual for this time, for this special room had become one of the most important new spaces in the homes of the rich in the 1870s and 1880s.[98]

Godwin also designed a decorative cove for the conservatory of the McLaren house, another fashionable new room common in houses of the 1870s and 1880s.[99] Godwin envisioned this room, for which a signed and dated sketch still exists, with a peach color scheme and Japanese sparrows and stylized lilies (fig. 7-20).[100] He also worked on lighting fixtures for this commission, including: "Chandelier very light . . . Branch candle lights" and accessories.[101]

An unidentified sketch of a drawing room signed "E. W. G." and dated September 1873 (fig. 7-21) may have been made for this commission.[102] That Godwin worked on a drawing-room scheme for the McLaren commission is confirmed by a letter he sent to George Lock, dated September 17, 1873: "I sent you drawings including one of the Decorative Schemes for McLarens drawing room—if the Dado & main wall space are to be papers in stock you cd use as you suggest the Element papers below & the upper might be made with a frieze paper hung diagonally."[103] The furniture represented in this sketch also matches items

Fig. 7-20. E. W. Godwin. "Decoration for Cove in Conservatory—McLaren," 1873. Pencil and body color on tracing paper; 11⅜ x 28¾ in. (28.9 x 73 cm). Trustees of the Victoria and Albert Museum, London, E.511-1963.

ordered for this commission: easy chair, occasional table, cabinet, chandelier, mantel, and fireplace grate.[104]

Moreover, Godwin designed an "art panel" depicting a girl gathering roses for the mantelpiece of the drawing room. This is particularly significant since the sketch is inscribed: "The whole room is suggested by the Garden in the 'Romance of the Rose' therefore artists engaged in panels etc to be referred to Chaucer's poem."[105] Closer examination of this sketch reveals that it is for the mantelpiece wall, which is divided into four main sections: upper frieze or cove, lower frieze, filling, and dado. In the Godwin scheme the upper frieze has nearly square panels filled in with "a gold burnished sun in relief on vellum ground with blue centres." A triple band of gold woodwork separated upper and lower frieze. The lower frieze was composed of rectangular panels outlined in gold and filled with scrolling foliage in "raised plaster work painted pale copper red on gold ground" around circular forms. A triple line of gold, vellum, and blue with a gold rod to hang pictures with black hooks demarcated the lower frieze from the filling. The main section of the wall was composed of a series of diagonal foliate scrolls making "gold & black patterns on dark vellum ground." The chair rail was made of "burnished gold panel[s] with red or black ornament" interspersed with mirrors and lettering taken from Chaucer's "Romaunt of the Rose." Another triple band of woodwork made of rosewood, ivory, and black separated chair rail from dado. The dado was composed of a series of panels, some filled with flowers, such as daisies and narcissus, and others with lattice. The skirting board was a double band of rosewood and gold. This elaborate design for a drawing room was typical of the many complicated decorative schemes favored by Aesthetic designers of this period.

Other decorative works for the McLaren residence included the design of the drawing-room ceiling, wall decoration for numerous rooms, a sunflower frieze for an unidentified room, three fireplace panels for one mantel, two fireplace panels for another, and a selection of appropriate wallpapers.[106]

Collinson and Lock: Grey Towers

The second large Collinson and Lock commission was for Grey Towers (fig. 7-22), recently identified by Ian Dungavell as a large Gothic Revival house in Nunthorpe, south of Middlesbrough, built for William Randolph Innes Hopkins, the mayor of Middlesbrough from 1866 to 1868.[107] Six years after the building was completed, Hopkins commissioned the London decorating firm of Collinson and Lock to redecorate the interior, and Godwin worked on the project from April 1873 to July 1874, designing more than twenty-

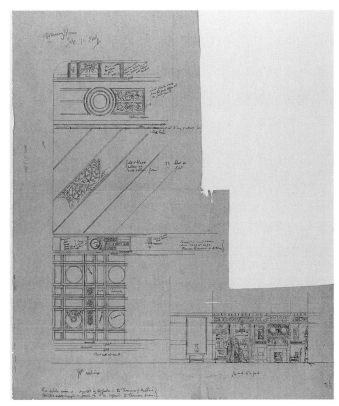

Fig. 7-21. E. W. Godwin. Scheme of decoration for a drawing room, inspired by Chaucer's "Romance of the Rose," ca. 1873–76. Pen and ink on tracing paper; 24⅜ x 19⅝ in. (62.0 x 50.0 cm). Trustees of the Victoria and Albert Museum, London, AAD 4/16 - 1988. *Checklist no. 52*

five pieces of furniture and extensive wall and ceiling decorations. An entry in his diary of April 1873 mentions "designs for house in Yorkshire,"[108] and a month later his assistant wrote, "Parcel of designs (Grey Towers decn) from Mr. G for C & L. Traced same."[109] Godwin's cash books for this month indicate that this parcel included designs for five separate rooms, two ceilings, and what he called powderings.[110] By June he was working on the drawing room, planning its general arrangement as well as specific pieces of furniture, including a cabinet and mantel.[111]

In September Godwin designed a mantel, chandelier, sofa, "pan cabinet," and easy chair.[112] In October he produced armchairs and an animal case and, in November, more armchairs, valance and wood cornice, music cabinet, occasional table, enamel-tile cabinet, glass for the drawing-room windows, angle cabinet with panels illustrating the seasons, and a series of four art panels also with the "seasons" theme.[113] In January he recorded an order for a table and made sketches for bedroom furniture.[114] The next entries are from April; these are for a coffee table, lady's

Fig. 7-22. John Ross. Grey Towers, Nunthorpe, Middlesbrough, Cleveland. Built 1865–67. Photographed in 1994. Long empty, the house was recently discovered to have had a Godwin-designed interior. National Monuments Record.

Fig. 7-23. Remains of the wall decoration designed by Godwin in 1874 for the entrance hall, Grey Towers. Photographed in 1993.

Fig. 7-24. A fragment of wall decoration, designed by Godwin in 1874, in a first-floor bedroom, Grey Towers. Photographed in 1993.

table, hanging cabinet, footstool, and chair.[115] The last entry, for a handle and lock plate, appears in July.[116]

Grey Towers still stands, albeit in a ruined state, but patches of the wall decoration give an idea of Godwin's intentions.[117] The decorations, mostly stenciled, show Godwin working in the popular Anglo-Japanese style. The entrance hall decoration is comprised of a stenciled pattern of powderings featuring a stylized bamboo leaf and rose medallions in the filling of the wall (fig. 7-23). A border of diagonal shapes forms the chair rail above the plain dado. The two-story Great Hall with large staircase reveals a stenciled dado featuring lattice decoration in red and pale blue with circular *mon* (crests) placed at the intersections. The frieze consists of red and yellow floral *mon* along a green vine on a white ground. As the staircase continues to the first-floor landing, this frieze becomes the dado and the main part of the wall is then decorated with red dragons on a yellow ground.

In the dining room the filling of the wall was covered with a plain earth-toned paper, and a purplish dado surmounted by a pattern of a "cockerel's comb set within a stylized bird's eye form."[118] It is banded by a line of yellow and then a line in a deep earth tone. This simple yet decorative treatment was probably a compromise between the highly patterned rooms that were becoming popular at this time and the more austere decoration that Godwin favored and displayed in his own interiors.

The decoration of the bedrooms also reveals a more restrained treatment. The walls were covered with a simple muted pattern and a stenciled border. The best preserved of the bedrooms was painted with a muted pale orange and mottled texture, with a frieze of flowers with three petals bordered by an orange ribbon (fig. 7-24).

The most elaborate decorative ensemble was used in the drawing room, the most formal room in a house at this time. The connecting anteroom had roundels with gilded peacocks (fig. 7-25), while the drawing room had a corresponding stenciling with peacocks alternating with five-petaled white flowers on a blue ground within a gilded lattice design. Godwin would produce a similar scheme in his designs for wall and ceiling decoration illustrated in Watt's *Art Furniture* catalogue of 1877 (fig. 7-26). The dado of the drawing room was composed of rectangular panels of light green, bordered by a light yellow band with symmetrically placed, petaled *mon*.

To relate to the Anglo-Japanese wall decoration for Grey Towers, Godwin designed furniture of Japanese inspiration. Two sketches for Japanese-style coffee tables, annotated "Grey Towers" in Godwin's hand, are in the Victoria and Albert Museum (fig. 7-27).[119] One table has an open lattice decoration, a low shelf, and a rounded top, and the other is smaller, with a cabinet section fronted by sliding doors, a low shelf, and flattened top. Both tables were two feet, four inches high, with thin, squared legs, angled struts, and delicate inlay work.

Other drawings in Godwin's sketchbooks for furniture

Fig. 7-25. A fragment of wallpaper with peacocks, designed by Godwin in 1874 for the drawing room at Grey Towers. Photographed in 1993.

Fig. 7-26. E. W. Godwin. "Wall Decoration and Frieze. Ceiling Decoration." From William Watt, *Art Furniture* (1877), pl. 14. The Mitchell Wolfson Jr. Collection, The Wolfsonian-Florida International University, Miami Beach, Florida, TD 1990.40.62.

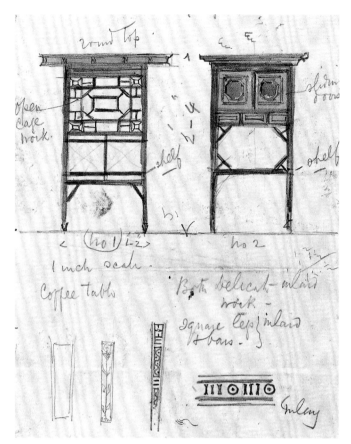

Fig. 7-27. E. W. Godwin. Design for coffee tables for Grey Towers. 1874. Pencil and colored washes; 8 x 5 in. (20.3 x 12.6 cm). Trustees of the Victoria and Albert Museum, London, E.487-1963.

Fig. 7-28. E. W. Godwin. The Virtues, ca. 1867. From "Figures designed for wall paintings at Dromore Castle," *Architect* (London) 7 (8 June 1872): 300 and illus.

Fig. 7-29. E. W. Godwin. The figure of "Liberality," part of the mural at the top of the Grand Staircase, Midland Grand Hotel (now the Saint Pancras Chambers), London, 1877. Photographed after restoration in 1995.

from this commission reveal bold outlines and Oriental-inspired cornices reminiscent of his Anglo-Japanese pieces of the late 1860s.[120] In contrast to his earlier furniture designs, however, these pieces have fuller proportions and make a greater use of curving lines, as can be seen in the aggressive sweep of the top surface of the corner cabinet with its arched rib forms. This enlargement of proportions was probably the result of the greater scale of the Grey Towers rooms.

The Midland Grand Hotel

Godwin continued to work in the Anglo-Japanese style of decoration through the 1870s. In 1877, however, he also revived the Gothic-style painted figural decoration that he had proposed for the dining room at Dromore Castle. He intended it this time for the vaulted ceiling decoration of the grand staircase of the Midland Grand Hotel (now called Saint Pancras Chambers) in London.[121] Originally designed by Sir George Gilbert Scott in 1867, this important building was owned by the Midland Railway Company whose trains ran into the adjacent terminus. The firm of Gillow and Company would provide much of the furnishing and decoration, and they employed Godwin to design ceiling decoration. His ledger books indicate that he visited the hotel on January 10, 1877, for a consulting fee of £5.5s.0d, and on January 12 he sent Gillow's a "roll of cartoons as agreed," for £50.0s.0d. and four heads, two borders, and a shield, which were sent on January 16 for the sum of £8.8s.0d.[122] The decorations have recently been restored. The team working on them has credited them to Gillow and Company but erroneously ascribes their design to Andrew Benjamin Donaldson.[123] The scheme is a reworking of the "eight virtues" frieze that Godwin and Henry Stacy Marks had originally designed in 1867 for Dromore Castle. The sketches for Dromore (fig. 7-28) are almost identical to the restored decoration at the Midland Grand Hotel (fig. 7-29). Not only has Godwin reproduced the figures of the virtues, but he has included the same japaneseque fruit trees, dragon, and radiating sun motifs. He has also reproduced a heraldic shield motif from the Dromore commission, replacing the beasts and emblems of the Limerick family with the appropriate arms of the cities served by the Midland Railway and the Wyvern, the heraldic beast that was the symbol of the Midland Railway (fig. 7-30).[124] In keeping with the Gothic-Revival interior, a border of medieval disks ran along the bottom of the figural representations.

The Butterfly Suite

Godwin returned to his more overtly Japanese style with an 1877 commission from William Watt to design a group of Anglo-Japanese furniture and Watt's stand at the Exposition Universelle in Paris in 1878 (see fig. 4-9). Godwin asked Whistler to collaborate with decorative painting, and the result was the Butterfly Suite. The austere stand was predominantly decorated in tones of yellow, prompting Whistler to call the group a "Harmony in Yellow and Gold," by which the suite is also known. Whistler painted the lower half of the dado of the stand with a cloud motif and the rectangular panels of the upper section with scattered chrysanthemum petals and butterflies on a yellow ground. The dado and wall were separated by a cluster of peacock feathers on a gold-painted wall. The same painted decoration was continued on the back shelves of the combined cabinet-and-fireplace which was the central feature of the display.

Fig. 7-30. E. W. Godwin. The heraldic shield and Wyvern, part of Godwin's design for mural decoration, Midland Grand Hotel (now the Saint Pancras Chambers), London, 1877. Photographed during restoration in 1995.

A detailed description of the suite, given in the *New York Tribune*, reveals the other components of the decoration:

> Against a yellow wall is built up a chimney-piece and cabinet in one; of which the wood, like all the wood in the room, is a curiously light yellow mahogany . . . . The fireplace is flush with the front of the cabinet; the front panelled in gilt bars below the shelf and the cornice, inclosing tiles of pale sulphur; above the shelf a cupboard with clear glass and triangular open niches at either side, holding bits of Kaga porcelain, chosen for the yellowishness of the red, which is characteristic of that ware; the frame of the grate brass; the rails in polished steel; the fender the same. Yellow on yellow, gold on gold everywhere. The peacock reappears, the eyes and the

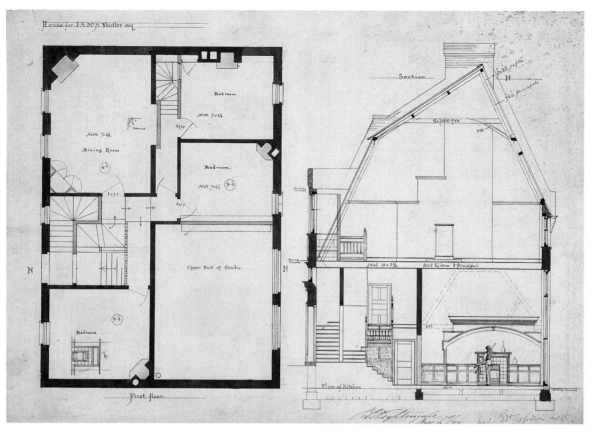

Fig. 7-31. E. W. Godwin. The White House, 35 Tite Street, Chelsea, London: first-floor plan and section, 1877. Pen and ink, watercolor, and pencil; 15¼ x 21¾ in. (38.7 x 55.4 cm). Trustees of the Victoria and Albert Museum, London, E.542-1963. *Checklist no. 84*

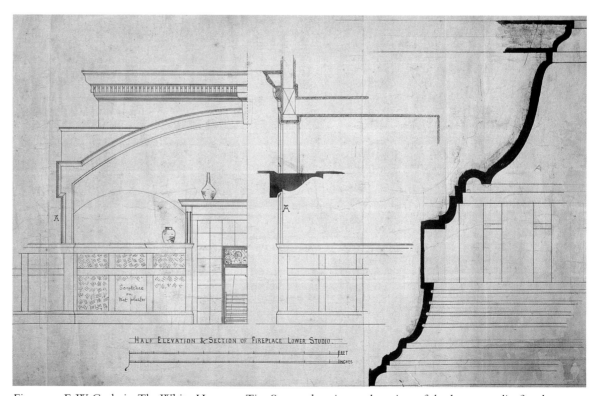

Fig. 7-32. E. W. Godwin. The White House 35 Tite Street: elevation and section of the lower-studio fireplace, 1878. Pen and ink, watercolor and pencil; 14⅞ x 22⅞ in. (37.8 x 58 cm). Trustees of the Victoria and Albert Museum, London, E.543-1963 (recto).

breast-feathers of him; . . . here the feather is all gold, boldly and softly laid on a gold-tinted wall. The feet to the table legs are tipped with brass, and rest on a yellowish brown velvet rug. Chairs and sofas are covered with yellow, pure rich yellow velvet, darker in shade than the yellow of the wall and edged with yellow fringe. The framework of the sofa has a hint of the Japanese which faintly, but only faintly, suggests itself all through the room.[125]

Although the reporter from New York thought that Japanese influence was only faintly suggested, many of the room's chief features were derived from Oriental design. Its yellow color scheme, display of Kaga porcelain, elegant rectilinear furniture, and painted decoration of peacock feathers, cloud motifs, and chrysanthemum petals were all expressive of Godwin and Whistler's joint knowledge of Japanese decorative arts. The ensemble was one of the most discussed and controversial exhibits, reinforcing the rage for Japanese decorative arts that was becoming a mania in Great Britain and America.

The White House

The Butterfly Suite may have provided some of the design concepts used in Whistler's new house, known as the White House, on Tite Street in London, which Godwin designed in 1877–78 (fig. 7-31 and see fig. 6-52).[126] Although this residence no longer exists and no photographs from Whistler's brief occupancy of the house appear to have survived, some of the architectural details gleaned from drawings in the Victoria and Albert Museum suggest a house with Japanese-inspired interiors. A half elevation and section of the fireplace in the ground floor studio, dated October 24, 1878, shows a mantelpiece contained within a low arch, which is crowned by a Greek cornice creating a shallow inglenook (fig. 7-32).[127] This drawing also reveals that the lower section of the wall had paneled woodwork or shelves upon which Whistler's collection of blue-and-white china was probably displayed. The back panels of these shelves were treated with "scratches on wet plaster" to emulate Chinese matting or plaited rattan. The fireplace grate was decorated with circular *mon* of the type that Thomas Jeckyll designed for the firm of Barnard, Bishop and Barnard of Norwich. That Godwin used Jeckyll's Anglo-Japanese grates for this room is confirmed in a letter from Whistler to Godwin, dated March 22, 1878, in which Whistler asks Godwin to visit the builder about "the Jeckyll stoves for the rooms. Some of them have come and he doesn't know where they are to go."[128] Another drawing of an elevation with a section of the ground floor specifies that the staircase was made

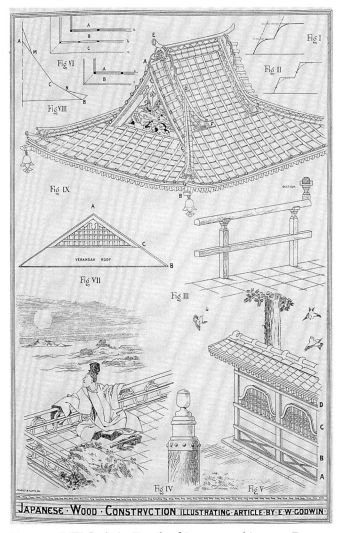

Fig. 7-33. E. W. Godwin. Details of Japanese architecture. From Godwin, "Japanese Wood Construction" (12 February 1875): 189.

of latticework sections with a newel post inlaid with a band of ivory.[129] Similar forms, derived from Japanese architecture, were reproduced by Godwin in "Japanese Wood Construction," a series of articles he wrote in 1875 (fig. 7-33).[130]

A drawing of the dining room shows a mantelpiece and cabinet designed by Godwin (fig. 7-34).[131] The mantelpiece is similar to that for the studio, with rows of square tiles, a Greek dentilated cornice, and a surround of rectangular panels. An unusual design element here is the insertion of rectangular glass panels at the top sides of the mantel. The overmantel was composed of a mirror with a matching Greek cornice, surmounted by a cabinet with two niches for the display of porcelain. In overall form the mantelpiece resembles the Butterfly Suite of 1877–78. In addition, a drawing for a built-in hanging cupboard with surrounding shelves also exists (fig. 7-35).[132] It exhibits the same rectilinear outline, play of solid and void, and paneled doors of the ebonized sideboard of 1867.

The color schemes and other furnishings for the White House can be reconstructed from the memories of visitors, one of whom recalled that a color scheme similar to that of the Butterfly Suite was incorporated in Whistler's drawing room: "... I found myself in a large terra cotta coloured room with white woodwork very plainly furnished and very unused .... The furniture consisted of a table and some large low chairs and a couch, covered to the ground in terra cotta serge. I had expected to find the furniture very severe in design, but to my surprise found no designs at all save what was necessary for comfort."[133] A drawing in one of Godwin's sketchbooks in the Victoria and Albert Museum indicates that the table mentioned may have been of a hexagonal shape.[134]

Another visitor, the painter Edwin Austin Abbey, also commented on the decoration of the drawing room: "His house ... is queer on the inside ... you tumble down about six steps into a large low-ceilinged room ... Here is matting on the floor and many cosy chairs, and a big table, an alcove with a big fireplace; at the end a piano, and over it Whistler's great portrait of Irving as Philip II. On the walls are framed proofs of Whistler's etchings."[135]

A lengthy description by Mrs. Julian Hawthorne, a reporter for *Harper's Bazaar*, gives us some idea of the decoration and furnishing of the studio and the dining room: "The walls of the studio were colored a sort of gray flesh tint—a singularly cold and unsympathetic

hue."[136] In another room, "there was no other color beside yellow. But it would be impossible to describe the subtle variations which had been played upon it; how the mouldings, the ceiling, the mantelpiece, the curtains, and the matting on the floor enhanced and beautified the general harmony .... This was picked out with yellow in the mouldings, cornice, etc., with a result extremely satisfactory and charming. All the decoration was entirely free from anything in the way of pattern or diaper; the color was laid smoothly and broadly on the hard finished plaster, and the effect depended solely upon the contrast and disposition of the tints."[137]

Whistler's friend and biographer T. R. Way also recalled the dining room with its "low-pitched ceiling, walls distempered in a rather dark green-blue, with simple straight yellow curtains by the window, and very plain cane-seated chairs painted a bright yellow. A white cloth was on the table, with some pieces of blue and white upon it; and on the bare wall opposite the window one small square hanging pot. I think Japanese, so perfectly placed as to fill its wall."[138]

Harper Pennington commented somewhat humorously on the sparsity of furnishings, writing that Whistler's "furniture was limited to the barest necessities and frequently, too few of those. Indeed some wit made what was called his 'standing joke' about poor Jimmy's dearth of seats. Once Dick (Corney) Grain said when shaking hands before a Sunday luncheon, 'Ah,! Jimmy, glad to see you playing before such a full house!' glancing around the studio with his large protruding eyes in search of something to sit on.

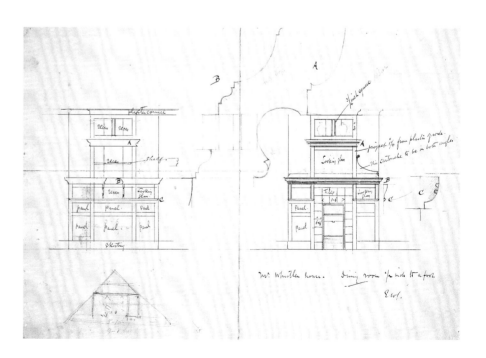

Fig. 7-34. E. W. Godwin. Design for dining room mantelpiece and corner cabinet for the White House, 1878. Ink and pencil on paper; 11 x 15 3/16 in. (28 x 38.6 cm). Trustees of the Victoria and Albert Museum, London, E.548-1963.

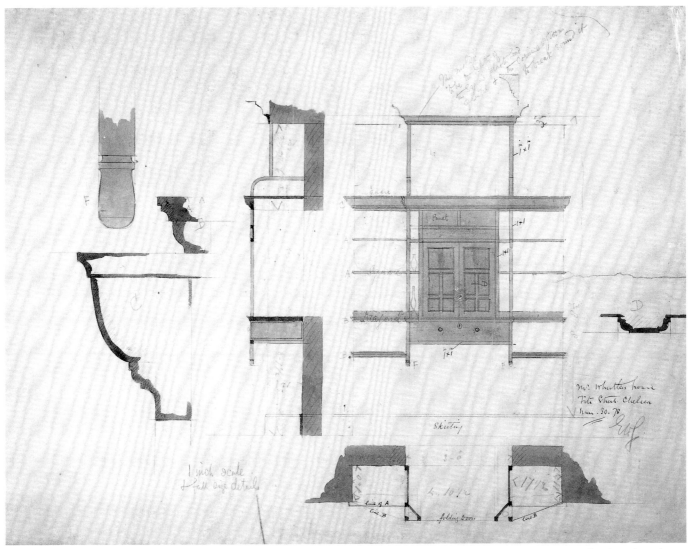

Fig. 7-35. E. W. Godwin. Design for a built-in hanging cupboard for the White House, dated March 30, 1878. Pencil, ink, and wash on paper; 15¾ x 20¼ in. (40 x 51.3 cm). Trustees of the Victoria and Albert Museum, London, E.550-1963.

'What do you mean' said Whistler. 'Standing room only' replied the actor. The studio could boast only four or five small cane-seated chairs (always requisitioned for the dining room on Sundays) and the most uncomfortable bamboo sofa ever made. Nobody, except some luckless model, sat upon it twice."[139]

This spartan approach in Godwin's interior design was also noted by Sadakichi Hartmann, another visitor, who wrote, "His rooms were meant for the photographer and not for human habitation."[140] This criticism was later leveled at many progressive designers of the early twentieth century. The disregard for domestic comfort may be viewed as a reaction to Victorian taste. In his writings Godwin stated that he never liked anything suggesting laziness, an attitude shared by Whistler, who is quoted by his friend

Mortimer Menpes as saying, "If you want to be comfortable go to bed."[141]

The "philosophy of comfort" was one of the key design factors in the furnishing of the Victorian interior. This attention to comfort expressed itself in the heavy, bulging upholstery; warm color schemes; dense, abundant furnishing fabrics and carpets; and the accumulation of objects and curios. Victorian taste equated the over-furnished, over-cluttered interior with domestic comfort, security, and good taste. In contrast a Godwin interior had the appearance of being executed for a very small amount of money—the ultimate rejection of the Victorian ideal that sought to project security through considerable expenditures of money.[142]

Fig. 7-36. E. W. Godwin. Staircase in Frank Miles's house, 44 Tite Street, Chelsea, London, 1879. Photographed in 1972.

Fig. 7-37. E. W. Godwin. Studio inglenook in Frank Miles's house, 44 Tite Street, Chelsea, London, 1879. Photographed in 1972.

44 Tite Street

The house and studio that Godwin built for Frank Miles in Tite Street (1878–79; see fig. 6-56) presents another Japanese-inspired interior with pale, distempered walls, bare wood floors covered with carpets, and sparse furnishings. Surviving architectural details, among them the paneled wall dados, the stair railing with latticework design and brass-capped finials (fig. 7-36), and the inglenooks with rounded lintels, show unmistakable Japanese-inspired design details (fig. 7-37).[143] Godwin may even have used actual

Japanese accessories in its interior furnishings, such as Japanese panels in a door frame. On December 14, 1878, Miles wrote to Godwin about such a treatment: "I will go in for one door with the Japanese work . . . . I have no doubt they are very beautiful & will be very effective: you must decide which door to put them in."[144]

In a letter to Miles dated May 22, 1879, Godwin specified a color scheme very similar to that used for Whistler's White House—lemon yellow, blue, light brown, dark green, and light pink.[145] Godwin was very involved in the

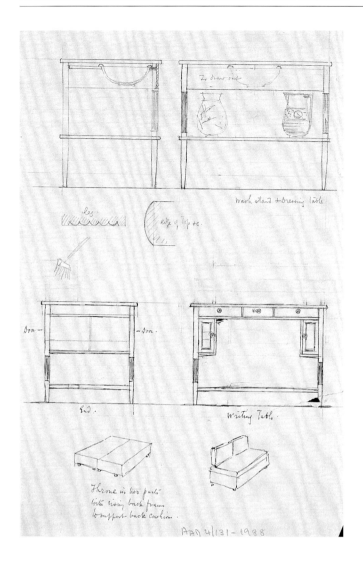

Fig. 7-38. E. W. Godwin. Designs for washstand and dressing table, daybed, and writing table for Frank Miles's house and studio, 44 Tite Street, Chelsea, London, dated July 1879. Pencil, pen and ink on paper; 12⅞ x 7¾ in. (32.7 x 19.7 cm). Trustees of the Victoria and Albert Museum, London, AAD 4/131-1988.

selection and mixing of these colors. A diary entry for June 20, 1879, reads: "All morning mixing colors at Miles' house."[146] This color scheme was very unlike the bilgey greenish tones so common in Aesthetic interiors. In fact Miles annotated Godwin's letter, writing, "as you make no mention of any of the sage or olive greens or duck egg I suppose you leave these tones for furniture hangings & c."[147]

Godwin proposed an austere studio setting with ivory-colored woodwork, white walls, and a deeper ivory-colored ceiling.[148] Chinese matting covered the floor. The minimal furniture included a "studio Chair light," a "Coffee table light," and a daybed of deal on french rollers and covered "with the same stuff as the curtains."[149] A drawing for this daybed (fig. 7-38) is inscribed, "Throne in two parts with rising back frame to support back cushion."[150]

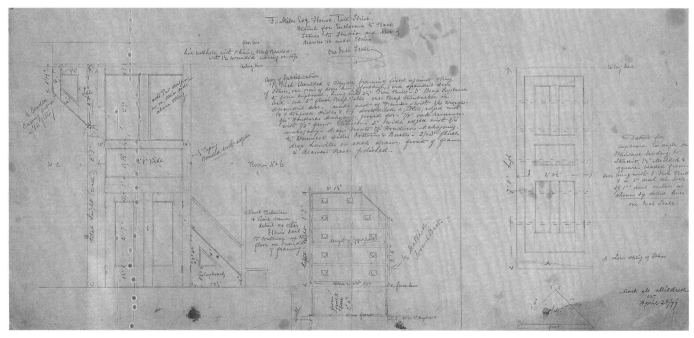

Fig. 7-39. E. W. Godwin. Design for a "nest of drawers" to fit beneath the stairs in Frank Miles's house, 44 Tite Street, Chelsea, London, 1879. Pencil, pen and ink with yellow crayon; 12¹³⁄₁₆ x 26¹⁵⁄₁₆ in. (32.7 x 68.5 cm). Trustees of the Victoria and Albert Museum, London, E.570-1963.

Fig. 7-40. E. W. Godwin. Frank Miles's house and studio: back elevation and transverse section, ca. 1878. Pen and ink, watercolor and pencil; 14¾ x 20⅛ in. (37.5 x 51.2 cm). Trustees of the Victoria and Albert Museum, London, E.557-1963. *Checklist no. 91*

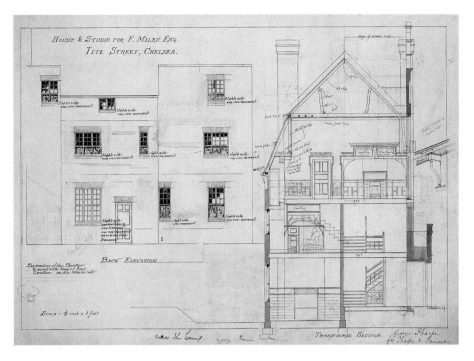

The stairs of the studio were to be covered with felt. Godwin designed a nest of drawers of Honduras mahogany with thin splayed legs to sit under these stairs (fig. 7-39).[151]

The austere approach to studio design practiced by Godwin, Whistler, and Miles was unusual in an age when most artists had studios that contained as many objects as their domestic interiors. Victorian artists lavishly appointed their working quarters with luxurious fabrics, elaborate pieces of furniture, and a profusion of antique casts, books, and assorted bric-à-brac.[152] In contrast, Godwin's and Whistler's studios with their plain walls and uncluttered appearance prefigured the stark, light-filled studios of the twentieth century.

The staircase and hall at 44 Tite Street were painted in shades of ivory, its ceiling a light brown. An umbrella stand and a square hall carpet of old Turkey work was part of the original decoration. The main stairs were finished in the way they had been for Whistler.[153] A back elevation (fig. 7-40) shows that the dado was treated with "the scratches on wet plaster," in imitation of matting, similar to plasterwork found in Whistler's house.[154] An annotated drawing for the staircase reveals that there was a "teak newel" and a bannister of "polished birch."[155] The stairs and balustrade were made of deal, with "polished and lacquered" brass finials.[156]

For the drawing room Godwin proposed another yellow color scheme with "walls and ceilings toned golden yellow and wood cinnamon." The master bedroom was in blue and gray with "wood blue, walls gray, blue-green ceiling,"[157] and with a minimum of furnishings: a four-foot brass bedstead, a washstand and toilet set, a writing table with drawers that could be locked,[158] an armchair, and a painted fireplace fender with brass mounts.[159] Blue cretonne curtains in a Japanese bird pattern with a blue lining covered the windows and blended in with the blue background color. The bare floor was stained dark.[160]

That Godwin designed furniture for this bedroom is confirmed by a surviving drawing showing a washstand and dressing table, and by a writing table that matches the Godwin description (see fig. 7-38).[161] The drawing indicates that Godwin was still designing severely rectilinear furniture with minimum ornament and decoration in 1879. Some softening of the outline, however, was achieved through a slightly rounded leg on the washstand and writing table.

The kitchen was painted a functional white and furnished with a three-legged, round deal table, three old Windsor chairs, and white china. For the storage of kitchenware, Godwin designed a large dresser with three drawers, three shelves, and "japanned wooden knobs."[162] He left no item of the furnishings to chance. An estimate for furnishing portions of Frank Miles's house includes a teapot, house pail, and wine sieve among many other less-than-glamorous items for the kitchen.[163]

Studio for Princess Louise

While designing the studio houses on Tite Street, Godwin also created an artist's studio in the gardens of Kensington Palace for Princess Louise, daughter of Queen Victoria. The princess was a sculptress and a friend of many of the artists who exhibited at the Grosvenor Art Gallery, including Whistler and Burne-Jones.[164] Photographs of the studio (see fig. 6-59) show a one-story brick building with tiled gambrel roof and large north windows looking out onto a garden. It was an inexpensive building with an anteroom and large central room. Godwin was paid 35 pounds for the

Fig. 7-41. E. W. Godwin. Interior of Princess Louise's studio, Kensington Palace, London, 1878. Photographed ca. 1940, after alterations had been made. National Monuments Record.

design plus an extra five pounds for what he called "Extra attendance."[165]

Correspondence relating to this commission reveals a concern for keeping expenditures low. In a letter to Princess Louise dated August 31, 1878, Godwin points out that the use of deal for the shutters to the windows would cost less than "old oak panels . . . for if the latter arrangement be adopted the framing must be in oak & the cost will be £90 to £24."[166] Although Godwin proposed an elaborate mantelpiece for the studio with a coved plaster cornice and Japanese lintel,[167] photographs of the interior show a simple mantel with tiled hearth and sloping hood. The upper portion of the walls and ceiling were paneled with horizontal wainscot (fig. 7-41), which according to the specifications was to be made of teak from East India.[168]

Commissions of the Eighties

The decade of the 1880s was a period of intense activity for Godwin. Although he spent a great deal of his time during this decade on theatrical productions, interior design commissions were also abundant. His diaries and sketchbooks list interior design schemes for ten clients: Lady Sinclair, Lady Feversham, Lady Shrewsbury, Charles Coghlan, Gwladys, Countess of Lonsdale, the Reverend Batson, Lillie Langtry, R. C. Woodville, Oscar Wilde, and Hermann Vezin. Unfortunately, little documentary evidence survives to be able to adequately describe most of these commissions. However, the design schemes for Oscar Wilde, Reverend Batson, Lady Shrewsbury, and Hermann Vezin provide enough evidence to reconstruct some of Godwin's interior design work of the 1880s.

10 Lancaster Place, London

In 1882 Godwin redecorated American actor Hermann Vezin's house in London at 10 Lancaster Place, Westminster. He selected paint colors and wallpapers, designed cabinetwork, ordered furniture from William Watt, and made architectural modifications. He also designed floorcloths for the sum of £10.[169] Estimates reveal that Godwin used a horizontal division of the wall surfaces with paint and paper that was identical to his work in the early 1870s for Collinson and Lock and for some of his own interiors.[170] Dubbed "the dado style" by the decorators Rhoda and Agnes Garrett, this treatment remained popular well into the 1880s in Great Britain.[171] Ceiling treatments became more elaborate in the 1880s, however, and paper was used to cover it; the largely white expanse was no longer considered fashionable.

The dining room of Vezin's house was papered with a combination of unidentified papers from James Toleman and Sons.[172] One paper was used on the walls above the skirting, and another as a frieze and on the ceiling. The cornice was painted with the darkest tone of the ceiling paper, and the woodwork, including the skirting, was painted a terracotta red. A new chimneypiece had four painted panels and silvered and beveled glass, which, according to a preliminary sketch, was circular (fig. 7-42).[173] The sketch also suggests a ledge running around the room and shows a Queen Anne–style window with a built-in window seat that Godwin designed as a major feature of the room. To blend in with the color scheme, chintz window curtains in terracotta red were used.[174]

The hall and staircase walls were papered above the

dado with Godwin's red "Greek" paper manufactured by Toleman. The woodwork and three-foot, six-inch dado were painted dark brown to match the darkest tone of the paper, and the stairs were painted to match this woodwork. The ceiling was sized, lined, and then distempered a straw color, and the skylight was cleaned and repaired.

The master bedroom in the Vezin apartment was done in a rose-colored scheme. Painted, rose-colored woodwork matched the wallpaper, which was of an unidentified pattern by Scott Cuthbertson and was installed to within a few inches of the ceiling. The ceiling itself was distempered.

Bedroom furniture, a major component of this commission, included "two wardrobes & chest of drawers . . . with outside framing . . . of Hondorus [sic] Mahogany, . . . all the rest to be of pine." One of the wardrobes had plate glass in the door.[175] The cabinetwork, which was made by the cabinetmaker C. Greaves of 40 Queens Road, Chelsea, was Sheraton style, with rectilinear lines, paneled decoration, and a curved apron to the bottom of the chest of drawers. A sketch for the Vezin bedroom shows the plan for this cabinetwork with an unusual angled hanging wardrobe (fig. 7-43). It is annotated, "this top piece to be screwed to the ceiling line and the wood ceiling of wardrobe to be fitted against top so as to get as much height as possible in wardrobe."[176] Previous wardrobe specifications stressed modest height dimensions and movability to facilitate cleaning.

The desire for a more sanitary environment led to another design solution in the 1880s: fitted furniture schemes, especially in bedrooms. This had been popularized by architect Robert Edis in *Healthy Furniture and Decoration* (1884). In the same year, the *Cabinet Maker* magazine praised fitted furniture, calling it "a new departure in the history of home furnishings."[177] Space limitations have been another factor in the development of built-in furniture; by the 1880s space in homes "was now quite often a premium in fashionable surroundings."[178]

The Vezin sitting room had a papered ceiling with distempered cornice. Godwin had the lintels cut away to install blinds, and he refixed the moldings. The housekeeper's bedroom was also papered but only over two-fifths of the wall. The kitchen was painted white with buff-colored woodwork and four-foot, six-inch dado. The ceiling and upper part of the walls were white limed. The boxroom and scullery were also painted white.

52 Frith Street

The white color schemes used in the service areas of the Vezin apartment would dominate the decoration of the

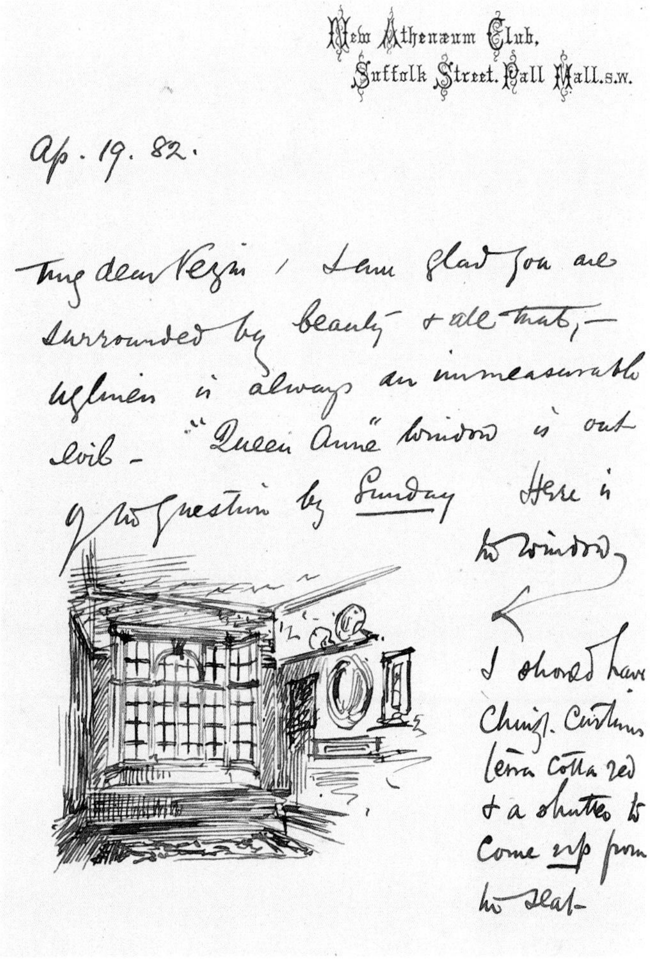

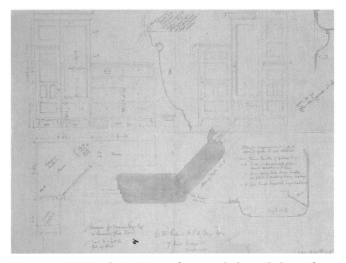

Fig. 7-42. Letter to Hermann Vezin from E. W. Godwin with a sketch of a window scheme for Vezin's residence at 10 Lancaster Place, Westminster, London, dated April 19, 1882. Trustees of the Victoria and Albert Museum, London, AAD 4/422-1988.

Fig. 7-43. E. W. Godwin. Design for a wardrobe and chest of drawers for Hermann Vezin's residence at 10 Lancaster Place, Westminster, London, 1882. Pencil and light red wash on tracing paper; 15 x 20⅛ in. (38 x 51 cm). British Architectural Library Drawings Collection, RIBA, London, Ran 7/J/5 (2).

Fig. 7-44. Oscar Wilde's house at 16 Tite Street, Chelsea, London. Interior redecorated by Godwin in 1884–85. Photographed ca. 1910.

London home of the Reverend A. Batson. In the fall of 1884 Godwin decorated the Batson home at 52 Frith Street, Soho, and, befitting the home of a minister, it was Godwin's most economical makeover. Notes in his sketchbooks provide clues about the low-cost furnishings as well as the predominantly white coloring.[179] The taste for white walls was shared by William Morris, who wrote: ". . . if we really care about art we shall not put up with 'something or other' but shall choose honest whitewash instead, on which sun and shadow play so pleasantly . . . ."[180] These white color schemes herald the all-white compositions of such progressive designers as Voysey and Mackintosh in the late 1880s and 1890s, as well as those of the Modern movement.[181]

The front room of the first floor, however, was designed in a more traditional color scheme, with the woodwork, frieze, and ceiling painted white and the main part of the wall covered with a gold paper. This arrangement may have been part of the revival of interest in Adam and Empire styles, which were sweeping Western Europe and America in the 1880s and 1890s.[182] Whistler would also favor white and gold in his interior design work of the 1880s and 1890s. A reviewer for *Art Age* remarked on the

beauty of one of Whistler's white-and-gold schemes: "I have lately seen a drawing room . . . one of his most successful harmonies in white and gold. The walls were pale golden, a rug of a darker shade lay on the floor, white and gold cretonne covered the furniture and covered the windows."[183]

Both the front and back rooms of the second floor were executed in tones of white with a white limed ceiling and white overmantel. The filling of the wall was papered with an unidentified wallpaper. Brass knobs were added to the shutters, and brass rods were installed for hanging curtains and blinds. Window seats were ordered.[184] The floors were stopped, stained, and varnished, and covered with Scinde rugs.

For the reception rooms Godwin ordered the most economical and utilitarian of furnishings: eighteen Sussex chairs from Messrs. West and Cottier, Hambledon, Henley on Thames, both with and without arms for the sum of 5/- and 8/ each[185] and "four Tables Richmond pattern as designed by Capt. Atkinson" from Messrs. Hughes & Co in highly polished ash with brass bolts at £2.12s.6d. each.[186] Other furnishings listed in his sketchbooks included a secretary, sofa, two easy chairs, umbrella stand, dining table, convex mirror, and Cairene screens for the windows.[187] For the bedroom, Godwin ordered a brass bedstead, washstand, wardrobe, a chest of drawers with a mirror glass, and three chairs. Godwin approved of economical furnishings, affirming that "the greatest-utility-at-the-least-cost principle is the only sure and certain road to beauty whether in furniture or architecture."[188]

16 Tite Street

One of Godwin's last decorating commissions was for 16 Tite Street, a four-story house in red brick with a large bay window, which he redecorated for his friend Oscar Wilde and Wilde's new wife, Constance, in 1884–85 (fig. 7-44).[189] Because Wilde was a promoter of Aesthetic decoration and lectured extensively on the "House Beautiful," it was particularly important that the decoration of this house reflect the owner's progressive taste. In December 1884 Wilde wrote to Godwin: "The house must be a success—do just add the bloom of colour to it in curtains and cushions."[190]

Godwin again based a color scheme on variations of a single color. He distempered the walls of all the rooms, eliminating patterned wallpapers. The entrance hall had white walls tinted with yellow to match the yellow ceiling, white woodwork, and a gray dado. A beaten iron lantern hung from the ceiling, and two white-framed engravings, *Apollo and the Muses* and *Diana and Her Nymphs Bathing*, on the walls. A white silk curtain separated the hall from the staircase,[191] which was painted white, with yellow walls and ceiling, and like the hall, a gray dado. The stairs themselves were covered with gold-colored matting.

The dining room was a study in white, with high-polished white walls. Adrian Hope, a visitor to the Wilde home, recalled that "the white paint (as indeed all the paint used about the house) was of a high polish like Japanese lac-querwork."[192] A green-blue Morris carpet with a white pattern covered the floor, and white curtains with yellow silk embroidery hung in the windows.[193] Godwin designed an entire suite of white furniture for the dining room, including a sideboard (fig. 7-45), which was a complicated storage piece with a combination of open and closed com-partments, reeded edging, and a lower cupboard section raised off the floor.[194] The piece was meant to stand a little higher than the picture rail so that its flat cornice could double as a display shelf for the large pieces of blue-and-white and yellow porcelain that decorated the room. God-win also designed white dining-room chairs of Greek inspiration, upholstered in white plush with blue and yel-low accents. A narrow deal shelf, painted white, circled the room and served as a buffet table for entertaining. Wilde called it "a sort of Japanese arrangement of shelves—but very tiny."[195] Notes in Godwin's sketchbooks indicate that the dining room also contained a "corner easy lounge & chest for [the storage of] table cloths Decanters &c. locked up."[196]

One visitor remarked that the arrangement of the dining-room furniture gave one the impression that "the centre of the room was an open space instead of being absorbed by the customary huge table laden with refresh-ment, and gave an impression of greater size and lightness to the room."[197] Wilde was so taken with the beauty of this room and its furniture that he wrote to Godwin thanking him "for the beautiful designs of the furniture. Each chair is a sonnet in ivory, and the table is a masterpiece in pearl."[198]

For the front drawing room, Godwin devised a scheme of white, yellow, and pink, with white woodwork. This color scheme had been used by Whistler a decade earlier, in 1866, in his drawing room at 2 Lindsey Row, and it can be conveyed by the background of Whistler's *Sym-phony in Flesh-Colour and Pink: Portrait of Mrs. Frances Leyland* (1871–74; fig. 7-46). A section of Japanese leather paper was inserted into the ceiling, the only use of paper in the entire decoration. A bronze plaque of a girl, sculpted by John Donoghue, illustrating Wilde's poem "Requiescat," hung in the center of an overmantel designed by Godwin. A sketch of this overmantel (fig. 7-47) shows that it had a rectangu-lar beveled glass panel below the main panel and two side

panels decorated with thin vertical panels of bronze to cor-respond to the Donoghue plaque.[199]

For the rear drawing room, which Wilde used as a smoking room, a green color scheme was introduced, with pale green distempered walls, ceiling, and "cornice walls green darker." Whistler may even have had a hand in this color scheme, since he is credited with designing the pale green ceiling. Anna de Brémont, a visitor to the Wildes' home, recalled the ceiling to be "of 'exceeding beauty' that Oscar spoke of . . . , with much pride as being a master-piece of design by Whistler."[200] It had two gold dragons at the corners with multicolored japanesque peacock feath-ers.[201] The walls were hung with various white-framed art-works by Wilde's friends and contemporaries, as well as a framed manuscript of a Keats sonnet. Anna de Brémont remarked on the room's exotic furnishings with its "Eastern decorations, Oriental divans and Moorish casements."[202] A surviving sketch of one of these casements shows that Godwin designed them with square lattices inset with

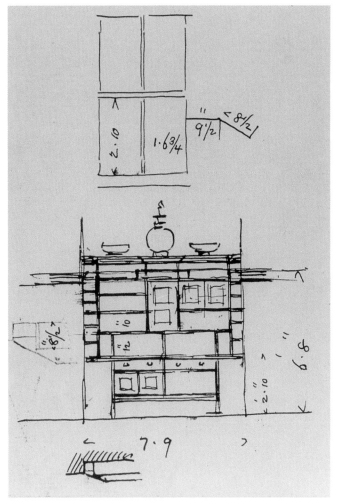

Fig. 7-45. E. W. Godwin. Design for a sideboard for Oscar Wilde, 16 Tite Street, Chelsea, London, 1884. Pen and ink on paper; 30 x 21⅜ in. (76.2 x 54.3 cm). The Hyde Collection, New Jersey.

Fig. 7-46. James McNeill Whistler. *Symphony in Flesh Colour and Pink: Portrait of Mrs. Frances Leyland*, 1871–74. Oil on canvas; 77⅛ x 40¼ in. (195.5 x 102.2 cm). Frick Collection, New York.

crosses, in imitation of Moorish work.[203] Because the house looked out "on a slum,"[204] the casements were meant to block the view as well as to give the room an exotic touch. A glass-bead curtain hung before the door and heavy serge curtains on brass rods covered the windows, "giving the room a rather mysterious look," recalled Oscar's son Vyvyan.[205]

Godwin designed a Japanese-style couch that Wilde called "exquisite"[206] and the Oriental divans, which stood against the wall on either side of the marble mantelpiece. They were angled and adorned with cushions; "queer little Eastern tables" sat in front.[207] Other furnishings included a Chippendale table, curule armchair, three white-lacquered straight-back chairs,[208] and a white painted piano, which stood in one corner of the room.[209] A small green bronze figure of Narcissus was displayed on the mantelpiece and a bust of Augustus Caesar, in the corner.

A note in Godwin's sketchbooks, dated December 11, 1884, gives some indication of the furnishings for the drawing room: "l light chair 2 Easy chairs table for tea [all in] white. Look out—greeny dull gold thick silk for curtains and covers thin for sashes."[210] On the back of a sketch by Beatrice Godwin of Constance Wilde, now in the Hunterian Art Gallery, Glasgow, is another sketch of what may be the Wilde drawing room designed by Godwin (fig. 7-48).[211] If so, it adds a new feature to the collective description pieced together by Wilde's biographers: Regency convex mirrors, which were common in Aesthetic interiors of the 1870s and 1880s and extensively used by Godwin.

For the library Godwin developed a Turkish or Moorish scheme, a decorating theme that was considered ad-

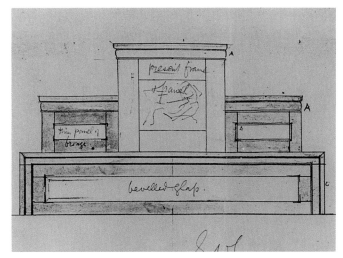

Fig. 7-47. E. W. Godwin. Overmantel design for Oscar Wilde, 1884. Pen and ink on paper; 30 x 21⅜ in. (76.2 x 54.3 cm). The Hyde Collection, New Jersey.

vanced taste at this time. The lower walls were painted a dark blue, and the upper parts of the walls, the cornice, and the ceiling were pale gold color. The woodwork was a golden brown. Over the doorway lines from Shelley were inscribed in gilt, red, and blue lettering.[212] As in the back drawing room the window was covered with a wood screen copied from a Moorish pattern and by a glass-beaded hanging. A large antique mahogany writing table, which had once belonged to Thomas Carlyle,[213] and a carved wood mantelpiece dominated the room. Low divans with corresponding ottomans lined the walls. Lanterns, a

Fig. 7-48. Attributed to Beatrice Godwin. Sketch of an interior, possibly Oscar Wilde's drawing room at 16 Tite Street, Chelsea, London, ca. 1884. Ink on paper; 14⅛ x 9 in. (36 x 23 cm). Hunterian Art Gallery, Glasgow, Birnie Philip Bequest, no. 46408 (verso).

Moorish-style inlaid table, and Eastern hangings also provided exotic touches. Wilde's copies of the Greek classics and his other books were displayed in a large glass-fronted bookcase to the right of the fireplace.[214] A cast of Hermes by Praxiteles stood on a red stand in the corner.[215] On the walls the various artworks included Japanese prints.

Ironically, the bedrooms on the second floor were in pink and blue schemes, the traditional gendered code of colors. The front bedroom, belonging to Constance Wilde, had pink-painted walls and apple green woodwork and ceiling, while the back bedroom, Oscar Wilde's room, was dark blue, with a cornice and ceiling of a pale greenish blue.

On the third floor the front room was painted white with a yellow ceiling. The back study was in shades of red: the lower part of the walls were painted a "red russet brown," and the upper part of the walls and ceiling, "a grayish-pink-red."[216]

The distinctive color schemes of 16 Tite Street depended on the most artistic combination of pure colors, which made a great impression on Wilde. In a letter of 1885 he criticized the all-prevading use of patterned William Morris wallpapers and extolled the virtues of plain painted walls. Although he does not acknowledge Godwin

directly, he described Godwin's work when he wrote, "I have seen far more rooms spoiled by wallpapers than anything else . . . My eye requires in a room a resting-place of pure colour . . . the only papers I use now are the Japanese gold ones . . . with these and with colour in oil and distemper a lovely house can be made . . . Anybody with a real artistic sense must see the value and repose of pure colour."[217]

•

The house for Constance and Oscar Wilde was the last of Godwin's forays into interior design. Godwin died in 1886, but his influence continued to be felt by a whole new generation of designers. His obituary in the *British Architect* recognized the profound impact Godwin had had on nineteenth-century tastes: "Long before any attempt was made to popularise art, he recognised that houses need not be ugly to be comfortable. We are still, alas! in an age of stucco and bastard art but the little that has been done to beautify our domestic surroundings is mainly due to him."[218]

•

Note: Most published sources are cited below in shortened form (author's last name, abbreviated title, date of publication); full references will be found in the bibliography. Frequently cited archives are abbreviated below; for a key to the abbreviations, also see the bibliography.

1. V&A AAD, 4/23-1988: 16–7.

2. Watt, *Art Furniture* (1877): viii.

3. Harbron, *Conscious Stone* (1949): 33.

4. E. A. Craig, *Gordon Craig* (1968): 34.

5. Ibid.

6. Thornton, *Authentic Decor* (1984): 313.

7. Godwin, "My House 'In' London," part 4 (5 August 1876): 73.

8. Ibid., part 5, (12 August 1876): 86.

9. [Godwin], "Furniture" (15 June 1872): 1–2; quoted in Aslin, *E. W. Godwin* (1986): 7.

10. See e.g., *The Gough Family*, 1741 (private collection), reproduced in Saumarez-Smith, *Eighteenth-Century Decoration* (1993): 171, pl. 157.

11. See Wainwright, "Dark Ages of Art Revived" (June 1978): 95–117.

12. All quotations in this paragraph are from Godwin, "My Chambers and What I Did to Them," part 2 (8 July 1876): 19.

13. Terry, *Ellen Terry's Memoirs* (1932): 38.

14. There is evidence that importers of Oriental and Turkey carpets were doing business in London already in the 1840s. Clive Wainwright identifies Mr. Cardinal, Levant Warehouse, Great St. Helens Bishopsgate, as a source for the purchase of Turkey carpets in London as early as 1842. Wainwright, *Romantic Interior* (1989): 60.

15. Godwin, "My House 'In' London," part 4 (5 August 1876): 72.

16. Godwin, "My Chambers and What I Did to Them," part 1 (1 July 1876): 5.

17. Banham, MacDonald, and Porter, *Victorian Interior Design* (1991): 95.

18. Ibid.

19. Godwin, "My House 'In' London," part 1 (15 July 1876): 34.

20. Godwin, "My Chambers and What I Did to Them," part 1 (1 July 1876): 4.

21. Ibid., pp. 4–5; and ibid., part 2 (8 July 1876): 18–19.

22. I am indebted to Joanna Banham for this information.

23. "House at Northampton" (7 January 1871): 10 and illustration.

24. For more information and illustrations of the early production of William Morris wallpapers, see Lesley Hoskins, "Wallpaper," in *William Morris*, ed. Parry (1996): 206–7.

25. Eastlake, *Hints on Household Taste* (1868): 123–26.

26. Latimer, "Division of the Wall" (1987–88): 18.

27. "Wall Decorations" (8 May 1874): 492–93 and illus. [504–5].

28. Godwin, "My Chambers and What I Did to Them," part 2 (8 July 1876): 19.

29. Ibid., part 1 (1 July 1876): 4.

30. See Banham, MacDonald, and Porter, *Victorian Interior Design* (1991): 12, fig. 4.

31. Godwin, "My Chambers and What I Did to Them," part 1 (1 July 1876): 5.

32. Ibid.

33. Ibid.

34. Ibid.

35. Ibid.

36. Ibid.

37. V&A PD, E.273-1963: 22.

38. This presumably refers to the Oriental-type rugs painted by Jan Van Eyck in *The Madonna Enthroned with St. Michael and the Donor*, dating from about 1430–31, and *The Madonna of Canon Georg van der Paele*, dated 1436, reproduced by nineteenth-century carpet manufacturers such as Harland and Fisher. It is not possible to determine whether the rugs represented in the Van Eyck paintings are actual Oriental specimens or Western reproductions. See Ydema, *Carpets and Their Datings* (1991): 8–9.

39. E. A. Craig, *Gordon Craig* (1968): 39.

40. Quoted in Wilkinson, "Edward William Godwin and Japonisme" (1987): 193. The use of ebonized furniture is a complicated issue. Important historical prototypes were the Tudor-style turned ebony chairs of the second half of the eighteenth century and most of the nineteenth century. Collectors believed they were of Tudor origin and considered them appropriate for the furnishing of Romantic interiors. For more information on the nineteenth-century trend for ebony furniture, see Wainwright, "Only the True Black Blood" (1985): 250–55.

41. I am indebted to Clive Wainwright for this information.

42. For more information on Fourdinois see Ledoux-Lebard, *Le mobilier français* (1989): 208.

43. London International Exhibition, *Official Catalogue* (1862): 338–39.

44. Godwin, "My Chambers and What I Did to Them," part 2 (8 July 1876): 19.

45. For the pictures, see V&A PD, E.230-1963: 13, 22; for the matting, see ibid., p. 4.

46. V&A AAD, 4/9-1980: 66, dated 19 February 1868.

47. For more information on the shops and bazaars selling Oriental objects in London in the 1860s and 1870s, see Wilkinson, "Edward William Godwin and Japonisme" (1987): 52–56.

48. Terry, *Ellen Terry's Memoirs* (1932): 71; quoted in Wilkinson, "Edward William Godwin and Japonisme" (1987): 155.

49. Godwin, "My House 'In' London," part 5 (12 August 1876): 86.

50. RIBA Drawings, Ran 7/B/1 (79), dated 27 July 1866.

51. Ibid., Ran 7/B/1 (13).

52. Ibid., Ran 7/B/1 (90).

53. Godwin, "On Some Buildings I Have Designed" (29 November 1878): 211; quoted in Reid, "Dromore Castle" (1987): 122.

54. RIBA Drawings, Ran 7/B/1 (91).

55. Ibid., Ran 7/B/1 (81).

56. Ibid., Ran 7/B/1 (67).

57. Reid, "Dromore Castle" (1987): 135.

58. RIBA Drawings, Ran 7/B/1 (73).

59. This piece was actually built; it was sold in the sale of Dromore's contents in 1949, lot no. 260, catalogued as "Large Austrian Oak Sideboard with Arms of the Earl of Limerick." See De Courcy, *Dromore Castle* [1949]. It was subsequently cut up and one portion remained in the hands of the Mc Mahon family until the late 1950s.

60. Some of these chairs are in the Victoria and Albert Museum (circ. 719-1966, circ. 720-1966, circ. 721-1966).

61. One of these tables is now in the personal collection of Paul Reeves of London. It has since been reduced in size. De Courcy, *Dromore Castle*, lots 257 and 258.

62. RIBA Mss, GoE/1/7/4.

63. [Godwin], "The Article 'Maison' in M. Viollet le Duc's [*sic*] Dictionnaire" (25 May 1872): 267–68.

64. RIBA Drawings, Ran 7/B/1 (67).

65. RIBA Mss, GoE/1/7/4 Dromore Castle, Specifications of Furniture.

66. Bristol Museums and Art Gallery, *Furniture by Godwin* (1976), acc. no. N4503.

67. RIBA Mss, GoE 1/7/4 Dromore Castle.

68. Wilkinson, "Edward William Godwin and Japonisme" (1987): 158–59.

69. A copy of the "Sister Arts" lecture is in V&A AAD, 4/561-1988.

70. These dressing tables are now divided between the Museé d'Orsay, Paris, acc. no. OAO 1280, and a private collection in London.

71. RIBA Drawings, Ran 7/L/5, 10, 12, 14.

72. V&A PD, E.234-1963: 72.

73. V&A PD, E.235-1963: 13.

74. E.g., Bristol Museums and Art Gallery, acc. no. N4501.

75. V&A PD, E.231-1963: 63.

76. See Lesley Hoskins, "Wallpaper," in *William Morris*, ed. Parry (1996): 206–7, figs. L1 and L3.

77. Unattributed quotations in this section are from the series, the part previously cited.

78. Godwin, "My House 'In' London," part 1 (15 July 1876): 34.

79. See A. Adams, "Architecture in the Family Way" (1992).

80. Boger and Boger, *Dictionary of Antiques* (1967): 157.

81. Godwin, "My House 'In' London," part 2 (22 July 1876): 45–46.

82. Ibid., part 4 (5 August 1876): 73.

83. V&A PD, E.233-1963: 37.

84. Godwin, "My House 'In' London," part 4 (5 August 1876): 73.

85. Ibid.

86. Ibid.

87. Ibid., part 3 (29 July 1876): 58–59.

88. For more information on the use of plants in interior design and their optimal incorporation in the home in Victorian England, see Clive Wainwright, "Rustic Adornments" (10 April 1986): 936–38; and idem, "The Garden Indoors," in *The Garden*, ed. John Harris (1979): 166–72.

89. Godwin, "From the House-Top" (26 August 1876): 112.

90. Godwin, "My House 'In' London," part 3 (29 July 1876): 59.

91. All information about the bedroom is from ibid., part 5 (12 August

1876): 86.

92. Ibid., part 6 (19 August 1876): 100.

93. Ibid., pp. 100–1.

94. Godwin's diary for 23 September 1873 refers to a visit to the "McLaren House Addison Road, Kensington fee paid" (V&A AAD, 4/1-1980).

95. V&A PD, E.234-1963: 50.

96. V&A AAD, 4/13-1980 n.p. "Collinson & Lock."

97. V&A PD, E.234-1963: 18.

98. Thornton, *Authentic Decor* (1984): 20.

99. Gere, *Nineteenth-Century Decoration* (1989): 102.

100. Signed and dated "E. W. G. Nov. 29.73," inscribed with color notes and "Decoration for Cove in Conservatory—McLaren," V&A PD, E.511- 1963.

101. For the lighting fixtures, see V&A PD, E.234-1963: 6.

102. V&A AAD, 4/16-1988. Godwin's ledgers for September 1873 reveal that he spent a great part of the month working on the McLaren commission. In particular, an entry for wall decoration (13 September) and a general design fee for McLaren house (23 September) would place this commission at or about the date of the unidentified sketch (V&A AAD, 4/13-1980 n.p, "Collinson & Lock," September 1873).

103. V&A AAD, 4/23-1988: 93–94.

104. For the grate, see V&A AAD, 4/13-1980 n.p., "Collinson & Lock," September 1873.

105. The use of a Chaucer text may have been derived from Morris. Morris and Co. would design an embroidered frieze for the dining room of Rounton Grange, Northallerton, North Yorkshire based on this same poem in the late 1870s. The figures were drawn by Burne-Jones. For an illustration see Banham, MacDonald, and Porter, *Victorian Interior Design* (1991): 85.

106. For the drawing-room ceiling, wall decoration, and sunflower frieze, see V&A PD, E.234-1963: 6; for the fireplace panels and painted panel, see V&A AAD, 4/13-1980 n.p. "Collinson & Lock" 25 September 1873; for the wallpapers, see ibid.

107. Dungavell, "A Lost House Rediscovered" (1992).

108. V&A AAD, 4/1-1980, 22 April 1873.

109. Ibid., 17 May 1873.

110. V&A AAD, 4/13-1980 n.p., "Collinson & Lock."

111. Ibid., June 1873.

112. Ibid., September 1873.

113. Ibid., October/November 1873.

114. Ibid., January 1874.

115. Ibid., April 1874.

116. Ibid., July 1874.

117. Purslow, "A Seminal Discovery" (1995): 3–5. The details relating to Grey Towers have been taken from this article.

118. Ibid., p. 4.

119. V&A PD, E.487-1963. These two designs relate to an order of 10 April 1874 in Godwin's ledger (V&A AAD, 4/13-1980 n.p., "Collinson & Lock").

120. V&A PD, E.234-1963: 40, 41.

121. I am indebted to Michael Whiteway of Haslam and Whiteway for this information.

122. V&A AAD, 4/12-1980, "Messrs Gillow & Co Oxford Street."

123. Free leaflet passed out on 14 and 15 September 1996 entitled, "Open House: A Celebration of London's Architecture."

124. Ibid.

125. Smalley, "a Harmony in Yellow and Gold" (6 July 1878): 2.

126. Much of the information regarding the White House is derived from Weber Soros, "Whistler as Collector" (1987).

127. V&A PD, E.543-1963.

128. Letter A105 in the Whistler Collection, Glasgow University Library, Glasgow, Department of Special Collections.

129. V&A PD, E.544-1963.

130. Godwin, "Japanese Wood Construction," part 5 (12 February 1875): 173–74; part 6 (19 February 1875): 200–202.

131. V&A PD, E.548-1963.

132. V&A PD, E.550-1963.

133. Library of Congress, Rosenwald Collection, box 1977.

134. V&A PD, E.244-1963: 4.

135. Lucas, *Edwin Austin Abbey* (1921): 80.

136. Hawthorne, "Mr. Whistler's New Portraits" (15 October 1881): 658–59.

137. Lucas, *Edwin Austin Abbey* (1921): 80.

138. Way, *Memories of James McNeill Whistler* (1912): 63.

139. Pennington's comments were originally published in *McClure's Magazine* 8, p. 374; cited in Eddy, *Recollections and Impressions of James A. McNeill Whistler* (1903): 112.

140. Ibid., p. 114.

141. Menpes, *Whistler As I Knew Him* (1904): 128.

142. For more information on the philosophy of comfort and patterns of consumption in nineteenth-century decoration, see Grier, *Culture and Comfort* (1988).

143. Girouard, "Chelsea's Bohemian Studio Houses," part 2 (23 November 1972): 1372.

144. V&A AAD, 4/158-1988.

145. V&A AAD, 4/159, 160-1988.

146. A detailed estimate for furnishing the house and studio outlines many of the colors and items of furniture that Godwin chose (V&A AAD, 4/159-1988).

147. V&A AAD, 4/159, 160-1988.

148. V&A AAD, 4/132-1988.

149. V&A PD, E.248-1963: 72–73.

150. V&A AAD, 4/131-1988.

151. V&A PD, E.570-1963.

152. For more information on artists' studios of the Victorian period see Joanna Banham, "Palaces of Art," in *Victorian Interior Design* by Banham, MacDonald, and Porter (1991): 131–55.

153. Godwin wrote, "studio stairs covered with felt Main stairs Dº [ditto] Whistler's stuff (V&A PD, E.248-1963: 72–73).

154. Wilkinson, "Edward William Godwin and Japonisme" (1987): 328.

155. V&A PD, E.567-1963.

156. RIBA Mss, GoE 1/12/1, estimate of works to be done in the Erection of a House in Tite Street for Frank Miles.

157. Godwin, letter to Frank Miles, dated 22 May 1879, V&A AAD, 4/159-1988.

158. V&A PD, E.248-1963.

159. V&A AAD, 4/132-1988.

160. V&A AAD, 4/132-1988.

161. V&A AAD, 4/131-1988.

162. RIBA Mss, GoE/1/12/1.

163. V&A AAD, 4/132-1988.

164. For more information on Princess Louise, see Wake, *Princess Louise* (1988).

165. "H.R.H. the Princess Louise, Marchioness of Lorne," 1878, V&A AAD, 4/12-1980 n.p.

166. Letter to Princess Louise dated 31 August 1878, V&A AAD, 4/189-1988.

167. V&A AAD, 4/188-1980.

168. RIBA Mss, GoE 1/10/3 (G/LO. 3/3).

169. V&A AAD, 4/3-1988.

170. Work for H. Vezin; verso: list of estimates Messrs. Belham's account, 26 July 1882, V&A AAD, 4/3-1988.

171. Garrett and Garrett, *Suggestions for House Decoration* [1876]: 56.

172. Godwin designed wallpapers for the firm of James Toleman and Sons, 170 Goswell Road, London, from 1874 to 1880.

173. V&A AAD, 4/422-1988.

174. Ibid.

175. V&A AAD, 4/426-1988.

176. RIBA Drawings, Ran 7/J/5.

177. Banham, MacDonald, and Porter, *Victorian Interior Design* (1991): 166.

178. Thornton, *Authentic Decor* (1984): 319.

179. V&A PD, E.264-1963: 48−49.

180. Vallance, *William Morris* (1986): 84.

181. For further information on the development of white color schemes, see Wigley, *White Walls* (1995).

182. For more information on the revival of Empire taste in England, see Collard, *Regency Furniture* (1985): 245−52.

183. *Art Age* 36 (June 1886). A copy can be found in the Library of Congress, Pennell Collection, Whistler clippings.

184. V&A PD, E.264-1963: 48−49.

185. G. Sharpe from F. Granger, 28 November 1884, V&A AAD, E.4/437-1988.

186. Letter to Messrs. Hughes & Co., dated 17 November 1884, V&A AAD, 4/436-1988.

187. V&A PD, E.264-1963: 56−57.

188. Godwin, "My House 'In' London," part 6 (19 August 1876): 100.

189. Reconstruction of Godwin's "House Beautiful" scheme is possible through analysis of the large cache of surviving letters between architect and client, sketches, the bankruptcy sale catalogue, notes in Godwin's sketchbooks, and recollections of visitors.

190. Hyde, *Oscar Wilde* (1975): 176.

191. Bankruptcy Sale catalogue, reprinted in Munby, ed. *Poets and Men of Letters* (1971): 386.

192. Quoted in Gere and Whiteway, *Nineteenth-Century Design* (1993): 328.

193. See Ellmann, *Oscar Wilde* (1988): 257−58.

194. This sketch of this piece is now in The Hyde Collection, Four Oaks Farm, Somerville, New Jersey.

195. Hyde, *Oscar Wilde* (1975): 97.

196. V&A PD, E.264-1963: 68.

197. Hyde, "Oscar Wilde and His Architect" (March 1951): 175.

198. Ibid.

199. Ellmann, *Oscar Wilde* (1988): 258.

200. Comtesse Anna Dunphy de Brémont, *Oscar Wilde and His Mother: A Memoir* (London: Everett, 1911): 89.

201. Ellmann, *Oscar Wilde* (1988): 257−58.

202. De Brémont, *Oscar Wilde* (1911): 88; cited above, n. 224.

203. The Hyde Collection, Four Oaks Farm, Somerville, New Jersey.

204. Adrian Hope, quoted in Gere and Whiteway, *Nineteenth-Century Decoration* (1993): 328.

205. Hyde, "Oscar Wilde and His Architect" (March 1951): 176.

206. Ibid.

207. Adrian Hope, quoted in Gere and Whiteway, *Nineteenth-Century Decoration* (1993): 328.

208. Ellmann, *Oscar Wilde* (1988): 257.

209. Hyde, *Oscar Wilde* (1975): 97.

210. V&A PD, E.264-1963: 67.

211. I am indebted to Margaret McDonald for showing me this sketch. Hunterian Art Gallery, cat. No. 46408, Birnie Philips Bequest.

212. The inscription read: "Spirit of Beauty! Tarry still awhile, They are not dead, thine ancient votaries, Some few there are to whom thy radiant smile Is better than a thousand victories" (quoted in Ellmann, *Oscar Wilde* [1988]: 257).

213. Bankruptcy Sale catalogue, lot 171, reprinted in Munby, ed., *Poets and Men of Letters* (1971): 386.

214. Hyde, *Oscar Wilde* (1975): 96.

215. Winwar, *Oscar Wilde* (1941): 137.

216. Hyde, *Oscar Wilde* (1975): 175.

217. Quoted in Wilkinson, "Edward William Godwin and Japonisme" (1987): 341; and Henderson, *William Morris* (1967): 206.

218. Quoted in Banham, MacDonald, and Porter, *Victorian Interior Design* (1991): 116.

Fig. 8-1. E. W. Godwin. Corner cabinet called "Lucretia," 1873. Made by Collinson and Lock; painted panels by Charles Fairfax Murray. Rosewood with painted panels, brass hardware; 75 x 32 x 23 in. (190.5 x 81.3 x 58.4 cm). The Detroit Institute of Art, Founders Society Purchase, European Sculpture and Decorative Arts General Fund, Honorarium and Memorial Gifts Fund, 1985 (1985.1). *Checklist no. 49*

CHAPTER 8

THE·FURNITURE·OF·E. W. GODWIN

S U S A N   W E B E R   S O R O S

Although E. W. Godwin was trained as an architect, his fame in the twentieth century rests more on his designs for furniture (fig. 8-1) than on his numerous architectural commissions. Art historian and critic Nikolaus Pevsner writes that Godwin was "more a designer than an architect,"[1] and indeed Godwin's Anglo-Japanese furniture, particularly his ebonized sideboard of about 1867, are considered major monuments of nineteenth-century design history. During a period of some twenty-five years, he designed at least four hundred pieces of furniture, some for his own use, others for exclusive private patrons or public and ecclesiastical commissions, as well as for the commercial trade. Godwin worked in all the historicist styles that popular taste demanded. He executed furniture in Gothic; Georgian, Cottage, and Queen Anne styles; Anglo-Greek; Anglo-Egyptian; and Jacobean or Old English styles, as well as in the Anglo-Japanese he is credited with originating and popularizing. Unlike the work of many of his contemporaries, however, Godwin's output rarely falls into the category of reproduction of historical work or excessive eclecticism. Whatever style he pursued or source he consulted, he always interpreted it his own distinctive way. As he explained: "It is easy enough to make up furniture in *direct imitation* of any particular style . . . . What I have endeavoured to secure in design, has rather been a modern treatment of certain well-known and admired styles."[2]

As did William Kent, Robert Adam, and other eighteenth-century architect-designers, and A. W. N. Pugin

and William Burges in his own century, Godwin believed that every detail of a building—the interior as well as the exterior—should be under the control of the architect. He expounded this unified approach to design in a lecture entitled "The Sister Arts and their Relation to Architecture," prepared for the Bristol Society of Architects in 1863.[3] Its central thesis was that the arts of painting, sculpture, and architecture were no longer dependent on each other as they had been in the Middle Ages, and that unless reunited under the control of a unifying spirit, they would not continue to flourish. He warned architects that "when each room and each article of furniture shall be found to be but resolutions of the same key-note . . . *then* may we hope to have an art of our own."[4]

Early Church Furniture

Godwin's first opportunity to realize his concept of stylistic unity came with his church commissions. Much of Godwin's restoration and redecoration work, including church furniture designed by him, still survives. Two of these projects provide the earliest documented Godwin furniture: the church of Saint Grada, Grade, Cornwall (restored 1860–63; fig. 8-2) and the church of Saint Wynwallow, Landewednack, Cornwall (restored 1860). Executed in reformed Gothic style, the furniture shows the influence of the architect-designer A. W. N. Pugin, particularly his structural Gothic work.[5] Like Pugin, Godwin studied the timber-frame construction of medieval architecture, making measured

Fig. 8-2. E. W. Godwin. Saint Grada Church, Grade, Cornwall: nave and chancel roofs, chancel desks, nave seats and chancel seats, 1861. India ink, red pen, and brown wash; 20 x 13 in. (50.8 x 33 cm). British Architectural Library Drawings Collection, RIBA, London, Ran 7/A/4 (7). *Checklist no. 8*

Fig. 8-3. Interior of Saint Grada Church, Grade, Cornwall, showing chancel pews designed by E. W. Godwin, 1860–63. Photographed in 1998.

Fig. 8-4. Saint Grada Church, Grade, Cornwall, showing the chancel desks designed by E. W. Godwin in 1860-63. Photographed in 1998.

Fig. 8-5. The nave at Saint Wynwallow Church, Landewednack, Cornwall, showing chancel seats designed by E. W. Godwin in 1860. Photographed in 1998.

drawings at actual structures throughout in his travels.[6]

Godwin also designed broad, severe forms with the revealed construction, structural supports, and use of solid wood that had been popularized by Pugin twenty years earlier. The oak chancel pews of the Grade church, for example, are stripped of all ornament (fig. 8-3). The revealed tenons at their ends and the vertical planking of their backs emphasize their structured orientation. The only concession to decoration is the pierced, sexfoil design in the arm of the seating form. The overriding architectural quality of this furniture is expressed even more fully in the chancel desks (fig. 8-4), with their sawtooth edges and Y-shaped braces with revealed tenons that echo the timber framing of the roof. Comparable structural Gothic furniture is seen in Godwin's designs—particularly the pews—for the church of Saint Wynwallow, Landewednack, Cornwall. A new structural form, however, is introduced in the seats made for the chancel but used in the nave. They have a crossed X-brace stretcher, another device borrowed from Pugin and ultimately derived from medieval sources (fig. 8-5).

Northampton Town Hall

Godwin continued to demonstrate his taste for severe, structural forms in the design of the interior furnishings for his first major architectural commission, Northampton Town Hall (1861–64; see fig. 6-1). Influenced by John Ruskin's *Stones of Venice* (1853) and the more amply illustrated *Brick and Marble in the Middle Ages: Notes Of A Tour in the North of Italy* by George Edmund Street (1855), Godwin produced a town hall in Italian Gothic style, with an interior that took its cue from the exterior architecture.

According to Godwin's ledger of September 21, 1863, he received an order to prepare designs for the town hall furniture at 10-percent commission.[7] The pieces were to be made by the London firm of Green and King, 23 Baker Street, who advertised themselves as artists and decorators. The firm had already been engaged to work on some of the building's painted decoration, including the main hall's elaborately painted roof trusses.[8] Godwin's contribution was extensive: he designed everything from hall stands to cupboards. Similar in design to his earlier church furnish-

Fig. 8-6. The Council Chamber, Northampton Town Hall, as originally designed by E. W. Godwin in 1863–64, set for a corporation banquet in ca. 1890. Northamptonshire Record Office, P/3852. *Checklist no. 12b*

Fig. 8-7. E. W. Godwin. The "Godwin Room" (formerly Council Chamber), Northampton Guildhall (formerly Town Hall), as restored by Roderick Gradidge and Christopher Boulter in 1992. Photographed in 1998. *Checklist no. 12a*

Fig. 8-8. E. W. Godwin. Councillor's Chair designed for Northampton Town Hall, 1865. Oak with inlaid decoration, green leather upholstery, with brass nails and brass castors; 29⅜ x 21⅝ x 20¼ in. (74.5 x 55 x 51.5 cm). Northampton Borough Council.

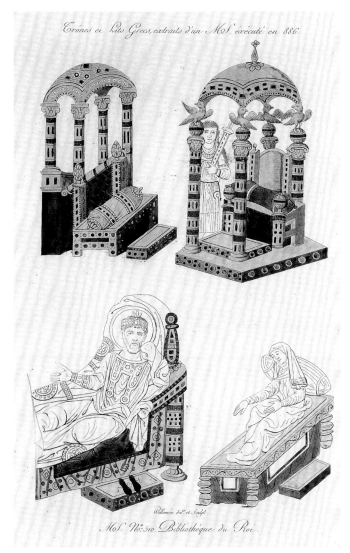

Fig. 8-9. Nicolas Xavier Willemin. "Trônes et Lits Grecs." From Willemin, *Monuments français* (1839): vol. 1, pl. 14.

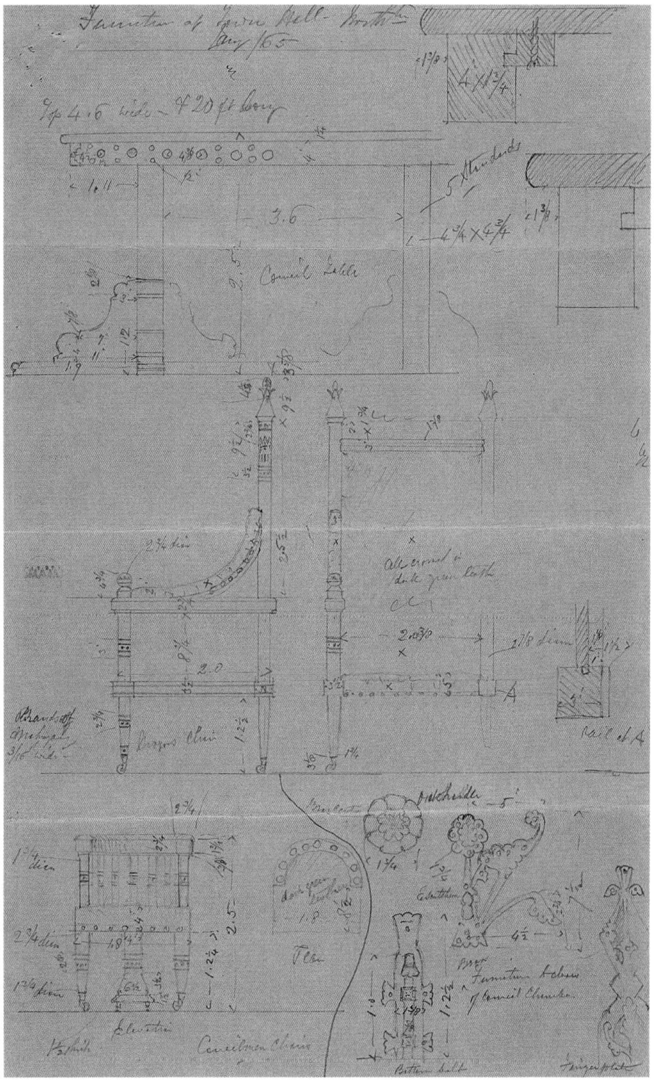

Fig. 8-10. E. W. Godwin. Designs for furniture for Northampton Town Hall: Mayor's Chair, Councillor's Chair, trestle table, and door hardware, 1865. Pencil on writing paper; 8⅜ x 13¼ in. (21.2 x 33.7 cm). Trustees of the Victoria and Albert Museum, London, E.619-1963. *Checklist no. 13*

ings, these were massive pieces of oak furniture in the reformed Gothic style.

The Council Chamber furniture (figs. 8-6 and 8-7), which is still in use in its original setting today, is the earliest documented Godwin furniture made for a nonecclesiastical setting. The large-scale, solid, roughly worked forms, vividly invoke the spirit of the Middle Ages, when furniture was still made by the carpenter and joiner to correspond to heavily fortified architectural settings.[9]

The councillors' chairs, with their semicircular back rails, spindle supports, and rounded legs inlaid with black circles of wood framed by a double row of horizontal bands, are deceptively simple in appearance (fig. 8-8). Their stylized forms, however, indicate a designer very much

aware of furniture history. They recall the barrel-backed throne chairs that originated in the ancient world and survived into the Middle Ages. Godwin could have seen such round-back chairs in medieval illuminated manuscripts, either in the collection of the British Museum or among the volumes owned by his friend and fellow architect, William Burges. Godwin himself was a consummate antiquary and as often as possible went to original sources for inspiration. An illuminated manuscript of the fifteenth century, shown in Nicolas Xavier Willemin's *Monuments français* (1839), depicts two solidly built circular chairs that may have been the prototype for Godwin's councillor's chair.[10] Moreover, Willemin's illustrations of "Trônes et Lits Grecs, extraits d'un Ms. éxécuté en 886" (fig. 8-9) and

Fig. 8-11. E. W. Godwin. Mayor's Chair for Northampton Town Hall, 1865. Made by Green and King. Oak with inlaid decoration, upholstered in red leather, with brass nails and brass castors; 67¾ x 30¾ x 24½ in. (172 x 78 x 62.5 cm). Northampton Borough Council. *Checklist no. 14*

Fig. 8-12. E. W. Godwin. Chief Magistrate's Chair, 1865. Made by Green and King. Oak, leather upholstery, brass castors; 81⅛ x 29¾ x 28¾ in. (206 x 75.5 x 73 cm). Northampton Borough Council.

"Siège bibliothéque Imperiale," taken from a plate entitled "Instrumens de musique en ornament (Bible de Charles-le-chause Ms. du milieu du IXme Siècle)," were probably the source for Godwin's Greek-inspired inlay design of stripes and circles. The introduction of the unusual bird's-tail, single rear-leg support is a design solution borrowed from the back stool or *sgabello* hall chair that was popular in fifteenth-century Italy. Godwin would again experiment with un-

usual rear-legged solutions in his Eagle Chair for Dromore Castle and many of his library chairs reproduced in Watt's *Art Furniture* catalogue.[11]

Surviving designs for the Northampton commission, as well as extant examples, indicate that these chairs were originally designed to be placed on four castors for ease in movement and to be covered in green leather tacked with a row of nail heads. The choice of green leather and nail-head decoration suggests the influence of Pugin, who used green as the principal color in furnishing the House of Commons, including green leather upholstery and rows of nail heads for the House of Commons chair from 1850.[12]

Other pieces from the Northampton commission also demonstrate informed borrowing and adapting of historical prototypes. The mayor's chair, for example, with its floriated finials is based on a medieval precedent (figs. 8-10 and 8-11). In general outline, it resembles the fourteenth-century Coronation Chair of Westminster Abbey, although Godwin's design for the chief magistrate's chair (fig. 8-12) with its crocketed triangular back splat is even closer to this specimen. The council tables in the Councillor's Chamber and the tables in the room beyond the Mayor's Names Gallery (fig. 8-13) point to fifteenth-century trestle tables such as those from the Great Hall, Penshurst, Kent, which are illustrated in T. F. Hunt's *Exemplars of Tudor Architecture*

Fig. 8-13. E. W. Godwin. Side table for Northampton Town Hall, 1865. Made by Green and King. Oak; 35 x 71¾ x 29¾ in. (89 x 182 x 55.5 cm). Northampton Borough Council.

Adapted to Modern Habitations . . . (1836).[13] The bench currently in the hallway of the Council Chamber staircase (originally designed for the Court Room), with its Y-braces and roughly hewn framework, recalls the fixed benches and tables of medieval type in the hall of Winchester College.[14]

Examined as a whole, Godwin's many designs for the Northampton commission reveal him to be capable of executing a wide range of different forms to meet the various requirements of the town's administrative center. He created more than fifty pieces of furniture, all slightly different but possessing an overriding stylistic unity.

Dromore Castle

Godwin's ability to design significant furnishing schemes was demonstrated in the domestic sphere with his commission for Dromore Castle in County Limerick (1866–69)

for the third earl of Limerick (see fig. 6-32). Godwin designed furniture, interiors (see chap. 7), metalwork, and tiles for this commission, a great deal of which still survives, as do detailed documents and specifications. Although Godwin used an Irish Vernacular Gothic style for the exterior of the castle, the interior reveals a more eclectic approach, with a combination of Gothic, Celtic, Chinese, and Japanese features. The furniture ranged from simple, lightweight bedroom chairs to an elaborate inlaid chess table (see fig. 7-13). Some of these pieces were made by the London firm of William Watt, but most were executed by Reuben Burkitt and Company of Cleveland Road in Wolverhampton.[15] Godwin's ledgers reveal that he received a 10-percent commission on this furniture, which included a £260 bill from William Watt and a £894.7s.6d bill from Reuben Burkitt.[16] That Reuben Burkitt supplied the vast majority of the furniture and not William Watt, as has been

Fig. 8-14. E. W. Godwin. Corner washstand designed for Dromore Castle, County Limerick, Ireland, 1870. Made by Reuben Burkitt and Company. Pine, raffia panels, marble top, brass fittings and castors; 59½ x 24¾ in. (151 x 63 cm). Private collection.

Fig. 8-15. E. W. Godwin. Side chair for Dromore Castle, County Limerick, Ireland, 1869. Made by William Watt. Oak, leather upholstery with gold stamped pattern, and brass nails; 42½ x 18¼ x 18⅞ in. (108 x 46.5 x 48 cm). Museum für Kunst und Gewerbe, Hamburg, 1967.262. *Checklist no. 26*

assumed up to now, is further confirmed by a letter from Godwin to William Burges in which he asks for an arbitration on his design fees.[17] Moreover, another letter proves the Burkitt–Dromore furniture connection beyond a doubt. It states: "The little doors containing pierced work in Buffet will be sent to Wolverhampton & made right."[18] An account sent to Lord Limerick also reveals that the hardware was supplied by the firm of Hart and Son, Wych Street, off the Strand, London and Birmingham, and by another firm, Benham and Froud, 40-42 Chandos Street, Charing Cross, London, both well-known metalsmiths.[19]

Although Japanese influence begins to permeate the design at Dromore Castle, it is difficult to know whether Godwin intended the overall aesthetic to be Japanese or medieval. Godwin himself was well aware of shared design elements between these two cultures. In "Japanese Wood Construction," a two-part article he wrote for the *Building News* in 1875, Godwin noted certain similarities between Japanese and medieval craftsmanship. Of Japanese door paneling he wrote, "the doors are single or double framed, and boarded between like our own Mediaeval examples."[20] And Godwin compared Japanese parapets and balustrades to "the wave parapet found in fourteenth century churches in our own country" and "different kinds of plain balustrading which are closely related to the various examples of old English paling."[21]

Godwin's incorporation of Japanese motifs into Gothic-style furniture at Dromore Castle was not unusual for the time. Architect-designers such as William Eden Nesfield and Thomas Jeckyll were also following this practice in the 1860s. Fellow medievalist and friend William Burges, who had been collecting Japanese and Chinese objects as well as medieval artifacts since the mid-1850s, reviewed the International Exhibition of 1862 for *Gentleman's Magazine*, writing of the relationship between Gothic and Japanese art: "If . . . the visitor wishes to see the real Middle Ages, he must visit the Japanese Court," which he called "the real Medieval Court of the Exhibition."[22] Whether Godwin visited this exhibition is not certain, but he had been aware of Japanese art for a decade by the date of the Dromore commission. Godwin biographer Harbron wrote that when Godwin "was able to please himself, his designs had a Japanese character. . . . He had, from 1860 onward, devoted as much time to the study of Japanese art and its principals [*sic*] as . . . he had employed upon mediaeval research."[23]

Certainly the sparseness of ornament, the rectilinear outline, and the use of natural wood grain are suggestive of both traditions. However, the choice of the wainscot oak, the architectural solidity of many of the case pieces, and the

Fig. 8-16. E. W. Godwin. One of a pair of wardrobes made for Dromore Castle, 1870. Made by Reuben Burkitt and Company. Pine with brass fittings and castors; 95½ x 60⅛ x 14 in. (241.5 x 152.5 x 35.2 cm). Private collection.

medievally inspired hardware of ringed pulls with circular escutcheon plates, shared by all the pieces, strongly point to a medieval tradition. This blurring of design sources had already been noted by a contemporary reviewer when he wrote: "Mr. Godwin . . . appears to be perplexed by a divided duty between Ireland and Japan, with an occasional leaning to the Mediaeval glories of Europe."[24]

An analysis of several of the surviving pieces from this commission reveals a spare, reformed Gothic style with Japanese details. A corner washstand made of pine in a stripped-down Gothic style has panels of plaited rattan inserted in its triangular pediment (fig. 8-14). This triangular framework corresponds to the timber framing of pointed arch and supporting truss used in the castle's interior.[25] The plaited rattan, however, refers to a Japanese source. In fact, similar specimens of rattan had been displayed in the Japanese Court at the 1862 Exhibition.[26] An oak escritoire has three sliding doors in the cupboard section above its hinged writing flap in imitation of sliding *shoji* panels.[27]

Fig. 8-17. E. W. Godwin. Design for dining-room sideboard and wall decoration, Dromore Castle, County Limerick, ca. 1869. Sepia pen and wash; 9⁹⁄₁₆ x 12¹⁄₁₆ in. (23.4 x 30.7 cm). British Architectural Library Drawings Collection, RIBA, London, Ran 7/B/1 (73). *Checklist no. 25*

Other pieces show less pronounced Japanese influence and more Gothic detailing. A wainscot-oak chair with ring-turned uprights and carved leonine heads has gold-stamped decoration in the form of medieval disks on its leather upholstery.[28] The side chairs from this suite are covered in the same gilded leather upholstery (fig. 8-15). A pair of wardrobes made of pine (fig 8-16), attributed to this commission on the basis of their door fittings, have Gothic details, including a castellated cornice, studded brass banding extending around each side, and lock plates with central escutcheons and ring handles reminiscent of the Gothic armoires from Bayeux and Noyon cathedrals. Godwin most likely had seen these cabinets illustrated in W. Eden Nesfield's *Specimens of Mediaeval Architecture . . .*[29] Similar examples, dating from about 1500, could be found in England at the chapel at York Minster.[30]

Godwin had obviously studied Gothic furniture originals, but he adapted the designs to nineteenth-century methods of production and patterns of use. He dispensed with the boarded construction and the painted decoration of many Gothic examples. Instead, he introduced modern cabinetmaking, with neatly integrated paneled doors, well-fitted shelves and drawers, and revealed woodgrains. He also dealt with issues of adaptability and function, mounting the square-sectioned legs on castors for easy movement and placing the bottom drawer several inches from the floor for easy cleaning. Bookcases from this commission, of which six identical examples have survived, also display a strongly medieval flavor with pierced triangular end brackets, arched bracket supports, and vertically paneled backboards.[31]

Chinese details also appear in some of the Dromore Castle pieces. An ebonized chess table, for example, which was part of a large suite of drawing-room furniture, had side panels of lattice-type decoration that point to Chinese latticework (see fig. 7-14).[32] Similar latticework panels can be found on many Ming and Qing dynasty forms, including

234

couches and daybeds (see fig. 3-8), narrow tables, bookshelves, and clothes racks.[33] The inward-curling feet of the large oak sideboard designed for the dining room (fig. 8-17)[34] come from the hoof-shaped feet or cabriole legs common to Chinese hardwood table and seating forms of the Ming dynasty (see fig. 3-8).[35] Godwin even mentions a Chinese prototype when giving specification for the upholstery for the drawing room: "yellow satin in colour like that known in China as Imperial yellow."[36]

Anglo-Japanese Furniture

Godwin intensified his exploration of Japanese design elements with the simple, functional furniture he produced for his own use, while he was fulfilling the Dromore Castle commission. The most famous of these pieces was his 1867 ebonized Anglo-Japanese sideboard, which would be made in several versions over the next twenty years (see fig. 4-1). With its gridlike, rectilinear form, complicated interplay of solid and void, and lack of superfluous ornament, this piece fulfilled the intentions Godwin had set out for himself in designing appropriate furniture for his own use. He wrote of this experience some ten years after the fact:

> When I came to the furniture I found that hardly anything could be bought ready made that was at all suitable to the requirements of the case. I therefore set to work and designed a lot of furniture, and, with a desire for economy, directed it to be made of deal, and to be ebonized. There were no mouldings, no ornamental metal work, no carving. Such effect as I wanted I endeavoured to gain, as in economical building, by the mere grouping of solid and void and by a more or less broken outline.[37]

This sideboard would be reproduced in William Watt's 1877 *Art Furniture* catalogue, along with many pieces in Godwin's Anglo-Japanese style. He would design a wide range of pieces in this style, from sofas to hanging wardrobes, in the 1860s and 1870s. He described them as "more or less founded on Japanese principles"[38] rather than actual furniture forms. There was very little precedent for Western forms within Japanese specimens since stands, small cabinets, trays, lanterns, hibachi, and folding screens were the only furniture forms to be found in a Japanese interior.

Godwin's study of Japanese arts and crafts probably began in the late 1850s. In 1862 he decorated his Bristol house with Japanese prints on the walls and an array of Oriental objects throughout, many of which he had bought in and around Bristol. He was probably aware of the Japanese Court at the International Exhibition of the same year and

was a collector of Japanese artifacts. An inventory in one of his diaries reveals that he owned Japanese furniture, textiles, ceramics, and bronzeware, in addition to Japanese prints, in the late 1860s.[39] He also began to study contemporary photographs of Japan and foreign accounts of travelers to Japan. Unlike Christopher Dresser, who visited Japan in 1876–77, Godwin never had the opportunity to travel to the Far East and had to rely on what was imported into England or reported in the newspapers and journals. His sketchbooks reveal that both Hokusai's *Manga* and Aimé Humbert's *Le Japon illustré* (1870) were rich sources for furniture forms and architectural details.[40]

A walnut tea table with shaped flaps and a stepped lower shelf (in The Metropolitan Museum of Art, New York; see fig. 3-1), is one of Godwin's most overtly Japanese designs. Its various elements—asymmetrical arrangement of shelves, latticework stretchers, angled joints bound with tooled brass braces, and rectangular legs encased in gilded brass *sabots*—point to the influence of Japanese design. A gong on stand designed by Godwin about 1875 (see fig. 3-15) also shows unmistakable Japanese influence. The lattice panels at the bottom of the stand are reminiscent of Japanese latticework, the top rail or lintel is based on Shinto shrine *tori* gates, and the top edges are covered with brasswork attached with rivets similar to that found on Japanese cabinets.

Not all of Godwin's Anglo-Japanese work, however, derived its features from Japanese specimens. Chinese hardwood furniture of the Ming and early Qing dynasties seemed to play an even greater role in this furniture than it had at Dromore. Godwin's ledgers indicate that he owned pieces of Chinese furniture as well as Chinese accessories, including a carved wooden screen.[41] Not only were a number of details of Chinese furniture adapted, such as the spiral or cloud-shaped feet used in the buffet at Dromore Castle, but certain Chinese forms were appropriated as well. Two that are particularly prevalent are the Chinese *kang*, or couch, which seems to have been the prototype for his sofa design,[42] and the Chinese compound wardrobe which Godwin used for his double wardrobe form. A comparison of a Ming couch-bed with lattice railings[43] and a Godwin mahogany sofa or settee (see figs. 3-8 and 3-9) reveals many interesting similarities. The most obvious are the rather deep seat proportions, the latticed side railings that curve down to meet the front legs, and the boxlike platform elevated high above the floor. The straight legs on castors, upholstered back splat and seat, and upright back posts with ball finials, however, are features of Western furniture.

In the Chinese bedroom, two identical wardrobes usually stand next to each other and Godwin found this

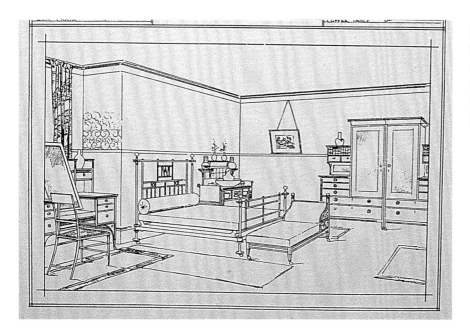

Fig. 8-18. E. W. Godwin. Design for a bedroom. From Watt, *Art Furniture* (1877): pl. 15 (detail). The Mitchell Wolfson Jr. Collection, The Wolfsonian–Florida International University, Miami Beach, Florida, TD 1990.40.62.

Fig. 8-19. E. W. Godwin. Wardrobe, ca. 1868. Made by William Watt. Pine, mirror glass insert, turned-wood knobs; 82⅞ x 47⅜ x 18⅝ in. (210.4 x 120.4 x 47.2 cm). Bristol Museums and Art Gallery, Bristol, N4505. *Checklist no. 37*

Chinese compound wardrobe particularly suited to Western use.[44] His sketchbooks contain many designs for combined wardrobes/chests of drawers meant to be made in pairs. Wardrobes made in pairs were used in his own bedroom, which he described in the *Architect* in 1876: "My wardrobe was a compound design—half chest of drawers and half hanging wardrobe—and, like the trouser patterns of some years ago, required a pair to show the complete design."[45]

William Watt's *Art Furniture* catalogue illustrates a bedroom furnished with a pair of matching wardrobes, mirror images of each other (fig. 8-18). A similar single wardrobe in the Bristol Museums and Art Gallery may have been one of two that were used by Godwin himself (fig. 8-19). What is interesting about the relationship of the Godwin wardrobes to their Chinese prototypes is that Godwin decided to adopt their modular arrangement. The Godwin wardrobe has been fabricated in components that can easily be taken apart and reassembled. The pine example in Bristol is made up of four separate elements—chest of drawers, hanging wardrobe, bookcase, and cornice. Each section is identified with its own William Watt label (fig. 8-20).

Fig. 8-20. William Watt label affixed to back of a wardrobe (fig. 8-19) designed by Godwin and made ca. 1868 for his own use.

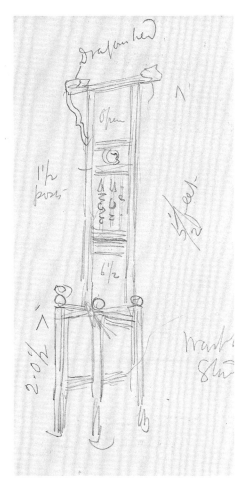

Fig. 8-21. E. W. Godwin. Sketch of a Chinese washstand, ca. 1877. Sketchbook. Pencil on paper; 5⅝ x 3¼ in. (14.3 x 8.2 cm). Trustees of the Victoria and Albert Museum, London, E.247-1963: 31.

Fig. 8-22. E. W. Godwin. Center table, ca. 1878. Made by Collinson and Lock. Macassar ebony veneer, rosewood, ivory inlay, brass castors; 27 x 27 x 27 in. (68.6 x 68.6 x 68.6 cm). Private collection: Sheri Sandler. *Checklist no. 93*

Godwin's adaptation of Chinese forms to suit Western furniture needs is also evident in his design for center tables. These tables, which constituted one of the major pieces of drawing-room furniture in the Victorian period, bear a striking resemblance to the Chinese hardwood stands used for lanterns or water basins in the Ming period.[46] That Godwin was aware of the Chinese forms is confirmed by the appearance of one of these stands in his sketchbooks. Annotated "Wash Hand Stand," it shows a typical Ming period stand with carved towel rack (fig. 8-21).[47] Godwin's octagonal center table for Collinson and Lock (fig. 8-22) is a multilegged form with radiating stretchers similar to a Ming-dynasty washstand.[48]

Godwin may have also been influenced by the bamboo and cane furniture from China that was sold in London throughout the nineteenth century.[49] With its lightweight construction and rectilinear outline, it appealed to Godwin's sense of austere design. He even owned some of it and, in describing his London drawing room in 1867, mentioned "four Japanese cane arm-chairs from Baker Street."[50] Nowhere is the influence of bamboo furniture more apparent than in the music bookcase or canterbury he designed for his own use in 1876 and which is currently in the Ellen Terry Memorial Museum (fig. 8-23). With its rounded, splayed legs, incised ring decoration, and rounded moldings, the piece simulates bamboo furniture. Godwin even designed wicker chairs, some of which were illustrated in the Watt catalogue (fig. 8-24). They have split-caned seats and backs and lightweight frames with incised ring decoration in imitation of bamboo.

In addition to adapting Asian features and motifs to Western forms, Godwin sometimes incorporated actual Chinese and Japanese fragments and accessories into his furniture designs. A walnut cabinet in the Victoria and Albert Museum has Japanese carved boxwood floral panels as well as ivory *netsuke* in the form of monkeys as its handles (see

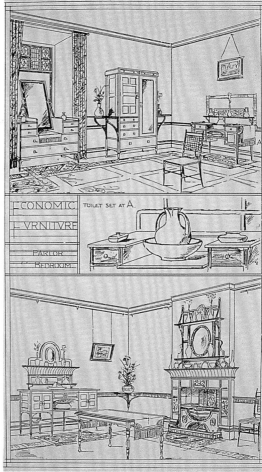

Fig. 8-23. E. W. Godwin. Music canterbury, ca. 1876. Made by William Watt. Walnut, brass fittings; 24⅛ x 20⅝ x 14⅛ in. (61.2 x 52.3 x 36 cm). Collection of the National Trust, Ellen Terry Memorial Museum, Smallhythe Place, Tenterden, Kent (SMA/F/83).

Fig. 8-24. E. W. Godwin. "Economic Furniture: Parlor, Bedroom." From Watt, *Art Furniture* (1877): pl. 16. The Mitchell Wolfson Jr. Collection, The Wolfsonian-Florida International University, Miami Beach, Florida, TD1990.40.62.

fig. 3-11). His celebrated sideboard in the Victoria and Albert Museum has panels of embossed Japanese leather paper in its upper and lower cupboard doors (fig. 8-25). Such panels, originally intended for wallpaper, were sold in the London galleries and bazaars that specialized in Asian arts and crafts in the 1860s and 1870s. Another version of the sideboard, now in the Bristol Museums and Art Gallery, has fragments of Japanese watercolors in the upper left cupboard doors, depicting a stylized Japanese floral arrangement with a hovering butterfly.[51] Descriptive notes from Watt's *Art Furniture* catalogue indicate that this sideboard also had an "Oriental curtain of gold embroidery on yellow satin"[52] that hung over the right cupboard. A photograph of the sideboard, taken in 1920 in the Chelsea sitting room of Ellen Terry, reveals that this curtain was embroidered with two addorsed peacocks.[53] Oriental accessories were arranged on its many display surfaces, blending with the decorative additions of curtain and watercolor panels.

Japanese lacquerwork also made its way into Godwin's cabinetwork. He designed a series of cabinets for Collinson and Lock with pieces taken from actual Japanese boxes and articles of furniture. Cannibalized fragments appear on a cabinet, for example, in a photography of the Collinson and Lock display at the Philadelphia Centennial Exhibition in 1876 (fig. 8-26). An annotated drawing for this cabinet in Godwin's sketchbook reveals that actual lacquer panels of a Japanese box framed in ebonized satinwood were inserted into the cabinets.[54] His sketchbooks also reveal that Japanese panels were used in many of his mantels and cabinets in the 1870s.[55] He also inserted a Japanese panel in the door frame of the house/studio he designed for artist Frank Miles in 1878.[56]

Tiled, Painted, and Stenciled Work

Godwin's adornment of furniture was not strictly limited to Asian accessories. He also incorporated Western adaptations of Asian designs into his furniture forms. Chief among these were the blue-and-white tiles he installed in some of his furniture forms, particularly dressing tables and overmantels. This was part of the general trend to incorporate artistically decorated tiles into furniture forms as diverse as chairs, sideboards, and plant stands in the 1870s and 1880s. Tiles were particularly suitable for the backs of washstands and dressing tables, and the tops of tables, for they were both easy to clean and durable. Godwin even designed some of the actual tiles. His ledger books and articles in the architectural press indicate that he worked for both Minton and Hollins, Stoke-on-Trent, Staffordshire[57] and Messrs. Wilcock and Company of Burmantofts, Leeds.[58] A Godwin dressing table or washstand in the Bristol Museums and Art Gallery has blue-and-white Minton tiles in a Persian-style floral pattern for its splashboard (see below, fig. 8-30). An Anglo-Japanese table illustrated by Elizabeth Aslin has Minton tiles on its top surface.[59]

Godwin's decorative work embraced far more than Asian arts and crafts. Painted panels in a Pre-Raphaelite style became especially popular in his designs of the 1870s. As the mid-nineteenth century taste for carved decoration declined, painted panels became the fashionable mode of decoration in art furniture of the 1870s and 1880s.[60] With rare exceptions, the painted panels incorporated in Godwin's furniture continue the predilection for classical scenes with figures. These were painted by a number of different artists, including Charles Fairfax Murray, Charles Glidden,[61] and Godwin's wife Beatrice.

The "Lucretia Cabinet" in the Detroit Museum of Arts is the most famous of Godwin's cabinets with painted figural decoration (see fig. 8-1). This rosewood corner cabinet was designed for the Collinson and Lock display at the Paris Exposition Universelle of 1878. Its painted decoration was carried out by Pre-Raphaelite painter and collector Charles Fairfax Murray.[62] The central panel, inscribed *Lucre-*

Fig. 8-25. E. W. Godwin. Sideboard, ca. 1867. Made by William Watt. Ebonized mahogany, silver-plated fittings, embossed Japanese leather paper inserts; 70⅛ x 63⅞ x 22 in. (178 x 162 x 56 cm). Trustees of the Victoria and Albert Museum, London, Circ. 38-1953.

Fig. 8-26. The Collinson and Lock stand at the Philadelphia Centennial Exhibition, 1876. Godwin designed the standing cabinet on the left, slightly behind the curtain. The Free Library of Philadelphia.

tia and initialed *CFM*, depicts the legendary Roman figure, recounted by Livy, who was raped by Sextus, son of Tarquin the Proud, and then committed suicide.[63] The cabinet's two smaller side panels depict two of the Virtues: Castitas (Chastity) and Fortitudo (Fortitude).

Beatrice Godwin, who married Godwin in 1876, was a painter and designer in her own right.[64] She is thought to have painted the four panels that are inset in the upper cupboard section of another cabinet, known as the "Four Seasons Cabinet" (see fig. 3-23), which is in the Victoria and Albert Museum.[65] These Pre-Raphaelite figures are after Godwin's designs symbolizing the twelve months.[66] Godwin would reuse these figures in the *British Architect Kalendar* of 1881.[67] With their earthtone colors of red, ocher, and brown on a gilt background, the panels blend with the cabinet's golden satinwood veneers and brass hardware.

In addition to painted figural representations, Godwin incorporated stenciled floral and abstract ornament into his furniture designs, particularly those pieces with an ebonized finish. This probably was a less expensive alternative to the painted panels. Chrysanthemum *mon* (crests) were a favorite motif and can be found stenciled in gold on the small doors of an ebonized hanging bookcase now in a private collection (fig. 8-27). The bookcase was a popular Godwin

design, and many versions of it are located in public and private collections throughout the world.

Circular medallions derived from Irish illuminated manuscripts were another favorite decoration for Godwin and were often stenciled onto the upper cupboard doors of Godwin's ebonized sideboards. One example, now in the Die Neue Sammlung, Munich (fig. 8-28), and another, which belonged to Alice and Wilfred Meynell, have this stenciled work (see fig. 4-11).[68]

Reformed Gothic Furnishings

It would be misleading to stress Asian influence in Godwin's work, for he continued to design reformed Gothic-style furniture for both ecclesiastical and domestic commissions throughout his career. In a letter to the firm of Collinson and Lock, dated July 30, 1873, he chastises them for "declining to work out medieval furniture & so meet the demand that is made by clergy & others on this style."[69] In 1877 Godwin designed Gothic-style church furnishings for Watt's *Art Furniture* catalogue. It was described as "Design for stalls & c. for choirs or private chapel."[70] As late as 1880, when Gothic-style domestic furniture was no longer fashionable, Godwin illustrated "A Gothic Table For a Drawing Rm"

Fig. 8-27. E. W. Godwin. Hanging bookcase, ca. 1867–85. Made by William Watt. Ebonized mahogany decorated with gold painted *mon* and brass fittings; 62⅜ x 32¹/₁₆ x 52 in. (158.4 x 81.5 x 132.1 cm). Private collection: Gary Kemp. *Checklist no. 38*

Fig. 8-28. E. W. Godwin. Sideboard, ca. 1867. Made by the Art Furniture Company. Ebonized deal, stenciled decoration, silver-plated fittings; 67⅜ x 60¼ x 18⅞ in. (171 x 153 x 48 cm). Die Neue Sammlung, Staatliches Museum für angewandte Kunst, Munich, 417/93.

alongside a "Queen Anne 'Over-Door'" in the *Building News*.[71] The commentator for the *Building News* remarked that this six-sided center table with its openwork tracery decoration was "an unusual subject just now for illustration" but one that had "an air of freshness about it." This was not an isolated event, for Godwin's sketchbooks reveal his unflagging interest in medieval-style furnishings. A Gothic-style cabinet with pointed tracery arches and painted panels is one of many examples in his sketchbooks from the late 1870s.[72]

Georgian Furniture

Georgian furniture without doubt had an impact on Godwin's design. His earliest home in Bristol, in 1862, was furnished with "carefully selected Antique furniture . . . a reversion to the taste of the eighteenth century."[73] Godwin's appreciation of Georgian furniture continued into the 1870s when he redecorated his London dining room "with a bow-fronted sideboard, Chippendale chairs, flap tables,

cabinets, bookcases, and a little escritoire, all of admirable colour, design and workmanship."[74]

The soberness of execution, rectilinear conception, beauty of proportion, lightness of form, and optimal use of woodgrain were all features of mid-to-late-Georgian furniture that appealed to Godwin. A mahogany spindle-leg tea table that Godwin designed in 1877 shows unmistakable Sheraton influence (fig. 8-29).[75] Its slender, turned legs, rectilinear stretchers, folding top, shaped apron support, and mahogany wood recall the "spider-leg" tea tables popular in England in the 1760s.[76] Godwin's sketchbooks reveal that he consulted Sheraton's *Cabinet Maker* in the British Museum in May 1876.[77]

Godwin's "Four Seasons Cabinet" (see fig. 3-23) also exhibits explicit Georgian characteristics. With its satinwood veneer, thin elegant proportions, splayed feet, reeded moldings, and open shelves, it resembles the open-shelved dwarf bookcases popular in the last decade of the eighteenth century. The top section, however, has Japanese

Fig. 8-29. E. W. Godwin. Tea table, 1877. Made by William Watt. Mahogany; 28 x 33¾ x 31¾ in. (71 x 85.7 x 80.5 cm). Private collection.

features: bell-shaped windows filled with brass latticework and horizontal top railings with metal-tipped finials. These resemble the Japanese architectural details Godwin included in "Japanese Wood Construction" in 1875.[78] Despite these Japanese elements, the overall effect of the cabinet is Georgian.

Design Concerns: Hygiene and Other Issues

Although Godwin explored many design idioms over his career, he had a predilection for thin, spindly forms devoid of carved ornament. This was in keeping with one of his major design concerns: hygienic, dust-free environments furnished with pieces that would not attract dirt and germs and could easily be cleaned and moved. This concern for domestic hygiene was a frequent theme in his writing. In an article for the *Globe* in 1872, he described the domestic household as "a tainted atmosphere with the seeds of disease in every crevice and corner."[79] A few years later, in an article on the furnishing of his own house in London in 1876, he wrote that: "cleanliness . . . I take to be the first consideration in all domestic design."[80]

Godwin's phobia for dust and dirt reflected the popular germ theory then circulating in London and other English cities.[81] Two cholera epidemics in London, in 1832 and 1848, and the incredibly high death rate of the working classes in the cities led to an increased awareness of the need to keep the Victorian household clean. Godwin's concern with cleanliness may have also been spurred on by his own chronic health problems, which ultimately led to his premature death.

Godwin's interest in hygiene prompted design modifications in his furniture. Castors, essential features of many of his designs from the 1860s, enabled pieces to be moved so that an entire room could be thoroughly cleaned. The castors he included in many of his chair designs, as well as on his large case pieces, vary in material—brass, white ceramic, black ceramic—and in size, reflecting the many different models available for sale in the nineteenth century. Two brands of castors Godwin used were produced by Cope of Birmingham and Parry of Manchester.[82]

In keeping with this concern for sanitation, Godwin's case pieces, particularly those for bedrooms, are generally austere in design with little or no ornament to attract germs and dust. They are usually lower than is customary, so that their tops can be dusted frequently and easily, and the bottom drawer or section is raised off the floor and castors are included to facilitate cleaning. His pine wardrobe (see figs. 8-18, 8-24) exhibits all these modifications.

Godwin's designs for beds also reflect his dedication to domestic hygiene. Examples in his sketchbooks[83] and in Watt's *Art Furniture* catalogue (see figs. 8-18 and 8-24) are made of minimal sections of brass, without testers or curtains, and mounted on castors so that the bedroom could be easily scrubbed and cleaned without dust-catching fabrics and surfaces.

Washstands and dressing tables were also minimally decorated and therefore easily scoured. In furnishing his own bedroom, Godwin recommended a "dressing table and wash stand of plain light wood, deal or birch or ash, neither oiled nor varnished, and designed with plain surfaces so as to be capable of being cleaned and scrubbed like the kitchen table."[84] A Godwin washstand currently in the Bristol Museums and Art Gallery (fig. 8-30) may have been the one he described in his own bedroom.[85] With its simple yet elegant lines, undecorated surfaces, large castors, white marble top, and splash board of blue-and-white tiles, it fulfilled Godwin's recommendations for a piece of furniture that was both plain and sanitary.

Godwin's upholstered pieces similarly reflect his concern for a hygienic household. Godwin abhorred the overstuffed seating forms that were often used in mid-Victorian bedrooms and drawing rooms. He described them as "arrangements of laziness" that assumed "an almost tyrannical position."[86] In contrast, his settees and other up-

Fig. 8-30. E. W. Godwin. Washstand, ca. 1870 Made by William Watt. Pine, white marble top, mirror glass, blue and white ceramic tiles, brass fittings, and white ceramic castors; 63⅞ x 36 x 19⅞ in. (162.4 x 91.5 x 50.5 cm). Bristol Museums and Art Gallery, Bristol (N4506).

holstered pieces have enough upholstery to render them functional, but not enough padding to be totally inviting. The lattice-sided settee he designed for Dromore Castle and put into commercial production with the firm of William Watt has the minimum of upholstery in its seating cushion, while the back is mostly left open except for a rectangular support with three modestly padded sections (see fig. 3-9).

Chairs with caned seats and backs could easily be cleaned, and their flat surfaces would not collect dust or germs. Godwin designed many caned-seat chairs in differ-

Fig. 8-31. E. W. Godwin. Anglo-Japanese side chair (one of a pair), ca. 1875. Probably made by William Watt. Ebonized wood with cane seat; 39 x 16⅞ x 16⅛ in. (99 x 43 x 41 cm). Musée d'Orsay, Paris, OAO 1302. *Checklist no. 70*

ent styles during his career. One example is the lightweight Anglo-Japanese side chair now in the Musée d'Orsay (fig. 8-31). His popular Jacobean or Old English chairs, first designed in 1867, also had caned seats (fig. 8-32), as did an Anglo-Greek chair of the 1880s (fig. 8-33). Leather was another popular upholstery material for Godwin, especially for dining chairs and library chairs. Leather was particularly suitable for these two rooms where the smell of food or cigars might permeate the cloth fabric. His dining chairs for Dromore Castle were covered in a stamped leather (see fig. 8-15), as were many of his chairs for the library illustrated in Watt's *Art Furniture* catalogue.[87] He would use the same stamped leather design for an easel (fig. 8-34), possibly for Dromore Castle in about 1870.[88]

What is ironic is that with all this attention to a germ-free environment, Godwin designed cabinets that typically show a plethora of small shelves—and even whole pieces—for the display of knickknacks. Hanging shelves on which a great number of objects could be displayed were favorite designs of Godwin. Many hanging bookcases survive; two are in the Bristol Museums and Art Gallery.[89] Other objects designed for the display of bric-à-brac include mantelpieces

Fig. 8-32. E. W. Godwin. "Old English or Jacobean" chair, ca. 1867. Made by William Watt. Ebonized wood, cane seat; 33 x 21 x 19⅜ in. (83.8 x 53.3 x 49.5 cm). Private collection.

Fig. 8-33. E. W. Godwin. "Greek" side chair, ca. 1885. Made by William Watt. Ash with cane seat; 39¾ x 14 x 16¾ in. (101 x 35.6 x 42.6 cm). Private collection. *Checklist no. 103*

with many projecting shelves and case pieces for "the exhibition of works of art, and the display of articles de virtu."[90]

Godwin realized, however, that there was a tendency to overload these pieces with art objects. He stressed the importance of displaying a few well-selected items. In an article he wrote on mantelpieces, he complained that "there are those whose *furore* for 'collecting' has entirely outrun their artistic judgement, and whose mantelpieces are liter-

ally nothing more nor less than repetitions of the upper part of the vernacular kitchen dresser—a vulgar heap of costly china, where the close proximity of pot and plate interrupt the full appreciation of one and the other."[91]

Much of Godwin's furniture has a thin, spindly look, perhaps the result of his belief that a room should be dominated by fixed architectural features, not furniture or movables. Godwin wrote: "In a well-balanced properly-

Fig. 8-34. E. W. Godwin. Easel, ca. 1870. Probably made by William Watt or Reuben Burkitt and Company. Ebonized wood, brass fittings, and leather with stamped pattern in gold, 65¾ x 35¾ x 52 in. (167 x 91 x 132 cm). The Mitchell Wolfson Jr. Collection, The Wolfsonian-Florida International University, Miami Beach, Florida, TD 1989.149.2.

ordered room, the details of windows, doors, mantelpieces, and, indeed, of all distinctly architectural fixtures, should be always bolder than the details of the furniture or moveables."[92] Turning away from the monumental, heavily decorated pieces that were so much a part of popular Victorian taste, Godwin wrote: "I venture to deny the existence of any satisfactory reasons for producing such weighty furniture or such heavy 'decoration.'"[93] Lightness of construction became one of the leitmotifs of his furniture design: "The construction is as light as is consistent with the strength required."[94] This lighter, more practical treatment anticipates the themes of modern furniture design.

Unlike William Morris, who looked back to the medieval way of craftsmanship and had ambivalent attitudes toward machinery, Godwin had no qualms about designing for the many art manufacturers who made some use of the machine to mass-produce goods for the ever-expanding middle-class market. Godwin's ledgers and diaries in the Victoria and Albert Museum indicate that he worked for the London firms of Cox and Son, Gillow and Company, W. A. and S. Smee, James Peddle, Waugh and Sons, and William Watt. In addition, Collinson and Lock paid him a monthly retainer from 1872 to 1875 and authorized individual payments for special commissions.[95]

He shared at least one view with Morris, however, by having a certain nostalgia for the elevated status and accomplished decorative work of the artists of the Middle Ages and Renaissance. Godwin tells us that the medieval artist "filled up the whole of his time for some years in painting and decorating furniture, seats, beds, caskets, &c."[96] Moreover, like Morris, Godwin grappled with the dilemma of affordability throughout most of his working life. In his architectural commissions it would take the form of parson's houses, a plan for cooperative housing, and affordable housing for residents of Bedford Park. His early experience with the Art Furniture Company taught him to take the exigencies of economic conditions seriously.[97] He was associated with the firm in 1867, but it went out of business

Fig. 8-35. E. W. Godwin. "Parlour Furniture." Drawn by Maurice B. Adams. From *Building News* 37 (31 October 1879): 522 and illustration [531].

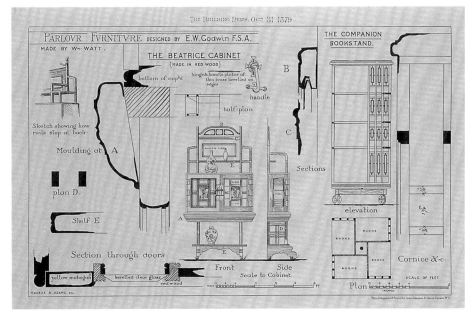

in 1868 because its furniture was beyond the economic reach of its clientele. The need to produce well-designed furniture at an affordable price became one of Godwin's primary aims. In writing of his experiences in designing his first pieces he recalled that he had "designed a lot of furniture, and, with a desire for economy, directed it to be made of deal, and to be ebonised."[98]

This concern with matters of economy carried through the advertising and promotional materials linked with his work through the 1870s and 1880s. In his preface to the *Art Furniture* catalogue published in 1877, he admonished his manufacturer William Watt to "continue . . . producing furniture of refined design, of good workmanship, of reasonable cost" (p. iii). In fact, plate 16 of the catalogue, entitled "Economic Furniture," shows pieces for the parlor and bedroom, which Godwin describes in the text as being "designed for single people living in small chambers."[99] An illustration of furniture in the *Building News* (18 December 1885) late in his career was entitled "Working Drawings of Inexpensive Furniture By E. W. Godwin F.S.A."[100] Obviously, furniture that could be economically produced was still at the forefront of his design agenda even at the end of his career.

In addition to matters of economy, the functional role of the pieces he designed was another concern. To this end Godwin incorporated multipurpose mechanisms into his furniture forms. His music stool, illustrated in plate 12 of the William Watt's *Art Furniture* catalogue, had a mechanism to raise its seat, both to accommodate the size of the player and to store music. His bookstand, made for William Watt and illustrated in the *Building News* (fig. 8-35), had what the reviewer called "a novel contrivance having four sides, and turning on a centre which stands on a tripod, so that a con-

siderable number of books may be consulted by a reader who may be sitting at a writing table, without quitting his seat."[101]

The most common multipurpose addition by Godwin was the hinged shelf found on many of his cabinet forms and tables, ranging from the classic sideboard (see fig. 4-1) to the Anglo-Japanese table (see fig. 3-1). The concept of hinged shelves, resting on swinging flaps, originated with the pembroke tables of the eighteenth century. Their purpose was to provide extra surface space when needed. Eighteenth-century cabinet makers also experimented with and incorporated a great range of mechanisms to expand the comfort of their products and to appeal to the taste for novelty. This quest for comfort and ingenuity continued throughout the nineteenth century. It was not the comfort aspect that so concerned Godwin, however, but rather the functional impact of such mechanisms on traditional furniture forms.

Godwin's views on utility were interrelated with cost effectiveness. He wrote that "the greatest-utility-at-the-least-cost principle is the only sure and certain road to beauty . . . in furniture."[102] To Godwin, pretension was a sure road to failure, as it reflected the "vulgar desire of exhibiting money's worth."[103] He admired the plain unadorned table, the three-legged stool, the plate rack, the dresser and hanging shelves often used in the kitchen, forms that had not changed since the Middle Ages. The Windsor chair was the only new form of furniture he admired, since according to Godwin it "was an innovation supported by genuine merit."[104]

Cottage and Queen Anne Styles

Godwin's admiration for well-designed kitchen furniture

Fig. 8-36. E. W. Godwin. Cottage cabinet, ca. 1874. Made by Collinson and Lock. Mahogany with brass fittings; 50 x 66 x 16⅞ in. (127 x 167.5 x 43 cm). Private collection: Sheri Sandler. *Checklist no. 51*

may have been the source of inspiration for a group of furniture he called "Cottage" style, designed for the firm of Collinson and Lock in 1873–74. This simple furniture was part of the so-called Queen Anne movement, an eclectic revivalist mix of styles that had little to do with the architecture and interiors of Queen Anne's time.

Godwin's sketchbooks and ledgers are full of drawings and commissions for furniture in this Cottage style: from angled cabinets, sideboards, and hanging cabinets to washstands, tables, and even couches.[105] A mahogany cabinet from 1874 (in a private collection), however, is the only extant piece so far that has been identified as part of this

group of furnishings made for Collinson and Lock (fig. 8-36). The cabinet is based on a drawing in his sketchbooks annotated "Cottage drawg rm cabt."[106] With its broad forms, heavy proportions, and minimum of ornament, it appears to be an abstracted version of his reformed Gothic furniture of the 1860s. Ornament is limited to a series of ribbed grooves and turned spindles. The brass hardware consists of the same ring pull handles and rectangular back plates with keyholes that he used on some of his Gothic Revival pieces for Dromore Castle. What is different, however, is the incorporation of curvilinear elements into its overall form. The strictly rectilinear outline of such pieces as his dressing table or sideboard has been softened to include beautifully curved lines, particularly in the side panels with their round-arched bottom openings.

Godwin revived this series of furnishings for William Watt in 1876. His sketchbooks are rich in designs for almost identical forms. One drawing from this group, annotated "Cheap deal Furniture," shows a low cabinet bookcase, as well the dressing table with mirror glass[107] and the drawing-room cabinet he had designed earlier for Collinson and Lock.[108]

With Godwin's interest in plain, well-designed furnishings, it is surprising that only one piece of Queen Anne furniture appears in *Art Furniture*. This is a design for a "Cabinet in the Queen Anne Style" illustrated in plate 12, "Drawing Room Furniture." With its broken pediment, dentilated cornice, molded doors, numerous shelves and brackets, and tapered legs, it features many of the favorite motifs of this style.[109] Although the Queen Anne style was not a favorite of Godwin's, he designed a number of houses in this manner in the 1870s, notably the Gillow Mansions on the Thames Embankment in 1878 and the first houses for the "Queen Anne" community of Bedford Park in 1876. The furnishing style seemed to be more popular in the late 1870s and early 1880s, which may account for the lack of examples in the Watt catalogue. A drawing-room suite by Shoolbred and Company illustrated in the *Cabinet Maker* in August of 1880 was described as designed in "the prevailing style of the day, a free treatment of Queen Anne."[110] And a Godwin "Queen Anne 'Over-Door'" illustrated in the *Building News* the same year was described as being in accord "with the present taste in furniture matters."[111]

Anglo-Greek Furniture

Although his Anglo-Japanese designs were most popular, Godwin also designed Anglo-Greek furniture for the trade. A ledger entry from 1876 reveals that Godwin was then creating a line of Anglo-Greek furniture for Waugh and Sons,[112] although none of these has yet surfaced. Drawings of Grecian-style furniture in Godwin's sketchbooks give us some idea of these pieces. Klismos-type chairs (fig. 8-37) and thrones with cut-out legs and inlaid decoration appear, as do tables of tripod form.[113] Godwin also designed floor cloths, wallpapers, and ceramics (see fig. 11-3) to outfit a total Anglo-Greek interior.

Several years later, in the 1880s, when he was working on a Greek play, he resurrected the Greek theme and designed a line of Anglo-Greek chairs that were marketed commercially by William Watt. They were made in several versions including one with arms, upright laths in the splat, and variations of legs, from turned to "cut square." An

Fig. 8-37. E. W. Godwin. Chairs in the Greek style, ca. 1873–76. Sketchbook (detail). Pencil and color shadings; 5⅝ x 3⅝ in. (14.3 x 9.3 cm). Trustees of the Victoria and Albert Museum, London, E.229-1963: 109.

oak example with upholstered seat and back and turned decoration on the legs is in the Victoria and Albert Museum (see preface, fig. ii), while an American private collection contains an ash example with caned seat and plain legs (see fig. 8-33). Sketches in Godwin's notebooks in the Victoria and Albert Museum indicate that these were inspired by his studies of antiquities in the British Museum and by nineteenth-century texts on ancient Greek art. One such sketch, dated about 1883, shows a stool taken from the Elgin Marbles at the British Museum with a similar rounded leg, and the same sketch includes a couch from the *Dictionnaire des Arts Grecques* published in Paris in 1873.[114] Moreover, Godwin's fascination with Greek furnishings led him to write an article on the ancient Greek home, published in a contemporary journal, *The Nineteenth Century*, in 1886.[115]

William Watt was only one of the firms that showcased Grecian-style furniture by Godwin. Another firm, W. A. and S. Smee, 6 Finsbury Pavement, London, also manufactured Grecian-style chairs designed by Godwin in the 1880s as did the firm of James Peddle.[116] A Smee chair, now in the Wolfsonian Collection in Miami Beach, Florida, shows unmistakable Greek influence, with a sloped back rest, turned legs, and double seat rails.[117]

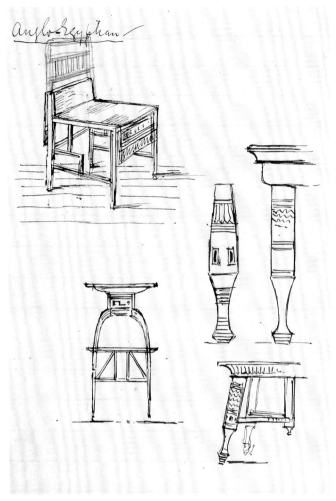

Fig. 8-38. E. W. Godwin. "Anglo-Egyptian" furniture, ca. 1872–79. Sketchbook. Pen and ink and pencil on paper; 5 ¾ x 3 ¹⁵⁄₁₆ in. (24.6 x 10 cm). Trustees of the Victoria and Albert Museum, London, E.233-1963: 53.

Anglo-Egyptian Furniture

Godwin's interest in ancient cultures led him to the study of Egyptian artifacts and yet another design mode or theme. In 1876 he designed a whole range of Anglo-Egyptian furniture for Waugh and Sons.[118] Based on Egyptian forms Godwin studied and sketched in the British Museum,[119] this group of furniture included pieces for the drawing room, bedroom, and even office.[120] Although it has not been possible to identify any of the actual pieces, drawings inscribed "Anglo-Egyptian" in Godwin's sketchbooks reveal austere, thronelike side chairs with elongated uprights and lateral stretchers, an occasional table with dished top and

angled supports, and a writing table with splayed legs, incised decoration, and angled stretchers (fig. 8-38).[121]

Godwin's interest in Egyptian furniture, however, probably began a decade earlier when unmistakable Egyptian details begin to appear in his designs. Angled stretchers and turned, splayed legs reminiscent of those in the Thebes stools and tables at the British Museum are in the design for an ebonized coffee table he originally created for his own use in 1867. It was made by both William Watt and Collinson and Lock (fig. 8-39). Egyptian-inspired details, such as angled underframing and ring-turned legs, reappeared in an oak dressing table he designed for himself about 1879, which is in the Ellen Terry Memorial Museum.[122] The most obvious Egyptian borrowing, however, occurs in his Eagle chair of 1869, which resembles the ceremonial thrones of dynastic Egypt with their animal-leg supports. The stylized wings of the goddess Ra are carved into the top rail panel of the chair reproduced in plate 11 of *Art Furniture*.[123]

Old English or Jacobean Style Furniture

With characteristic versatility Godwin created notable designs in the so-called Old English or Jacobean style that was popular in the 1870s. It was part of an English national desire to rediscover its past, which had begun with the Romantic interiors of the first half of the nineteenth century.[124] This is hardly surprising when one considers Godwin's longstanding interest in the plays of Shakespeare, which he pursued in his architectural journalism as well as his work in the theater. A design for a sideboard in one of Godwin's sketchbooks, dated July 30, 1876,[125] may be for a piece put in production for William Watt and illustrated in plate 15 of Watt's *Art Furniture* Catalogue under the title "Old English or Jacobean." With its turned cup-and-cover supports, tiered form with deep lower display shelf mounted on feet, and fluted cornice, the sideboard recalls late-sixteenth-century oak cupboards. That Godwin studied surviving examples firsthand is confirmed by the many drawings of furniture details in his sketchbooks from the same period. These show quite detailed studies of Jacobean specimens, among them carved and gadrooned baluster supports.[126]

Although certainly not the most original of his styles, Godwin's Jacobean furniture must have been quite popular. Of the sixteen plates in William Watt's *Art Furniture* showcasing furniture, four illustrated furniture in the Jacobean style. What is different about Godwin's rendition of this style is the reduction in scale and proportions intended to suit the smaller rooms of Victorian homes as well as the more modern and functional modes of living. A review of some of Godwin's Old English or Jacobean

Fig. 8-39. E. W. Godwin. Coffee table, ca. 1872-75. Made by Collinson and Lock. Ebonized mahogany; 27¼ x 20⅛ x 19⅝ in. (69 x 51 x 50 cm). Private collection: Gary Kemp. *Checklist no. 41*

Fig. 8-40. E. W. Godwin. Designs for "Old English or Jacobean Furniture." From *Furniture Gazette* n.s. 6 (19 August 1876): following 112, and subsequently published in Watt, *Art Furniture* (1877): pl. 15.

Fig. 8-41. E. W. Godwin. "Old English or Jacobean" armchair, ca. 1867. Made by William Watt. Ebonized wood, upholstered seat; 34½ x 20½ x 20½ in. (87.5 x 52 x 52 cm). Private collection: Gary Kemp. *Checklist no. 42*

Fig. 8-42. E. W. Godwin. "The Shakespere [*sic*] Dining-Room Set." From *Building News* (11 November 1881): 634.

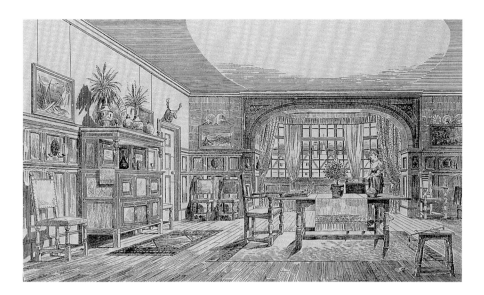

dining-room furniture in the *Furniture Gazette* of August 1876 (fig. 8-40) mentions the lighter-than-usual proportions: "This 'Old English' or Jacobean dining-room furniture, is given mainly for the purpose of showing how even this somewhat costly and heavy style may be treated as to preserve all its artistic characteristics and yet be reasonably light."[127] Godwin's intention to design Old English–style furniture with more modest proportions than the original pieces is reiterated in an article in which he criticizes the fashion for Early English furniture with "massive" proportions and questions the "reasons for producing such weighty furniture." But with a change in dining habits, appropriate body type, and architectural settings, the "style of furniture suited for our dining-rooms should also be light."[128]

Thus, a lightweight, round oak armchair, which Godwin called "Old English or Jacobean" is one of his recommended dining chairs (fig. 8-41). Godwin described these chairs as "light enough for a child to carry, and strong enough for a child to clamber on."[129] This chair, one of Godwin's most popular designs, was illustrated in plate 15 of the Watt catalogue of 1877. In the descriptive notes to the catalogue, Godwin informs us that it was taken from an "old English example."[130]

Godwin's Jacobean-style dining tables were also smaller in scale than their prototypes and often had leaves that could extend their dimensions. The massive dining table "capable of accommodating at least fourteen people" was not suitable to the requirements of modern life which, Godwin tells us, normally involved seating "only four people at a time."[131] Thus, the three Godwin Jacobean-style dining tables illustrated in William Watt's *Art Furniture* catalogue are all diminutive in scale, ranging from just three feet, six inches to seven feet in length.[132] Godwin's Jacobean-style buffets followed this trend and ranged in size from six feet to seven feet, six inches.[133] Godwin also

designed these to be manageable in size to the point that they could "be moved easily in any direction by one pair of hands."[134]

Godwin's interest in the Jacobean period continued into the 1880s with his "Shakspere [*sic*] Dining-Set," an oak dining suite in Jacobean style for William Watt. An 1881 illustration of this suite appeared in the *Building News*, where it was described grandly as having been "chiefly taken . . . from the original furniture, which is said to be either in the possession of Shakespeare's family at the present time, or known to have belonged to him."[135] This suite included court cupboard, farthingale chair and side chairs, trestle stool, and planked dining table "held together by a grooved ledge at either end" (fig. 8-42).[136]

The farthingdale chairs were quite popular. One is the Ellen Terry Memorial Museum at Smallhythe Place, Kent, and an almost identical example is now in a private collection (fig. 8-43). The pieces come closer to reproductions of historical styles than any of Godwin's other schemes of decoration, leading one contemporary reviewer to comment that "there is something clever in thus capturing those who dote on the antique by certified modern reproductions."[137] Another reviewer was less charitable in his critique:

A popular architect looks up a chair attributed to Shakespeare, finds some more old furniture to match, and then reproduces the lot under the title of "the Shakespeare dining-room set." The room certainly makes a capital picture from an antiquarian point of view: whether the furniture comfortably meets the requirements of a modern dining room is another question, which does not matter much.[138]

The Shakespeare chair was extremely popular and was reproduced by many other furniture manufacturers. In

Fig. 8-43. E. W. Godwin. "Shakespeare" armchair, ca. 1881. Made by William Watt. Oak; 40½ x 24 x 20 in. (103 x 61 x 50.8 cm). Collection of Paul Reeves, London. *Checklist no. 119*

1885 a commentator in the *Cabinet Maker And Art Furnisher* noted that " . . . Shakespeare's chair . . . has been frequently reproduced of late—thanks, in the first instance, to Mr. E. W. Godwin—and much used in halls and libraries."[139] An article in another issue of the same journal observed that "Mr. Watt seems still to find it worth while to adhere to that thoroughly English Shakespearian furniture which Mr. Godwin designed expressly for him some years ago."[140]

Promotion of Godwin's Designs

Godwin's reputation and influence as a furniture designer spread with the publication of his designs for furniture in the *Building News*, especially between 1871 and 1886, as well as in William Watt's *Art Furniture* catalogue, first published in London in 1877 (see fig. 3-18). This volume made his designs available to an even greater audience. Twenty lithographs of Godwin's historicist work, in addition to his Anglo-Japanese designs, were included. The reviewers took notice and endorsed this collection of designs for their readers.[141] In fact the catalogue was so popular that a second printing was issued the following year.

Godwin's popularity as a furniture designer is further confirmed by the extensive copying and plagiarizing of his work by the commercial trade. In the preface of Watt's *Art Furniture*, Godwin complained that many of the designs he had produced for William Watt some nine or ten years earlier had "fortunately secured such attention as to be copied by others in the trade . . . . A marked example of this is the square coffee table . . . . [I am] meeting it almost wherever I go,—in private houses, in show-rooms, in pictures, and in books, very prominently in the frontispiece of Miss Garrett's 'Suggestions for House Decoration' (Macmillan's 'Art at Home' series)."[142] Plagiarized Godwin coffee tables appear in contemporary trade catalogues, advertisements, and illustrations in the art and architectural journals of the time. Although the overall shape is basically the same, the proportions and treatment of the details differ. A comparison of a Godwin original (see fig. 8-39) with a copy by Bruce and Smith, for example, reveals a different spacing of the angled spindles, less pleasing proportions, and thicker turned legs.[143] Another version by D. Blythe Adamson and Company, 55 and 57 Wilson Street, Finsbury Square, London, was reproduced in the *Cabinet Makers' Pattern Book* (1877–79) printed by Wyman and Sons as supplements to the *Furniture Gazette*. It also exhibits similar variations in proportions and details.[144] It is no wonder that Godwin wrote that the "lines and dimensions of the different parts of what seems to be a very simple bit of furniture constitute its beauty and its art—if it has any. But I have seen the lines changed, the proportions altered, until that which I had regarded as a beauty became to me an offense and an eyesore."[145] Other pieces extensively copied by the trade included his caned chair (see fig. 8-31)[146] and his Old English or Jacobean chair (see figs. 8-32, 8-41).[147]

International Exhibitions

The display of Godwin's works at some of the leading international exhibitions also helped bring his furniture designs to the attention of the general public and the trade.[148] Godwin's work was first exhibited at the Collinson and Lock stand of the Vienna Exhibition of 1873 where he was represented by five pieces in different styles as well as the design for the exhibition stand itself.[149]

Fig. 8-44. E. W. Godwin. Design for chairs for the Vienna Exhibition of 1873. Pen, ink, and pencil on tracing paper; 13⅜ x 17½ in. (34 x 44.5 cm). Collection of the National Trust, Ellen Terry Memorial Museum, Smallhythe Place, Tenterden, Kent, SMA D.24. *Checklist no. 50*

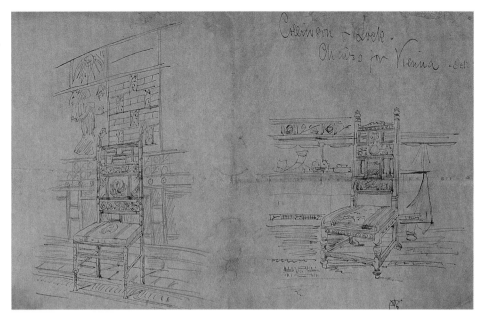

Fig. 8-45. E. W. Godwin. The "Butterfly Cabinet," 1878. Made by William Watt; painted decoration by James McNeill Whistler. Mahogany, glass, ceramic tiles, brass fittings; 119¼ x 74¾ in. (303 x 190 cm). The Hunterian Art Gallery, Glasgow, Scotland.

Drawings in his sketchbooks indicate that he designed a Jacobean sideboard in oak,[150] and a cabinet bookstand or *bibliothek* in ebonized wood with gold, "sparingly applied."[151] In addition, a design survives for two chairs (fig. 8-44), inscribed "Collinson & Lock Chairs for Vienna— Oct '73," in the Ellen Terry Memorial Museum.[152] One of these chairs is in the Anglo-Japanese style while the other is a Jacobean adaptation. Godwin's diary for March 20, 1873, mentions a visit to "Mr. Lock re Vienna Table partics," so obviously a table was part of the exhibition installation as well.[153]

Godwin's work must have had a sizable following, for Collinson and Lock again exhibited an Anglo-Japanese cabinet by him at the Philadelphia Centennial of 1876, and a Godwin rosewood cabinet (see fig. 8-1) and octagonal table with ivory inlay (see fig. 8-22) were shown at the Paris Universal Exhibition of 1878, although by this time Godwin was no longer exclusively designing for the firm.

It was Godwin's Butterfly Suite, however, designed for the firm of William Watt specifically for the Paris Exposition Universelle of 1878 that gained him the greatest international prominence (see fig. 4-9). The Butterfly Suite, conceived by Godwin and painted by Whistler (whose monogram was a butterfly), attracted worldwide press attention. A drawing by Godwin dated "Paris 22 September 1877" in the Victoria and Albert Museum[154] represents the combination fireplace and cabinet with shelves, which were part of this extensive suite that also included lightweight chairs, occasional tables, a sofa, and a case for music.[155]

The modified Butterfly Cabinet is in the collection of the Hunterian Art Gallery, Glasgow (fig. 8-45).[156] The doors and central panels of the cabinet have a Japanese cloud motif and butterflies on a primrose ground. The mahogany panels are sprinkled with butterflies and chrysanthemum petals in gold. This painted decoration, horizontal in orientation, softens the cabinet's strong vertical design. Whistler's painted additions also provide a degree of animation to an otherwise ponderous, massive piece of furniture.

A "lounging chair," with a wheel-shaped arm (fig. 8-46), from this suite is now in a private collection.[157] The design was illustrated in the *Building News*, but the actual chair is slightly different from the illustration.[158] The bottom stretcher and a padded headrest have been eliminated. The *Building News* described the chair as being exhibited with a cushion of "yellow plush" and being available in varia-

Fig. 8-46. E. W. Godwin. Easy chair, ca. 1876. Made by William Watt. Ebonized wood, upholstery, brass castors; 32 x 23 x 31 in. (81.3 x 58.4 x 78.7 cm). The Brant Foundation, Greenwich, Connecticut. *Checklist no. 81*

tions, including added spindles in the arm "if four, as shown, are thought insufficient."[159]

This suite caused a sensation in the international press. Many reviewers criticized it for being impractical and flimsy. One commentator for the *Magazine of Art*, for example, wrote that some of this furniture seemed "rather slight for everyday use," and described its color scheme as "this 'agony' in yellow."[160]

In spite of the many negative reviews, there was also a great positive reception. An earlier comment in the *Society of Arts Artisan's Report* (1878) cited the suite of furniture "designed to an original style by Mr. Godwin."[161] The *British Architect and Northern Engineer* commended "the exhibit of Wm. Watt . . . a very pleasant harmony of color. Chairs, mantlepieces, settees, & c. are all in pale yellowish mahogany, light and even elegant in form . . . the general scheme of colour, which is excellent . . . the manner in which the panel decoration is, as it were, carried through on to the wall, is ingenious and suggestive."[162] The *New York Tribune* (July 6, 1878) commented on "the carpentry as light as if the long fingers of a saffron-faced artist had coaxed it into shape."[163] In any event, this controversial exhibit produced an unprecedented amount of news coverage which spread interest in Godwin's designs.

International Clientele

By the 1870s Godwin had attracted many clients from beyond his national boundaries. Hermann Muthesius wrote that Godwin's work was studied and admired in Germany and Austria at a time when English work was not well-considered.[164] Upon seeing his furniture at the International Exhibition in Vienna in 1873, Prince Esterhazy of Vienna commissioned him to design some chairs and a ceiling through the firm of Collinson and Lock. Godwin may even have traveled to Vienna for this commission: a sketchbook design for an armchair is annotated "chair for Esterhazy via Collinson and Lock Oct '73 Ordered in Vienna"; another page is annotated "Met Lock Golden Lamb Hotel Leopold Strasse Vienna Oct 18 1873."[165]

By the same time, Godwin's influence had spread to America, where his commissions through Collinson and Lock included one from James Goodwin for his residence in Hartford, Connecticut.[166] A note in Godwin's sketchbook confirms the identity of "Mr. Goodwin—America. Perspective sketch of an octagonal centre table. Mantel glass & shelves 6.1/8 chimney breast height 11.6."[167] Godwin's ledgers for Collinson and Lock record that he designed "a mantelpiece (America)" in December of 1873 and "a table (America)" in January of 1874 for Collinson and Lock.[168] Moreover, surviving photographs of the Hartford

residence in 1873 show that Godwin's bamboo-patterned wallpaper hung on the walls of the dining room (see fig. 10-24).[169]

That the Goodwins imported English wallpaper and furniture is not surprising since many rich Americans at this time were doing so. The American market was a developing sphere of economic activity for Collinson and Lock, and in 1876 they exhibited at the Philadelphia Centennial. Although Godwin has been credited in the past with designing most of the pieces for their exhibition stand (see fig. 8-26),[170] period photographs and reviews reveal that Godwin only designed the Anglo-Japanese cabinet ornamented with panels taken from actual Japanese boxes, and the sketch for this cabinet indicates that it had been designed by Godwin some two years earlier, in July 1874, when he was still working exclusively for Collinson and Lock.[171] By the time of the exhibition, he was no longer under contract, which may explain why more of his pieces were not shown. In any case, Godwin had a strong following in America, which was increased by the publication of Watt's *Art Furniture* catalogue in 1877. Twelve of its plates appeared a year later in the American periodical, the *Art-Worker*,[172] and soon Godwin's creations resonated through the American design world, attracting the attention of American architects, decorators, and designers.[173]

Godwin's work had a wide international following. His designs were copied in India in the 1880s by local manufacturers, including the Bombay Art Manufacturing Company.[174] There is also evidence that copies of his designs reached Australia through the firm of Cottier and Company, Art Furnishers, who opened branches in Sydney and Melbourne in the 1870s.[175] In addition, an advertisement for Cullis Hill and Company in the *Melbourne Bulletin* in May 1885 shows pieces taken from plate 12 of Watt's *Art Furniture*.[176]

Godwin did not tie himself morally or aesthetically to any one style. His furniture demonstrates an original and distinctive output very definitely his own, and he practiced what he described as "judicious eclecticism."[177] He believed that the way to the future was through the study of the past, but his antiquarian interests and scholarship never dictated the forms of his design work; they informed and enriched. He studied more recent design traditions from different parts of the world, including Japan, but he used the design repertory of each culture in highly original ways to produce work that appealed to contemporary sensibilities.

Godwin's designs were always rooted in the need for forms of furniture appropriate for modern living. He experimented with modular and fitted furniture, which would only become widely popular in the mid-twentieth century.[178] He grappled with problems of affordability, utility, and function, concerns that would preoccupy many designers throughout the twentieth century, from Josef Hoffmann in Austria to Alvar Aalto in Finland and Charles and Ray Eames in the United States. Questions of hygiene as it was understood in the period also entered Godwin's design consciousness, resulting in furniture without dust-catching ornament and often mounted on castors so that the surrounding room could be easily cleaned. His concern for cleanliness and simplicity, rooted in the health-reform movements of the period,[179] was paralleled in the design preferences of the Arts and Crafts movement, with its emphasis on simplicity. Nevertheless, Godwin was one of the few designers of his day to consistently campaign, through his writings as well as his designs, for more hygienic furnishings and homes. He had similiar "modern" concerns about the size, weight, and cost of furniture for contemporary homes.

Godwin's own unique style thus issued from both a consideration of the present and an admiration for the past. He encouraged students to study all styles and civilizations. He warned them not to work in one particular style and counseled them if ever asked in which style they worked to reply "my own."[180] He wrote, "When we have learnt more the past . . . and then, building on that foundation, we may attain beauty for ourselves without any slavish imitation of past forms, working earnestly towards that goal, and leaving the name of our work and its true estimate to the only fit judge—*posterity*."[181]

•

Note: Most published sources are cited below in shortened form (author's last name, abbreviated title, date of publication); full references will be found in the bibliography. Frequently cited archives are abbreviated below; for a key to the abbreviations, also see the bibliography.

1. Pevsner, *Pioneers* (1960): 62.

2. Watt, *Art Furniture* (1877): viii.

3. RIBA Mss, GoE/7/8/2; a copy is also in V&A AAD, 4/561-1988.

4. Ibid.

5. Clive Wainwright, "Furniture," in *Pugin*, ed. Atterbury and Wainwright (1994).

6. Godwin drew from the reformed Gothic works of both G. E. Street and William White, two architects who also worked in Cornwall in the late 1840s and early 1850s. Godwin first discovered Street's work in 1853, when "the view of his design for Cuddesdon College, published in the *Illustrated News* of 28 April 1853 . . . first attracted me, then a student, to this accomplished architect" (Harbron, "Edward Godwin" [1945]: 48). Street's church of St. Mary, Par, in Cornwall (1848–49), his restorations of the church of St. Probus (1849), and the church of Ss. Peter and Paul at Shevoick in Cornwall (1851) reveal functionalist interiors and furnishings derived from Pugin's church commissions (Hitchcock, "G. E. Street in the 1850s" [December 1960]: 145–71). William White's restoration and refurnishing of the church at Gerrans in Cornwall (1849), also demonstrate the structural orientation prevalent in Pugin's designs (Atterbury and Wainwright, eds., *Pugin* [1994]: 16). For more information on William White, see S. Muthesius, *High Victorian Movement* (1972): 53–54.

7. V&A AAD, 4/9-1980: 43.

8. Aslin, *E. W. Godwin* (1986): 11.

9. Mercer, *Furniture* (1969): 53–60.

10. Willemin, *Monuments français* (1839): vol. 1, pls. 52, 14, 9.

11. See Watt, *Art Furniture* (1877): pls. 2, 11.

12. Atterbury, ed., *A. W. N Pugin* (1995): 322–23.

13. Hunt, *Exemplars of Tudor Architecture* (1836): pl. xxxi.

14. See Eames, *Furniture in England, France and the Netherlands* (1977): pl. 70A.

15. Kelly's Directories, *Post Office Directory of Birmingham* (1868), lists "Burkitt, Reuben and Co. hardware merchants, Cleveland Road."

16. V&A AAD, 4/10-1980: 87.

17. In a letter to William Burges dated 4 August 1871 Godwin lists the total amount of the furniture as £1154.7s.6d, the amount of Watts and Burkitt's bills combined. This letter also lists some of the items, including "sideboard, Table, Chairs (easy & others), Sofas, bookcases, chess table (with animals carved) wardrobe with decoration" (V&A AAD, 4/22-1988: 60–62). Since the specifications for furniture for William Watt still exist in the RIBA (Mss, GoE/1/7/4), it is possible to deduce that at least the wardrobe, table, sideboard, and bookcases were made by Burkitt.

18. Letter from F. V. Hart (Godwin's assistant) to Godwin, dated 2 November 1869, V&A AAD, 4/184-1988.

19. The Hart and Son's bill was for £206.16s.0d, while the Benham and Froud bill was for £274.9s.7d (V&A AAD, 4/22-1988: 69–70).

20. Godwin, "Japanese Wood Construction," part 6 (19 February 1875): 200.

21. Ibid., part 5 (12 February 1875): 173.

22. Burges, "The International Exhibition" (July 1862): 10–11.

23. Harbron, *Conscious Stone* (1945): 78.

24. "Wall-papers" (11 October 1872): 291.

25. RIBA Drawings, Ran 7/B/1 (7).

26. Haslam, "Some Furniture from Dromore Castle" (May/June 1993): 26.

27. For this escritoire see Gere and Whiteway, *Nineteenth-Century Design* (1962): 133, pl. 160.

28. For this chair, see ibid., p. 134, pl. 163. The chair is in the Victoria and Albert Museum. For the pine wardrobes, also see Christies (London), *British Decorative Arts from 1880* (5 February 1992): 54, lot. 127.

29. Nesfield, *Specimens of Mediaeval Architecture* (1862). This was a text that Godwin bought as Honorary Secretary to give as the Bristol Society of Architects students' prize for the best measured drawing, which was awarded to W.V. Gough in 1864. The prize was described as "Nesfield's Sketches in France and Italy." Minutes of a meeting held 4 May 1864, Bristol Society of Architects.

30. Eames, *Furniture in England* (1977): pl. 4, cat. 3.

31. Aslin, *E. W. Godwin* (1986): 43, pl. 10.

32. RIBA Drawings, Ran 7/B/1 (55).

33. Wang Shixiang, *Classic Chinese Furniture* (1991): 39.

34. RIBA Drawings, Ran 7/B/1 (73).

35. For examples of Ming hardwood furniture with these types of feet see Wang Shixiang and Evarts, *Masterpieces from the Museum of Classical Chinese Furniture* (1995): pls. 4, 47.

36. RIBA Mss, GoE/1/7/3.

37. E. W. Godwin, "My Chambers," part 1 (1 July 1876): 5.

38. Watt, *Art Furniture* (1877): viii.

39. Wilkinson, "Edward William Godwin and Japonisme" (1987): 154.

40. His article, "Japanese Wood Construction," was largely taken from these two well-illustrated sources (Godwin, "Japanese Wood Construction," part 5 [12 February 1875]: 173–74 and 189; part 6 [19 February 1875]: 200–201 and 214). He also made frequent visits to the library of the British Museum, which had one of the major collections of Japanese books, manuscripts, and drawings in England. Some notes in his sketchbook are annotated "Douglass [*sic*] Jap. Book Dept. BM" (V&A PD, E.226-1963: 63) referring to Robert Kennaway Douglas, Keeper of the Department of Oriental Printed Books and Manuscripts of the British Museum (Wilkinson, "Edward William Godwin and Japonisme" [1987]: 146).

41. "List of articles of Vertu in large office," V&A AAD, 4/10-1980: n.p.

42. Wilkinson, "Edward William Godwin and Japonisme" (1987): 174.

43. Ellsworth, *Chinese Hardwood Furniture* (ca. 1982): pl. 76.

44. Clunas, *Chinese Furniture* (1988): 79.

45. Godwin, "My Chambers," part 1 (1 July 1876): 5.

46. Wilkinson, "Edward William Godwin and Japonisme" (1987): 178.

47. V&A PD, E.243-1963: 31.

48. Wang Shixiang, *Classic Chinese Furniture* (1991): fig. 170.

49. Walkling, *Antique Bamboo Furniture* (1979): 29. Bamboo furniture from China was imported into England in vast quantities and sold in the Oriental warehouses and bazaars that Godwin frequented. It was also exhibited in the Chinese sections of the international exhibitions after 1851.

50. Godwin, "My Chambers," part 1 (1 July 1876): 5.

51. Bristol Museums and Art Gallery, no. N4507.

52. Watt, *Art Furniture* (1877): viii.

53. "Two Interiors at the House of Miss Ellen Terry" (October 1920): 52.

54. V&A PD, E.478-1963.

55. See V&A PD, E.480-1963.

56. Letter from Frank Miles to Godwin, 14 December 1878, V&A AAD, 4/158-1988.

57. "Minton & Hollins," V&A AAD, 4/12-1980, n.p.

58. "Rambling Sketches," part 14 (2 September 1881): 444–45.

59. Aslin, *E. W. Godwin* (1986): 67, pl. 39.

60. Aslin, *Nineteenth Century Furniture* (1962): 60.

61. Classical panels illustrating Jason, Medea, Actaeon, Hercules, and Aesculapius can also be found on the bottom half of a stained oak bookcase of 1871 that has been separated from its upper structure, one of a series that Godwin designed for the collector Dr. George Bird. This relates to an entry in Godwin's ledger books for 27 September 1871 which lists "Bird Dr Bookcase des . . . ." (V&A AAD, 4/10-1980: f. 93, "Sundries"). In these panels, the palette is pale peach, green, and blue predominating. Dudley Harbron has identified the painter as Charles Glidden, who he described as "a brilliant young artist . . . who died when he was twenty" (Harbron, *Conscious Stone* [1945]: 82).

62. For more information on Charles Fairfax Murray, see Barrington, "Copyist, Connoisseur" (November 1994): 15–21; and Robinson, "Burne-Jones, Fairfax Murray" (November 1975): 348–51.

63. J. Hall, *Dictionary of Subjects* (1979): 259.

64. For more information on Beatrice Godwin, later to become Beatrice Whistler, wife of James McNeill Whistler, see MacDonald, *Beatrice Whistler* (1997).

65. "Four Seasons Cabinet," Victoria and Albert Museum, W.15-1972.

66. Aslin, *E. W. Godwin* (1986): pl. 74.

67. V&A PD, E.533-536-1963.

68. Die Neue Sammlung, Museum für Angewandtke Kunst, Munich, 417/93; Vallance, "Furnishing and Decoration of the House," part 4 (April 1892): 112.

69. Letter to Collinson and Lock, dated 30 July 1873, V&A AAD, 4/23-1988: f. 62–4.

70. Watt, *Art Furniture* (1877): viii.

71. "Furniture by E. W. Godwin" (5 November 1880): 528 and 534.

72. V&A PD, E.233-1963: 43.

73. Harbron, *Conscious Stone* (1945): 33. Godwin shared this unusual appreciation for Georgian furniture with the Pre-Raphaelite painter Dante Gabriel Rossetti, who furnished his Chelsea house in 1862 with an assortment of eighteenth-century furniture mixed with Japanese ceramics and other period furnishings.

74. Godwin, "My Chambers," part 2 (8 July 1876): 19.

75. Blairman and Sons, *Furniture* (1994): fig. 17. A signed and dated drawing for this table (RIBA Drawings, Ran 7/N/14) tells us that it was made in September 1877 for Paris. Perhaps it was meant to be exhibited on William Watt's stand for the Paris Exposition Universelle of 1878.

76. An elegant mahogany example from about 1765 at the Vyne, Hampshire, shares a great many similarities with the Godwin table and may have been the kind of slender so-called flap table that served as a prototype (illustrated in Macquoid and Edwards, *Dictionary of English Furniture* [1986]: 240, fig. 26).

77. V&A PD, E.279-1963: insert between 4 and 6.

78. Godwin, "Japanese Wood Construction," part 5 (12 February 1875): 189; part 6 (19 February 1875): 214.

79. Godwin, "Furniture" (15 June 1872): 1–2.

80. Godwin, "My House 'In' London," part 2 (22 July 1876): 45.

81. Canadian Centre for Architecture, *Corpus sanum* (1991).

82. A sofa designed by Godwin in a private collection has Cope of Birmingham brass castors. A drawing of table legs with attached castors appears in Godwin's sketchbooks annotated "Parrys direct bearing castor City Rd. Manchester" (V&A PD, E.233-1963: 49).

83. For example, V&A PD, E.233-1963: 15.

84. Godwin, "My House 'In' London," part 5 (12 August 1876): 86.

85. Bristol Museums and Art Gallery, no. N4506.

86. Godwin, "My House 'In' London," part 5 (12 August 1876): 86.

87. Watt, *Art Furniture* (1877): pl. 11.

88. Wolfsonian-Florida, TD 1989.149.2.

89. Bristol Museums and Art Gallery, nos. 4501 and 4510. For an illustration of no. 4501 see Aslin, *E. W. Godwin* (1986): 71, pl. 44.

90. "Cabinet for Objets du Virtu [*sic*]" (5 March 1886): 376.

91. Godwin, "Mantlepieces" (3 June 1876): 353.

92. Ibid.

93. Godwin, "My House 'In' London," part 3 (29 July 1876): 58.

94. Ibid., p. 59.

95. V&A AAD, 4/11-1980: f. 32 and n.p., and AAD, 4/13-1980: n.p.

96. Watt, *Art Furniture* (1877): iii.

97. "Art Furniture" (5 June 1868): 375.

98. Godwin, "My Chambers," part 1 (1 July 1876): 5.

99. Watt, *Art Furniture* (1877): viii.

100. "Working Drawings of Inexpensive Furniture by E. W. Godwin" (18 December 1885): 1011 and illus. 1008–9.

101. "Parlour Furniture" (31 October 1879): 522 and illus. 531.

102. Godwin "My House 'In' London," part 6 (19 August 1876): 100.

103. Ibid.

104. Ibid.

105. Entries for 9 April 1873, "Cott table"; 25 February 1873, "Cott. couch"; 25 February 1873, "Cott. sideboard"; 28 March 1873, "Cott. hanging cabt."; 10 April 1874, "Cott. L, cab."; 10 April 1874, "cott. Dr. rm cab," V&A AAD, 4/13-1980, n.p., "Collinson & Lock."

106. V&A PD, E.235-1963: 32.

107. Compare sketches in V&A PD, E.233-1963 101 for Collinson and Lock with E.235-1963: 7 for William Watt.

108. For a sketch of this cabinet, see V&A PD, E.233-1963: 101.

109. Girouard, *Sweetness and Light* (1977): 132.

110. Agius, *British Furniture* (1978): 45.

111. "Furniture by E. W. Godwin" (5 November 1880): 528 and illus. 534.

112. "Messrs Waugh & Son." and "Constable & Waugh & Son," V&A AAD, 4/12-1980 n.p. This line included a buffet, mantelpiece, hanging cabinet, a so-called lady's companion, and even Anglo-Greek office furniture.

113. V&A PD, E.229-1963: 109, 83.

114. V&A PD, E.472-1963.

115. Godwin, "Greek Home According to Homer" (June 1886): 914–22.

116. A drawing in his sketchbooks is annotated "Greek Furniture Peddle Dec. 1880" (V&A PD, E.229-1963: 114).

117. Wolfsonian-Florida, no. 85.11.14.

118. Entries in Godwin's diary from November 1876 corroborate the fact that he was designing Anglo-Egyptian furniture for Waugh and Sons (V&A AAD, 4/2-1980, diary 1874 and 1876, eg. 23 November 1876).

119. V&A PD, E.278-1963; illustrated in Aslin, *E. W. Godwin* (1986): 80, pl. 62.

120. V&A AAD, 4/12-1980: n.p., "Messrs Waugh & Son."

121. V&A PD, E.233-1963: 53.

122. For an illustration of this dressing table, see Aslin, *E. W. Godwin* (1986): 74, pl. 50.

123. Lever, *Architects' Designs* (1982): 81.

124. For more information on the antiquarian craze in the first half of the nineteenth century, see Wainwright, *Romantic Interior* (1989).

125. V&A PD, E.233-1963: 41.

126. Ibid., p. 3.

127. "Old English Furniture" (19 August 1876): 112 and illus.

128. Godwin, "My House 'In' London," part 3 (29 July 1876): 58.

129. Ibid., p. 59.

130. Watt, *Art Furniture* (1877): viii. Simon Jervis points out that cane-seated armchairs such as these were derived from ebonized country models in the Sheraton and Regency traditions (Jervis, "'Sussex' Chairs in 1820" [1974], p. 99).

131. Godwin, "My House 'In' London," part 3 (29 July 1876): 58.

132. The walnut dining table in plate 16 is 3 feet, 6 inches by 5 feet; the oak table in plate 15 is 4 feet and the oak table in plate 7 is 7 feet by 3 feet 6 inches. These measurements are listed in the annotated price list that accompanied each catalogue. Godwin's own copy is in the Victoria and Albert Museum, London (V&A AAD, 4/508-534-1988).

133. The smallest is a 6-foot oak buffet in plate 16; the largest is the oak buffet in plate 7 which measured 7 feet, 6 inches.

134. Godwin, "My House 'In' London," part 3 (29 July 1876): 59.

135. "The Shakespeare Dining-Room Set" (11 November 1881): 626 and illus. 634.

136. Ibid. Some pieces survive at the Ellen Terry Memorial Museum, Smallhythe Place, Kent, the country home of Ellen Terry: an oak far-thingale chair based on a late sixteenth-century *caqueteuse* decorated with rows of chip carving, a dining table with trestle supports, and side chairs with lion-headed back supports recalling Flemish examples.

137. "The love of old things" (1 December 1881): 103.

138. "Our Museum" (1 April 1882): 187.

139. "Furniture and Decoration at the Royal Albert Hall" (1 December 1885): 142.

140. "At Kensington" (1 April 1885): 183.

141. The reviewer in the *Building News* called it "a rather choice collection of designs for domestic furniture . . . [that] display a decided taste for the truthful and simple in workmanship . . . . We recommend the furnisher of a new house to consult Mr. Watt's suggestive guide" ("Art Furniture" [24 August 1877]: 174). The critic of the *Furniture Gazette* also praised the Watt furniture catalogue, writing that "we can unhesitatingly recommend to our readers as good examples of the styles now mostly sought after" ([Review], *Art Furniture* [25 August 1877]: 145).

142. Watt, *Art Furniture* (1877): iii.

143. Illustrated in C. Spencer, ed., *Aesthetic Movement* (1973): 34, no. 14.

144. "Drawing room Furniture Manufactured by D. Blythe Adamson & Co." (13 April 1878): pl. 67.

145. Watt, *Art Furniture* (1877): iii.

146. See Joy, ed., *Pictorial Dictionary* (1977): 251. It was still being copied in 1884 by Heal and Son.

147. An example is in the Victoria and Albert Museum, London, Circ. 643-1962. It was copied by Collier and Plucknett of Warwick.

148. For more information about the influence of the International Exhibitions, see Greenhalgh, *Ephemeral Vistas* (1988).

149. "English Art Furniture at the Vienna Exhibition" (22 May 1873): 1–2. A drawing in Godwin's sketchbooks illustrates the paneled room with carved frieze that he designed for Collinson and Lock (V&A PD, E.234-1963: 79). An account in the *Amtlicher Bericht* of 1873 reveals that it was paneled in a dark wood and had a frieze made of oblong pieces of wood in which "in each one, one could see a branch blooming or weighed down with fruit, and fluttered by insects and birds, each one of another type of plant . . . in the . . . extraordinary effective, stylistic fashion of Japanese art" (Centralcommission des Deutsches Reiches, *Amtlicher Bericht* [1873]: 471–72).

150. V&A PD, E.229-1963: 47.

151. Aslin, *E. W. Godwin* (1986): 15.

152. Ellen Terry Museum, SMA/D/24.

153. Diary of 1873, V&A AAD, 4/1-1980. He was also responsible for the decoration (V&A AAD, 4/13-1980 n.p. "Collinson & Lock"; February 8, 1873, "Decn Vienna 3-3-0").

154. V&A PD, E.233-1963: 98.

155. Much of this information on the Butterfly Suite comes from Weber, "Whistler as Collector" (1987).

156. The Butterfly Cabinet was sold at auction to the University of Glasgow for £8,400. See Christie's (London), *Victorian Objects of Art Sculpture and Furniture*, sales cat. (4 October 1973), lot 196.

157. The Virginia Museum of Fine Arts owns the lightweight Anglo-Japanese side chair shown in the contemporary photograph (acc. no. 96.99).

158. "Anglo-Japanese Furniture," (14 June 1878): 596.

159. Ibid.

160. "The Paris Universal Exhibition," part 5 (1878): 113. The negative comments were echoed in the *Society of Arts Artisans' Report* (1879). A copy is in the "Butterfly Cabinet" curatorial file of the Hunterian Art Gallery, Glasgow.

161. *Society of Arts Artisans' Report* (1878).

162. Day, "Notes on English Decorative Art," part 3 (12 July 1878): 15–16.

163. Smalley, "Harmony in Yellow and Gold" (6 July 1878): 2.

164. H. Muthesius, *English House* (1979): 157.

165. V&A PD, E.234-1963: 20, 25. Also see Aslin, *E. W. Godwin* (1986): 57, pl. 26.

166. It was a High Victorian Gothic mansion built by the amateur architect Reverend Francis Goodwin and English emigré architect Frederick Clarke Withers in 1871–74. See Howe et al., *Herter Brothers* (1994): 166–69.

167. V&A PD, E.234-1963: 50.

168. V&A AAD, 4/13-1980 n.p., "Collinson & Lock."

169. See Bolger Burke, *In Pursuit of Beauty* (1986): 68–69.

170. Aslin, *E. W. Godwin* (1986): 68, pl. 40.

171. For the cabinet see also Gere and Whiteway, *Nineteenth-Century Design* (1993): 164; for the sketch see V&A PD E.478-1963.

172. "Art Furniture by E. W. Godwin, F.S.A.," parts 1–9, *Art-Worker* (New York) (February–October 1878).

173. Aslin has identified Godwin's influence in the furniture of American architect H. H. Richardson, notably his designs for library furniture at Woburn, Massachusetts, from 1878. Richardson's wheel-shaped, spindle-armed, sloping-back oak armchair with sunflower petals and cross stretchers (Aslin, *E. W. Godwin* [1986]: 65, pl. 35) resembles Godwin's design for an easy chair with stretchers in plate 8 of the Watt catalogue (Aslin, *E. W. Godwin* [1986]: 15). The Anglo-Japanese work of Herter Brothers from the late 1870s also shows the influence of Godwin's furniture designs. A comparison of the ebonized cherry side chair (ca. 1877–79) with a Godwin side chair made for the dining room of Dromore Castle reveals a similar design approach, characterized by lightweight rectilinear construction, elongated uprights, stretchers underneath the seat, ring-turned front legs, and splayed back rear legs (Howe et al., *Herter Brothers* [1994]: 193). A wing cabinet owned by the dealer Meg Caldwell in New York, probably designed by the firm of A. H. Le Jambre of Philadelphia, is the most overt example of Godwin's influence on American design. At first glance it appears identical to Godwin's wing cabinet in William Watt's *Art Furniture* catalogue (plate 8). Closer examination reveals too many differences to make a Godwin attribution credible.

174. Andrews, "Curious Case of the Godwin Sideboard," *Antique Collecting* (September 1985): 46.

175. Bolger Burke, *In Pursuit of Beauty* (1986): 414–15.

176. Cullis Hill and Company, *Melbourne Bulletin* (15 May 1885): 7; Watson, *Godwin Variations* (1994), n. 4.

177. Godwin, "Friends in Council: No. 40" (30 December 1881): 655.

178. Richard Riemerschmidt designed modular furniture, or what he called "build-on" furniture, in the first decade of the twentieth century. See Heskett, *German Design* (1986): 97.

179. For more information on hygiene and health reform during this period, see Wohl, *Endangered Lives* (1983).

180. Godwin, "On Some Buildings I Have Designed" (29 November 1878): 211.

181. "The New European Style" (6 March 1874): 269.

Fig. 9-1. E. W. Godwin. "Butterfly" Brocade, ca. 1874. Made by Warner, Sillett and Ramm. Jacquard woven silk; 34¹⁄₁₆ x 21⁹⁄₁₆ in. (86.5 x 55 cm). Trustees of the Victoria and Albert Museum, London, T.152-1972. *Checklist no. 54*

CHAPTER 9

E·W·GODWIN·AND·TEXTILE·DESIGN

LINDA PARRY

E. W. Godwin's interest in textiles was both passionate and academic. He appreciated the dramatic effects they added to an interior—as window drapery, as upholstery on couches and chairs, and as hangings on walls or across stage sets. He used textiles in many of his decorative schemes for churches, public buildings, private homes, and theatrical productions. As one of the major decorators and arbiters of taste of his or any other generation, Godwin influenced textile designs and their implementation, which encouraged a wider and more imaginative use of textile furnishings. Despite his knowledgeable appreciation for the media, however, his output as a textile designer is surprisingly meager.

Godwin's sketchbooks, now in the collection of the Department of Prints and Drawings at the Victoria and Albert Museum, show that he devoted considerable time to producing repeating patterns for printed and woven textiles (fig. 9-1), linoleum floor coverings, and carpets in a wide range of styles. Furthermore, his diaries and correspondence list contacts with various furnishers and textile manufacturers concerning production. It has not been possible, however, to trace the number of Godwin's designs that actually reached the production stage. Few examples can be positively identified and, of the small group of his designs that survive as fabrics, only his so-called "Anglo-Japanese" style is evident. In quantity and range these are no match for his work in other areas of the decorative arts—furniture and wallpaper design, in particular—and they give an incomplete picture of his interests and talents as a textile designer.

Despite the lack of evidence, a study of Godwin's ideas and designs for decorative schemes shows an understanding that came from observation of the past and from knowledge accumulated through an almost manic study of historic artifacts and records. With the exception of A. W. N. Pugin, William Burges, and William Morris, few other nineteenth-century designers had such an understanding of textiles. All four men arrived at this point through observation and by equipping themselves with a wide range of historical and aesthetic sources.

Many more textile furnishings are attributed to Godwin than is likely to be the case. Because he was one of the foremost designers in the Anglo-Japanese manner, there is a tendency to identify any pattern showing the influence of Japan as his work.[1] However, in this field, Godwin's contemporary Bruce J. Talbert was far more prolific, and his style more commercial. Consequently, it is likely that Talbert, rather than Godwin, was responsible for designing the majority of surviving textiles of this type. Stylistically, it is possible to separate the work of the two men despite their similar training and influences.[2] Godwin's patterns tend to have a geometric framework. Motifs are often taken directly from traditional Japanese devices, and the coloring and structure of his repeating patterns depend on the simplicity and purity of "solid and void" (as he described it)[3] that he most admired in Japanese work. On the other hand, Tal-

Fig. 9-2. Attributed to Bruce James Talbert. Textile, ca. 1876. Made by Cowlishaw, Nichol and Company. Jacquard woven silk; 93 ½ x 56 ½ in. (237 x 143.5 cm). Trustees of the Victoria and Albert Museum, London, T.10-1990.

bert's patterns (fig. 9-2) are conceived with a different view of the East. Using less formal, meandering repeats he combined elements of Japanese pattern, such as stark color contrasts, with a naturalistic, Western rendition of foliage, fruit, and flowers. None of his patterns could be mistaken for anything other than British work, and his clever use of new and exotic shapes within an acceptable, traditional format proved popular with the general public. Godwin's highly original creations were for a more avant-garde audience.[4]

Godwin's early artistic interests influenced his mature style as a commercial designer, and this was strongly manifest in his textile work. It is immediately apparent in studying his early years that his Japanese-inspired work, with which he is chiefly associated today, was not his only preoccupation but one of many interests. His early fascination for classical and Gothic decoration was matched by his interest in many non–Western cultures. This factor is as important to his development as a designer and user of textiles as to his work in all other spheres.

In line with such contemporaries as William Eden Nesfield, Richard Norman Shaw, Burges, and Talbert, Godwin was fascinated by the Middle Ages. He devoured all manner of existing published information on the architecture and decoration of the period but was not content simply to rely on secondary sources. Documentation in the form of early court inventories, paintings, tombs, brasses, and, wherever possible, surviving architecture and interiors were studied, and his claim to have examined all the medieval illuminated manuscripts in the British Museum shows a greater enthusiasm than most.[5] Illuminated manuscripts proved particularly useful to him, providing a source

for formal figurative compositions and dress. In his design for a costume for *Rienzi* (fig. 9-3), for example, he may have based the fabric on motifs in a British Museum manuscript as he did for several other costumes in the presentation book.[6] His sketches from the actual manuscripts also show repeating patterns taken from initial letters and page borders, as well as from the decoration on robes and heraldic banners.[7]

These references supplied a general stock of ideas and provided Godwin with inspiration for textile designs and suggestions for displaying or representing fabrics in interiors. Of particular interest was the effect of painting draped textiles on walls as shown in a number of manuscripts.[8] This form of decoration was first sketched by Godwin in a design for Northampton Town Hall between 1861 and 1862 (see fig. 6-16).[9] A similar effect was used in the restoration of the fourteenth-century parlor of the Vicar's Hall at Wells in Somerset, which was completed by Godwin's close friend Burges in 1864. Godwin and Burges worked closely at this time and shared ideas. Godwin's executed scheme at Northampton did not include the painted draped textiles, but he continued to sketch them into town hall designs as late as 1872.[10] Contemporary photographs of Burges's decoration provide a close parallel (fig. 9-4).[11] The types of pattern Godwin used on painted representations also appear on actual curtains. These usually show banded, heavyweight fabric with quatrefoil and geometric motifs representing a kind of textile admired by Godwin and used by him throughout his career as wall coverings and room dividers, in addition to conventional curtains.

The use of painted representations of cloth as a dec-

Fig. 9-3. E. W. Godwin. Designs for costumes for W. G. Wills'
Rienzi, ca. 1880-85. Pencil and watercolor on paper; 10¼ x
6¼ in. (26 x 16 cm). The Board of Trustees of the Victoria and
Albert Museum, London, S.114-1998. *Checklist no. 144*

orative feature originated in the ancient world, another of
Godwin's formative artistic influences.[12] Although he
entered the battle between the merits of medieval and classical design, which waged throughout the nineteenth century, as an ardent supporter of the Gothic Revival, he came
to believe that the two styles were symbiotic, stating: "The
best work of the thirteenth century . . . approximates in
feeling to Greek Art; earnest studies of the best Gothic
work of the thirteenth century, will lead us, step by step,
back to Greek work."[13] By using painted curtains he was to
prove this point.

Godwin was eager to acknowledge the historical
sources of many of these ideas, although most of his work

was clearly inspired by, rather than copied directly from, the
originals. This is very clear in a sketch in the Victoria and
Albert Museum (fig. 9-5),[14] which is quaintly inscribed
"Early 15th century." Only the draped cloth behind the
cabinet comes close to the original. The eclectic furniture
is far closer to Burges's rendition of the reformed Gothic
style than to late-medieval examples.

The assimilation of ideas from early sources involved
Godwin in detailed studies of textiles, which, in the case of
medieval tapestries and embroideries, had survived in large
numbers.[15] The Flemish tapestries in particular, which he
saw in various private and public collections, supplied him
with numerous patterns and became a rich source of information for historical costume. Through close study Godwin
concluded that embroidery provided the quickest and most
practical means of applying pattern to cloth. A page from
one of the sketchbooks used by Godwin between 1855 and
1869 includes drawings taken from examples of "Opus
Anglicanum," the internationally famed English profes-

Fig. 9-4. William Burges's painted hangings, designed in 1864,
can be seen in this view of the restored parlor at Vicar's Hall in
Wells, Somerset. From a sketch by O. Jewett in John Henry
Parker, *Illustrations of the Architectural Antiquities of the City of
Wells* (London: James Parker, 1866): pl. 7.

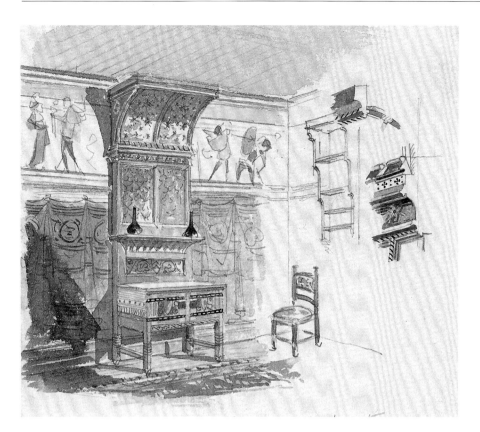

Fig. 9-5. E. W. Godwin. An interior design inscribed "Early 15th century," ca. 1880. Pencil and watercolor on paper; 9¹³⁄₁₆ x 5⁵⁄₁₆ in. (23.4 x 15.1 cm). Trustees of the Victoria and Albert Museum, London, E.378-1963.

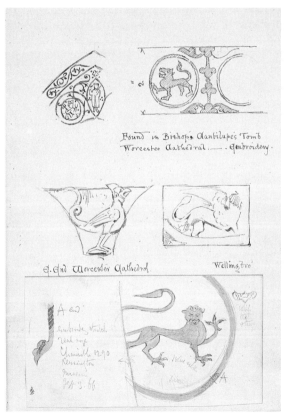

Fig. 9-6. E. W. Godwin. Details of English medieval embroidery, ca. 1866. Sketchbook. Pencil and watercolor on paper; 9 x 6⅜ in. (22.9 x 16.2 cm). Trustees of the Victoria and Albert Museum, London, E.269-1963: 5.

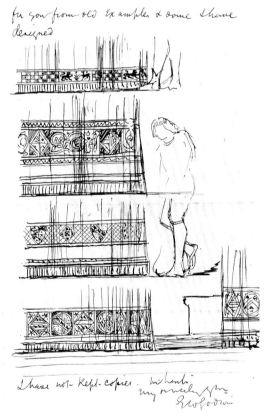

Fig. 9-7. E. W. Godwin. Drapery designs for Dromore Castle, County Limerick, Ireland, ca. 1868–71. Pen and ink on paper; 8⅜ x 5⁵⁄₁₆ in. (21.3 x 13.5 cm). From an album belonging to Lord Limerick. Courtesy of Lord Limerick.

266

Fig. 9-8. E. W. Godwin. Designs for banners for the chapel at Dromore Castle, County Limerick, Ireland, ca. 1868–71. Pencil and watercolor; 6 3/16 x 3 1/2 in. (15.8 x 8.8 cm). Trustees of the Victoria and Albert Museum, London, E.365-1963.

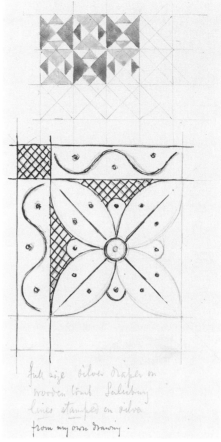

Fig. 9-9. E. W. Godwin. Diaper patterns, ca. 1867. Pencil, ink and watercolor; 8 13/16 x 6 1/16 in. (22.3 x 15.3 cm). Trustees of the Victoria and Albert Museum, London, E.285-1963: 15.

sional needlework of the thirteenth and fourteenth centuries (fig. 9-6).[16] The page depicts part of a bishop's mitre and a decorative border from a tomb in Worcester cathedral, as well as sketches of the Clare Chasuble, a late-thirteenth-century ecclesiastical vestment, which had been acquired by the South Kensington Museum in 1864.[17] Not content with a general drawing of the overall repeating design, Godwin went to great lengths to represent the embroidery technique. In a detail of one small area he shows the direction of the couching stitches that hold the gold threads in place. This close observation of a difficult, yet eminently effective form of embroidery points to more than idle antiquarian curiosity. He had already produced designs for embroidered church furnishings and knew the potential of the technique.[18] His drawings indicate that he was exploring different forms to achieve medieval-looking results in a contemporary project, such as the furnishing of Dromore Castle in Ireland, built for Lord Limerick from 1866 to 1873.

Unfortunately, no original textiles from Dromore have been traced,[19] although existing drawings show that Godwin intended to supply his client with various types of furnishings. For the house he designed carpets (see fig. 7-9) and two forms of hangings: heavy decorated fabrics to be used as drapery or on walls and lighter, plain curtains with applied heraldic borders (fig. 9-7).[20] For the chapel Godwin suggested banners. Two sketches now in the Victoria and Albert Museum show both figurative and repeating patterns for these (fig. 9-8).[21] For one banner Godwin turned again to early historical references.[22] The pattern, showing a repeating diaper motif, was originally taken from carving on a wooden tomb at Salisbury (fig. 9-9). Ironically, the original carving represents embroidered decoration on a robe.

Godwin's existing designs for hangings for the house[23] show his desire to re-create a strong baronial effect in keeping with the Gothic vernacular style of architecture (see fig. 6-33). The horizontal and diagonal banding, a major feature of these textiles (see figs 7-7, 7-9) represents a development

Fig. 9-10. The Summer Smoking Room at Cardiff Castle, designed by William Burges from 1866 to 1872. Photographed ca. 1900. Courtesy of Cardiff Castle.

Fig. 9-11. E. W. Godwin. Drapery design for Cowlishaw, Nichol and Company. From "Designs for Curtain Materials," *Furniture Gazette* 5 (15 April 1876): following 242.

Fig. 9-12. E. W. Godwin. Design for "Butterfly" Brocade, ca. 1874. Pencil and watercolor; 14½ in x 12¼ in (37 x 31 cm). Purchased through The Art Foundation of Victoria with the assistance of J. B. Were and Sons, Governor, 1989. National Gallery of Victoria, Melbourne P108/109. *Checklist no. 53*

from his earlier proposed painted decoration at Northampton. The designs are further refined by the colors and patterns of heraldic devices. The sources for some small-scale repeats for carpets and for the background designs of curtain valances and hangings are noted on his Dromore designs,[24] yet his use of heraldry in these examples is purely decorative despite his strong academic interest in the subject and the copious lists of arms and standards in his sketchbooks.[25]

Apart from woven carpets, all other patterned textiles designed for Dromore were probably intended for embroidery, the technique most likely to have produced the effects Godwin wished to achieve.[26] To carry out his exacting designs for church banners, Godwin is likely to have called on the considerable skills of Jones and Willis of Covent Garden, a firm renowned for ecclesiastical and ceremonial embroidery. Godwin had already used this firm for earlier church work, including a frontal designed in 1862 for the church of Saint Wynwallow, Landewednack, Cornwall.[27] Jones and Willis were noted for the excellence of their decorations on dress uniforms and other regalia and particularly adept at the difficult technique of padded gold work, an effect Godwin had seen and admired in the medieval work displayed at South Kensington. This type of embroidery is suggested in the drawing of the geometric banner design for Dromore.

It is difficult to determine where the curtains intended for the house were made. Contemporary work by Burges, however, may give some insight into their appearance. Recently discovered embroidered furnishings designed by Burges for Cardiff Castle,[28] a commission started in 1866, resemble Godwin's designs for Dromore, and it may be assumed that the Dromore designs would be executed in a similar way. A surviving set of the hangings made for Cardiff Castle, which can be seen in a nineteenth-century photograph of the Summer Smoking Room (fig. 9-10), are made of heavy wool serge. Decoration is applied in the form of bands of contrasting wool fabric with embroidered motifs in silk and wool. This applied technique is taken directly from late-medieval embroidery and was first revived in the nineteenth century by the architect George Edmund Street, for church furnishings.[29] It was also the technique chosen in the early 1860s by William Morris for wall hangings at Red House.[30] Whereas Burges and Morris used wool serge to create a quasi-medieval appearance, Street generally preferred the richer background effect of velvet for his frontals. It is possible that Godwin also decided upon this more refined finish for Dromore: certainly he is known to have used velvet to cover some of

the drawing-room chairs.[31] The Cardiff Castle embroideries are competently worked but suggest amateur rather than commercial production. Unfortunately, it is not known who was responsible for carrying out the work for Cardiff Castle or Dromore, or, in fact, whether Godwin's textile schemes were ever fully realized.

Following his early great successes as the architect of public and domestic buildings, Godwin expanded his arena of operations into the manufacturing world, and by 1872 he was selling individual designs through agents and directly to decorators and manufacturers. His sketchbooks, diaries, and ledgers for the decade after 1872 record a wide range of designs, including textiles and floor coverings, for a number of commercial clients. Most significantly, there is evidence of direct contact with two important weaving firms: Cowlishaw, Nichol and Company, a well-respected Manchester company known for its heavy wool hangings (erroneously described as "tapestries"),[32] and Warner and Ramm, a firm of silk weavers newly established in Spitalfields, East London.

In a sketchbook used in the mid-1870s, Godwin gives the sizes of pattern repeat required by the Manchester firm for their looms: "Patterns for C.N. & Co should be 7" across and any height 63" wide for silk brocade 54" wide 9" across tapestry."[33] This suggests that rather than allowing designers freedom to choose, the firm specified the size of the pattern to be woven on their looms. This encompassed nine repeats in each loom width for silk fabric and seven for the narrower, wool fabric. It is probable that Cowlishaw, Nichol used a number of Godwin's patterns. An entry in Godwin's ledger for July 15, 1874, shows that they owed him a total of £29.8.0 for "Designs for Stuffs."[34] A slightly later entry, noting consultancy work for the same weaving firm but without charge, suggests a reworking or amending of these patterns for production. Unfortunately only one of these designs, illustrated in both the *Furniture Gazette* and the *Building News* of 1876, is known today (fig. 9-11).[35]

Benjamin Warner trained as a textile designer at the Spitalfields School of Design and in 1870 set up a firm manufacturing woven silks. By 1874, the year he first had commercial dealings with Godwin, his company was known as Warner, Sillett and Ramm (Sillett left a year later), and its factory had recently moved from Spitalfields to Hollybush Gardens, Bethnal Green. Warner's ability as a weaver was matched by his skills in recognizing and encouraging a number of talented, young, avant-garde designers and purchasing their work. Godwin produced designs for the company over a two-year period from September 1874 to October 1876; Godwin's last diary entries mentioning

Fig. 9-13. E. W. Godwin."Large Syringa," ca. 1874. Made by Warner, Sillett and Ramm. Jacquard woven silk; 54½ x 42 in. (138.4 x 106.7 cm). Trustees of the Victoria and Albert Museum, London, T.153-1972. *Checklist no. 56*

Fig. 9-14. E. W. Godwin. "Small Syringa," ca. 1874. Made by Warner, Sillett and Ramm. Jacquard woven silk; 34¼ x 62⅝ in. (87 x 159 cm). Trustees of the Victoria and Albert Museum, London, T.154-1972. *Checklist no. 55*

Fig. 9-15. Attributed to E. W. Godwin. "Dahlia," ca. 1874. Made by Warner, Sillett and Ramm. Jacquard woven silk; 41 ⅝ x 34 ¾ in. (105.7 x 88.2 cm). Trustees of the Victoria and Albert Museum, London, T.148-1972.

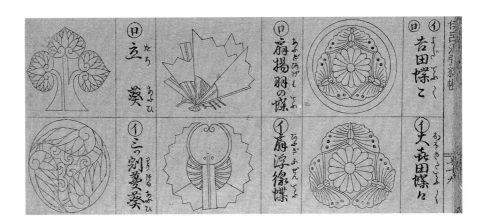

Fig. 9-16. Page from a nineteenth-century book of Japanese crests. Trustees of the Victoria and Albert Museum, London, Far East Department Library.

Warner and Ramm were in September and October 1876 and record reminder letters, suggesting late payments by Warner's for work completed.[36]

Only three Warner silks can be identified today as Godwin's work[37]: "Butterfly Brocade" (see fig. 9-12 and fig. 9-1)[38]; and "Large Syringa" (fig. 9-13) and "Small Syringa" (fig. 9-14), which are small and large versions of the same pattern. These designs show Godwin's mature, Anglo-Japanese style—a mixture of traditional repeating forms and popular Aesthetic motifs. "Dahlia" (fig. 9-15), another silk woven at Warner's at the same period, may also be his work. The pattern's formalism is similar to the other identified examples, and the motif of chrysanthemums surrounded by butterflies is taken directly from a book of Japanese crests (fig. 9-16), a copy of which Godwin almost certainly owned and used as the source for a number of other repeating designs.[39]

Godwin designed many "curtains," a term he uses in his account books, which suggests woven fabrics produced specifically for furnishing companies rather than manufac-

Fig. 9-17B

Fig. 9-17A,B. Attributed to E.W. Godwin. Two samples of woven furnishing fabric, ca. 1870. Made by J.W. and C. Ward. From a sample book. Woven silk, wool, and cotton; A, 8⅛ x 5⅝ in. (208 x 144 cm); B, 5¼ x 6½ in. (13.5 x 16.5 cm). Trustees of the Victoria and Albert Museum, London, scrapbook T.97-1953.

turers. As early as 1871 he provided drawings for curtains for a bookcase for "Dr. Bird,"[40] part of a commission for the bookcase which would have been ordered directly by the furniture company. His silk design, "Butterfly Brocade," was commissioned by the London decorating firm of Collinson and Lock, for whom he also designed patterns for printed fabrics, carpets,[41] and wool cloths.[42] Although it has not been established which contractor Collinson and Lock employed to manufacture their heavy furnishings, there is a strong possibility that the weavers were J. C. and W. Ward of Halifax in Yorkshire.[43] A group of thirty-five small samples woven by Ward's was acquired by the Victoria and Albert Museum in 1953 and includes patterns attributed to Christopher Dresser[44] and Talbert. Other Aesthetic designs in the collection show strong stylistic similarities to Godwin's work (fig. 9-17).

Godwin's increasing experience of commercial manufacture in the 1870s encouraged a new pragmatism in his attitude toward interiors. The design of floor coverings, for instance, was given greater consideration than in the past. Although he usually preferred plain wood boards or Indian matting covered with Oriental rugs in his own homes, his sketchbooks show a number of repeating designs that were possibly intended for machine-woven carpets and oil-cloths (fig. 9-18).[45] Only one commission, two carpet patterns for an "Anglo-Greek" bedroom suite for Waugh and Son of Tottenham Court Road,[46] gives any idea of Godwin's designs for commercial production. Most of the sketchbook patterns are formal, using repeating devices of the type found in fifteenth-, sixteenth- and seventeenth-century Italian and Spanish silks (fig. 9-19). Studies made by Godwin from historical examples (probably drawn in the South Kensington Museum), and a reference to Franz Bock, one of the leading textile historians and dealers of the day, are also noted by him in his sketchbooks.[47]

In September 1876 Godwin published his ideas on floor coverings in an article entitled "Floorcloths" in the *Architect*. He restated his preference for using existing Eastern products, writing that "the plainer fabrics of the East . . . whether in matting, carpets or curtain stuffs, are almost so invariably good that . . . it matters little which we take."[48] He went on to criticize British design and to itemize those elements that could be improved. Patterns should be nondirectional and never attempt three-dimensional effects. He further believed that colors should be restricted to no more than six per design, and pattern repeat sizes should be six inches or less, even smaller than those used for Cowlishaw, Nichol's woven curtaining. The effect of such

Fig. 9-18. E. W. Godwin. Design for a floor covering for Waugh and Son, 1876. Pencil and watercolor on paper; 3 ¹⁵⁄₁₆ x 6 in. (10 x 15.2 cm). Trustees of the Victoria and Albert Museum, London, E.241-1963: 33.

a small regular repeat over a large area would have been surprisingly ordinary, despite the originality of the design itself. This may be the reason why no examples of this type of work by Godwin have been identified, despite a number having been made and offered for sale by an agent identified as "Constable."[49]

Godwin's use of textiles in interiors was both sporadic and varied, but nearly always original. He was not content to use them simply because it was expected, nor to fill a house with them if it was not appropriate. Frequently he selected plain blinds for windows, for example, rather than elaborate curtains.[50] Although it is difficult to determine how much consideration was given to clients in the choice of furnishings, it is clear that Godwin's chosen style at any given time controlled not only the general arrangement and decoration but also individual features, such as curtains and carpets, which would supply the effects required. In some interiors the need for color was supplied by plain hangings in which texture, either in the form of heavy, majestic wools, lightweight printed cottons, lustrous silks, or luxuriant velvets, provided these effects. For furnishings Godwin first looked at what was already available in the shops and chose commercial production if it suited his purposes. Unlike his contemporary William Morris, he did not decry

Fig. 9-19. E. W. Godwin. A repeating ogee device sketched from a fifteenth-century Spanish woven silk in the South Kensington Museum collection, ca. 1874–75. Sketchbook. Pencil on paper; 5 ⁹⁄₁₆ x 3 ¼ in. (14.2 x 8.2 cm). Trustees of the Victoria and Albert Museum, London, E.239-1963: 41.

273

Fig. 9-20. E. W. Godwin. Unexecuted design for the Italian library at Castle Ashby, ca. 1872–83. Pencil, pen and ink, and red/brown crayon; 5 13/16 x 10 1/8 in. (14.8 x 25.7 cm). Trustees of the Victoria and Albert Museum, London, E.499-1963.

most modern manufacture as worthless. His schemes did not rely on the sole use of contemporary textile manufacture but on a mix of old and new artifacts from all parts of the world. Such a miscellany dominated the decorating style he used for his own and others' houses, appealing to a new generation of collectors and travelers.

Whereas it is impossible to study Godwin's use of textiles in interiors, as no schemes have survived, published accounts in articles, biographies, and Godwin's own letters and designs show the variety of this work. For his own homes, Godwin's arrangements were highly original. Sir Johnston Forbes-Robertson recounts that the drawing-room walls of Godwin's residence at Taviton Street had a dado of straw-colored matting, and "above the dado were white walls and the hangings were of cretonne, with a fine Japanese pattern in delicate blue-grey. The chairs were of wicker with cushions like the hanging."[51] To find existing stocks of imported Japanese, printed cottons (these were probably of indigo blue with resist-dyed patterns) and matting was not as difficult at that time as might be imagined. In 1872 Kelly's *Post Office Directory* listed no fewer than eighteen merchants importing Chinese and Japanese goods.[52]

Although Godwin recycled many ideas about house decoration throughout his career, a comparison of his 1860s designs for Castle Ashby with later commissions for Hermann Vezin and Oscar Wilde shows how his use of textile furnishings developed. His designs for the proposed Italian Library at Castle Ashby included heavy wool drapery (fig. 9-20).[53] In a letter of December 23, 1867, he suggested curtains across the upper half of the height of the bookcases, believing that they would provide "a most jolly division of the length of the room."[54] The effect, had the room been built, would have been solemn, in line with the purpose of the library, but also very dark. In complete contrast were Godwin's 1880s decorations for various properties in London. For Vezin's house at 10 Lancaster Place, Westminster, there were few textiles and a much lighter effect was gained by using plain printed-cotton curtains of a very fashionable terracotta red.[55] Unfortunately, the pattern was not recorded in his papers.

Textiles used by Godwin in the decoration of Oscar Wilde's house in Tite Street reveal attempts to establish different moods for each of the three main reception rooms. The conventional effect of sumptuousness in the drawing room was achieved with thick silk curtains and upholstery;

for the dining room, a more avant-garde effect was gained with a Morris machine-woven carpet in green and blue, and white hangings embroidered in yellow silk. The style chosen for the library was based on Eastern exoticism, with beaded curtains and cushions strewn on upholstered divans.[56]

In his search for endless varieties of furnishings and dress materials, Godwin developed an extensive knowledge of commercial suppliers. His theater notes and accounts are sprinkled with the names of silk merchants, linen drapers, trimmings suppliers, and dyers. He also became a customer of large furnishing shops such as Morris and Company, Liberty's, and Lewis and Allenby, and he purchased from firms for which he also worked. In line with a new commercialism seen in his work beginning in the 1870s, Godwin had developed a closer commercial relationship with London furnishers, even to the extent of providing stock designs for rooms. A group of these were published by the firm of William Watt in 1877 (see fig. 7-1). These illustrations, which are the only means of judging Godwin's work in context, show a conventional use of textiles as window hangings or room dividers, with diagonally striped heavy wool curtains reminiscent of his designs for Dromore Castle and Castle Ashby.

Godwin used fabric on furniture for upholstery or

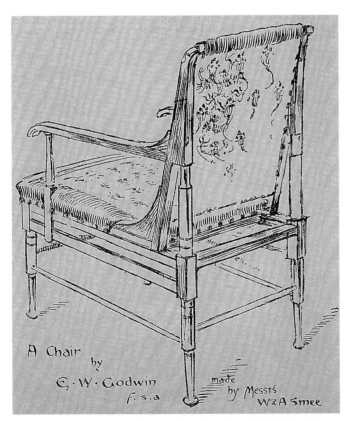

Fig. 9-21. A suggestion of one of Godwin's textile designs for his furniture is seen in this sketch in the *British Architect*. From "The Furniture Trades Exhibition," part 2 (11 May 1883): 236.

Fig. 9-22. E. W. Godwin. Sketch of Aesthetic dress of 1880, derived from a cartoon by George DuMaurier, part of a set of drawings probably for *Dress and Its Relation to Health and Climate*, 1880. Pencil and pen on paper; 6.5 x 5⅛ in. (16.5 x 13 cm). Trustees of the Victoria and Albert Museum, London, Archive of the Theatre Museum (Blythe House), S.190-1998.

hangings on or behind cabinets and buffets. As seen in his sketches and in contemporary illustrations, this use shows his work at its most commercial (fig. 9-21). However, there is little to separate his ideas from those advocated by Robert W. Edis and Eastlake or seen in the work of Talbert, Shaw, or T. E. Collcutt. Nor are the furnishings individual enough in appearance to suggest that they were special designs.

Existing documentation shows that Godwin became an avid buyer of all types of textiles although it is difficult to identify items he was acquiring for use in his homes and those that were perhaps purchased to form a pattern reference collection. He bought mostly Chinese and Japanese textiles and items of costume, but a group of six sketchbook patterns labeled "Indian," and others taken from Islamic sources, show that his interests were not restricted to the Far East.[57]

His use of exotic patterns and textures in his interiors was well known and admired, and his expertise was called on for both commercial and charitable purposes. On January 17, 1884, Liberty and Company's "Historic and Artistic Studios" entered into an agreement with Godwin for "professional aid" at a rate of £1.1s per hour ("not to exceed six hours in any week") with a commission of three percent on any sales resulting from his personal introduction of clients.[58] Whereas it has always been assumed that "professional aid" referred exclusively to Godwin supplying ideas for artistic dress (fig. 9-22), there is a strong possibility that advice on other aspects of textiles was part of the arrangement. From its foundation, Liberty's had concentrated on the sale of Oriental goods, especially carpets and embroideries, with occasional exhibitions of historical tex-

tiles. Before opening the shop in 1875, Lasenby Liberty had worked in the Oriental Warehouse of Farmer and Rogers, a firm from which Godwin purchased many items used in his interiors.[59] Subsequently Godwin became a client of Liberty's.

Further evidence of Godwin's reputation as a consultant comes in a letter asking him to advise on the use of "artistic decoration or any novel suggestions you may make" for embroideries worked by Bulgarian and Turkish refugees. These were part of a large collection being sold by Lady Charlotte Schreiber on behalf of the refugees and already on display at two Regent Street shops, Liberty's and Lewis and Allenby's.[60]

Godwin's increasing involvement in stage design toward the end of his life illustrates his use of fabrics in a different sphere. His stage sets included many of the effects he had learned by decorating private homes, and the striped curtains first selected for the medieval-inspired Dromore interiors reappeared draped across the center of the set

Fig. 9-23. Costumes and set designed by E. W. Godwin for John Todhunter's play *Helena in Troas*, 1886. Photograph; 6¾ x 9⅞ in. (17.2 x 25.2 cm). Trustees of the Victoria and Albert Museum, London, S.168-1998. *Checklist no. 150*

for the 1886 production of *Helena in Troas* (fig. 9-23 and see fig. 12-49). Probably due to financial constraints, the curtain was not specially designed but purchased from Cowtan, the London decorators.⁶¹

Godwin's great achievements as a designer, the versatility and range of his interior schemes, and his passionate interest in history combined to make him one of the most significant artistic personalities of the nineteenth century.

His textile designs, however, have been sadly neglected until now. It cannot be claimed that this work greatly affected the development of textile design in the late nineteenth century or of the industry as a whole, but his work in this field was an important component of his career. His selection and use of textiles in domestic interiors reveal a knowledgeable and original talent. It is time that this important aspect of his work gains the recognition it rightly deserves.

•

Note: Most published sources are cited below in shortened form (author's last name, abbreviated title, date of publication); full references will be found in the bibliography. Frequently cited archives are abbreviated below; for a key to the abbreviations, also see the bibliography.

1. Elizabeth Aslin attributed the woven silk "Nagasaki" to Godwin (Aslin, *Aesthetic Movement* [1969]: 125, pl. 75). However, details from the archives of Warner Fabrics and a comparison of style suggest that this is the work of B. J. Talbert.

2. Talbert trained as an architect, and, like Godwin, his early decorative work shows a simplified or "reformed" version of European Gothic design.

3. Godwin, "My Chambers and What I Did to Them," part 2 (8 July 1876): 5.

4. Warner and Sons existing production ledgers from 1884 (V&A TD, T.610–626–1972) list details of a number of Anglo-Japanese silks woven throughout the 1880s and 1890s. Some are by B. J. Talbert, but only a few of the recognized Godwin designs are present in these orders.

5. This claim was made by Godwin in a letter to W. C. Angus dated 13 August 1884, V&A TA, Godwin collection, box 3, Costume Society letterbook.

6. British Library, 6.E.ix; Godwin's sketch, V&A TA, Godwin collection, box 9.

7. Godwin's references to specific manuscripts are in the form of bibliographical lists as well as individual sketches showing repeating patterns. These are usually geometric motifs but more familiar devices such as butterflies, used in Godwin's later work, are also noted (see, e.g., British Library, Ad. Ms. 27695, verso p. 9, 11).

8. Of the manuscripts listed by Godwin there are various images of draped textiles in this manner. These include a banded and lightly patterned cloth draped behind an image of the Virgin (British Library, 6.E.IX) and a set of bed hangings in red with a valance of blue, white, and green bands (British Library, Harley 4431). His sketchbooks have further references including a sketch inscribed "unfold on this or the others—BIB.REX.I.D.X. (BM) (c.1200)" (V&A PD, E.285-1963).

9. On Godwin's drawing (fig. 6-16; V&A PD, E.592-1963) there is some ambiguity as to whether the impression of drapes on the wall and inscription "curtains at back" mean actual cloth or painted representations. It is likely that the latter was intended. This interpretation has also been placed on the drawings by Roderick Gradidge and Christopher Boulter of the firm of Farlow and Boulter in their recent restoration of Northampton Guildhall.

10. See, e.g., "Leicester Municipal Buildings" (13 January 1872): 24. The plate shows a transverse section of the Borough Court of Godwin's competition design, with painted or perhaps real curtains hanging along the wall.

11. For contemporary photographs of the entire restoration scheme in the Vicar's Hall, see John Henry Parker, *Illustrations of the Architectural Antiquities of the City of Wells* (London: James Parker and Co., 1866). I am very grateful to Michael Whiteway for allowing me to study his copy of this publication and for providing the illustration (fig. 9-4).

12. Godwin's sketchbook notes from the British Museum are not confined to medieval decoration and show that he studied work from many parts of the ancient world, including Nineveh, Athens, Corinth, Smyrna, and Rhodes. I am grateful to Catherine Arbuthnott for the benefits of her research in this area.

13. Godwin, "Studios and Mouldings" (7 March 1879): 261, quoted in Crook, *William Burges* (1981): 50, n. 31.

14. V&A PD, E.378-1963.

15. By 1866 South Kensington Museum had already acquired ten important medieval tapestries. See "Concordance" in George Wingfield Digby, *Victoria and Albert Museum: The Tapestry Collection, Medieval and Renaissance* (London: HMSO, 1980).

16. V&A PD, E.269-1963:5.

17. V&A 673-1864.

18. For example, an altar frontal was made by Jones and Willis for Godwin's restoration and refurnishing of the Church of Saint Wynwallow, Landewednack, in Cornwall in 1862 (V&A AAD, 4/9-1980:51).

19. The catalogue of the house sale held 19–21 October 1949 gives scant reference to textile furnishings among the hundreds of other items (De Courcy, *Dromore Castle* [1949]).

20. A page from an album owned by Lord Limerick shows four designs for the lighter curtains. Borders were to be at the lower edging of the drapes, just above a fringe. Godwin's inscription claims "from old examples & some I have designed." I am grateful to Aileen Reid for allowing me to study her photograph of this drawing.

21. V&A PD, E.365-1963 and E.367-1963. The former is inscribed "See for Angels pt. Decorations of Dromore Chapel."

22. V&A PD, E.285-1963:15.

23. RIBA Drawings, Ran 7/B/90 and 91.

24. Ibid., Ran 7/B/1 (91). See fig. 7-9 in this volume.

25. Several sketchbooks show drawings of identified English and French medieval standards and devices, including those used at Agincourt (e.g. V&A PD, E. 279-1963, et al.).

26. Aileen Reid suggests the curtains were woven by Warners but this is unlikely (Reid, "Dromore Castle" [1987]: 113–42). The designs would have been difficult to adapt to a loom, and the firm was not established until 1870.

27. Ledger, V&A AAD, 4/9-1980: 51-52: "The Reverend P.V. Robinson, Landewednack, Helstone (sic)." Jones and Willis was paid £6.1.8.on 1 September 1862. Two other church frontals, designed by Godwin in March 1862, are also likely to have been made by the firm (V&A AAD, 4/9-1980): 45-46.

28. I am indebted to Matthew Williams of Cardiff Castle for sharing these discoveries with me. For the Burges embroideries made for Cardiff Castle, see Matthew Williams, "Gorgeously Arrayed in Blue and Gold," Country Life (5 March 1998): 56–59.

29. The door curtain of the Summer Smoking Room in Cardiff Castle is almost identical in design and technique to a sedilia hanging, designed by Street in 1850 for Saint John's Church, Hollington, in Staffordshire. See Parry, ed., William Morris (1996): 234, no. M.3.

30. Ibid., p. 236, nos. M.6, (M.7).

31. Specification for the furniture made for Dromore Castle by William Watt, RIBA Mss, GoE/1/7/4.

32. Godwin referred to the firm as "CN & Co." They are first listed in ledger entry dated 15 July 1874, V&A AAD, 4/11-1980: 18-19; and sketchbook dated 1875, V&A PD, E.236-1963. The firm traded from 23 Portland Street, Manchester, and the Ashenden Works, Blackley. These two addresses probably represented offices and factory, respectively. They produced a variety of woven fabrics, and a recurring advertisement in issues of the Furniture Gazette (1874) boasts "Brocades, Cotelines, Tapestries, Cashmeres, Terries, Reps, Borderings, Tablecloth &C." See also "Designs for Curtain Materials" (15 April 1876): 241; and "Manchester Work and Workers XXL," Manchester Record Office, n.d., which describes the factory and states that there was also a machine embroidery section located there.

33. V&A PD, E.236-1963: 49.

34. An order for "W. Jones," V&A AAD, 4/11-1980: 18-19.

35. "Designs for Curtain Materials" (15 April 1876): 242. "Curtain Fabrics" (31 March 1876): 318, 320–21.

36. Diary for 1874 and 1876, V&A AAD, 4/2-1980, entries for 14 September and 6 October 1876.

37. Apart from the three examples catalogued here, in recent years Warner's has attributed two further silk designs—"Swallow" and "Ely"—to Godwin, although no substantive proof is available. Neither design has strong stylistic characteristics linking them to Godwin's work. A letter in the archive suggests that the original design for "Swallow" was signed by an "Ed Godwin," but when sold in the "Warner's Archive Sale" (Christie's, 10 July 1972, lot 147), the catalogue entry describes it as "in the style of Godwin."

38. The paper design for "Butterfly Brocade" was kept by the firm until 1972 when it was sold at auction: Christie's, 10 July 1972, lot 127; resold at Christie's 13 December 1988, lot 163; now in the National Gallery of Victoria, Melbourne.

39. Many of these books were bought in London at the time and were particularly favored by artists and designers. One book of Japanese crests is in the Hunterian Art Gallery, Glasgow. Part of the Birnie Phillip bequest, it is known to have belonged to Godwin's wife Beatrice. I am grateful to Martin Hopkinson, former curator of the Hunterian, for this information. The central circular motif of a magnolia flower set against five leaves seen in "Butterfly Brocade" (fig. 9-1) and in a design woven by J. C. & W. Ward (fig. 9-6) is also from this book; Godwin's sketches of these motifs appear on a page of a sketchbook, V&A PD, E.280-1963:9, "Powderings or Crests" (see fig. 10-6).

40. This was Dr. George Bird of Welbeck Street, London. "Sundries," 27 September 1871, V&A AAD, 4/10-1980:93. A charge of £4.4s is noted.

41. In Godwin's cashbook recording work for Collinson and Lock (V&A AAD, 4/13-1980, n.p.) an entry dated 17 February 1873 notes designs for "Print for curtain" and two entries for "Dining Room carpet." A charge of £3.3s was levied for each. His diary for 30 July 1873 states "Sent C&L alternative details for 3 designs & sketch for chintz" (V&A AAD, 4/1-1980).

42. Cashbook entry dated 10 March 1873 records designs for "Curtain stuff" and "Apple leaf curtain" for Collinson & Lock (V&A AAD, 4/13-1980: n.p.).

43. A long-established company, they received honorable mention for their exhibits at the 1851 Great Exhibition (Class 12 and Class 15) and consistently registered designs throughout the nineteenth century (see BT 43 and BT 44, representations and registers [Class 11 and 12], Public Record Office, Kew, London).

44. For details of the Dresser attributions, see Halen, Christopher Dresser (1990): 94–95.

45. Most examples of this type are in his sketchbook, V&A PD, E.241-1963.

46. Ledger entries for 8 August and 31 October 1876 for "Messrs Waugh & Son, 65 Tottenham Court road," V&A AAD, 4/12-1980.

47. V&A PD, E.233-1963: 104, 133; and V&A PD, E.341-1963.

48. Godwin, "Floorcloths" (2 September 1876): 128.

49. Godwin's diary for 3 October 1876 states, "Mr Constable took designs of floorcloths (5 for £10.10.0) away to sell." On 25 October a further entry mentions "Constable at Club (with Lowenthal) told me he had sold 2 of my floorcloth patterns" (V&A AAD, 4/2-1980).

50. For example, in sketchbook V&A PD, E.235-1963: 51, Godwin lists the items needed for the decoration in 1874 of 27 Gordon Square for Philip Jordan, including sixteen linen blinds and rollers.

51. Johnston Forbes-Robertson, A Player under Three Reigns (Boston: Little Brown, 1925): 66, quoted in Harbron, Conscious Stone (1949): 95.

52. Kelly's Directories. Post Office (London) Directory (1872).

53. V&A PD, E.497–499-1963. These designs show Godwin's familiar diagonal patterning.

54. Letter from E. W. Godwin to Lady Alwyne dated 23 December 1867, Compton Family Documents, Castle Ashby, Northampton.

55. Letter from E. W. Godwin to Hermann Vezin dated 19 April 1882, V&A AAD, 4/442-1988.

56. V&A PD, E.264-1963: 67, 68; See also Hyde, "Oscar Wilde and His Architect" (March 1951): 175–76; and Ellmann, Oscar Wilde (1988): 56–59.

57. Godwin sketchbook, V&A PD, E. 241-1963: 21–31.

58. A photocopy of this agreement is among unregistered papers on file at the Victoria and Albert Museum.

59. Just a year after Liberty's was opened, Godwin wrote about it as part of his "Afternoon Strolls" series. Godwin, "A Japanese Warehouse" (23 December 1876): 363. He particularly recommended their embossed papers and fans.

60. Letter to E. W. Godwin from Evelyn Beerbohm, writing on behalf of Lady Charlotte Schreiber, dated 12 September 1884, V&A TA, Godwin collection, box 7.

61. Godwin's account of costs of the 1886 production of *Helena in Troas* at Hengler's Circus includes the information that the curtain stuff was ordered from Cowtan and Sons at a cost of five pounds (ibid., box 6).

Fig. 10-1. E. W. Godwin. Design for "Bamboo" wallpaper, 1872. Watercolor on tracing paper; 21¼ x 21¼ in. (54 x 54 cm). Trustees of the Victoria and Albert Museum, London, E. 515-1963. *Checklist no. 65*

CHAPTER 10

E·W·GODWIN·AND
WALLPAPER·DESIGN

JOANNA BANHAM

B y 1872, the year E. W. Godwin issued his first designs for wallpapers, he had already established a successful architectural practice in London and had begun to make a name for himself as a designer of innovative Anglo-Japanese interiors and furniture. Godwin's involvement with wallpaper design lasted about a decade, during which time he provided patterns for several of the country's leading paper stainers, including Jeffrey and Company (fig. 10-1), James Toleman and Sons, and Lightbown Aspinall, as well as Collinson and Lock and William Watt, two of England's best-known art furniture houses. Much of the evidence for this work is to be found in Godwin's sketchbooks which contain approximately fifty designs for patterns. His ledgers, letter books, and diaries also contain many scattered references to transactions with manufacturers and to specific projects, but only a fraction of Godwin's actual wallpapers have survived in the form of printed patterns. Four papers, for example, were registered at the Patent Office, seven were illustrated in William Watt's *Art Furniture* (1877), and five appear in manufacturers' logs. The remainder exist only as sketches, and as yet it is not possible to establish exactly how many of his designs went into commercial production. What is clear, however, is that for a short but significant period of his career, Godwin maintained a strong interest in wallpaper design and pioneered a highly original Anglo-Japanese style whose individuality was in sharp contrast to the mass of commercially produced work.

Godwin's wallpapers were made during a period when the wallpaper industry in Britain was booming. Widespread mechanization by many of the larger wallpaper firms in the 1850s and 1860s and the repeal of the last remaining taxes on printed papers in 1861 resulted in huge increases in production and dramatic reductions in costs.[1] Increased production was matched by an unparalleled growth in consumer demand. Rising living standards and higher wages—particularly among the professional classes—and a series of speculative building booms encouraged greater spending on items such as household furnishings and decoration, the acquisition of which was an important indicator of social status. In addition, numerous new products were coming onto the market, including washable papers, embossed decorations, and imitation leathers, making wallpapers a commodity available to suit virtually every taste and income, and every area of the home.

Godwin's work was pitched at the upper end of the market, where the majority of patterns were still printed by hand, using techniques that had changed little since their introduction in the late seventeenth century. The design was engraved on the surface of a large rectangular wooden block, which was then inked with pigment and laid face down on the paper for printing. Polychrome patterns necessitated the use of several blocks, and each color had to dry before the next one could be applied.[2] It was a painstaking and labor-intensive process.

Stylistically, the designs for this clientele were dominated by two main trends. The first consisted of patterns

Fig. 10-2. James Huntington. French-influenced English wallpaper, ca. 1860. From Sugden and Edmondson, *History of English Wallpaper* (1926): pl. 103.

Fig. 10-3. A. W. N. Pugin. Wallpaper for Captain Washington Hibbert used at Bilton Grange, Warwickshire, 1848. Trustees of the Victoria and Albert Museum, London, E. 108-1939.

strongly influenced by French examples, comprising showy renditions of trailing fruit and floral motifs, virtuoso imitations of textiles and upholstery effects, and elaborate revivals of historical styles, especially Louis Quinze and Louis Seize (fig. 10-2). The designs were often extremely complex, and the treatment of the motifs was highly realistic, incorporating naturalistic colors, detailed drawing, and much use of illusionistic devices, such as perspective and light and shade. The second trend reflected the impact of mid-century design reformers, such as A. W. N. Pugin and Owen Jones, who had decried the illusionism of French styles as a moral and aesthetic sham. Objecting particularly to the exaggerated realism and meretricious detail characteristic of such work, they argued for patterns that would complement rather than disguise the flat, solid wall. Their ideas spawned a plethora of quasi-medieval or geometric designs founded on "correct" principles that featured stylized forms derived from historic ornament or conventionalized forms of nature. These were printed in bright, primary colors and arranged in simple, regular repeats (fig. 10-3). Allied to this trend was a move within progressive circles toward a more stylized, two-dimensional treatment of floral and foliate motifs similar to that pioneered by William Morris and other designers belonging to a second generation influenced by the Gothic Revival.

Although much space was devoted to the superiority of these reform styles in the design press, their appeal among consumers was clearly limited. The records of the decorating firm Cowtan and Sons for the 1860s and early 1870s indicate that the majority of its aristocratic and upper-class clientele still preferred "French"-influenced designs. Trailing florals, chintz patterns, and imitation textiles continued to dominate the hand-printed wallpapers issued by most of the larger manufacturers during this period.[3]

Godwin frequently expressed a preference for light colors and simple designs. It is hardly surprising, therefore, that when he came to look for wallpapers in 1867 for his London apartment in Albany Street, Regent's Park, he found little to tempt him in the range of designs that were then available. "I went to the paper stainer's works," he wrote, and "I dropped in at every shop I passed where papers were exhibited; and I turned over patterns by the thousand. There was plenty of bright colouring; but I could not find it anywhere combined both with simplicity and delicacy or refinement. In a word, wherever a wallpaper was bright, it was more than a thousand chances to one that it was crude."[4] His frustration was alleviated only by "recourse to a house distinguished then, and which has since become very distinguished indeed for its artistic 'tone.'"[5] The "house" to which he refers was almost certainly that of Morris, Marshall, Faulkner and Company. Godwin had already suggested examples of their wallpapers for Dromore Castle and had used their output at Rheinfeldon, Northamptonshire, in 1867–68.[6] For his own rooms he selected Morris's "Diaper" wallpaper for the dado in the sitting room and entrance hall, his "Fruit" pattern in the drawing room (fig. 10-4), the "Trellis" paper in the dining room, and the "Venetian" pattern in the bedroom.[7] Although a dissatisfaction with contemporary work may have sparked an initial interest in wallpaper design, it was not until October 1871, when Godwin was approached by Metford Warner, a partner in Jeffrey and Company, that he actually began designing wallpapers himself.

First established as Jeffrey, Wise and Company in 1836, Jeffrey and Company was a well-respected firm of London paper-stainers.[8] The innovative nature of the company was evident from its early days: at the beginning of the 1840s they were credited with being one of the first London firms to install a cylinder printing machine and were listed in the trade press as the "sole maker"[9] of an early type of washable paper developed by James Crease and Son earlier in the century. By 1851 Jeffrey's was printing private commissions for the exclusive London upholsterers and decorators, Jackson and Graham, and was also importing French papers in association with Robert Horne, another paper-stainer, who became a partner about 1842. Jeffrey and Company was awarded a medal for its display at London's International Exhibition of 1862, and in 1864 they merged with Holmes and Aubert, moving into Holmes's Islington premises and acquiring the stock of high-quality handprints, flocks, and leaf-metal papers. Shortly afterward in 1865, Jeffrey and Company won the job of printing Owen Jones's wallpapers for the viceroy's palace in Cairo, Egypt, commissioned by Jackson and Graham. By the time Metford Warner joined the firm in 1866, Jeffrey's reputation for quality had attracted the attention of William Morris whose designs they printed beginning in 1864. They also printed several designs by Christopher Dresser in 1867, and the firm's main exhibit at the Paris Exposition Universelle of that year was an eye-catching pilaster decoration by Owen Jones.

Godwin's introduction to Warner may have come through William Burges who was also commissioned to produce designs for Jeffrey and Company around this time. Warner himself declared that he was spurred on to approach the two after reading Charles Eastlake's criticisms of the wallpaper industry in *Hints on Household Taste* (1868). In notes for a lecture read before the Art Workers' Guild on December 4, 1896, Warner recalled, "I felt keenly his [East-

Fig. 10-4. William Morris. "Fruit" wallpaper (also known as "Pomegranate"), ca. 1866. Block-printed paper; 27 x 19¾ in. (68.6 x 50 cm). Trustees of the Victoria and Albert Museum, London, E.446-1919.

lake's] remark in the first edition that 'the Manufacturer (if any are to be found so disinterested) must first inform themselves of the best sources from which good designs may be originally obtained, because at present they seem to be derived from the very worst'."[10] Metford Warner went on to describe how Eastlake's book had encouraged him to seek designs from new sources. "I sought an interview with the writer, in which I endeavoured to point out to him that the fault was not so much the want of enterprise on the part of the manufacturer as the lack of good designs . . . [and] it also made me think that if such fresh designs could not be obtained from the trade designer, artists who had not previously been engaged on such work might be willing to do so. It was in this way I obtained the assistance of William Burges, E W Godwin and Albert Moore."[11]

Warner's decision to employ leading architects, none of whom had previously designed wallpapers, was virtually unprecedented. Until then manufacturers (including Jeffrey's) had relied either on anonymous freelance designers or, more frequently, on the men who cut their printing

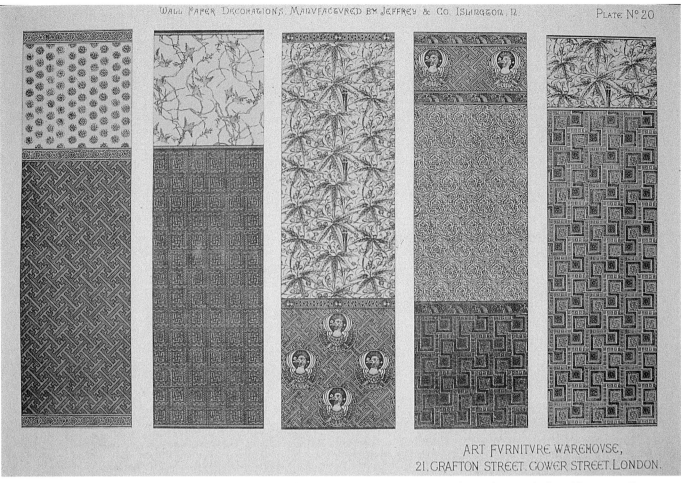

Fig. 10-5. Wallpapers designed by E. W. Godwin. From William Watt, *Art Furniture* (1877), pl. 20. The Mitchell Wolfson Jr. Collection, The Wolfsonian–Florida International University, Miami Beach, Florida, TD1990.40.62.

blocks for the provision of designs. These men also called themselves "Pattern-Drawers," and as a means of obtaining work, they often gave a price for the block-cutting alone, "the drawing being thrown in to the bargain as a sort of bait."[12] The main advantage of this arrangement was that the patterns were cheap and easy to produce, but the disadvantage was that they had little "artistic feeling" and were generally "lacking in originality."[13] In commissioning well-known figures such as Burges, Godwin, and Moore, as well as Eastlake himself, Warner not only aimed to avoid these pitfalls but also hoped to raise the status of wallpapers within artistic circles and to improve the general awareness of their decorative potential. In 1873 Warner successfully lobbied for Jeffrey's architect-designed papers to be shown at the Fine Arts Exhibition in London's Albert Hall. This was the first time wallpapers had been included in an exhibition that was not of industrial goods; Jeffrey's was awarded a medal for their display, and the occasion represented an important step in wallpaper being accepted as a branch of the decorative arts.

Initially, responses to this approach were mixed. Warner remembered, for example, "that the public did not appreciate all that was attempted . . . and both Artist and Manufacturer had to put up with severe rebuffs."[13] Some observers were concerned that "gentlemen not accustomed to such work" might not understand the practical requirements of wallpaper production, which included attention to the numbers of blocks required, the size and nature of the repeat, and the costs involved in introducing many colors.[14] In the long run, however, the policy paid off, and by the mid- and late 1870s numerous other firms were employing artists and architects, and the association of "Art" with wallpapers had become widespread. Jeffrey's went on to commission work from Walter Crane, A. J. Brophy, Bruce Talbert, and many others. As pioneers in this sphere, Jeffrey and Company not only secured a position well ahead of other "Art" manufacturers but also became firmly established in the eyes of the public and of design critics as the leading producers of "Artistic" wallpapers for a discerning market.

Fig. 10-6. E. W. Godwin. Crests and other motifs, ca. 1870. Sketchbook. Pencil and watercolor; 9 x 6½ in. (22.9 x 16.5 cm). Trustees of the Victoria and Albert Museum, London, E.280-1963: 9. *Checklist no. 60*

The first mention of Godwin's wallpapers occurs in a ledger entry headed "Messrs. Jeffrey & Co." and dated October 26, 1871, which records "3 designs for papers taken away," for which he received £10.10.0, and his first working drawings were made in 1872 and payments for a further five designs followed in November and December of that year and January of the next.[15] This group of patterns were printed as wallpapers called "Peacock," "Bamboo," "Sparrows," and "Manji," as borders called "Sparrows" (fig. 10-8) and "Peacock's Feather," and as fillings called "Geometric" and "Floral" (fig. 10-5). Selected examples were exhibited at the annual meeting of the Society of Architects in June 1872 and at the 1873 Fine Arts Exhibition in London. Contemporary observers were quick to note the strong Japanese influence in the designs. "Mr. Godwin has gone beyond most people's notions of the boundaries of civilisation," declared a writer in the *Building News*, "and has added Japan to the list of authorities worth copying,"[17] while the critic in the *Globe and Traveller* commented on Godwin's "close adherence and elaboration of Japanese forms."[18]

The early 1870s marked a high point in British artists' interest in Japan, and as the decade progressed the influence of Japanese art rapidly began to infiltrate the work of certain commercial manufacturers. Godwin's enthusiasm for this subject was firmly established well before this time. He had been one of a small band of architects and artists, including Burges and Dresser, and William Eden Nesfield, as well as James McNeill Whistler and Albert Moore, who had championed an appreciation of Japanese art in the late 1850s and early 1860s. Godwin's designs for furniture and interiors had begun to incorporate Oriental features from about 1868. His first designs for wallpapers reveal a particular fascination with the stylized forms of Japanese crests or *mon* and a page in a sketchbook of about 1870 contains a sheet of approximately twenty "powderings—or crests," several of which provided motifs for his wallpaper designs (fig. 10-6).[19] The precise source for this sheet is not recorded, but many of the designs have recently been identified as deriving from Aimé Humbert's *Le Japon illustré* which was first published in 1870 and which was one of the

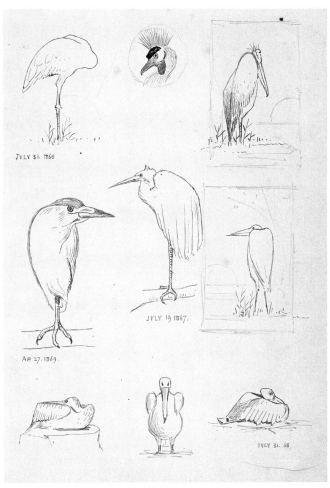

Fig. 10-7. E. W. Godwin. Sketches of birds, including a crowned crane, ca. 1867–69. Sketchbook. Pencil, red ink, black ink. Trustees of the Victoria and Albert Museum, London, E.272-1963: 1.

Fig. 10-8. Aimé Humbert. A crest, or *mon*, with two sparrows. From Humbert, *Le Japon illustré*, vol. 1: 392.

Fig. 10-9. E. W. Godwin. Design for "Sparrows" border and "Floral Medallion" filling, 1872. Pencil on tracing paper; 13⅞ x 16⅞ in. (35.1 x 43 cm). Trustees of the Victoria and Albert Museum, London, E.514-1963. *Checklist no. 63*

most comprehensive and influential of the contemporary textbooks on Japan.[20] The peacock *mon* featured in the middle of the top row of Godwin's drawing, for example, is a version of the stylized crane that appears on the wall in Humbert's engraving of the library at Yedo. This motif was combined with a sketch of a crowned crane drawn from life (fig. 10-7),[21] which Godwin had made when he was working on designs for Dromore around 1869 to form the central motif in the "Peacock" paper. Similarly, the crest

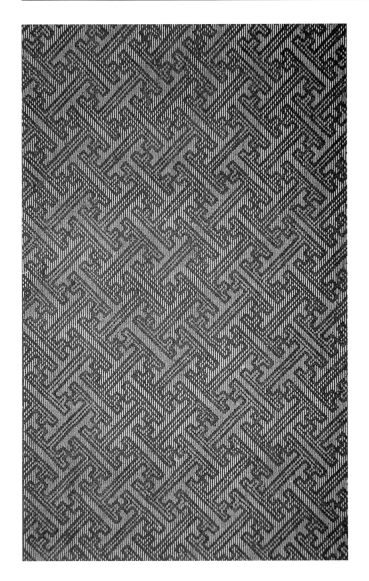

Fig. 10-10. E. W. Godwin. "Manji" wallpaper. From William Watt, *Art Furniture* (1877), pl. 20 (detail). The Mitchell Wolfson Jr. Collection, The Wolfsonian–Florida International University, Miami Beach, Florida, TD 1990.40.62.

containing two facing sparrows was closely related to the sparrow *mon* illustrated in the first volume of Humbert's work (fig. 10-8), and it appears again in the design for the "Sparrow" border (fig. 10-9), above a filling containing a version of the Imperial chrysanthemum *mon*. Other papers of this period show that Godwin was also looking at other sources for Japanese-style ornament. The cross pattern featured in the "Geometric" filling was a variation on a traditional Japanese motif illustrated in many nineteenth-century pattern books, while the diagonal "H" pattern that appears in the "Manji" paper (fig. 10-10) and again in the background to the "Peacock" paper (fig. 10-11) was derived from both Japanese and Celtic ornament. Godwin also studied *mon* in Albert Jacquemart's *Histoire de la Céramique* (1873) which is mentioned by name in one of his sketch-books.[22] He made further studies of birds such as the lively sparrows in the "Sparrows and Bamboo" paper from Hokusai's *Manga*.[23]

But despite the literal nature of these borrowings, Godwin's wallpapers involved much more than a superficial

Fig. 10-11. E. W. Godwin. "Peacock" wallpaper, ca. 1873. Made by Jeffrey and Company. Block-printed wallpaper; 26½ x 19¼ in. (67.2 x 48.9 cm). Manchester City Art Galleries, 1934.22/19iii.
Checklist no. 67

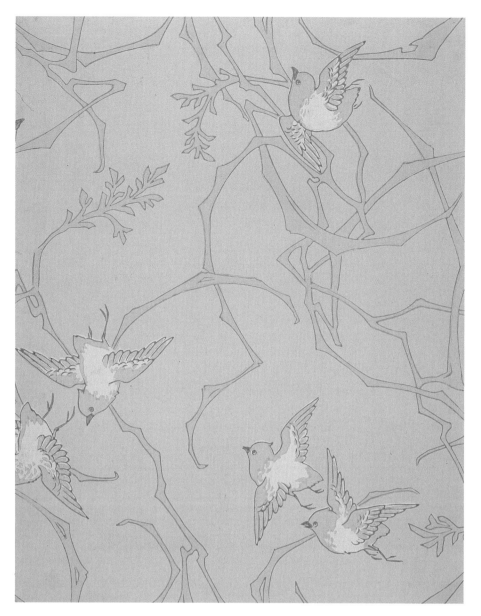

Fig. 10-12. E. W. Godwin. "Sparrows and Bamboo," 1872. Made by Jeffrey and Company. Block-printed wallpaper; 13⅞ x 16⅞ in. (35.1 x 43 cm). Manchester City Art Galleries, 1934.22/37viii. *Checklist no. 61*

Fig. 10-13. E. W. Godwin. Design for wallpaper, 1876–78. Sketchbook. Pencil and watercolor; 6 x 3¹⁵⁄₁₆ in. (15.2 x 10 cm). Trustees of the Victoria and Albert Museum, London, E.241-1963: 45.

grafting of Japanese forms onto Western designs. The bold, naturalistic treatment of the large sprays of leaves in the "Bamboo" pattern (see fig. 10-1), for instance, represents a much freer and more inventive interpretation of Japanese motifs than is to be found in the work of other designers, such as Dresser and Talbert, who were also experimenting with Japanese sources and Japanese-style wallpapers at this date. Moreover, the loose and seemingly random placement of the birds in the "Sparrows and Bamboo" paper (fig. 10-12) suggests a keen understanding of the asymmetrical nature of Japanese art. Asymmetry rapidly became one of the qualities most closely associated with the Anglo-Japanese style and by the end of the 1870s the use of off-center arrangements had become so commonplace as to represent something of a cliché in commercially produced work. But in 1872, the introduction of this feature was ambitiously unconventional and new. The critic for the *Building News* described Godwin's pattern as "the only *irregular* arrangement we are acquainted with,"[24] and in comparison with the strict, almost mathematical symmetry of wallpapers by designers such as Owen Jones, the freshness and asymmetry of Godwin's work must have appeared highly original and suggested exciting new possibilities for two-dimensional design.

Color also played an important role in Godwin's appreciation of Japanese art, and many of his designs for wallpapers feature subtle combinations of clear, bright tones of the kind to be found in Japanese prints. The drawing for the "Bamboo" pattern (see fig. 10-1), for example, is a dazzling mixture of strong oranges, reds, and greens against a soft yellow background, while other sketches and designs include combinations of bright blues and yellows, and soft reds, greens, purples, and whites, which appear strikingly fresh in comparison with the harsh and somber tones characteristic of much contemporary work (fig. 10-13).[25] But Godwin himself was often dissatisfied with the crudeness of the results produced by manufacturers, and in a discussion of his "Manji" pattern he described how his original colors were altered in the printing process: "I had [it] printed in three ways—green, blue, red—showing on the drawing the colours I wished to see reproduced, carefully copied from Japanese work. As, however, I used transparent water-colour, the manufacturer was not much to blame for printing a green, blue and red of his own, and which, I need hardly say, were very harsh translations of my Japanese tones. The green, instead of being merely quiet, was dull, if not dirty; the blue and red, instead of being pleasantly bright, were positively violent."[26]

To some extent these modifications must have resulted from the thick, impasto distemper pigments used in

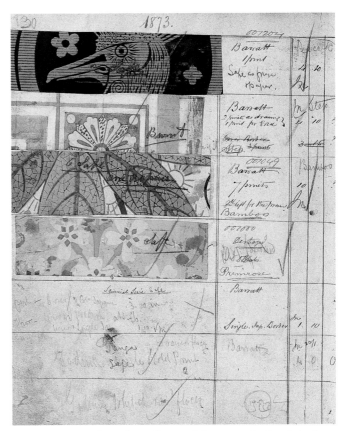

Fig. 10-14. Page from the Jeffrey and Company logbook (vol. 1, no. 2, p. 130), with samples of E. W. Godwin's wallpapers, "Peacock" (top) and "Bamboo" (third from top), 1873. Block-printed wallpaper, paper, pen and ink notations; 12⅝ x 10¼ in. (32 x 26 cm). Arthur Sanderson & Sons Limited. *Checklist no. 68*

the printing of wallpapers, but they were also undoubtedly due to the manufacturers' desire to capitalize on the contemporary taste for tertiary tones. An examination of the samples in the Jeffrey and Company logs illustrates how many of Godwin's designs were printed in several colorways, ranging from bright blues, pinks, and yellows to drab greens and browns (fig. 10-14).[27] Elsewhere Godwin describes how he repeatedly had to compromise his preference for light tones in favor of a "gloomier style" to satisfy the "apostles of the tertiary creed."[28] Despite the fact that his name was often associated with such tones, he remained vehement in his opposition to the dingy khakis and olive greens that became synonymous with "Art" wallpapers and Aesthetic taste and which he regarded as not only unattractive but also unhealthy and unwholesome.

The mid-1870s was one of the busiest periods in Godwin's career. He was producing designs not only for wallpapers but also for painted decoration, textiles, tiles, and stained glass. His exclusive contract with Collinson and Lock was presumably terminated in late 1874 or early 1875

Fig. 10-15. E. W. Godwin. Designs for ceiling wallpapers. From William Watt, *Art Furniture* (1877), pl. 9. The Mitchell Wolfson Jr. Collection, The Wolfsonian–Florida International University, Miami Beach, Florida, TD1990.40.62.

Fig. 10-16. E. W. Godwin. "Star" wallpaper, 1876. Made by William Watt. Block-printed wallpaper; 22 x 29½ in. (56 x 75 cm). Public Record Office, United Kingdom, BT/43/101 Part 1 No. 302033. *Checklist no. 73*

after the firm complained that a paper similar to one of Godwin's designs for them was being sold by Jeffrey and Company,[29] who conveniently also cut the blocks for Collinson and Lock's designs, and he began working for several other firms including William Watt, Lightbown Aspinall, and James Toleman and Sons. Several of the early Japanese-style patterns were illustrated in Watt's *Art Furniture* (1877; see fig. 10-5), along with two designs for ceiling papers (fig. 10-15), and a decoration for a dado. A year earlier Watt had registered another three designs—"Star," "Apple," and "Queen Anne" (figs. 10-16, 10-17, 10-18)—at the Patent Office in London. About the same time, Godwin made contact with Lightbown Aspinall,[30] one of Britain's largest paper-stainers, who were known primarily for their machine-prints and whose factory was based in Pendleton,

Lancashire. Unfortunately, no records of Godwin's work for this firm survive, but given that they were also printing designs by Dresser during this period, it is reasonable to suppose that they were eager to expand their range of architects' designs.

Godwin's association with James Toleman appears to have been both more productive and more long-lasting than his collaboration with Lightbown Aspinall. Comparatively little is known about Toleman's history. The firm appears in the London Post Office Directories as Colleau and Toleman, trading at 170 Goswell Street and 72 Upper Whitecross Street, in 1844, and shortly afterward the name was changed to James Toleman and Sons. After the introduction of machine-printing, Toleman's acted as merchants for machine-printed goods while still producing their own

Fig. 10-17. E. W. Godwin. "Apple"
wallpaper, 1876. Made by William Watt.
Block-printed wallpaper; 20⅞ x 22⅟₁₆ in. (53
x 56 cm). Public Record Office, United
Kingdom, BT/43/101 Part 1, No. 301929.
Checklist no. 74

Fig. 10-18. E. W. Godwin. "Queen Anne"
wallpaper, 1876. Made by William Watt. Block-
printed wallpaper; 19⅟₁₆ x 22⅟₁₆ in. (49 x
56 cm). Public Record Office, United
Kingdom, BT/43/101 Part 1 No. 302278.
Checklist no. 75

range of high-quality handprints. During the 1870s and
1880s they gained a reputation for their dado papers and
were credited with being the first firm to devise a form of
staircase dado that followed the rake of the stairs.[31] Godwin
is recorded as having first sold them designs for papers in
1874.[32] A further ten payments were made, the latest in
1880, and several small drawings in Godwin's sketchbooks
of the mid- and late 1870s are annotated "Gane," the name
of Toleman's agent.[33]

Many of the patterns of this period indicate that Godwin was moving toward a more complex style of design and
was beginning to experiment with a variety of sources in
addition to his favored Anglo-Japanese. Anglo-Japanese
elements continued to appear in the form of stylized bird
feathers, flowers, and fret motifs, but they are allied more

closely to studies from nature. The most markedly naturalistic features emerge in designs such as the "Daisy" and
"Iris" friezes of 1877 (figs. 10-19, 10-20). Certain wall and
ceiling patterns made for William Watt, such as the "Apple"
and "Star" papers (see figs. 10-16, 10-17), contain naturalistic, bold leaf and flower motifs incorporating flat areas of
color with dark outlines that are similar to the work of
Lewis F. Day. A number of "Queen Anne"-style designs—
a wall pattern for Watt (see fig. 10-18) and some sketches for
frieze and ceiling patterns of about 1877[34]—also reveal an
interest in eighteenth-century sources, which is paralleled
in Godwin's furniture of this date (see chap. 8). A series of
designs in his sketchbooks, with titles such as "Indian,"
"Algerian," "Eastern," "Pompeian," and "Anglo-Greek"
(1877–78), indicate that he was also looking at a range

Fig. 10-19. E. W. Godwin. Designs for "Daisy" and "Moth" friezes, 1876-78. Sketchbook. Pencil and watercolor; 6 x 3 ¹⁵⁄₁₆ in. (15.2 x 10 cm). Trustees of the Victoria and Albert Museum, London, E.241-1963: 53.

Fig. 10-21. E. W. Godwin. Design for "Egyptian" frieze, March 1877. Sketchbook. Pencil and watercolor; 6 x 3 ¹⁵⁄₁₆ in. (15.2 x 10 cm). Trustees of the Victoria and Albert Museum, London, E.241-1963: 71.

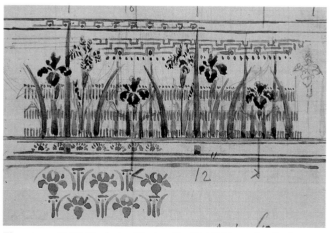

Fig. 10-20. E. W. Godwin. Design for "Iris" frieze, April 1877. Sketchbook. Pencil and watercolor; 6 x 3 ¹⁵⁄₁₆ in. (15.2 x 10 cm). Trustees of the Victoria and Albert Museum, London, E.241-1963: 79.

of more exotic styles.[35] An "Egyptian" frieze (fig. 10-21) with its pattern of stylized papyrus plants is particularly reminiscent of Dresser's work,[36] while the "Indian" and "Pompeian" designs (fig. 10-22)[37] exhibit something of the geometry and symmetry of Owen Jones. Among the most frankly Aesthetic of Godwin's designs of this date is an Anglo-Greek staircase dado (fig. 10-23) made up of square and rectangular compartments containing branches of fruit and leaves, interspersed with panels of classical ornament, rising out of a Greek urn of the kind featured in paintings by Moore.[38]

The majority of Godwin's wallpapers were issued as components within the frieze-filling-dado scheme, a decorative device widely adopted in artistic circles in the 1870s and 1880s that consisted of three or more patterns arranged in horizontal bands one above the other around the room.[39] The dado occupied the space between the skirting and chair rail and usually rose to three or four feet from the floor. Above this came the filling, which provided a background for pictures hung from the picture rail, and above

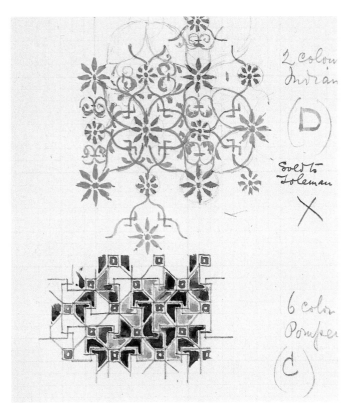

Fig. 10-22. E. W. Godwin. Designs for "Indian" and "Pompeian" wallpapers, August 1876. Sketchbook. Pencil and watercolor, pen and ink; 6 x 3 ¹⁵/₁₆ in. (15.2 x 10 cm). Trustees of the Victoria and Albert Museum, London, E.241-1963: 39.

Fig. 10-23. E. W. Godwin. Design for "Anglo-Greek" dado wallpaper, 1876-78. Sketchbook. Pencil and watercolor, pen and ink; 6 x 3 ¹⁵/₁₆ in. (15.2 x 10 cm). Trustees of the Victoria and Albert Museum, London, E.241-1963: 7.

the picture rail was the frieze. There were many variations on this basic format, and articles on design frequently discussed the most suitable patterns and the most artistic ways for them to be arranged. Most authorities agreed, however, that the colors and materials in each section should be complementary, and that the colors should be graduated from the skirting to the ceiling—the higher up the wall, the lighter in color.

Godwin seems to have favored a twofold division of the wall, incorporating a high dado surmounted by a wide frieze. He used this arrangement in the decoration of his London chambers in 1867,[40] and several versions appear in an engraving of his wallpapers illustrated in *Art Furniture* (see fig. 10-5). His dado papers, like the "Peacock" and "Manji" patterns, were generally dark and stylized in keeping with the notion that the dado should serve as a background for furniture and lend stability to the rest of the patterns on the wall, while his frieze papers, such as the "Sparrows" and "Bamboo" (see fig. 10-1) patterns, were lighter and less formal and sometimes included pictorial elements.

Godwin also designed a number of ceiling papers using flat stylized motifs arranged in multidirectional patterns that could be viewed from any part of the room. In time, however, he became increasingly concerned about the disturbing effect of including too much pattern in a room. Describing the redecoration of his apartment in 1872, he criticized the tendency of "decorators to indulge their customers not merely with two but with three papers—for dado, wall and frieze"[41] and recalled how he opted first for a painted dado and patterned frieze, before finally banishing wallpaper altogether in favor of panelled dados and painted walls.[42]

Fig. 10-24. "Bamboo" wallpaper in the dining room of James Goodwin, Hartford, Connecticut. Photographed in the late nineteenth century. Harriet Beecher Stowe Center, Hartford, Connecticut.

Godwin's writings of this period also reveal his deep antipathy toward conventional styles of decoration. In his articles for the *Architect* in July and August 1876 he criticized the grained woodwork and imitation marble or granite wallpapers typically used in contemporary stairways, passages, and halls as gloomy and unhygienic, recommending instead plain cream-colored walls above a stenciled dado.[43] Similarly, he considered "nothing more offensive than the flock papers and woollen hangings" which represent "the usual surroundings of an Englishman's dining table" because of their propensity to retain dirt and odors.[44] The satin wallpapers and white-and-gold color schemes fashionable in many French-style middle-class drawing rooms were also roundly condemned as fussy and pretentious,[45] while he regarded bedrooms as places solely for repose and therefore advised a simple distemper treatment with no positive color and "no patterns of any kind to distract the tired or sick brain."[46]

Unfortunately, no records for the sales of Godwin's wallpapers survive, and there is scant evidence to show exactly how and where they were used. Certain examples were used in Godwin's own commissions for interiors and his letters and diaries include mention of papers supplied for

several clients including Lord Cowper, John Wingate McLaren, the Honorable Slingsby Bethel, Hermann Vezin, and Lady Shrewsbury. But other records, such as Cowtan and Sons' order books, indicate few requests for Godwin's designs, and, in comparison with sales of Walter Crane's papers to the same clientele, demand for Godwin's work appears to have been quite slight.[47] One reason for their limited appeal was surely the novel and uncompromisingly Oriental appearance of the early designs. Metford Warner described how Godwin's and Burges's designs were initially regarded as "rather mad,"[48] and he also recalled an anecdote in which Godwin's landlady refused to allow the decorator to hang his "Peacock" paper while Godwin was away, on the grounds that it looked far too bizarre for Godwin to have approved the choice of design.[49] Nevertheless, Jeffrey and Company continued to keep Godwin's wallpapers in stock throughout the 1870s and 1880s, and his work was included in a new pattern book issued in 1883, which was advertised as containing "80 of the most successful patterns brought out during the last few years."[50]

Examples of Godwin's work also apparently sold well in the United States. Several rolls of the "Bamboo" paper were hung in the parlor of Major Goodwin's house in Connecticut (fig. 10-24). The fashionable status of this pattern was demonstrated by its illustration in the January 1884 issue of New York's *Decorator and Furnisher*.[51] By this date, Anglo-Japanese patterns formed a standard part of most commercial manufacturers' ranges. While more sophisticated examples might combine seminaturalistic motifs with a meandering Aesthetic style, the majority consisted of tightly patterned compositions of circles, squares, and rectangles, filled with an assortment of Eastern or Western ornament, arranged in a studiedly asymmetrical fashion and printed in dull golds, greens, and browns. Both styles represented a radical dilution of the principles upon which Godwin's work was based, and he disapproved strongly of the misappropriation and misapplication of Japanese designs and motifs. Writing again in the *Architect* in 1876, he railed against the "slavish copying of Japanese books for details" and "the way in which Japanese 'bits' are being worked up into modern English manufacture," declaring "the Japanese have taught us much, and deserve better at our hands than for us to trace one of their artists' designs for a sword hilt and sow it at 4-inch regular intervals all over our walls."[52] His own designs for wallpapers were both more original and altogether more authentic in their reflection of the true spirit of Japanese design.

Note: Most published sources are cited below in shortened form (author's last name, abbreviated title, date of publication); full references will be found in the bibliography. Frequently cited archives are abbreviated below; for a key to the abbreviations, also see the bibliography.

1. The national output had risen from 1,222,753 rolls in 1834 to 32,000,000 in 1874 while prices for machine-printed papers had dropped to as little as a few pence a yard. For a discussion of British wallpapers in the mid- and late-19th century, see Banham, "English Response" (1994): 132–49.

2. A detailed account of the block-printing process appears in Christine Woods, "A Chip off the Old Block," *Traditional Interior Decoration* (London) (April/May 1988): 84–95.

3. The Cowtan and Sons wallpaper log books are in V&A PD, E.43-97-1939.

4. Godwin, "My Chambers," part 1 (1 July 1876): 4.

5. Ibid.

6. "House at Northampton" (7 January 1871): 10.

7. Godwin, "My Chambers," part 1 (1 July 1876): 4–5. Godwin does not identify these designs by name but his descriptions match the Morris patterns cited of this date.

8. The firm underwent several changes of name: to Jeffrey and Wise in 1839; Jeffrey, Wise and Horne in 1842; Horne and Allen in 1843; and Jeffrey, Allen and Co. in 1847, finally becoming Jeffrey and Co. in 1858. See Christine Woods, "Jeffrey & Co.," in *Encyclopedia of Interior Design*, vol. 1, ed. Banham (1997): 652–55.

9. Ibid.

10. Metford Warner, manuscript notes for a lecture given to the Art Workers Guild (4 December 1896), p. 71, V&A National Art Library.

11. Metford Warner, "Some Victorian Designers," manuscript read at the Design Club (24 November 1909), pp. 8–9, V&A National Art Library.

12. Frederick Aumonier, "Wallpapers, their Manufacture and Design," in *The Decorators' and Painters' Magazine* (1895): 102.

13. Metford Warner, "Some Victorian Designers," manuscript read at the Design Club (24 November 1909), p. 11, V&A National Art Library.

14. Metford Warner, manuscript notes for a lecture given to the Art Workers Guild (4 December 1896), p. 71, V&A National Art Library.

15. "Wall Papers" (27 June 1872): 6.

16. Godwin ledgers (26 October 1871), V&A AAD, 4/10-1980: 89; and ibid., p. 5.

17. "Wall-Papers" (11 October 1872): 291.

18. "Wall Papers" (27 June 1872): 6.

19. Godwin sketchbook, V&A PD, E.280-1963: 9.

20. Wilkinson, "Edward William Godwin" (1987): 225–26.

21. Godwin sketchbook, V&A PD, E.272-1963: 1.

22. V&A PD, E.234-1963:73. Godwin notes, "Hist. of Ceramic Art by Albert Jacquemart." See Albert Jacquemart, *History of the Ceramic Art: A descriptive and philosophical study . . .* , trans. Mr. B. Palliser (London, 1873).

23. Wilkinson, "Edward William Godwin" (1987): 258.

24. "Wall Papers" (11 October 1872): 291.

25. Most of Godwin's watercolor sketches for textiles and wallpaper are in one of his sketchbooks: V&A PD, E.241-1963.

26. Godwin, "My Chambers," part 2 (8 July 1876): 19.

27. Jeffrey and Company logbooks, in the Design Archive, Arthur Sanderson and Sons Ltd., Uxbridge, England.

28. Godwin, "My Chambers," part 1 (1 July 1876): 4.

29. Godwin letterbook, vol. 2, letter from Godwin to Collinson and Lock, dated 5 November 1874, V&A AAD, 4/23-1988: 137–40.

30. For a concise history of this firm, see Sugden and Edmondson, *History of English Wallpaper* (1926): 215–18. Godwin diary, entry for 10 October 1876, V&A AAD, 4/2-1980. The entry records, "wrote Lightbown & Aspinall."

31. Sugden and Edmondson, *History of English Wallpaper* (1926): 232.

32. Godwin diary, entry for 28 February 1874, V&A AAD, 4/2-1980. A payment of £5.0.0. from Toleman is recorded.

33. E.g., Godwin sketchbook, July 1878, V&A PD, E.241-1963: 81; ibid., 31 July 1878, p. 83; ibid., "The Shield Pattern," undated.

34. E.g., Godwin sketchbook, V&A PD, E.241-1962: 5, 69, 73.

35. Godwin sketchbook, V&A PD, E. 241-1963: 22–31, "Indian"; ibid., p. 35, "Algerian" and "Anglo-Greek"; ibid., p. 77, "Eastern"; ibid., p. 29, "Pompeian."

36. Ibid., p. 71.

37. Ibid., p. 29.

38. Ibid., p. 7.

39. For a full discussion of this scheme, see Latimer, "Frieze, Filling and Dado" (1985).

40. Godwin, "My Chambers," part 1 (1 July 1876): 4–5.

41. Ibid., part 2 (8 July 1876): 19.

42. Godwin, "My House 'In' London," part 1 (15 July 1876): 34.

43. Ibid., part 2 (22 July 1876): 45.

44. Ibid., part 3 (29 July 1876): 58.

45. Ibid., part 4 (5 August 1876): 72–73.

46. Ibid., part 5 (12 August 1876): 86.

47. The Cowtan books include samples of the "Sparrows" border ordered for Kelsey Manor, Herts., and Headfort House, Co. Meath, in 1875; the "Sparrows and Bamboo" paper ordered for Madeley Manor, Newcastle, in 1877 .

48. Metford Warner, "Some Victorian Designers," manuscript read at the Design Club (24 November 1909), p. 12, V&A National Art Library.

49. Metford Warner, manuscript notes for a lecture given to the Art Workers Guild (4 December 1896), p. 72, V&A National Art Library.

50. Jeffrey and Company presscuttings, V&A PD, E.42A(1-3)-1945.

51. Lynn, *Wallpaper in America* (1980): 386, fig.16-15.

52. Godwin, "My Chambers," part 2 (8 July 1876): 19.

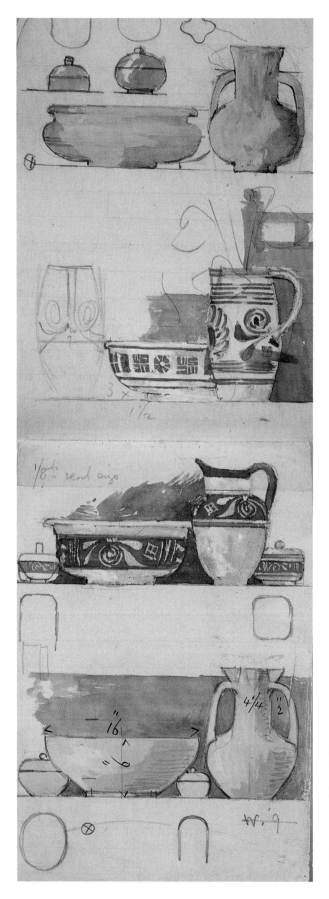

Fig. 11-1. E. W. Godwin. Designs for toilet sets, ca. 1876. Sketchbook. Watercolor and pencil, annotations in pencil and in pen and ink; [page 26] 5⅞ x 4 in. (15 x 10.3 cm), [page 27] 5¾ x 3¹⁵/₁₆ in. (14.6 x 10 cm). Trustees of the Victoria and Albert Museum, London, E.233-1963: 26-27. *Checklist no. 77*

CHAPTER 11

E·W·GODWIN·AND·CERAMICS·

CATHERINE ARBUTHNOTT

Godwin's exploration of the decorative arts extended to ceramics. His sketchbooks and surviving architectural drawings are filled with ceramic forms (fig. 11-1). Bowls, plates, jugs, and vases are sketched onto designs for mantelpieces, around plate rails, and on any design for furniture that could conceivably display pottery. This signature of Godwin's drawing style did not go unnoticed. In 1877 architect and designer Maurice B. Adams, in a lecture on the history of architectural illustration, mentioned an illustration dating from 1784 that included "pots on the shelves à la Godwin."[1]

Although Godwin was never wealthy enough to be a serious collector of ceramics, he was in the forefront of the fashion for "blue and white," as it was satirized by *Punch*. He may have owned Japanese or Chinese porcelain as early as 1858,[2] which was about the time Ellen Terry recalled seeing "an impressive collection of blue china" in Godwin's home in Bristol.[3] Two lists survive of Godwin's own collection.[4] Both date from the 1860s, before his financial troubles of 1873 and 1874, when items of value belonging to him were seized by the bailiffs. The lists include pots referred to as "Nankin" and "Jap" or "Japanese" and "Chinese." Most spectacularly there is a Chinese Imperial Yellow pot bought from Wareham of Leicester Square, who dealt in Oriental ceramics. In the first list, it is valued at nine pounds and in the second, later, list at twelve pounds. Also very valuable were "2 blue pots (Nankin)," which were worth eight guineas at the time of the earlier list and were

valued at twelve pounds by the time of the second list. Godwin described the Imperial Yellow pot as one of the yellow notes in the dining room of his London Chambers in 1867, along with two smaller yellow jars from Cannes and some yellow-green plates.[5] These were displayed against the black wood and gold curtain of the famous prototype sideboard in ebonized deal.

Godwin did not restrict himself to collecting ceramics. He also designed some original pieces of domestic ware, although the actual production was limited, an outgrowth of his furniture practice. He created a series of jug-and-basin sets (also called toilet sets, or ewer-and-basin sets), to complement his designs for washstands. The earliest known set dates from 1873 and was for Collinson and Lock.[6] One of Godwin's sketchbooks of 1873 includes a pencil drawing of a jug and basin standing on integral feet, which was probably the preliminary design.[7] There is no hint in the drawing as to the decoration of the set, but a table jug design of a similar date (fig. 11-2) shows a peculiar synthesis of Japanese and Geometric Greek motifs.[8] The Japanese *mon* with two facing sparrows was used by Godwin in wallpaper designs (see fig. 10-8 and checklist no. 64) at about this time and was reused in the Collinson and Lock decoration of the conservatory at 69 Addison Road, Kensington, for J. W. McLaren in 1873.[9] It is possible that the toilet set was also designed for McLaren.

A year later, in 1874, Godwin wrote an article on opportunities for women architects at the request of Emily

Fig. 11-2. E. W. Godwin. Design for a table jug, ca. 1873. Sketchbook. Pencil on lined paper; 5 11/16 x 3 5/8 in. (14.4 x 9.3 cm). Trustees of the Victoria and Albert Museum, London, E.229-1963: 108.

Faithfull, editor of the magazine *Women and Work*.[10] In it he described the "chief features" of his own practice, which included painting on cabinets, walls, and ceilings, wallpaper designs, and tile designs, but of domestic ceramics there was no mention. It was not until about 1875 that Godwin returned to designing jug-and-basin sets, this time for the William Watt firm. Two pages torn from a sketchbook, one dated 1875, show designs for jugs and bowls "after Greek vases" (fig. 11-3).[11] Godwin does not inscribe his precise sources on these sheets, but in 1875 while researching Greek costumes and properties for his series of essays, "The Architecture and Costume of Shakespere's Plays," he had made sketches from Hamilton's book on vases and had spent time in the British Museum looking at the collection of Greek ceramics.[12]

Four designs for toilet sets in a sketchbook dating from 1872 to 1879 continue the Greek theme (see fig. 11-1).[13] Two of them, colored blue and cream or white, are decorated with a Greek floral meander. The jug on page twenty-

seven of the sketchbook is inspired by an archaic East Greek oinochoe, dating from 600–550 B.C., which was acquired by the British Museum in 1867.[14] Godwin copied the shape of this jug and enclosed the meander in a blue border extending around each item in the set.

All four of these sets were probably made for William Watt, although only one of them can be definitely identified as part of Watt's production. This set, marked "W.9," reappears in a sketch of a washstand designed for Watt, dated July 22, 1876 (see fig. 2-14).[15] It is also illustrated in plate 16 of Watt's *Art Furniture* catalogue (see fig. 8-24).[16] The set of jug, basin, soap dish, and shaving dish is undecorated and colored a quiet earthenware brown, which gives a workmanlike, functional impression. The shape of the jug is far

Fig. 11-3. E. W. Godwin. Designs for jugs and bowls after Greek vases, ca. 1875. Pencil, pen and ink, watercolor on paper torn from a sketchbook; 5 3/4 x 3 1/4 in. (14.5 x 8.3 cm). Trustees of the Victoria and Albert Museum, London, E.471-1963: verso.

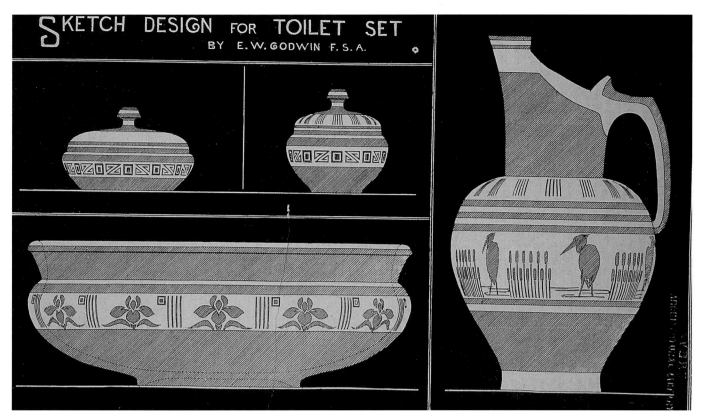

Fig. 11-4. E. W. Godwin. "Sketch Design for Toilet Set." From *British Architect* 11 (14 February 1879): illus.

from simple, however, having two handles, a rim pulled out to form four spouts, and an impractical, low center of gravity, which would make it difficult to pour when full.

In September and October 1876 there are several entries in Godwin's diaries that suggest he was looking for new outlets for his decorative designs.[17] On October 6, 1876, Godwin wrote to the firm of William Brownfield and Sons, a leading Staffordshire pottery.[18] It was a good choice for Godwin. His letter met with a quick response, and by November 24 he was writing to Mr. E. Brownfield (one of the sons) "for 5 guinea for fee for Ewer &c he took away," and on November 27 Godwin acknowledged the receipt of a check from the firm.[19]

In Godwin's ledger the design is identified as a "toilet set (Anglo Greek)."[20] Although Brownfield registered a toilet set called "Olympus" in 1877,[21] the transfer print of a peacock on the jug of the set looks far more like a design by J. Moyr Smith or Christopher Dresser than by Godwin. The shape fails to match any in Godwin's sketchbooks. In fact no set designed by Godwin can be positively identified among the Brownfield production of the time, although a design by Godwin for a toilet set published in the *British Architect* on February 14, 1879, may be his design for Brownfield (fig. 11-4).[22] Once again, the set displays a

synthesis of styles: the soap and shaving dishes have a Greek zigzag motif; the bowl is decorated with conventionalized iris flowers divided by vertical parallel lines which give it a Greek "feel." The jug borrows its shape directly from a Greek vase sketched by Godwin in about 1875[23] (see fig. 11-2), although its stork decoration has a distinctly Oriental flavor.

The only three-dimensional ceramic pieces associated with Godwin to have surfaced are a pair of red earthenware vases with sgraffito decoration on cream slip (fig. 11-5). The name of the potter is unknown, although the color of the clay suggests a West Country origin (Devon and Cornwall), as does the technique of sgraffito, which has been associated with West Country potteries for centuries.[24] This tradition was continued in the nineteenth century, notably by Devon potters such as Edwin Beer Fishley of Fremington and James Brannam of Barnstable.[25]

The two earthenware pots are fine examples of "Art Pottery." The roughness of the glaze and the avoidance of a factory-perfect shape and surface make clear that these are craft objects with no taint of the machine. The potter's signature on the bases is an illegible scrawl but above this monogram are clearly incised the initials "J.G. + E.W.G." If this were not enough identification, almost every motif

Fig. 11-5. Attributed to E. W. Godwin. Pair of vases with sgraffito decoration, ca. 1877. Red earthenware with cream slip glaze, 7½ x diam. 8½ in. (19 x diam. 21.6 cm). Paul Reeves, London. *Checklist no. 58*

on the two vases is culled from Godwin's range of decorative designs, mainly those published by William Watt in his catalogue of 1877. The front cover of the catalogue provides a particularly rich seam of motifs for mining: the stork, the open fans, and the roundels, which are used on both vases, are all taken from this page. Next to the stork on one of the vases is an image of Godwin's much-plagiarized coffee table, about which he had complained in the preface to the catalogue. To underline the joke, the word "KAWPHYRITE" has been inscribed vertically beside the table, surely a phonetic spelling of "copyright."[26] These vases may have been owned by Godwin himself, as the joke would have misfired with anyone outside his circle of friends. Indeed, when the vases first appeared at auction, "kawphyrite" was assumed to be the name of the maker.[27] The vases are evidently display items. The light-hearted decorative references to the Watt catalogue date them to after 1877, the year of publication. They do not appear in any of Godwin's diaries or ledgers, but since Godwin's diary for 1878 is missing this absence of documentation does not undermine their attribution. A single clue as to their possible use is provided by a published source. A writer in the *Furniture Gazette* mentions that earthenware of "Old Flem-

ish or Early English design" was used by William Watt to dress the Godwin furniture displayed at the International Electric exhibition at the Crystal Palace in 1882.[28] This inexact stylistic designation could characterize these rough-glazed earthenware pots, with their restrained color and sgraffito decoration—a technique that could certainly be described as "Early English"—and their bulbous shape, which seems to quote from traditional West County harvest jugs.[29]

Godwin's designs for tiles are better documented than those for his jugs and basins. Architectural ceramics were a natural design field for an architect, particularly for one who wished to be responsible for a building in its entirety, outside and in.[30] Godwin's earliest commissions were for tile pavements, for which he designed the overall floor rather than individual tiles. The earliest mention of tiles is in 1854, when Godwin suggested plain encaustic tiles for the floor of Saint Philip and Saint Jacob's Church, Bristol, in his report on the condition and restoration of the church.[31] Godwin's ledgers do not cover the period from 1853 to 1858, and so the earliest identifiable pavement by Godwin, at Saint Christopher's Church, Ditteridge, Wiltshire, may not be his first pavement design. The ledger entry

Fig. 11-6. E. W. Godwin. Paved chancel floor at Saint Christopher's Church, Ditteridge, Wiltshire, 1860–61. Made by Minton and Hollins. Photographed in 1998.

for this church in 1860 included twenty pounds paid to Minton Hollins and Company.[32] This firm had been in the forefront of the medieval revival, producing characteristic, inlaid tiles from about 1840. The paved chancel floor at Ditteridge is a striking design, composed of red, black, and buff yellow tiles of different shapes and sizes (fig. 11-6). The red-and-black triangular pattern at the sides of the design consists of a mosaic of six-inch tiles, halved diagonally, with some halved again. A foliage meander surrounds square encaustic tiles which are set at a diagonal to the east-west direction of the pavement. The eye cannot follow a single line of tile edges. The sparing use of patterned tiles combined with the bold colors and the breaking up of the direction of the squares and rectangles make this one of Godwin's most striking pavements. It is, however, rather overwhelming in the tiny twelfth- and thirteenth-century church.

For the chancel in the church of Saint Grada, Grade, Godwin designed a very different type of pavement in 1862. It is simple and unobtrusive, consisting of blocks of square red encaustic tiles bordered by thin slips of black and green, set once again at a diagonal to the direction of the

walls of the church (see figs. 8-3, 8-4).[33] These two types of designs for pavements—the vividly colored and patterned type at Ditteridge and the nearly monochrome pavement at Grade—developed in parallel during the 1860s and early 1870s.

The most dramatic scheme of the first type was designed for the Council Chamber at Northampton Town Hall in about 1863 or 1864 (fig. 11-7).[34] Once again Godwin uses triangular tiles, a quarter the size of the six-inch square, and sets them in a mosaic pattern within larger squares at a diagonal to the room and bordered in black. He introduces simple patterned tiles at the intersections of the design and adds decorative edges with rows of dots which pick up the motif of the horizontal bands of inlaid decoration on the tables he designed for the room (see fig. 8-10). The colors are black, red, and buff, with the addition in the corridor of some strips of blue, bordering the central square of the design. This central square includes more elaborate patterned tiles. One displays a shield with the arms of the town, and the others consist of a circular motif with a central star shape surrounded by conventionalized foliage. Unlike the work at Ditteridge, the pavement at Northamp-

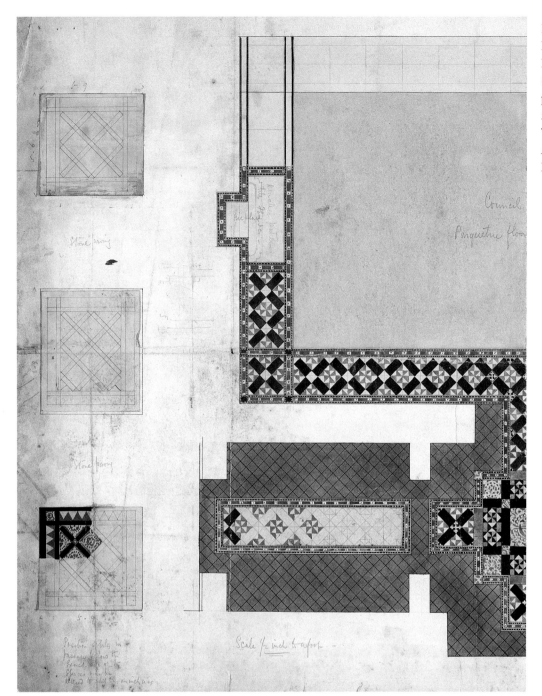

Fig. 11-7. E. W. Godwin Design for pavement at Northampton Town Hall (detail), ca. 1863-64. Pencil, pen and ink, watercolor; 19 x 28⅜ in. (48.2 x 72 cm). Trustees of the Victoria and Albert Museum, London, E.598-1963.

ton complements rather than overwhelms the furniture and decoration. This is partly owing to Godwin's decision to use tiles only as a border around a central oak floor. This restraint, in the most important room of a grand civic building, shows Godwin beginning to integrate his designs so that individual notes within an interior balance and enhance each other.[35]

Godwin's simple monochrome pavements such as the one at the church of Saint Grada evolved in the 1860s and early 1870s. He used a more complicated version of this type of pavement for the chapel and Grand Staircase (fig. 11-8) at Dromore Castle in 1869,[36] and in the entrance hall at Beauvale House in 1873 (fig. 11-9), although cream-colored slips replaced the black and green slips used at Grade. The slips mark out intricate linear patterns, quite unlike the block patterns at Ditteridge and Northampton. At Beauvale these are somewhat akin to a Greek maze pattern, although a series of sketches on squared paper, which survive in an album at the Ellen Terry Memorial Museum, Smallhythe Place, Tenterden, suggest that Godwin was looking at Greek, Japanese, Celtic, and medieval English sources for these pavements (fig. 11-10). Sketches in this album include several versions of the Greek key and maze, Japanese *manji* pattern, and other Japanese patterns taken

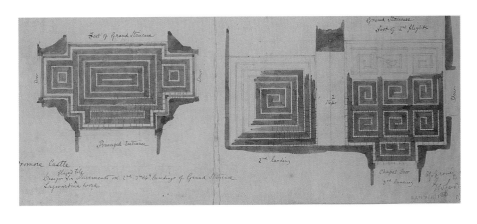

Fig. 11-8. E. W. Godwin. Design for tile pavements for the second, third and fourth landings of the Grand Staircase, Dromore Castle, County Limerick, Ireland, 1869. Pencil, brown and grey washes, Indian ink; 6⅜ x 15⅝ in. (16.2 x 39.7 cm). British Architectural Library Drawings Collection, RIBA, London, Ran 7/B/1 (85).
Checklist no. 30

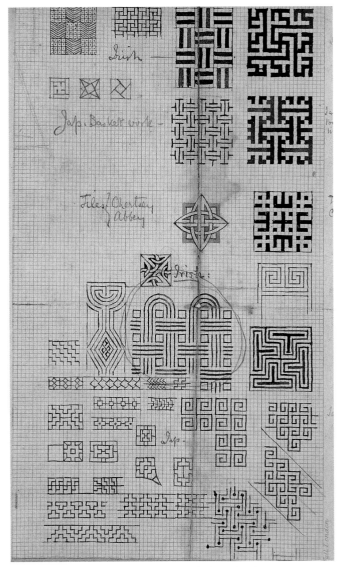

Fig. 11-9. E. W. Godwin. Tile pavement in the entrance hall at Beauvale House, Newthorpe, Nottinghamshire, 1873. Probably made by William Godwin of Lugwardine. Photographed in 1998.

Fig. 11-10. E. W. Godwin. Sketches of tile and other patterns from various sources, ca. 1867–74 (date of album). Pencil, black and red ink on squared paper; 10⅝ x 5 in. (27 x 12.7 cm). Collection of the National Trust, Ellen Terry Memorial Museum, Smallhythe Place, Kent.

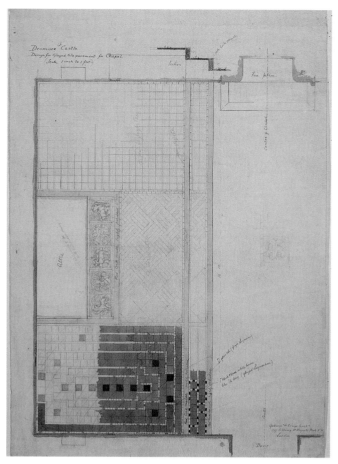

Fig. 11-11. E. W. Godwin. Design for glazed tile pavement in the Chapel, Dromore Castle, County Limerick, Ireland, 1869. India ink, pencil, colored washes; 22 x 15⅜ in. (56 x 39 cm). British Architectural Library Drawings Collection, RIBA, London, Ran 7/B/1 (83).

from basketwork. Others are labeled "Irish" and two further sketches are marked "Tiles, Chertsey Abbey."[37] The earlier chapel pavement at Dromore of 1869 (fig. 11-11) is more elaborate than the Beauvale example. At Dromore the white linear pattern is deliberately set off center within the rectangular spaces to the left and right of the altar, a design feature that is enhanced by the placement of square black tiles down the middle of the linear pattern. The area in front of the altar consists of rectangular tiles laid diagonally. Immediately in front of the altar are five patterned tiles, with the Lamb of God depicted in the center and symbols of the four evangelists to the left and right.

Godwin's ledgers and letter books refer to a number of other commissions for pavement designs. These include an early domestic commission at Ivywell House, Ivywell Road, Bristol, for a solicitor named A. Henderson, dated 1860,[38] and a pavement of Minton tiles at the Church of Saint Wynwallow, Landewednack, in 1861.[39] Godwin occasionally designed pavements that reused old tiles. In a letter of 1871 to Rev. A. J. Ross, the incumbent of Saint Philip's Church, Stepney, Godwin wrote: "with my own hands I placed the old tiles in a pattern which we could have been proud to shew . . . imagine my state of mind to find that without a word to me the tiles had been rearranged after a churchwarden's pattern!"[40] The elaborate and colorful pavements at Saint Botolph's Church, Northfleet, mix old and new tiles: the old are arranged in the nave, and the new in the chancel. Godwin also made a design for the tiling of the

Fig. 11-12. E. W. Godwin. Chancel pavement at Saint Botolph's Church, Northfleet, Kent, 1862. Maker unknown. Photographed in 1998.

Fig. 11-13. E. W. Godwin. Design for tiles for Dromore Castle, County Limerick, Ireland, ca. 1868–71. Pen and ink on tracing paper; 5 11/16 x 10¼ in. (14.5 x 26.1 cm). From an album belonging to Lord Limerick. Courtesy of Lord Limerick.

lower part of the walls of the chancel of this church.[41] Here he introduced tiles depicting Saint Botolph kneeling before an elaborate canopied chair and holding a crown. The floor in the chancel at Saint Botolph's Church is a particularly interesting combination of linear and block pattern types of pavement designed by Godwin (fig. 11-12). Most of the floor consists of plain red tiles set in squares with black tile borders, but a central strip of pavement running from the nave to the altar adds blocks of decorated tiles in green, buff, red, and brown, enclosed by colorful patterned borders.

Godwin's earliest design for an individual tile dates from about 1863 for Northampton Town Hall. A drawing of the lower part of the walls of the Council Chamber shows that Godwin intended to use tiles as a band of decoration at the level of the seats in the stone recesses beside the fireplaces. The drawing is annotated: "all tiles glazed ½ inch thick with pattern as above or of one to be approved by the Architect."[42] These were not executed. A near contemporary photograph of the Council Chamber shows that the walls were painted rather than tiled (see fig. 8-6).[43] Godwin's first executed tile designs were made in 1868 for Dromore Castle by William Godwin (no relation) of Lugwardine, a firm whose speciality was the manufacture of encaustic tiles to medieval designs.

E. W. Godwin was in contact with William Godwin by 1866, at which date the firm supplied tiles to Godwin and Crisp for the floor of Stockland Bristol Church near Bridgwater.[44] Godwin's designs for two encaustic tiles for the fireplaces at Dromore are preserved in an album in the possession of Lord Limerick. They depict a lion and hart (fig. 11-13) and are inscribed, "to be made by Godwin of Lugwardine, Herefordshire" and "Yellow pattern on red ground." The strongest evidence that these are Godwin's first executed designs for tiles comes in a letter of December 21, 1868, from William Godwin, in which he writes, "Dromore Castle: The drawing from which a 4 inch Tile

is to be made requires to be rather larger to allow for the shrinkage in the firing of the Tile. As the enlarging of patterns requires to be done with the greatest nicety to get the proper proportions of each part I have enclosed a tracing shewing the proper size required. I shall take it as a particular favour if you will please sketch in the pattern."[45] There is a strong implication that Godwin never had to produce a full-size tile design before this time. It is an important point, as the encaustic tiles within the fireplaces at Northampton Town Hall, which date from about five years earlier, include a tile depicting a lion within a circle with fleur-de-lis at the corners. This is almost identical in pattern to the lion designed by Godwin for Dromore. The Northampton lions, however, are weakly drawn and lack definition. It is quite possible that Godwin chose the Northampton tiles from the stock of a manufacturer and later remembered and improved the motif for his own design for Dromore. A photograph of about 1947 shows the tiles in situ in the ruined drawing-room fireplace at Dromore (see fig. 7-10). Godwin had grouped them in a horizontal band running the width of the fireplace.[46] The same tiles were used in the dining-room and billiard-room fireplaces.[47]

Dromore Castle was intended to be the complete design, with exterior and interior under the control of a single architect-designer. At Beauvale House, Godwin was not as fortunate in his client, who did not require Godwin to design every last feature of the building.[48] The tiles on the floor of the fireplaces, for example, were selected by Godwin from the stock of William Godwin of Lugwardine.[49] The standard of these tiles prompted an exasperated postscript to a letter dated August 2, 1873, in which Godwin asked, "How is it the designs for encaustic tiles kept in stock by Minton, yr self & Maw are so commonplace that we (artist) Architects can never adopt them?"[50] The tile surrounds to the fireplaces were selected from the stock of Messrs Hart and Company of Wych Street, Strand.[51] God-

Fig. 11-14. Tile in the Anglo-Japanese style in the drawing room fireplace, Grey Towers, Nunthorpe, Middlesbrough, Cleveland, 1873. Maker unknown. Photographed in 1994. Dorman Museum, Middlesbrough.

win was dissatisfied with these, too, writing a note on a page of his sketchbook, "At Beauvale Sep 16. 73. . . . Tiles of grates beastly. . . . not like what I saw? pale nasty blue dull [nasty] red. 1 yellow right in color only."[52]

In spite of these disappointments, Godwin continued to select tiles from the stock of a variety of manufacturers for his interiors. An unusual Anglo-Japanese set of tiles by an unknown manufacturer were installed by Godwin in the drawing room fireplace at Grey Towers in 1873, a Collinson and Lock commission for the ironmaster William Randolph Innes Hopkins (see chap. 7). Designed in a faux-naive style, each tile shows a musician dressed in a loosely interpreted Japanese kimono with bird and sun motifs (fig. 11-14).[53] The misinterpretation of Japanese dress makes it unlikely that they were designed by Godwin, that connoisseur of correct costume, who had already bought a genuine kimono from Farmer and Rogers in the 1860s.[54]

At the White House in 1878 Whistler asked Godwin to use tiles that are described as "those plain simple yellow ones that Watt has from Doulton."[55] These may have been the tiles subsequently used for the fireplace of the "Butterfly Cabinet" for the Watt stand at the Paris Exposition Universelle of 1878.[56] A firm called Burkes supplied the "all white mosaic" for the hall of A. Stuart Wortley's studio in Tite Street (see fig. 6-58),[57] and a letter of March 11, 1884, indicates that pale-red tiles with a rough glaze manufactured by William Godwin of Lugwardine were used for the bedroom and dining-room fireplaces of Elmleigh, a house built for Joseph Shuttleworth at Dallington Park, Northampton.[58] Other tiles used in the vestibule at Elmleigh were bought from Minton.[59]

Godwin's 1874 article for *Woman and Work* named tile design as a feature of his practice.[60] He made a number of designs for tiles that were not associated with any particular architectural commission. Of those recorded in his sketchbooks, two (figs. 11-15, 11-16)[61] combine geometric patterns similar to those recorded in the pages of the album at the Ellen Terry Memorial Museum, with motifs taken from Japanese crests that Godwin sketched in about 1870 on a page headed "powderings—or crests" (see fig. 10-6).[62] A third design is adapted from a border he sketched in 1866 in the British Museum from the Arundel Psalter.[63] The manufacturers of these tiles, if any, are not recorded.

In 1880 and 1881 Godwin approached several firms with suggestions for tile designs.[64] His diary entry for March 10, 1881, notes that he was "With Minton Hollins & Co re tile designs. Offering 24 for the same price Edis pd for his birds."[65] Over the next few days Godwin added six further designs to the twenty-four.[66] The whole set included twelve "Bird" tiles, twelve "Months," four "Seasons," and designs for "Day" and "Night," for which Godwin was paid £94.10.0; that is, 3 guineas for each design.[67] Godwin's designs for these tiles do not survive, although a drawing in a sketchbook of 1874 may indicate the kind of design he sent to Minton (fig. 11-17). It shows a female head against the background of a sunburst representing day and a veiled and crowned male head representing night.[68]

A total of six Minton tiles that may be by Godwin have surfaced. Three of the "Seasons" (fig. 11-18) appear on a set of tiles in poses identical with those of the figures in a stained-glass panel which has been identified as the work of the maker G. E. Cooke, with whom Godwin had connections.[69] These three tiles have some superficial similarities with Godwin's "Kalendar" drawings for the *British Architect*.[70] Three "Bird" tiles made by Minton are likely to be by Godwin (fig. 11-19). Godwin sketched a number of birds "from the life," transcribing these drawings into a special "bird" sketchbook, which contains many examples of small British birds such as the ones shown on these tiles.[71] A swallow on one of the tiles is very similar to that of a design for stained glass found among Godwin's papers.[72] Although these tiles can be tentatively attributed to Godwin, there is no body of ceramic work by him available for comparison.

Fig. 11-16. E. W. Godwin. Design for tiles, ca. 1870–73. Pencil and blue wash; 9 x 6¼ in. (22.9 x 15.8 cm). Trustees of the Victoria and Albert Museum, London, E.380-1963.

Fig. 11-15. E. W. Godwin. Design for tiles and a frieze, ca. 1870–73. Pencil and watercolor; 9⅜ x 6 in. (23.8 x 15.2 cm). Trustees of the Victoria and Albert Museum, London, E.377-1963.

Fig. 11-17. E. W. Godwin. Designs for "Day," "Night," and "Death," 1873. Sketchbook. Pencil and pen and ink; 5½ x 3¼ in. (13.9 x 8.3 cm). Trustees of the Victoria and Albert Museum, London, E.234-1963: 29.

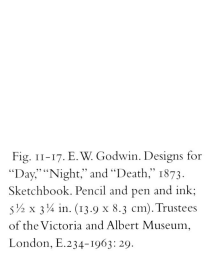

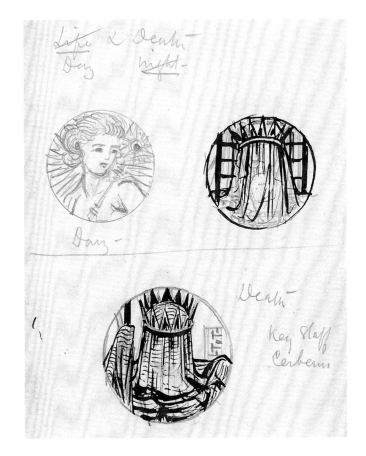

Fig. 11-18. Attributed to E. W. Godwin. Tiles decorated with figures representing three of the seasons, 1881. Made by Minton and Hollins. Glazed ceramic. Private collection.

Fig. 11-19. Attributed to E. W. Godwin. Tiles from a set decorated with birds, ca. 1881. Made by Minton and Hollins. Glazed ceramic; 6 x 6 in. (15.2 x 15.2 cm). Paul Reeves, London. *Checklist no. 59*

A short paragraph in the *British Architect,* published only eight days after Godwin's meeting with the Minton representatives, records that "Messrs Minton, Hollins, & Co. have in preparation a series of art tiles from the designs of E. W. Godwin, F.S.A., which is not unlikely to produce some sensation in the aesthetic world."[73] Unfortunately they did not. Godwin attempted to sell a further set of designs to Minton in November 1881, writing in his diary "left 4 winds & virtues at Mintons Conduit st.,"[74] but there is no matching payment in his cash accounts for this year or the next, implying that Minton refused to buy.

In 1881 Godwin was also in contact with Wilcock and Company of Burmantofts, Leeds.[75] His introduction to the firm may have been through the architect Maurice B. Adams, with whom Godwin had collaborated on a book of designs for conservatories in 1880.[76] Adams was a friend of James Etches Holroyd, the manager of Wilcock and Company, who began to transform the firm from a manufacturer of salt-glazed bricks and sanitary tubes to an art pottery in about 1880.[77] Who approached whom is not recorded, but an article in the *British Architect* of September 2, 1881, suggests that "Messrs. Wilcock have laid themselves out to not

Fig. 11-20. E. W. Godwin. "Bird" tiles. Part of a set designed for Burmantofts Furnace Works, Leeds. Drawn by T. Raffles Davison for *British Architect*. From "Rambling Sketches," part 14 (2 September 1881): illus.

only obtain a wide choice of subjects, but to get it in the best market,"[78] implying that the firm had requested designs from Godwin. Several examples of Wilcock's production were illustrated in the same issue of the journal, including three designs for "Bird" tiles by Godwin (fig. 11-20), which, according to the article, "take the palm for quaintness and invention, . . . The humour and delicacy of these designs are in the originals very charming."[79] These naturalistic depictions of birds and their surrounding foliage are similar to the Minton "Bird" tiles, but very different from the bulk of Godwin's known production of decorative designs using bird motifs. For this reason, even though the *British Architect* identified E. W. Godwin as the designer, it has been suggested that the designs may have been made by Godwin's wife Beatrice.[80] Her papers contain dozens of sketches of small birds similar to the ones in question.[81]

Godwin's diary entry for April 9, 1881, records that he sold a total of eight designs for "Bird" tiles to James Holroyd of Wilcock and Company for which he was paid a total of twenty-four pounds.[82] Only one tile of the set has survived and been identified (fig. 11-21). This shows a bird against a background of spiky pine needles; it is relief molded from plastic clay and finished in a dark blue-green glaze.[83]

The tiles at Dromore have vanished from the now derelict building. No toilet sets made for William Watt, Collinson and Lock, or Brownfield and Sons have been identified, and only a handful of the tiles manufactured by Minton and Wilcock have surfaced. Although ceramic design was only a small part of Godwin's decorative design and architectural practice, the survival rate of these pieces has been disappointing. At their best, Godwin's designs for

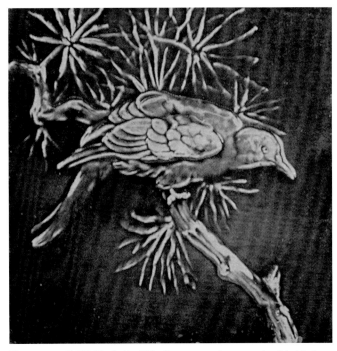

Fig. 11-21. E. W. Godwin. Tile from a set decorated with birds, 1881. Made by Wilcock and Company. Relief molded with dark blue-green glaze. From Thomas, *Victorian Art Pottery* (1974): 229, fig. 107.

ceramics show him as a most brilliantly eclectic and versatile artist, creating an effortless synthesis of styles from a wide variety of sources, while his concern for even this small detail of decorative effort within his buildings confirms the claim of one of his obiturists that he was an "architect of all the Arts."[84]

Note: Most published sources are cited below in shortened form (author's last name, abbreviated title, date of publication); full references will be found in the bibliography. Frequently cited archives are abbreviated below; for a key to the abbreviations, also see the bibliography.

1. M. B. Adams, "Architectural Association" (26 January 1877): 53.

2. For a discussion of the dates at which Godwin began to collect Japanese objects, see Wilkinson, "Edward William Godwin" (1987): 17.

3. E. A. Craig, *Gordon Craig*, (1968): 34.

4. Both lists occur in Godwin's ledgers: for one see V&A AAD, 4/9-1980: n.p.; and for the other, headed "List of articles of Vertu in large office," see V&A AAD, 4/10-1980: n.p., undated.

5. Godwin, "My Chambers," part 1 (1 July 1876): 5.

6. The set is referred to in his ledger for that year but without any indication of the client. See "Collinson and Lock" entry for 17 September 1873, V&A AAD, 4/13-1980: n.p.

7. V&A PD, E.234-1963: 3. This sketchbook is dated August to December 1873. A note at the end (fol. 73) indicates that one of Godwin's sources for his ceramic shapes may have been Albert Jacquemart, *History of the Ceramic Art: A descriptive and philosophical study . . .* , trans. Mr. B. Palliser (London, 1873).

8. V&A PD, E.229-1963: 108. Although this sketch of a table jug is itself undated, sketches on neighboring pages are dated 1873. The motif of star shapes within vertical parallel lines on the neck is much used on East Greek middle Geometric pottery, such as a krater from Camirus, Rhodes, dating from about 790–745 B.C., in the British Museum (GR.1861.4-25.51).

9. For an illustration of wallpaper design, see "Wall Decorations" (8 May 1874): 504; for design for the decoration of a conservatory for J. W. McLaren, see V&A PD, E.511-1963; and for a similar use of the sparrow motif, see V&A PD, E.512-1963.

10. "Industrial Education Bureau" (6 June 1874): 5.

11. V&A PD, E.398-1963, dated 1875; V&A PD, E.471-1963 verso, undated.

12. Godwin, "Architecture and Costume of Shakespere's plays: The Greek Plays" part 3 (22 May 1875): 299. In this article Godwin describes his visits to the vase rooms of the British Museum and also refers to the book by Sir William Hamilton, *Collection of engravings from ancient Vases* (1791–95). Godwin made further detailed sketches from this book in about 1881, in his sketchbook, V&A PD, E.282-1963.

13. V&A PD, E.233-1963: 26–27.

14. For Godwin's sketch of a portion of this jug, see V&A PD, E.473-1963 verso. The jug itself is in the British Museum, Blacas Collection (GR.1867.5-8.925).

15. V&A PD, E.233-1963: 35, dated 22 July 1876.

16. Watt, *Art Furniture*, (1877): pl. 16.

17. He contacted the following: Howard and Sons, "offering co-operation in inlay wood" (diary entry for 18 September 1876, V&A AAD, 4/2-1980); Marshall and Eton of Bethnal Green Road, "suggesting designs" (diary entry for 14 September 1876, ibid.); and the wallpaper firm Lightbown and Aspinall (diary entry for 10 October 1876, ibid.). He also came to an arrangement with an agent, a Mr. Constable, who took designs away to sell in exchange for 10 percent commission and who may have introduced Godwin to the firm of Waugh and Sons, for whom Godwin designed furniture, floorcloths, and wallpapers in 1876–77 (diary entries: Constable's fees, 29 September 1876, ibid.; contact with Waugh and Son, 6, 10, 12, 17, October and 8, 9, 23 November 1876, ibid.).

18. "Wrote . . . Brownfield & Sons," diary entry for 6 October 1876, ibid. Founded in 1836 Brownfield mainly produced earthenware and stoneware until about 1871, after which it began to compete in the lucrative china market with Minton and Hollins, Wedgwood, Copeland, and others. In 1876, the year Godwin first contacted Brownfield, the firm had displayed a large collection of china and other pottery at the Philadelphia Centennial Exhibition. For a history of the firm and their production, see Peake, *William Brownfield* (1995). Elizabeth Aslin identifies Brownfield as the makers of ceramics for William Watt, which would imply that Godwin's introduction to Brownfield was through his connection with Watt (Aslin, *E. W. Godwin* [1986]: 31, n. 48). Although possible, Watt's records do not survive and there is no mention of Watt in the surviving Brownfield papers at Keele University or in the possession of the ceramics historian T. H. Peake.

19. Diary entries for 24 and 27 November 1876, V&A AAD, 4/2-1980.

20. "Sundries," 9 November 1876, "Messrs Brownfield for toilet set (Anglo Greek) 5.5," ledger, V&A AAD, 4/12-1980: n.p.

21. The jug was illustrated in Peake, *William Brownfield* (1995): 166. The set was registered at the patent office on 10 October 1877 as nos. 315104–5.

22. "Sketch Design for Toilet Set" (14 February 1879): 72 and illus.

23. V&A PD, E.471-1963 verso.

24. See Godden, *British Pottery* (1971): 16–17. Godden illustrates several examples of West Country sgraffito-decorated earthenware, including pieces dating from 1764 and 1778.

25. The Fishley family began making pottery in Barnstable in the late eighteenth century. Edwin Beer Fishley's career and his work, including sgraffito-decorated earthenware using clay described as "a rich madder brown," was discussed in Francesca M. Steele, "Fremington Pottery," *Art Journal* (January 1900): 28–29. I am grateful to Richard Bryers for this information.

James Brannam of Barnstable won a bronze medal at the 1851 Great Exhibition in London for his display of jugs and vases made from local red clay, covered with white slip and decorated with patterns scratched through the slip to expose the dark body. Brannam's son Charles would later invent "Barum ware." This firm had strong links with the dealers Howell and James of Regent Street, London. Liberty's of Regent Street also sold Barum ware. See. F. Lloyd Thomas, *Victorian Art Pottery* (London: Guildart, 1974): 103–6.

26. I am grateful to Richard Bryers for providing detailed information about the sources of the motifs on these pots.

27. I am grateful to Paul Reeves for this information.

28. "Domestic Electric Lighting" (1 April 1882): 202.

29. For West Country harvest jugs see Godden, *British Pottery* (1971): pls. 22, 23.

30. See, e.g, Godwin's letter to Earl Cowper dated 1 April 1873, V&A AAD, 4/23-1988: 16-17. Godwin writes, "in each house I have built I have had the pleasure of regarding it as my own work entirely; down, or rather up, to its coloured decoration."

31. Draft report of St. Philip's Tower, dated 22 August 1954, V&A AAD, 4/237-1988.

32. Ledger, V&A AAD, 4/9-1980: 15–16.

33. Ibid., 25–26. The ledger entry is for "Art designs for Pave't & glass." for which Godwin was paid five guineas.

34. Design for the pavement of the Council Chamber at Northampton Town Hall, V&A PD, E.598-1963.

35. It is not known whether this pavement was executed. A near-contemporary photograph (P/3852) in the Northamptonshire Record Office does not show the floor. The present tiled decoration to Godwin's design was added during the restoration by Roderick Gradidge in 1992. See M. Hall, "Modern Gothic" (1993): 48–51.

36. RIBA Drawings, Ran 7/B/1 (83-88), designs for the pavements at Dromore. The chapel pavement is Ran 7/B/1 (83).

37. Album, Ellen Terry Museum. For discussion of the then newly discovered tiles at Chertsey Abbey see William Burges, "What We Learn from the Chertsey Tiles," *Builder* 6 (1858): 502–4; see also Crook, *William Burges* [1981]: 265.

38. Ledger, V&A AAD, 4/9-1980:19–20.

39. Ledger, V&A AAD, 4/9-1963: 21–22.

40. Letter from E. W. Godwin to Rev. A. J. Ross dated 28 September 1871, letterbook, V&A AAD, 4/22-1988: 104–105.

41. Ledger, V&A AAD, 4/9-1980: 45–46. The entry includes a sum of three guineas for the design for the encaustic floor and a further three guineas for the designs of the encaustic wall lining and "Dallage."

42. V&A PD, E.614-1963.

43. Northamptonshire Record Office, P/3852.

44. Henry Crisp sent sketches for the pavement to the incumbent of Stockland Bristol, Rev. A. Daniel in July 1866, writing "you will observe our object has been simplicity of design throughout" (Proctor and Palmer, letter no. 338). However, this was a little disingenuous. In an earlier letter to W. Godwin of Lugwardine, Crisp asked the manufacturer to provide a "suggestive sketch" for the tiling. His instructions had suggested "plain tiles arranged in simple patterns with borders" for the aisles porch, tower, and organ chapel, and ornamental tiles for the chancel (ibid., letter no. 324, dated 5 July 1866).

45. V&A AAD, 4/180-1988, letter from William Godwin of Lugwardine to E. W. Godwin, dated 21 December 1868.

46. I am grateful to Brendan McMahon for lending me his copy of this photograph.

47. RIBA Drawings, Ran 7/B/1 (40). This drawing is annotated: "*Note the tiles with red markings are to have alternate pattern of Lion & Hart in yellow on red ground. glazed. (Godwin's) Those not marked to be plain red glazed.*"

48. Godwin was driven to protest that "[I]n each house I have built I have had the pleasure of regarding it as my own work entirely; down, or rather up, to its coloured decoration . . . you will not I hope entertain the thought that I have assumed a responsibility either novel or unusual to me." (letter from E. W. Godwin to Lord Cowper dated 1 April 1873, V&A AAD, 4/23-1988: 16–17).

49. Letter from E. W. Godwin to William Godwin of Lugwardine dated 30 July 1873, letterbook V&A AAD, 4/23-1988: 61.

50. Letter from E. W. Godwin to William Godwin of Lugwardine, dated 2 August 1873, ibid., fol. 69.

51. Letter from E. W. Godwin to Hart and Sons, dated 30 July 1873, ibid., fol. 60.

52. V&A PD, E. 234-1963: 4.

53. Examples of these tiles are in the Dorman Museum, Middlesbrough.

54. List of Japanese, Chinese, and other objects owned by Godwin, V&A AAD, 4/9-1980: n.p.

55. Letter from James McNeill Whistler to E. W. Godwin, annotated received 22 March 1878, Glasgow University Library, Whistler 9105.

56. William Watt wrote to Godwin in January 1878 suggesting that Godwin should see the tiles and the covering of the easy chair selected for Paris (V&A AAD, 4/19-1988).

57. Diary entry for 11 January 1879, V&A AAD, 4/4-1980.

58. Letter from E. W. Godwin to John Watkin, dated 11 March 1884, V&A AAD, 4/77-1988.

59. Letter from E. W. Godwin to John Watkin, dated 19 November 1883, V&A AAD, 4/67-1988.

60. "Industrial Education Bureau" (6 June 1874): 5

61. V&A PD, E. 377-1963 and ibid., E.380-1963.

62. V&A PD, E.280-1963: 9

63. For this third design, see V&A PD, E.377-1963; for Godwin's sketch of the border from the Arundel Psalter, see V&A PD, E.285-1963:9. Another sketch from the Arundel Psalter on the same page is dated in pencil, "Ap.26.66."

64. These letters are recorded in Godwin's diaries; see, e.g., entry for 21 June 1881, V&A AAD, 4/6-1980. He states, "Wrote letters to Martin, Webb & Maw & Co with Marks D [illegible] & Co re tile designs."

65. Diary entry for 10 March 1881, V&A AAD, 4/6-1980. Edis is Col. Robert Edis, a friend and occasional architectural collaborator with Godwin, and an author (see Edis, *Decoration and Furniture of Town Houses* [1881]).

66. "12 months 4 seasons day & night & 12 birds," diary entry for 14 March 1881, V&A AAD, 4/6-1980.

67. Cash account, diary entry dated 15 March 1881, ibid.

68. V&A PD, E.234-1963: 29.

69. Private collection, Brighton. A stained-glass panel with identical figures was made by G. E. Cooke, a stained-glass manufacturer with links to Frederick Vincent Hart, Godwin's assistant of the late 1860s and early 1870s. F. V. Hart and Cooke collaborated on a number of stained-glass windows. Cooke may be responsible for the making of the east window at All Saint's Church, Winterbourne Down, to Godwin's design.

70. In 1880 Godwin designed a "Kalendar" for the *British Architect* with figures representing each month that was published in 1881. Although some of these figures were reused in the "Four Seasons Cabinet" now in the V&A, they cannot have been the prototypes for the Minton "Months," because an entry in Godwin's cash account describes these designs not as figures but as heads (cash account, entry dated 15 March 1881, V&A AAD, 4/6-1980).

71. V&A PD, E.272-1963.

72. V&A PD, E.517-1963.

73. "Messrs. Minton, Hollins, & Co." (18 March 1881): 143.

74. Diary entry dated 29 November 1881, V&A AAD, 4/6-1980.

75. Cash account and diary entries for 15 March and 14 April 1881, ibid.

76. Messenger and Company, *Artistic Conservatories* (1880; reprint 1978).

77. For Maurice B. Adams's connection with Wilcock and Company, see Victoria Bergesen in *Encyclopaedia of British Art Pottery: 1870-1920* (London: Barrie and Jenkins, 1991): 48–52.

78. "Rambling Sketches," part 14 (2 September 1881): 444-45 and illus.

79. Ibid.

80. See MacDonald, *Beatrice Whistler* (1997): 28-29.

81. Ibid.

82. "To Islington gave Holroyd of Wilcock & Co. designs for tiles (8) ordered at £3 each," diary entry for 9 April 1881, V&A AAD, 4/6-1980.

83. A photograph of this tile was illustrated in Thomas, *Victorian Art Pottery* (1974): 229, fig. 107. The present whereabouts of this tile is unknown.

84. Campbell, "The Woodland Gods" (November 1888): 2.

Fig. 12-1. E. W. Godwin. Design for costumes for the Provost's guards and the Abbot in W. G. Wills's *Juana*, 1881. Pencil, pen and ink and watercolor; 10⅞ x 6⅞ in. (27.5 x 17.5 cm). Trustees of the Victoria and Albert Museum, London, S.102-1998. *Checklist no. 122*

CHAPTER 12

E·W·GODWIN·AND DESIGN·FOR·THE·THEATER

FANNY BALDWIN

E.W. Godwin was first and foremost an architect, bringing related knowledge and abilities to his work in the theater. His skills were those of a trained draftsman, and he had the ability to work imaginatively in three-dimensional form. At a personal level his interest in historical costume had begun when, as a child, he had spent hours copying, coloring, and cutting out the costumed figures from magazine reproductions of the illustrations in *A History of British Costume from the Earliest Period to the Close of the Eighteenth Century* by the playwright, antiquary, and scene designer James Planché.[1] This interest in costume later developed into costume design (fig. 12-1) and grew to encompass archaeological and historical buildings, decoration, furniture, objects, and manners. Godwin also brought to his work in the theater a love of Shakespeare's plays, a delight in theatergoing, an advanced capacity for writing and research, the ability to persuade, and a shrewd intellectual mind. His approach to stage design was fired by a philosophy of visual truth, realized through accuracy in re-creation of the appearance of the original, a perfect illusion of reality to be assimilated by the audience for their edification and aesthetic appreciation.

The decades before Godwin began his work in the theater had seen a gradual transition away from the use of standard and stock scenery. There had also been a move away from using a mixture of dress from the wardrobes of the players as well as from costumiers. Actuality on stage had increased with the appearance of real water, horses, dogs, furniture. Although Godwin was part of a line of scenic reformers, in company with James Planché, William Macready, Samuel Phelps, Charles Kean, and Charles Fechter,[2] his view that nothing less than full scenic and costume research and realization would do was new in its comprehensiveness and rigor. This view had crystalized long before he had any practical involvement in the staging of plays.

Commentator and Critic

Godwin's earliest theatrical work was as a commentator and critic. As a student he had read Shakespeare plays aloud with friends and had regularly attended the Theatre Royal, Bristol.[3] From October 1862 to October 1864 he submitted a series of articles entitled "Theatrical Jottings," signed "G," to Bristol's *Western Daily Press*. In these he commented on current productions in Bristol, Bath, and London, criticizing the inaccuracies of dress, scenery, gesture, and delivery that he observed.[4]

By the end of "Jottings," Godwin had formulated a rationale for the correct historical appearance of the stage picture. "The use of scenery, dress, and other accessories directly implies an intention to reproduce the original scene, and consequently an error in either of these vitiates the whole result."[5] He also prescribed the role of the audience: "We do not go to the theatre to hear passionate recitations and funny speeches, but to witness such a performance as will place us as nearly as possible in the position of spectators of the original scene or of the thing represented and

Fig. 12-2. E. W. Godwin. Designs for costumes and properties for *Hamlet*, ca. 1874–1886. Pencil, watercolor, pen and ink (in a bound volume of essays and illustrations); 12½ x 8 5⁄16 in. (31.8 x 21.2 cm). Trustees of the Victoria and Albert Museum, London, Archive of the Theatre Museum (Blythe House) S.173-1998. *Checklist no. 107*

so gain information of man, manners, customs, costumes, and countries."[6] This coincides with the contemporary view that the audience was invisible, looking at the stage picture through the proscenium frame.

There were many social and technical developments during the previous decades which together had contributed to the pictorialization of the Victorian stage. These included new experiences of peering into brightly lit scenes—the invention of the stereoscope in 1832, magic lanterns and colored slides, and even the pastime of window-shopping. The camera had been in use professionally since 1840; advances in printing ensured increasing numbers of illustrations in books and magazines; and there were new art galleries to visit. More painters were designing for the newly built theaters, with scenic artists in London and the major cities producing skilled and complex work. The Grieves family of scenic artists added moving panoramas across the back of the stage at Covent Garden beginning in 1820, while dioramas, with three-dimensional effects from the lighting of two transparent surfaces, were in use in Regents Park in 1823.

After 1830 the practice developed of rendering famous paintings on stage as tableaux at the ends of scenes or acts, the term for this in stage directions being "picture." To accommodate additional patrons, managers were abandoning the projecting stage, thus removing the one area where actors came "into" the auditorium. Finally, elaborate proscenium arches, decorated act-drops, sumptuous curtaining, and blazing footlights further separated the audience, rendering them spectators rather than participants at the drama. In "Jottings" Godwin bore witness to the audience being instructed, their visual assimilation of a faithful realism enabling them to share another time, another place.

Adherence to the period, location, and status of the characters in the text not only provided an authentic context for the action, it also represented a form of truth, a theme that Godwin developed more fully in his series of thirty articles (fig. 12-2), "The Architecture and Costume of Shakespere's [sic] Plays," published in the Architect between October 31, 1874, and June 26, 1875.[7] He wrote:

> There are three ways (indeed where are there not?) of representing stage plays. First, they may be governed by the period of the story, that is, of course, where the story has any historical foundations; or, second, they may be made to obey the internal evidence, or, in other words, the period at which they were written; and third, there may be no governing of any kind, but actor and actress, stage manager and scene painter, may be left to do as they please.[8]

This confident opening to Godwin's series of Shakespeare articles summarizes, with a nice touch of humor, his order of merit for principles of stage design. He considered the third way ludicrous; the second was sufficient only when realization of the first was impossible or irrelevant, or the play was contemporary. The primary purpose of the articles was to establish the historical basis for the first, and, in his view, the correct way of staging: to depict as accurately as possible the period and location of the story of the play. Throughout his life Godwin deviated little from this primary approach, although his concept of authenticity was to expand as he became involved in theater productions and with theater professionals.

Godwin was by no means the first to suggest the application of antiquarian research to stage design. J. P. Kemble was fascinated by the medieval period and his scenic artist, William Capon, meticulously sketched Gothic buildings and London streets for Kemble's various medieval productions on the vast stage of the rebuilt Drury Lane Theatre from 1800 and Covent Garden from 1809. Kemble's brother Charles employed James Planché, Fellow of the Society of Antiquaries and a Herald,[9] to design a landmark production of King John at Covent Garden in 1823. Costumes were inspired by contemporary effigies, sculpture, coats of arms, and heraldic seals. For the first time an entire cast was appropriately dressed, not just the leads. Throughout the 1830s Planché was responsible for Mme Lucia Vestris's scene painters and dressmakers, first at the Olympic Theatre and then at Covent Garden, where he continued his research and reform, his costume publications clearly influencing Godwin.

Perhaps Godwin's most immediate antiquarian predecessors were Charles Kean and his team of scenic artists at the Princess's Theatre—Frederick Lloyds, William Gordon, J. Dayes, the Grieves (father and two sons), and William Telbin (Sr.). During the 1850s this team used many archaeological and historical sources, such as: recent Assyrian discoveries for the reconstruction of ancient Nineveh in the 1852 production of Sardanapalus; the architecture of Hampton Court Palace for Henry VIII in 1885, along with a moving panorama based on drawings of London made in 1543 and also many costumes taken from Holbein's portraits. Details from Etruscan vases were used for The Tempest in 1857 and locational drawings for The Merchant of Venice in 1858. Kean was elected a Fellow of the Society of Antiquaries in 1857 for his antiquarian services to the theater.

Nothing as comprehensive as Godwin's approach in his Shakespeare articles, however, had yet been adopted. Godwin began each essay by assessing the evidence for dating the period of the play and noting any textual anachronisms.[10] He then decided on the number of sets necessary for staging, repeating locations where the descriptions of them were generalized in order to hold down the potential costs.[11] Next he discussed the architectural styles appropriate for the sets, commenting on suitable materials and the correct scale. He considered the costumes, suggesting the types of cloth, the ornamentation, the details of patterning, and the accessories that correctly matched the status or calling of each character.[12] He even gave guidance on research times and study locations, suggesting, for example, that a knowledge of Greek chitons, their material, cut, styles, sleeves, girdles, and border designs could be acquired with two days of study at the British Museum.[13]

The methodology recommended by Godwin was exemplified by his own practice. His priority was first to study the actual locations and buildings, whenever possible, or their equivalents. Then he scoured museums and galleries for primary sources—monuments, sculpture, heraldry, coins, furniture, tapestry, vases, manuscripts, costumes, and paintings.[14] This was supplemented by the study of scholarly books.[15] To prevent accusations of pedantry he states in the second article, "I wish it to be clearly understood that I am not advocating the reproduction in dramatic representation of every old feature which we may exhume in the course of our researches. The poet has a licence."[16] He also writes that "The architect should understand something of the requirements of the stage and of the *business* of the action."[17]

Godwin's Shakespeare articles imply a knowledge of stagecraft that he probably acquired from Ellen Terry after she came to live with him in 1868. He is, for example, aware

of some of the financial limitations of theater managers and the constraints within which scenic artists, carpenters, lighting men, property makers, costumiers, and perruquiers had to work.

In the series Godwin explores relevant secondary topics. He pleads against fluctuations of scale in architectural set pieces. "There is no need for the audience to see a cardboard model of the *whole* interior of the Abbey," he writes caustically, for *Henry IV.* He cautions that "Wherever possible the scale of the mimic scene should be equal to that of the real one."[18] Deploring the practice of expecting actors and actresses to supply all or part of their own costumes,[19] he remarks that "we continually see the most harsh and violent discord,"[20] and he is witty about the ungainly movements of players who have not been sufficiently rehearsed in their apparel: "Every movement of their bodies says plainly 'this is a very telling sort of dress, and no doubt it must arrest attention; but I never wore anything like it before'."[21] Each of these irritations bore a common hallmark—inaccuracy, thus a lack of truth.

First Commissions, 1875–76

In 1862 Kate and Ellen Terry joined James Henry Chute's company at the Bristol Theatre and Godwin invited them to play-readings at his home in Portland Square. When Ellen was engaged to play Titania in *A Midsummer Night's Dream* at the Theatre Royal, Bath, in March 1863, Godwin designed, cut out, and helped sew a dress appropriate for the Greek references in the play.[22] Ellen seems not to have worn the costume on stage, however, as Godwin's review of the play attacks the costume she did wear: "the ballet girl's

Fig. 12-3. Designs for costume and musical instruments for *The Merchant of Venice,* ca. 1880. Ink and watercolor on paper; 6⅜ x 8¾ in. (16.3 x 22.2 cm). Trustees of the Victoria and Albert Museum, London, Archive of the Theatre Museum (Blythe House), S.84-1998. *Checklist no. 113*

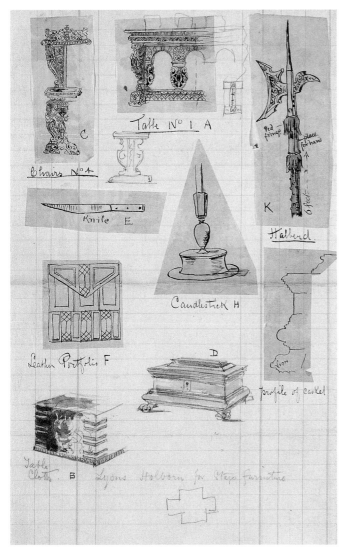

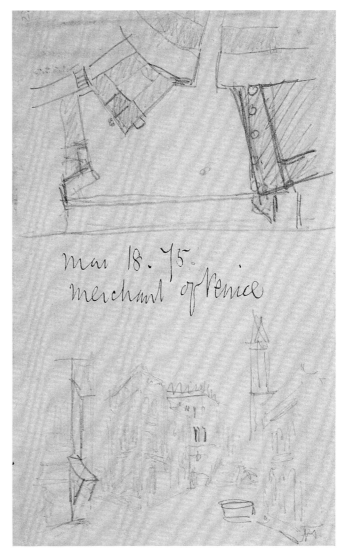

Fig. 12-4. E.W. Godwin. Designs for properties for *The Merchant of Venice*, 1880. Ink wash and pencil on tracing paper; 12¾ x 8⅛ in. (32.5 x 20.5 cm). Trustees of the Victoria and Albert Museum, London, Archive of the Theatre Museum (Blythe House) S.80-1988. *Checklist no. 109*

Fig. 12-5. E.W. Godwin. Preparatory sketches for stage sets for *The Merchant of Venice*, 1875. Sketchbook. Pencil, pen and ink; 3⅜ x 5⅞ in. (8.5 x 14.8 cm). Trustees of the Victoria and Albert Museum, London, E.236-1963: 27. *Checklist no. 108*

attire is not the costume for Titania and no artist would think of so draping his figure."[23]

Godwin and Terry's daughter, Edy Craig, indicates that he designed dresses for Ellen twelve years later when she played Juliet and Rosalind during Charles Calvert's Manchester season in 1874, but again Godwin's designs were not used.[24] Godwin's first two professional commissions for advisory work in the theater were for productions of Shakespeare plays: they gave him the opportunity to put into practice the suggestions he had made in his associated Shakespeare articles.

The first of these commissions was in 1875 for Squire and Marie Bancroft's *Merchant of Venice* at the Prince of Wales Theatre. Mrs. Bancroft persuaded Ellen Terry to act

Portia and secured Godwin's services as historical advisor. In their memoir, *Recollections of Sixty Years*, the Bancrofts tell how they took their scenic artist, George Gordon, to Venice to sketch waterways and buildings, while paintings by Titian and Veronese were studied for the costumes (fig. 12-3).[25]

They play down Godwin's contribution. The program note acknowledging his "valuable aid in archaeological research" was inserted only on George Gordon's insistence.[26] The locations and the artists studied by the Bancrofts and Gordon, however, were those Godwin had included in his two essays on the play in the Shakespeare series of articles. Furthermore an inventory of scenery, properties (fig. 12-4), and costumes compiled by Godwin

Fig. 12-6. E. W. Godwin. Costume design for a Senator and Attendant in *The Merchant of Venice*, ca. 1880. Ink and watercolor on paper with pencil notes; 6⅜ x 8¾ in. (16.3 x 22.2 cm). Trustees of the Victoria and Albert Museum, London, Archive of the Theatre Museum (Blythe House) S.82-1998. *Checklist no. 111*

for a later client match those used by the Bancrofts.[27] Two of Godwin's sketchbooks[28] include numerous drawings for the production, including a scene plan and elevation dated March 18, 1875, a month before the first night (fig. 12-5). Ink and watercolor drawings by Godwin of costumes for *The Merchant of Venice* (figs. 12-6, 12-7) were later published in the *British Architect,* and the text with the published illustrations states that these were used in the Bancroft production. Since Godwin wrote to the *Times* disclaiming responsibility for the dresses, however, it must be concluded that while he advised the scenic artists, either he wished the costumier to receive credit, or his own drawings were refinements for the later client and for publication.[29]

The response of critics to *The Merchant of Venice* was mixed. Some referred to the "series of brilliant pictures" and to costumes "found remarkable for their antiquarian accuracy, the characters being likened to portraits having stepped down from their frames" (fig. 12-8).[30] Others commented on the disproportion of parts of the architecture in comparison with the characters and how the audience had laughed at the archaeologically correct apparel.[31]

The second of Godwin's early commissions associated with his "Shakespeare" articles was for John Coleman's 1876 production of *Henry V*. Godwin was acknowledged in the program in phraseology implying scholarly authenticity: "The entire archaeology of the Play has been under the

Fig. 12-7. E. W. Godwin. Costume designs, probably for Portia in *The Merchant of Venice*, ca. 1880. Ink and watercolor on paper; 6⅜ x 8¾ in (16.3 x 22.2 cm). Trustees of the Victoria and Albert Museum, London, Archive of the Theatre Museum (Blythe House), S.83-1998. *Checklist no. 112*

Fig. 12-8. E. W. Godwin. Costume designs for the Doge in *The Merchant of Venice* and a plan of the Doge's Court, ca. 1880. Ink and watercolor on paper; 6⅜ x 8¾ in. (16.3 x 22.2 cm). Trustees of the Victoria and Albert Museum, London, Archive of the Theatre Museum (Blythe House), S.81-1998. *Checklist no. 110*

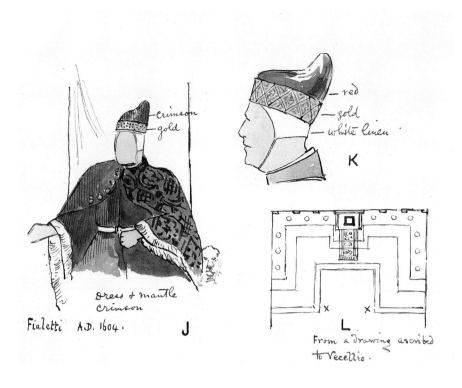

superintendence of Mr E. W. Godwin FSA."[32] Three of Godwin's sketchbooks are almost entirely devoted to preparatory drawings.[33] They include sketches of Shallow's House and of the Jerusalem Chamber (fig. 12-9) as well as studies of French and English medieval costume, armor, and heraldry from manuscripts, bronzes, and books by Planché and the antiquary Eugène Emmanuel Viollet-le-Duc. Godwin's diary entries show how he tried to make his presence felt during the preparation of the mise-en-scène. He attended rehearsals, communicated with Coleman about inaccuracies he had observed, and made last-minute deliveries of further sketches. Nevertheless, on the eve of the first performance he "Wrote Coleman list of absurdities witnessed last night."[34]

Before the run Godwin had published "*Henry V*: An Archaeological Experience" in the *British Architect* for "the

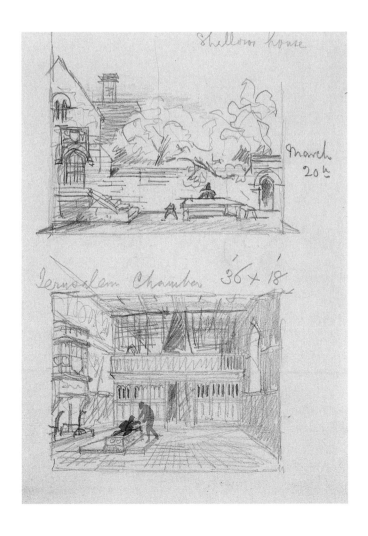

Fig. 12-9. E. W. Godwin. Set designs for *Henry V,* showing Shallow's House and the Jerusalem Chamber, ca. 1875–76. Sketchbook. Pencil and watercolor; 7⅛ x 5¼ in. (18.1 x 13.2 cm). Trustees of the Victoria and Albert Museum, London E.279-1963: 7. *Checklist no. 114*

Fig. 12-10. E. W. Godwin. Costume designs for Othello and Cassio in *Othello*, 1880. Pen and ink on paper; 8 x 5¼ in. (20.3 x 13.2 cm). Trustees of the Victoria and Albert Museum, London, Archive of the Theatre Museum (Blythe House), S.94-1998. *Checklist no. 115*

Fig. 12-11. E. W. Godwin. Costume designs for Desdemona and an unidentified male character in *Othello*, 1880. Pen and ink on paper; 8⅛ x 6⅜ in. (20.5 x 16.1 cm). Trustees of the Victoria and Albert Museum, London, Archive of the Theatre Museum (Blythe House), S.95-1998. *Checklist no. 116*

instruction of young architects and embryo antiquaries who may have the ambition to direct the archaeology of future revivals."[35] After the opening William Burges published a letter listing some erroneously designed items of costume, indicating that they cannot have been sanctioned by Godwin and inviting him to "write a critique in his own style upon his own (?) costume in *Henry V*."[36] Godwin complied with "*Henry V*: A Theatrical Experience"[37] discussing the way in which his contribution had been altered or ignored. He cited numerous examples of incorrect scenery, heraldry, costume, and properties that he had observed during the ten visits to the theater recorded in his diaries.[38] In his critique he specifically exempts the scene painter George Gordon from his charges, but without overtly blaming Coleman, he implies that the manager is at fault for insufficient attention and stringency in his dealings with the cast. The experience was still rankling in 1885 when Godwin recalled how the accurate drawings he had made, including two almost full-size Abbey piers for one scene, had been rejected: "Mr Coleman would have the whole church in almost toy-like proportion."[39]

Thus Godwin's first theater work, in two moderately received productions, was disheartening. He paid tribute to the intelligence of "artists, tradesfolk and mechanics" but stressed their resentment toward interference from any outsider. He also made it clear that although he had spoken out about the inaccuracies that had come to his attention before the opening, of most "I saw nothing until the night of public production."[40] After these disappointing early commissions there was a hiatus in Godwin's theater work of nearly five years.

Design Consultant, 1880–83

In 1880 Godwin began to write theatrical criticism again, contributing a "Theatrical Jottings" column to the *British Architect*. The series commenced with a substantial review of Richard Wagner's 1840 opera, *Rienzi*, which was revived by the Carl Rosa Opera Company at Her Majesty's Theatre. Later articles this same year returned to a Shakespearean theme, with Godwin's discussion and costume designs for *The Merchant of Venice, As You Like It, Romeo and Juliet*, and *Othello*.[41] His essay, "The Costumes of Romeo and Juliet,"

Fig. 12-12. E. W. Godwin. Costume design for
Hermann Vezin as Hamlet, 1881. Pen and Ink on
paper; 9⅛ x 6⅛ in. (23.1 x 15.5 cm). Trustees of
the Victoria and Albert Museum, London,
Archive of the Theatre Museum (Blythe House),
S.85-1998. *Checklist no. 117*

see little or no resemblance. Actresses will not dress in
Medieval costume as they should." This was because, in the
main, they still preferred to look fashionable according to
contemporary aesthetic values, a practice deplored by Godwin in his earlier Shakespeare articles.

Meanwhile, in "The Costumes of Othello," in the
British Architect,[45] Godwin published some of the drawings
he had made for Mrs. Bateman's *Othello*, which had opened
in September 1880 at Sadlers Wells. The program acknowledged that he had advised on scenery, costumes, and properties. In the essay Godwin's concern for accuracy is
evident. He chose primary sources for his costumes that
would correct and militarize the more usual civilian appearance of the male characters in the play. Godwin's sketchbooks[46] for this production show that, as with the Juliet
costumes for Wallis, his sources were largely pictorial. The
sumptuous costumes were described in the *Portfolio*: Othello wore a "deep scarlet and amber brocade" taken from
Cesare Vecellio (fig. 12-10).[47] Desdemona wore gray plush,
blue velvet, and pearls, taken from Jost Amman (fig. 12-11).
The American actor Hermann Vezin, who played Iago, wore

was published at the time of his acceptance of a commission
to design three costumes based on Giotto frescos for Juliet,
to be played by an actress named Miss Wallis. The commission was matched by one from the actor R. B. Mantell,
who ordered designs for Romeo and Orlando costumes.[42]
A year later, in July 1881, *Romeo and Juliet* was staged at the
Olympic Theatre with Mantell and Wallis in the title roles.
From an unsigned review in the *British Architect*,[43] which
was probably written by Godwin, it can be inferred that
Mantell used his Godwin-designed costumes, while Wallis
did not: "Mr Mantell is the first Romeo we have ever seen
who looked like a Montague (Montecchi) of Verona during the first quarter of the fourteenth century . . . with
some small exceptions such as shirt, shoes, and sword hilt,
we are glad to see the actor has followed the archaeologist."[44] It is significant that shirts, shoes, and swords were
precisely the kinds of costume and property that actors were
expected to provide from their own professional wardrobes,
with varying degrees of authenticity as a result. The same
review was more critical of Wallis's appearance: "Referring
to illustrations we published we are sorry to say we could

Fig. 12-13. E. W.
Godwin. Costume
design for Hermann
Vezin as Hamlet,
1881. Pen and ink
and watercolor on
paper; 9½ x 4⅜ in.
(24.0 x 11.0 cm).
Trustees of the
Victoria and Albert
Museum, London,
Archive of the
Theatre Museum
(Blythe House),
S.86-1998.
Checklist no. 118

Fig. 12-14. Scenes from *The Cynic* by Herman Merivale as it was performed at the Globe Theatre, London, January 14, 1882. From *Illustrated Sporting and Dramatic News* (21 January 1882).

a yellow silk cloak lined with black.[48] The Doge was dressed in crimson velvet, gold and white, while the members of his council wore red and black. The critic in the *Portfolio* described the whole effect as "a Venetian picture put on the stage."[49]

Vezin soon privately commissioned more costumes from Godwin for his lead in *Hamlet*, which opened at Sadlers Wells in February 1881.[50] The *British Architect* published two lively drawings by Godwin of Vezin in a costume (figs. 12-12, 12-13), which was described by the *Chronicle* as being an unexpected "short tunic of black, heavily braided in gold" worn with a jaunty cap, in strong contrast with the more usual long velvet cloak and funereal plumes worn by other Hamlets. The critic in the *Sunday Times* was conservative and found the effect "ungainly and clumsy-looking."[51] Vezin evidently approved of the result, as he asked for Godwin's help in designing or advising on several later costumes. These included costumes for the character Claude Melnotte in *The Lady of Lyons*, produced at the Gaiety Theatre in January 1882,[52] and for characters in *The Cynic*, a Faustian melodrama set in the contemporary period, billed as the "Shadow of an Old Legend in Modern Life." It opened on January 14, 1882, at the Globe Theatre and reviewers found the play dull, but the stage sets and costumes compelling (fig. 12-14). The *British Architect*'s reviewer, probably Godwin himself, fussed that the Abbey ruins, much praised by others, "tipped en masse whenever they were sat on" and that the two interiors were "distinctly bad," especially Count Lestrange's chambers. Clearly, Godwin had little sympathy with the symbolic coloring so enjoyed by the reviewer for *The Play*: "a luxurious room of our own period, decorated and furnished in the traditional Mephistophelean hues of black and red."[53]

Vezin later asked Godwin to oversee the costumes for *The Merchant of Venice* in his staging of the play as a benefit matinee on November 30, 1883, at the Gaiety Theatre. On November 17 Vezin had written jokingly to Godwin, "Will you take as little trouble as your conscience will allow to make the play presentable as far as costume is concerned."[54] Remuneration was subsequently proffered "for cab hire, anxiety of mind and archaeological distress at Jessica's dress. You will be pleased to hear that *she* thought it a great success and that her husband fell in love with her de novo . . ."[55] Yet another actress had determined to look fashionable rather than correct to the time of the story of the play.

It was precisely against this kind of free-for-all that Godwin had argued in his Shakespeare articles, with "actor and actress, stage manager and scene painter . . . left to do as they please."[56] Nevertheless, the early 1880s saw Godwin creating costumes for an increasing number of individual actors and actresses, rather than costuming and designing whole productions as he had, theoretically at least, in his Shakespeare articles. In May 1883, for instance, he provided an actor named Oates with designs for Hamlet costumes for a fee of five guineas,[57] and a series of letters to Godwin of 1881 from the young actor George Alexander[58] aptly illustrate the increasing pressure on the designer's time from individual professionals. This was the result of their growing awareness of his expertise and of a perceptible swing toward historical and archaeological accuracy in the theater as a whole.[59] Alexander's letters thank Godwin for a positive review in the *British Architect*,[60] ask him for a introduction to the actor-manager Henry Irving, request his advice on costume, and thank him for his responses in the form of sketches of wigs and costumes and advice regarding dealings

Fig. 12-15. "The Death of Synorix," a scene from Tennyson's play *The Cup*, as it was performed at the Lyceum Theatre, London, January 3, 1881. Henry Irving played Synorix and Ellen Terry (center) was Camma, her costume designed by E. W. Godwin. From *Illustrated London News* (5 February 1881).

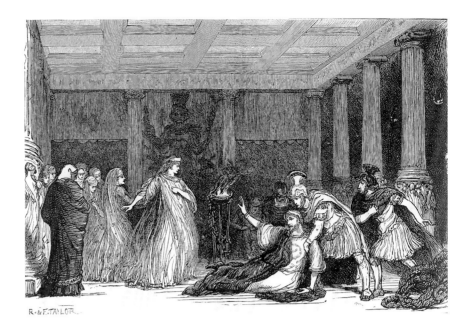

with the perruquier Willy Clarkson and costumier Victor Barthe.

The stringencies of an actor's life are glimpsed when Alexander, asking Godwin to design several costumes for him, writes, "You will, I am sure, see the necessity of my doing the thing as reasonably as possible. . . . I am quite dependent on my profession for a living . . . Every dress I have will be paid for out of hardly earned savings from a not over large salary."[61] His letters represent a conscientious actor's desire to make his working wardrobe accurate, while financial constraints such as those mentioned by Alexander continued to mature Godwin's understanding of real theater practice as distinct from the ideals, theories, and research of detached design.

Alexander's request for an introduction to Irving is significant, as Godwin's most prestigious commission to date had been his costumes for the character Camma, played by Ellen Terry, in Irving's production of Tennyson's play *The Cup*, which opened on January 3, 1881, at the Lyceum Theatre. This was the first play for which Irving had commissioned outside designers, and the resulting mise-en-scène was the work of a team of experts.

The play, which told the dramatic story of Camma's revenge on the Tetrarch Synorix for the killing of her husband, Sinnatus, was set in Asia Minor in about 300 B.C., with scenes in Greek-influenced Galatia. James Knowles, architect of Tennyson's house and editor of the *Nineteenth Century*, was given responsibility for designing the two interiors—a room in the Tetrarch's house and the Temple of Artemis.[62] Terry persuaded Irving to invite Godwin to design her dresses, while Alexander Murray, assistant keeper of Greek antiquities at the British Museum, advised on other costumes and properties. Godwin also designed a ver-

sion of the cup itself, and Ellen later had a replica made which was presented to Tennyson on the hundredth night: "I had it made in silver from Mr Godwin's design—a three-handled cup, pipkin-shaped, standing on three legs."[63] During preparation of the play Godwin found an unexpected ally in the Lyceum's versatile master carpenter who was named Arnott. For one of Ellen's togas, Arnott personally dyed yards of raw silk the required saffron yellow and block-printed the border in black and red, to create the effect of a more costly silk and rich embroidery than Irving could have afforded.[64]

The reviewer in the *British Architect*,[65] probably Godwin, criticized Knowles' Temple of Artemis, arguing the case for the focal statue to be encircled by columns rather than boxed "like the tabernacle of the Jews." Other misapprehensions included Murray's leopard-skin costume for Irving's character Synorix in the first act, which the anonymous reviewer likened to the dress of an African refugee or Robinson Crusoe. The literati, including artists such as Lawrence Alma-Tadema and critics, were unanimous in praise for the atmospheric scenery and lighting, which kept the play running to full houses.

At this time the Lyceum was becoming famous for its lighting plans. Of particular interest to Godwin would have been the Lyceum scenic artists' practice of using scale models to design the color, proportion, and lighting effects of a production. Irving also was in the habit of holding gas- and lime-lighting rehearsals with the scenic artists and costume designers in attendance. Ellen Terry records the effect of the lighting in the Temple scene of *The Cup* (fig. 12-15): "The gigantic figure of the many-breasted Artemis, placed far back in the scene-dock, loomed through a blue mist, while the foreground of the picture was in yellow light."[66]

The opportunity of being even a transient contributor to the vibrant and experimental, artistically and commercially successful Lyceum team was an invaluable boost to Godwin's work in the theater, and the lessons in lighting he must have learned there later bore fruit in his work for the actor-manager Wilson Barrett at the Princess's Theatre.

In early September 1880 Godwin had received a letter from Wilson Barrett asking him to provide a sketch for some stage properties. These were probably used in Barrett's production of *Mary Stuart*, adapted by the Hon. Lewis Wingfield from Schiller as Barrett sent the Godwins two stall tickets for a performance of the play at the Court Theatre on October 11.[67] This commission was the forerunner to Godwin's professionally successful working relationship with the actor-manager. Godwin's close friend, the Irish dramatist William G. Wills was at this time writing a new drama, *Juana*, which had been commissioned by the Polish actress Helena Modjeska. Godwin's diary shows that he was

yellow turned up white

Ceremony Dress

CARLOS

Fig. 12-16. E. W. Godwin. Costume designs for Don Carlos of Narcisso in W. G. Wills's *Juana*, 1881. Pencil, pen and ink, and watercolor on paper; 11 x 7⅛ in. (28 x 18 cm). Trustees of the Victoria and Albert Museum, London, Archive of the Theatre Museum (Blythe House), S.103-1998. *Checklist no. 123*

pressed into service by Wills as advisor, reader, scribe, supplier of several dinners, and social companion at the London Zoo.[68] When the text was completed, Wills asked Godwin to perform the reading of the play aloud to Modjeska and Wilson Barrett. Both were sufficiently impressed for Barrett to accept the play for production the following year. Barrett later asked Godwin to design the scenery, costumes (fig. 12-16), and properties in collaboration with his scenic artists William Beverley, Stafford Hall, and Walter Hann.[69]

This was a comprehensive commission and Godwin's diary records study trips to museums, including the National Gallery, visits to the costumier and to a sale of armor, meetings, and rehearsals.[70] His sketchbook[71] contains a checklist of designs passed to Barrett between March 29, and April 14, 1881, demonstrating both the intense pressure of the work and the variety of items needed (figs. 12-17, 12-18, and see fig. 12-1). It includes three scene designs and drawings for sixty-one of the costumes and properties. Godwin records that after one trip to the British Museum he went straight back to the theater and drew a full-size bell and a hand-loom in the property room.[72] When the play opened at the Court Theatre on May 7, 1881, the program noted that Godwin had sought to achieve unity of time and place—1496 in Toledo—by creating the mise-en-scène from one source, "a very fine illuminated work made for Isabella of Castile."[73]

To Wills's intense dismay, the tragedy was described in various reviews as ghastly, bloodthirsty, tedious, gloomy, oppressive, and full of horror, and despite Godwin's immediate rallying visit, Wills withdrew the play for revision. Godwin was unscathed by this. The mise-en-scène was considered "beautiful" and "magnificent" by the same reviewers, who, significantly, called it "fully up to the Lyceum standard,"[74] Irving's Lyceum being the yardstick by which other theaters' productions were assessed. The *World* carried a letter from Godwin recording that some of the costumes had not been designed by him,[75] yet in the sixth article of his series entitled "Archaeology on the Stage" for the *Dramatic Review*, written four years later, Godwin said that of all the plays with which he had been involved, the properties for *Juana* had been best realized from his designs.[76]

Another of Wills's plays for which Godwin made designs was *Rienzi*, based on the novel by Bulwer, Lord Lytton, and completed in 1882–83 after Wills had returned from a prolonged visit to Italy. Wills may have been inspired to write the play by a lavish production of Richard Wagner's 1840 opera of the same name, which had been revived by the Carl Rosa Company at Her Majesty's Theatre in 1880 and was reviewed by Godwin in the *British Architect*.[77]

Fig. 12-17. E. W. Godwin. Costume design for the Provost of Toledo in W. G. Wills's *Juana*, 1881. Pencil and watercolor on paper; 10⅝ x 6½ in. (27 x 16.5 cm). Trustees of the Victoria and Albert Museum, London, Archive of the Theatre Museum (Blythe House), S.100-1998. *Checklist no. 120*

Fig. 12-18. E. W. Godwin. Costume designs for Don Carlos of Narcisso and friend in W. G. Wills's *Juana*, 1881. Pencil and watercolor on paper; 10⅞ x 6⅞ in. (27.5 x 17.5 cm). Trustees of the Victoria and Albert Museum, London, Archive of the Theatre Museum (Blythe House), S.101-1998. *Checklist no. 121*

Juana had been short-lived; *Rienzi* was neither published nor produced, although in 1887 Wills received eight hundred pounds from Irving for the rights to use the script.[78] It may have been in the hope of securing a second Lyceum commission with Irving that Godwin prepared a presentation book in about 1883 of detailed and delicate drawings in pencil and watercolor of his designs for costumes and sets for the play (see fig. 9-3). These were researched from manuscripts in the British Museum which "have been examined minutely and compared with frescos, sculptures and other 14th century authorities."[79]

The research was always meticulous, and the spread of subjects on which Godwin made himself an expert for the purposes of accurate representation of the time and place of a play, extraordinary. The autumn of 1881, for example, found him responding to a commission from the actress and manager Mary Siddons for the design of *Queen and Cardi-*

nal, a new play by Walter S. Raleigh. He was given responsibility for supervising the scenic artists and for all the costumes except Anne Boleyn's,[80] which had already been prepared from sketches by the Hon. Lewis Wingfield. A preview in the *British Architect*, possibly written by Godwin, remarks that "contemporary portraits of Anne Boleyn and of nearly every character in the play, exist, and no doubt the Hon. Lewis Wingfield will have as carefully copied Anne's as Mr Godwin has the others."[81]

Godwin made himself equally at home in the world of ancient antiquities. In May 1883 he met with Sir Charles Newton, keeper of classical antiquities at the British Museum, to discuss costumes and properties for *The Tale of Troy*,[82] an amateur production designed by Frederick Leighton, president of the Royal Academy, and Sir Edward Poynter, another eminent Royal Academy classicist, and mounted by Professor George Warr to raise money for

Fig. 12-19. Costume design for Richard Orchardson in Robert Buchanon's *Storm Beaten*, 1883. Pen and ink, pencil and watercolor on paper; 9⅝ x 6⅛ in. (24.5 x 15.5 cm). Trustees of the Victoria and Albert Museum, London, Archive of the Theatre Museum (Blythe House), S.161-1998. *Checklist no. 127*

Fig. 12-21. Costume design for Sally Marvel in Robert Buchanon's *Storm Beaten*, 1883. Pencil and watercolor on tracing paper with pen and ink inscriptions; 7½ x 6½ in. (19.0 x 16.5 cm). Trustees of the Victoria and Albert Museum, London, Archive of the Theatre Museum (Blythe House) S.159-1998. *Checklist no. 125*

Fig. 12-20. E. W. Godwin. Costume design for Kate Christianson in Robert Buchanon's *Storm Beaten,* 1883. Pencil and watercolor on paper; 8⅞ x 5¼ in. (22.7 x 13.5 cm). Trustees of the Victoria and Albert Museum, London, Archive of the Theatre Museum (Blythe House), S.158-1998. *Checklist no. 124*

London University's "Lectures to Ladies." Godwin was present at three rehearsals,[83] probably invited by Newton, who had been asked by Warr to advise on costumes and properties. The combination of Newton, Warr, Leighton, and Poynter was formidable;[84] either the invitation was a courtesy to an interested friend or Godwin's increasing knowledge of stagecraft and his translation of antiquarian theory into theatrical practice made his advice desirable.

A production in the same year, 1883, was important for Godwin's development as a designer for the theater. This was Robert Buchanon's *Storm Beaten*, which opened on March 14 at the Adelphi, a theater famous for its spectacle. For the production, Godwin had designed late-eighteenth-century dress (fig. 12-19), which he had researched at the British and South Kensington museums, and at the Painted Hall at Greenwich.[85]

The play opened with rustic scenes of a May festival (figs. 12-20, 12-21) and pastoral ballet followed by dramatic events unfolding on the *Miles Standish*, a ship bound for America. A fire started on board and towering icebergs drifted toward the doomed vessel. Realistic sound effects provided the creaking and wrenching of her timbers amid the shrieks of her passengers and crew. The next scene found the ship crushed in the ice, and the protaganists stranded on an ice floe. The ship heaved, ice-falls slid into the sea, and a dual was fought as the floe broke up and a pink and silver aurora borealis waxed and waned on the horizon. The villain was plunged into the icy water, and the play concluded with Christmas on a lonely island and a tableau dream. An enthusiastic audience brought William Beverley, the scenic artist, a tremendous call to the foot-lights. The play was copiously reviewed[86] with Godwin's costumes found pleasing (fig. 12-22).

The scenic mounting of *Storm Beaten* was unlike any previous setting for Godwin's work, and it established a precedent for his later design and stage management. At the end of 1883 Godwin was commissioned by Wilson Barrett to design the entire production of *Claudian* which was to open at the Princess's Theatre on December 6.

There seems little doubt that Beverley's work in *Storm Beaten* had turned Godwin's imagination toward the kinds of spectacle that could be produced through lighting and atmospheric effects and through movement within the set itself. Until this time Godwin's scenery had been static, conceived solely in architectural terms, and the relation of the acting to the scenery had been one of correct usage of the places depicted, according to the historical period. Beverley's histrionics, with the sets and actors interactive, and

Fig. 12-22. Scenes from Robert Buchanon's *Storm Beaten,* as it was performed at the Adelphi Theatre, London, March 14, 1883. From *Illustrated Sporting and Dramatic News* (24 March 1883): 40.

Fig. 12-23. E. W. Godwin. Costume designs for an attendant and a Frank in W. G. Wills and Henry Herman's *Claudian*. From Godwin, "*Claudian*: A Few Notes" (1883). Trustees of the Victoria and Albert Museum, London, Archive of the Theatre Museum (Blythe House), S.153-1998. *Checklist no. 128*

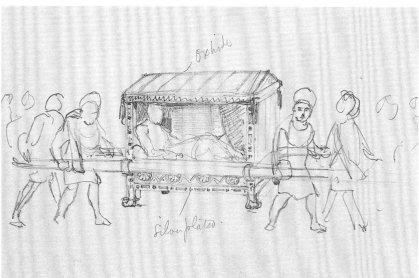

Fig. 12-24. E. W. Godwin. Design for a litter for W. G. Wills and Henry Herman's *Claudian*, 1883. Pencil on paper; 4½ x 6⅞ in. (11.4 x 17.6 cm). Trustees of the Victoria and Albert Museum, London, Archive of the Theatre Museum (Blythe House), S.157-1998. *Checklist no. 132*

Fig. 12-25. "Claudian Barrett Refusing Byzantium's 'Barrer'." Wilson Barrett dressed as Claudian rejects Godwin's prop in a cartoon lampooning Godwin's antiquarian authority. From *Illustrated Sporting and Dramatic News* (22 December 1883): 369.

perhaps also Godwin's memory of Rosa's production of *Rienzi* in 1880, in which there had been a scene of Rome on fire with columns falling, had given him new territory to explore.

The prologue of *Claudian* was set in Byzantium in A.D. 362, while the rest of the play took place a century later. In his article "Archaeology on the Stage No. 5" (1885), Godwin classified the period as "one of transition from decayed classic to a new form of art through the union of the classic with the rude splendour of barbaric nations,"[87] and in the next article in the series he admitted that the

drawings were "more than usually heavy to prepare."[88] His research is detailed in an open letter to Barrett published in the *British Architect* on December 7, 1883, with the same text published as a pamphlet (fig. 12-23).[89]

Godwin wrote that "three distinct phases of art" were apparent in Constantinople of the period, the most useful visual sources of information for these being the reliefs on the Column of Theodosius II and the interior of the basilica of Junius Bassus (A.D. 317–40).[90] For costume, he added other sources: sculpture, coins, catacomb paintings, mosaics, and ivories. He acknowledged Signor Niccolini of the

National Museum of Naples "for a series of large photographs illustrating the only known portrait of a Roman litter in existence."[91] Barrett, for reasons of personal dramatic effect, however, chose not to use Godwin's litter for his first entry on stage (fig. 12-24). The *Illustrated Sporting and Dramatic News* published a cartoon showing the actor firmly refusing the offer of a primitive wheelbarrow by a perplexed yokel (fig. 12-25).[92]

The period, Godwin wrote,[93] was "distinguished for gorgeous display" including costly silks and "boots and shoes gilded and enriched with embroideries, gold, jewels and cameos." Clothes were layered (fig. 12-26): "the rich man wore two or three tunics, all displayed," and so did the horses. There was opulence in jewelry, with fine work in gemstones and colored metals. Godwin dealt in his text

with military and civilian styles, the appearance of the poor, and the intricacies of female classical dress. Eleven illustrations accompanied the text.

Godwin's sketchbook and notebooks include many studies of costume and armor copied from Greek vases in the British Museum and from scholarly books (fig. 12-27).[94] Details abound, such as eleven ways of wearing girdles and belts (fig. 12-28), which in the production itself became an excellent way of individualizing the "supernumeraries" on stage. Some drawings show decorated sandals and shoes.[95] That these were actually produced is confirmed by an account in the *Stage* of a visit to W. H. Davies in Bow Street, where the writer observed colored and jeweled sandals (fig. 12-29) labeled for the actors in this production.[96] Godwin's administrative paperwork and drawings show the com-

Fig. 12-26. E. W. Godwin. Costume design for an unidentified character, possibly Claudian, in W. G. Wills and Henry Herman's *Claudian*, 1883. Pencil and watercolor on tracing paper; 6¼ x 3¼ in. (16 x 8.3 cm). Trustees of the Victoria and Albert Museum, London, S.155-1998. *Checklist no. 130*

Fig. 12-27. E. W. Godwin. Costume design for a female supernumerary in W. G. Wills and Henry Herman's *Claudian*, 1883. Watercolor on paper; 14 x 9⅞ in. (35.5 x 25 cm). Trustees of the Victoria and Albert Museum, London, Archive of the Theatre Museum (Blythe House), S.154-154A-1998. *Checklist no. 129*

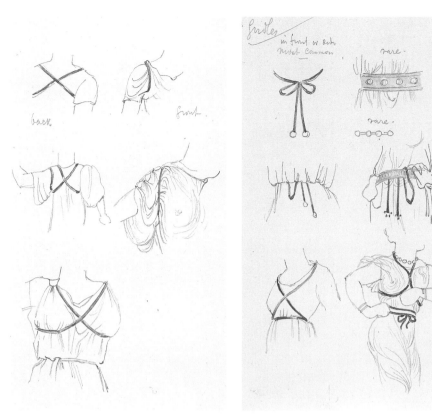
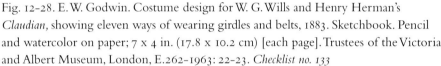
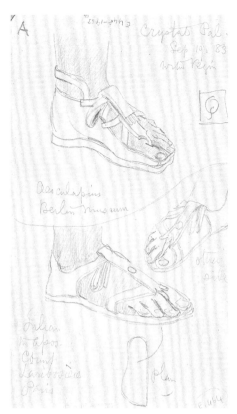

Fig. 12-28. E. W. Godwin. Costume design for W. G. Wills and Henry Herman's *Claudian,* showing eleven ways of wearing girdles and belts, 1883. Sketchbook. Pencil and watercolor on paper; 7 x 4 in. (17.8 x 10.2 cm) [each page]. Trustees of the Victoria and Albert Museum, London, E.262-1963: 22–23. *Checklist no. 133*

Fig. 12-29. E. W. Godwin. Designs for sandals for W. G. Wills and Henry Herman's *Claudian*, 1883. Pencil on paper; 5½ x 3 3/16 in. (14 x 8.1 cm). Trustees of the Victoria and Albert Museum, London, E.448-1963. *Checklist no. 134*

plexity of fitting out the large cast according to the stylistic influences he had researched (fig. 12-30).[97] Materials were ordered from Liberty's; two costumiers, Barthe and Auguste, were contacted and the Princess's Theatre wardrobe and properties departments worked around the clock. The scenery was the responsibility of Walter Hann and Stafford Hall, who were architectural specialists, and William Telbin, a landscape painter.

Barrett delayed the opening of the play by a week in order to perfect the special effects.[98] From the first night, audiences flocked to *Claudian*, and all the major journals ran reports and illustrations.[99] The prologue showed a busy slave market and street scene with full-size columns, steps, walls, and monuments in "solid" (papier-mâché) relief, with trees, hills, and the Bosporus in the distance. This scene included one of three tableaux in the play, which gave the audience the opportunity to compare the stage pictures with the Academy paintings of Alma-Tadema. Godwin had incorporated a realistic diversity of status and style into his scene of street life, seen not only in the dresses, but in the "archaeological" aspects of the "stage business." This would

have included personal interaction, precedence, ritual, and processions.

The realization of the spectacular earthquake in act 3 was the result of teamwork. *Modern Society* described the collapse of Claudian's palace with its "appearance of great solidity, the arches and pillars being particularly massive looking," and the reviewer wrote that "the effect was terrorising. With a mighty upheaval the walls, pillars and arches shook, then split up and fell with a crash; and in a quarter of a minute, the magnificent palace was reduced to a fearful desolation amid which Claudian stood pale, dignified and unharmed. It was perfect, and the audience would fain have had on authors, actors, machinists and scene-painters then and there..."[100] Gentler scenes included atmospheric effects in evocative landscapes: a sunny vineyard, a gloomy cave, a blue sea, and a wooded ravine with effects of sun, rain, and mist, and the final moonlit view of the shattered city (fig. 12-31).

Claudian was important for Godwin's work for the theater. For the first time he had formally influenced the movement and grouping of actors. He had designed scenery that would, itself, change realistically in front of the audience. He had worked effectively with a leading actor-manager, three experienced scenic artists, a master carpenter, theater machinists, lighting men, wardrobe, costumiers, and perruquier. He was undoubtedly established in both public and professional opinion as an influential theater designer.

Designer-Manager: Pastoral Plays, 1884–86

Although *Claudian* had been a turning point in Godwin's career as a theater designer, Wilson Barrett's refusal to use both the archaeologically correct litter and one of the costumes Godwin had designed for him,[101] showed where the ultimate authority in the production lay. The years 1884 to 1886 saw Godwin testing a new role in the theater—that of designer-manager.

Godwin had been thinking about his role since at least 1881 when he had been a founding member of the Society of English Players. Planned as a joint stock company and initiated by a group of theatrical and literary friends, the society set out to promote dramatic art, create a school for young actors, and found a cooperative company that would stage productions for mutual benefit. Godwin was made art director. The organizational and financial logistics, in the face of the professional obligations of its leading members, proved too severe, however, and the enterprise collapsed, notwithstanding the investment of a great deal of enthusiasm and time.[102]

By 1884 Godwin had met Lady Archibald Campbell, an Aesthetic socialite with royal connections, through their mutual friend James McNeill Whistler. Lady Archie, as she was known, decided to present open-air performances for charity, of the forest scenes from *As You Like It*, in the wood-

Fig. 12-30. E. W. Godwin. Costume design for an unidentified character, possibly one of Claudian's attendants, with a diagram showing how to drape a mantle, 1883. Pencil and watercolor on tracing paper; 8¼ x 5½ in. (21.1 x 14 cm). Trustees of the Victoria and Albert Museum, London, Archive of the Theatre Museum (Blythe House) S.156-1998. *Checklist no. 131*

Fig. 12-31. Scenes from W. G. Wills and Henry Herman's *Claudian,* as performed at the Princess's Theatre, December 6, 1883. From "Sketches from *Claudian*," *Illustrated London News* (15 December 1883): 573.

Fig. 12-32. The forest scenes from *As You Like It*, as performed at Coombe House, New Malden, Surrey, July 22, 1884. Godwin is sketched in a vignette, center right. From the "*As You Like It* at Coombe House," *Illustrated Sporting and Dramatic News* (2 August 1884): 530.

lands at Coombe House in Surrey (fig. 12-32). She planned to play Orlando, with a supporting cast of amateur enthusiasts, and asked Godwin to take sole charge of designing the piece and directing the players. The success of the production in 1884 and its revival in 1885 prompted the creation of the Society of Pastoral Players, under the patronage of the Prince of Wales, with a committee and a subscribing membership.[103] A financial agreement was signed between Godwin as director and Lady Archibald as president, which specified that, for managing the plays in the open air, Godwin would "be remunerated by payment of a sum equal to one half the net profits and that his duties shall be those usually undertaken by theatrical managers."[104]

Although Godwin had earlier researched and designed fifteenth-century costumes for *As You Like It* for

his *British Architect* drawings,[105] he made new designs for the Pastoral Players production. Significantly, in the Shakespeare articles, he had omitted to discuss the design of landscape scenes.[106] Perhaps it was the fact that he could now bring a mature experience of the stage to this task that generated his radical exploitation of the setting.

Among many other journals, the *Era* described the scene: the audience sat on tiers of benches within a small rectangular enclosure made by stretching green fabric between tree trunks; "at the summons of a shrill whistle, the fourth side of the rectangle was suddenly let down, disclosing the open wood which was only separated from the theatre itself by a narrow belt of moss planted with ferns where the footlights would have been . . ."[107] Godwin had visited Coombe earlier and jotted down plans of his proposed site, noting the position of trees and spaces.[108] The audience saw a winding glade of lime trees with greensward beyond.[109] To the right and to the left were roughly stacked piles of firewood. Fallen trunks provided picturesque settings and a tall tree lent a central focus. The critic of the *National Review* glimpsed a hind's shelter, and noticed the "twitter of birds and glitter of butterflies . . . flocks and distant bleating, all things native and natural."[110] The writer in *Truth* remarked, "horns blew, dogs barked, huntsmen wandered here and there, boys strolled in and out of the trees, the characters came on as if they had been walking in the park . . ."[111]

Of the 1885 revival of the Pastoral Players' *As You Like It*, Oscar Wilde wrote, "Through an alley of white hawthorne and gold laburnum we passed into the green pavillion, the air sweet with the odour of lilac and with the blackbird's song."[112] Rosalind and Celia's dresses were in russet tones, Orlando in golden-green, and Phoebe in violet. Wilde appreciated the color palette, eminently representative of the Aesthetic movement, but found Phoebe's Liberty silk dress and stockings inappropriately grand, and Touchstone's motley, and Rosalind's bridal dress too glaring.

The Foresters' costumes, however, were universally praised. Writing in the *Woman's World* in 1888, Lady Archie remembered that Godwin had contrasted the apparent age and condition of their "high hunting boots and by-cocket caps, the dull velvets and worn leather" with "the newer habits of those 'young gentlemen of estate',"[113] a telling touch of realism (fig. 12-33).

Spurred on by the critical success of *As You Like It*, Godwin and Lady Archie produced a second play in 1885: John Fletcher's *The Faithfull Shepherdesse*, which was revised and adapted by Godwin[114] for performance by the Pastoral Players in Coombe Woods. Lady Archie was cast as the hero, Perigot, Princess Helen of Kappurthala as Amoret, and Hermann Vezin as the Sullen Shepherd. This cast was supported by shepherds, shepherdesses and satyrs. There was a full orchestral score including songs and dances written by the Reverend A. Wellesley Batson and performed by a chorus of more than forty singers hidden in the wood.

The play was visually complex, with its classical context and English pastoral symbolism. Godwin's antiquarian research produced a giant statue of Pan (fig. 12-34)[115] and

Fig. 12-33. Cast members dressed as Foresters for *As You Like It*, 1884. Trustees of the Victoria and Albert Museum, London, Archive of the Theatre Museum (Blythe House), S.164-1998.

Fig. 12-34. A shepherd and shepherdess with the statue of Pan in a scene from E. W. Godwin's adaptation of John Fletcher's play *The Faithfull Shepherdesse*, Coombe Wood, Surrey, 1885. The "curtain ditch" is in the foreground. Trustees of the Victoria and Albert Museum, London, Archive of the Theatre Museum (Blythe House), S.167-1998.

Fig. 12-35. The characters Perigot and Amoret driving an oxcart in a scene from E. W. Godwin's adaptation of John Fletcher's play *The Faithfull Shepherdesse*, Coombe Wood, Surrey, 1885. 5⅝ x 8⅝ in. (14.3 x 22 cm). Trustees of the Victoria and Albert Museum, London, Archive of the Theatre Museum (Blythe House), S.166-1998. *Checklist no. 146*

Fig. 12-36. Scenes from *Hamlet* as performed at the Princess's Theatre, London, October 16, 1884. From "*Hamlet,*" *Illustrated London News* (1 November 1884): 428.

an altar, both from British Museum sources. He also researched classical choreography for sacred circle dances. In pursuit of realism, he found an operational ox-cart (fig. 12-35) and designed pan pipes, crooks, baskets, and furry padded tights for the satyrs. He acquired two heifers to draw the cart, borrowed sheep, goats, and pigeons to fill the stage area and background, but he drew the line at Lady Archie's suggestion that he increase the number of satyrs, bring in trained dogs, and order a hundred butterflies. He explained, "As theres not the remotest chance of clearing 1/. [sic] out of the Coombe Plays do not I beg you ask me to involve anyone in more debts than already face us."[116] The menagerie amused the reviewers. *Truth*'s theater critic spotted that all had not been easy with the animals: "the

only performers who somewhat make a mess of it are the sheep, who last Saturday declined to appear, owing, as I was told, to a dispute with the oxen."[117]

Management of the players also proved testing, with Princess Helen failing to attend rehearsals, and D'Arcy Ferris, the chorus leader, falling out with Batson. Godwin also had to respond to a problematic aftermath to the play, including the financial demands from suppliers and exorbitant expense claims from participants.[118] The actors and other theater colleagues appear to have been in no doubt, however, about Godwin's authority and managerial skills as their letters, affectionately addressing him as Earl, Duke, King, Manager, and Master, demonstrate.[119]

Reviewers of *The Faithfull Shepherdesse* agreed that

although the piece was overlong, it was visually spectacular, with its incense-burning altar, the statue of Pan with festoons of lilac and laburnum (see fig. 2-23), and the rustic well with its waterlilies. The *Era* chose to emphasize Godwin's choreographed naturalism and pictorial composition. The reviewer described "crowds of skin-clad shepherds and shepherdesses in flowing robes, now grouping themselves round the trees in rhythmic dance, while in the far background, satyrs slipped in and out chasing one another, and vexing the shepherds by clashing cymbals. When in the midst of all this, Amoret and Perigot came riding down the glade in a gilded chariot drawn by a pair of heifers, and the Priest of Pan with his attendant thurifers advanced to the altar with their hands outstretched in blessing on the crowd, the picture was of ideal beauty: a canvas of Alma-Tadema suddenly touched to life."[120]

The final Pastoral Players production involving Godwin was also his final theatrical production.[121] *Fair Rosamund*, a play sensitively adapted by Godwin from Tennyson's *Becket*, was performed by a cast of professionals supporting Lady Archie as Rosamund, in the woods belonging to the Villa Cannizaro at Wimbledon, London, in the summer of 1886. Brief descriptions were written by the reviewers of Rosamund's dress of delicate blue, the black robes of the chanting monks, and what the *Theatre* described as "the dull and lumpish costume of the British yokel of the twelfth century."[122] Audiences were satisfied, but the novelty of pastoral theater had worn off with other pastoral productions being staged in imitation of Lady Archie's.[123]

The 1870s and 1880s had seen a fierce ongoing debate about whether scenic realism detracted from the drama, poetry, and language of a play. The reviewer in the *Era* called this the "Battle between the Realists and the Idealists," in his review of the Pastoral Players' 1885 performance of *As You Like It*.[124] The debate had been fueled by the visit in 1881 of the Meiningen Company, which Godwin himself had favorably reviewed in the *British Architect*.[125] Godwin had praised the Meiningen Company's finely rehearsed crowd scenes and "natural" acting, their detailed movements and facial expressions taken from everyday life rather than the English emphasis on the language of the play with supporting symbolic gesture.[126]

For many, the entertainment provided by the Pastoral Players was simply a delightful way to pass a summer's afternoon, but others recognized that the boundaries of theatrical realism had been significantly extended. There was no picture-frame proscenium or box set. The scenery was real and the audience was part of it. Space and time were used naturally, the characters making their way through the trees, reposing in the bracken or moving to join the hunt in the distance. There were chance elements of sunlight and cloud, breeze in the foliage, patterns of woodsmoke, birds, and butterflies. The actors too were natural. *Truth* noted an "entire absence of all conventionality," and the *Era* confirmed that "the performers were able to abstract themselves from all reference to the spectators."[127] That this naturalism was sought and tutored by Godwin is confirmed by Lady Archie, "he urged more than ever upon the actor . . . the necessity that the ordinary *techniques* of the stage must be held by him subordinate and sacrificed to pictorial and realistic effect."[128] Godwin had even worn a friar's costume at rehearsals in order to move among the actors without disturbing the illusion of reality (see fig. 1-16).[129]

Stage "realism" encompassed both the stage action and the mise-en-scène. The Meiningen Company had confirmed for Godwin what was achievable with the first, and he had made a deliberate effort to direct the actors to be as natural as possible. The Pastoral Plays inevitably extended the boundaries of the stage, and some critics were quick to recognize a loss to drama. Oscar Wilde, representing the Idealists, wrote of *The Faithfull Shepherdesse*, "The whole thing was an exquisite piece of tom foolery, . . . What one wants to see upon a stage, whether of boards or grass, is art, not nature; nature bores us, and is extremely monotonous, where she is not absolutely repulsive."[130]

Designer-Manager: Archaeological and Historical Realism, 1884–86

As manager of the Pastoral Players, Godwin was able to exploit the freedom of the open-air setting and the amateur status of most of his actors to achieve a visual naturalism. At the same time he was involved in the design of a number of professional productions for Wilson Barrett and others, in which he developed his ideas on archaeological and historical realism. One of these was *Hamlet*, which opened in October 1884 at the Princess's Theatre with the expert scene-painting team of Beverley, Telbin, Hall and Hann to help Godwin create the mise-en-scène (fig. 12-36).

On opening day, the journal *Life* published an interview with Godwin, revealing his preparation and working methods. Godwin had made a special visit to Copenhagen, and in the Museum of Northern Antiquities had been "allowed to handle the curiosities, etc., make full-size drawings of weapons, adornments, etc., so that they could be exactly copied."[131] In the library he had studied the appearance of the Danes, their hair, moustaches, and beard styles, headgear and footwear, adornments and weapons. There are several sketchbooks, tracings, and drawings that show his

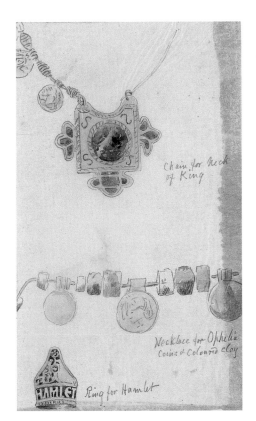

Fig. 12-37. E. W. Godwin. Design for jewelry for *Hamlet*, 1884. Pencil and watercolor on paper; 9⁵⁄₁₆ x 6¼ in. (23.7 x 15.9 cm). Trustees of the Victoria and Albert Museum, London, Archive of the Theatre Museum (Blythe House), S.92-1998. *Checklist no. 140*

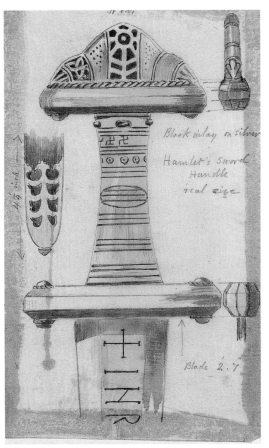

Fig. 12-38. E. W. Godwin. Design for Hamlet's sword handle, 1884. Pencil and watercolor on paper; 10 x 6¼ in. (25.5 x 16 cm). Trustees of the Victoria and Albert Museum, London, Archive of the Theatre Museum (Blythe House), S.91-1998. *Checklist no. 139*

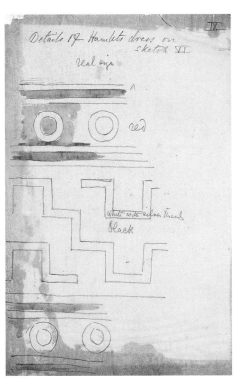

Fig. 12-39. E. W. Godwin. Details of a costume design for Hamlet, 1884: Pencil and watercolor on paper; 10 x 7⅛ in. (25.5 x 18.1 cm). Trustees of the Victoria and Albert Museum, London, Archive of the Theatre Museum (Blythe House), S.90-1998.

research and costume designs for the characters (figs. 12-37, 12-38, and 12-39).[132] Back in London, throughout the play's preparation, he responded to a stream of requests from the workshops for details of properties, furniture, and additional costume.[133]

During the interview Godwin paid tribute to Hann's detailed architectural studies. Hann's watercolor design of

Fig. 12-40. Walter Hann. Set design for the interior of the Palace in *Hamlet*, 1884. Pen and ink and watercolor on paper; 11⅜ x 18⅞ in. (29 x 47.8 cm). Trustees of the Victoria and Albert Museum, London, E.898-1966. *Checklist no. 142*

Fig. 12-41. E. W. Godwin. Design for a costume for Ophelia in *Hamlet*, 1884. Pencil and watercolor on paper; 9⅞ x 6¼ in. (25 x 15.8 cm). Trustees of the Victoria and Albert Museum, London, Archive of the Theatre Museum (Blythe House), S.88-1998. *Checklist no. 137*

Fig. 12-42. E. W. Godwin. Design for a costume for Polonius in *Hamlet*, 1884. Pencil and watercolor on paper; 9⁹⁄₁₆ x 6¹¹⁄₁₆ in. (24.3 x 17 cm). Trustees of the Victoria and Albert Museum, London, Archive of the Theatre Museum (Blythe House), S.93-1998. *Checklist no. 141*

Fig. 12-41.

Fig. 12-42.

the interior of the palace (fig. 12-40), shows stone walls, pillars, semicircular arches, beamed roof and rustic wooden furniture.[134] Godwin also explained one of his innovations: he had set the play-within-the-play scene in the castle garden. "There is a garden portal and the curtain is hung between two trees, where there is a little stage up three steps. The whole court are spread around the garden . . . plenty of torches and a reflection of the moon in the sea.

The advice to the players will be spoken in a front scene, which courtiers cross on their way to the play."[135] Here speaks the designer of the open air *As You Like It*. Here too is the practical man of the theater, deploying a drop scene behind which the stagehands and lighting men could reset the scene, winch down a cut sky cloth, and light burning torches.

Critics assessed both the authenticity and the originality, while audiences waited in suspense to see the ghost. It appeared as a projected transparency, gray-veiled, gliding along the battlements. Both the *Era* and the *Stage* proved surprisingly reactionary about the costumes (figs. 12-41 and 12-42), the former concluding that "archaeologically correct costumes are occasionally grotesque, and sometimes border on the ridiculous," and the latter writing that "some of the costumes are positively ugly."[136]

Godwin's next commission from Wilson Barrett was for the design of *Junius: or the Household Gods*, by Bulwer,

Lord Lytton. Set in Imperial Rome, it gave Godwin an opportunity to re-create the classical world in his mise-en-scène (figs. 12-43 and 12-44). Although the play was found to be boring and ran for fewer than thirty nights, the mounting was deemed impressively realistic. The *Times* described it as "*le dernier mot* of the stage carpenter. That once humble functionary may be said to have been supplanted by the stage architect."[137] The reviewer went on to describe the solidly built palaces, temples, and interiors.

The prolific writer and theater theorist Percy Fitz-

Fig. 12-43. A scene from act 2 in Bulwer, Lord Lytton's *Junius*, as performed at the Princess's Theatre, London, February 26, 1885. From *Illustrated Sporting and Dramatic News* (14 March 1885).

Fig. 12-44. Walter Hann. Set design for the Palace of Tarquin in Bulwer, Lord Lytton's *Junius*, 1885. Watercolor and ink; 13⅜ x 16⅞ in. (34 x 43 cm). Trustees of the Victoria and Albert Museum, London, E.904-1966. *Checklist no. 143*

Fig. 12-45. Scenes from Sydney Grundy and Wilson Barrett's *Clito*, as performed at the Princess's Theatre, London, May 1, 1886. From "Scenes from *Clito*," *Illustrated Sporting and Dramatic News* (15 May 1886): 262–63.

gerald provides a glimpse of the staging techniques at the Princess's Theatre: "Grand solemn masses of colour and shadow, stately columns, 'built-up' pediments, gorgeous lustrous furniture, succeeded each other scene after scene, and most effective was the mysterious fashion in which one melted, as it were, into the other, without discordant groanings, heavings and flappings, and rattling of wheels and cordage, with which huge masses of scenery have to be hauled away.[138] Godwin's easy collaboration with the same scenic artists, property makers, carpenters, and machinists as for *Claudian* resulted in a high standard of theater professionalism.

In his review of *Junius: or the Household Gods* Percy Fitzgerald also wrote an eulogistical defence of Godwin's ability to transcend dry antiquarianism. This ability was tested by Barrett's next production, *Clito*, an original tragedy written by Sydney Grundy and by Barrett himself,

which opened at Princess's Theatre on May 1, 1886. *Clito* was set in Athens of 404 B.C. The complicated plot concerned the doomed young sculptor Clito who, entering a competition, fell in love with his model, the beautiful, wicked and shameful Helle. Most critics found the violence and immorality of the story to be too much, and Vezin wrote to Godwin, "It is a *very poor play* . . . and [Barrett] finishes with an appendix several pages in length after the Athenian mob has plunged innumerable daggers into his inexhaustible lungs . . . the mise-en-scène is exquisite but I cannot believe the play will draw."[139] However, the respected theater critic Clement Scott, assessing the production in the *Illustrated London News*, wrote, "Mr Godwin, the learned archaeologist, and the modern professors of stage management have combined to tone down the glaring colors of the text . . . the excited mobs of indignant Athens, the exquisite ease and luxury of Helle's home, the sweetly scented fumes of incense, the lutes, the slaves, the plashing fountains, and the gorgeous apparel of old Athenian life, have been effectively introduced to gild the bitter pill of human depravity. . . ."[140]

Drawings of scenes from the play in the *Illustrated Sporting and Dramatic News* show Clito's studio, the canopied hall in Helle's palace, Helle's room and the street scene, with a breathtaking landscape of Athens beyond (fig. 12-45). The reviewer found Godwin's costumes "not in all cases as becoming as they are correct. One of the ugliest modes of dressing the hair is chosen for Miss Eastlake [Helle], while the airy costume worn by Clito on the occasion of his evening call must, we should think, make his representative very uncomfortable indeed."[141] The *Queen* reported a minor injury to Barrett: "One of the Athenian mob assembled in the fifth act of the Princess's play having stabbed him in the arm . . . the frequency of these accidents in theatrical performances should undoubtedly warn those concerned against the use of such weapons as are now employed in stage representations. Realism in these matters is quite unnecessary, and, indeed, is fraught with danger as to require strict suppression."[142] The *Queen* was evidently in the Idealists' camp in the battle between the Realists and the Idealists.

A week after the opening of *Clito*, another play on which Godwin had advised was performed, at the Grand Theatre. This was *The Cenci* by Shelley, directed by John Todhunter for the Shelley Society. A conventional, Italian Renaissance mise-en-scène from theater stock had been used for the play, with very little input from Godwin. *The Cenci*, a sixteenth-century legend based on the dark deeds of Count Cenci of Rome, who was played by Vezin, caused moral outrage. Critics wrote even stronger reviews than they had for *Juana*, describing the play as unsavory, immoral, ghastly, gruesome, hideous, objectionable, unnecessary, repulsive, and, at four hours' duration, monotonous.[143]

The mid-1880s saw Godwin's interest in the classical world increasing. Although a good Gothic architect in his youth, he had become increasingly interested in the art, architecture, and theater of the Greeks. *Clito*'s Athenian setting was the forerunner of a much more ambitious project: that of staging *Helena in Troas* written by J. John Todhunter based on the play by Sophocles. It opened on May 17, 1886, at Hengler's Circus, an arena which was normally leased for equestrian and circus events.

The project had been under consideration for some time. By July 1885, Godwin had invited his friend the actress Lillie Langtry to play the part of Helena, as in a reply to him that month she accepts provisionally, "*if* the part is as good an acting one as the other ladies" and adds "if I have a the-

atre at that time will lend it—to the cause."[144] In September she wrote to thank him for designs for a gilded wig and a bordered dress. These items were almost certainly ordered for the grueling, sixteen-week autumn tour of provincial cities with her repertory company.[145] She wrote again in December, having received a copy of the script of *Helena in Troas*. Her letter went straight to a weak area of the script: "Don't you feel that the scene between Hecuba and Helen wants variety as far as Hecuba is concerned. She seems to be harping on one string all the time."[146] Her letters to Godwin are delightfully flirtatious.

Lillie Langtry did not, in the end, appear in *Helena in Troas*. Helena was played by Alma Murray, Oenone by Maud Beerbohm Tree to her husband Herbert's Paris, Hecuba by Lucy Roche, and her tire-woman by the painter Louise Jopling, while Helena's handmaidens were Constance Wilde, the wife of Oscar, and Miss Hare. Priam was played by Vezin, the Archer by H. Paget, and the chorus of fifteen was led by Miss Kinnaird. Langtry's offer of a theater, if she had one, also came to nothing. Instead, Godwin leased Hengler's Circus.[147] His sketchbook contains the plan of a Greek theater from Professor Mahaffy's *History of Greek Literature* and a sectional drawing of Hengler's.[148] On a printed plan Godwin made colored annotations reducing the number of seats to allow for his stage.[149] His signed watercolor, *Proposed Alterations to Mss Hengler's Cirque for Greek Play March 1886* shows the final plan and scenic elevation (fig. 12-46), countersigned by builders and the scenic artist Walter Hann.[150]

The program explained that Godwin had made no attempt to reproduce the scenery and costume at the supposed time of the siege of Troy but had tried to reproduce the stage that an audience would have witnessed in Sophocles' time. A decade earlier in his Shakespeare series of articles, he had considered this second way of staging plays inferior to the first, preferring the staging to be governed by the period of the story rather than by the period at which the play was written. For *Helena in Troas*, he drew the audience into the scheme: they would be in the position of a classical audience, in a sense part of the "reality" he was attempting to create.

Audiences were entranced. The arena floor was covered with a painted oilcloth showing tessellated marble and in the center was an altar of Dionysus raised on a low dais. A platform stage, reached by steps, preceded Hann's elevation, "A Portion of the Palace of Priam on the Walls of the Citadel in front of the Tower of Paris." Within this were the three entrances of the classical Greek stage, the central one used by the chief actor, in this case a vestibule with bronze doors to the apartment of Helen and Paris, while left and

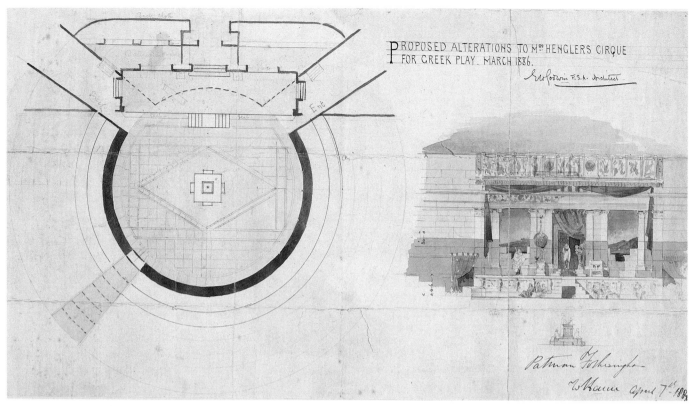

Fig. 12-46. E. W. Godwin. Hengler's Circus, London: plan of the arena and elevation of the stage showing alterations proposed for the staging of John Todhunter's *Helena in Troas*, 1886. Pencil, pen and ink, ink wash, and watercolor; 10⅝ x 18¾ in. (26.9 x 47.7 cm). Trustees of the Victoria and Albert Museum, London, E.632-1963. *Checklist no. 148*

Fig. 12-47. A cartoon depicting Godwin as the ringmaster at Hengler's Circus, London. From "*Helena in Troas,*" *Illustrated Sporting and Dramatic News* (29 May 1886): 327.

right, for supporters and opponents, entrances opened onto the battlements with the blue Hellespont and purple hills beyond. Properties comprised a marble chair, altar, and gilded statue of Aphrodite while colored plaques decorated the platform base. The snake motif, displayed on a shield that hung on the palace facade,[151] was also printed on the yellow playbills and quoted in a cartoon published by the *Illustrated Sporting and Dramatic News*. This showed a clown, in snake-decorated costume, begging Godwin as ringmaster not to repeat his takeover of Hengler's (fig. 12-47).[152]

The leading characters had a difficult task with the unexciting plot where the only dramatic highlight was the shriek from Oenone as she leapt suicidally from the battlements. The chorus, however, contributed a new and essential element. Entering from a lower door, they filed in to form sculptural groups within the arena, around the altar, or upon the steps, conveying their comment in song and dance. According to Louise Jopling, whom Godwin had asked to coach a small group, the poses on the steps were taken from the Parthenon frieze (see fig. 2-22).[153] It was a new and intriguing experience for the audience to see these players so near to them, unprotected by the proscenium arch or footlights, indeed representing the people present at the drama.

The dresses were considered beautiful. Godwin's sketchbook includes preparatory drawings of costumes, properties, and notes on Greek music; his designs included details for the costumier.[154] Helen wore a golden satin chiton with a himation of white gauze with gold and scarlet embroidery, and golden jewelry. Hecuba was dressed in dark gray, Oenone in a misty grey-blue, Priam in clear black, red, gray and white (fig. 12-48), and Paris wore an elaborately embroidered costume in red. The chorus wore sleeveless white linen chitons and short mantles, their long flowing hair bound by gold fillets. These costumes were re-created from Godwin's detailed notes from *The Iliad* and *The Odyssey* and from his numerous, needle-sharp copies of figures on Greek vases supplemented by detailed notes from *The Iliad* and *The Odyssey*.[155]

The audiences included members of the Royal Family, Henry Irving, Ellen Terry, Oscar Wilde, Frederick Leighton, and Alma-Tadema, whose name had so frequently been cited in describing Godwin's work.[156] *Helena in Troas* generated more reviews than any of Godwin's other productions, and the reviewers assessed all aspects of the visual, literary, historical, musical, kinetic, and even the olfactory experience (fig. 12-49).[157] The consensus was that while the script was a little protracted, the experience was artistic, educational, and moving. Clement Scott in the *Illustrated London News* was critical of the acting, which for him outweighed the mise-en-scène,[158] but Constance Wilde summarized more typically in the *Lady*, "Mr Godwin can throw the glamour of art over the accuracy of archaeology," and in her review for the *Theatre* she high-

Fig. 12-48. E. W. Godwin. Costume design for the character Priam in John Todhunter's *Helena in Troas*, 1886. Pencil and watercolor on paper; 9⅞ x 6⅛ in. (25 x 15.5 cm). Trustees of the Victoria and Albert Museum, London, Archive of the Theatre Museum (Blythe House), S.152-1998. *Checklist no. 149*

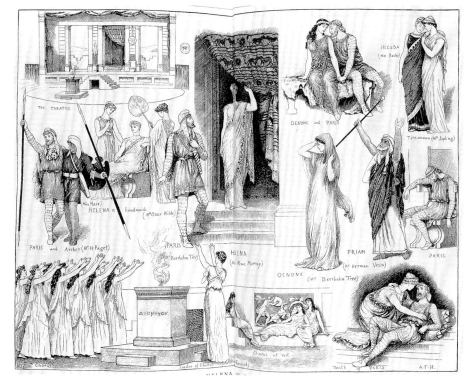

Fig. 12-49. Scenes from John Todhunter's *Helena in Troas*, as performed at Hengler's Circus, London, May 17, 1886. From "*Helena in Troas*: Sketches," *Queen* (5 June 1886): 264–66.

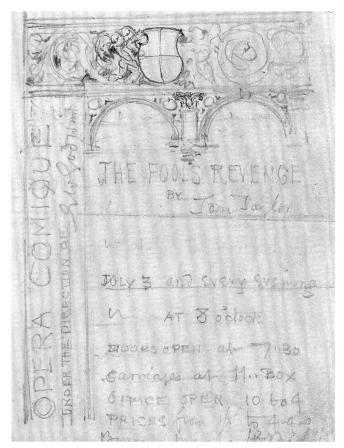

Fig. 12-50. E. W. Godwin. Design for the program for Tom Taylor's play *The Fool's Revenge*, 1886. Pen and ink and pencil; 5⅞ x 4½ in. (15 x 11.5 cm). Trustees of the Victoria and Albert Museum, London, Archive of the Theatre Museum (Blythe House), S.96-1998. *Checklist no. 151*

lighted the effect of the chorus, including the ending where "there was a strange sense of sorrow in the 'Dead March' of these broken-hearted girls as they slowly moved from our sight and faded away like phantoms of some sad dream, from which we wake in tears."[159]

The critical success of *Helena in Troas* led Godwin to over-reach himself. He decided to speculate and, with two society sisters, Miss Steer and Mrs. Mackintosh, he leased the Opéra Comique for a revival of T*he Fool's Revenge* (figs. 12-50 and 12-51) set in the French Renaissance. He commissioned Hann as scenic artist, Vezin and W. Herbert as the only professional actors, and he added a cast of amateurs including the two sisters. The play opened on July 3, 1886, to catastrophic reviews. Godwin had made a series of poor management decisions: the play was sombre and inappropriate for the venue; with the exception of Vezin and Herbert, the actors were poor; it was hot (the temperature reached eighty degrees); and the holidays had begun. "The public stage is not the place for these desperate experiments," admonished the *Illustrated Sporting and Dramatic News*.[160]

John Coleman, perhaps still smarting from Godwin's criticism of *Henry V* in 1876, now retaliated in the *Dramatic Review*, finding the scenery commonplace and the dresses so pretty that Godwin had missed his vocation (figs. 12-52 and 12-53). He berated the tedious delays in the scene-shifting and lack of stage management exemplified by an exit from one side of the stage to fetch a ladder and entry with it from the other, and he commented on a dummy carried on at one point which caused "much merriment." Complaining that Godwin "appears here, there and everywhere," he crescendoed with, "let us now take our hats off to *Godwin*, the renowned; *Godwin*, the architect and archaeologist,

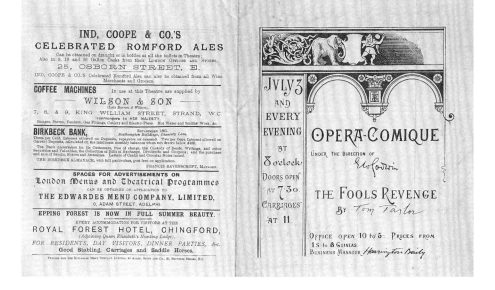

Fig. 12-51. Program for Tom Taylor's play *The Fool's Revenge*, 1886. 6¾ x 11¼ in. (17.3 x 28.5 cm). Trustees of the Victoria and Albert Museum, London, Archive of the Theatre Museum (Blythe House), S.97-1998. *Checklist no. 152*

Fig. 12-52. E. W. Godwin. Costume designs for the character of the Fool, Bertuccio, and for an unidentified character in Tom Taylor's play *The Fools Revenge*, 1886. Pencil and watercolor on paper; 7⅞ x 6⅜ in. (20 x 16.1 cm). Trustees of the Victoria and Albert Museum, London, Archive of the Theatre Museum (Blythe House), S.99-1998. *Checklist no. 154*

greater artistic importance . . . the people, technically un-learned of knowledge, are not so earnest in the pursuit of information as he is himself. He has sought to give them a lesson when they came to him for amusement, and they have gone away disappointed. . . . "[163] That the play was a financial as well as a critical disaster can be deduced from Godwin's list detailing the salaries and overheads for the four nights of the run.[164]

Godwin's Contribution to Stage Design

Godwin had learned theatercraft the hard way—through practice. His first commissions gave him the opportunity to present his research, but he found it frustrating to be isolated from production practices and to find his designs treated as a stimulus rather than as a blueprint. However, because he offered archaeological and historical authenticity, the cachet of a Fellow of the Society of Antiquaries, and the ability to

Fig. 12-53. E. W. Godwin. Costume design for the character of the Page, Ascanio, in Tom Taylor's play *The Fool's Revenge*, 1886. Pencil and watercolor on paper; 8⅛ x 4½ in (20.6 x 11.6 cm). Trustees of the Victoria and Albert Museum, London, Archive of the Theatre Museum (Blythe House), S.98-1998. *Checklist no. 153*

Godwin the manager and stage manager; *Godwin* the scene-painter and inventor of the Pastoral Player; *Godwin* the Great Man Milliner!"[161]

In the same issue, a review entitled "Archaeology or Art," signed by "Lys," discussed Godwin's visual style and countered the manifesto which Godwin had outlined in 1864 in the *Western Daily Press*. "We do not go to the theatre to hear passionate recitations and funny speeches," Godwin had written, "but to witness such a performance as will place us as nearly as possible in the position of spectators of the original scene or thing represented and so gain information of man, manners, customs, costumes, and countries."[162] Lys, looking at the failure of *The Fool's Revenge*, disagreed. "In his zeal for archaeological correctness," wrote Lys, "and in his devotion to minute realism, [Godwin] has allowed himself to forget matters of far

345

publish his complaints in the journals to which he regularly contributed if his work was by-passed, he became respected as an agent for change.

It was unsurprising that his theories of visual realism increasingly included the art of acting. The Bristol "Jottings," the Shakespeare essays, and the *British Architect* articles all included attention to the players' deportment, management of their costumes, and stage business. With *Claudian*, *Hamlet*, *Junius*, and *Clito*, Barrett's managerial support and the teamwork at the Princess's ensured histrionic and visual integration of a high order. Godwin ensured that the movement and gestures of the actors, their grouping and physical use of the set, became part of an authentic mise-en-scène.

In the pastoral plays and *Helena*, Godwin originated and tested a unique role—that of designer-manager. It is significant that in these productions, archaeological straitjacketing, although never far away, partially receded in the face of a more poetic view of the truth. *Truth*, nevertheless, reported of *The Faithfull Shepherdesse*, that "every lady and gentleman had to submit to a severe inspection from Mr Godwin; they had been taken by him to the British Museum to study the fall of drapery and Greek hairdressing, and if a fold was out of place, or there was a petticoat too much, the offender was sternly ordered to rectify the mistake."[165]

Godwin's enthusiasms and abilities were, in one sense, very much of their time. The Victorian age provided a context of interest in antiquity and historical research. Royal Academicians Frederick Leighton, George Watts, Lawrence Alma-Tadema, Edward Poynter, John William Waterhouse, Albert Moore, and Edward Burne-Jones were prominent in the classical revival, which had been fueled by the earlier enthusiasms of participants in the Grand Tour and by the recent excavations of Heinrich Schliemann in Crete and Asia Minor, and Ernst Curtius at Olympia. History painters Paul Falconer Poole, James Linton, William Yeames, Alfred Elmore, and Edwin Abbey provided images of national, literary and domestic drama. Amateur dramatics, charades, masques, tableaux, and costume balls combined in a lexicon of middle-class and upper-class social activity in which Godwin's later work was at home.

It is in the studied "naturalism" of the pastoral plays and, above all, in *Helena in Troas*, that we see a mature theater manager. Godwin's painstaking copies from vases in the British Museum, study of antiquarian books, exhaustive examination of *The Iliad* and *The Odyssey*, discourse with scholars, knowledge of classical revivals at the universities[166] and the writing of his impressive article, "The Greek House According to Homer" for the *Nineteenth Century* in 1886,[167] generated an inner experience of the world of Helen and of Troy which enabled him to transcend archaeological realism in this play.

Two of Godwin's friends pay the most perceptive tributes to his work in the theater. Oscar Wilde wrote of *Helena*, "the historical accuracy that underlies the visible shapes of beauty that he presents to us, is not by any means the distinguishing quality of the completed work of art. This quality is the absolute unity and harmony of the entire presentation, and presence of one mind controlling the most minute details, and revealing itself only in that true perfection that hides personality."[168] Lady Archie wrote, "Poet of architects and architect of all the arts, he possessed that rare gift, a feeling for the very essence of Beauty wherever and whenever it was to be found. The arts seemed to yield their secrets to him, and for him Nature opened her scroll, while with exquisite spirit of choice, and delicate tact of omission, he would, from both of these worlds of wonder, select all congruous elements of beauty and of strength and combine them into works of perfect symmetry and right proportion."[169]

Note: Most published sources are cited below in shortened form (author's last name, abbreviated title, date of publication); full references will be found in the bibliography. Frequently cited archives are abbreviated below; for a key to the abbreviations, also see the bibliography.

1. Harbron, *Conscious Stone* (1949): 6–7; Planché, *History of British Costume* (1834) This book was the result of a decade of study (Planché, *Recollections and Reflections* [1872]: 223); it was updated in 1847 and ran to later editions, including a retitled version in 1874 (*British Costume: A Complete History*).

2. Managements (listed with relevant years) referred to are: Lucia Vestris at the Olympic, 1830s; William Macready, Covent Garden, 1837–39; Samuel Phelps, Sadlers Wells, 1843–62; Charles Kean, Princess's Theatre, 1850–59; Charles Fechter, Lyceum Theatre, 1863–67. A crucial role was also played by scenic artists (listed with their life dates): Philip de Loutherbourg (1740–1812); John Henderson Grieve (1770–1845) and his sons, Thomas (1799–1882) and William (1800–1844); David Roberts, RA (1796–1864); Clarkson Stanfield, RA (1793–1867); Frederick Lloyds (1818–94); William Telbin Sr. (1813–1873) and many others.

3. For information on Godwin's theatrical interests during the period in Bristol, see Harbron, *Conscious Stone* (1949): chaps. 1–3.

4. "Theatrical Jottings" appeared in the *Western Daily Press* from October 1862 to October 1864. See also Barker, "Terrys and Godwin in Bristol" (Autumn 1967): 27–43.

5. Godwin, "Theatrical Jottings" (11 October 1864): 2.

6. Ibid.

7. The articles deal with thirty-two plays, each based on historical research. The text approximates 90,000 words and includes twelve diagrammatic architectural stage plans. Six are diagonally angled to the proscenium, each showing two elevations, three being interiors and three open places. Four plans show outside venues and are loosely clustered in a semicircle around the proscenium. Two plans, one interior and one exterior, are square-on to the proscenium. Within the plans are a variety of levels, angles, and open loggias.

8. Godwin, "Architecture and Costume of . . . *Hamlet*" (31 October 1874): 224.

9. A Herald is an officer with specialist knowledge responsible for providing information and advice in the drawing or deciphering of coats of arms according to genealogies.

10. The opening article, "Architecture and Costume of . . . *Hamlet*," establishes the approach. Thirteen examples of Elizabethan items and practices are recorded, which would have been unknown in the Danish Court of 1012, to which date, on historical grounds, Godwin ascribes the play.

11. When possible Godwin proposes one scene per act, many totals are reduced to five or eight scenes including the dramatist's thirty-six for *Antony and Cleopatra*. The difference in costs between Elizabethan and Victorian stage mounting is striking.

12. Details of patterning are examined, such as the use of spirals, chevrons, dots, or interlacing in *Hamlet* (Godwin, "Architecture and Costume of . . . *Hamlet*" [31 October 1874]: 225); or the extent of slashing on the court fashion 1521–33 in *Henry VIII* (Godwin, "Architecture and Costume of . . . *Henry VIII*" [6 March 1875]: 134.

13. Godwin, "Greek Plays," part 3 (22 May 1875): 299.

14. Recommended as most useful were the South Kensington Museum, the British Museum, the National Gallery, and the Royal Academy.

15. Particularly reliable resources proved to include: Parker and Turner, *Some Account of Domestic Architecture in England . . .* (1851); Augustus Charles Pugin, *Specimens of Gothic Architecture* (1850); Verdier and Cattois, *Architecture civile et domestique* (1855–57); Viollet-le-Duc, *Dictionnaire Raisonné du Mobilier Francais* (1858–75); Quicherat, *Histoire du Costume en France* (1875); G. E. Street, *Brick and Marble Architecture of Italy* (1855) and Vecellio, *Degli Habiti antichi et moderni* (1855).

16. Godwin, "Architecture and Costume of . . . *Romeo and Juliet*" (14 November 1874): 252.

17. Godwin, "Architecture and Costume of . . . *Twelfth Night*" (24 April 1875): 240.

18. Godwin, "Architecture and Costume of . . . *Henry IV*, Part I" (23 January 1875): 46.

19. Cyril Bowen, *Practical Hints on Stage Costume* (London and New York: Samuel French, ca. 1880). Bowen provides guidance on the repertoire of costumes and properties that a professional actor should possess to equip himself for work.

20. Godwin, "Architecture and Costume of . . . *Merry Wives of Windsor*" (2 January 1875): 3.

21. Godwin, "Architecture and Costume of . . . *Much Ado About Nothing*" (24 April 1875): 241.

22. Terry, *Story of My Life* (1908): 46. The actress writes, "This was the first lovely dress that I ever wore and I learned a great deal from it."

23. Godwin, "Theatrical Jottings" (11 March 1863): 4.

24. Terry, *Ellen Terry's Memoirs* (1933): 74.

25. On return, five scenes and three act-drops were selected and massive plaster columns created for the interiors.

26. Bancroft and Bancroft, *Bancrofts: Recollections of Sixty Years*, (1909): 201, 205. Cf, "Programme," for *The Merchant of Venice*, performed 17 April 1875 at The Prince of Wales Theatre. (V&A TA). Unless otherwise acknowledged, all programs referred to are held in the V&A TA.

27. Correspondence and documents, July 1880–August 1881, V&A TA., Godwin collection, box 6: Godwin, Costings for *The Merchant of Venice*; "Scenery for The Merchant of Venice—Four set scenes as designed by E. W. Godwin FSA and as carried out at the Prince of Wales Theatre London for Mr and Mrs Bancroft"; "Properties and Furniture for the above"; "Costume complete: for the above . . . "; pencil and watercolor sketches for *The Merchant of Venice*. The items were part of Godwin's response to John Barber, approached by a royal client in Hyderabad for quotations on supply of a stage and fittings, scenery, costumes, and properties for a selection of plays. There is no evidence of purchase.

28. Godwin sketchbooks, V&A PD, E.236-1963 and E.250-1963,

29. [Godwin,] "Costume of the *Merchant of Venice*" (13 February 1880): 74–75 and illus. following p. 78. See also Godwin, Letter to the *Times* (23 April 1875): 10, in which Godwin disclaims responsibility.

30. "The Prince of Wales' Theatre" (19 April 1875): 3.

31. For example, W. H. W. [W. H. White], "The Prince of Wales Theatre" (23 April 1875): 471–72.

32. Program for *Henry V*, V&A TA, Godwin collection, box 9. The scene painters were again George Gordon and William Harford.

33. Godwin sketchbooks, V&A PD, E.279-1963, E.239-1963, and E.240-1963. Godwin opens one of these sketchbooks (E.279-1963) with the comment, "Prepared this play in winter of 1875–76."

34. Godwin diary entries for 8 September–9 October 1876, V&A AAD, 4/2-1980; and notes entitled "*Henry V* Queries," dated 2 September 1876, V&A TA, Godwin collection, box 7.

35. Godwin, "*Henry V*: An Archaeological Experience" (9 September 1876): 142–43.

36. William Burges, "'Henry V' at the Queen's Theatre" (23 September 1876): 188.

37. Godwin, "*Henry V*: A Theatrical Experience" (30 September 1876): 192–94.

38. Diary entries for 16, 19, 22, 26, and 27 September; for 2, 7, 9, 10, 14 October; and for 4 November, V&A AAD, 4/2-1980.

39. Godwin, "Archaeology on the Stage," part 2 (22 February 1885): 53. There were seven parts in the series, which was published in the *Dramatic Review* from 8 February to 24 October 1885.

40. Godwin, "*Henry V*: A Theatrical Experience," (30 September 1876): 194.

41. Godwin, "Costume of T*he Merchant of Venice*" (13 February 1880): 78 and illus.; idem, "Sketches of Costume for *As You Like It*" (26 March 1880), 150 and illus.; idem, "The Costumes of *As You Like It* (23 April 1880): 196; idem, "The Costumes of *Romeo and Juliet* (21 May 1880): 247.

42. Wallis had played the leading role in *Ninon* by Wills in February at the Adelphi, and Godwin had visited her backstage (Godwin diary entries for 7 and 9 February and 30 March 1880, V&A AAD, 4/5-1980). Godwin charged Wallis and Mantell 5 pounds, payable on delivery (ibid.).

43. [Godwin], Notes on Current Events, "Mr. R. B. Martell . . . " and "We understand Miss Wallis obtained . . . " (1 July 1881): 330.

44. Ibid.

45. Godwin, "Costume of *Othello*" (15 October 1880): 176.

46. Godwin sketchbooks, V&A PD, E.250-1963 and E.252-1963.

47. Burges lent a copy of Vecellio, *Degli Habiti antichi et moderni* (1855) to Godwin while he was writing the Shakespeare essays.

48. Vezin subsequently asked Godwin to design costumes for *Macbeth*. See letters from H. Vezin dated 12 April and 7 September 1880, V&A TA, Godwin collection, box 6; see also Godwin's sketches for *Macbeth* from the Bayeux Tapestry, in his 1880 sketchbook, V&A PD, E.251-1963.

49. Art Chronicle, "At Sadlers' Wells . . ." (November 1880): 186.

50. For a preview and review of *Hamlet*, see Notes on Current Events, "Mr Hermann Vezin will appear . . ." (4 February 1881): 64; idem, "Mr Vezin made his appearance . . ." (4 March 1881): 115 and illus.; "Mr. Vezin as Hamlet" (15 March 1881): 192−93.

51. Undated cuttings entitled "Sadlers Wells" from the *Chronicle* and "Mr Herman Vezin's Hamlet" from the *Sunday Times*, V&A Theatre Museum. Godwin's ledger shows receipt of five guineas for the design (ledger entry for 31 January 1881, V&A AAD, 4/12-1980). See also Vezin's lively correspondence on the acquisition of the gold braid in a letter dated 24 May 1881, V&A TA, Godwin collection, box 6.

52. *The Lady of Lyons* was performed as a benefit matineé for the widows and orphans of the Metropolitan Fire Brigade, on 18 January at the Gaiety Theatre. Vezin asked Godwin if he might study "free gratis for nothing" designs Godwin has already made for Melnotte (letter of 31 December 1882, V&A TA, Godwin collection, box 6). In return Vezin sent thanks and stalls tickets (letter dated 1 January 1883, ibid.). See also advance notice of the production in the *Era* (13 January 1883): 16.

53. [E. W. Godwin], "Theatrical Notes," *The British Architect* (27 January 1882): 40; "Sitting at a Play" (19 January 1882): 101.

54. Hermann Vezin, letter dated 17 November 1883, V&A TA, Godwin collection, box 6.

55. Hermann Vezin, letter dated 4 December 1883, ibid.

56. Godwin, "Architecture and Costume of . . . *Hamlet*" (31 October 1874): 224..

57. Godwin diary entry dated 4 May 1883, V&A AAD, 4/8-1980.

58. George Alexander letters, May−October 1881, V&A TA, Godwin collection, box 7.

59. Godwin's first theater work for 1884 was a commission for the costumes of *She Would and She Would Not* by Colley Cibber, set in Madrid (costume designs, V&A TA, Godwin collection, box 9) It was a benefit matineé for Kate Vaughan who played the lead. Reviewers were sadly dismissive of the poor elocution of Vaughan's supporting cast, and one paper printed enigmatically, "The dresses for the most part: [*sic*] the mounting of the piece decidedly perfunctory" (unattributed review; V&A TA, Godwin collection, box 9); see also the *Stage* (13 June 1884): 14; and the *Referee* (8 July 1884). Kate Vaughan had arranged a stalls ticket for Godwin and afterward, in a letter, she enclosed his fee and said she was pleased he liked her performance, assuring him that she would recover his costume sketches from the costumier and return them to him. (Kate Vaughan letters dated 4 June 1884 and n.d. [ca. 5 June 1884], V&A TA, Godwin collection, box 7). Vezin commissioned costumes from Godwin for his role in *Secret Service* as the elderly Michael Perrin (Godwin sketchbook, V&A PD, E.265-1963). The play, adapted by Planché was produced by Kate Vaughan at Her Majesty's Theatre, opening on 15 October 1885. The *Era* thought "the costumes were especially noticeable for the taste and care displayed in their execution" ([17 October 1885]: 8). Godwin's solution to the era of Bonaparte had been to take inspiration from a painting by Watteau. It is not clear whether *Secret Service* or *The Eumenides*, a student production at Cambridge University opening on 1 December, represented Godwin's last stage work of 1885. Evidence suggests that he had an advisory role in the Cambridge production: among his papers are several copies of the cover of the *Illustrated London News* ([12 December 1885]: 597) on which scenes and costumes are shown; and a letter from

a staff-member of the Fitzwilliam Museum touches on his guidance of the play (V&A TA).

60. [E. W. Godwin], Notes on Current Events, "It 'ud take a fortnight . . ." (22 April 1881): 203. The unsigned review describes Alexander as being "pre-eminently promising . . . he has learnt much and is of the stuff good actors are made of." The young actor was later to become the celebrated actor-manager, Sir George Alexander, evidence of Godwin's discerning eye.

61. George Alexander letters, 4 September 1881, V&A TA, Godwin collection, box 7.

62. See Bram Stoker; *Personal Reminiscences of Henry Irving*, vol. 1 (London: William Heinemann, 1906): 205.

63. Terry, *Story of My Life* (1908): 199. A photograph of Ellen Terry (V&A, Theatre Museum) shows this cup; however it conflicts with the two-handled goblet on stem and base shown in a watercolor of "the cup" tipped into a manuscript of *The Cup*, which was annotated and owned by Tennyson (Tennyson Research Centre, Lincoln). For a possible third design, see the *Illustrated London News* (5 February 1881): 124 illus. The goblet has a curved integral stem and base, without handles.

64. Terry, *Story of My Life* (1980): 170−71.

65. [E. W. Godwin], "The mounting of Mr. Tennyson's classical play . . ." (14 January 1881): 16.

66. Terry, *Story of My Life* (1908): 196. Three unsigned detailed watercolors of the stage sets, possibly by their designer James Knowles, are tipped into Tennyson's copy of the script (Tennyson Research Centre, Lincoln).

67. Wilson Barrett letters dated 15 September and 2 October 1880; V&A TA, Godwin collection, box 1; program for *Mary Stuart* (11 October 1880), annotated by Godwin, ibid., box 2. Mary was played by Helena Modjeska.

68. Godwin diary entries for 17 October−13 December 1880, V&A AAD, 4/5-1980; diary entry for 28 March 1881, V&A AAD, 4/6-1980. See also Wills, *W.G. Wills* (1898): 184.

69. Ibid. After the reading Wills celebrated by giving Godwin a five pound "consultation" fee. *Juana* opened at The Court Theatre on 7 May 1881.

70. Godwin diary entries dated 29 March−7 May 1881, V&A AAD, 4/6-1980.

71. Godwin sketchbook, V&A PD, E.253-1963.

72. Godwin diary entry for 22 April 1881, V&A AAD, 4/6-1980.

73. Program for *Juana*, 7 May 1881, The Court Theatre, V&A TA, Godwin collection, box 1. For comment on scenes and some costumes, see "Mr. Wills' powerful play or rather tragedy of *Juana* . . . ." (13 May 1881): 245.

74. G. A. S., "The Playhouses," *The Illustrated London News* (14 May 1881): 471; (21 May 1881), p. 495; "The Court" (14 May 1881): 6; "The Court" (13 May 1881): 7.

75. Godwin, "Letter to Atlas from E. W. Godwin" (11 May 1881): 13. Godwin's letter was a response to report in the *World* on Modjeska's failure to wear accurate copies of Godwin's designs (Atlas [pseud.], "What the World Says" [4 May 1881]: 14).

76. Godwin, "Archaeology on the Stage," part 2 (22 February 1885): 53.

77. Godwin, "Theatrical Jottings: No. 1, *Rienzi* at Her Majesty's Theatre" (30 January 1880): 50.

78. Wills, *W. G. Wills* (1898): 188−96. The fee was standard for this well-known playwright; Godwin's diary for 1883 records £800 passed to Wills by Barrett for *Claudian* (V&A AAD, 4/8-1980).

79. Around the time of writing a review of Carl Rosa's *Rienzi*, Godwin started a series of costume sketches from Italian sources in the British

Museum, also compiling lists of information with the reference "Wills Rienzi" (Godwin's sketchbook for 1880, V&A PD. E.251-1963). The presentation book with pencil and watercolor drawings was prepared a few years later. It includes sets, costumes, color notations, and a list of his source manuscripts in the British Museu (V&A TA, Godwin collection, box 9). This presentation book, entitled "RIENZI 1350 Studies for Costume Etc by E.W. Godwin FSA 1880-" also includes designs for *The Merchant of Venice* (1883). For a large watercolor of the elevation of Rienzi's house in Rome by Godwin, see Godwin's architectural drawing, "Elevation of Rienzi's House Rome," n.d., RIBA Drawings, Ran 7/N/22-7.

80. Mrs Scott Siddons and Mr. McMahon, letters dated October 1881, V&A TA, Godwin collection, box 7..

81. Theatrical Notes. "Mr. Godwin has been retained . . ." (21 October 1881): 522. That the Hon. Lewis Wingfield's costumes for Anne Boleyn were taken from Holbein is confirmed by a reviewer (see "Sitting at a Play" (3 November 1881): 13. Wingfield was a trained painter and professional costume designer.

82. Godwin diary entry dated 22 May 1883, V&A AAD, 4/8-1980.

83. Godwin diary entries dated 23, 25, and 26 May 1883, ibid.. Godwin attended the performance on 6 June. The venue was Cromwell House, home of Sir Charles Freake.

84. For attributions and discussion of the design for *The Tale of Troy*, see Baldwin, "Victorian Artists and Stage Design" (1991).

85. Godwin bartered for an ongoing fee of two pounds a week for the duration of the season in addition to twenty pounds for thirty-two sheets of designs (Godwin and Robert Buchanon, letters dated January 1883, V&A TA, Godwin collection, box 7; costume designs for *Storm Beaten*, ibid., box 1). See also Godwin diary entries dated 4 January–14 March 1883, V&A AAD, 4/8-1980.

86. See any of the contemporary journals (e.g., *Times, Daily News, Era, Stage, Play, Illustrated London News, Illustrated Sporting and Dramatic News*, etc.) for March–May 1883.

87. Godwin, "Archaeology on the Stage," part 5 (19 September 1885): 60–61.

88. Ibid., part 6 (10 October 1885): 92–93.

89. Godwin, "A Few Notes on the Architecture and Costume of . . . *Claudian*," (7 December 1883): 268–69, and illus. This open letter to Wilson Barrett was also issued as a pamphlet (Godwin, *"Clauidian"* [1883]).

90. Godwin's source for the column is given as Claude François Menéstrier, *Description de la belle et grande Colonne historiée, dressée à l'honneur de l'Empéreur Théodore* (Paris, 1702). His source for the church included drawings by Antonio Giamberti da Sangallo, made in the early sixteenth century (Godwin, "A Few Notes on the Architecture and Costume of . . . *Claudian*," [7 December 1883]: 268–69.

91. Godwin, *"Claudian"* (1883): 3.

92. "Claudian Barrett refusing Byzantium's 'Barrer'" (27 December 1883): 369. On the cart is the legend, "E.W. Godwin FSA Maker." See also "Princess's Theatre" (7 December 1883): 3.

93. Godwin, *"Claudian"* (1883): 3.

94. Godwin sketchbook, V&A PD E.262-1963; Godwin notebooks, RIBA Mss, GoE/5/1–3 (G/GR.2/4, 6-10, 19 and 20).

95. Eleven ways of wearing a girdle, V&A PD, E.262-1963; decorated sandals and shoes, ibid., E.448-1948.

96. "Theatrical Trades: Boots and Shoes" (16 November 1883): 8–9.

97. Preparatory documents and designs for *Claudian,* 1883, V&A TA, Godwin collection, boxes 1 and 3.

98. This was reported in the *Era* (1 December 1883): 5.

99. E.g., reports in: *Era, Stage, Theatre, Play, Modern Society, Daily News, Illustrated Sporting and Dramatic News,* and *Illustrated London News.* For detailed descriptions of the mise-en-scène, probably written by Godwin, see [Godwin], "The first act of *Claudian*. . . ."] (14 December 1883): 277; and [Godwin], "The third act of *Claudian* . . . ." (28 December 1883): 300.

100. "*Claudian* at The Princess's" (15 December 1883): 47.

101. See, e.g., [Godwin] "A Few Notes on . . . *Claudian*" (7 December 1883): 268; "Princess's Theatre" (7 December 1883): 3; "Before and Behind the Curtain" (15 December 1883): 13.

102. See various papers of the Society, including prospectus, minute book, and letters, V&A TA, Godwin collection, box 6.

103. For the wide variety of archives of *As You Like It* (1884 and 1885), *The Faithful Shepherdesse* (1885), *Fair Rosamund* (1886), and the Society of Pastoral Players (1884–86), see V&A TA, Godwin collection, boxes 5, 6, 7, and 9.

104. Lady Archie reserved right of approving expenditure and Godwin was to have a secretary to keep accounts and Box Office (memorandum of agreement between Lady Archibald Campbell and Godwin, 17 October 1884, V&A TA, Godwin collection, box 5).

105. Godwin sketchbooks, V&A E.253-1963 and E.264-1963; Godwin, "Sketches of Costume for *As You Like It* (26 March 1880): 150 and illus.

106. For an invaluable discussion of the neglect of rural scenes in Godwin's Shakespeare articles, see Souder, "E.W. Godwin and the Visual Theatre" (1976): 25–26.

107. "Shakespeare under the Greenwood Tree" (26 July 1884): 8. There were many other reviews in numerous newspapers and journals.

108. Godwin sketchbook, V&A PD E.264-1963.

109. Guests in May 1885 included the Princess of Wales and their children; the Duke of Saxe Meiningen and his wife; Prince Edward of Saxe Weimar; and James MacNeill Whistler and Frederick Leighton.

110. Austin, "In the Forest of Arden" (September 1884): 128.

111. "Rosalind in the Wood" (31 July 1884): 174–75.

112. O. Wilde, "*As You Like It*" (6 June 1885): 296–97.

113. Campbell, "Woodland Gods" (November 1888): 5.

114. Last witnessed in 1668, the five-act play was cut to three by Godwin with Wills's assistance. Some of the bawdier scenes were omitted and language sanitized for Victorian sensibilities.

115. Godwin's drawing of Pan labeled from the Bronze Room of the British Museum, with annotation giving the height of the head as 2 feet excluding horns, RIBA Mss, GoE 5/3 (G/GR/109).

116. Draft of a letter from Godwin to Lady Archibald Campbell dated 22 June 1885, in reply to her memo, V&A TA, Godwin collection, box 5.

117. Scrutator [pseud.], "The Coombe Shepherdesses" (2 July 1885): 13–14.

118. Archives include Godwin's preparation and prompt copy of the play, Batson's score published by Novello, account sheets and numerous letters (V&A TA, Godwin collection, boxes 5, 6, and 7). See also letter from Godwin to G. Sharpe dated 2 April 1885 and headed, "Auditorium at Coombe," V&A AAD, 4/443-1988.

119. See letters from H. B. Tree, A. W. Batson, A. Bourchier, Lucy Roche, V&A TA, Godwin collection, box 7.

120. "The Pastoral Players," *Era* (4 July 1885): 12.

121. Although Godwin's obituary, ("The Late E. W. Godwin," *Building News* 51 [15 October 1886]: 589) refers to "the tableaux vivants given at Prince's Hall, Picadilly" and "arranging of *Bachelors* when brought out at the Opera Comique" as Godwin's final theatrical work, Professor Warr's *Tale of Troy* (1883 and 1886) and *The Story of Orestes* (1886) did not credit

Godwin among the list of Royal Academy and Royal Institute designers of these productions (see Baldwin, "Victorian Artists and Stage Design" [1991]: 221–46), and no corroborative evidence has been located to date to suggest that Godwin arranged *Bachelors* at the Opera Comique in August 1886.

122. Thiselton, "*Fair Rosamund*" (1 September 1886): 170–72.

123. On performances of pastoral plays see, e.g., "The Pastoral Players," (4 July 1885): 12., and on performances of the forest scenes from *As You Like It* at Charlton Park and The Holly Trees, Colchester, see *The Era* (7 August 1886): 7.

124. "The Pastoral Players," *The Era* (6 June 1885): 9.

125. [E. W. Godwin], Notes on Current Events, "To the Meiningen court company . . ." (10 June 1881): 289–91; idem, Notes on Current Events, "*Julius Caesar* as performed" (17 June 1881): 302–3.

126. The Meiningen Company, founded by Duke George of Saxe-Meiningen, toured Europe between 1874 and 1890. They stressed artistic unity and ensemble playing, giving extra rehearsal time to crowd scenes so that mass movement was broken up by characteristic action for individuals. They were also known for costume research, diagonal staging, and a variety of stage levels. Innovative in Germany, these approaches had already been introduced in England by Charles Keen in the 1850s. Godwin advocated simiar practices in his "Shakespere [sic]" articles of 1874–75.

127. "Rosalind in the Wood" (31 July 1884): 174–75; "Forest Scenes of . . . *As You Like It*" (26 July 1884): 8.

128. Campbell, "Woodland Gods" (November 1888): 3.

129. Photographs, V&A TA, Godwin collection, box 9. Godwin's responsibility had been considerable. He had designed stage, auditorium, costumes, and properties, managed, and rehearsed forty-four actors and twenty-one backstage staff, helped to publicize the production, and kept the accounts (list in a Godwin sketchbook, V&A PD, E.265-1963).

130. O. Wilde, "Pastoral Players: *The Faithfull Shepherdesse*" (1 August 1885): 4.

131. "*Hamlet* at the Princess's" (16 October 1884): 312.

132. Godwin sketchbooks, V&A PD, E.263-1963 and E.252-1963. A further sketchbook is held by the RIBA (Mss, GoE/7/8 [G/GR.2/1 and 26/10]), which includes a list inside the cover of designs posted or taken to Barrett between 2 July and 8 September 1884. Many of the leaves in this sketchbook have been removed are are now held in V&A TA, Godwin collection, box 1.

133. Eight letters and cards to Godwin from theater personnel, including E. H. B. Lyne, requesting various properties and dress designs for *Hamlet* in 1884, V&A TA, Godwin collection, box 1.

134. Walter Hann, design for interior of the palace for *Hamlet*, 1884, V&A PD, E.898-1966.

135. "*Hamlet* at the Princess's" (16 October 1884): 312.

136. "*Hamlet* at the Princess's" (18 October 1884): 8; "Princess's" (24 October 1884): 14. Godwin's financial reward was a fee of seventy pounds with ten shillings per night above one hundred nights (note in Godwin's sketchbook, V&A PD, E.262-1963).

137. The Theatres, "Princess's" (2 March 1885): 10. Scenes included a street in Rome with the Temple of Jupiter, the old ruined Temple of Romulus, the house of Colatinus, and Hann's sumptuous, marbled Palace of Tarquin (Walter Hann, design for setting for Junius, 1885, V&A PD, E.904-1966). See also Godwin's drawings labeled "Household Gods" which may have been used for the idols in Junius, RIBA Mss, GoE/5/- (G/GR.81) .

138. Fitzgerald, "Junius" (22 February 1885): 72.

139. Hermann Vezin, letter dated 8 May 1886, V&A TA, Godwin collection, box 6.

140. C. Scott, "Playhouses" (8 May 1886): 476.

141. "Scenes from *Clito*" (15 May 1886): 262–63; "*Clito*: Edmund Barnard" (8 May 1886): 141–42; see also illustrations. "Some scenes from *Clito*" (4 May 1886): 11.

142. "Drama: Between the Acts" (22 May 1886), p. 563.

143. See, e.g., "Performance of T*he Cenci*" (8 May 1886): 13; "*The Cenci*: Greek Plays" (14 May 1886): 16; and Wedmore, "Review of T*he Cenci*" (15 May 1886): 352.

144. Lillie Langtry, letter dated 20 July 1885, V&A AAD 4/172-1988.

145. Lillie Langtry, letter dated 6 September 1885, V&A AAD 4/174-1988. The repertoire comprised *The Lady of Lyons* by Lord Lytton, *She Stoops to Conquer* by Oliver Goldsmith, *School for Scandal* by Christopher Sheridan, *Peril* by Sardou adapted by Stephenson and Scott, and *A Young Tramp* by William G. Wills.

146. Lillie Langtry, letter dated 14 December 1885, V&A AAD 4/175-1988.

147. Godwin sketchbook containing a draft of a letter to Mr. C. Hengler hoping to lease the building on inexpensive terms if it were normally closed in May, V&A PD E.265-1963. See also various letters concerning the adaptation of the building, V&A TA, Godwin collection, box 8..

148. Godwin sketchbook, V&A PD E.265-1963.

149. Godwin adaptation of a commercial printed plan entitled "Henglers Grand Cirque," 1886, V&A TA, Godwin collection, box 8.

150. Godwin's "Proposed Alterations to Mss Hengler's Cirque for Greek Play March 1886," V&A PD, E.632-1963. The builder was Patman Fotheringham.

151. Godwin's drawings of weaponry copied from Greek vases in the British Museum, including two with the snake motif used in *Helena in Troas*, RIBA Mss, GoE/5/- (G/GR.2/19 and 20).

152. For the cartoon captioned "Oh if yer please Mr Godwin. . . . ," see Our Captious Critic, "*Helena in Troas*" (29 May 1886): 327.

153. Jopling, *Twenty Years of My Life* (1925): 289–90.

154. Godwin sketchbook, V&A PD E.265-1963. See also costume design for Priam, V&A TA, Godwin collection, box 8.

155. Files of Godwin's notes and drawings of costume, some in color, copied from Greek vases in the British Museum and books at the Society of Antiquaries, London, RIBA Mss, GoE/5/- (especially G/GR.2/4,6-10, 19 and 20).

156. Leighton's model, Dorothy Dene, had a part in the chorus. Alma-Tadema's work was increasingly renowned after he exhibited 287 pictures in the Grosvenor Gallery in 1882 and made annual contributions at the Royal Academy; Godwin's stage work was sometimes described in the press as "Alma-Tademaesque."

157. See, among others, reviews in the *Era* (22 May 1886): 14; *Stage* (21 May 1886): 15–16; *Illustrated Sporting and Dramatic News* (22 May 1886): 295; ibid. (29 May 1886): 327; *Illustrated London News* (29 May 1886): 566; *Queen* (5 June 1886): 626; *Dramatic Review* (22 May 1886): 161–62.

158. C. Scott, "Greek Plays" (22 May 1886): 524.

159. W. C. K. Wilde, "*Helena in Troas*" (20 May 1886): 389; idem, "*Helena in Troas*" (1 June 1886): 331–35.

160. [Review of T*he Fool's Revenge*] (10 July 1886): 495.

161. Coleman, "*The Fool's Revenge*" (7 August 1886): 11–12. For further examples of staging problems, see the review in the *Era* (10 July 1886): 14.

162. Godwin, "Theatrical Jottings" (11 October 1864): 2.

163. Lys, [pseud.], "Archaeology or Art" (7 August 1886): 13–14.

164. Godwin entries totaling nearly £128 on printed Opera Comique Salary List for *The Fool's Revenge*, n.d. [1886], V&A TA, Godwin collection, box 1.

165. Scrutator [pseud.], "The Coombe Shepherdesses," *Truth* (2 July 1885): 13–14.

166. The university revivals included: *The Agamemnon* (Oxford, 1880); *The Tale of Troy* (London, 1883); *Eumenides* (Cambridge, 1885); and *The Story of Orestes* (London, 1886).

167. Godwin, "The Greek Home According to Homer" (June 1886): 914–22. See also RIBA Mss, GoE/5/1/–, and related letters.

168. O. Wilde, "*Helena in Troas*" (22 May 1886): 161–62.

169. Campbell, "Woodland Gods" (1888): 3.

Fig. 13-1. William Rothenstein. *Edward Gordon Craig as Hamlet*, 1896. Oil on canvas; 36 ¾ x 24 ⅛ in. (93.6 x 61.3 cm). Trustees of the Victoria and Albert Museum, London, Theatre Museum (Blythe House), S.1056-1984.

CHAPTER 13

THE·GENETIC·LEGACY

LIONEL LAMBOURNE

Although Godwin's son Edward Gordon Craig (1872–1966; fig. 13-1) was only three years of age when his parents separated in 1875, the career and character of the father was to have a profound effect on the life of the son. Both men had a love-hate relationship with the theater, for neither found lasting satisfaction in acting itself, but both formulated philosophies of stage presentation that affect the production of plays to this day.

The filial attitudes of two of Godwin's three children were vastly different. Edith Craig (1869–1947), Godwin's daughter, who was aged six at the time of the breakup, came to hate her father after he left, probably because his attempt to abduct her left lasting scars. Gordon Craig recalled with horror: "I shall ever remember one day in 1878 she asked me if I would like to see a portrait of my father—whom I had not seen since I was three years old and could not remember—and instantly she whipped out a terrible drawing someone had made for her, of a fiend with long teeth and claws and a tail, and said "There—that's him!"[1]

Edith, known as Edy, became an ardent feminist, fiercely distrustful of men, and the center of a colony of avant-garde women with a culture of their own. Her life, evoked in Virginia Woolf's last novel, *Between the Acts*, as the character "Miss La Trobe," was to end in the creation of the Ellen Terry Memorial Museum at Smallhythe in Kent. Her brother Gordon Craig was to become the theatrical prophet and seer whose experiments with nonrepresentational stage setting and atmospheric nonrealistic lighting

have passed into the general vocabulary of twentieth-century theater.

Of his father and their relationship, Craig wrote in his late twenties in 1901: "he who failed so much when he had the gifts to succeed—he is remembered as a failure—and they say 'see his son—another failure—like father like son' This won't do."[2] Craig tried to compensate for his father's lack of recognition by republishing the series of articles entitled The Architecture and Costume of Shakespeare's Plays, which had originally appeared in the *Architect* in 1875. They were presented in Craig's own important theatrical journal, the *Mask*, during the 1910s. This act of filial piety is surprising when it is remembered that Craig was himself always opposed to painstaking historical accuracy in productions of Shakespeare, but loyalty to his lost father seems to have persuaded him that his father's theories were indeed extremely radical. He particularly admired the way in which "my father had transformed the Circus into a Greek Theatre, giving a quite different new shape to the stage. A long, and not very high proscenium—but the eye could go up, following the high lines *behind* the proscenium—few borders or flapping cloths—that's original . . . . I'll inherit that, I thought . . . it seemed to me quite a big fortune."[3]

In *A Note on the Work of E. W. Godwin*, published in the *Mask*, Craig quoted from Godwin's 1875 review of pictures in the Royal Academy: "The accessories in pictures, whether on canvas or on the stage, should be altogether wrong or wholly right." Craig wrote approvingly that "the

Fig. 13-2. Edward Gordon Craig as a young man, 1897. Photograph, with pen and ink alterations made by Ellen Terry, possibly to stress the resemblance to E. W. Godwin. Collection of the National Trust, Ellen Terry Memorial Museum, Smallhythe Place, Kent.

suggestion that they may be altogether 'wrong,' that is to say, incorrect, is very illuminating for it shows that he [Godwin] realized that in the art of the theatre accuracy of detail is of no importance whatever provided it be entirely inaccurate . . . the producer's role was to represent the purely imaginative realm of the poetic drama removed from all realities, furnished and peopled with purely imaginative forms."[4]

Such sentiments are of course far more akin to Craig's own theories on the theater than those of his father. Half a century later in Craig's autobiographical memoirs, *Index to the Story of My Days* (1957), written at the age of eighty-four, he looked back at the early events of his long and romantic life: "Every other boy I knew had his mother *and* father. Not having mine—not hearing of mine—this grave sensation of *something being wrong* grew and grew into a fixed sort of small terror with me."[5]

He brooded over the "might have been" if his mother Ellen Terry and father E. W. Godwin had stayed together, fantasizing that they could have revolutionized the English stage. Deprived himself of a "remembrance of things past" like any child who has not known one of his parents, he

wondered what his father was like and speculated on the genetic cocktail of filial resemblance revealed in his own face (fig. 13-2). Like most young actors, Craig was intrigued by his own physical appearance, and the feminine cast of countenance which in Elizabethan times he speculated would have enabled him to play all the female roles in Shakespeare.[6] Craig kept wondering about his father's appearance, humorously regretting that "I was born with my father's chin. There was not very much of it."[7] Although dissatisfied with his chin, he was pleased to have inherited his father's nose.[8] When playing the role of the aged Edward IV in Irving's 1896 production of *Richard III* at the Lyceum, Craig even tried to become his father. As he described it, he "decided to make-up so as to look like E. W. G. for which I secured a photograph. It seems I managed to make up all right and I looked very like him."[9] Later in life, after retiring from acting, Craig wrote: "I came to have my father's eyelids too. His eyelids drooped down over his eyes—a hooded hawk—so he had the appearance of being conceited; but I very much doubt whether he was so."[10] Craig even produced an illustration to accompany these remarks (fig. 13-3). From his father Craig also "inherited his capacity to fall in love as easily as the White Knight falls off his horse."[11]

Throughout his life Craig mused obsessively over his fascination for the role of Hamlet and the play itself. As a young actor he had played the part at the age of twenty-two. He saw himself as Hamlet and his father as the Ghost, while Ophelia was all the silly girls who had fallen in love with him. He wrote of the mysterious hold that the role had on him:

Fig. 13-3. Edward Gordon Craig. Idealized portrait of his father, E. W. Godwin. From *The Mask* (October 1910).

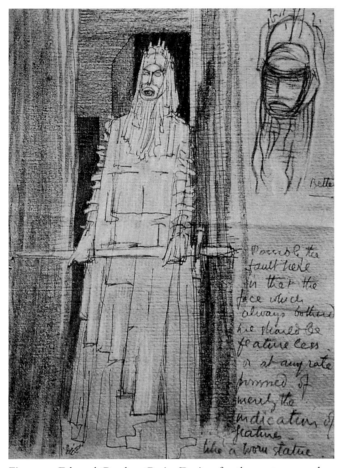

Fig. 13-4. Edward Gordon Craig. Design for the costume and mask of the Ghost in *Hamlet*, 1910. Collection, Österreichische Nationalbibliothek, Vienna.

Fig. 13-5. Edward Gordon Craig. Isadora Duncan, 1905. Collection of the National Trust, Ellen Terry Memorial Museum, Smallhythe Place, Kent.

Hamlet was not only a play to me nor he a role to be played—I somehow or other lived Hamlet day by day. Since I was so much like Hamlet myself I *had* to—not only were my weaknesses his, but his situation was almost mine. I too had lost a father— I too saw my mother married to another—I exaggerated these things then and supposed my stepfather might well have poisoned him in his orchard at Harpenden as he slept. And sleeping, vanished. For one day I perceived that he was not there any longer—I needed him—and he only came in darkest visions . . . and thus it came about that he grew in grandeur and immensity—a spectre and a reality, if truth be that, a possession—a patrimony—a blessing.[12]

The blessing became a burden, an obligation, almost a curse for Craig during the years in which he labored on

his famous production of the play, held in 1911 at the Moscow Art Theatre. It was one of the most influential theatrical events of the twentieth century. In it Craig's conception of the Ghost is of interest, for on the design sketch (fig. 13-4), he wrote: "Possibly the fault here is that the face which always bothered me should be featureless or at any rate possesses merely the indications of features like a worn statue."[13]

The opportunity for Craig to mount the production came about as a result of his love affair with the dancer Isadora Duncan (1878–1927; fig. 13-5) who called him "a creature like Shelley, made of fire and lightening."[14] They met in 1904 in Berlin, and their daughter Deirdre was born in Holland in 1906.[15] This was a very creative period for Craig, from which came a tremendous outpouring of work and ideas. In 1907 they separated, mainly because they realized that neither of them could give up their art for the other. Isadora remained convinced of Craig's genius, and

Fig. 13-6. Edward Gordon Craig. Design for a scene from *Hamlet*, 1907. Etching; 6½ x 4⅛ in. (16.5 x 10.5 cm). Trustees of the Victoria and Albert Museum, London, E.147-1922.

while performing in Moscow, she encouraged Constantin Stanislavsky, director of the Moscow Arts Theatre, which was famous for its productions of Chekhov, to invite Craig to Moscow. Stanislavsky offered Craig *carte blanche* in his choice of plays, and Craig chose *Hamlet*, although later he came to regret this as a major error.

Stanislavsky, in his memoirs, *My Life in Art,* described how Craig worked, using a model stage and "simple screens which could be placed upon the stage in endless combinations. They hinted at architectural forms, corners, niches, streets, aided by the imagination of the spectator" (fig. 13-6).[16] Stanislavsky further wrote that "The interplay of darkness and light was to symbolize the struggle in *Hamlet* between death and life. All this was wonderfully pictured in the sketch, but I, as the stage director, could not bring it to life on the stage."[17]

The court scene was particularly spectacular, a glittering cloth of gold streaming downstage from the king and queen, enveloping the figures of the fawning, corrupt courtiers whose heads and shoulders protruded through slits in the cloth like so many gravestones in a golden graveyard. Down in front the solitary black figure of Hamlet sat alone, part of a great shadow. Although difficulties with language caused many problems, Stanislavsky regarded the production as a success, as "an event without parallel in the history of the theatre . . . it was presented more than four hundred times."[18]

Craig's ideas were widely reported and blatantly appropriated by other designers throughout the world. Craig himself, perhaps recalling his father's production of *Helena in Troas*, which had been admired by W. B. Yeats, gave a set of his model screens to Yeats and Lady Gregory from which they made full scale versions for Yeats's *Plays for an Irish Theatre*. The screens remained in use at the Abbey Theatre until a fire in 1951.

The mobile stage, the white movable screens, and the dramatic use of light and dark that was so central to Craig's theatrical credo, are usually said to derive from his study of

Fig. 13-7. Edward Gordon Craig. Stage setting labeled "The Herald," 1907. Proof for etching; 8³⁄₁₆ x 5¹³⁄₁₆ in. (20.8 x 14.8 cm) Trustees of the Victoria and Albert Museum, London, E.92-1922.

Fig. 13-8. Helen Craig. Portrait of her father, Edward Anthony Craig with a ca. 1955 photograph of his father, Edward Gordon Craig, also by Helen Craig, 1968. Courtesy of Helen Craig

Serlio's *Five Books of Architecture* and his decision to create a "scene" so mobile that it might move in all directions (fig. 13-7). These ideas can also perhaps be traced back to his fixation on his lost father, which dominated his early years, finding perhaps its clearest expression in a dream that Craig recorded in the notebook, "Confessions 1900—1901—1902":

> One night I thought that I saw and spoke with my father. Although I had never seen him whilst he lived I fancied him in my dream that his face was as familiar to me as Mother's—But it was terribly sad. We sat on boxes that floated on a calm sea. At times . . . standing on his floating box he would pour out a torrent of praise and love addressed to his lost lady, my mother . . . All the time his eyes would rain tears which ran down into the salt water and spread round him in rings of crimson, purple and black which with the green of the sea combined to make the most pleasing effect that delighted us (my father and myself) exceedingly. We were both astonished at the colours for after all said he "they cannot be tears of blood" and laughed—and I replied "nor coloured tears, father."[19]

Craig's dream continues in the same vein until, after hearing "strange old English airs, madrigals and glees," he concludes: "I looked around me. The sea, the boxes, my father—had all disappeared—and there in front of me sat thousands and thousands of gods and goddesses as in a huge theatre . . . All the walls were made of white wood and everyone was dressed in white."[20]

In his eighties Gordon Craig enjoyed reading the biography of Godwin by Dudley Harbron.[21] Of it he wrote: "Mr Harbron's book on E. W. G. is carefully done, and only after much patient research. Most of the information it contains was unknown to me—but I knew the truth about E. W. G. through my blood and bones."[22] His knowledge also came from the self-induced memories of the work of his father in the theater which they both loved.

Gordon Craig's son Edward (Teddy) Craig (1905–1998; fig. 13-8) played an important part in British film design. As a boy he lived for a time with Ellen Terry in Kent, before joining his father in Rome as "pupil assistant," helping to produce the *Mask* and to assemble the "International Exhibition of Theatre Art and Craft." He began his independent career working under the name of Edward Carrick, determined to get by on his own merits, under a different name. He considered that the movie camera rather than the stage could best convey the effects and theories about light and movement advocated by his father. His own film career was to include a wide range of popular productions ranging from musicals by Gracie Fields to horror films with Bette Davis, and wartime propaganda films such as *Target for To-night* (1941) and *Fires Were Started* (1943). In 1937 he founded Britain's first film school, and later wrote an influential book, *Art and Design in the British Film* (1948), based on an important exhibition at the Victoria and Albert Museum. He wrote a major biography of his father, entitled *Gordon Craig: The Story of his Life*, after his father's death in 1968.[23] And so the genetic legacy continues, proving the truth of Sherlock Holmes's observation: "Art in the blood can take strange forms."

Note: Most published sources are cited below in shortened form (author's last name, abbreviated title, date of publication); full references will be found in the bibliography. Frequently cited archives are abbreviated below; for a key to the abbreviations, also see the bibliography.

1. E. G. Craig, *Ellen Terry* (1931): 59

2. From notebook entitled "Confessions 1901—1902—1903—," quoted in E. A. Craig in *Gordon Craig* (1968): 142.

3. E. G. Craig, *Ellen Terry* (1931): 125.

4. Godwin, "Notes on the Costume in the Pictures at the Royal Academy" (29 May 1875): 315.

5. E. G. Craig, *Index* (1957): 48.

6. Ibid., p. 130.

7. Ibid., p. 10.

8. Ibid., p. 130.

9. Ibid., p. 181.

10. Ibid., p. 130.

11. Ibid., p. 10.

12. Ibid., pp. 162, 163.

13. Inscribed on the drawing, Osterreichische National Bibliothek, Vienna, H.R. 13195a.

14. Isadora Duncan, *My Life* (New York: Boni and Liveright, 1927), chap. 19.

15. Deirdre was tragically drowned in the Seine in Paris in 1913 (E. A. Craig, *Gordon Craig* [1968]: 285).

16. Constantin Stanislavski, *My Life in Art*, trans. J. J. Robbins (Boston: Little, Brown, 1924), 511.

17. Ibid., p. 519.

18. Ibid., p. 524.

19. Quoted in E. A. Craig, *Gordon Craig* (1968): 141, 142.

20. Ibid., p. 142.

21. Harbron, *Conscious Stone* (1949).

22. E. G. Craig, *Index* (1957), 14.

23. E. A.. Craig, *Gordon Craig* (1968).

•CHRONOLOGY•
•CHECKLIST OF THE EXHIBITION•
•BIBLIOGRAPHY•

·CHRONOLOGY·

The Life and Career of
Edward William Godwin (1833–1886)

Compiled by Susan Weber Soros

Much of the information below has been taken from Godwin's own diaries, journals, letters, and drawings, most of which are now in the Victoria and Albert Museum, London, and the Royal Institute of British Architects, London. Other records of his architectural work exist in the Procter and Palmer archives, Clevedon, near Bristol. In these papers, Godwin offers tantalizing hints of projects that have otherwise defied detection, and although every effort has been made to attach an address or client name to these projects, many records remain incomplete. Contemporary periodicals were also useful in compiling this chronology. For architectural work, dates separated by dashes indicate the beginning and end of a project, from initial design to completion. Dates separated by slants indicate that Godwin worked intermittently on the project over this period of time. The present status of a building is given at the end of the entry whenever possible. Actual dates of demolition, however, are largely omitted because a great deal of uncertainty surrounds them. For architectural work during the years of Godwin's partnership with Henry Crisp, the firm name is listed at the end of the entry; in most cases, however, Godwin alone was responsible for the design.

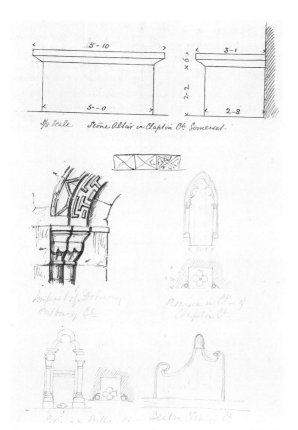

Fig. C1. E. W. Godwin. Page from a sketchbook: antiquarian sketches, ca. 1849. Pencil, pen and ink, sepia wash; 6¾ x 9¼ in. (17.3 x 23.5 cm). Trustees of the Victoria and Albert Museum, London, E.267-1963. *Checklist no. 3*

1833
May 26—Edward William Godwin born at 12 Old Market Street, Bristol to William and Ann Jones Godwin.

n.d.
Attends Exley's School, Cotham, Highbury, Bristol.

1846
September 12—His father, William Godwin, dies.

1848
Begins to take detailed notes and make measurements of medieval remains in and around Bristol (fig. C1).

ca. 1848
Articled to William Armstrong, City Surveyor, Architect and Civil Engineer at 7 Brunswick Square, Bristol.

1850
Assists William Armstrong with the conversion of the Dominican Friary in Bristol to a Quaker school.

1850–51
Student member of the Bristol Society of Architects.

1851
Holidays with fellow apprentice architect James Hine to study ruins and architectural sites in Cornwall. Member of the Archaeological Institute, London. Co-authors and co-illustrates *The Architectural Antiquities of Bristol and Its Neighbourhood* with W. C. Burder and James Hine.

ca. 1852

Establishes his own architectural practice in Bristol.

1852–53

First commission, to design a small Gothic school, Trinity Branch School, in Easton near Bristol for Rev. D. Cooper (demolished).

1853, 1859–60

Restores and refurnishes the church of Saint John, Littlehempston, Devonshire, for Rev. Fitz-Henry Hele.

1854

Establishes his own office, as architect and surveyor, at 1 Surrey Street, Bristol. Makes preliminary design for his own cottage at Colerne. Co-supervises, with Rev. Gilbert Heathcote, the excavation of a Roman villa near Colerne in Wiltshire. September— Exhibits drawings, with descriptions, of a Roman tesselated pavement found at Colerne and some fragments of pottery as part of a group exhibition at the Temporary Museum at the New Town Hall, Chippenham, Wiltshire.

1854, 1859–61

Designs additions and furnishings for the rectory, restores the nave, and refurnishes the church of Saint Christopher, Ditteridge, Wiltshire, for Rev. W. N. Heathcote.

1854–55, 1861

Restores and refurnishes the church of Saint John the Baptist, Colerne, Wiltshire, for Rev. H. F. Atherley.

1854–71

Restores and refurnishes the church of Saint Philip and Saint Jacob, Bristol (with James Hine; subsequently with Henry Crisp).

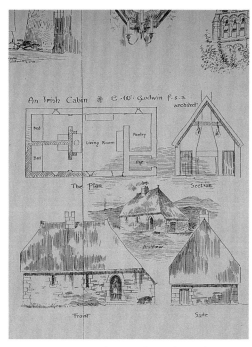

Fig. C2. E. W. Godwin. "The Cabin of an Irish Patriot." From "Rambling Sketches . . . No. 1," *British Architect* 15 (25 February 1881).

1856

Designs a factory on Merchant Street, Bristol, for horsehair merchant James Smith (demolished).

1856–58

Spends two years in Ireland where he and his brother Joseph Lucas, a civil engineer, work on a competition for a proposed railway bridge in Londonderry (not executed).

1856–57

Designs a number of small cottages (fig. C2) with attached pigsty in Ireland.

1857–60

Designs Saint Baithen's Church, St. Johnstown, County Donegal, Ireland. This is the first illustration of a completed architectural project by Godwin to be published (see the *Builder* [9 May 1857]).

1857–61

Designs a small church, Saint Columcille, in West Town, Tory Island, County Donegal, Ireland.

ca. 1857–61

Designs All Saints Church, Newtowncunningham, County Donegal, Ireland.

1858

Returns to Bristol and resumes his practice. Plans and surveys a house for Miss Elizabeth L. Sale, 4 Portland Street, Kingsdown, Bristol. Designs a proposed Italian Villa with Tower (with James Hine). Designs a proposed Roman Catholic school in Jersey (with James Hine). Submits competition design for Town Hall, Newton Limvaddy, Ireland.

1858–59

Meets fellow architect William Burges and begins a friendship that would continue until Burges's death in 1881. Godwin probably sees Burges's collection of Japanese objects and prints. Designs a factory at 104 Stokes Croft, Bristol, for Perry and Sons, manufacturers of carriages and harnesses (later known as Anderson's Warehouse).

1858–60

Restores and designs windows for Saint Paul de Leon Church, Staverton, Devon, for Rev. H. F. Atherley.

1858–61

Designs Western College, Plymouth, Devon (with James Hine).

1859

Surveys and reports on 203 Tottenham Court Road, London, for Miss Harwood. Designs a proposed house in Birmingham (with James Hine). Designs a proposed Conservatory Dome (with James Hine). Designs a proposed tower, Christ Church, Plymouth, Devon (with James Hine). Designs a granite drinking fountain, King Street, for Mr. W. D. Wills of Portland Square, Bristol (demolished.). Makes a report and arbitration for a greenhouse for Mr. G. Halkert and Mr. R. M. Bryant, Swansea, Wales. Submits competition design for a New Tabernacle for the Reverend Spurgeon's Chapel at Newington, London (unpremiated). November 1—

Fig. C3. E. W. Godwin. The Great Hall, Northampton Guildhall (formerly known as Northampton Town Hall), 1861–64. Photographed in 1998.

Marries Sarah Yonge, the daughter of Rev. William Clarke Yonge of Henley-on-Thames, Oxfordshire. The newlyweds live at Brighton Villa, Richmond Road, Upper Montpelier, Bristol.

1860
Wins competition design for the proposed Saint Philip and Jacob's Schools, Mary Bush Lane, Bristol (with J. A. Clark). (The building as it exists today has been much altered.) Designs new furnishings and a wood gate for the churchyard of the church of Saint Wynwallow, Landewednack, Cornwall, for Rev. Vyvyan Robinson. Makes alterations and interior decoration of Ivywell House, 9 Ivywell Road, Bristol, for Mr. A. Henderson, a solicitor, of 501 Broad Street, Bristol (with J. A. Clark). Unspecified designs for Rosenbery Exchange Bank (with James Hine). Submits competition design for Clifton College, Bristol, and secures third premium.

1860–62
Designs Nos. 10 and 11 Rockleaze, Sneyd Park, Bristol, for Mr. H. J. Brown, solicitor, of Corn Street, Bristol (with J. A. Clark).

1860–63
Restores and refurnishes Saint Grada Church, Grade, Cornwall, for Rev. F. C. Jackson.

1861
Designs a proposed bank at Exeter, Devon (with James Hine). Submits competition design for Market and Schools, Ilfracombe, Devon.

1861–64
Wins competition design and builds the new Town Hall, Northampton (fig. C3). Design includes furniture and decorations.

1862
Submits competition design for a college, Malvern, Hereford and Worcester. Moves with his wife to 21 Portland Square, Bristol, where he decorates and furnishes the interior with Persian rugs laid over the bare wood floors, a few artfully placed Japanese prints on the walls, and selected pieces of Georgian furniture placed against plainly colored wall. Restores and refurnishes the church of Saint Botolph, Northfleet, Kent, including the design of the east window and the sedilia (fig. C4), for Rev. G. Akers. Makes alterations of premises at 4 Ashley Place, Westminster, London, for Mr. Thomas Turner. Submits competition design for Preston Town Hall, Lancashire. Makes alterations to house in Abingdon Street, Northampton, for Pickering Phipps.

1862–63
Designs panels for Theatre Royal, Bath.

1862–64
Designs the apse, cloister, and tower, and the pulpit desk, for Highbury Chapel, Bristol, which was originally designed by Butterfield in 1842–43. Designs the accompanying Highbury Chapel Schools.

1862–65
Writes occasional reviews, called "Jottings" and signed "G," of theatrical productions in Bristol and London for the *Western Daily Press*.

1862–72
Elected Fellow of the Society of Antiquaries.

Fig. C4. E. W. Godwin. Sedilia in the church of Saint Botolph, Northfleet, Kent, 1862. Photographed in 1998.

1862–73

Elected Fellow and Honorary Secretary and Librarian of the Bristol Society of Architects.

1863

Holidays with wife Sarah in France to study Gothic architecture in Amiens, Paris, and Chartres. Designs a dress for Ellen Terry for the character of Titania in James Chute's production of *A Mid-*

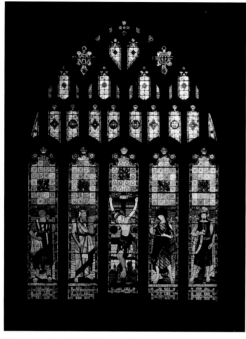

Fig. C5. E. W. Godwin. The east window, Saint Philip's Church, Bristol, 1864. Photographed in 1998.

summer Night's Dream at the Theatre Royal, Bath, first performed on March 4. (The costume is not used.) Submits competition design for a proposed cathedral of Saint Finn Barr in Cork, Ireland. (The competition is won by Burges.) Submits a competition design for Cheltenham Parish Church, Gloucestershire. Writes a lecture for the Bristol Society of Architects, "The Sister Arts and their relation to Architecture."

1864

Forms a partnership with architect Henry Crisp, and they open a joint office in Godwin's house at 21 Portland Square, Bristol, as Godwin and Crisp. Surveys the Vicarage, Almondsbury, Glos., for Lady Emile Gray and the Reverend Murray Browne (Godwin and Crisp). Submits a competition design for a new town hall at East Retford, Nottinghamshire, and wins a premium (Godwin and Crisp). Submits a competition design for Chester Town Hall, Chesire, and wins second premium (Godwin and Crisp). Submits competition design for Rochdale Town Hall, Greater Manchester (Godwin and Crisp). Submits competition design for Hull Exchange, Lincolnshire (Godwin and Crisp). Designs a tombstone, curb, and rails for the grave of Rev. S. E. Day at Almondsbury, Glos., for his widow Lady Emile Gray (Godwin and Crisp). Designs a stained-glass window (fig. C5) for the east end of Saint

Philip's Church, Bristol, in memory of Rev. S. E. Day (Godwin and Crisp). Surveys and reports on the restoration of Bristol Cathedral, formerly the Abbey Church of Saint Augustine (Godwin and Crisp). Establishes a Bristol Society of Architects committee to study the setting up of a "Students Class" to facilitate the passing of exams at the Royal Institute of British Architects (R.I.B.A).

1864/66

Designs All Saints School, Church Road, Winterbourne Down, Glos., for Rev. F. W. Greenstreet (Godwin and Crisp). (This building was converted to a house in 1966.)

1864–67

Wins design competition and builds Congleton Town Hall in Cheshire (Godwin and Crisp).

1865

Godwin and Crisp relocate their office to Rupert Chambers, 2 Quay Street, Bristol. Designs a memorial window to honor Rev. Henry Gray at Almondsbury Church, Glos., for Lady Emile Gray and Viscount Glentworth (Godwin and Crisp). May 3— Sarah Godwin dies after a long illness. Writes *A Handbook of Floral Decoration for Churches* (fig. C6), published by J. Master's and Sons, London. Searches for a possible site for the Bristol New Theatre for the Bristol New Theatre Company. Designs St. Martin's Villas, 43–44 Billing Road, Northampton, for Pickering Phipps (Godwin and Crisp). Travels with William Burges to Ire-

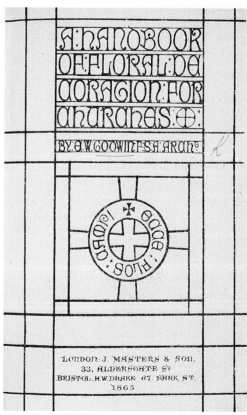

Fig. C6. E. W. Godwin. Frontispiece for *A Handbook of Floral Decoration for Churches* (1865) Furniture and Woodwork Department, Victoria and Albert Museum, London.

land to visit Conway. Visits Roman ruins and medieval sites in Somerset with Lord and Lady Limerick in preparation for Dromore Castle project. October—Establishes a London office at 23 Baker Street, Portman Square, London, leaving Crisp to manage the Bristol office. Submits competition design for Cheltenham College Boarding Houses, Glos. (Godwin and Crisp). Submits competition design for Wolverhampton New Town Hall, West Midlands (Godwin and Crisp). Completes work begun by fellow architect S. B. Gabriel, at the request of Gabriel's widow. The projects include Crews Hole Schools, Saint John's Church, Clifton, and a greenhouse at Clevedon (Godwin and Crisp).

1865–66
Submits competition design for restoration and addition to Stroud Church, Glos. (Godwin and Crisp). Completes work begun by fellow Bristol architect T. S. Hack, at the request of Hack's widow, including Princes Building, Clifton, and Stockland Bristol Church, near Bridgwater, Somerset (Godwin and Crisp).

1865/67
Makes a preliminary design for the Tea Warehouse for Messrs. Polglase, Small Street, Bristol (Godwin and Crisp).

1866
Assists William Burges with his drawings for the New Law Courts competition, Strand in London. Designs stained-glass windows (fig. C7) for church of All Saints, Winterbourne Down, Glos. (Godwin and Crisp). Makes preliminary design for proposed church in Easton, Bristol, for Rev. D. Cooper (Godwin and Crisp). Makes preliminary design for proposed church at Grafton, Torquay, Devon (Godwin and Crisp). Submits competition design for West of England Dissenters' Proprietary School, Taunton, Somerset (Godwin and Crisp). Submits competition design for proposed Manchester Town Hall (Godwin and Crisp).

1866–
Designs wallpaper for Metford Warner of Jeffrey and Company, 64 Essex Road, Islington, London.

1866–67
Submits competition designs for the proposed Assize Courts, Bristol. Godwin and Crisp awarded first, second, and third premiums (not executed according to Godwin's designs.)

1866–67
Designs workshops and offices at Lawrence Hill, Bristol, for the Bristol Wagon Works Company (Godwin and Crisp).

1866–69
Designs parish room, Village Hall, Westbury-on-Trym, Bristol (Godwin and Crisp).

1866/71
Makes preliminary design for a house in London for Percy J. Waite (Godwin and Crisp).

1866–73
Designs and decorates Dromore Castle, County Limerick, Ireland, and accompanying stables and cottage for the 3rd Earl of Limerick (Godwin and Crisp). (The building is now in ruins.)

ca. 1867
Becomes a member of the Arts Club, London.

Fig. C7. East window in the church of All Saints, Winterbourne Down, Glos., 1866. Photographed in 1998.

1867
Again submits competition designs for the proposed Assize Courts, Bristol. This was the third competition held for this project. Godwin and Crisp awarded second premium. Designs two new wards, post-mortem room, and morgue for the Royal Infirmary, Bristol (Godwin and Crisp). (The work is much altered today.) Converts a chapel in Unity Street, Bristol, to create Saint Philip's Dining Hall (Godwin and Crisp). Designs a buffet for Mr. J. W. Wilson of Gothenburg, Sweden. Relocates the London office of Godwin and Crisp to 197 Albany Street, Regents Park, London. Designs Anglo-Japanese sideboard, coffee table, chair with caned seat and back, and other furniture for his London chambers.

1867/71
Designs furniture (buffet, table, chairs) for Mr. Thomas Wells of 14 Manchester Square, London. Designs furniture for Mr. J. Passmore Edwards, 31 Tavistock Street, London.

1867–70
Designs Glenbeigh Towers, County Kerry, Ireland, including main house and stables, for Hon. Roland Winn (Godwin and Crisp; the buildings are now in ruins).

1867–86
Designs furniture, wallpapers, and other furnishings for the firm of William Watt, 21 Grafton Street, Gower Street, London.

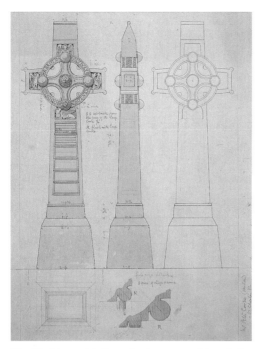

Fig. C8. Memorial Cross for the graves of Annabelle, Dowager Viscountess Glentworth and the Hon. Lady Caroline E. J. B. Pery, Kensal Green Cemetery, London, ca. 1869. Sepia pen and wash, pencil details, red pen labeling; 13 ¹³⁄₁₆ x 10 ⅝ in. (35.1 x 26.2 cm). British Architectural Library Drawings Collection, RIBA, London, Ran 7/C/8. *Checklist no. 31*

1868

Begins a six-year illicit liaison with actress Ellen Terry. Godwin decorates their residence, which is known as the Red House, Gustard Wood Common near Harpenden, Hertfordshire. Makes preliminary designs for the restoration and redecoration of the Walton Parish Church, near Clevedon, Somerset, for Rev. W. Hautenville (Godwin and Crisp). Makes a preliminary design for a church and school at Knowle, Bristol, for Rev. H. N. Turton (Godwin and Crisp). Designs a proposed tower and wall for Ashridge, near Little Gaddeston, Hertfordshire, and a school at Studham, Bedfordshire, for Lady Marion Alford. Surveys premises in Anerley, London, for Charles Lane, a solicitor (Godwin and Crisp). Designs two shops with flats above at 74 and 76 Stokes Croft, Bristol, for Rev. R. W. Gotch (Godwin and Crisp; the site as it exists today is altered). Restores the stonework and designs stained glass for the west window of Collingtree Church, Northamptonshire. Designs a cottage in Collingtree, Northamptonshire, for Pickering Phipps (Godwin and Crisp). Designs a post office at Glenbeigh, County Kerry, Ireland, for Hon. Roland Winn, (Godwin and Crisp). Designs cottages at Wedmore, Somerset (Godwin and Crisp).

1868–69

Designs additions to Saint Philip and Saint Jacob's Schools, Bristol (Godwin and Crisp). Surveys and makes alterations to houses in Chelsea and Bayswater, London, for Mr. E. C. Sterling. Designs Rheinfeldon House on Billing Road, Northampton, for Picker-

ing Phipps (Godwin and Crisp; demolished). Designs gatehouse, two lodges, walls and gateway for kitchen garden, and gates to the Chase at Castle Ashby, Northamptonshire, for the Marquess of Northampton (Godwin and Crisp). Designs furniture for the Art Furniture Company, 25 Garrick Street, Covent Garden, London.

1869

April 8—Godwin's mother, Ann Jones Godwin, dies. Designs an ebonized cabinet/desk for C. L. Lane, a solicitor. Designs Mitre Works exhibition buildings in Wolverhampton, West Midlands, for F. C. Clark (Godwin and Crisp). Designs a monumental cross (fig. C8) for Kensal Green Cemetery, London, commissioned by the third Earl of Limerick for the graves of Anabella Dowager Viscountess Glentworth, and the Honourable Lady Caroline E. J. B. Pery (Godwin and Crisp). Designs the proposed Irish Constabulary Barracks for the Earl of Limerick, County Kerry (Godwin and Crisp). Designs a stained-glass window for Charles C. Dix, possibly for Mamhilad, Monmouthshire, Wales (Godwin and Crisp). Designs a proposed parish church, possibly for Horfield Road, Bristol (Godwin and Crisp). Designs a Memorial Cross for Coalpit Heath, Bristol (Godwin and Crisp). December 9—A daughter, Edith (Edy), is born to Godwin and Terry. She later calls herself Edith Craig, and in 1887 she is christened with the name Edith Geraldine Alisa Craig.

1869–70

Designs an enlarged cottage, new coach house, and stables at Cherry Orchard Farm, Westbury-on-Trym, Bristol, for George Smith (Godwin and Crisp).

1869–74

Submits competition design for Plymouth Town Hall, Devon, as consulting architect with Hine and Norman (damaged in World War II).

Fig. C9. E. W. Godwin. "Stables, Treherne House, Hampstead." From *Architect* (London) 5 (10 June 1871).

1870

Designs an apiary for the kitchen garden, Castle Ashby, Northamptonshire (Godwin and Crisp). Makes alterations to Polglase and Company Warehouse, Stephen Street, Bristol (Godwin and Crisp).

1870–71

Designs stables and new rectory for Little Gaddesden, Hertsfordshire, for Rev. Charlton George Lane (Godwin and Crisp; much altered). Designs alterations to Saint Philip's Church, Stepney, London (fig. C10).

Fig. C10. "St. Philip's Church, Stepney, Showing Alterations Designed by E. W. Godwin, F.S.A." From *Architect* (London) 6 (23 December 1871).

1870–72

Designs stables (fig. C9) for John Fletcher, Esq., at Treherne House, West End Road, Hampstead, London (Godwin and Crisp; demolished).

1871

January 18—Partnership with Crisp comes to an end. Designs hall and window decoration for Henry Christian at 197 Albany Street, Regents Park, London. Makes designs for alterations and redecorations (including stained glass, painting, sculpture) to the church of Saints Peter and Paul, Little Gaddesden, Hertfordshire. Makes preliminary designs for the decoration of east end and a stained-glass window for Oxford

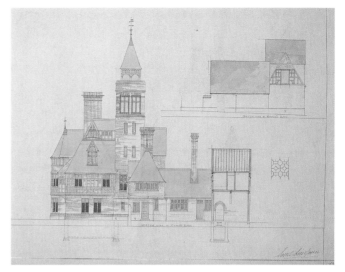

Fig. C11. Beauvale House, Newthorpe, Nottinghamshire: northeast elevation, ca. 1872–73. India ink, colored washes, and pencil details, 16 x 22 in. (40.6 x 55.9 cm). British Architectural Library Drawings Collection, RIBA, London, Ran 7/D/8 (10). *Checklist no. 44*

Chapel, Vere Street, London, for Rev. Ashley. Submits competition designs for proposed Leicester Municipal Buildings and takes first premium (not executed according to Godwin's designs). Submits competition design for proposed Winchester Town Hall, Hampshire, and takes second premium. (The first-place winner reused Godwin's plan of Northampton Town Hall.) Designs proposed stables, coach house, and conservatory probably for Rheinfeldon, Billing Road, in Northampton for Pickering Phipps. Designs proposed garden gymnasium in the Japanese style for an unidentified client.

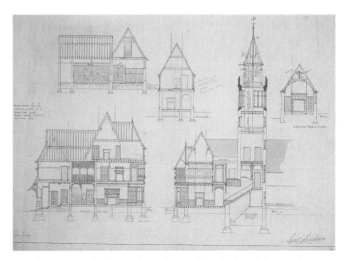

Fig. C12. Beauvale House, Newthorpe, Nottinghamshire: sections, ca. 1872–73. India ink, colored washes, and pencil details; 16 x 22 in. (40.6 x 55.9 cm). British Architectural Library Drawings Collection, RIBA, London, Ran 7/D/8 (11). *Checklist no. 45*

1871, 1874

Designs furniture and interior decoration for Dr. George Bird, 49 Welbeck Street, Cavendish Square, London.

1871–72

Designs a new home for himself and Ellen Terry, called Fallows Green, Sun Lane, Harpenden, Hertfordshire (demolished).

1871–73

Designs Beauvale House (figs. C11, C12) and its gardens, near Eastwood, Nottinghamshire, for Earl Cowper.

1872

January 16—A son, Edward (Teddy) is born to Godwin and Ellen Terry. He later calls himself Edward Henry Gordon Craig. Relocates his office to 29 Craven Street, London. Exhibits fourteen architectural drawings at Church Congress, Nottingham. Submits competition design for the proposed Houses of Parliament, Berlin, Germany (with Robert W. Edis). Submits competition design for the proposed Saint Ann's Heath Lunatic Asylum, Surrey (with J. P. Seddon). Makes plans for the restoration of the pedestal figures for the Shrine of Saint Amphibalus discovered at Saint Albans, Hertfordshire. May—Exhibits architectural drawings at the Royal Academy of Arts, including those for Municipal Buildings, Leicester. Designs three cottages at Melbourne Hall, Derbyshire, for Earl Cowper.

1872–73

Designs a small house for Mr. William in Hixon, Staffordshire, for the estate of Lord Ferrers.

1872–74

Enters into a design agreement, with monthly retainer, with Collinson and Lock, Art Furnishers, 109 Fleet Street, London.

1873

Holidays in Bayeux, Lisieux, and Saint-Lô, France. Submits competition design for the City Hall and County Building, Chicago, Illinois. Designs the decoration for house and conservatory at 69 Addison Road, Kensington, London, for John Wingate McLaren, commissioned by Collinson and Lock. Designs the decoration for Grey Towers, Nunthrope, Middlesbrough, for William Randolph Innes Hopkins, commissioned by Collinson and Lock (Grey Towers is now in ruins). Decorates the hallway of a club in Eastbourne, East Sussex, for Collinson and Lock. Designs a Parson's house known as The Manse at 128 Moorgreen, Moor Green, Nottinghamshire, with accompanying furniture and stables, for Earl Cowper. Designs a proposed Greek church, Notting Hill, London. Designs a proposed theater on Oxford and Hanway streets, Westminster, London. Designs five pieces of furniture and installation for Collinson and Lock exhibition stand at the Vienna Universal Exhibition. Designs chairs and ceiling decoration for Prince Esterhazy of Vienna, son of the ambassador to England, commissioned by Collinson and Lock. Travels to Vienna to meet George Lock at the Vienna Universal Exhibition. Submits competition design for the proposed Parliament House, Pietermaritzburg, Natal. Submits competition design for a proposed Unitarian Congregational church, High Pavement, Nottingham. Submits competition design for the proposed Sunderland Town Hall, Tyne and Weir, Durham. Acts as consulting architect for Robert Edis's competition design for proposed new schools at Battersea, School Board of London. Designs furniture for Mr. Smalley, Cherlin Place, Hyde Park, London, commissioned by Collinson and Lock. Designs bay window for Count Pallfy of Hungary, commissioned by Collinson and Lock.

1873–74

Designs a mantelpiece and octagonal center table for James Goodwin of Hartford, Connecticut, commissioned by Collinson and Lock.

1874

Godwin and Terry move to 20 Taviton Street, Gordon Square, London, and Godwin decorates the rooms. Relocates office to 6 John Street, Adelphi Chambers, London. Makes alterations to a church in Croydon, London. Designs a "Co-operative Home" based on E. M. King's proposed specifications and requirements published in the *Building News* (24 April 1874). Writes a series of articles on his travel through Normandy for the *Building News*. June—Collaborates with Whistler on the installation of Whistler's works at 48 Pall Mall, London, where a brown color scheme was complemented by colored screens and pottery. Designs Anglo-Egyptian as well as Anglo-Greek furniture and decorations for Waugh and Sons, 65 Tottenham Court Road, London. Designs fabrics for Cowlishaw, Nicol and Company, 23 Portland Street, Manchester. Designs fabrics for Warner and Ramm, 9 Newgate Street, London, and Hollybush Gardens, Bethnal Green Road, London. Writes a series of thirty-three articles on Shakespeare's plays for the *Architect*. Establishes contact with Christopher Dresser. Decorates house at 27 Gordon Square, London, for Mr. Philip Jordan. Designs a series of Cottage-style furniture for Collinson and Lock.

1874–77

Designs furniture and a Jacobean library and painted panels for Gillow and Company of Oxford Street, London.

1874–80

Designs wallpapers for James Toleman and Sons, 170 Goswell Road, London.

1875

Designs a block of two semidetached cottages (52 and 54 Moorgreen) and makes alterations to a farmhouse (31 Moorgreen) at Moor Green, near Eastwood, Nottinghamshire, for Earl Cowper. Designs Old Oaks Farm, a farmhouse and dairy, at Moor Green, Nottinghamshire, for Earl Cowper. Designs a monument to Bishop Coke, Hereford Cathedral, Hereford and Worcester. Designs a proposed curate's house at Bagthorpe, Selston, Nottinghamshire. Submits competition design for Paisley Town Hall, Renfrewshire, Scotland. Serves as historical consultant for the Bancrofts' production of *The Merchant of Venice,* starring Ellen Terry as Portia and first performed at the Prince of Wales Theatre on April 17. Godwin and Ellen Terry separate. Establishes a combined office and home at 34 Essex Street, Strand, London.

1875–78
Designs corner houses and semidetached pairs of houses for the Bedford Park Estate, Turnham Green, Chiswick, London. Corner houses are at 1, 2, 37, 39, The Avenue; 2, 35, 37, Woodstock Road; 1, 2, Queen Anne's Grove; and 10 Bedford Road. Semidetached houses are at 3 and 5, The Avenue; 7 and 9, The Avenue; 12 and 14, The Avenue; 16 and 18, The Avenue.

1876
January 4—Marries Beatrice Philip, a pupil in his office. Relocates his office to 8 Victoria Chambers, Westminster, London. October 1—A son, Edward (the same name given to his illegitimate son with Ellen Terry) is born to Godwin and Beatrice. He is known as Ted or Teddy. Collinson and Lock displays Godwin's Anglo-Japanese cabinet at the Philadelphia Centennial Exhibition. Designs the Monkey Cabinet, for William Watt. Designs ceramics for William Brownfield and Sons, Cobridge, Staffordshire. Writes a six-part series of articles entitled "My House 'In' London" and a two-part article entitled "My Chambers and What I Did to Them" for the *Architect*. Designs cartoons for Cox and Sons, 3 Southampton Street, Strand, London. Acts as archaeological superintendant, including design of costumes, props, and scenery, for John Coleman's production of Shakespeare's *Henry V*, first performed at the Queen's Theatre, Long Acre, on September 16. Submits competition design for Byron Memorial, London. Designs furniture and floor cloths for Waugh and Sons, 65 Tottenham Court Road, London. Designs a proposed theater, Panton Street, Westminster. Submits competition design for Free Library and Art Gallery, Southport, Merseyside. Submits competition design for Free Library and Museum, Derby, Derbyshire. Submits competition design for Esclusham Church near Wrexham for Rev. J. Dixon. Makes preliminary design for a townhouse for Mr. J. W. Wilson of Gothenburg, Sweden, through an agent named Constable. Designs reredos for an unidentified church in Monkton Wyld, Dorset, for Rev. B. M. Camm. Designs interior (painted ceiling, mantelpiece, and fireplace) for photographer Frederick Hollyer, 9 Pembroke Square, Kensington, London.

1876, 1881
Designs a proposed theater, Northumberland Avenue, Westminster, London.

1877
Submits competition design for Wakefield Town Hall, West Yorkshire. Submits competition design for Vestry Hall, Kensington, London (with J. P. Seddon). Submits competition design for lodge and buffet for recreation ground, Sydenham, London. Submits competition design for Baths and Wash Houses, Manchester. Submits competition design for Barrow-in-Furness Town Hall and Public Offices, Cumbria. Submits competition design for Reading Town Hall, Berkshire. Designs Hunt's Hill Cottages, 259 and 260 Willey Lane, Moor Green, near Eastwood, Nottinghamshire, for Earl Cowper. Designs a new masthead for the *British*

Architect. Wins competition design and builds the Nottingham Church Cemetery Chapel, Mansfield Road, Nottinghamshire (demolished). The first edition of William Watt's catalogue, *Art Furniture from designs by E. W. Godwin, F.S.A. and others, with hints and suggestions on domestic furniture and decoration* is published in London by B. T. Batsford. Designs proposed licensed restaurant in Battersea Park, London. Submits competition design for boat and club house on the banks of the River Thames at Putney, London, for the Thames Boathouse Company. Submits competition design for a hotel in Coventry, West Midlands. Designs frieze decoration for Gillow and Company, for the vaulted ceiling of the main staircase of the Midland Grand Hotel, adjacent to Saint Pancras Station, London. Submits report on Caenwood Towers for Gillow and Company, London. Submits competition design for Judge's Lodgings, Swansea, Wales. Designs Chaucerian costumes for Gillow and Company.

1877–78
Designs 4, 5, and 6 Chelsea Embankment, Kensington, London, for Gillow and Company.

1877–79
Designs and decorates the White House, 35 Tite Street, London, for James McNeill Whistler (demolished).

1878
January—Creates decoration for a masked ball, using purchases from Liberty, for an unidentified client. Submits competition

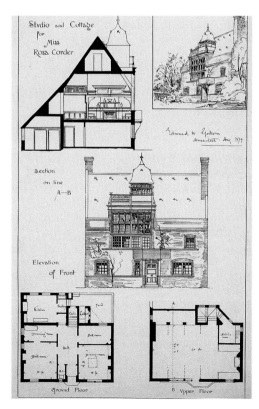

Fig. C13. E. W. Godwin. "Studio and Cottage for Miss Rosa Corder." From *British Architect* 12 (3 October 1879).

design for Yarmouth Municipal Offices, Norfolk. Collaborates with Whistler on the Butterfly Suite for William Watt's stand at the Paris Exposition Universelle. Jeffrey and Company exhibit Godwin's wallpaper designs and Collinson and Lock exhibit his furniture at the Paris Exposition Universelle. Designs a double house and studios, known as Chelsea Lodge, for Archibald Stuart Wortley and Carlo Pellegrini at 60 Tite Street, London (demolished). Submits competition design for the Oratory, Brompton Road, Kensington, London. Holidays in Bruges, Ostend, Antwerp, Liège, Cologne, and along the Rhine River. The second edition of William Watt's *Art Furniture* catalogue is published. Designs an overmantel and color scheme for the rooms of artist Frederick Sandys at 1 Spencer Street, London. Plates from Watt's *Art Furniture* catalogue are published in an American journal called the *Art Worker: A Journal Devoted to Art-Industry* (February–August).

1878–79

Designs a studio/house at 44 Tite Street, London, for Frank Miles. Designs a studio for Her Royal Highness Princess Louise, a sculptor, in the garden at Kensington Palace, London (demolished).

1879

Makes alterations and additions to Chelsea Lodge (60 Tite Street, London) for the Hon. Slingsby Bethel (demolished). Designs a proposed London cottage and studio for Rosa Corder (fig. C13), an animal painter. Submits competition design for City of London Schools, Victoria Embankment. Designs a proposed monument to Lord Northbrook with sculpture by Joseph Edgar Boehm. Submits competition design for Devonport Public Hall, Devon. Submits competition design for a cemetery layout, Derbyshire. Designs a proposed conservatory for conservatory manufacturer Messenger and Company, Laughborough. Decorates Captain Frederick Campbell's home at 22 Ovington Square, London. Designs font, pulpit, and choir stalls for Saint Wilfred's Church, Eppington, Derbyshire. Designs furniture for dramatist and painter W. G. Wills, including six bird panels and six spray panels for the mantelpiece, two dressing tables, and a hanging cabinet.

1879–83

Designs new house and studio, Canwell House, for Archibald Stuart Wortley, at 29 Tite Street, London (demolished).

1879–84

Establishes an Art Club for the *British Architect* and judges designs submitted by students; the winners are published in the journal.

1880

Designs a proposed People's Palace, including a panoramic theater and exhibition galleries at the Savoy Palace, Victoria Embankment, London (with J. P. Seddon). Designs a proposed hotel at Birchington, Kent (with J. P. Seddon). Messenger and Company publishes *Artistic Conservatories, and Other Horticultural Buildings . . . from Rough Sketches by E. W. Godwin, F.S.A. and from Designs and Drawings by Maurice B. Adams*. Designs proposed Lancaster Club and Residences, The Embankment, Westminster, London, for the Metropolitan Mansions Company. Submits

competition design for a town hall in Pietermaritzburg, Natal. Submits competition design for a town hall in Southampton, Hampshire. Designs Nurnberg series of furniture for William Watt. Designs costumes for the leading roles in Mrs. Bateman's production of Shakespeare's *Othello*, first performed at Sadler's Wells Theatre on September 20. Advises on the decoration of Rorkes Gallery, 35 Parliament Street, London, being furnished by Liberty's. September—Travels to Antwerp and other cities in Belgium. Relocates his office to Saint Stephen's Palace Chambers, London. Designs Greek-style furnishings for the London firm of James Peddle.

1880–81

Designs an illustrated calendar for the *British Architect*.

1880–81

Designs some of the costumes for Mr. R. B. Mantell's role in *Romeo and Juliet* at the Olympic Theatre. Designs the new proposed stage, scenery, properties, furniture, and costume for a theater in Hyderabad, India, for the Nizam of Hyderabad, through the consulting engineer and agent, John Barber and Company of Leeds.

1881

Makes the preliminary design for the Comedy Theatre, near Fountain Court, Strand, London. Makes the preliminary design for the Savoy site, The Embankment, Westminster, London. Designs the "Shakespeare" dining-room suite for William Watt. Designs costumes for American actor Hermann Vezin for Isabel Bateman's production of *Hamlet* at the new Sadler's Wells Theatre, London, first performed on February 28. Designs Ellen Terry's costumes for Henry Irving's production of *The Cup* by Tennyson, first performed at the Lyceum, London, on January 3. April—Designs an early English reception room for William Watt's display at an exhibition of the Domestic Lighting Company, Victoria Cross Rooms, Crystal Palace, London. Designs scenery, costumes, and property for Wilson Barrett's production of *Juana* by W. G. Wills, first performed at the Court Theatre, London, on May 7. Designs scenery and dresses for Mrs. Mary Siddon's production of Walter S. Raleigh's *Queen and Cardinal*, first performed at the Theatre Royal, Haymarket, on October 26. May—Designs stone aedicule for a life-size marble statue of an angel by Joseph Edgar Boehm at the back of the conservatory at Castle Ashby, Northamptonshire, commemorating the fourth marchioness of Northampton. August—William Watt exhibits Godwin's furniture at the "Decorative Art Exhibition" held at the premises of Mr. T. J. Gullick of 103 New Bond Street, London. Designs ceramic tiles for Minton and Hollins Company, Stoke-on-Trent. Designs wall coverings for the Papyrotile Company, 14 Holborn Viaduct, London. August—Designs wall coverings for the stand of the Papyrotile Company in a furniture exhibition at Islington, London. Designs ceramic tiles for Messrs. Wilcock and Company, Burmantofts Furnace Works, Leeds, West Yorkshire. Becomes a member of Saint Stephens Art Society in London and serves on the newly formed permanent exhibitions committee. Designs furniture for Mr. Michaels, 54 Carnivall Gardens, London, commissioned by William Watt. Participates in founding the Society of English Players and is elected art director. Submits preliminary specifications for the decoration and furnishing of a studio in Kensington, London, for painter R. Caton Woodville.

1881–82

Designs new entrance facade and makes alterations to the premises of the Fine Art Society, 148 New Bond Street, London. Submits competition design for the Museum of Science and Arts, and the National Library buildings in Dublin, Ireland. Designs a proposed London house and interiors for actress Lillie Langtry.

1881–85

Designs Tower House, 46 Tite Street, London, a block of four studio flats.

1882

Relocates his office to 7 Great College Street, Westminster, London. His brother Joseph Lucas Godwin dies in Northern Ireland, and in March Godwin designs a memorial for him. Designs a proposed scheme to build three houses in Melbury Road, Holland Park, London, as a speculative venture. Designs a proposed housing estate for the Wish Farm Estate, Brighton, West Sussex, and proposed premises for the Brighton Club and Cafe Royal, 77 West Street, Brighton, West Sussex. Decorates and furnishes 10 Lancaster Place, Westminster, London, for Hermann Vezin. Decorates and makes alterations to 37 Lowndes Square, Westminster, and accompanying stable, for Lady Shrewsbury. Designs the interior of a house in Lennox Gardens, Kensington and Chelsea, London, for Gwladys, Countess of Lonsdale. Decorates 40 King Street, Soho, London, for Lady Sinclair. Decorates 19 Belgrave Square, London, for Lady Feversham. April—Exhibits the Shakespeare dining-room suite for William Watt's stand at the "Building Exhibition," Agricultural Hall, London. Designs a room and cabinet for William Watt for Charles Coghlan Esq., 54 Ladbroke Road West, London. Designs the proposed Wyndham Theatre, London. June—Opens new offices 7 Great College Street West, London. Executes survey for a house at 13 Fountain Court, London, for Mr. C. Ford Webb. Designs a proposed building for the Learned Societies, London. Submits competition design for the Durban Town Hall, Natal. Submits competition design for municipal buildings, Middlesbrough. Makes alterations to and partly refurnishes a church for Rev. W. Ormsby at Clarens, Switzerland. Designs the costumes for Hermann Vezin's production of *The Cynic* by Herman Melville, first performed at the Royal Globe Theatre, London, on January 14.

1882–83

Designs Elmleigh, with coach house and stables, at Dallington Park, Harleston Road, Northampton, for J. Shuttleworth, a tea merchant.

1882–84

Participates in the founding of the Costume Society and is elected honorary secretary.

1883

Designs a proposed office for Nottingham, Nottinghamshire. Submits competition design for the proposed Brisbane Town Hall, Australia. Designs proposed stables for Lord Dysart. Makes preliminary design for a monument to Charles I, Charing Cross, Westminster, London. Makes preliminary design for a monument to Victor Emmanuel. Designs a monument to Lady Florence Chapman (sculpture by Joseph Edgar Boehm). Designs a monument to Lady Joddrell, wife of Rev. W. Joddrell (sculpture by Joseph Edgar Boehm). Designs a proposed renovation scheme for the Connaught Theatre, London, for T. Knox Holmes. Designs a proposed New Theatre at 106 Strand, London. Designs a proposed municipal building, including two police courts, for West Derby, Merseyside. Does survey work for Mr. Parsons at Risley Hall, Derbyshire. Designs costumes for Robert Buchanon's *Storm Beaten*, first performed at the Royal Adelphi, London, on March 13. Costume advisor for Hermann Vezin's benefit matinee production of Shakespeare's *Merchant of Venice* at the Gaiety, London, on November 30. Designs Wilson Barrett's production of Henry Hermann and W. G. Will's *Claudian*, first performed at the Princess's Theatre, London, on December 6. Designs costumes for Henry Irving's proposed production of *Rienzi* adapted by W. G. Wills from the novel by Bulwer, Lord Lytton; it was to have been shown at the Lyceum Theatre, London. Designs Hermann Vezin's costume for the character of Claude Melnotte in John Hollingshead's production of the *Lady of Lyons* by Bulwer, Lord Lytton,

Fig. C14. E. W. Godwin. Costume design for Claudius, king of Denmark, in *Hamlet*, 1884. Pencil and watercolor on mounted tracing paper; 9½ x 5⅝ in. (24.1 x 14.3 cm). Trustees of the Victoria and Albert Museum, London, S.89-1998. *Checklist no. 138*

Fig. C15. "Lady Jane Seymour: Historic Dress at Liberty's Studios by E. W. Godwin, F.S.A." From *British Architect* 21 (13 June 1884).

first performed at the Gaiety, London, on January 18. Designs furniture for Messrs. W. A. and S. Smee, 89 Finsbury Pavement, London, exhibited at the "Furniture Trades Exhibition," London. Designs a book cover for *The Costume Society: Part 1.*

1883–84
Writes *Dress and its Relation to Health and Climate* for the organizers of the "Health Exhibition," London. Designs a pedestal for the bronze statue of William Tyndale by Joseph Edgar Boehm, Victoria Tower Gardens, Westminster, London.

1884
February—Designs an English fifteenth-century room for William Watt's stand at the exhibition of furniture, Royal School of Art Needlework, South Kensington, London. May—Jeffrey and Company exhibits Godwin wallpapers at the London International and Universal Exhibition. Designs costumes for Kate Vaughan's production of Colley Cibber's *She Would and She Would Not*, first performed at the Prince's Theatre, London, on June 5. Serves as production manager and designer of the forest scenes for the Pastoral Player's open-air production of Shakespeare's *As You Like It*, first performed in the woods at Coombe House, New Malden, Surrey, on July 22. Travels to Copenhagen, Denmark, to visit the Museum of Northern Antiquities and to research the setting of *Hamlet*. Designs Wilson Barrett's production of *Hamlet* (fig. C14), first performed at the Princess's Theatre, London, on October 16. Makes a preliminary design for the front facade and entrance to McLean's Fine Art Gallery at 7 Haymarket, London. Becomes consultant to Liberty's of London newly opened Dress Studios (fig. C15). Decorates and furnishes the

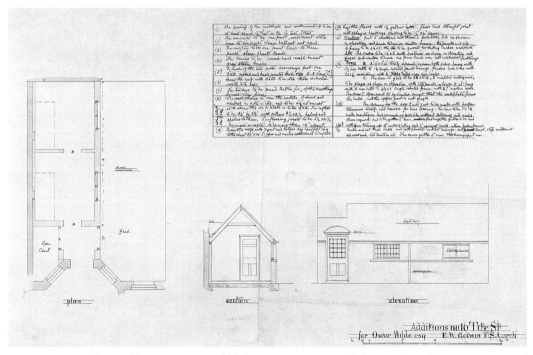

Fig. C16. E. W. Godwin. Additions to Oscar Wilde's house, 16 Tite Street, Chelsea, London: elevation, section, and plan, ca. 1884. Pen and ink, watercolor; 13¾ x 20⅞ in. (35 x 53 cm). Trustees of the Victoria and Albert Museum, London, E.575-1963. *Checklist no. 102*

Clergy House, 52 Frith Street, Soho, London, for Rev. A. Wellesley Batson. Submits competition design for the Liverpool Cathedral. Makes a preliminary design for a theater and shops in Manchester for Charles Spencer.

1884–85

Remodels and decorates 16 Tite Street (fig. C16; now 34 Tite Street), London, for Oscar and Constance Wilde.

1885

Displays architectural drawings, including *A Town Church*, in the "Exhibition of Architectural Drawings" at the R.I.B.A. Designs Wilson Barrett's production of *Junius* by Bulwer, Lord Lytton, first performed at the Princess's Theatre, London, on February 26. Serves as production manager and designer of the Pastoral Players' open-air production of *The Faithfull Shepherdesse* by John Fletcher (adapted by Godwin), first performed in the woods at Coombe House, New Malden, Surrey, on June 27. Designs a proposed auditorium at Coombe, New Malden, for Lady Archibald Campbell. Designs Hermann Vezin's costumes for Kate Vaughan's production of *Secret Service*, adapted by James R. Planche and first performed at Her Majesty's, London, on October 15. Designs J. W. Clark's student production of Aeschylus's *The Eumenides*, performed at Cambridge University before December 12. Designs Greek-style chairs for William Watt.

1885–86

Makes alterations and repairs to the Rookeries, Ramsbury, Wiltshire, including repair of main house, stables, and coach house, for Francis Cunningham Batson.

1885–87

Representatives of William Watt and Company continue to produce furniture to Godwin designs after the death of William Watt.

1886

Designs Wilson Barrett's production of Sydney Grundy and Wilson Barrett's *Clito*, first performed at the Princess's Theatre, London, on May 1. Jointly produces and advises on design (with John Todhunter) on the Shelley Society's production of P. B. Shelley's *The Cenci* performed at the Grand Theatre, Islington, London, on May 7. Designs the program for a production of *The Fool's Revenge* by Tom Taylor at the Opera Comique, London. Writes "The Greek Home according to Homer," published in the *Nineteenth Century*, James Knowles's monthly magazine. Serves as production manager and designs costumes, properties, and sets for *Helena in Troas,* adapted from Sophocles by John Todhunter and first performed at Hengler's Circus, London, on May 17; adapts Hengler's Circus to create a Greek theater. Serves as production manager and designer of *The Fool's Revenge*, adapted by Tom Taylor and first performed at the Opera Comique, London, on July 3. Serves as production manager and designer of Rosen's *Bachelors*, adapted by Robert Buchanan and Hermann Vezin and first performed at the Opera Comique, London, in August. Serves as production manager and designer of the Pastoral Player's open-air production of *Fair Rosamund*, adapted by Godwin from Tennyson's play *Beckett* and first performed on July 20 at Cannizaro Woods, Wimbledon, Surrey. October 6—Dies at the age of fifty-three from complications following surgery to remove kidney stones and is buried at Northleigh, near Witney, in Oxfordshire.

CHECKLIST·OF·THE·EXHIBITION

Most of the objects in the exhibition are illustrated elsewhere in the catalogue. Figure numbers in parentheses after each title refer the reader to the essays and the chronology. In the dimensions height precedes width precedes depth. In the references, citations are given in short form: author's last name, shortened title, and year of publication. Full citations are given in the bibliography: For sources by Godwin, see "E. W. Godwin's Writings and Published Drawings"; for all other sources, see "Secondary Sources Plus Period Sources and Illustrations of Godwin's Work." Square brackets around "Godwin" as author indicate that the writing is attributed to him on the basis of records (including the architect's ledgers) in the Archive of Art and Design and the Department of Prints and Drawings at the Victoria and Albert Museum, London. Page numbers in square brackets indicate illustrations.

1. Gong and Stand *(fig. 3-15)*
ca. 1875
Probably made by William Watt
Oak and iron frame, bronze gong, wood striking stick
32½ x 17¾ x 17⅛ in. (82.6 x 45.1 x 43.5 cm)

National Museums and Galleries on Merseyside, Walker Art Gallery 1994.17

References: Phillips (London), *British, Continental* (13 October 1992): lot 255, illus.; Gere and Whiteway, *Nineteenth-Century Design* (1993): 156, pl. 193; National Art-Collections Fund, *National-Art Collections Fund Review* (1994): no. 4043; Soros, "E. W. Godwin" (1998): 58, fig. 32, cat. no. 403.

2. Godwin in Medieval Dress *(left; fig. 1-7)* **and Playing Chess** *(right)*
ca. 1861–65
Photograph
Left, 3 x 1¾ in. (7.6 x 4.4 cm); right, 3¾ x 2 in. (8.3 x 5.1 cm)
Inscription: [recto] "Copied"; [verso, in Ellen Terry's hand], "*About 1860* - Purple Velvet Coat - dull Red Tights and Hood"

Collection of the National Trust, The Ellen Terry Memorial Museum, Smallhythe Place, Kent, SMA PH: 122

Reference: Holding, "The Late E. W. Godwin, F. S. A." (22 October 1886): 371.

3. Sketchbook
Open to antiquarian sketches *(fig. 2-1 and Chronology, fig. C1)*
ca. 1849
Pencil, pen and ink, sepia wash
Page trim, 6¾ x 4⅝ in. (17.3 x 11.7 cm)
Inscription: "Bracket / Lower Garden; Gargoyle from / Stroud Church. (Upper) / Garden); Weston in / Gordano.; Crocket; E Window / W in G; Pinnacle from / Bristol Cath.; Stone Altar in Clapton Ch. Somerset; Impost of Doorway / Portberry [sic] Ch; Piscina in Cp - of / Clapton Ch.; Piscina in Portberry [sic] Ch.; Seat in Clapton Ch." [and additional inscriptions]

The Board of Trustees of the Victoria and Albert Museum, London, E.267-1963

References: Godwin "On some Buildings . . ." (29 November 1878): 210; Harbron, *Conscious Stone* (1949): 3.

4. *The Architectural Antiquities of Bristol and Its Neighbourhood*, by E. W. Godwin, James Hine, and William Burder
Open to plate 3, "The Church of St Mary, Redcliffe: Doorway, North Porch" *(fig. 2-2)*
Drawn by E. W. Godwin; engraved by William Corbett Burder
Published: Bristol, 1851
Bound book
With binding, 15 x 11¼ in. (38 x 28.5 cm); page trim, 14⅝ x 10⅝ in. (37.1 x 27 cm)

The Board of Trustees of the Victoria and Albert Museum, London, NAL 33 E.82

References: Godwin and Hine, *The Architectural Antiquities of Bristol and Its Neighbourhood by James Hine and E. W. Godwin,* pamphlet (Bristol: March 1850) in RIBA Mss GoE/3/5/1; Harbron, "Edward Godwin," (August 1945): 48–49; Harbron, *Conscious Stone* (1949): 10–11.

5. Saint Grada Church, Grade, Cornwall *(fig. 6-10)*
Ground plan, elevation of east end, transverse section through porch, section looking east
1861
India ink, red pen, and colored washes
13 x 20 in. (33 x 50.8 cm)
Inscription: [recto] "Grade Church - / Cornwall / *January 1861*.; Ground Plan.; East End.; Porch.; Section looking East.; E W Godwin Archᵗ. / Montpelier Bristol" [and additional inscriptions]; [verso] "Grade Church"

British Architectural Library Drawings Collection, RIBA, London, Ran 7/A/4 (2)

References: Godwin "Notes on Some of the Churches," part 1 (September 1861): 234–38; Pevsner, *Cornwall* (1970): 73–74.

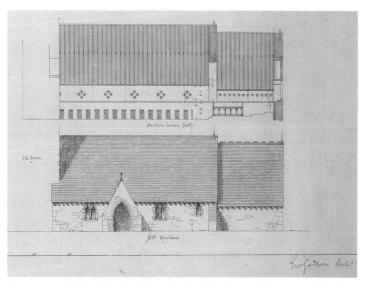

Cat. no. 6. Saint Grada Church, Grade, Cornwall: section looking north, south elevation, ca. 1861. India ink, red pen, and colored washes; 13 x 20 in. (33 x 50.8 cm). British Architectural Library Drawings Collection, RIBA, London, Ran 7/A/4 (3).

6. Saint Grada Church, Grade, Cornwall

Section looking north, south elevation
ca. 1861
India ink, red pen, and colored washes
13 x 20 in. (33 x 50.8 cm)
Inscription: "GRADE CHURCH, CORNWALL.; Section looking North; Old Tower; Soth [sic] Elevation; E W Godwin Arch'" [and additional inscriptions]

British Architectural Library Drawings Collection, RIBA, London, Ran 7/A/4 (3)

References: see no. 5

7. Designs for Saint Grada Church, Grade, Cornwall *(fig. 6-11)*

East window and stained glass
ca. 1861
India ink, red pen, and colored washes
20 x 12^{13}⁄₁₆ in. (50.8 x 32.5 cm)
Inscription: "GRADE CHURCH. CORNWALL.; A.2; East Window ; Edw W Godwin Arch^t." [and additional inscriptions]

British Architectural Library Drawings Collection, RIBA, London, Ran 7/A/4 (5)

References: see no. 5

8. Designs for Saint Grada Church, Grade, Cornwall *(fig. 8-2)*

Nave and chancel roofs, chancel desks, nave seats, and chancel seats
ca. 1861

India ink, red pen, brown wash
20 x 13 in. (50.8 x 33 cm)
Inscription: "GRADE CHURCH. CORNWALL.; A.4; ROOFS/Nave Chancel.; See Suplimentary [sic] drawing/ C I.; Front of Chancel Desks; Nave Seats; Chancel Seats; Edw W Godwin Archt." [and additional inscriptions]

British Architectural Library Drawings Collection, RIBA, London, Ran 7/A/4 (7)

References: see no. 5; Soros, "E.W. Godwin" (1998): 38–40.

9. Photograph of Northampton Guildhall (formerly Northampton Town Hall), taken from St. Giles' Square *(fig. 6-1)*

Photographed in 1998
David Allison

References: "New Town Hall" (13 April 1861): 8; "Northampton Town Council" (20 April 1861): 6; "Northampton Town-Hall" (27 April 1861): 282; "Northampton Town Hall" (27 April 1861): 7; "New Town Hall" (27 April 1861): 7; "'Circumspice' versus 'Non Nobis Domine'" (4 May 1861): 3; "Northampton Town Hall Competition" (4 May 1861): 5; "New Town Hall" (4 May 1861): 5; "Northampton Town Hall" (11 May 1861): 3; "New Town-Hall Movement" (25 May 1861): 5; "Ground Plan of Town Hall" (8 November 1861): 892–93; "View of the Town Hall," ibid., "New Town-hall, Northampton" (2 October 1863): 748 and [749]; *Guide to the New Town Hall* (1864); "Sculpture, New Town-Hall" (10 November 1865): 788 and [795]; *Account of the Town Halls* (1866); Godwin "On Some Buildings . . ." (29 November 1878): 210–11; *Descriptive Guide* (1881); Campion, *Northampton Town Hall* (1925); Harbron, *Conscious Stone* (1949): 26–31; Reynolds, *Northampton Town Hall* (1956, 1974); Glazebrook, *History of Northampton's Town Halls* (1970); Cunningham, *Victorian and Edwardian Town Halls* (1981): 132–33, 193 fig. 89; M. W. Brooks, *John Ruskin* (1987): 210–11; *Northampton Remembers* (1989); M. Hall, "Modern Gothic" (4 February 1993): 48–51; Cruickshank, "Good Godwin" (August 1993): 74–79.

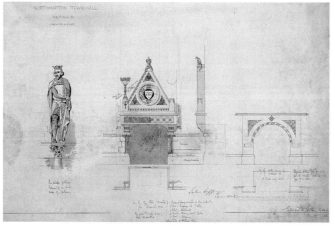

Cat. no. 10. Design of details for Northampton Town Hall: statue of King Edward I; plans, elevations, and sections of fireplaces, 1861. Pen and ink, watercolor and pencil; 20¹⁄₁₆ x 28¼ in. (51 x 71.7 cm). Trustees of the Victoria and Albert Museum, London, E.594-1963.

Cat. no. 15. Ceremonial trowel for Northampton Town Hall, 1861. Birmingham, unknown maker. Silver gilt with ebony handle; L. 11¼ in. (28.6 cm). The Trustees of the British Museum, London, 1980, 2-3,1.

10. Designs for Northampton Town Hall

Statue of King Edward I; plans, elevations, and sections of fireplaces
1861
Pen and ink, watercolor and pencil.
20⅟₁₆ x 28¼ in. (51 x 71.7 cm)
Inscription: :"NORTHAMPTON TOWN-HALL. DETAILS; The statue of King / Edward I on west / side of balcony; no 2. of these mantels / for Council room; John Jeffrey / Town Clerk; John Watkin; Edward W Godwin Architect / Bristol 1861." [and additional inscriptions]

The Board of Trustees of the Victoria and Albert Museum, London, E.594-1963

References: see no. 9; Reid, "Dromore Castle" (1987): 135, fig. 24; Soros, "E. W. Godwin" (1998): 166–67, fig. 166, cat. no. 102, fig. 1, cat. no. 103, fig. 4.

11. Northampton Town Hall *(fig. 6-16)*

Sections through the Great Hall and Court Room
1861
Pen and ink, watercolor and pencil
19⁵⁄₁₆ x 27¹⁵⁄₁₆ in. (49.1 x 71 cm)
Inscription: "John Watkin; Thomas Brawn; John Jeffrey / Town Clerk; Edward W Godwin Arch^t" [and additional inscriptions].

The Board of Trustees of the Victoria and Albert Museum, London, E.592-1963

References: see no. 9; Cruickshank, "Good Godwin" (August 1993): 79, fig 10.

12a. View of the "Godwin Room" (former Council Chamber), Northampton Guildhall *(fig. 8-7)*

Restored by Roderick Gradidge and Christopher Boulter, 1992
Photographed in 1998
David Allison

References: see no. 9; M. Hall, "Modern Gothic" (4 February 1993): 48–51.

12b. The Council Chamber, Northampton Town Hall *(fig. 8-6)*

Photographed ca 1890
Modern print from a photograph pasted in an album of ca. 1890. The table is set for a corporation banquet.

Northamptonshire Record Office, P/3852

References: see no. 9

13. Designs for Furniture for the Council Chamber, Northampton Town Hall *(fig. 8-10)*

1865
Pencil on writing paper
8⅜ x 13¼ in. (21.2 x 33.7 cm)
Inscription: [recto] "Furniture of Town Hall North^ton, Council Table; Mayor's Chair; Councilmen (*sic*) Chairs; Furniture to doors of Council Chamber; Doorhandle; Escutcheon; Bottom bolt; finger plate; Jan^y/65" [and additional inscriptions]; [verso]: "1865 / Plan of Council / Chamber & Lavatory / to do; Detail of Furniture / Council Chamber" [and additional inscriptions]

The Board of Trustees of the Victoria and Albert Museum, London, E.619-1963

References: Harbron, *Conscious Stone* (1949): 26–31; Aslin, *E. W. Godwin* (1986): 25, 35, pl. 1; Cooper, *Victorian and Edwardian Decor* (1987): 140, pl. 321; Cruickshank, "Good Godwin" (August 1993): 74–79; Soros, "E. W. Godwin" (1998): 40–44, cat. no. 100 fig. 1, cat. no. 101 fig. 1, cat. no. 200 fig 1.

14. Mayor's Chair for Northampton Town Hall *(fig. 8-11)*

1865
Made by Green and King
Oak with inlaid decoration, upholstered in red leather, with brass nails, and brass castors
67¾ x 30¾ x 24½ in. (172 x 78 x 62.5 cm)

Northampton Borough Council

References: Aslin, *E. W. Godwin* (1986): 25, 35, pl. 2; M. Hall, "Modern Gothic" (4 February 1993): 51, pl. 10; Soros, "E. W. Godwin" (1998): 41–43, no. 101, fig. 11.

15. Ceremonial Trowel for Northampton Town Hall

1861
Birmingham, unknown maker
Silver gilt with ebony handle
L. 11¼ in. (28.6 cm)
End of handle engraved: "PP"
Inscription: [in Black Letter script] "Presented to the worshipful Mayor of Northampton, Pickering Phipps. Esq. by the Town Council, on the occasion of his laying the Foundation Stone of the New Town Hall. Oct.22.1861"

The Trustees of the British Museum, London, 1980, 2-3,1

References: Collins, *Toward Post-Modernism* (ca. 1987): 21, fig. 11; Rudoe, *Decorative Arts* (1991): 51–52, 148, pl. 3.

16. Congleton Town Hall, Cheshire

Perspective drawing
ca. 1864
Watercolor and body color
20⅞ x 13³⁄₁₆ in. (53 x 33.5 cm)
Inscription: [verso] "E.W.G.; Congleton town Hall"

Cat. no. 16. Congleton Town Hall, Cheshire: perspective drawing, ca. 1864. Watercolor and body color; 20⅞ x 13³⁄₁₆ in. (53 x 33.5 cm). Trustees of the Victoria and Albert Museum, London, E.626-1963.

The Board of Trustees of the Victoria and Albert Museum, London, E.626-1963

References: "Congleton Town Hall" (16 July 1864): 528–30; "Congleton Town Hall" (6 January 1865): 8, 16, [10, 13]; Godwin, "On Some Buildings"(29 November 1878): 211; Head, *Congleton, past and present* (1887; reprint, 1987): 138–42; Harbron, "Edward Godwin," (August 1945): 49, illus.; Harbron, *Conscious Stone* (1949): 41, 49–50; Stevens, ed., *History of Congleton* (1970): 92–107; Pevsner and Hubbard, *Cheshire* (1971): 183–84; S. Muthesius, *High Victorian Movement* (1972): 125–26; Physick and Darby, *Marble Halls* (1973): 133–34, cat. no. 85, [28]; Service, *Edwardian Architecture* (1975): 58, fig. 2; Cunningham, *Victorian and Edwardian Town Halls* (1981):133–34; Lambourne, *Aesthetic Movement* (1996): 154, illus.; T. A. T. Robinson, "Congleton Town Hall" (n.d.).

17. Congleton Town Hall, Cheshire
(fig. 6-19)
Competition drawing: longitudinal section of hall, section through tower, and other sections
ca. 1864
India ink, red pen, colored washes, gold
18¹³⁄₁₆ x 25³⁄₁₆ in. (47.8 x 64 cm)
Inscription: "CONGLE / TON:TO / WN: HAL / L: SECTI / ON A.B.; SECTION O.P.; SECTION M.N.; SECTION R.S.; Charles Burkitt; E.W. GODWIN F.S.A. F.R.I.B.A." [and additional inscriptions]

British Architectural Library Drawings Collection, RIBA, London, Ran 7/A/9 (7)

References: see no. 16

18. Bristol Assize Courts *(fig. 6-21)*
Front elevation after a competition drawing of 1866
1871
India ink, sepia pen, and wash, mounted on blue card
13 x 16⅞ in. (33 x 42.9 cm)
Inscription: :"TEN HUNDRED AND SIXTY SIX: / A.D. 1871; 1st Premium Bristol Assize Courts.; E W Godwin"

British Architectural Library Drawings Collection, RIBA, London, Ran 7/A/11 (1)

References: "The Bristol Assize Courts Competition" (10 August 1866): 533; "Bristol Assize Courts" (30 August 1866): 4; "The Assize Courts Competition" (1 September 1866): 4; "Godwin and Crisp's Designs . . ." (21 April 1871): 297 and illus.; "Winchester Guildhall &c."

(19 May 1871): 386 and illus.; Harbron, "Edward Godwin" (August 1945): 49, illus.; Harbron, *Conscious Stone* (1949): 55–56; Service, *Edwardian Architecture* (1975): 59, fig. 3; Gomme, Jenner, and Little, *Bristol* (1979): 429.

19. Aerial Photograph of Dromore Castle, County Limerick
ca. 1949
Modern print

Courtesy of Mrs. Nancy Tierney

References: Godwin, "Dromore Castle, Co. Limerick" (29 March 1867): 222 [224–25]; ibid. (1 November 1867): 755, [758–59]; *Irish Builder* (15 December 1868): 357–58; "Dromore Castle" (21 March 1873): 330 and [339]; Godwin, "On Some Buildings" (29 November 1878): 210–11; "Dromore Castle, Co. Limerick" (15 January 1900): 239 and illus.; Fleming, "Historic Irish Mansions" (24 August 1940); Bence-Jones, "An Aesthete's Irish Castle" (12 November 1964): 1275, fig. 4; de Breffny and Ffolliott, *Houses of Ireland* (1975): 217–18; Richardson, *Gothic Revival Architecture in Ireland* (1983): 693–701; Reid, "Dromore Castle" (1987): 113–42; Fitz-Gerald, Griffin, and Robinson, *Vanishing Country Houses* (1988): 103; Somerville-Large, *Irish Country House* (1995): 289, figs. 26 a–b.

20. Design for Wall Decoration, Dromore Castle, County Limerick *(fig. 3-6)*
ca. 1869
Watercolor and pencil
5⁵⁄₁₆ x 7½ in. (13.5 x 19 cm)

The Board of Trustees of the Victoria and Albert Museum, London, E.491-1963

References: see no. 19; "Figures designed for Wall Paintings . . ." (8 June 1872): 300 and illus.; "Decorations of Dromore Castle" (4 April 1873): 390 and [402]; Aslin, *E.W. Godwin* (1986): 23, 65, col. pl. 2; N. B. Wilkinson, "Edward William Godwin" (1987): 159, fig. 36; Banham, MacDonald, and Porter, *Victorian Interior Design* (1991): 111, col. pl. 115; Lambourne, *Aesthetic Movement* (1996): 162, illus.; Soros, "E.W. Godwin" (1998): 163–64, fig. 164.

21. Design for the Drawing Room Wall, Dromore Castle, County Limerick *(fig. 7-11)*
ca. 1869
India ink, red and blue pen, colored washes, pencil.
23¼ x 19³⁄₁₆ in. (59.1 x 48.7 cm)
Inscription: "Walls for Drawing room; White"

British Architectural Library Drawings Collection, RIBA, London, Ran 7/B/1 (80)

References: see nos. 19, 20

22. Design for a Chess Table for Dromore Castle, County Limerick *(fig. 7-13)*
ca. 1869
India ink and colored washes
13 x 19½ in. (33 x 49.5 cm)
Inscription: "Chess Table (scale 2 in to one foot) / mahogany ebonized and Boxwood piercings; Pierced work in ends (full size); Elevation of end; Elevation of Side; Detail of Table top full size; Section at C.D. full size; Full size at A; Full size at B; Candle stand; Well; Real ebony and Boxwood squares; Butt Hinge / from top to / bottom; Candle / Stand; the same thickness / as drawer; Drawer"

British Architectural Library Drawings Collection, RIBA, London, Ran 7/B/1 (55)

References: see no. 19; Lever, *Architects' Designs for Furniture* (1982): 79, fig. 55; Aslin, *E.W. Godwin* (1986): 26, 40, pl. 6; Reid, "Dromore Castle" (1987): 136; Lambourne, *Aesthetic Movement* (1996): 158, illus.; Soros, "E.W. Godwin" (1998): 51, fig. 24.

23. Designs for Furniture for Dromore Castle, County Limerick *(fig. 7-12)*
ca. 1869
India ink and brown wash
12⅞ x 19¹¹⁄₁₆ in. (32.8 x 50 cm)
Inscription: [recto] "Plan of Card table; Plan of arm chair / No 1; front of Whatnot; Side of Whatnot; CARD TABLE; CHESS TABLE.; Side of Arm Chair / no 2; Plan of arm chair No 2; Plan of chair; Full drawing of end of sofa; working drawing of Table; thickness ?required; £3"; [verso] "SET C"

British Architectural Library Drawings Collection, RIBA, London, Ran 7/B/1 (53)

References: Lever, *Architects' Designs for Furniture* (1982): 79–80, pl. 56; Aslin, *E.W. Godwin* (1986): 26, 41, pl. 7; Soros, "E.W. Godwin" (1998): 168–69, fig. 172.

24. Settee *(fig. 3-9)*
ca. 1869–85
Made by William Watt
Mahogany, upholstered back and seat, brass castors
35 x 66⅛ x 22⅞ in. (89 x 168 x 58.1 cm)

Private collection, Courtesy of The Fine Art Society, Plc.

References: Watt, *Art Furniture* (1877): pl. 15; Fine Art Society, *Aesthetic Movement* (1972): no, 285; Royal Academy of Arts, *Victorian and Edwardian Decorative Art* (1972): no. D19; Bristol Museums and Art Gallery, *Furniture by Godwin and Breuer* (1976): no. 3 (similar settee); Sotheby's, *Art Nouveau* (31 March 1977): lot 435 (similar settee); Gere and Whiteway, *Nineteenth-Century Design* (1993): 134, pl. 161 (similar settee); Soros, "E. W. Godwin" (1998): 60, fig. 34 (similar settee), 80, 93, 168, cat. no. 114.1.

25. Design for Buffet and Wall Decoration for the Dining Hall, Dromore Castle, County Limerick *(fig. 8-17)*

ca. 1869
Sepia pen and wash
9³⁄₁₆ x 12¹⁄₁₆ in. (23.4 x 30.7 cm)
Inscription: "Chastity; Industry"

British Architectural Library Drawings Collection, RIBA, London, Ran 7/B/1 (73)

References: "Dromore Castle" (20 August 1870): 104 and illus.; "Figures designed for Wall Paintings" (8 June 1872): 300 and illus.; Bence-Jones, "An Aesthete's Irish Castle" (12 November 1964): 1277, fig. 10 (similar image); S. Muthesius, *The High Victorian Movement* (1972): 205, fig. 157; Lever, *Architects' Designs for Furniture* (1982): 60, pl. xii, 79, fig. 54; Aslin, *E. W. Godwin* (1986): 26, 38, pl. 4; Cooper, *Victorian and Edwardian Decor* (1987): 120, 122, fig. 289 (similar piece); Yorke, *English Furniture* (1990): 120, illus. Barbican Art Gallery and Setagaya Art Museum, *Japan and Britain* (1991): 116, fig. 102; Soros, "E. W. Godwin" (1998): 164–65, fig. 165.

26. Side Chair for Dromore Castle, County Limerick *(fig. 8-15)*

1869
Made by William Watt
Oak, leather upholstery with gold stamped pattern and brass nails
42½ x 18¼ x 18⅞ in. (108 x 46.5 x 48 cm)

Museum für Kunst und Gewerbe, Hamburg, 1967.262

References: De Courcy, *Dromore Castle* [1949]: 7, lot. 257; Victoria and Albert Museum, *English Chairs* (1970): pl. 123 (similar chair); Aslin, *E. W. Godwin* (1986): 26, 42, pl. 9 (similar chair); Reid, "Dromore Castle" (1987): 137; *Aesthetic Movement* (1994): 326; Howe et al., *Herter*

Brothers (1994): 194, illus. (similar chair); Spielmann, *Die Jugenstil-Sammlung* (1996): 50; Soros, "E. W. Godwin" (1998): 80, 166–67, cat. no. 110 (similar chair).

27. Design for Ceiling Decoration for Dromore Castle, County Limerick *(fig. 6-34)*

1868 or 1871
India ink, colored washes, gouache
19¹⁄₁₆ x 23¼ in. (48.5 x 59 cm)
Inscriptions: [recto] "DROMORE CASTLE No. II DECORATIONS / Plans of Ceilings / Drawing Room. (g.); Plan of Drawing room ceiling C. / The letters shown where the patterns are to be repeated; Music Room (w); Plan of Music room ceiling / in spaces D only one red circle to be used.; This moulding to apply to ribs of all the principal rooms; Godwin: / 197 Albany St Regents Park N.W. / Jan 1868" [and additional inscriptions.]; [verso] "18th Dec. 71"

British Architectural Library Drawings Collection, RIBA, London, Ran 7/B/1 (82)

References: Bence-Jones, "An Aesthete's Irish Castle" (12 November 1964): 1276, fig. 9; Reid, "Dromore Castle" (1987): 135–36, fig. 26; Soros, "E. W. Godwin" (1998): 162, fig. 66.

28. Design for Curtain Fabric for Dromore Castle, County Limerick *(fig. 7-7)*

ca. 1869–70
Pencil and colored washes
7 x 10 in. (17.7 x 25.4 cm)
Inscription: "Fabrics for Dromore 1/6th full size; Gold; red"

British Architectural Library Drawings Collection, RIBA, London, Ran, 7/B/1 (90)

References: See no. 26; Reid, "Dromore Castle" (1987): 129; Soros, "E. W. Godwin" (1998): 161–62, fig. 160.

29. Design for Textiles for Dromore Castle, County Limerick *(fig. 7-9)*

ca. 1869–70
Pencil, colored washes
8½ x 6¹¹⁄₁₆ in. (21.5 x 17 cm)
Inscription: "Dromore Castle Patterns; Rana; Quarter by Wyatt; Border red white; Blanket; oil cloth; Carpet; Valence; Nevill; Carpet; ?Merley; White stars / on red; white & blue; Glanville"

British Architectural Library Drawings Collection, RIBA, London, Ran 7/B/1 (91)

References: Reid, "Dromore Castle" (1987): 131–32, fig. 20; Soros, "E. W. Godwin" (1998): 162, fig. 162.

30. Design for Tile Pavements for Dromore Castle, County Limerick *(fig. 11-8)*

1869
Pencil, brown and gray washes, India ink, labeling
6⅜ x 15⅝ in. (16.2 x 39.7 cm)
Inscription: "Dromore Castle / Design for glazed tile Pavements on 2nd. 3rd & 4th landings of Grand Staircase / Lugwardine Work; Foot of Grand Staircase / Principal Entrance; Grand Staircase / foot of 2nd flight; Chapel door / 3rd landing; 2nd landing; approved. / 14.69 (sic) / E W Godwin"

British Architectural Library Drawings Collection, RIBA, London, Ran 7/B/1 (85)

References: Reid, "Dromore Castle" (1987): 129; Soros, "E. W. Godwin" (1998): 160, fig. 157a.

31. Design for a Memorial Cross, Kensal Green Cemetery, London *(Chronology, fig. C8)*

ca. 1869
Sepia pen and wash, pencil details, red pen labelling
13¹³⁄₁₆ x 10⅝ in. (35.1 x 26.2 cm)
Inscription: "ss set back from / the face of the large / Circle; R flush with the large / Circle; Mr. Peter Cooke (Builder) / 57 Chester St / Kennington Rd Lambeth." [and additional inscriptions]

British Architectural Library Drawings Collection, RIBA, London, Ran 7/C/8

32. Photograph of Glenbeigh Towers, County Kerry *(fig. 6-35)*

Photographed before 1914
William Lawrence
Modern contact print from a glass plate
Inscription: "CASTLE WHYNN. GLENBEIGH. 2813. W.L."

Lawrence Collection, National Library of Ireland, Dublin, W.L. 2813.

References: "Glenbeigh Towers" (13 May 1871): 248–49 and illus.; *Irish Builder* (28 August 1902): 1378 and illus.; Fuller, *Omniana* (1916): 203–204; Richardson, *Gothic Revival Architecture in Ireland* (1983): 692–93; Fitz-Gerald, Griffin, and Robinson, *Vanishing Country Houses* (1988): 82–83; Bence-Jones, *Guide to Irish Country Houses* (1990): 136.

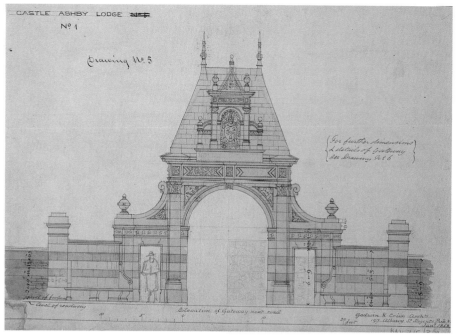

Cat. no. 35. Central Gateway, South Avenue Lodges, Castle Ashby, Northamptonshire: elevation, 1868. India ink and colored washes with pencil detail; 10⅞₆ x 14¹¹⁄₁₆ in. (26.5 x 37.4 cm). British Architectural Library Drawings Collection, RIBA, London, Ran, 7/C/3 (29).

33. "Railway Lodge," Castle Ashby, Northamptonshire (fig. 6-36)
Front elevation
1867
India ink and colored washes
21¾ x 15 in. (55.3 x 38.2 cm)
Inscription: "CASTLE ASHBY / LODGE NO 2; FRONT ELEVATION; Geo Scriven / John Watkin; GODWIN & CRISP. ARCHTS / 197 ALBANY ST REGENTS PARK N.W./ NOV^BR 1867"

British Architectural Library Drawings Collection, RIBA, London, Ran 7/C/3 (14)

References: "North Lodge at Castle Ashby" (10 June 1871): 302 and illus.; Godwin "On Some Buildings . . ." (29 November 1878): 211; Jackson-Stops, "Castle Ashby . . ." (6 February 1986): 314–15; M. Hall, "Chinese Puzzle" (25 July 1991): 78–81.

34. South Lodges and Gateway, Castle Ashby, Northamptonshire
(fig. 6-38)
Front elevation
1869
India ink and colored washes
10¹⁄₁₆ x 38¼ in. (25.6 x 97.2 cm)

Inscription: [recto] "SOUTH LODGES CASTLE ASHBY / CONTRACT B Drawing no. 2 / R. M Bryant; Elevation next road; Godwin & Crisp Archts. / 197 Albany St Regents Park N.W. / May 1869" [and additional inscriptions]; [verso] "CASTLE ASHBY"

British Architectural Library Drawings Collection, RIBA, London, Ran 7/C/3 (51)

References: see no. 33; "Gateway to the South Avenue . . ." (21 October 1871): 202 and illus.; "Lodge at Castle Ashby" (7 March 1873): 272 and illus. [279].

35. Central Gateway, South Avenue Lodges, Castle Ashby, Northamptonshire
Elevation
1868
India ink and colored washes with pencil detail
10⅞₆ x 14¹¹⁄₁₆ in. (26.5 x 37.4 cm)
Inscription: "CASTLE ASHBY LODGE / No. 1 / Drawing No. 5; Elevation of Gateway next road; for further dimensions / & details of Gateway / see Drawing no. 6; level of footway; level of roadway; Godwin & Crisp Archts. / 197 Albany St Regents Park N.W. / Jany 1868" [and additional inscriptions]

British Architectural Library Drawings Collection, RIBA, London, Ran, 7/C/3 (29)

References: see no. 34.

36. The Red House, Gustard Wood Common, Wheathampstead, Hertfordshire (fig. 7-5)
Perspective drawing and floor plans
ca. 1868
Watercolor, pencil, pen and ink
8⅞ x 11⅛ in. (22.7 x 28.2 cm)
Inscription: "Large Van Eyck Carpet.; Large Turkey carpet; red curtains; deal table / with drawers; Turkey rug; Large / wood beds^t; Small Van / Eyck / Carpet; Brass / Bedstead; 1 pr. blue curtains; Blue curtains." [and additional inscriptions]

The Board of Trustees of the Victoria and Albert Museum, London, E.273-1963

References: Terry, *Ellen Terry's Memoirs* (1933): 65–69, 74; E. A. Craig, *Gordon Craig* (1968): 38–40; Strickland, "Ellen Terry's six years 'exile'" (July 1970): 29; Clutterbuck, "Ellen Terry's 'exile'" (November 1970): n.p.; N. B. Wilkinson, "Edward William Godwin" (1987): 151–52, fig. 30; Reid, "Homes Fit for Hera" (10 December 1992): 38, fig. 6; Soros, "E. W. Godwin" (1998): 154–59, fig. 155.

37. Wardrobe (fig. 8-19)
ca. 1868
Made by William Watt
Pine, mirror glass insert, turned wooden knobs
82⅞ x 47⅜ x 18⅝ in. (210.4 x 120.4 x 47.2 cm)
Enameled William Watt labels affixed to back of hanging section, to chest of drawers, and to book shelf sections of wardrobe
Inscription: [in pencil on inside of wardrobe door in Ellen Terry's hand] "This my bedroom at Farm E.T."

Bristol Museums and Art Gallery, Bristol, N4505

References: Watt, *Art Furniture* (1877): pl. 15; Bristol Museums and Art Gallery, *Furniture by Godwin and Breuer,* exh. cat. (1976): no. 11; Aslin, *E. W. Godwin* (1986): 30, 71, pl. 45; N. B. Wilkinson, "Edward William Godwin" (1987): 190; Soros, "E. W. Godwin" (1998): 60–61, fig. 36, cat. no. 302.

38. Hanging Bookcase (fig. 8-27)
ca. 1867–85
Made by William Watt
Ebonized mahogany decorated with gold-painted *mon* (crests) and brass fittings

62⅜ x 32 1/16 x 52 in. (158.4 x 81.5 x 132.1 cm)

Private collection: Gary Kemp

References: Watt, *Art Furniture* (1877): pl. 6; Bristol Museums and Art Gallery, *Furniture by Godwin and Breuer,* exh. cat. (1976): no. 8 (similar bookcase); Fine Art Society, *Spring '94,* exh. cat. (1994): 36, fig. 47 (similar bookcase); Soros, "E. W. Godwin" (1998): 71–72, fig. 63 (similar bookcase), cat. 315.1.

39. *"Fallows Green," Harpenden, Hertfordshire* (fig. 6-30)
Johnston Forbes-Robertson
ca. 1873
Oil on board
5 x 6¾ in. (12.7 x 17.2 cm)

Collection of the National Trust, The Ellen Terry Memorial Museum, Smallhythe Place, Tenterden, Kent, SMA P.138

References: Brandreth, *Harpenden in Old Picture Postcards* (1983): pl. 25; Melville, *Ellen and Edy* (1987): 53, illus.; Soros, "E. W. Godwin" (1998): 170–72.

40. *"Fallows Green," Harpenden, Hertfordshire* (fig. 6-31)
Johnston Forbes-Robertson
ca. 1873
Oil on board
4½ x 6½ in. (11.4 x 16.5 cm)

Collection of the National Trust, The Ellen Terry Memorial Museum, Smallhythe Place, Tenterden, Kent, SMA P. 139

References: E. A. Craig, *Gordon Craig* (1968): 41, illus.; Strickland, "Ellen Terry's six years 'exile'" (July 1970): 29; Woolfe, "Smallhythe Place, Kent" (30 August 1990): 78, fig. 1; Melville, *Ellen Terry and Smallhythe Place* (1997): 8, illus.; Soros, "E. W. Godwin" (1998): 170–72.

41. **Coffee Table** (fig. 8-39)
ca. 1872–75
Made by Collinson and Lock
Ebonized mahogany
27¼ x 20⅛ x 19⅝ in. (69 x 51 x 50 cm)
Stamped "Collinson and Lock 7001" on underside of table top

Private collection: Gary Kemp

References: Soros, "E. W. Godwin" (1998): 105, cat. no. 210.

42. **"Old English or Jacobean" Armchair** (fig. 8-41)
ca. 1867–85
Made by William Watt
Ebonized wood, upholstered seat
34½ x 20½ x 20½ in. (87.5 x 52 x 52 cm)
Enameled William Watt label affixed to the underside of chair

Private collection: Gary Kemp

References: Watt, *Art Furniture* (1877): pl. 15; Bridgeman and Drury, eds., *Encyclopaedia of Victoriana* (1975): 56, illus. (similar chair); Fine Art Society, *Architect-Designers,* exh. cat. (1981): 32, fig. 26 (similar chair); Aslin, *E. W. Godwin* (1986): 27, 49, fig. 15 (similar chair); Tilbrook, *Truth, Beauty and Design* (1986): fig. 60 (similar chair); Soros, "E. W. Godwin" (1998): 111–12, no. 107.

43. **Beauvale House, Newthorpe, Nottinghamshire** (fig. 6-40)
Southwest elevation and details of glazing patterns
ca 1872–73
India ink, colored washes with pencil details
16 x 22 in. (40.7 x 55.8 cm)
Inscription: "BEAUVALE. S.W. ELEVATION; Dormer; iron / casement; lead / flashing; 2 courses of tiles deep / Small Bay; no lead; Windows at side of / Small Bay ½ in. scale; A.B. These Two patterns of / Glazing are not to occur in the / same windows; secret gutter; E W Godwin; Saml Simpson"

British Architectural Library Drawings Collection, RIBA, London, Ran 7/D/8 (8)

References: "Beauvale, Nottinghamshire" (3 July 1874): 8 and illus. [30–31]; "Beauvale: Mr. E. W. Godwin, Architect" (10 July 1874): 58; Pevsner, *Nottinghamshire* (1951): 34; Mark Girouard, "Beauvale" in *The Country Seat,* ed. Colvin and Harris (1970): 262–66; Girouard, *Victorian Country House* (1979): 329–34, fig. 321; N. B. Wilkinson, "Edward William Godwin" (1987): 284–86; Esher, *Glory of the English House* (1991): 170.

44. **Beauvale House, Newthorpe, Nottinghamshire** (Chronology, fig. C11)
Northeast elevation
ca. 1872–73
Inscription: "8; DATUM LINE. or Ground Line.; E W Godwin; Saml Simpson"
India ink, colored washes with pencil details
16 x 22 in. (40.6 x 55.9 cm)

British Architectural Library Drawings Collection, RIBA, London, Ran 7/D/8 (10)

References: see no. 43.

45. **Beauvale House, Newthorpe, Nottinghamshire** (Chronology, fig. C12)
Sections
ca. 1872–73
India ink, colored washes with pencil details
16 x 22 in. (40.6 x 55.9 cm)
Inscription: "SECTION THRO' KITCHEN; E W Godwin; Saml Simpson" [and additional inscriptions]

British Architectural Library Drawings Collection, RIBA, London, Ran 7/D/8 (11)

References: see no. 43.

Cat. no. 46a–c. Designs for stained-glass roundels representing floral motifs, ca. 1873. Watercolor; 9¾ x 8⅛ in. (24.8 x 20.7 cm); 9 11/16 x 7 13/16 in. (24.6 x 19.9 cm); 9½ x 8⅛ in. (24.2 x 20.7 cm). Trustees of the Victoria and Albert Museum, London, E. 519-521-1963.

46. Designs for Stained-Glass Roundels Representing Floral Motifs

ca. 1873
Watercolor
9¾ x 8⅛ in. (24.8 x 20.7 cm);
9¹¹⁄₁₆ x 7¹³⁄₁₆ in. (24.6 x 19.9 cm);
9½ x 8⅛ in. (24.2 x 20.7 cm)

The Board of Trustees of the Victoria and Albert Museum, London, E. 519-521-1963

References: Mark Girouard, "Beauvale" in *The Country Seat*, ed. Colvin and Harris (1970): 265, fig. 178; Girouard, *Victorian Country House* (1979): 322, fig. 319; Aslin, *E. W. Godwin* (1986): 25, 71, fig. 14.

47. Minister's House, Moor Green, Nottinghamshire *(fig. 6-44)*

Plans, elevations, and details
ca. 1873
India ink and colored washes with pencil details on tracing paper
17½ x 24 in. (44.5 x 61 cm)
Inscription: "Ministers House Moorgreen / Nottingham Scale 8ft to 1 inch; Details and specification of cottages / to apply to this except shown here / in detail to be different / Doors to closets under roof may / be placed at M.M; S.E. ELEVATION; S.W ELEVATION; N.W. ELEVATION; N.E. ELEVATION; GROUND PLAN; BASEMENT PLAN; Window; ROOF PLAN; Shutters for windows marked only."

British Architectural Library Drawings Collection, RIBA, London, Ran 7/E/2 (1)

References: "A Parsonage for £550" (6 March 1874): 256, [263, 266–67]; Greeves, "London's First Garden Suburb" (7 December 1967): 1526; Mark Girouard, "Beauvale" in *The Country Seat*, ed. Colvin and Harris (1970): 266, n. 5; N. B. Wilkinson, "Edward William Godwin" (1987): 286–87.

48. Design for a Detached Corner House, Bedford Park, Chiswick, London *(fig. 6-49)*

Plans and elevation
1875
Pencil, pen and ink
11 x 17½ in. (27.9 x 44.4 cm)
Inscription: "Bedford Park / For Corner Plot 50' x 75'; 1st floor; 2nd floor; E. W. Godwin Archt. / Sep 1875" [and additional inscriptions]

The Board of Trustees of the Victoria and Albert Museum, London, E.577-1963

References: "Bedford-Park Estate . . . " (22 December 1876): 622; Harbron, *Conscious Stone* (1949): 110; Greeves, "London's First Garden Suburb" (7 December 1967): 1524–9; Aslin, *Aesthetic Movement* (1969): 49–50; Greeves, *Bedford Park* (1975): fig. 68; Harbron, "Edward Godwin" in Edwardian Architecture, ed. Service (1975): 60, fig. 4; Bolsterli, *Early Community* (1977): 45–59; Girouard, *Sweetness and Light* (1977): 160-62; Stamp and Amery, *Victorian Buildings of London* (1980): 156–57; A. M. Edwards, *Design of Suburbia* (1981): 61–64; Pendleton, "Bedford Park" (1981): 16–44; Harper Smith and Harper Smith, *Middle Class Townlet* (1992); Stamp and Goulancourt, *English House* (1986): 206-207; N. B. Wilkinson, "Edward William Godwin" (1987): 287–89.

49. Corner Cabinet *(fig. 8-1)*

1873
Made by Collinson and Lock
Painted panels by Charles Fairfax Murray ("CFM" inscribed on Lucretia panel)
Rosewood with painted panels, brass hardware
75 x 32 x 23 in. (190.5 x 81.3 x 58.4 cm)
Stamped: "Collinson and Lock" inside third drawer; "Edwards and Roberts" inside top drawer

The Detroit Institute of Art, Founders Society Purchase, European Sculpture and Decorative Arts General Fund, Honorarium and Memorial Gifts Fund, 1985 (1985.1)

References: Kinchin, "Collinson and Lock" (May 1979): 51–52, fig. 8; Aslin, *E. W. Godwin* (1986): 17, 30, nos. 18, 42; Cooper, *Victorian and Edwardian Decor* (1987): p. 141, pl. 330; Hoare, "Lost and Found" (March 1983): 31, illus.; Detroit Institute of Art (1985): 32, fig. 23; Barnet, "From the Middle Ages to the Victorians" (December 1986): 505; Bolger Burke, *In Pursuit of Beauty* (1986): 150-51, fig. 5.9; Darr, "European Sculpture and Decorative Arts" (June 1988): 500, fig. 115; Soros, "E. W. Godwin" (1998): 69, fig. 56, cat. no. 322.

50. Design for Chairs *(fig. 8-44)*

1873
Pen, ink, and pencil on tracing paper
13⅜ x 17½ in. (34 x 44.5 cm)
Inscription: "Collinson & Lock. / Chairs for Vienna Oct '73."; [monogram signature] EWG

Collection of the National Trust, Ellen Terry Memorial Museum, Smallhythe Place, Tenterden, Kent, SMA D.24

References: Aslin, *E. W. Godwin* (1986): 28, 58, pl. 27; Cooper, *Victorian and Edwardian Decor* (1987): 129, figs. 208–9; Soros, "E. W. Godwin" (1998): 122, fig. 133.

51. Cottage Cabinet *(fig. 8-36)*

ca. 1874
Made by Collinson and Lock
Mahogany with brass fittings
50 x 66 x 16⅞ in. (127 x 167.5 x 43 cm)

Private collection: Sheri Sandler

References: Soros, "E. W. Godwin" (1998): 89–90, fig. 88, cat. no. 324.

52. Decorative Scheme for a Drawing Room *(fig. 7-21)*

ca. 1873–76
Pen and ink on tracing paper
24⅜ x 19⅝ in. (62 x 50 cm)
Inscription: "Inscription round room / lines 2289 to 2292 / Chaucers Romaunt of the Rose; blue; This is a nearly square panel / in plane / with a gold burnished / sun in relief / on vellum ground / with blue centres; gold; raised plaster work / painted pale copper red / on gold ground ; gold; vellum colours; gold rod to hang pictures / black hooks; gold & black / patterns on / dark vellum ground / or blue on / gold; burnished / gold / panel / with red on / black ground / Ivory / & gold / ornament; mirror; ivory; rosewood; black; Ebony & gold bars across / mirror; Labyrinth; Daisy; Narcissus; ¼ inch to a foot"

The Board of Trustees of the Victoria and Albert Museum, London, AAD 4/16-1988

References: Aslin, *E. W. Godwin* (1986): 16, 88, pl. 72; Soros, "E. W. Godwin" (1998): 184–86. fig. 180.

53. Design for "Butterfly" Brocade *(fig. 9-12)*

ca. 1874
Pencil and watercolor, on paper with overlapping flap
14½ in x 12¼ in. (37 x 31 cm)

Purchased through The Art Foundation of Victoria with the assistance of J. B. Were and Sons, Governor, 1989. National Gallery of Victoria, Melbourne, P108/109

References: Gere and Whiteway, *Nineteenth-Century Design* (1993): 157, pl. 195.

54. "Butterfly" Brocade *(fig. 9-1)*

ca. 1874
Made by Warner, Sillett and Ramm
Jacquard woven silk
34¹⁄₁₆ x 21⁹⁄₁₆ in. (86.5 x 55 cm)

The Board of Trustees of the Victoria and Albert Museum, London, T.152-1972

References: Aslin, "E. W. Godwin and the Japanese Taste" (December 1962): 34, 91; Goodale, *Weaving and the Warners* (1971): 54, no. 15; Lubell, *Textile Collections of the World*, vol. 2 (1976): 61, fig. 24; D. King, ed., *British Textile Design,* vol. 3 (1980): xxiv, no. 74; Aslin, *E. W. Godwin* (1986): 34, 91, pl. 76; Galeries nationales du Grand Palais, *Japonisme* (1988): 187, fig. 210; Parry, *Victoria and Albert Museum's Textile Collection* (1993): 23, 64, fig. 75; Lambourne, *Aesthetic Movement* (1996): 152, illus.

55. "Small Syringa" *(fig. 9-14)*
ca. 1874
Made by Warner, Sillett and Ramm
Jacquard woven silk
34¼ x 62⅝ in. (87 x 159 cm)

The Board of Trustees of the Victoria and Albert Museum, London, T.154-1972

References: D. King, *British Textile Design* vol. 3, (1980): xxiv, no. 71; Parry, *Victoria and Albert Museum's Textile Collection* (1993): 23, 63, fig. 72.

56. "Large Syringa" *(fig. 9-13)*
ca. 1874
Made by Warner, Sillett and Ramm
Jacquard woven silk
54½ x 42 in. (138.4 x 106.7 cm)

The Board of Trustees of the Victoria and Albert Museum, London, T.153-1972

References: Goodale, *Weaving and the Warners* (1971): 54, no. 17; Tilbrook, *Truth, Beauty and Design* (1986): fig. 62; Sato and Watanabe, *Japan and Britain* (1991): 116–17, fig. 109 (similar fabric).

57. Sideboard *(fig. 4-1)*
ca. 1877
Made by William Watt
Ebonized mahogany with brass pulls and hinges, glass panels
72½ x 100½ x 19¾ in. (184.2 x 255.3 x 50.2 cm)

Private collection

References: Agius, *British Furniture* (1978): 64, pl. 70 (similar sideboard); Cooper, *Victorian and Edwardian Decor* (1987): 140, fig. 324 (similar sideboard); Barnet and Wilkinson, *Decorative Arts 1900*, exh. cat. (1993): no. 11; Gere and Whiteway, *Nineteenth-Century Design* (1993): 134–35, pl. 164; Reeves, "Anglo-Japanese Buffet" (1994): 37, fig. 2; Watson, *The Godwin Variations* (1994): 1–8; Watson, "Not Just a Sideboard" (Spring–Summer 1997): 63–84; Soros, "E. W. Godwin" (1998): 52, cat. no. 301.5.

58. Pair of Vases *(fig. 11-5)*
Attributed to E. W. Godwin
ca. 1877
Red earthenware with cream slip glaze.
Each vase, 7½ x 8½ x 8½ in.
(19 x 21.6 x 21.6 cm)
Inscription: [on the side of one vase]
"KAWPHYRITE"
Marks: [incised on bases] "J.G. + E.W.G.";
[potter's initials illegible]

Paul Reeves, London

Reference: Bryers, "Unique and Important Pair of Red Earthenware Vases" (ca. 1996).

59. "Bird" Tiles *(fig. 11-19)*
Attributed to E. W. Godwin
ca. 1881
Made by Minton and Hollins
Glazed earthenware
Each tile (3 in all), 6 x 6 in.
(15.2 x 15.2 cm)

Paul Reeves, London

References: "Messrs. Minton, Hollins, & Co . . . " (18 March 1881): 143.

60. Sketchbook
Open to drawings of crests and other motifs *(fig. 10-6)*
ca. 1870
Pencil and watercolor
9 x 6½ in. (22.9 x 16.5 cm)
Inscription: "Powderings - or Crests; Mikado; The ?white / should be / larger."

The Board of Trustees of the Victoria and Albert Museum, London, E.280-1963: 9

References: Humbert, *Le Japon illustré* (1870); Aslin, "E. W. Godwin" (December 1962): 779, fig. 1; Aslin, *E. W. Godwin* (1986): 33–34, 90, pl. 75; N. B. Wilkinson, "Edward William Godwin" (1987): 254; Lambourne, *Aesthetic Movement* (1996): 157, illus.

61. "Sparrows and Bamboo" Wallpaper *(fig. 10-12)*
1872
Made by Jeffrey and Company
Block-printed wallpaper
13⅞ x 16⅞ in. (35.1 x 43 cm)

Manchester City Art Galleries, 1934.22/37viii

References: "Wall-Papers" (11 October 1872): 291, [286–87]; George, *Modern Wall Decoration* (1893): 5; Watt, *Art Furniture* (1877): pl. 20; Sugden and Edmondson, *History of English Wallpaper* (1925): pl. 117; Whitworth Art Gallery, *A Decorative Art,* exh. cat. (1985): 53, fig. 40; N. B.

Wilkinson, "Edward William Godwin" (1987): 257–58, fig. 141; Banham, MacDonald, and Porter, *Victorian Interior Design* (1991): 112–13, fig 117.

Cat no. 62. Page from a Jeffrey and Company logbook (vol. 1, no. 2, p. 118), showing Godwin wallpapers: "Sparrows and Bamboo," "Jeddo," and "Plait," 1872. Block-printed wallpaper, paper, pen and ink notations; 12 ⅝ x 10 ¼ in. (32 x 26 cm). Arthur Sanderson and Sons Limited.

62. Page from a Jeffrey and Company Logbook
Vol. 1, no. 2, p. 118, showing Godwin wallpapers: "Sparrows and Bamboo," "Jeddo," and "Plait"
1872
Block-printed wallpaper, paper, pen and ink notations
12⅝ x 10¼ in. (32 x 26 cm)

Arthur Sanderson and Sons Limited

References: "Wall-Papers" (11 October 1872): 291, [286–87]; "Wall Decorations" (8 May 1874): 492–93, [504–5].

63. Design for "Sparrow" Border and "Floral Medallion" Filling
(fig. 10-9)
1872
Pencil on tracing paper
13⅞ x 16⅞ in. (35.1 x 43 cm)
Inscription [verso]: "Wallpaper Design / for Jeffrey Islington 1872 / Illustrated the Building News / May 8 1874"

The Board of Trustees of the Victoria and Albert Museum, London, E.514-1963

References: "Wall Decorations" (8 May 1874): 492–93 and [504–5]; Watt, *Art Furniture* (1877): pl. 20; Harbron, *Conscious Stone* (1949): 81; Aslin, *E. W. Godwin* (1986): 34, 92, pl. 78.

Cat. no. 64. E. W. Godwin. Design for wallpaper (or tiles): frieze with Japanese sparrow design, ca. 1872. Pencil and watercolor with pen and ink notes on tracing paper; 12 x 15 in. (30.5 x 38 cm). Trustees of the Victoria and Albert Museum, London, E.512-1963.

64. Design for Wallpaper Frieze or Tiles

ca. 1872
Pencil and watercolor with pen and ink notes on tracing paper
12 x 15 in. (30.5 x 38 cm)
Inscription: "White or / Blue Ground; Blue or / White ground; Repeat Bird"

The Board of Trustees of the Victoria and Albert Museum, London, E.512-1963

References: Oman and Hamilton, *Wallpapers* (1982): 330, fig 970.

65. Design for "Bamboo" Wallpaper

(fig. 10-1)
1872
Watercolor on tracing paper
21¼ x 21¼ in. (54 x 54 cm)
Inscription: [recto] "WALL DECORATION by / E. W. Godwin / November 1872"; [verso] "Wall Decoration, November 1872."

The Board of Trustees of the Victoria and Albert Museum, London, E.515-1963

References: "Wall Decorations" (8 May 1874): 492–93, [504–5]; Watt, *Art Furniture* (1877): pl. 20; Harbron, *Conscious Stone* (1949): 81; Aslin, *Aesthetic Movement* (1969): 28, pl. 16, 63–64; Fine Art Society, *Architect-Designers* (1981): 32, illus.; Teynac, Nolot, and Vivien, *Wallpaper* (1982): 153, illus.; J. Hamilton, *Introduction to Wallpaper* (1983): 30, pl. 32; Aslin, *E. W. Godwin* (1986): 25, col. pl. 16, dust jacket; *British Design* (1987): 44, pl. 27; N. B. Wilkinson, "Edward William Godwin" (1987): 255–56, fig. 137; Lambourne, *Aesthetic Movement* (1996): 157, illus.

66. Design for "Peacock" Wallpaper

(fig. 3-12)
ca. 1872
Watercolor and pencil on tracing paper
13¾ x 10½ in. (35 x 26.8 cm)
Inscription: "To be printed in the / pale or ground tint on / the darkest or line tint / the second that for the / making of the feathers ; E.W.G."

The Board of Trustees of the Victoria and Albert Museum, London, E.513-1963
References: "Wall Decorations" (8 May 1874): 492–93 and illus. [504–5]; Watt, *Art Furniture* (1877): pl. 20; *Magazine of Art* 1 (1878–79): 90; Sugden and Edmondson, *History of English Wallpaper* (1925): pl. 123; Entwisle, *Wallpapers of the Victorian Era* (1964): fig. 39, pl. 22; Oman and Hamilton, *Wallpapers* (1982): 330–31, fig. 971; Aslin, *E. W. Godwin* (1986): 34, 91, pl. 77; N. B. Wilkinson, "Edward William Godwin" (1987): 225–26, 255–56; Galeries nationales du Grand Palais (1988): 187, fig. 209.

67. "Peacock" Wallpaper *(fig. 10-11)*

ca. 1873
Made by Jeffrey and Company
Block-printed wallpaper
26½ x 19¼ in. (67.2 x 48.9 cm)

Manchester City Art Galleries, 1934.22/19iii

References: George, *Modern Wall Decoration* (1873): 5; "Wall Decorations" (8 May 1874): 492–93 and illus. [504–5]; Watt, *Art Furniture* (1877): pl. 20; *Magazine of Art*, 1 (1878–79): 90; Sugden and Edmondson, *History of English Wallpaper* (1925): pl. 123; Harbron, *Conscious Stone* (1949): 83, illus.

(similar piece); Entwisle, *Wallpapers of the Victorian Era* (1964): fig. 39; Aslin, *Aesthetic Movement* (1969): 120, fig. 73 (similar piece); N. B. Wilkinson, "Edward William Godwin" (1987): 225–26; Banham, MacDonald, and Porter, *Victorian Interior Design* (1991): 112, fig. 116; Lambourne, *Aesthetic Movement* (1996): 59, illus.

68. Page from a Jeffrey and Company Logbook *(fig. 10-14)*

Vol. 1, no. 2, p. 130, showing Godwin wallpaper: "Peacock" and "Bamboo"
1873
Block-printed wallpaper, paper, pen and ink notations.
12⅝ x 10¼ in. (32 x 26 cm)

Arthur Sanderson and Sons Limited

References: "Wall Decorations" (8 May 1874): 492–93 and illus. [504–5].

69. Anglo-Japanese Designs *(fig. 3-21)*

ca. 1875
Pen and ink, with watercolor
7⅞ x 11⅝ in. (20 x 29.5 cm)
Inscription: "Anglo Japanese. Designs by E W Godwin"

The Board of Trustees of the Victoria and Albert Museum, London, E.482-1963

References: Lasdun, *Victorians at Home* (1981): 108, illus.; N. B. Wilkinson, "Edward William Godwin" (1987): 246–47; Galeries nationales du Grand Palais, *Japonisme* (1988): 224–25, [230]; Sato and Watanabe, *Japan and Britain* (1991): 116, fig 104; Jacobson, *Chinoiserie* (1993): 205. Miyajima, *British Design at Home* (1994): 61, no. 38.

70. Anglo-Japanese Side Chair *(fig. 8-31)*

ca. 1875
Probably made by William Watt
Ebonized wood with cane seat; one of a pair
39 x 16⅞ x 16⅛ in. (99 x 43 x 41 cm)

Musée d'Orsay, Paris, OAO 1302

References: Phillips, *British, Continental* (13 October 1992): lot 255; Gere and Whiteway, *Nineteenth-Century Design* (1993): 156, 171, illus.; Tokyo Metropolitan Art Museum, *Modernité* (1996): 180, cat. no. 120; Musée d'Orsay, *De l'Impressionisme à l'Art Nouveau* (1996): 106; Soros, "E. W. Godwin" (1998): cat. no. 123.

71. Table with Folding Shelves *(fig. 3-1)*

ca. 1872
Probably made by Collinson and Lock
Walnut with gilt brass fittings

29⁷⁄₁₆ x 16 x 32⅛ in. (74.7 x 40.6 x 81.5 cm)

The Metropolitan Museum of Art, New York, Purchase, Rogers Fund; Margaret A. Darrin Gift; Gift of Ogden Mills, by exchange; Gift of Bernard Baruch, by exchange; Anne Eden Woodward Foundation and Friends of European Sculpture and Decorative Arts Gifts, 1991 (1991.87).

References: Cooper, *Victorian and Edwardian Decor* (1987): 140–41, pl. 326; N. B. Wilkinson, "Edward William Godwin" (1987): 226–28; Metropolitan Museum of Art, "Recent Acquisitions" (Fall 1991): 32; Reid, "Homes Fit for Hera" (10 December 1992): 39, fig. 8 (similar piece); Gere and Whiteway, *Nineteenth-Century Design* (1993): 153, pl. 188; Gruber, *Art décoratif* (1994): 245; Soros, "E. W. Godwin" (1998): 58, 87–88, cat. no. 211.

72. *Art Furniture, from Designs by E. W. Godwin, F.S.A., and Others, with Hints and Suggestions on Domestic Furniture and Decoration,* by William Watt
Open to the frontispiece and title page
(fig. 3-18; see also figs. 3-7, 3-18, 4-3, 7-1, 7-26, 8-18, 8-24, 10-5, 10-10, 10-15)
Published by B. T. Batsford, London
1877
Bound book
8⅛ x 12¼ in. (20.4 x 31 cm)

The Mitchell Wolfson Jr. Collection, The Wolfsonian-Florida International University, Miami Beach, Florida, TD1990.40.62

References: "Art Furniture," part 2 (24 August 1877): 174; "*Art Furniture from Designs* . . . " (25 August 1877): 145; "Art Furniture by Edward W. Godwin" (October 1878): pl. 76; Lancaster, "Oriental Contributions to Art Nouveau" (December 1952): 300, fig. 1; Symonds and Whineray, *Victorian Furniture* (1962): 77, fig. 86; Aslin, *E. W. Godwin* (1986): 26–27, 44–45, pl. 11.

73. "Star" Wallpaper *(fig. 10-16)*
1876
Made by William Watt
Block-printed paper
22 x 29½ in. (56 x 75 cm)

Public Record Office, United Kingdom, BT/43/101 Part 1, No. 302033

References: Aslin, *E. W. Godwin* (1986): 34, 95, pl. 84; Lambourne, *Aesthetic Movement* (1996): 157, illus.

74. "Apple" Wallpaper *(fig. 10-17)*
1876
Made by William Watt
Block-printed paper
20⅞ x 22¹⁄₁₆ in. (53 x 56 cm)

Public Record Office, United Kingdom, BT/43/101 Part 1, No. 301929

References: Aslin, *E. W. Godwin* (1986): 34, 95, pl. 83.

75. "Queen Anne" Wallpaper *(fig. 10-18)*
1876
Made by William Watt
Block-printed paper
19⁵⁄₁₆ x 22¹⁄₁₆ in. (49 x 56 cm)

Public Record Office, United Kingdom, BT/43/101 Part 1, No. 302278

76. Sketchbook
Open to design sketches for "Anglo-Greek" and "Algerian" wallpapers
ca. 1876–78
This page: pencil, red ink, and pen on paper *(also see figs. 10-13 and 10-19–10-23)*
With binding, vertical opening, 6¹⁄₁₆ x 3¹⁵⁄₁₆ in. (15.3 x 10 cm); page trim, 6 x 3¹⁵⁄₁₆ in. (15.2 x 10 cm); Inscription: "Anglo-Greek. / 2 colour. / Sold / Waugh; Algerian / 3 color [*sic*]"

The Board of Trustees of the Victoria and Albert Museum, London, E.241-1963: 35

References: Watt, *Art Furniture* (1877): pl. 2.

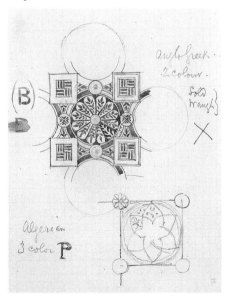

Cat. no. 76. Page from a sketchbook: design sketches for "Anglo-Greek" and "Algerian" wallpapers, ca. 1876–78. Pencil, red ink, and pen on paper; 6 x 3¹⁵⁄₁₆ in. (15.2 x 10 cm). Trustees of the Victoria and Albert Museum, London, E.241-1963: 35.

77. Sketchbook
Open to pages 26 and 27, designs for toilet sets probably for William Watt *(fig. 11-1)*
ca. 1876
These pages: watercolor and pencil, annotations in pencil and in pen and ink
Each page (vertical): 6 x 4 in. (15.2 x 10.3 cm)
Inscription: [page 27] "1/8 real size; W.9" [and additional inscriptions]

The Board of Trustees of the Victoria and Albert Museum, London, E.233-1963: 26–27

References: Watt, *Art Furniture* (1877): pl. 16; Aslin, *E. W. Godwin* (1986): 13, 31, 73, pl. 48.

78. Nottingham Church Cemetery Chapel, Nottingham *(fig. 6-12)*
Competition drawing: perspective view from the northeast
1877
Sepia pen and wash
12³⁄₁₆ x 7¾ in. (30.9 x 19.7 cm)
Inscription: "E. W. Godwin F.S.A. Archt."

British Architectural Library Drawings Collection, RIBA, London, Ran 7/E/8 (10)

References: "Competition for Cemetery Chapel . . . " (3 August 1877): 99; "Nottingham Church Cemetery Competition" (24 August 1877): 99; "Nottingham Church Cemetery Competition . . . " (23 November 1877): 254, illus.; Godwin, "On Some Buildings . . . " (29 November 1878): 211.

79. Preliminary Design, Possibly for the Leicester Municipal Buildings Competition *(fig. 6-22)*
ca. 1871–73
Pen and ink, pencil and watercolor
12⅞ x 10⅞ in. (32.7 x 27.7 cm)

The Board of Trustees of the Victoria and Albert Museum, London, E.633-1963

References: Cunningham, *Victorian and Edwardian Town Halls* (1981): 50, 52–53 135, 142.

80. Design for a Town Hall, probably Kensington Vestry Hall, London
(Introduction, fig. iv)
1877
Pencil and watercolor, pen and ink
10⅜ x 8 in. (26.5 x 20.3 cm)
Inscriptions: [recto] "18,000"; [verso] "1877"

The Board of Trustees of the Victoria and Albert Museum, London, E.634-1963

References: Aslin, *Aesthetic Movement*
(1969): 87, pl. 57; Girouard, *Sweetness and
Light* (1977): 76, 82–84, facing p. 15
col. pl. 2; Cunningham, *Victorian and
Edwardian Town Halls* (1981): 133–34 n. 8
[228], 142.

81. Easy Chair *(fig. 8-46)*
ca. 1876
Made by William Watt
Ebonized wood with upholstered seat,
back, and arms, brass castors
32 x 23 x 31 in. (81.3 x 58.4 x 78.7 cm)
Label: [underside of seat] ivory disk
with Patent Office Registration dated
14 November 1876

The Brant Foundation, Greenwich,
Connecticut

References: "Anglo-Japanese Furniture,
Paris Exhibition" (14 June 1878): 596;
Harris, "Pieces of the Past" (1983): 11;
Hoare, "Lost and Found" (July 1983): 31;
Phillips, *Art Nouveau* (5 July 1984): lot. 305;
Aslin, *E. W. Godwin* (1986): 29, 64, pl. 34;
Fine Art Society, *Spring 1986* (1986): 29
no. 34, 64 [illus.]; Cooper, *Victorian and
Edwardian Decor* (1987): 122, pl. 290; N. B.
Wilkinson, "Edward William Godwin"
(1987): 250–51; Fine Art Society, *Spring
1989* (1989): 63 [ill]; Johnson, *Phillips Guide
to Chairs* (1989): 96; Soros, "E. W. Godwin"
(1998): 131, figs. 140–41, cat. no. 125.

82. "The William Watt Stand at the Paris Exposition Universelle of 1878" *(fig. 4-9)*
1878
Photograph (modern print)

The Board of Trustees of the Victoria and
Albert Museum, London

References: Aslin, "Furniture Designs of
E. W. Godwin" (October 1967): 10, fig. 10;
R. Spencer, *Aesthetic Movement* (1972):
[58]; Aslin, *E. W. Godwin* (1986): 28, 59,
pl. 28; Soros, "E. W. Godwin" (1998): 125.

83. The White House, 35 Tite Street, Chelsea, London *(fig. 6-52)*
Front elevation; first design, rejected by
the Metropolitan Board of Works, London
1877
Watercolor, pen and ink, and Chinese
white
15¼ x 21⅞ in. (38.6 x 55.5 cm)
Inscription: "Tite St. FRONT
ELEVATION of House for J.A.Mc.N.
Whistler Esq Chelsea; WINDOWS ¼
REAL SIZE; B. Nightingale/ Novr
6th/77; Edw W Godwin F.S.A. Archt. /
(no. 1.) Sep. 77." [and additional
inscriptions]

The Board of Trustees of the Victoria and
Albert Museum, London, E.540-1963

References: Godwin, "On Some
Buildings . . . " (29 November 1878): 210–
11; Godwin, "Studios and Mouldings"
(7 March 1879): 261–62; "Some Facts
about 'The White House,' Chelsea"
(26 September 1879): 119; Harbron,
Conscious Stone (1949): 126–27, 129;
Chelsea Society, *Annual Report, 1962*
(1962): 22–32; Dudley Harbron, "Edward
Godwin" in *Edwardian Architecture,* ed.
Service (1975): 62 fig. 5; Girouard,
"Chelsea's Bohemian Studio Houses"
(23 November 1972): 1370, fig 1; Physick
and Darby, *Marble Halls* (1973): 88, no. 44,
illus.; Girouard, *Sweetness and Light* (1977):
179, fig. 165; M.W. Brooks, *John Ruskin*
(1987): 210–11; N. B. Wilkinson, "Edward
William Godwin" (1987): 316–22; Gere
and Whiteway, *Nineteenth-Century Design*
(1993): 151, pl. 186; Walkley, *Artists' Houses
in London* (1994): 85, fig. 61; Bendix,
Diabolical Designs (1995): 147–48, fig. 53.

84. The White House, 35 Tite Street, Chelsea, London *(fig. 7-31)*
First-floor plan and section
1877
Pen and ink, watercolor, and pencil
15¼ x 21¾ in. (38.7 x 55.4 cm)
Inscription: "House for J.A.Mc.N. Whistler
esq; First floor; Section; B. Nightingale
Nov 6th/77; (no 3) E W Godwin Archt."

The Board of Trustees of the Victoria and
Albert Museum, London, E.542-1963

References: see no. 83; Soros, "E. W.
Godwin" (1998): 196–97.

85. The White House, 35 Tite Street, Chelsea, London *(fig. 6-53)*
Front elevation and section through
ground floor; revised design, accepted by
the Metropolitan Board of Works, London
ca. 1877–78
Pen and ink
13 x 19¾ in. (33.1 x 50.3 cm)
Inscription: "House & Studio for
J.A.Mc.N. Whistler Esq. Chelsea.; section
through Ground Floor; E. W. Godwin
Archt."

The Board of Trustees of the Victoria and
Albert Museum, London, E.544-1963

References: see no. 83; Dudley Harbron,
"Edward Godwin" in *Edwardian
Architecture,* ed. Service (1975): 62, fig. 6;
Aslin, *Aesthetic Movement* (1969): 103,
pl. 64; R. Spencer, *Aesthetic Movement*
(1972): 56–57, illus. (similar drawing);
Girouard, *Sweetness and Light* (1977): 179,

fig. 166; Banham, MacDonald, and Porter,
Victorian Interior Design (1991): 150, fig.
156; Soros, "E. W. Godwin" (1998): 196,
fig. 198.

86. "The White House, 35 Tite Street, Chelsea, London" *(fig. 6-54)*
ca. 1963
Photograph

Chelsea Library, Local Studies Collection,
neg. no. B498

References: see no. 83.

87. Preliminary Designs for Houses for Messrs. Gillow, 4–6 Chelsea Embankment, London *(fig. 6-51)*
1877
Pencil and colored wash with Chinese
white
13¾ x 19¹⁄₁₆ in. (35 x 48.5 cm)
Inscription: "EWG / Janʸ 77." [and
additional inscriptions]

British Architectural Library Drawings
Collection, RIBA, London, Ran 7/G/1 (1)

References: "Houses on Thames
Embankment . . . " (15 February 1878): 76,
86; (15 March 1878): 122; (12 April 1878):
170; "New Houses at Chelsea . . . "
(15 March 1878): 264, [266–67]; "The
Chelsea Embankment" (11 April 1879):
373–74; "What a pity it is . . ." (18 April
1879): 162; Girouard, "Chelsea's Bohemian
Studio Houses" (23 November 1972):
1370; Girouard, *Sweetness and Light* (1977):
94; Walkley, *Artists' Houses in London*
(1994): 83.

88. Frank Miles's House and Studio, 44 Tite Street, Chelsea, London *(fig. 3-26)*
Front elevation, section, and plans; detail
of a settee and a drawer handle; design
rejected by the Metropolitan Board of
Works
1878
Pencil and watercolor
8⅝ x 19¼ in. (22 x 49 cm)
Inscription: "EWG/June 24 78" [and
additional inscriptions]

The Board of Trustees of the Victoria and
Albert Museum, London, E.553-1963

References: Godwin, "Studios and
Mouldings" (7 March 1879): 261–62;
"Artists' Houses, Chelsea." (14 May 1880):
234 and illus.; "House and Studio for
F. Miles, Esq." (11 June 1880): 282 and
illus.; Harbron, *Conscious Stone* (1949), 128;
Stamp and Amery, *Victorian Buildings of
London* (1980): 141–42, fig. a.; N. B.

Wilkinson, "Edward William Godwin" (1987): 326–29; Walkley, *Artists' Houses in London* (1994): 88, fig. 65; Lambourne, *Aesthetic Movement* (1996): 164, illus.

89. Frank Miles's House and Studio, 44 Tite Street, Chelsea, London
(fig. 6-55)
Front elevation; design rejected by the Metropolitan Board of Works, London
ca. 1878
Pen and ink, pencil, and watercolor
15¼ x 11⅜ in. (38.7 x 28.9 cm)
Inscription: "[F]OR F. MILES ESQ. / [TITE S]TREET, CHELSEA. / FRONT ELEVATION"

The Board of Trustees of the Victoria and Albert Muscum, London, E.556-1963

References: Girouard, "Chelsea's Bohemian Studio Houses" (23 November 1972): 1371, fig 4; Girouard, *Sweetness and Light* (1977): 182, fig. 167; Cooper, *Victorian and Edwardian Decor* (1987): 119, fig. 286; Banham, MacDonald, and Porter, *Victorian Interior Design* (1991): 151, pl. 157.

90. Frank Miles's House and Studio, 44 Tite Street, Chelsea, London
(fig. 6-56)
Front elevation; design accepted by the Metropolitan Board of Works, London
1878
Pen and ink, pencil, and watercolor
20⅛ x 14⅝ in. (51.2 x 37.3 cm)
Inscription: "HOUSE & STUDIO FOR F. MILES ESQ: ; Note. The panels tinted red & bracket over top panel wall will be provided / by Mr Miles & will be 4½ to 5 inches thick; witness John Leaming ; George Francis Miles ; George Sharpe / for Sharpe & Everard"

The Board of Trustees of the Victoria and Albert Museum, London, E.554-1963

References: Godwin, "Studios and Mouldings" (7 March 1879): 261–62; Harbron, "Edward Godwin" (August 1945): 51, illus.; Aslin, *Aesthetic Movement* (1969): 102, pl. 63; Girouard, "Chelsea's Bohemian Studio Houses" (23 November 1972): 1371, fig. 5; Girouard, *Sweetness and Light* (1977): 182, fig. 168; Stamp and Amery, *Victorian Buildings of London* (1980): 142, fig. b.; Stamp and Goulancourt, *English House* (1986): 186–87; N. B. Wilkinson, "Edward William Godwin" (1987): 326–29; Walkley, *Artists' Houses in London* (1994): 89, fig. 66.

91. Frank Miles's House and Studio, 44 Tite Street, Chelsea, London
(fig. 7-40)

Cat. no. 92. "Chelsea Lodge, 60 Tite Street, Chelsea, London," ca. 1935. Chelsea Library, Local Studies Collection.

Back elevation and transverse section
ca. 1878–79
Pen and ink, watercolor, and pencil
14¾ x 20⅛ in. (37.5 x 51.2 cm)
Inscription: "HOUSE & STUDIO FOR F. MILES ESQ. / TITE STREET, CHELSEA ; BACK ELEVATION ; TRANSVERSE SECTION; witness John Leaming / George Francis Miles; George Sharpe for Sharpe & Everard"

The Board of Trustees of the Victoria and Albert Museum, London, E.557-1963

References: see nos. 88, 89, and 90.

92. "Chelsea Lodge, 60 Tite Street, Chelsea, London"
ca. 1935
Photograph

Chelsea Library, Local Studies Collection

References: "House and Studio for A. Stuart Wortley Esq., at Chelsea (29 November 1878): 210 and illus.; Godwin, "Studios and Mouldings" (7 March 1879): 261–62; Lucas, *Edwin Austin Abbey* vol. 2. (1921): 341; Girouard, "Chelsea's Bohemian Studio Houses" (23 November 1972): 1373, fig. 9; Walkley, *Artists' Houses in London* (1994): 87, pl. 63.

93. Center Table *(fig. 8-22)*
ca. 1878
Made by Collinson and Lock
Macassar ebony veneer, rosewood, ivory inlay, brass castors
27 x 27 x 27 in. (68.6 x 68.6 x 68.6 cm)
Stamped: [underside of table top]
Collinson and Lock London

Private collection: Sheri Sandler

References: "Furniture at the Paris Exhibition" (7 September 1878): 159; Cooper, *Victorian and Edwardian Decor* (1987): 140, pl. 327; Soros, "E. W. Godwin" (1998): 62, 123, fig. 40, cat. no. 226.

94. Studio for Princess Louise, Kensington Palace, London
(fig. 6-60)
Plan, elevations, section, and perspective drawing
1878
Sepia and red pen, India ink, colored washes, and gouache
12½ x 19½ in. (31.8 x 49.6 cm)
Inscription: "STUDIO KENSINGTON PALACE for H.R.H. The Princess Louise; GROUND PLAN; SECTION N; NORTH SIDE; SECTION M; EAST END; E W Godwin. 1878. / Geo Stephenson"

British Architectural Library Drawings Collection, RIBA, London, Ran 7/F/2 (1)

References: Godwin, "Studios and Mouldings" (7 March 1879): 261–62; "H.R.H The Princess Louise's New Studio at Kensington" (3 December 1880): 240, [238]; Soros, "E. W. Godwin" (1998): 210–11, fig. 207.

95. "Studio for Princess Louise, Kensington Palace" *(fig. 6-59)*
ca. 1940
Photograph (modern print)

English Heritage, #K1978

References: see no. 94.

96. *Artistic Conservatories, and Other Horticultural Buildings Designed . . . from Rough Sketches by E. W. Godwin, F.S.A., and from Designs and Drawings by Maurice B. Adams, A.R.I.B.A.* by Messenger and Company
Open to plate 3 *(fig. 4-10)*
Published: B. T. Batsford, London, 1880
Bound book
13 x 8½ in. (33 x 21.5 cm)

The Board of Trustees of the Victoria and Albert Museum, London, NAL 31.G.Box VI, L746-1880

References: "Detached Conservatory" (8 May 1880): 323 and illus.; O'Callaghan, "The Fine Art Society and E. W. Godwin" (1976): 7, fig D.; N. B. Wilkinson, "Edward William Godwin" (1987): 271–72.

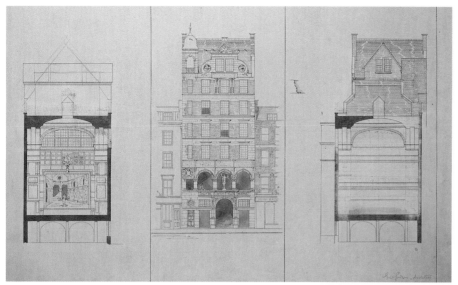

Cat. no. 97. "The Comedy Theatre," London: front elevation and cross sections showing stage and auditorium, 1881. India ink, sepia pen, India red and sepia washes; 20¹¹/₁₆ x 28⁹/₁₆ in. (52.5 x 72.5 cm). British Architectural Library Drawings Collection, RIBA, London, Ran 7/J/1 (13).

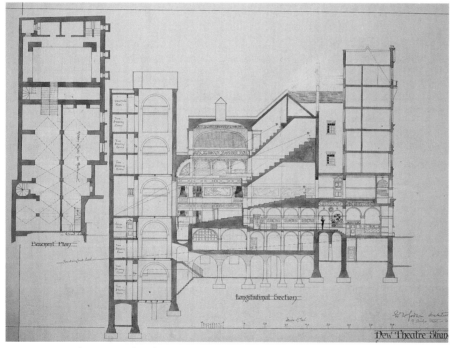

Cat. no. 98. "The Comedy Theatre," London: basement plan and longitudinal section, ca. 1881–82. India ink, blue and sepia pen, India red ink, and sepia washes, pencil details; 20¹¹/₁₆ x 28⅜ in. (52.5 x 72 cm). British Architectural Library Drawings Collection, RIBA, London, Ran 7/J/1 (14).

97. Design for "The Comedy Theatre," 106 Strand, London

Front elevation and cross sections showing stage and auditorium
1881
India ink, sepia pen, India red and sepia washes
20¹¹/₁₆ x 28⁹/₁₆ in. (52.5 x 72.5 cm)
Inscription: "THE COMEDY THEATRE 1881 [on front of building]; E W Godwin. Architect"

British Architectural Library Drawings Collection, RIBA, London, Ran 7/J/1 (13)

98. Design for "The Comedy Theatre," 106 Strand, London

Basement plan and longitudinal section
ca. 1881–82
India ink, blue and sepia pen, India red ink, and sepia washes, pencil details
20¹¹/₁₆ x 28⅜ in. (52.5 x 72 cm)
Inscription: "New Theatre Strand; Basement Plan; Longitudinal Section; Wardrobe / Floor; Two / Dressing / Rooms; Green / Room; Kitchen offices for Restaurant.; Strand Level; Fountain Court level; Edw W Godwin Architect / 9 Bridge Street Westm [sic]" [and additional inscriptions]

British Architectural Library Drawings Collection, RIBA, London, Ran 7/J/1 (14)

99. Tower House, 46 Tite Street, Chelsea, London (fig. 6-64)

Front elevation
ca. 1881–83
Pen and colored washes on tracing paper
25½ x 16¾ in. (64.8 x 42.5 cm)
Inscription: "Tower House Tite Street Chelsea. / front elevation; E.W. Godwin F.S.A. Architect" [and additional inscriptions]

British Architectural Library Drawings Collection, RIBA, London, Ran 7/G/6 (7)

References: Girouard, "Chelsea's Bohemian Studio Houses" (23 November 1972): 1374, fig. 12; Girouard, *Sweetness and Light* (1977): 178, 184–85; N. B. Wilkinson, "Edward William Godwin" (1987): 338; Walkley, *Artists' Houses in London* (1994): 153–54.

100. Sketchbook

Open to a sketch of a new facade for The Fine Art Society, 148 New Bond Street, London (fig. 6-62)
1881
Pencil, pen and ink
3¼ x 5¼ in. (8.3 x 13.3 cm)

The Board of Trustees of the Victoria and Albert Museum, London, E.254-1963: 42

References: Harbron, *Conscious Stone* (1949): 144; O'Callaghan, "The Fine Art Society and E. W. Godwin" (1976): 5–9; N. B. Wilkinson, "Edward William Godwin" (1987): 337; Lambourne, *Aesthetic Movement* (1996): 166–67; Casteras and Denney, *Grosvenor Gallery* (1966) : 149–50.

101. Preliminary Design for the Facade of McLean's Fine Art Gallery, London (fig. 6-63)

1884
Pencil, watercolor, Chinese white

19⅝ x 11⅞ in. (50 x 30.2 cm)
Inscription: "McLEAN / FINE ART
GALLERIES; 7; FOUNDED / 1811;
E W Godwin"

The Board of Trustees of the Victoria and
Albert Museum, London, E.629-1963

References: N. B. Wilkinson, "Edward
William Godwin" (1987): 342–44;
Lambourne, *Aesthetic Movement* (1996):
153, illus.

102. Additions to Oscar Wilde's House, 16 Tite Street, Chelsea, London *(Chronology, fig. C16)*
Elevation, section, and plan
ca. 1884
Pen and ink, watercolor
13¾ x 20⅞ in. (35 x 53 cm)
Inscription: "Additions no 16 Tite St / for
Oscar Wilde esq E.W.Godwin F.S.A. arch^t;
plan; section; elevation" [and additional
inscriptions]

The Board of Trustees of the Victoria and
Albert Museum, London, E.575-1963

References: Harbron, *Conscious Stone*
(1949): 164–65; Hyde, "Oscar Wilde and
His Architect" (March 1951): 175–76;
Aslin, *E. W. Godwin* (1986): 18; N. B.
Wilkinson, "Edward William Godwin"
(1987): 339–42; Soros, "E. W. Godwin"
(1998): 218–28.

103. "Greek" Side Chair *(fig. 8-33)*
ca. 1885
Made by William Watt
Ash with caned seat
39¾ x 14 x 16¾ in. (101 x 35.6 x 42.6 cm)

Private collection

References: Barnet and Wilkinson,
Decorative Arts 1900 (1993): 13, pl. 2; Gere
and Whiteway, *Nineteenth-Century Design*
(1993): 155, pl. 191; Soros, "E. W. Godwin"
(1998): 80, fig. 80, 100–101, cat. no. 135.

104. Front Cover and Plate 3 from *The Costume Society: Part 1* *(fig. 2-19)*
1883
Pen and ink (from a bound book)
15⅜ x 11⅜ in. (39 x 29 cm)

The Board of Trustees of the Victoria and
Albert Museum, London, 980452

References: "Illustrations of Costume . . ."
(21 May 1880): 246 and illus.; "Persons of
taste have long been annoyed . . ." (28
September 1882): 5; "The recently formed
Costume Society . . . " (1 December
1882): 570; "Perseus Slaying the Gorgon"
(26 June 1885): 1004; Godwin, *Dress and Its
Relation to Health and Climate* (1884): 36,

figs. 25, 26; Harbron, *Conscious Stone*
(1949): 161; Pearson, *Beerbohm Tree* (1956):
37–40; Baldwin, "Victorian Artists" (1991):
531–34.

105. *Dress and Its Relation to Health and Climate* by E. W. Godwin
Open to sketches of eighteenth- and
nineteenth-century dress *(fig. 2-17)*
1884
Bound book
11 x 8½ x ¼ in. (28 x 21.5 x 1 cm)

The Board of Trustees of the Victoria and
Albert Museum, London, NAL 24.C.64 /
L660-1884

References: "*Dress and Its Relation to
Health and Climate*" (25 July 1884): 119–21;
Harbron, *Conscious Stone* (1949): 164–65;
also see fig. 2-17 in this volume.

106. Costume Design, possibly for Liberty and Company *(fig. 2-20)*
ca. 1884
Pencil and watercolor on paper
7⅝ x 4⅜ in. (19.3 x 11 cm)
Inscription: [recto] "Statue / by EWG.;
12th Century / Chartres; gold lions on
silk / found in / tomb of 12 / cent. notre
Dame / Paris; c 1130; another / neck;
laced at back; silk or c of gold; Elastic
tissue; Bodice of Statue / of Door Notre
Dame / de Corbeil now / at St. Denis sd.
to be / Clothilde laced / at back.; V[iollet]
le D[uc].; Silk crèpée; real / neck;
sleeve tied up / untied would / trail on
ground; pleated; button" [and additional
inscriptions]; [verso] "sleeve of Queen
Clothilde reaches to just below the knee
edged like a f[? illegible] see fig in Shaw."

The Board of Trustees of the Victoria and
Albert Museum, London, S.191-1998

References: Godwin, *Dress and Its Relation
to Health and Climate* (1884): 34, fig. 20;
Liberty and Company, *Fancy Dress* (n.d.),
no. 7 and illus.; Liberty and Company,
"Liberty" Collection of Costume Design
(1893): n.p., illus. ["Clothilde"].

107. "The Architecture and Costume of Shakespere's [*sic*] Plays"
Open to drawings of costumes and
properties for *Hamlet* *(fig. 12-2)*
ca. 1874–86
Leather-bound book; pencil, watercolor,
pen and ink
With binding, 12½ x 8⁵⁄₁₆ in. (31.8 x
21.2 cm)
Inscription: [this page] "HAMLET; Claud.
B.iv –(c.1006–20 / (966); CLAUD. B. IV;
sometimes / 3 cross pieces; Tib. C.VI /
Macbeth.; Cleop / C.VIII; Bronze /
Amulet / 21 turns / in 1 foot; Trumpet /

Cleop C.VIII; Ethelwulf's ring / in Medal
Room. Br. Mus.; king has an / attendant
to / protect him / with a second / shield;
CLEOP.CVIII; Claud B.IV; Reaches just /
below knee; gold / lined; open; Painted
blue / on blue; VESP. AVII.966."
The Board of Trustees of the Victoria and
Albert Museum, London, S.173-1998

References: The volume comprised essays
written by E. W. Godwin and originally
published in *Architect* (London) between
31 October 1874 and 26 June 1875;
Godwin, "The Architecture and Costume
of Shakespere's [*sic*] Plays: *Hamlet*"
(31 October 1874): 224–25.

108. Sketchbook
Open to a preparatory set design for *The
Merchant of Venice* *(fig. 12-5)*
1875
Inscription: "Mar 18. 75 / Merchant of
Venice"
Pencil, pen and ink on metallic surfaced
paper
3⅜ x 5⅞ in. (8.5 x 14.8 cm)

The Board of Trustees of the Victoria and
Albert Museum, London, E.236-1963: 27

References: Godwin, "Architecture and
Costume of Shakespere's [*sic*] Plays"
(27 March 1875): 182; ibid. (3 April 1875):
196–97; "Prince of Wales' Theatre"
(19 April 1875): 3; "Prince of Wales'
Theatre" (19 April 1875): 6; "Theatres,
Prince of Wales" (19 April 1875): 8;
W. H. W. [William Henry White] "Prince
of Wales's Theatre" (23 April 1875): 471–
72; Godwin, "Archaeology on the Stage"
(22 February 1885): 53; Bancroft, *The
Bancrofts* (1909): 201, 205; Tree, *Thoughts
and After thoughts* (1913): 44; Terry, *Ellen
Terry's Memoirs* (1933): 82–88; Harbron,
Conscious Stone (1949): 103–13; Steen, *A
Pride of Terrys* (1962): 139–40; E. A. Craig,
Gordon Craig (1968): 45–46; Stokes,
"Resistible Theatres" (1972): 35, 38–39;
Souder, "E. W. Godwin" (1976): 43–49,
132; Lambourne "Pyrrhic Success"
(2 October 1986): 1024; Baldwin,
"Victorian Artists" (1991): 144–48,
pl. 7; Lambourne, *Aesthetic Movement*
(1996): 162.

109. Designs for Properties for *The Merchant of Venice* *(fig. 12-4)*
1880
Ink wash and pencil on tracing paper
12¾ x 8⅛ in. (32.5 x 20.5 cm)
Inscription: "*Table No 1A; Chairs No. 4*; C;
Knife E; *Halberd*; red / fringe; place / for
hand; 6 feet; Candlestick H; Leather
Portfolio F; profile of casket; D; Table /
Cloth. B; Lyons Holborn for Stage
furniture."

The Board of Trustees of the Victoria and Albert Museum, London, S.80-1988

References: see no. 108; Godwin, "Costume of *The Merchant of Venice*" (13 February 1880): 74–75, [78–81].

110. Designs for *The Merchant of Venice* (fig. 12-8)
Costume for the Doge of Venice; plan of the Doge's Court
ca. 1880
Ink and watercolor on paper
6⅜ x 8¾ in. (16.3 x 22.2 cm)
Inscription: "II.; Fialetti AD. 1604.; Dress and mantle / crimson; From a drawing ascribed / to Vecellio." [and additional inscriptions]

The Board of Trustees of the Victoria and Albert Museum, London, S.81-1998

References: see nos. 108 and 109.

111. Costume Designs for *The Merchant of Venice* (fig. 12-6)
For a Senator and an Attendant
ca. 1880
Ink and watercolor on paper with pencil notes
6⅜ x 8¾ in. (16.3 x 22.2 cm)
Inscription: "III.; J. AMMAN.; *One of the Senators* / 3 Magistrates / Chiefs of Council of 10 the / same with *plain* red gown; PAGANO / after / TITIAN; attending before / the Doge." [and additional inscriptions]

The Board of Trustees of the Victoria and Albert Museum, London, S.82-1998

References: see nos. 108 and 109.

112. Costume Designs for *The Merchant of Venice* (fig. 12-7)
Probably for Portia
ca. 1880
Ink and watercolor on paper
6⅜ x 8¾ in. (16.3 x 22.2 cm)
Inscription: "VIII.; J. AMMAN.; VECELLIO."

The Board of Trustees of the Victoria and Albert Museum, London, S.83-1998

References: see nos. 108 and 109.

113. Designs for Costumes and Musical Instruments for *The Merchant of Venice* (fig. 12-3)
ca. 1880
Ink and watercolor on paper
6⅜ x 8¾ in. (16.3 x 22.2 cm)
Inscription: "VI.; M.PAGANO after TITIAN; TINTORET; K.S.M.; VERONESE; K.S.M."

The Board of Trustees of the Victoria and Albert Museum, London, S.84-1998

References: see nos. 108 and 109.

114. Sketchbook
Open to set designs for Shallow's House and the Jerusalem Chamber in *Henry V* (fig. 12-9)
ca. 1875–76
Pencil and watercolor
7⅛ x 5¼ in. (18.1 x 13.2 cm)
Inscription: "Shallows house / March 20th / Jerusalem Chamber 36'x 18'"

The Board of Trustees of the Victoria and Albert Museum, London, E.279-1963: 7

References: Godwin, "*Henry V*: An Archaeological Experience." (9 September 1876): 142–43; "*Henry V* at the Queens" (18 September 1876): 10; Burges, "*Henry V* at the Queen's Theatre" (23 September 1876): 188; Godwin, "*Henry V*: A Theatrical Experience." (30 September 1876): 192–94; Burges, "Archaeology on the Stage" (7 October 1876): 221; Godwin, "Archaeology on the Stage (14 October 1876): 224–25; idem, (21 October 1876): 238–40.

115. Costume Designs for *Othello* (fig. 12-10)
For Othello, Iago, and Cassio
1880
Pen and ink on paper
8 x 5¼ in. (20.3 x 13.2 cm)
Inscription: "OTHELLO; CASSIO"

The Board of Trustees of the Victoria and Albert Museum, London, S.94-1998

References: Godwin, "Architecture and Costume of Shakespere's [*sic*] Plays" (13 March 1875): 151–52; Godwin, "Costume of *The Merchant of Venice*" (13 February 1880): 74–75; Godwin, "Theatrical Jottings" (24 September 1880): 143; "New Sadler's Wells *Othello*" (14 September 1880): 4; Godwin, "Costume of *Othello*" (15 October 1880): 176 and illus.; "At Sadler's Wells Theatre *Othello* . . ." (November 1880): 186; Harbron, "Edward Godwin" (August 1945): 50, illus.; Stokes, "Resistible Theatres" (1972): 40; Baldwin, "Victorian Artists" (1991): 154–55, pl. 9.

116. Costume Designs for *Othello* (fig. 12-11)
For Desdemona and an unidentified male character
1880
Pen and ink on paper
8⅛ x 6⅜ in. (20.5 x 16.1 cm)

The Board of Trustees of the Victoria and Albert Museum, London, S.95-1998

References: see no. 115; Baldwin, "Victorian Artists" (1991): 154, pl. 10.

117. Costume Design for *Hamlet* (fig. 12-12)
For Hermann Vezin as Hamlet
1881
Pen and ink on paper
9⅛ x 6⅛ in. (23.1 x 15.5 cm)

The Board of Trustees of the Victoria and Albert Museum, London, S.85-1998

References: Godwin, "The Architecture and Costume of Shakespere's [*sic*] Plays: *Hamlet*" (31 October 1874): 224–25; "Mr. Herman Vezin will appear . . ." (4 February 1881): 64; "Mr. Vezin made his appearance . . ." (4 March 1881): 115; Godwin, "Mr. Vezin as Hamlet: Costume by E. W. Godwin F.S.A." (15 April 1881): 192, illus.; Baldwin, "Victorian Artists" (1991): 185–89.

118. Costume Design for *Hamlet* (fig. 12-13)
For Hermann Vezin as Hamlet
1881
Pen and ink and watercolor on paper
9½ x 4⅜ in. (24 x 11 cm)
Inscription: "Copyright"

The Board of Trustees of the Victoria and Albert Museum, London, S.86-1998

References: see no. 117; Godwin, "Mr. Vezin as Hamlet: Costume by E. W. Godwin F.S.A." (15 April 1881): 193, illus.

119. "Shakespeare Armchair" (fig. 8-43)
ca. 1881
Made by William Watt
Oak
40½ x 24 x 20 in. (103 x 61 x 50.8 cm)

Paul Reeves, London

References: "The Shakespeare Dining Room Set" (11 November 1881): 626 [634]; "The love of old things . . ." (1 December 1881): 103; "Pen and Ink Notes" (1 April 1882): 181–84; "Our Museum" (1 April 1882): 187–88; Aslin, *E. W. Godwin* (1986): 33, 84, pl. 68 (similar chair); Soros, "E. W. Godwin" (1998): 113–16, fig. 125, cat. no. 132.1.

120. Costume Design for W. G. Wills's *Juana* (fig. 12-17)
For the Provost of Toledo
1881
Pencil and watercolor on paper
10⅝ x 6½ in. (27 x 16.5 cm)

Inscription: "JUANA XV; The Provost; jewel & gold cord.; Mr Darley; EWG."

The Board of Trustees of the Victoria and Albert Museum, London, S.100-1998

References: "The Theatres: Court Theatre" (8 April 1881): 4; "Mr. W. G. Wills' tragedy of *Juana* . . ." (22 April 1881): 203; "The preparation of Mr. Wills' new play . . ." (4 May 1881): 14; "The Theatres" (9 May 1881): 10; "*Juana* at the Court Theatre" (9 May 1881): 3; ". . . is only to be commended to . . ." (11 May 1881): 11; Godwin, "Letter to Atlas . . ." (11 May 1881): 13; "Court" (13 May 1881): 7; "Mr. Wills' powerful play . . ." (13 May 1881): 245; "The Court" (14 May 1881): 6; "Theatres" (14 May 1881): 470–71; Scrutator [pseud.], "*Juana*" (19 May 1881): 676; "The Playhouses" (21 May 1881): 495; W. G. Wills, "*Juana*": *A Tragedy in Four Acts* (1881); Godwin, "Archaeology on the Stage" (10 October 1885): 92–93; F. Wills, *W. G. Wills* (1898): 184; Stokes, "Resistible Theatres" (1972): 41; Baldwin, "Victorian Artists" (1991): 158–60, 481–82.

121. Costume Designs for W. G. Wills's *Juana* (fig. 12-18)
For Don Carlos of Narcisso
1881
Pencil and watercolor on paper
10⅞ x 6⅞ in. (27.5 x 17.5 cm)
Inscription: "Juanna [*sic*]; caps of officials; EWG; 1st / act; Carlos / 1st scene / without / falcon chain / or hat but / white / skull cap.; Friend of / Carlos in / undress.; Note/ Fur lining turned down as collar / & turned up as cuffs. / There may be fur border to the skirt / which need not touch the ground.; Badelaire worn / by civilians & / sometimes by / priests.; CARLOS."

The Board of Trustees of the Victoria and Albert Museum, London, S.101-1998

References: see no. 120.

122. Costume Design for W. G. Wills's *Juana* (fig. 12-1)
For the Provost's guards and the Abbot
1881
Pencil, pen and ink and watercolor - page in two pieces
10⅞ x 6⅞ in. (27.5 x 17.5 cm)
Inscription: "JUANA XIX; Iron or / steel / pellets.; semi transparent; Provosts guards. / helmet lined red; grey fur; white; white; The Abbot; EWG."

The Board of Trustees of the Victoria and Albert Museum, London, S.102-1998

References: see no. 120.

123. Costume Designs for W. G. Wills's *Juana* (fig. 12-16)
For Don Carlos of Narcisso
1881
Pencil, pen and ink and watercolor on paper
11 x 7⅛ in. (28 x 18 cm); page in two pieces
Inscription: "III; yellow turned / up white; EWG; ceremony dress; CARLOS; J. Forbes Robertson."

The Board of Trustees of the Victoria and Albert Museum, London, S.103-1998

References: see no. 120.

124. Costume Design for Robert Buchanon's *Storm Beaten* (fig. 12-20)
For Kate Christianson
1883
Pencil and watercolor on paper
8⅞ x 5¼ in. (22.7 x 13.5 cm)
Inscription: "Kate Christianson / Queen of the May.; *EWG*; silk petticoat & hose & / ribbands / muslin Dress / straw hat" [and additional inscriptions]

The Board of Trustees of the Victoria and Albert Museum, London, S.158-1998

References: Buchanan [*sic*], *God and the Man: A Romance* (1881); "Adelphi Theatre" (17 March 1883): 5; "London Theatres. The Adelphi: *Storm Beaten*" (17 March 1883): 6; "*Storm Beaten* at the Adelphi" (5 May 1883): 442, and illus.; Fitzgerald, "On

Scenic Illusion and Stage Appliances" (18 March 1887): 457–58; Stokes, "Resistible Theatres" (1972): 43; Baldwin, "Victorian Artists" (1991): 161–64.

125. Costume Design for Robert Buchanon's *Storm Beaten* (fig. 12-21)
For Sally Marvel the Dairy Maid
1883
Pencil and watercolor on tracing paper with pen and ink inscriptions
7½ x 6½ in. (19 x 16.5 cm)
Inscription: "*Sally Marvel the Dairy Maid*; Prologue; Sally Marvel; *May day*; Act I." [and additional inscriptions]

The Board of Trustees of the Victoria and Albert Museum, London, S.159-1998

References: see no. 124.

126. Costume Design for Robert Buchanon's *Storm Beaten*
Costume for Jabez Greene, a Shepherd
1883
Pencil and watercolor on tracing paper
6¼ x 6¾ in. (16 x 17 cm)
Inscription: [in ink] "*Jabez Greene*; Act I" [and additional inscriptions]

The Board of Trustees of the Victoria and Albert Museum, London, S.160-1998

References: see no. 124.

127. Costume Design for Robert Buchanon's *Storm Beaten* (fig. 12-19)
For Richard Orchardson, the Squire's son
1883
Pen and ink, pencil and watercolor
9⅝ x 6⅛ in. (24.5 x 15.5 cm)

Cat. no. 126. Costume design for *Storm Beaten*: the character Jabez Greene, a shepherd, 1883. Pencil and watercolor on tracing paper; 6¼ x 6¾ in. (16 x 17 cm). Trustees of the Victoria and Albert Museum, London, S.160-1998.

Inscription: "1770; length of / cloak / added / for III; silk Velvet [crossed out] suit of apple green. gilt buttons / & gold trimming; Waistcoat yellow / Hose very pale apple green; Richard Orchardson" [and additional inscriptions]

The Board of Trustees of the Victoria and Albert Museum, London, S.161-1998

References: see no. 124.

128. "Claudian": A Few Notes on the Architecture and Costume: A Letter to Wilson Barrett, Esq. by E. W. Godwin

Open to a page of costume designs for an Attendant and a Frank (fig. 12-23)
Privately printed: London, 1883
Thread-stitched pamphlet
8⅝ x 10⅞ in. (22 x 27.5 cm)

The Board of Trustees of the Victoria and Albert Museum, London, S.153-1998

References: "Mr. Wilson Barrett, in endeavouring . . ." (7 December 1883): 264; "The Costumes for Claudian by E.W. Godwin, F.S.A" (7 December 1883): 267 and illus.; Godwin, "A Few Notes on . . . Claudian" (7 December 1883): 268–70 and illus; "Princess's Theatre" Daily News (7 December 1883): 3; "Princess's Theatre" Times (London) (7 December 1883): 6; "Claudian" (7 December 1883): 4; "Claudian at the Princess's Theatre" (7 December 1883): 6; "At the Play" (9 December 1883): 2; "The Theatre" (12 December 1883): 6; "Sitting at a Play: The Princess's" (13 December 1883): 69–70; "The peculiar characteristic . . ." (14 December 1883): 277; "Princess's" (14 December 1883): 14; "Before and Behind the Curtain" (15 December 1883): 13; "Sketches from Claudian . . ." (15 December 1883): 573; C. Scott, "Claudian (15 December 1883): 574; "Claudian at the Princess's" (15 December 1883): 47; "The Drama" (15 December 1883): 377; "The Theatres" (15 December 1883): 765–66; [Godwin], "The first act of Claudian . . ." (21 December 1883): 290; "Scenes from Claudian" (22 December 1883): 384; ibid. (29 December 1883): 396; ibid. (5 January 1884): 420; ibid. (12 January 1884): 444; [Godwin], "The third act of Claudian . . ." (28 December 1883): 300; C. Scott, "Claudian" (1 January 1884): 43–49; "Notes on Claudian" (1 April 1884): 218–20; "Bijou Portraits, no. 64 . . ." (12 April 1884); Godwin, "Archaeology on the Stage" (19 September 1885): 60–61; ibid. (10 October 1885): 92–93; O. Wilde, "The Truth of Masks" in Intentions (1930), 1067, 1075; Harbron, "Edward Godwin" (August 1945): 52; Harbron, Conscious Stone (1949): 170–71; E. A. Craig, Index to the Story of

My Days (1957): 58; Stokes, "Resistible Theatres" (1972): 43–45, 61–62; Souder, "E. W. Godwin" (1976): 56–61, 136–38, illus.; Lambourne, "Pyrrhic Success" (2 October 1986): 1025; Baldwin, "Victorian Artists" (1991): 164–72, 205; Lambourne, Aesthetic Movement (1996): 163, illus.

129. Costume Design for W. G. Wills and Henry Herman's Claudian

(fig. 12-27)
For a female supernumerary
1883
Watercolor on two sheets of paper
14 x 9⅞ in. (35.5 x 25 cm)

The Board of Trustees of the Victoria and Albert Museum, London, S.154-154A-1998

References: see no. 128; Godwin, "Claudian": A Few Notes . . . (1883): 1, illus.; Godwin, Dress and Its Relation to Health and Climate (1884): 32, fig. 13.

130. Costume Design for W. G. Wills and Henry Herman's Claudian

(fig. 12-26)
For an unidentified character, possibly Claudian
1883
Pencil and watercolor on tracing paper
6¼ x 3¼ in. (16 x 8.3 cm)
Inscription: "red / with gold / pattern / & colored / medal / portraits; white; gold."

The Board of Trustees of the Victoria and Albert Museum, London, S.155-1998

References: see no. 128.

131. Costume Design for W. G. Wills and Henry Herman's Claudian

(fig. 12-30)
For an unidentified character, possibly one of Claudian's attendants, with diagram showing how to drape a mantle
1883
Pencil and watercolor on tracing paper
8¼ x 5½ in. (21.1 x 14 cm)
Inscription: "2 costu[mes] / in 2 diff[erent] / colors; way [of] / putting / on the / mantle; make this / . . . embroidery not too exp[ensive?] / for a / . . . [G]entleman; EWG "

The Board of Trustees of the Victoria and Albert Museum, London, S.156-1998

References: see no. 128.

132. Design for a Litter for W. G. Wills and Henry Herman's Claudian (fig. 12-24)

1883
Pencil on paper

4½ x 6⅞ in. (11.4 x 17.6 cm)
Inscription: "oxhide; silver plated"

The Board of Trustees of the Victoria and Albert Museum, London, S.157-1998

References: see no. 128; Godwin, "A Few Notes on . . . Claudian" (7 December 1883): 268; "Princess's Theatre" (7 December 1883): 3; "Before and Behind the Curtain" (15 December 1883): 13; Cartoon. "Claudian Barrett refusing Byzantium's 'Barrer' " (22 December 1883); Stokes, "Resistible Theatres" (1972): 44; Souder, "E. W. Godwin" (1976): 57; Baldwin, "Victorian Artists" (1991): 166.

133. Sketchbook

Open to costume designs for W. G. Wills and Henry Herman's Claudian, showing eleven ways of wearing a girdle (fig. 12-28)
1883
Pencil and watercolor on metallic surfaced paper
Page trim: 7 x 4 in. (17.8 x 10.2 cm)
Inscription: "Girdles; in front or side / most common; rare; back; front"

The Board of Trustees of the Victoria and Albert Museum, London, E.262-1963: 22–23

Cat. no. 136. Costume design for Hamlet: the character Gertrude, Queen of Denmark, 1884. Pencil and watercolor on mounted tracing paper; 9⅞ x 6⅛ in. (25 x 15.6 cm). Trustees of the Victoria and Albert Museum, London, S.87-1998.

References: see no. 128; Lambourne, "Pyrrhic Success" (2 October 1986): 1025, fig. 4; Baldwin, "Victorian Artists" (1991): 167; Lambourne, *Aesthetic Movement* (1996): 163, illus.

134. Design for Sandals for W. G. Wills and Henry Herman's *Claudian* (fig. 12-29)
1883
Pencil on paper
5½ x 3³⁄₁₆ in. (14 x 8.1 cm)
Inscription: "Crystal Pal. / Sep 19.83 / with Vezin; Aesculapius / Berlin Museum; other side; Julian / the apos[tate]. / Count Laribosiere / Paris ; plan"

The Board of Trustees of the Victoria and Albert Museum, London, E.448-1963

References: see no. 128; "Theatrical Trades: Boots and Shoes" (16 November 1883): 8–9; Godwin, "A Few Notes on . . . *Claudian*" (7 December 1883): 269; Baldwin, "Victorian Artists" (1991): 167–68.

135. Godwin (third from right) **and Cast Members of *As You Like It*, Coombe Wood** (fig. 1-16)
1884
Photograph on card
6 x 11⅝ in. (15.3 x 29.5 cm)
Inscription. verso: "As You Like It Coombe House 1884 Vezin Fulton Marshall Godwin Tapley Eaton Atkinson Hilton Ponsonby A. Yorke; EWG"

The Board of Trustees of the Victoria and Albert Museum, London, S.163-1998

References: "At the Play: *As You Like It* in a Wood" (26 June 1884): 61–62; "Under the Greenwood Tree" (26 July 1884): 4–5; Chit Chat. "It was on a Wednesday afternoon . . ." (25 July 1884): 12; "Shakespeare under the Greenwood Tree" (26 July 1884): 8; "*As You Like It*, Under the Trees" (29 July 1884); "The Lovers of novelty . . . " (30 July 1884): 13; "Rosalind in the Wood" (31 July 1884): 174–75; "*As You Like It*, at Coombe House" (2 August 1884): 530; "The Saturday Performance of *As You Like It* . . . " (2 August 1884): 5; "Theatricals in the Open Air . . . " (9 August 1884): 132; Austin, "In the Forest of Arden" (September 1884): 1 "Our Omnibus Box" (1 September 1884): 160; Campbell, "The Woodland Gods" (November 1888): 1–7; Beerbohm, "1880" (January 1895): 280; O. Wilde, "The Truth of Masks" in *The Complete Works of Oscar Wilde* (1990): 1076; Harbron, "Edward Godwin" (August 1945): 52; Harbron, *Conscious Stone* (1949): 167–68; Stokes, "Resistible Theatres" (1972): 47–50;

Souder, "E. W. Godwin" (1976): 66, 68–80; Lambourne, "Pyrrhic Success" (2 October 1986): 1025; Baldwin, "Victorian Artists" (1991): 172–84, pl. 17; Lambourne, *Aesthetic Movement* (1996): 167.

136. Costume Design for *Hamlet*
For Gertrude, Queen of Denmark
1884
Pencil and watercolor on mounted tracing paper
9⅞ x 6⅛ in. (25 x 15.6 cm)
Inscription: "Pattern of ?desired / on stuff gold on red or silver on blue for change; circles 2½ inches / diameter.; gold; gold Bracelets; Veil 4½ yds / long 1 yard wide / to 1½ yards; mantle / a circle / 4ft diam[eter]; gold on yellow; *The Queen*; Under dress of thick gold / [illegible] white silk with thin / Plates of gold applied on border / Mantle of red silk / veil of fine white wo[rk?]; gilded Leather; 'Good Hamlet cast thy nighted colour off'" [Quotation from Act 1 Scene 2 of the play]

The Board of Trustees of the Victoria and Albert Museum, London, S.87-1998

References: Godwin, "Architecture and Costume of Shakespere's [sic] Plays: *Hamlet*" (31 October 1874): 224–25; "*Hamlet* at the Princess's: An Interview with Mr. E. W. Godwin, F.S.A." (16 October 1884): 312; "*Hamlet* at the Princess's" (17 October 1884): 5; "*Hamlet* at the Princess's Theatre Last Night" (17 October 1884): 6; "On Thursday night . . ." (18 October 1884): 6–7; "*Hamlet* at the Princess's" (18 October 1884): 6; "Drama. The Week, Princess's *Hamlet*" (18 October 1884): 505; "Dramatic and Musical Gossip. Mr. Wilson Barrett's adaptation . . ." (19 October 1884): 2; "Princess's" (24 October 1884): 14–15; [Review] (25 October 1884): 128; "The Playhouse's *Hamlet* at the Princess's" (25 October 1884): 391; C. Scott, "The New *Hamlet*" (1 November 1884): 243–54; "*Hamlet* at the Princess's Theatre" (1 November 1884): 428; Harbron, "Edward Godwin" (August 1945): 52; Harbron, *Conscious Stone* (1949): 171; Stokes, "Resistible Theatres" (1972): 44–45; Souder, "E. W. Godwin" (1976): 62–67; Lambourne, "Pyrrhic Success" (2 October 1986): 1025; Baldwin, "Victorian Artists" (1991): 185–89.

137. Costume Design for *Hamlet*
(fig. 12-41)
For Ophelia
1884
Pencil and watercolor on mounted tracing paper
9⅞ x 6¼ in. (25 x 15.8 cm)

Inscription: "Veil 4 yards long 1 yard to 1½ yds wide; silver grey / veil; Ivory Box of / jewels; Over dress / When the over / dress is dropped / it hangs loose / about the feet / in folds on / the ground ./ front side & / back; veil; This yellow Pattern is a / favorite [sic] one & / is found on a / large number of / contemporary drawings; under dress pale green- / blue; all wool; laced leather; '*Ophelia*'; 'My lord, I have remembrances of yours.'" [Quotation from Act 3, scene 1 of the play]

The Board of Trustees of the Victoria and Albert Museum, London, S.88-1998

References: see no. 136.

138. Costume Design for *Hamlet*
(Chronology, fig. C14)
For Claudius, King of Denmark
1884
9½ x 5⅝ in. (24.1 x 14.3 cm)
Pencil and watercolor on mounted tracing paper
Inscription. verso : "ivory staff; fringe & / border / of coat; 'The King drinks to Hamlet.'" [Quotation from Act 5, scene 2 of the play]

The Board of Trustees of the Victoria and Albert Museum, London, S.89-1998

References: see no. 136.

139. Design for Hamlet's Sword Handle (fig. 12-38)
1884
Pencil and watercolor on mounted tracing paper
10 x 6¼ in. (25.5 x 16 cm)
Inscription: "Front; side; Black inlay on silver; Hamlet's sword / Handle / real size; 4¼ inch; Blade 2' 7'"

The Board of Trustees of the Victoria and Albert Museum, London, S.91-1998

References: see no. 136.

140. Design for Jewelry for *Hamlet*
(fig. 12-37)
For Claudius, Ophelia, and Hamlet
1884
Pencil and watercolor on mounted tracing paper
9⁵⁄₁₆ x 6¼ in. (23.7 x 15.9 cm)
Inscription. verso: "Chain for neck / of King; Necklace for Ophelia / coins and colored clay; Ring for Hamlet"

The Board of Trustees of the Victoria and Albert Museum, London, S.92-1998

References: see no. 136.

141. Costume Design for *Hamlet*
(fig. 12-42)
For Polonius
1884
Pencil and watercolor on mounted tracing paper
9⁹⁄₁₆ x 6¹¹⁄₁₆ in. (24.3 x 17 cm)
Inscription: "silver bracelet; grey / Mantle; *Polonius*; White wand / tipped and shod / with silver; 'Ophelia walk you here.'"
[Quotation from Act 3, Scene 1 of the play]

The Board of Trustees of the Victoria and Albert Museum, London, S.93-1998

References: see no. 136.

142. Set Design for the Interior of the Palace in *Hamlet* *(fig. 12-40)*
Walter Hann
1884
Pen and ink and watercolor on paper
11⅜ x 18⅞ in. (29 x 47.8 cm)
Inscription: "for Wilson Barrett Hamlet"

The Board of the Trustees of the Victoria and Albert Museum, London, E.898-1966

References: see no. 136; Baldwin, "Victorian Artists" (1991): 186 and pl. 20.

143. Set Design for *Junius, or the Household Gods*: the Palace of Tarquin *(fig. 12-44)*
Walter Hann
1885
Watercolor and ink
13⅜ x 16⅞ in. (34 x 43 cm)
Inscription: "scene from 'Junius' W Hann"

The Board of Trustees of the Victoria and Albert Museum, London, E.904-1966

References: Fitzgerald, "*Junius or the Household Gods*" (22 February 1885): 72; "*Junius or the Household Gods*" (28 February 1885): 8; "Princess's" (2 March 1885): 10; Baldwin, "Victorian Artists" (1991): 189–90.

144. *RIENZI 1350 Studies for Costume &c. by E. W. Godwin F. S. A. 1880-*
Open to designs for costumes and properties *(fig. 9-3)*
ca. 1880–85
Bound book; this page, pencil and watercolor on paper
Page trim: 10¼ x 6¼ in. (26 x 16 cm)
Inscription: [this page] "XI; A; B from / Tomb / S Antonio / Padua; inside / outside / C 27695"

The Board of Trustees of the Victoria and Albert Museum, London, S.114-1998

References: Baldwin, "Victorian Artists" (1991): 480, n.63.

145. A Scene from E. W. Godwin's Adaptation of John Fletcher's play *The Faithfull Shepherdesse*: Homage to Pan *(fig. 2-23)*
1885
Photograph on card
5¼ x 9½ in. (13.5 x 24.2 cm)

The Board of Trustees of the Victoria and Albert Museum, London, S.165-1998

References: Godwin, *The Faithfull Shepherdesse* (1885); Campbell, "*The Faithfull Shepherdesse*" (17 June 1885): 1031–42; "The Pastoral Players" *Evening Post* (29 June 1885); "The Pastoral Players" *Daily Telegraph* (29 June 1885): 3; "*The Faithfull Shepherdesse*" (2 July 1885): 17–18; "The Pastoral Players" (3 July 1885): 17; "Theatres" (4 July 1885): 11; "The Pastoral Players at Coombe House" (4 July 1885): 3 and frontispiece; "*The Faithfull Shepherdesse*," *Illustrated London News* (4 July 1885); "*The Faithfull Shepherdesse*," *Society* (4 July 1885): 20–22; Ignotus [pseud.], "Pastoral Players: *The Faithfull Shepherdesse*" (1 August 1885): 4; Campbell, "The Woodland Gods" (November 1888): 1–7; Woodville, *Random Recollections* (1914): 138; Harbron, "Edward Godwin" (August 1945): 52; Harbron, *Conscious Stone* (1949): 176; Stokes, "Resistible Theatres" (1972): 50–52; Souder, "E. W. Godwin" (1976): 81–106; Lambourne, "Pyrrhic Success" (2 October 1986): 1025; Baldwin, "Victorian Artists" (1991): 172, 178, 184–85; Lambourne, *Aesthetic Movement* (1996): 167, illus.

146. A Scene from E. W. Godwin's Adaptation of John Fletcher's play *The Faithfull Shepherdesse*: Perigot and Amoret Driving an Oxcart *(fig. 12-35)*
1885
Photograph
5⅝ x 8⅝ in. (14.3 x 22 cm)

The Board of Trustees of the Victoria and Albert Museum, London, S.166-1998

References: see no.145; Campbell, "The Woodland Gods" (November 1888): frontis.; Lambourne, "Pyrrhic Success" (2 October 1986): 1024, fig. 2.

147. "*The Faithfull Shepherdesse* by John Fletcher, adapted by E. W. Godwin"
Preparation copy open to costume designs for Amoret, Hobinal, and two other characters
1885
Printed text with ink, pen, pencil, and watercolor additions
8¼ x 6⅝ in. (21 x 16.8 cm)

Inscriptions: [with miscellaneous stage directions and corrections to the text]

The Board of Trustees of the Victoria and Albert Museum, London, S.189-1998

References: see no. 145.

148. Design for Alterations to Hengler's Circus, London *(fig. 12-46)*
Plan of the arena, and elevation of the stage
1886
Pencil, pen and ink, ink wash, and watercolor
10⅝ x 18¾ in. (26.9 x 47.7 cm)
Inscription: "PROPOSED ALTERATIONS TO Mˢˢ HENGLERS CIRQUE / FOR GREEK PLAY. MARCH 1886; E W Godwin F. S. A. Architect; Patman Fotheringham; W Hann April 7th 1886" [and additional inscriptions]

The Board of Trustees of the Victoria and Albert Museum, London, E.632-1963

References: "The Greek Theatre and *Helena in Troas*" (13 May 1886): 725–26; "The Performance in the Greek Theatre" (18 May 1886): 5; "*Helena in Troas* at Hengler's" (18 May 1886): 4; "The Greek Play at Hengler's Circus" (18 May 1886): 3; "*Helena in Troas*" (18 May 1886): 5; "A Greek Theatre in London" (18 May 1886): 5; "*Helena in Troas*" (18 May 1886): 5; "Our London Letter" (18 May 1886), 2 [*Cork Constitution*]; "Athens in London" (18 May 1886): 6; W. C. K. Wilde, "*Helena in Troas*" (20 May 1886): 389; Scrutator [pseud.], . *Helena in Troas*" (20 May 1886): 765; "A Greek Theatre in London" (21 May 1886): 818; "The Greek Plays: *Helena in Troas*" (21 May 1886): 15; O. Wilde, "*Helena in Troas*" (22 May 1886): 161–62; "The Drama: Between the Acts" (22 May 1886): 563; "*Helena in Troas*" (22 May 1886): 14; "Before and Behind the Curtain" (22 May 1886): 14; C. S., "Greek Plays" (22 May 1886): 534; "Drama: The Greek Plays" (22 May 1886): 689–90; "Greek Performances" (22 May 1886): 370; "Dramatic Notes" (22 May 1886): 2; "Dramatic and Musical Gossip: Hengler's Circus" (23 May 1886): 2; "*Helena in Troas* at the Greek Theatre" (23 May 1886): 7; "Mr. Todhunter's *Helena in Troas* . . . " (26 May 1886): 15; "Our Captious Critic. *Helena in Troas*" (29 May 1886): 327; W. C. K. Wilde, "*Helena in Troas*" (1 June 1886): 331–35; "*Helena in Troas*: Sketches Taken at the Greek Theatre Hengler's Circus" (5 June 1886): 624–26; "Hengler's Circus" (5 June 1886); Harbron, *Conscious Stone* (1949): 176–81; R. Spencer, *Aesthetic*

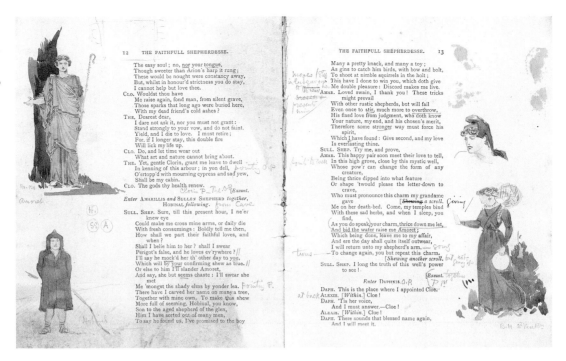

Cat. no. 147. "*The Faithfull Shepherdesse* by John Fletcher, adapted by E. W. Godwin": Preparation copy open to costume designs for the characters Amoret, Hobinal, and two others, 1885. Printed text with ink, pen, pencil, and watercolor additions; 8¼ x 6⅝ in. (21 x 16.8 cm). Trustees of the Victoria and Albert Museum, London, S.189-1998.

Movement (1972): 104–105, 110; Stokes, "Resistible Theatres" (1972): 52–56, 61, 64–66, 68; Souder, "E. W. Godwin" (1976): 107–27; Lambourne, "Pyrrhic Success" (2 October 1986): 1024–25; Baldwin, "Victorian Artists" (1991): 192–99; Jenkyns, *Dignity and Decadence* (1992): 303–306; Lambourne, *Aesthetic Movement* (1996): 168–70.

149. Costume Design for John Todhunter's *Helena in Troas*
(fig. 12-48)
For the character Priam
1886
Pencil and watercolor on paper
9⅞ x 6⅛ in. (25 x 15.5 cm)
Inscription: "PRIAM.; white; gold; chain of / Dionysos; Black / & / gold stars; White dress / & porphyry / mantle / bare arms; pattern / the long way of / the himation; ivory; Sandals & bare feet (fleshings)."

The Board of Trustees of the Victoria and Albert Museum, London, S.152-1998

References: see no. 148; Stokes, "Resistible Theatres" (1972): 54; Baldwin, "Victorian Artists" (1991): 197.

150. The Chorus in John Todhunter's *Helena in Troas*: Costumes and Set Designed by E. W. Godwin
(fig. 9-23)
1886
Photograph
6¾ x 9⅞ in. (17.2 x 25.2 cm)

The Board of Trustees of the Victoria and Albert Museum, London, S.168-1998

References: See no. 148; R. Spencer, *Aesthetic Movement* (1972): 104–5, illus.; Lambourne, "Pyrrhic Success" (2 October 1986): 1024, fig. 1; Baldwin, "Victorian Artists" (1991): 196; Lambourne, *Aesthetic Movement* (1996): 168–69, illus.

151. Program Design for Tom Taylor's Play *The Fool's Revenge*
(fig. 12-50)
1886
Pen and ink and pencil
5⅞ x 4½ in. (15 x 11.5 cm)
Inscription: "OPERA COMIQUE / UNDER THE DIRECTION OF E W Godwin; THE FOOL'S REVENGE / BY / Tom Taylor; July 3 and every evening / AT 8 o'clock / DOORS OPEN at 7.30 / carriages at 11 .. BOX / OFFICE OPEN 10 to 4 / PRICES from 1/s to 4 guin / Business Manager H Daily"

The Board of Trustees of the Victoria and Albert Museum, London, S.96-1998

References: "Opera Comique" (9 July 1886): 16; "Plays and Players" (10 July 1886): 18; [*The Fool's Revenge*] (10 July 1886): 495; (10 July 1886): 14; Coleman, "*The Fool's Revenge*" (7 August 1886): 11–12; Lys [pseud], "Archaeology or Art?" (7 August 1886): 13–14; Harbron, "Edward Godwin" (August 1945): 52; Harbron, *Conscious Stone* (1949): 181–82; Stokes, "Resistible Theatres" (1972): 56–57, 63; Souder, "E. W. Godwin" (1976): 43, 127; Baldwin, "Victorian Artists" (1991): 199–202, 487–490.

152. Program for Tom Taylor's Play *The Fool's Revenge* (fig. 12-51)
1886
Printed paper
6¾ x 11¼ in. (17.3 x 28.5 cm)

The Board of Trustees of the Victoria and Albert Museum, London, S.97-1998

References: see no. 151.

153. Costume Design for Tom Taylor's Play *The Fool's Revenge* (fig. 12-53)
1886
Pencil and watercolor on paper
8⅛ x 4½ in. (20.6 x 11.6 cm)
Inscription: "spear; & 2 Chamberlain / & 2 Servant / Manfred; Shoes.; Miss Hare"

The Board of Trustees of the Victoria and Albert Museum, London, S.98-1998

References: see no. 151.

154. Costume Design for Tom Taylor's Play *The Fools Revenge* (fig. 12-52)
For the character of the Fool, Bertuccio and an unidentified character
1886
Pencil and watercolor on paper
7⅞ x 6⅜ in. (20 x 16.1 cm)
Inscription: "Bertuccio / *Vezin*; Harl 3000 / 15th; all terra cotta / old gold & / vermilion; Ital. / 22.138; shoe.; EWG June; June 1886."

The Board of Trustees of the Victoria and Albert Museum, London, S.99-1998

References: see no. 151.

•BIBLIOGRAPHY•

Archives Consulted

*Abbreviations in **bold** represent the short form of citation used in the notes to the essays and checklist references.*

Bristol Society of Architects. Papers held by the architectural firm Whicheloe MacFarlane, Bristol.

Bristol Record Office, Bristol

British Library Mss
British Library Manuscripts Collection, London.

Chelsea Library, Local Studies Library, London.

Cheshire Record Office

Gillow Archives
City of Westminster Archives Centre, London. Gillow and Company Archives.

Compton Family Documents, Castle Ashby, Northamptonshire.

Corporation of London Records Office, London.

Craig Family. Papers. Private collection.

The Design Archive, Arthur Sanderson and Sons Ltd., Uxbridge, England.

Devon Record Office, Exeter.

Ellen Terry Museum
Collection of the National Trust, Ellen Terry Memorial Museum, Smallhythe Place, Tenterden, Kent.

The Free Library, Philadelphia, Pennsylvania.

Glasgow School of Art. Archives, Glasgow, Scotland.

Glasgow University Library, Glasgow, Scotland. Department of Special Collections, Whistler Collection.

Greater Manchester County Record Office.

Guildhall Library, Manuscript Division. Corporation of London.

Hulton Getty Photo Archive, London.

Hunterian Art Gallery, Butterfly Cabinet Curatorial Papers. Glasgow, Scotland.

Hyde Collection. Four Oaks Farm, Somerville, New Jersey.

Lambeth Palace Library, London. Records of the Incorporated Church Building Society.

Liberty Archives
City of Westminster Archives Centre, London. Liberty and Company Archives.

Library of Congress, Washington, D.C. Rosenwald Collection, Box 1977.

Library of Congress, Washington, D.C. Whistler Clippings, Pennell Collection, Volume 36.

London Metropolitan Archives.

Lothian Papers
Nottingham Record Office, Nottinghamshire. Lothian Papers.

Northampton Record Office, Northamptonshire.

National Library of Ireland, Dublin. Lawrence Collection.

National Monuments Record Centre. Royal Commission on the Historic Monuments of England, London and Swindon, England.

Plymouth and West Devon Record Office, Plymouth.

Proctor and Palmer
Henry Crisp. Papers held by Proctor and Palmer Architects (formerly Oatley & Brentnall), Clevedon, Somerset.

Public Record Office, Kew, Richmond, Surrey, England.

RIBA Mss
Royal Institute of British Architects, Manuscripts and Archives Collection, British Architectural Library, London.

RIBA Drawings
The Royal Institute of British Architects, Drawings Collection, British Architectural Library, London.

V & A AAD
Victoria and Albert Museum, London. Archive of Art and Design.

V & A PD
Victoria and Albert Museum, London. Department of Prints, Drawings, and Paintings.

V & A TA
Victoria and Albert Museum, London, Theatre Archive, Blythe House. E. W. Godwin collection (9 boxes of uncatalogued material).

Wolfsonian–Florida
The Mitchell Wolfson Jr. Collection, The Wolfsonian-Florida International University, Miami Beach, Florida.

E. W. Godwin's Writings and Published Drawings

Citations are arranged by publication date; books precede journal contributions. Square brackets around titles indicate articles that are unsigned but attributed to Godwin on the basis of records (including the architect's ledgers) in the Archive of Art and Design and the Department of Prints, Drawings and Paintings at the Victoria and Albert Museum, London. Page numbers in square brackets indicate illustrations.

1851

Godwin, Edward William, James Hine, and William Corbett Burder. *The Architectural Antiquities of Bristol and Its Neighbourhood.* Bristol: Burder, Hine, and Godwin, 1851.

1853

"Ancient Coffin-Slab in St. Philip's Church, Bristol." *Archaeological Journal* 10 (December 1853): 182–83.

"Notes, Historical and Architectural, of the Priory of Dominicans, Bristol." In *Memoirs Illustrative of the History and Antiquities of Bristol, and the Western Counties of Great Britain* . . . , by the Royal Archaeological Institute of Great Britain and Ireland. London: George Bell for the Archaeological Institute, 1853.

"Notes on Some Examples of Church Architecture in Cornwall." *Archaeological Journal* 10 (December 1853): 317–24.

1856

"Account of a Roman Villa Discovered at Colerne, in the County of Wilts." *Archaeological Journal* 13 (December 1856): 328–32.

1857

"An Account of the Church of St. John the Baptist, Colerne." *Wiltshire Archaeological and Natural History Magazine* 3, no. 9 (1857): 358–66.

"Answers to Queries: Earl's Meadows." Letter to the *Ulster Journal of Archaeology* 5 (1857): 163–64.

"Antiquarian Notes and Queries: 'Augustinians' and 'Augustine Canons.'" *Ulster Journal of Archaeology* 5 (1857): 157–58.

"Gothic and Classic." *Builder* 15 (28 March 1857): 176.

1858

"An Account of Ditchridge Church, Wilts." *Wiltshire Archaeological and Natural History Magazine* 4 (1858): 146–48.

"An Account of the Church of Biddeston St. Nicholas, Wilts." *Wiltshire Archaeological and Natural History Magazine* 4 (1858): 143–46.

"Notice of the Castle at Dudley." *Archaeological Journal* 15 (1858): 47–54.

"The Taunton Tower, or a Word for Restoration." *Builder* 16 (21 August 1858): 572.

1860

"The Court-House, Clapton-in-Gordano, Somersetshire." *Archaeological Journal* 17 (1860): 128–31.

1861

"Notes on Some of the Churches in the Deaneries of Kerrier and [P]enwith, Cornwall." Parts 1 and 2. *Archaeological Journal* 18 (September 1861): 231–52; (October 1861): 325–41.

"Notice of an Example of Domestic Architecture at Colerne, Wiltshire." *Archaeological Journal* 18 (June 1861): 125–27.

1862

"Excursion of the Bristol Society of Architects." *Western Daily Press* (20 August 1862): 3.

Theatrical Jottings in the *Western Daily Press*. "The New Burlesque" (16 October 1862): 4; (21 October 1862): 2; (30 October 1862): 2; (6 November 1862): 3; (15 November 1862): 3; "*Romeo and Juliet*" (24 November 1862) 3; (28 November 1862): 3; (1 December 1862): 3; "*Macbeth*" (4 December 1862): 2; (8 December 1862): 3; (17 December 1862) 4; "Christmas at the Theatre Royal: *Cinderella and the Cruel Sisters*" (26 December 1862): 4.

1863

"Bristol Cathedral." *Archaeological Journal* 20 (March 1863): 38–63.

"The Destroyed Monasteries of Bristol." *Western Daily Press* (16 February 1863): 3; (23 February 1863): 3.

Theatrical Jottings in the *Western Daily Press*. "*The Pantomime*" (3 January 1863): 4; "*The Little Treasure*" (7 January 1863): 2; (13 January 1863): 3; "The London Pantomime" (21 January 1863): 4; (27 January 1863): 3; (11 February 1863): 3; (17 February 1863): 2; (23 February 1863): 2 (26 February 1863): 2; (5 March 1863): 3; (11 March 1863): 4.

1864

"An Antiquarian Tramp through Old Bristol." *Western Daily Press* (10 September 1864): 4.

"The Churches of Somersetshire." *Building News and Engineering Journal* 11 (24 June 1864): 479–80.

["The Savoy Chapel, Strand."] *Building News and Engineering Journal* 11 (15 July 1864): 539.

"The Theatre." *Western Daily Press* (4 April 1864): 3.

"Theatre Royal, Bath: *The Merchant of Venice*." *Western Daily Press* (18 October 1864): 4.

Theatrical Jottings in *Western Daily Press*. (21 March 1864) 3; (5 April 1864): 3; (18 July 1864); (31 August 1864) 2; (6 September 1864): 3; (10 September 1864); (19 September 1864): 2; (22 September 1864): 3; (5 October 1864): 2; (11 October 1864): 2; "Drury Lane and the Lyceum Theatres" (2 November 1864): 2; "The Olympic" (9 November 1864): 3.

1865

A Handbook of Floral Decoration for Churches. London: J. Masters and Sons, 1865.

"Art Cliques." Parts 1–8 of 12. *Building News and Engineering Journal* 12 (15 September 1865): 642–43; (22 September 1865): 657; (29 September 1865): 673; (13 October 1865): 707; (20 October 1865): 725–26; (3 November 1865): 766–67; (1 December 1865): 843; (15 December 1865): 876.

"A Few Notes on Some Churches near Warwick." *Archaeological Journal* 22 (March 1865): 33–40.

["Plymouth."] *Building News and Engineering Journal* 12 (18 August 1865): 574–75.

1866

"Art Cliques." Parts 9–12 of 12. *Building News and Engineering Journal* 13 (19 January 1866): 33; (2 February 1866): 62–63; (9 March 1866): 146–47; (23 March 1866): 177–78.

"(Notes on) Painted Decoration(s)." Parts 1–8 of 12. *Building News and Engineering Journal* 13 (20 April 1866): 247–48; (4 May 1866): 282–83; (25 May 1866): 334–35; (22 June 1866): 405; (3 August 1866): 507; (10 August 1866): 526–27; (7 September 1866): 590; (16 November 1866): 756–58.

"Three Modern Architects." *Building News and Engineering Journal* 13 (30 November 1866): 799–800.

1867

"The Architectural Exhibition, 1867." *Building News and Engineering Journal* 14 (17 May 1867): 335–38.

"Dromore Castle." *Building News and Engineering Journal* 14 (29 March 1867): 222, 224–25; (1 November 1867): 755, [758–59].

"Leicester and Its Clock Tower Competition." *Building News and Engineering Journal* 14 (20 December 1867): 877–78.

"Mr Street on the Bristol Cathedral." *Building News and Engineering Journal* 14 (9 August 1867): 549–51.

"(Notes on) Painted Decoration(s)." Parts 9–11 of 12. *Building News and Engineering Journal* 14 (4 January 1867): 4–5; July 1867): 490–91; (18 October 1867): 715–17.

"The Photographs of the Architectural Photographic Association for 1867." Parts 1 and 2. *Building News and Engineering Journal* 14 (22 February 1867): 147–48; (1 March 1867): 164–66.

"St. Alban's Abbey Church Reviewed." *Civil Engineer and Architect's Journal* (1 April 1867): 117–19.

"A Paper Read by E. W. Godwin F.S.A. at the Country Meeting of the Waynflete Society in the Abbey of S. Albans on June 15, 1867." *The Annual Report of the Waynflete Society.* London: Waynflete Society, 1867.

1868

"(Notes on) Painted Decoration(s)." Part 12. *Building News and Engineering Journal* 15 (3 January 1868): 6–8.

1869

"The Architectural Association's Screen at the Exhibition, Conduit Street." *Architect* (London) 1 (15 May 1869): 253.

["Architecture at the Royal Academy."] *Architect* (London) 1 (8 May 1869): 242–43.

"Bradford Town Hall." Letter to *Architect* (London) 2 (27 November 1869): 266.

"Bradford Town Hall Competition." Letter to *Architect* (London) 2 (18 December 1869): 302.

"Foundation of S. Mary and S. Mark, Now the Mayor's Chapel, Bristol." In *Somersetshire Archaeological and Natural History Society. Proceedings during the Year 1867.* Vol. 14, part 1. Taunton: Frederick May, 1869.

"Mr. Marks's Work at the Gaiety Theatre," *Architect* (London) 1 (2 January 1869): 3–4.

"On Ancient Bristol." In *Somersetshire Archaeological and Natural History Society. Proceedings during the Year 1867.* Vol. 14, part 2. Taunton: Frederick May, 1869.

"The Royal Academy." *Architect* (London) 1 (1 May 1869): 229–30.

"The Royal Academy Exhibition." *Architect* (London) 1 (5 June 1869): 289–90.

1870

"Exeter Cathedral." *Architect* (London) 3 (11 June 1870): 286–88.

"Some Remarks on Mr. Smith's Article, 'The Consequences of the Gothic Revival.'" Letters to the *Architect* (London) 4 (9 July 1870): 24–25.

"The Decoration of St. Paul's Cathedral." *Architect* (London) 4 (23 July 1870): 43–44.

"St. Paul's Cathedral." *Architect* (London) 4 (30 July 1870): 57–58.

"Decoration of St. Paul's Cathedral." *Architect* (London) 4 (13 August 1870): 89.

1871

Review of *Architectural Drawings,* by William Burges. *Architect* (London) 5 (7 January 1871): 8–9.

"The Decoration of St. Paul's Cathedral." *Architect* (London) 6 (22 July 1871): 38–40.

"The New Law Courts." *Building News and Engineering Journal* 21 (28 July 1871): 73.

"The *Times* and the New Law Courts." *Architect* (London) 6 (30 September 1871): 164–66.

"Geoffrey Chaucer as Clerk of the King's Works." Parts 1 and 2. *Architect* (London) 6 (4 November 1871): 221–22; (11 November 1871): 233–34.

"The Gothic Revival." *Architect* (London) 6 (2 December 1871): 271–73, 278–79.

"The *Times* v. Architects." *Architect* (London) 6 (16 December 1871): 297.

["Art at the Theatre: *Pygmalion and Galatea* at the Haymarket."] *Architect* (London) 6 (16 December 1871): 301.

1872

"Spenser's Castles, &c." Parts 1 and 2. *Architect* (London) 7 (27 January 1872): 41–42; (3 February 1872): 54–55.

["Ancient Leadwork."] *Architect* (London) 7 (3 February 1872): 55.

"The *Times* and Others v. Street." *Architect* (London) 7 (10 February 1872): 65–67.

["Wall Painting."] *Architect* (London) 7 (24 February 1872): 87.

["Wall-Painting as Taught in the Mediaeval Mss."] *Architect* (London) 7 (2 March 1872): 101.

["Conventionalism in Art."] *Globe and Traveller* (London) (2 April 1872): 1–2.

"School Boards and Competitions." *Architect* (London) 7 (6 April 1872): 169–70.

["The Louvre"; "The Hotel Dieu, Paris."] *Architect* (London) 7 (20 April 1872): 199.

["Universal Exhibition in Paris"; "The Coming Paris Salon"; "Faience of Rouen."] *Architect* (London) 7 (20 April 1872): 200.

[Review of *The Means of Making a House Healthy and Comfortable,* by Henry J. Lanchester.] *Architect* (London) 7 (20 April 1872): 203.

"On the Architecture and Antiquities of the Western Part of the Province of Ulster." Parts 1–5. *Architect* (London) 7 (20 April 1872): 193–95; (4 May 1872): 222–25; (11 May 1872): 233–34; (18 May 1872): 248–49; (1 June 1872): 278–81.

"Some Remarks on the Shrine of S. Alban." *Architect* (London) 7 (27 April 1872): 207–9.

["New Villa Berlin"; "Churches by Mr. R. I. Withers, Architect."] Illustrations in the *Architect* (London) 7 (27 April 1872): 214.

["The Royal Academy."] *Architect* (London) 7 (4 May 1872): 222.

["The Buried Treasure."] *Architect* (London) 7 (4 May 1872): 225.

["Balliol College Chapel, Oxford"; "Oxford Museum"; "The London School Board: Competition for Schools, Johnson Street, Stepney."] Illustrations in the *Architect* (London) 7 (4 May 1872): 226.

["Mr. Gibson's Gift to the Royal Academy."] *Architect* (London) 7 (4 May 1872): 232.

["The Royal Academy: Architecture."] *Architect* (London) 7 (11 May 1872): 235–37.

["Professional Charges and Surveyors."] *Architect* (London) 7 (11 May 1872): 241.

["The American Institute of Architects."] *Architect* (London) 7 (18 May 1872): 250–51.

"The London School Board Competitions." *Architect* (London) 7 (25 May 1872): 265–66.

["The Article 'Maison' in M. Viollet Le Duc's [*sic*] *Dictionnaire.*"] *Architect* (London) 7 (25 May 1872): 267–68.

["The Rival Schools."] *Globe and Traveller* (London) (7 June 1872): 1–2.

["Ladies' Dress."] *Globe and Traveller* (London) (8 June 1872): 1–2.

["Furniture."] *Globe and Traveller* (London) (15 June 1872): 1–2.

"The 'British Architects.'" *Building News and Engineering Journal* 22 (21 June 1872): 505.

["Jewellery."] Parts 1 and 2. *Globe and Traveller* (London) (22 June 1872): 1–2; (26 June 1872): 1–2.

["Wall Papers."] *Globe and Traveller* (London) (27 June 1872): 6.

["Professional Tenderness."] *Building News and Engineering Journal* 22 (28 June 1872): 515.

["The Article 'Maison' in M. Viollet Le Duc's [*sic*] *Dictionnaire.*"] *Architect* (London) 7 (29 June 1872): 337–39.

[Reviews of *Moniteur des Architectes; Encyclopédie d'Architecture* (No. 8); and *Illustrated Handbook of the Scenery and Antiquities of South-Western Donegal.*] *Architect* (London) 7 (29 June 1872): 344.

"Modern Architects and Their Works." Parts 1–6. *Building News and Engineering Journal* 23 (5 July 1872): 13; (12 July 1872): 35; (26 July 1872): 67; (30 August 1872): 167; (6 September 1872): 187; (11 October 1872): 291–92.

["Chimneys and Chimney-Pots."] *Globe and Traveller* (London) (13 July 1872): 1–2.

["Domes."] *Architect* (London) 8 (13 July 1872): 19.

"Kilcolman." *Architect* (London) 8 (17 August 1872): 91–92 and illus.

"Proposed Asylum, S. Ann's Heath Competition." Letters to the *Building News and Engineering Journal* 23 (11 October 1872): 295–96 passim.

E. W. C. [*sic*] "Gothic Furniture." Letter to the *Building News and Engineering Journal* 23 (15 November 1872): 393–94.

1873

"The Secret Manufacture of Architecture." *Building News and Engineering Journal* 24 (7 February 1873): 145–46.

"Architectural Perspective." Letter to the *Building News and Engineering Journal* 24 (14 February 1873): 201.

"Edinburgh Cathedral Competition." Letter to the *Building News and Engineering Journal* 24 (21 February 1873): 231.

["Honour to Whom Honour Is Due."] *Building News and Engineering Journal* 24 (28 February 1873): 235.

"The Armoire, Bayeux Cathedral." *Building News and Engineering Journal* 25 (29 August 1873): 235 and [233].

"What Is a Baldacchino?" *Building News and Engineering Journal* 25 (26 September 1873): 351–52.

"The Works of Mr. R. Norman Shaw, A.R.A." *Building News and Engineering Journal* 25 (24 October 1873): 449–50.

1874

"Manoir D'Ango: Timber Work." *Building News and Engineering Journal* 26 (27 February 1874): 228 and [230].

"The New European Style." *Building News and Engineering Journal* 26 (6 March 1874): 269.

"The Manor-House of Ango, near Dieppe." *Building News and Engineering Journal* 26 (3 April 1874): 364 and [373].

"Chateau d'Ango." *Building News and Engineering Journal* 26 (10 April 1874): 390 and [392].

"Co-operative Home." *Building News and Engineering Journal* 26 (24 April 1874): 446 and [456–57].

"Architectural Education." *British Architect* 1 (22 May 1874): 1.

"Mr. E. W. Godwin's Sketches." *Building News and Engineering Journal* 26 (29 May 1874): 584 and [595].

"Industrial Education Bureau." *Women and Work* 1, no. 1 (6 June 1874): 5.

"Mr. E. W. Godwin on Lady Architects." *British Architect* 1 (12 June 1874): 378.

"Lady Architects." *Architect* (London) 11 (13 June 1874): 335.

"St. Gilles near St. Lô." *Building News and Engi-*

neering Journal 27 (3 July 1874): [22].

"What I Noted in Passing through Manchester and Liverpool." *Building News and Engineering Journal* 27 (10 July 1874): 55.

["The Grocers' Company Middle-Class School Competition."] *Building News and Engineering Journal* 27 (31 July 1874): 129–30.

"The Decoration of St. Paul's Cathedral." Parts 1 and 2. *Architect* (London) 12 (1 August 1874): 57–59; (7 August 1874): 179–80.

"Mr. E. W. Godwin's Measured Sketches: Shop and Stairs in House, St. Lô." *Building News and Engineering Journal* 27 (14 August 1874): 194 and [200].

"Some Notes of a Month in Normandy." Parts 1–4. *Building News and Engineering Journal* 27 (28 August 1874): 251–52; (11 September 1874): 307–8; (2 October 1874): 395–96; (13 November 1874): 572–73.

"Lisieux." *Building News and Engineering Journal* 27 (11 September 1874): 310 and [318].

"Lisieux Cathedral." *Building News and Engineering Journal* 27 (2 October 1874): 400 and [408].

"Belleville, near Dieppe." *Building News and Engineering Journal* 27 (23 October 1874): 488 and [499].

"Architecture and Costume of Shakespere's [sic] Plays." *Architect* (London) 12: *"Hamlet, Prince of Denmark"* (31 October 1874): 224–25; *"Romeo and Juliet"* (14 November 1874): 252–54; *"Cymbeline"* (21 November 1874): 267–69; *"King Lear* and *Macbeth"* (28 November 1874); *"King John"* (5 December 1874): 298–99; *"Richard II"* (12 December 1874): 314–15; *"Henry IV"* (19 December 1874): 331–32; *"Henry V"* (26 December 1874): 349–51.

"The Church of West Littleton." *Building News and Engineering Journal* 27 (13 November 1874): 576 and [587].

"Church near Dromore Castle." *Building News and Engineering Journal* 27 (25 December 1874): 752 and [760].

1875

"Architecture and Costume of Shakespere's [sic] Plays." *Architect* (London) 13: *"The Merry Wives of Windsor"* (2 January 1875): 2–3; *"Henry VI*–Part I" (23 January 1875): 46–47; *"Henry VI*–Part I, Continued" (30 January 1875): 60–61; *"Henry VI*–Part III" (6 February 1875): 73–74; *"Richard III"* (13 February 1875): 87–88; *"Henry VIII"* (27 February 1875): 116–17; *"Henry VIII,* Continued" (6 March 1875): 133–34; *"Othello"* (13 March 1875): 151–52; *"Two Gentlemen of Verona"* (20 March 1875): 168–69; *"Merchant of Venice"* (27 March 1875): 182–84; *"Merchant of Venice,* Continued" (3 April 1875): 196–97; *"The Taming of the Shrew"* (10 April 1875): 210–11; *"Measure for Measure"* (17 April 1875): 224–25; *"Twelfth Night"* (24 April 1875): 240–41; *"As You Like It"* (1 May 1875): 255–56; "The Greek Plays–I" (8 May 1875): 270–71; "The Greek Plays–II" (15 May 1875): 284–85; "The Greek Plays–III" (22

May 1875): 298–99; "The Greek Plays–IV" (5 June 1875): 328–29; "The Roman Plays–I. *Coriolanus"* (12 June 1875): 344–45; "The Roman Plays–II. *Julius Caesar"* (19 June 1875): 358–59; "The Roman Plays–III. *Antony and Cleopatra"* (26 June 1875): 372–73.

"Competitions and Professional Referees." *Architect* (London) 13 (9 January 1875): 15–17.

"Someries Castle." Illustration in the *Building News and Engineering Journal* 28 (22 January 1875): 90 and illus. [92].

"First Impressions on a Private View of the Dudley Gallery." *Building News and Engineering Journal* 28 (5 February 1875): 146–47.

"Japanese Wood Construction." Parts 5 and 6 of "Woodwork." *Building News and Engineering Journal* 28 (12 February 1875): 173–74 and [189]; (19 February 1875): 200–201 and [214].

[Obituary. "Professor Willis."] *Architect* 13 (6 March 1875): 134–35.

[Theatrical Jottings.] Parts 1 and 2. *Building News and Engineering Journal* 28 (19 March 1875): 311–12; (18 June 1875): 683–85.

"Specimens of Glazing." *Building News and Engineering Journal* 28 (19 March 1875): 316 and illus.

"The Ex-Classic Style Called 'Queen Anne.'" *Building News and Engineering Journal* 28 (16 April 1875): 441–42.

Letter to the *Times* (London) (23 April 1875): 10.

"Notes on the Costume in the Pictures at the Royal Academy." *Architect* (London) 13 (29 May 1875): 314–15.

"Wall Paintings in 1875: Mr. Armstrong and Mr. V. Prinsep." *Architect* (London) 14 (3 July 1875): 2–3.

"Architectura Vulgata." *Architect* (London) 14 (10 July 1875): 16–17.

"Curiosities of Architecture." *Architect* (London) 14 (17 July 1875): 30–31.

"Harold's Church at Waltham." *Architect* (London) 14 (24 July 1875): 42–45.

"Old English or Saxon Building." Parts 1–4. *Architect* (London) 14 (7 August 1875): 70–71; (14 August 1875): 84–85; (21 August 1875): 98–99; (28 August 1875): 112–14.

"Bristol." *Architect* (London) 14 (4 September 1875): 126.

"The Present Aspect of Decorative Painting." *Architect* (London) 14 (11 September 1875): 140–41.

"More Words on Saxon Architecture." *Architect* (London) 14 (18 September 1875): 154.

"The 'Improvement' of London Bridge." Letter to the *Architect* (London) 14 (25 September 1875): 179–80.

"The Cyclopaedia of Costume." *Architect* (London) 14 (16 October 1875): 208–9.

"The 'Mise-en-Scene' at the Lyceum." *Architect* (London) 14 (23 October 1875): 222.

"The Bayeux Tapestry." *Architect* (London) 14 (6 November 1875): 250–51.

"The *Daily News* versus Art." *Architect* (London) 14 (20 November 1875): 281–82.

"The Hope of the Family." *Architect* (London) 14 (18 December 1875): 342–43.

1876

"Some Stray Notes on the Modern Field of Art." *Architect* (London) 15 (1 January 1876): 2–3.

"A Painter and a Sculptor." *Architect* (London) 15 (15 January 1876): 30.

"Correspondence: The Walker Exhibition." *Architect* (London) 15 (22 January 1876): 58.

"*Frozen Music.*" *Architect* (London) 15 (5 February 1876): 76–77.

["Notes on English Mediaeval Architecture."] *Architect* (London) 15 (19 February 1876): 107–8.

"In the Studios of Some 'Outsiders.'" Parts 1 and 2. *Architect* (London) 15 (11 March 1876): 156–57; (18 March 1876): 172–73.

"A Church in the Way." *Architect* (London) 15 (25 March 1876): 190–91.

"The Popular Novelist on Art." *Architect* (London) 15 (8 April 1876): 221–22.

"Scraps for Students." Parts 1–6. *Architect* (London) 15 (15 April 1876): 237–38; (22 April 1876): 252–53; "Selection of Studies" (6 May 1876): 284–85; "The Office'" (13 May 1876): 303–5; "Competition and Clients" (20 May 1876): 320; "At Home" (27 May 1876): 338–39.

["Bristol Blunders."] *Architect* (London) 15 (29 April 1876): 267–68.

"Mantelpieces." *Architect* (London) 15 (3 June 1876): 353.

"Modern Dress." *Architect* (London) 15 (10 June 1876): 368.

"Greek Art at the Conference." *Architect* (London) 15 (24 June 1876): 396–97.

"My Chambers and What I Did to Them." Parts 1 and 2. *Architect* (London) 16, "Chapter 1: A.D. 1867," (1 July 1876): 4–5; "Chapter 2: A.D. 1872," (8 July 1876): 18–19.

"My House 'In' London." Parts 1–6. *Architect* (London) 16 (15 July 1876): 33–34; "The Hall" (22 July 1876): 45–46; "The Dining-Room" (29 July 1876): 58–59; "The Drawing-Room" (5 August 1876): 72–73; "The Bedrooms" (12 August 1876): 86; "Tops and Bottoms" (19 August 1876): 100–101.

"From the House–Top." *Architect* (London) 16 (26 August 1876): 112–13.

"Floorcloths." *Architect* (London) 16 (2 September 1876): 128.

"*Henry V*: An Archaeological Experience." *Architect* (London) 16 (9 September 1876): 142–43.

"Lintel Architecture." *Architect* (London) 16 (16 September 1876): 157.

"The Bell Turrets of North Wilts." *Architect* (London) 16 (23 September 1876): 174–75.

"*Henry V*: A Theatrical Experience." *Architect* (London) 16 (30 September 1876): 192–94.

"Odds and Ends about Construction." Parts 1 and 2. *Architect* (London) 16 (14 October 1876): 225–26; (28 October 1876): 248–49.

"Mr. Deschamps' Gallery." *Architect* (London) 16 (11 November 1876): 276.

"The Byron Memorial: A Sculptor's Competition." *Architect* (London) 16 (18 November 1876): 290–91.

"Unjust Competitions." *Architect* (London) 16 (9 December 1876): 335–36.

"Afternoon Strolls." *Architect* (London) 16 (23 December 1876): 363–64.

1877

["An Art Conversazione at the Hogarth."] *Architect* (London) 17 (6 January 1877): 5.

"The Exhibition of Works of the Old Masters." *Architect* (London) 17 (13 January 1877): 19–20.

["The Queen's Theatre."] *Architect* (London) 17 (20 January 1877): 36.

"Notes on Mr. Whistler's 'Peacock Room.'" *Architect* (London) 17 (24 February 1877): 118–19.

["Monastic Sites"; "Christian Grave Stones."] *British Architect and Northern Engineer* 7 (6 April 1877): 218.

"Architectural Poaching." *British Architect and Northern Engineer* 8 (13 July 1877): 16–17 and illus.

"Mural Decorations: Guffens and Others." *British Architect and Northern Engineer* 8 (3 August 1877): 54–55.

["Some New Competitions."] *British Architect and Northern Engineer* 8 (31 August 1877): 312–13.

"Temple Bar." Parts 1 and 2. *British Architect and Northern Engineer* 8 (19 October 1877): 189–90; (26 October 1877): title page.

"Cleopatra's Needle and Where to Place It." *British Architect and Northern Engineer* 8 (9 November 1877): 225–26.

"The Dudley Gallery." *British Architect and Northern Engineer* 8 (30 November 1877): 264.

["Can Greek Art Be Made Popular?"] *British Architect and Northern Engineer* 8 (28 December 1877): 311.

["Reading Town Hall Competition."] *British Architect and Northern Engineer* 8 (28 December 1877): 311–13.

1878

["To Our Readers."] *British Architect and Northern Engineer* 9 (4 January 1878): 1.

[Notes on Current Events. "It will be noticed . . . ."] *British Architect and Northern Engineer* 9 (4 January 1878): 8.

["Notes on Current Events."] *British Architect and Northern Engineer* 9 (11 January 1878): 20.

"The Abbey Church of St. Alban." *Athenaeum*, no. 2620 (12 January 1878): 62–63.

"A Few Words to Architectural Students." *British Architect and Northern Engineer* 9 (1 February 1878): 51.

["We learn from an American newspaper . . ."; "In the *Art at Home* series . . ."; "Mr. Stanley . . . ."] *British Architect and Northern Engineer* 9 (8 February 1878): 64.

["Architects' Rights."] *British Architect and Northern Engineer* 9 (8 February 1878): 63.

"Illustrations of Anglo–Saxon Art." Part 1. *British Architect and Northern Engineer* 9 (8 March 1878): 108 and [after 110].

["A Sculptured Frieze by N. Geiger"; "The Wellington Monument in St. Paul's."] *British Architect and Northern Engineer* 9 (22 March 1878): 131.

[Notes on Current Events. "We have just read . . ."; "The Superintendent . . . ."] *British Architect and Northern Engineer* 9 (22 March 1878): 132.

"Sir George Gilbert Scott." *British Architect and Northern Engineer* 9 (5 April 1878): 155–56.

["The Domestic Economy Congress."] *British Architect and Northern Engineer* 10 (5 July 1878): 1.

[Notes on Current Events. "There were three . . ."; "Why is it that . . ."; "Not content with . . ."; "A curiously picturesque town . . ."; "The new Kursaal . . ."; "A new corner house . . ."; "Ostend does not possess . . . ."] *British Architect and Northern Engineer* 10 (5 July 1878): 2.

[Notes on Current Events. "George Augustus Sala . . ."; "Architects are invited . . ."; "Where is Yeadon? . . ."; "Mr. Thomas C. Hine's . . ."; "As the Castle is . . ."; "Before quitting this museum . . ."; "Is it not quite time . . ."; "It is no doubt . . . ."] *British Architect and Northern Engineer* 10 (2 August 1878): 49–50.

["Roof Restoration."] *British Architect and Northern Engineer* 10 (16 August 1878): 69.

[Notes on Current Events. "The Mansfield Improvement Commissioners . . . ."] *British Architect and Northern Engineer* 10 (16 August 1878): 70.

["Japanese Building."] *British Architect and Northern Engineer* 10 (30 August 1878): 85.

["Waste in Every–Day House–Building."] *British Architect and Northern Engineer* 10 (20 September 1878): 109.

"On Some Buildings I Have Designed." *British Architect and Northern Engineer* 10 (29 November 1878): 210–12.

[Notes on Current Events. "We have authority . . . ."] *British Architect and Northern Engineer* 10 (6 December 1878): 217–18.

["The Dudley."] *British Architect and Northern Engineer* 10 (6 December 1878): 218.

1879

"A Suburban Church." *British Architect and Northern Engineer* 11 (3 January 1879): 6 and [after 6].

"An Example of Modern Domestic Architecture, Designed and Drawn by E. W. Godwin, F.S.A." *British Architect and Northern Engineer* 11 (3 January 1879): 6 and [after 6].

"A Suburban Church, Designed and Drawn by E. W. Godwin, F.S.A." Illustration in the *British Architect and Northern Engineer* 11 (3 January 1879).

[Notes on Current Events.] *British Architect and Northern Engineer* 11 (24 January 1879): 33–34.

"Examples of Ancient Irish Architecture by E. W. Godwin, F.S.A.: 1. Dysert." *British Architect and Northern Engineer* 11 (31 January 1879): 46, [after 46]; "2. Kilcolman" (21 February 1879): 84, [after 84]; "3. Kilbreedy" (7 March 1879): 104; [after 104]; 4. "St. Doulough, Church and Well" (14 March 1879): 114 [after 114].

"Studios and Mouldings." *Building News and Engineering Journal* 36 (7 March 1879): 261–62.

"The Architectural Association: The Designing of Studios." *Architect* (London) 21 (8 March 1879): 146.

["A Note on the Study of Greek Sculpture"; "Fact v. Theory."] *British Architect and Northern Engineer* 11 (11 April 1879): 151.

[Notes on Current Events.] *British Architect and Northern Engineer* 11 (2 May 1879): 181–82.

[Notes on Current Events. "The engraving of Mr. Whistler's portrait . . ."; "We wonder if it is true . . ."; "Reading at our leisure . . . ."] *British Architect and Northern Engineer* 12 (15 August 1879): 60.

[Notes on Current Events. "Among the names . . ."; "We are glad to find . . ."; "We hear that . . . ."] *British Architect and Northern Engineer* 12 (29 August 1879): 79.

[Notes on Current Events.] *British Architect and Northern Engineer* 12 (19 September 1879): 109–10.

"Some Facts about 'The White House,' Chelsea." *British Architect and Northern Engineer* 12 (26 September 1879): 119.

"Whistler v. Ruskin," *British Architect and Northern Engineer* 10 (29 November 1879): 207.

1880

Messenger and Company. *Artistic Conservatories, and Other Horticultural Buildings Designed . . . from Rough Sketches by E. W. Godwin, F.S.A., and from Designs and Drawings by Maurice B. Adams, A.R.I.B.A.* London: B. T. Batsford, 1880. Reprint, New York: Garland, 1978.

["Theatrical Jottings, No. I."] *British Architect and Northern Engineer* 13 (30 January 1880): 50–52.

[Notes on Current Events. "The Hon. Mrs. Brassey . . ."; "We inspected this week . . ."; "Mrs. Butler's (Miss Thompson) . . . ."] *British Architect and Northern Engineer* 13 (13 February 1880): 73.

["The Costume of *The Merchant of Venice*."] *British Architect and Northern Engineer* 13 (13 February 1880): 74–75.

["The Haymarket Theatre."] *British Architect and Northern Engineer* 13 (13 February 1880): 75–76.

["Theatrical Jottings, No. II."] *British Architect and Northern Engineer* 13 (13 February 1880): 77.

"Illustrations of Costume for *The Merchant of Venice*." *British Architect and Northern Engineer* 13 (13 February 1880): 78 and illus.

["Theatrical Jottings, No. III."] *British Architect and Northern Engineer* 13 (20 February 1880): 87.

["Theatrical Jottings, No. IV: Shakspere [sic] at the Imperial."] *British Architect and Northern Engineer* 13 (19 March 1880): 134.

"Examples of Ancient Irish Architecture by E. W. Godwin, F.S.A." Illustration in the *British Architect and Northern Engineer* 13 (19 March 1880).

[Notes on Current Events. "We are very glad . . ."; "Friday last was . . ."; "The French Gallery is . . ."; "Among other works . . ."; "The inquiry into . . ."; "Apropos of the same . . ."; "The shafts for the tunnel . . ."; "To Correspondents."] *British Architect and Northern Engineer* 13 (26 March 1880): 145.

["Theatrical Jottings, No. V: Shakspere [sic] at Sadler's Wells."] *British Architect and Northern Engineer* 13 (26 March 1880): 145–46.

"*British Architect* Art Club: 'An Architect's Table.'" *British Architect and Northern Engineer* 13 (26 March 1880): 147–48.

"Sketches of Costume for *As You Like It*." *British Architect and Northern Engineer* 13 (26 March 1880): 150 and illus.

[Notes on Current Events. "On Sunday and Monday . . ."; "Mr. Frank Dicksee has . . ."; "Mr. Ernest Parton . . ."; "A young landscape artist . . ."; "Mr. Robertson, the painter . . ."; "Mr. J. D. Watson illustrates . . ."; "Mr. J. Forbes Robertson is . . ."; "A young artist who is . . ."; "The splendour of harmony . . ."; "Mr. W. G. Wills . . ."; "Mr. F. Sandys has . . ."; "At the conversazione . . . ."] *British Architect and Northern Engineer* 13 (2 April 1880): 157.

["Theatrical Jottings, No. VI."] *British Architect and Northern Engineer* 13 (2 April 1880): 158.

[Notes on Current Events. "The gentlemen who manage . . ."; "Someone has written . . ."; "Mr. Stone . . ."; "The Fine Art Society . . . ."] *British Architect and Northern Engineer* 13 (9 April 1880): 169.

Godwin, Edward William, ed. Notes on Current Events. "Mr. Lehmann sends portraits . . ."; "Mr. Charlton's hunting scenes . . ."; "Mr. Herkomer . . ."; "Mr. Robert Barrett Browning . . ."; "Mr. Alfred Hunt . . ."; "Mr. P. R. Morris' (A.R.A.) picture . . ."; "D. Pettie, R.A., in his portrait . . ."; "'His Grace' is a small canvas . . ."; "Mr. Calderon . . ."; "Mr. Storey . . ."; "Mr. Richardson's (R.A.) picture . . ."; "Mr. G. H. Boughton . . ."; "'Amor Vincit Omnis,' a still unfinished canvas . . ."; "The Society of British Artists . . . ." *British Architect and Northern Engineer* 13 (9 April 1880): 169–70.

Godwin, Edward William, ed. "Society of British Artists: Suffolk Street Spring Exhibition." *British Architect and Northern Engineer* 13 (9 April 1880): 171.

"*British Architect* Art Club." *British Architect and Northern Engineer* 13 (9 April 1880): 174.

[Notes on Current Events. "The Hon. William Collins . . ."; "For the elevations . . ."; "There are architects . . ."; "To all which we . . ."; "The Architectural Association . . ."; "We ought not to omit . . ."; "Apart from politics . . ."; "Talking about M. P.'s . . ."; "The Exhibition of Building Appliances . . ."; "In the 'Theatrical Jottings' . . . ."] *British Architect and Northern Engineer* 13 (16 April 1880): 181–83.

["Theatrical Jottings, No. VII."] *British Architect and Northern Engineer* 13 (23 April 1880): 194.

"The Costumes of *As You Like It*." *British Architect and Northern Engineer* 13 (23 April 1880): 196.

[Notes on Current Events. "In deference to . . ."; "As we wandered through . . ."; "We are glad to hear . . ."; "The Society of Painters . . ."; "The best figure subject . . ."; "The landscapes this year . . ."; "Of two exquisitely lovely works . . ."; "We pass to the . . ."; "Architecture and building are . . ."; "Mr. H. C. Angell's 'Raspberries' . . ."; "Mr. George Smith of Coalville . . . ."] *British Architect and Northern Engineer* 13 (30 April 1880): 205.

["Theatrical Jottings, No. VIII."] *British Architect and Northern Engineer* 13 (30 April 1880): 206.

["The Grosvenor Gallery."] Parts 1–3. *British Architect and Northern Engineer* 13 (7 May 1880): 218–19; (14 May 1880): 231–32; (21 May 1880): 243–44.

"*British Architect* Art Club: Review of Designs, Series II." *British Architect and Northern Engineer* 13 (7 May 1880): 220–21.

["Theatrical Jottings, No. IX."] *British Architect and Northern Engineer* 13 (14 May 1880): 231.

[Notes on Current Events. "We are much obliged . . ."; "Mr. Street's letter . . ."; "Not content with obliterating . . ."; "Mr. F. W. Lawson exhibits . . ."; "We publish this week . . . ."] *British Architect and Northern Engineer* 13 (21 May 1880): 241–42.

[Notes on Current Events. "We shall watch with interest . . ."; "At the German Athenaeum . . ."; "We entertain no doubt . . ."; "But apart from the closed . . ."; "It is little use . . ."; "It is more or less a . . . ."] *British Architect and Northern Engineer* 13 (21 May 1880): 242–43.

"Illustrations of Costume by E. W. Godwin, F.S.A.: Romeo and Juliet." *British Architect and Northern Engineer* 13 (21 May 1880): 246 and illus.

"*British Architect* Art Club: A Fireplace and Mantel for a Small Room." *British Architect and Northern Engineer* 13 (21 May 1880): 246–47 and illus.

"The Costumes of *Romeo and Juliet*." *British Architect and Northern Engineer* 13 (21 May 1880): 247.

[Notes on Current Events. "To how many suicides . . ."; "The ground rent paid . . ."; "The inaugural supper . . ."; "So the amateurs . . ."; "The childish feebleness . . ."; "That a new House of Commons . . ."; "Mr. Pearson's design . . ."; "Viewed by the standard . . ."; "From the highest authority . . ."; "Madame Modjeska has concluded . . ."; "The Countess of Carnarvon's assembly . . ."; "Planché was Charles Kemble's antiquarian . . . ."] *British Architect and Northern Engineer* 13 (4 June 1880): 265–67.

[Notes on Current Events. "We heard the following . . ."; "A week or two ago . . ."; "We are glad to hear . . ."; "Even in one of the last . . ."; "We are glad to see . . ."; "The works of Viollet–le–Duc . . ."; "Talking of Paris . . ."; "Walking through the National Gallery . . . ."] *British Architect and Northern Engineer* 13 (11 June 1880): 277–78.

"The Royal Academy and the French Salon." Parts 1–3. *British Architect and Northern Engineer* 13 (11 June 1880): 279–80; (18 June 1880): 292–93; 14 (9 July 1880): 14.

[Notes on Current Events. "There has been exhibited . . ."; "The exhibition of the works . . ."; "All the drawings . . ."; "As exquisite examples . . ."; "Viollet–le–Duc's figure drawings . . ."; "On Tuesday evening . . ."; "The play over . . . ."] *British Architect and Northern Engineer* 13 (25 June 1880): 301–2.

["Theatrical Jottings, No. X."] *British Architect and Northern Engineer* 13 (25 June 1880): 304.

"*British Architect* Art Club: Review of Designs." *British Architect and Northern Engineer* 13 (25 June 1880): 305.

["Theatrical Jottings, No. XI."] *British Architect and Northern Engineer* 14 (2 July 1880): 3.

[Notes on Current Events. "Temple Bar is going . . ."; "Once more the question arises . . ."; "It is perhaps well . . ."; "Stroll in on . . ."; "There would be no . . ."; "We publish this week . . ."; "The salade . . . ."] *British Architect and Northern Engineer* 14 (23 July 1880): 31–34.

"*British Architect* Art Club: An Artist's Studio and Residence, by B in a Circle." *British Architect and Northern Engineer* 14 (23 July 1880): 36 and illus.

[Notes on Current Events. "What to do with our walls . . . ."] *British Architect and Northern Engineer* 14 (30 July 1880): 47–48.

"To Our Student Readers." Parts 1–3. *British Architect and Northern Engineer* 14 (30 July 1880): 48–49; (13 August 1880): 70; (27 August 1880): 95.

[Notes on Current Events. "Two of the members . . ."; "From Mr. Roger Smith's . . ."; "In the January number . . ."; "Gabriel Beranger busied himself . . ."; "There are many extracts . . . ."] *British Architect and Northern Engineer* 14 (6 August 1880): 56–58.

[Notes on Current Events. "Last Tuesday

morning . . ."; "Your ladyship . . ."; "We cannot go into . . ."; "One of these modern . . ."; "Messrs. Child's new bank . . ."; "The scene representing . . ."; "Another batch of letters . . . ."] *British Architect and Northern Engineer* 14 (13 August 1880): 67–68.

[Notes on Current Events. "We dined the other evening . . ."; The interior decorations . . ."; "The fourth illustration . . . ."] *British Architect and Northern Engineer* 14 (13 August 1880): 68–69.

[Notes on Current Events. "No doubt the First . . ."; "Mr. Raphael Tuck . . ."; "St. Stephen's Palace Chambers . . ."; "One great defect . . ."; "Another defect . . ."; "What an inartistic race . . . ."] *British Architect and Northern Engineer* 14 (20 August 1880): 79–81.

[Notes on Current Events. "Well done, Mr. Burnand! . . ."; "This is a single–handed . . ."; "The scene in Oxford–Street . . ."; "We gladly give publicity . . . ."] *British Architect and Northern Engineer* 14 (24 September 1880): 139–140.

["Theatrical Jottings, No. XII."] *British Architect and Northern Engineer* 14 (24 September 1880): 143.

[Notes on Current Events. "With Mr. Barry's report . . ."; "Even if the designs . . ."; "The next two paragraphs . . ."; "'Duty,' Mr. Barry says . . ."; "Again, the condition . . ."; "As to the merit . . ."; "The designs which appear . . ."; "'Partcullis' . . ."; "'Stet's' estimate . . ."; "We have received the following . . . ."] *British Architect and Northern Engineer* 14 (1 October 1880): 151.

"*British Architect* Art Club: Fifth List Award." *British Architect and Northern Engineer* 14 (1 October 1880): 155–56.

["Theatrical Jottings, No. XIII."] *British Architect and Northern Engineer* 14 (15 October 1880): 175–76.

"The Costume of *Othello*." *British Architect and Northern Engineer* 14 (15 October 1880): 176.

["Theatrical Jottings, No. XIV."] *British Architect and Northern Engineer* 14 (26 November 1880): 231.

"*British Architect* Kalendar" for 1881. *British Architect and Northern Engineer* 14 (3 December 1880).

Illustration. "Irish Sketches, by E. W. Godwin, F.S.A." *British Architect and Northern Engineer* 14 (3 December 1880): 239.

[Notes on Current Events. "When the Society of . . ."; "The Exhibition of . . . ."] *British Architect and Northern Engineer* 14 (17 December 1880): 255.

"A Lodge Gable by E. W. Godwin, F.S.A." Illustration in the *British Architect and Northern Engineer* 14 (17 December 1880): 260.

1881

[Notes on Current Events. "The Grosvenor Exhibition . . . ."] *British Architect and Northern Engineer* 15 (7 January 1881): 3.

"*British Architect* Art Club: Award on Sixth Series." *British Architect and Northern Engineer* 15 (7 January 1881): 7–8.

["The mounting of Mr. Tennyson's classical play . . ."; "Of the costumes . . . ."] *British Architect and Northern Engineer* 15 (14 January 1881): 16.

[Notes on Current Events. "The decorative designs . . ."; "Mr. Burne–Jones's outline . . ."; "The third group . . ."; "Mr. Whistler's 'Venice Pastels' . . . ."] *British Architect and Northern Engineer* 15 (28 January 1881): 43–44.

[Notes on Current Events. "We are glad to find . . . ."] *British Architect and Northern Engineer* 15 (4 February 1881): 59.

[Review.] *British Architect and Northern Engineer* 15 (4 February 1881): 62–63.

"Cottage for P. Phipps Esq., Collingtree, Northants." *British Architect and Northern Engineer* 15 (4 February 1881): [66].

"With Whistler's Critics." *British Architect and Northern Engineer* 15 (25 February 1881): 98–99.

"Messrs. Minton, Hollins, and Co. . . ." *British Architect and Northern Engineer* 15 (18 March 1881): 143.

"Peel Tower, Ireland." *British Architect and Northern Engineer* 15 (18 March 1881): [147].

"*British Architect* Art Club: Award on Seventh Series." *British Architect and Northern Engineer* 15 (1 April 1881): 173.

"Mr. Vezin as Hamlet." *British Architect and Northern Engineer* 15 (15 April 1881): [192 and 193].

"Sketches of Old Work." *British Architect and Northern Engineer* 15 (22 April 1881): 203 and [207].

"Friends in Council: No. 15, William Burges, A.R.A." *British Architect and Northern Engineer* 15 (29 April 1881): 213–15.

"What the World Says." Letter to the *World* (4 May 1881): 14.

"On the matter of stage costume . . . ." Letter to the *World* (11 May 1881): 114.

[Notes on Current Events. "So the great fight . . ."; "The house in Conduit–street . . ."; "In our remaining notes . . ."; "Gallery No. 2 opens . . ."; "'The Land of Streams' . . ."; "Gallery No. 3 . . ."; "'Cornfield' . . ."; "G. H. Boughton . . . ."] *British Architect and Northern Engineer* 15 (13 May 1881): 243–44.

"Church Tower with a Batter." *British Architect and Northern Engineer* 15 (13 May 1881): [244].

"Thatched Cottage 'Adapted to the Usages' from a Design by E. W. Godwin, F.S.A., Carried out in Glenbegh, Co. Kerry, 1870." Illustrations in the *British Architect and Northern Engineer* 15 (27 May 1881): 267.

[Notes on Current Events. "Sculpture in England . . ."; "From the architectonic point . . ."; "Excellent work as detached . . ."; "'A Moment of Peril' . . ."; "Messrs. Howell and James' exhibition . . ."; "But of all the right . . ."; "Albert Hill is another . . ."; "In the Prize Gallery . . ."; "In the large gallery . . ."; "Mr. McDowell . . ."; "To the Meiningen Court Company . . ."; "The scenery was limited . . ."; "Yet in spite of all . . . ."] *British Architect and Northern Engineer* 15 (10 June 1881): 287–91.

"*British Architect* Art Club: Eighth Series." *British Architect and Northern Engineer* 15 (10 June 1881): 297.

"*Julius Caesar*." *British Architect and Northern Engineer* 15 (17 June 1881): 302–3.

[Notes on Current Events. "An alderman . . ."; "The *Lion d'Or* . . ."; "The annual meeting . . ."; "The annual report contains . . ."; "The way they build studios . . ."; "When in Paris . . ."; "*Harper's Monthly Magazine* . . ."; "Mr. R. B. Mantell . . ."; "We understand Miss Wallis obtained . . . ."] *British Architect and Northern Engineer* 16 (1 July 1881): 328–31.

[Notes at the Salon. "Marat and the Reign . . . ."] *British Architect and Northern Engineer* 16 (1 July 1881): 331.

"Outline of Interior Decoration." *British Architect and Northern Engineer* 16 (1 July 1881): illus.

[Notes on Current Events. "'An Essay on the History' . . ."; "These essays . . ."; "This sartorial essay . . ."; "The performance given . . ."; "We have received a small . . ."; "The Meiningen Court Company . . ."; "'The Winter's Tale' . . ."; "The costume in 'The Winter's Tale' . . ."; "The only answer . . ."; "While we are on . . ."; "Mr. Tree was . . . ."] *British Architect and Northern Engineer* 16 (15 July 1881): 354–57.

"*Preciosa* and *The Winter's Tale*." *British Architect and Northern Engineer* 16 (15 July 1881): 356.

[Notes on Current Events. "The designs sent in . . ."; "Really decorative and more . . ."; "We have only this week . . ."; "By the catalogue . . ."; "(61) 'Le Menuisier,' . . ."; "(63) 'Summertime,' . . ."; "(154) By Achille Dien . . ."; "We reach in (286) . . ."; "H. Fantin (402) shows . . ."; "313, 377, 379 are the . . ."; "Last week we briefly . . ."; "In the discursus before us . . ."; "Contemporary with these . . ."; "It is not our custom . . ."; "One parting word to Mr. Scott . . ."; "The Irving Amateur Dramatic . . ."; "The Royalty Theatre opened . . ."; "Miss Florence St. John . . ."; "*As You Like It* at the . . . ."] *British Architect and Northern Engineer* 16 (22 July 1881): 365–70.

["Theatrical Notes."] *British Architect and Northern Engineer* 16 (29 July 1881): 379–80.

"Art Objects from a Private Collection." *British Architect and Northern Engineer* 16 (12 August 1881): 402 and illus.

[Notes on Current Events. "The suicide, by chloroform . . ."; "One cause of the lack . . ."; "The system of living . . ."; "Thus in a plan . . ."; "This indifference . . ."; "In last week's number . . ."; "But our *Academy* enlightener . . ."; "What becomes of . . ."; "At the rooms of . . ."; "We have received a letter . . .";"On Tuesday next . . . ."] *British Architect and Northern Engineer* 16 (2 September 1881): 437–38.

["Theatrical Notes."] *British Architect and Northern Engineer* 16 (2 September 1881): 439.

["Theatrical Notes."] *British Architect and Northern Engineer* 16 (9 September 1881): 449–50.

[Notes on Current Events. "Mr. J. A. McN. Whistler . . ."; "In the forthcoming seascape . . ."; "We have at last . . ."; "The value of this . . ."; "People talk a good deal . . ."; "Really it is too . . ."; "Seriously, however . . . ."] *British Architect and Northern Engineer* 16 (23 September 1881): 471.

["Theatrical Notes."] *British Architect and Northern Engineer* 16 (23 September 1881): 473–74.

"*British Architect* Art Club: Second Session, First Series." *British Architect and Northern Engineer* 16 (23 September 1881): 475.

[Notes on Current Events. "So the Dilletante [sic] Club . . ."; "A limited company . . ."; "In the new hotel . . ."; "So the Star Brewery . . . ."] *British Architect and Northern Engineer* 16 (30 September 1881): 485–86.

["Theatrical Notes."] *British Architect and Northern Engineer* 16 (30 September 1881): 486–87.

[Notes on Current Events. "So one of the most interesting . . ."; "Of the manor house . . . ."] *British Architect and Northern Engineer* 16 (7 October 1881): 496.

"Clapton Church, Somersetshire." *British Architect and Northern Engineer* 16 (21 October 1881): 519–20 and illus.

"*British Architect* Art Club: Second Session, Award on Second Series." *British Architect and Northern Engineer* 16 (4 November 1881): 547–49.

["Greek Houses, and Those Who Lived in Them."] *Builder* 41 (3 December 1881): 685–88.

[Notes on Current Events. "Who on earth is . . ."; "A winter exhibition . . ."; "J. D. Watson gives us . . ."; "We shall have something . . ."; "Who is the architectural . . ."; "The same number of . . ."; "We have received the . . ."; "'Before a Botticelli I am dumb,' says Maudle . . ."; "The *Fanfulla* of Rome . . ."; "It will occur to . . ."; "What is the matter . . ."; "We have received from . . . ."] *British Architect and Northern Engineer* 16 (9 December 1881): 612–13.

[Theatrical Notes. "On Saturday morning . . ."; "The opening of . . ."; "Indeed, one fault . . . ."] *British Architect and Northern Engineer* 16 (9 December 1881): 613–14.

British Architect and Northern Engineer. (16 December 1881): 632 and illus.

"Friends in Council: No. 40, A Retrospect." *British Architect and Northern Engineer* 16 (30 December 1881): 655–57.

[Notes on Current Events. "*The Year's Art* for 1882 . . ."; "Some of the figures . . . ."] *British Architect and Northern Engineer* 16 (30 December 1881): 657–58.

[Theatrical Notes. "Since our last notes . . .";

"'Foggerty's Fairy,' . . ."; "The Savoy Theatre . . . ."] *British Architect and Northern Engineer* 16 (30 December 1881): 658–59.

1882

[Notes on Current Events. "On Thursday . . ."; "The exhibition of works . . ."; "Gallery No. 1 contains . . ."; "Gallery No. 2 contains . . ."; "The large room . . . ."] *British Architect and Northern Engineer* 17 (6 January 1882): 2.

[Notes on Current Events. "Returning to the Royal . . . ;" "The Dutch masters . . ."; "In the large room . . ."; "There is a fine . . ."; "The last or fifth . . ."; "The *Art Journal* opens . . ."; "We take up the . . . ."] *British Architect and Northern Engineer* 17 (13 January 1882): 14.

"An Irish Sketch by E. W. Godwin, F.S.A." *British Architect and Northern Engineer* 17 (20 January 1882): [30].

"Fires in Theatres." *Building News and Engineering Journal* 42 (27 January 1882): 106–7.

"Irish Sketches by E. W. Godwin, F.S.A." *British Architect and Northern Engineer* 17 (3 February 1882): [52].

[Theatrical Notes.] *British Architect and Northern Engineer* 17 (3 February 1882): 53.

"*British Architect* Art Club: Second Session." *British Architect and Northern Engineer* 17 (10 March 1882): 117.

"Irish Sketches by E. W. Godwin, F.S.A." *British Architect and Northern Engineer* 17 (31 March 1882): [149].

"*British Architect* Art Club: Fifth Series." *British Architect and Northern Engineer* 17 (28 April 1882): 199.

1883

"Claudian," *A Few Notes on the Architecture and Costume: A Letter to Wilson Barrett Esq., by E. W. Godwin.* Pamphlet. London: privately printed, 1883. Copy in V&A TA, Godwin collection, box 1.

"*The Tale of Troy.*" Review in the *Royal Society of Painters in Water Colours* (1883).

"*British Architect* Art Club." *British Architect and Northern Engineer* 19 (19 January 1883): 32–33.

"A Few Notes on the Architecture and Costume of the Period of the Play of *Claudian,* A.D. 360–460." *British Architect and Northern Engineer* 20 (7 December 1883): 267–70 and illus.

["The first act of *Claudian* . . . ."] *British Architect and Northern Engineer* 20 (21 December 1883): 290.

["The third act of *Claudian* . . . ."] *British Architect and Northern Engineer* 20 (28 December 1883): 300.

"*British Architect* Art Club: Second Session, Analysis of Merit and Award." *British Architect and Northern Engineer* 20 (28 December 1883): 302–4.

1884

Dress and Its Relation to Health and Climate. Lon-

don: William Clowes and Sons for the Executive Council of the International Health Exhibition and for the Council of the Society of Arts, 1884.

[Notes on Current Events. "We propose to publish . . . ."] *British Architect and Northern Engineer* 21 (4 January 1884): 4.

[Notes on Current Events. "The exhibition of furniture . . . ."] *British Architect and Northern Engineer* 21 (22 February 1884): 86.

[Notes on Current Events. "Every archaeologist must be . . ."; "Previous to the Norman . . ."; "The circular keep . . ."; "The second part of the work . . ."; "Some of the notices . . ."; "Whether or not undue . . . ."] *British Architect and Northern Engineer* 21 (21 March 1884): 134.

[Notes on Current Events. "Of the detailed accounts . . ."; "But seriously . . ."; "The constructive works . . ."; "The Royal School of Art Needlework . . ."; "The arrangement of . . ."; "There is no insurmountable . . . ."] *British Architect and Northern Engineer* 21 (28 March 1884): 146.

"The New Admiralty and War Offices Competition." *British Architect and Northern Engineer* 21 (4 April 1884): 165.

"To Art Students." Parts 1–10 (two parts are numbered "Letter No. 4"). *British Architect and Northern Engineer* 21, "Letter No. 1" (2 May 1884): 215; "Letter No. 2" (9 May 1884): 225; "Letter No. 3" (16 May 1884): 238; "Letter No. 4" (30 May 1884): 262; "Letter No. 4 [sic]" (6 June 1884): 273; "Letter No. 5" (13 June 1884): 285; "Letter No. 6" (20 June 1884): 297; "Letter No. 7" (27 June 1884): 309–10; 22, "Letter No. 8" (4 July 1884): 1–2; "Letter No. 9" (11 July 1884): 13.

"My dear Atlas." Letter to the *World* (30 July 1884).

"Tenders: The Tower House, Chelsea." *Builder* 47 (2 August 1884): 179.

"Westminster Hall." Letter to the *Times* (London) (4 December 1884): 10. Reprinted in *Building News and Engineering Journal* 47 (5 December 1884): 902–3.

"The Restoration of Westminster Hall." Letter to the *Times* (London) (10 December 1884): 6.

"The Restoration of Westminster Hall." *British Architect and Northern Engineer* 22 (19 December 1884): 302–3.

1885

Godwin, Edward William, ed. *The Faithfull Shepherdesse, by John Fletcher. Adapted and arranged in Three Acts for the Open Air.* London: G. Hill, 1885.

"Archaeology on the Stage." Parts 1–7. *Dramatic Review* (8 February 1885): 19–20; (22 February 1885): 53; (7 March 1885): 84–85; (5 September 1885): 42; (19 September 1885): 60–61; (10 October 1885): 92–93; (24 October 1885): 112–13.

"The Tower House . . . ." *British Architect and*

Northern Engineer 23 (22 May 1885): 252.

"*British Architect* Special Correspondence." *British Architect and Northern Engineer* 24 (18 December 1885): 262.

1886

"Ancient Greek, Assyrian and Phoenician Furniture" [ca. 1886]. British Architectural Library Manuscripts Collection, Royal Institute of British Architects, London, MS GoE/5/1.

"The Greek House According to Homer: Its Furniture and the Costume of Its Inhabitants" [ca. 1886]. British Architectural Library Manuscripts Collection, Royal Institute of British Architects, London, MS GoE/5/1.

"Fine Art." Review of *Costume in England*, by F. W. Fairholt. *Academy* 29 (27 March 1886): 225–26.

"Dramatic and Musical Gossip." *Referee* (London) (23 May 1886).

"The Greek Home According to Homer." *Nineteenth Century* (London) 19 (June 1886): 914–22.

"The Home of an English Architect." Parts 1 and 2. *Art Journal* (June 1886): 170–73; (October 1886): 301–5.

1914

"A Lecture on Dress." *Mask* 6 (April 1914): 351.

Secondary Sources Plus Period Sources and Illustrations of Godwin's Work

Citations are arranged in alphabetical order. Page numbers in brackets indicate illustrations.

Account of the Town Halls, Old and New with Illustrations. Northampton: J. Taylor and Son, 1866.

Adams, Annmarie. "Architecture in the Family Way: Health Reform, Feminism, and the Middle-Class House in England, 1870–1900." Ph.D. diss., University of California at Berkeley, 1992.

———. *Architecture in the Family Way: Doctors, Houses, and Women, 1870–1900.* Montreal and Kingston: McGill-Queen's University Press, 1996.

Adams, James Truslow. *Empire on the Seven Seas: The British Empire: 1784–1939.* New York: Scribner's, 1940.

———. "Architects from George IV to George V." Part 2. *Journal of the Royal Institute of British Architects*, 3d ser., 19 (27 July 1912): 643–45.

Adams, Steven. *The Arts and Crafts Movement.* Baldock: Apple Press, 1987.

Adburgham, Alison. *Liberty's: A Biography of a Shop.* London: George Allen and Unwin, 1975.

"Adelphi Theatre." *Times* (London) (17 March 1883): 5.

Agius, Pauline. *British Furniture, 1880–1915.*

Woodbridge, England: Antique Collectors' Club, 1978.

Alcock, Rutherford. *Art and Art Industries in Japan.* London: Virtue, 1878.

———. *Catalogue of Works of Industry and Art, Sent from Japan.* London: William Clowes, 1862.

———. *The Capital of the Tycoon: A Narrative of Three Years' Residence in Japan.* New York: Harper, 1863.

Allwood, John. *The Great Exhibitions.* London: Studio Vista, 1977.

"Ancient Bristol." Letter to the *Architect* (London) 14 (11 September 1875): 151.

"An Ancient Lesson for Decorators." *Furniture Gazette*, n.s., 1 (25 October 1873): 460.

Andrews, John. "The Curious Case of the Godwin Sideboard." *Antique Collecting: The Journal of the Antique Collectors' Club* 20 (September 1985): 45–47.

———. *Victorian and Edwardian Furniture: Price Guide and Reasons for Values.* Woodbridge, England: Antique Collectors' Club, 1992.

"Anglo-Japanese Furniture, Paris Exhibition." *Building News and Engineering Journal* 34 (14 June 1878): 596 and [603].

Anscombe, Isabelle. "Furniture by Architects." *Connoisseur* 207 (May 1981): 60–61.

"The Archaeology of Shakespeare." *Globe and Traveller* (London), (16 November 1874): 1.

"Archaeology on the Stage." Letter to the *Architect* (London) 16 (7 October 1876): 221.

"Architects and Furniture." Letter to the *Furniture Gazette*, n.s., 2 (17 January 1874): 72–73.

"Architects and Their Judges." *British Architect and Northern Engineer* 11 (14 March 1879): 111.

"An Architect's Report on Furniture in the Vienna Exhibition." *Furniture Gazette*, n.s., 1 (19 July 1873): 229.

"An Architect's Residence." *Furniture Gazette*, n.s., 10 (30 November 1878): 375.

"The Architectural Art Classes." *Architect* (London) 6 (4 November 1871): 227.

"Architectural Association." *Building News and Engineering Journal* 26 (24 April 1874): 442–45.

"The Architectural Association: Architectural Illustration." *British Architect and Northern Engineer* 7 (26 January 1877): 53.

"The Architectural Association: The Designing of Studios." *Architect* (London) 21 (8 March 1879): 145–47.

"The Architectural Exhibition." Part 1. *Architect* (London) 1 (8 May 1869): 244–45.

"An Architectural Patchwork, 1880." *British Architect and Northern Engineer* 14 (3 December 1880): [240].

"Architectural Poaching." Letters to the *British Architect and Northern Engineer* 8 (20 July 1877): 35; (27 July 1877): 40.

"Architecture at the Royal Academy Exhibition." Part 1. *Building News and Engineering Journal* 22 (10 May 1872): 381–82.

"Architecture in Chicago." *Builder* 31 (31 May 1873): 432.

Art Age (June 1886). Copy in the Whistler Clippings. Volume 36, Pennell Collection. Library of Congress, Washington, D.C.

"Art and Artists." *Brooklyn Daily Times* (11 August 1888): 7.

"An Art Cabinet Designed by E. W. Godwin, F.S.A." *Building News and Engineering Journal* 50 (19 March 1886): 456 and [471].

"Art Furniture." *Building News and Engineering Journal* 15 (5 June 1868): 375.

"Art Furniture." Parts 1 and 2. *Building News and Engineering Journal* 33 (21 December 1877): 614 and [617]; (24 August 1877): 174.

"Art Furniture." *British Architect and Northern Engineer* 10 (13 September 1878): 104 and illus.

"Art Furniture by Edward W. Godwin, F.S.A." Parts 1–9. *Art Worker* (New York) 1 (February 1878): pls. 12, 13; (March 1878): pl. 22; (April 1878): pl. 30; (May 1878): pl. 37; (June 1878): pl. 46; (July 1878): pl. 53; (August 1878): pls. 60, 61; (September 1878): pl. 69; (October 1878): pl. 76.

"*Art Furniture from Designs by Edward W. Godwin, F.S.A., and others . . . , by Edward W. Godwin, et al.*" Review in the *Furniture Gazette*, n.s., 8 (25 August 1877): 145.

"Art Furniture Company, the 'Florence Cabinet,' Edward W. Godwin, Archt." *Building News and Engineering Journal* 21 (29 December 1871): [495].

"'Art' Furniture So-Called." *Furniture Gazette*, n.s., 11 (15 February 1879): 108 and illus.

Art Journal. *The Illustrated Catalogue of the Paris International Exhibition, 1878.* London: Virtue, 1878.

"'Artistic' Furnishing." *Furniture Gazette*, n.s., 5 (8 April 1876): 222.

"Artists' Houses, Chelsea." *British Architect and Northern Engineer* 14 (14 May 1880): 234 and illus.

"*As You Like It*, at Coombe House." *Illustrated Sporting and Dramatic News* (2 August 1884): 530.

"*As You Like It*, under the Trees." *New York Mirror* (29 July 1884).

Aslin, Elizabeth. *Nineteenth Century English Furniture.* London: Faber and Faber, 1962.

———. "E. W. Godwin and the Japanese Taste." *Apollo*, n.s., 76 (December 1962): 779–84.

———. "The Furniture Designs of E. W. Godwin." *Victoria and Albert Museum Bulletin* 3 (October 1967): 145–54. Reprint, London: Victoria and Albert Museum, 1970.

———. *The Aesthetic Movement: Prelude to Art Nouveau.* New York: Praeger, 1969.

———. "The Oriental Influence on the Decorative Arts in France and England." In *World Cultures and Modern Art: The Encounter of Nineteenth and Twentieth Century European Art and Music with Asia, Africa, Oceania, and Afro- and Indo-America.* Exh. cat. Munich: Bruckmann, 1972.

———. *E. W. Godwin: Furniture and Interior Decoration.* London: J. Murray, 1986.

———. "Japanese Influence on Nineteenth-Century Decorative Arts." In *The Decorative Arts in the Victorian Period,* edited by Susan M. Wright. London: The Society of Antiquaries, 1989.

"The Assize Courts Competition." Letter to the *Western Daily Press* (1 September 1866).

"At page 347 ante our correspondent . . . ." *British Architect and Northern Engineer* 16 (22 July 1881): 367.

"At Sadlers' Wells Theatre *Othello* has been put on the stage . . . ." *Portfolio* (London) 11 (November 1880): 186.

"At the Play." *Observer* (9 December 1883): 2.

"At the Play: *As You Like It* in a Wood." *Vanity Fair* (26 June 1884): 61–62.

"Athens in London." *St. James' Gazette* (18 May 1886): 6.

Atterbury, Paul, comp. *Aspects of the Aesthetic Movement, Including Books, Ceramics, Furniture, Glass, Textiles.* Exh. cat. London: Dan Klein, 1978.

Atterbury, Paul, ed. *A. W. N. Pugin: Master of Gothic Revival.* Exh. cat. New Haven and London: Yale University Press for The Bard Graduate Center for Studies in the Decorative Arts, 1995.

Atterbury, Paul, and Clive Wainwright, eds. *Pugin: A Gothic Passion.* Exh. cat. New Haven and London: Yale University Press in association with the Victoria and Albert Museum, 1994.

"Austen Breteton." *Theatre* (1 June 1886): 330–31.

Austin, Alfred. "In the Forest of Arden." *National Review* 4 (September 1884): 126–36.

Ayres, William F. *The Highbury Story, Highbury Chapel, Bristol: The First Fifty Years.* London: Independent Press, 1963.

Baker and Sons. *In Liquidation, "The White House," Tite Street, Chelsea: A Catalogue of the Remaining Household Furniture.* Sale cat. London, 18 September 1879.

Baldry, Alfred Lys. "The Growth of an Influence." *Art Journal* (February 1900) 46–47.

Baldwin, Fanny P. "Victorian Artists and Stage Design 1870–1905." Ph.D. diss., Courtauld Institute, London, 1991.

Bancroft, Squire, and Marie Bancroft. *The Bancrofts: Recollections of Sixty Years.* 1909. Reprint, New York: B. Blom, 1969.

Banham, Joanna, ed. *Encyclopedia of Interior Design.* London: Fitzroy Dearborn, 1997.

Banham, Joanna, Sally MacDonald, and Julia Porter. *Victorian Interior Design.* London: Cassell, 1991.

Barker, Kathleen. "The Terrys and Godwin in Bristol." *Theatre Notebook* 22 (October 1967–July 1968): 27–43.

———. *The Theatre Royal, Bristol, 1766–1966: Two Centuries of Stage History.* London: The Society for Theatre Research, 1974.

Barnet, Peter. "From the Middle Ages to the Victorians." *Apollo,* n.s., 124 (December 1986): 499–505.

Barnet, Peter, and Mary Ann Wilkinson. *Decorative Arts 1900: Highlights from Private Collections in Detroit.* Exh. cat. Detroit: The Detroit Institute of Arts, 1993.

Barr, James. *Anglican Church Architecture.* Oxford: J. H. Parker, 1842.

Barrington, Robert. "Copyist, Connoisseur, Collector: Charles Fairfax Murray (1849–1919)." *Apollo,* n.s., 140 (November 1994): 15–21.

"The Barrow-in-Furness Municipal Buildings Competition." Parts 1 and 2. *British Architect and Northern Engineer* 8 (21 December 1877): 299–300; (28 December 1877): 313–14.

Bascou, Marc. "Acquisitions: Dressing-table." *Revue du Louvre* 4 (October 1995): 92.

"Baths and Wash-Houses, New Islington, Manchester: Design by E. W. Godwin, F.S.A." *British Architect and Northern Engineer* 9 (4 January 1878): 8 and illus.

"Beauvale, Nottinghamshire." *Building News and Engineering Journal* 27 (3 July 1874): 8 and [30–31].

"Beauvale: Mr. E. W. Godwin, Architect." *Building News and Engineering Journal* 27 (10 July 1874): [58].

"The Bedford Park Estate, Chiswick." *Building News and Engineering Journal* 38 (30 January 1880): 124–25.

"Bedford Park Estate: Comical Criticism." Letter to the *Building News and Engineering Journal* 32 (2 February 1877): 134.

"Bedford-Park Estate, Turnham-Green." *Building News and Engineering Journal* 31 (22 December 1876): 621 and illus.

"Bedford Park Estate, Turnham Green." *Building News and Engineering Journal* 32 (12 January 1877): 36 and [43].

"Bedford Park Estate, Turnham-Green: Comical Construction." Letter to the *Building News and Engineering Journal* 32 (19 January 1877): 77.

"Bed-Room Furniture." *Building News and Engineering Journal* 37 (24 October 1879): 490 and [499].

Beerbohm, Max. "1880." *Yellow Book* 4 (January 1895).

"Before and behind the Curtain." *London Figaro* (15 December 1883): 13; (22 May 1886): 14.

Bence-Jones, Mark. "An Aesthete's Irish Castle: Dromore Castle, Co. Limerick." *Country Life* 136 (12 November 1964): 1274–77.

———. *A Guide to Irish Country Houses.* 2d rev. ed. London: Constable, 1990.

Bendix, Deanna Marohn. "James McNeill Whistler as a Designer: Interiors and Exhibitions." Ph.D. diss., University of Minnesota, 1992.

———. *Diabolical Designs: Paintings, Interiors and Exhibitions of James McNeill Whistler.* Washington, D.C.: Smithsonian Institution Press, 1995.

———. "Whistler as Interior Designer: Yellow Walls at 13 Tite Street." *Apollo,* n.s., 143 (January 1996): 31–38.

"Berlin Competition Designs." *Architect* (London) 7 (13 April 1872): 192.

Berman, Avis. "Antiques: Furniture by Architects." *Architectural Digest* 50 (March 1993): 164–67, 191–92.

"Bijou Portraits, No. 64: Mr. Wilson Barrett as Claudian." *Society* (12 April 1884).

H. Blairman and Sons. *Furniture and Works of Art.* London: H. Blairman and Sons, 1994.

Bloxham, Matthew. *The Principles of Gothic Architecture Elucidated by Question and Answer.* London: Whittaker, Treacher, and Co., 1829.

Bøe, Alf. *From Gothic Revival to Functional Form: A Study in Victorian Theories of Design.* Reprint of 1957 ed. New York: Da Capo Press, 1979. Originally the author's thesis, Oxford, 1954.

Boger, Louise Ade, and H. Batterson Boger. *The Dictionary of Antiques and the Decorative Arts.* New York: Scribner, 1967.

Bolger Burke, Doreen, et al. *In Pursuit of Beauty: Americans and the Aesthetic Movement.* Exh. cat. New York: The Metropolitan Museum of Art and Rizzoli, 1986.

Bolsterli, Margaret Jones. *The Early Community at Bedford Park: "Corporate Happiness" in the First Garden Suburb.* London: Routledge and Kegan Paul, 1977.

"Bradford Town Hall." Letters to *Architect* (London) 2 (4 December 1869): 279; (11 December 1869): 290.

Brandreth, Eric. *Harpenden in Old Picture Postcards.* Zaltbommel, Netherlands: European Library, 1983.

Brémont, Anna Dunphy, Comtesse de. *Oscar Wilde and His Mother: A Memoir.* London: Everett, 1911.

Breuer, Gerda, ed. *Arts and Crafts: Von Morris bis Mackintosh—Reformbewegung zwischen Kunstgewerbe und Sozialutopie.* Exh. cat. Darmstadt: Institut Mathildenhöhe, 1994.

"Brick Carving at Mr. A. S. Wortley's House at Chelsea." *British Architect and Northern Engineer* 14 (3 December 1880): [236].

Bridgeman, Harriet, and Elizabeth Drury, eds. *The Encyclopedia of Victoriana.* New York: Macmillan, 1975.

Brighton Museum and Manchester City Art Gallery. *The Inspiration of Egypt: Its Influence on British Artists, Travellers and Designers, 1700–1900.* Edited by Patrick Conner. Exh. cat. Brighton: Brighton Borough Council, 1983.

"Bristol Assize Courts." Letter to the *Bristol Times,* 30 August 1866, 4.

"The Bristol Assize Courts Competition." *Building News and Engineering Journal* 13 (10 August 1866): 533.

Bristol Museums and Art Gallery. *Furniture by Godwin and Breuer.* Exh. cat. Bristol: Bristol City Museum and Art Gallery, 1976.

Bristol Society of Architects. *First Annua*

Report, for the Year Ending May 1851. Copy in the archives of the architectural and engineering firm of Whicheloe MacFarlane, Bristol.

"Bristol Society of Architects." *Western Daily Press* (14 February 1863): 2.

"Bristol Society of Architects." *Building News and Engineering Journal* 11 (15 July 1864): 545–46.

"Bristol Society of Architects." *Western Daily Press* (6 August 1864): 2; (9 September 1864): 3.

"Bristol Society of Architects"; "Mediaeval Bristol." *Western Daily Press* (8 September 1864): 4.

"*British Architect* Art Club: Designs for a Shop Frontage." *British Architect and Northern Engineer* 13 (9 April 1880): 174 and illus.

"*British Architect* Art Club, E. W. Godwin, F.S.A., Assessor: First Session." *British Architect and Northern Engineer* 16 (19 August 1881): 420–21.

"*British Architect* Art Club: Third Session-Sixth Series, Award by E. W. Godwin, F.S.A." *British Architect and Northern Engineer* 22 (7 November 1884): 220.

"*British Architect* Cottage Competition." Part 2. *British Architect and Northern Engineer* 10 (26 July 1878): [40].

British Design—Konstindustri och Design, 1851–1987. Exh. cat. Stockholm: Nationalmuseum, 1987.

Britton, John. *Historical and descriptive accounts, with illustrations, of English Cathedrals.* Vol. 4, *Wells, Exeter, and Worcester.* Vol. 5, *Peterborough, Gloucester, and Bristol.* London: M.A. Nattali, 1836.

Bromfield, David John. "The Art of Japan in Late Nineteenth Century Europe: Problems of Art Criticism and Theory." Ph.D. diss., University of Leeds, 1977.

Brooks, Chris, and Andrew Saint, eds. *The Victorian Church.* Manchester: Manchester University Press, 1995.

Brooks, Michael W. *John Ruskin and Victorian Architecture.* New Brunswick, N.J.: Rutgers University Press, 1987.

Bryers, Richard. "A Unique and Important Pair of Red Earthenware Vases." Unpublished manuscript, ca. 1996.

Buchanon, Robert. *God and the Man.* London, 1881.

"The *Building News* Designing Club: Designs for a Small Stable." *Building News and Engineering Journal* 36 (20 June 1879): 703.

Burder, William Corbett, James Hine, and Edward William Godwin. *The Architectural Antiquities of Bristol and Its Neighbourhood.* Bristol: Burder, Hine, and Godwin, 1851.

Burg, Detlev von der, ed. *Pinakothek der Moderne: Eine Vision des Museums für Kunst, Architektur und Design des 20. Jahrhunderts in München.* Munich: Prestel, 1995.

Burges, William. Abstract of Diaries. Metalwork Department, Victoria and Albert Museum, London.

———. "The International Exhibition." *Gentleman's Magazine and Historical Review* 212, n.s., 12 (June 1862): 665; 213, n.s., 13 (July 1862): 3–12.

———. "The Japanese Court in the International Exhibition." *Gentleman's Magazine and Historical Review* 213, n.s., 13 (September 1862): 243–54.

———. "'Henry V' at the Queen's Theatre," *Architect* (London) 16 (23 September 1876): 188.

———. "Archaeology on the Stage." Parts 1 and 2. *Architect* (London) 16 (14 October 1876): 224–25; (21 October 1876): 238–40.

"Cabinet for Objects de Virtu." *Building News and Engineering Journal* 50 (5 March 1886): 376 and [390].

Calloway, Stephen. *The House of Liberty: Masters of Style and Decoration.* London: Thames and Hudson, 1992.

Camp, Michael, and Keith Hill. *The Windows of St. Botolph's, Northfleet.* Northfleet, England: St. Botolph's Parochial Church Council, 1992.

Campbell, Janey Sevilla. "The Faithfull Shepherdesse." *Nineteenth Century* (London) 17 (June 1885): 1031–42.

———. "The Woodland Gods." *Woman's World* (November 1888): 1–7.

Campion, S. S. *Northampton Town Hall: Its Story, Told by Itself.* Northampton: W. Mark, 1925.

Canadian Centre for Architecture. *Corpus sanum in domo sano: L'architecture du mouvement en faveur de la salubrité domestique, 1870–1914 / The Architecture of the Domestic Sanitation Movement, 1870–1914.* Exh. cat. Montreal: Canadian Centre for Architecture, 1991.

"Carved Brick Panels: Houses on the Chelsea Embankment for Messrs Gillow & Co by E. W. Godwin F.S.A., Architect, from full size drawings by Beatrice Godwin." *British Architect and Northern Engineer* 11 (9 May 1879): 194 and illus.

Casteras, Susan P., and Colleen Denney, eds. *The Grosvenor Gallery: A Palace of Art in Victorian England.* Exh. cat. New Haven and London: Yale Center for British Art and Yale University Press, 1966.

"*The Cenci*"; "Greek Plays in London." *Stage* (14 May 1886): 16.

Centralcommission des deutschen Reiches für die Wiener Weltausstellung, ed. *Amtlicher Bericht über die Wiener Weltausstellung im Jahre 1873.* 5 vols. Braunschweig: Wieweg, 1874–77.

Charles, R. "The International Exhibition." Letter to the *Furniture Gazette,* n.s., 1 (17 May 1873): 89.

"The Chelsea Embankment." *Building News and Engineering Journal* 36 (11 April 1879): 373–74.

Cherry, Bridget, and Nikolaus Pevsner. *Devon.* The Buildings of England. Harmondsworth, England.: Penguin Books, 1989.

Cheshire, David F. *Portrait of Ellen Terry.* Oxford: Amber Lane Press, 1989.

Chesneau, Ernest. "Le Japon à Paris." *Gazette des beaux-arts,* n.s., 18 (1878): 386.

Chisaburo, Yamada, ed. *Japonisme in Art: An International Symposium.* Tokyo: Committee for the Year 2001 and Kodansha International, 1980.

Chit-chat. "It was on Wednesday afternoon . . . ." *Stage* (25 July 1884): 12.

Christie's. *British Decorative Arts from 1880 to the Present.* Sale cat. London, 5 February 1992.

———. *Continental Decorative Arts from 1880 to the Present Day, British Decorative Arts from 1860 to the Present Day.* Sale cat. London, 8 June 1993, lots 104–106.

———. *British Decorative Arts from 1860.* Sale cat. London, 16 February 1994.

———. *British and Continental Decorative Arts from 1850 to the Present Day.* Sale cat. London, 2 May 1996, lot 23.

———. *The Chair.* Sale cat. London, 29 October 1997, lot 17.

"Circumspice versus 'Non Nobis Domine.'" Letter to the *Northampton Herald* (4 May 1861) 3.

"Civil List Pensions." *Pall Mall Gazette* (25 August 1887).

Clarke, Somers, Jr. "Bedford Park Estate." Letter to the *Building News and Engineering Journal* 32 (9 February 1877): 161.

"*Claudian* at the Princess's." *Modern Society* (15 December 1883): 47.

"*Claudian.*" *Pall Mall Gazette* (7 December 1883): 4.

"*Claudian* at the Princess's Theatre." *Daily Chronicle* (7 December 1883): 6.

"*Claudian* Barrett refusing Byzantium's 'Barrer.'" *Illustrated Sporting and Dramatic News* (27 December 1883): [369].

"Clifton College Competition." *Builder* 18 (15 December 1860): 804.

"*Clito*: Edmund Barnard." *Dramatic Review* (8 May 1886): 141–42.

Clunas, Craig. *Chinese Furniture.* Far Eastern Series, Victoria and Albert Museum. London: Bamboo, 1988.

Clutterbuck, Major R. G. "Ellen Terry's 'exile'." *Hertfordshire Countryside* 25, no. 139 (November, 1970).

Coleman, John. "The Fool's Revenge." *Dramatic Review* (7 August 1886): 11–12.

Collard, Frances. *Regency Furniture.* Woodbridge, Eng.: Antique Collectors' Club, 1985.

Collins, Michael. *Towards Post-Modernism: Design Since 1851.* London: British Museum Publications, 1987.

Collinson and Lock. *Sketches of Artistic Furniture, Manufactured by Collinson and Lock.* London, 1871.

Colomina, Beatriz. "The Split Wall: Domestic Voyeurism." In *Sexuality and Space,* edited by

Beatriz Colomina. Princeton Papers on Architecture. New York: Princeton Architectural Press, 1992.

Colvin, Howard, and John Harris, eds. *The Country Seat: Studies in the History of the British Country House Presented to Sir John Summerson on His Sixty-Fifth Birthday Together with a Select Bibliography of His Published Writings.* London: Allen Lane, The Penguin Press, 1970.

"Competition Designs for Lodge to the Proposed Recreation Ground, Sydenham." *Building News and Engineering Journal* 33 (28 September 1877): 301–2.

"Competition-Designs for the Rev. Mr. Spurgeon's Chapel: The Award of Premiums." *Builder* 17 (19 February 1859): 129–30.

"Competition for Cemetery Chapel: Nottingham Church Cemetery Company." *Building News and Engineering Journal* 33 (3 August 1877): 99.

"Competitions: Dublin Science and Art Museum." *Builder* (25 November 1882): 698.

"Competitions: Macclesfield Town Hall." *Builder* 22 (19 March 1864): 211.

"Competitions: Winchester Guildhall." *Builder* 29 (24 June 1871): 483.

The Concise Dictionary of National Biography: From the Beginnings to 1930. London: Oxford University Press, 1939.

"Congleton Town Hall." *Builder* 22 (16 July 1864): 528–30; *Building News and Engineering Journal* 12 (6 January 1865): 8 and [10, 13].

"Conversazione of the Architectural Association." *Architect* (London) 8 (2 November 1872): 247.

Cooper, Jeremy. "Victorian Furniture: An Introduction to the Sources." *Apollo,* n.s., 95 (February 1972): 115–22.

———. *Victorian and Edwardian Decor: From the Gothic Revival to Art Nouveau.* New York: Abbeville Press, 1987.

The Costume Society: Part 1. London: Costume Society, 1883. A copy is located in the Godwin papers in the Victoria and Albert Museum, Theatre Archive.

"Costumes for *Othello* from Sketches by E. W. Godwin, F.S.A." *British Architect and Northern Engineer* 14 (15 October 1880): [176].

"Cottage Studio." *British Architect and Northern Engineer* 12 (3 October 1879): 132 and illus.

"Court." *Stage* (13 May 1881): 7; *Era* (14 May 1881): 6.

Cowper, Katrine Cecilia Compton. *Earl Cowper KG: A Memoir by his Wife.* London: privately printed, 1913.

Craig, Edward Anthony [Edward Carrick, pseud.]. *Gordon Craig: The Story of His Life.* New York: Knopf, 1968; London: Victor Gollancz, 1968.

———. "E. W. Godwin and the Theatre." *Theatre Notebook,* no. 2 (1977).

Craig, Edward Gordon. *Ellen Terry and Her Secret Self.* London: Sampson Low, Marston, 1931.

———. *Index to the Story of My Days: Some Memoirs of Edward Gordon Craig, 1872–1907.* London: Hulton Press, 1957; New York: The Viking Press, 1957.

Craig, Maurice. *The Architecture of Ireland from the Earliest Times to 1880.* London: B. T. Batsford, 1989.

Crick, Clare. *Victorian Buildings in Bristol.* Bristol: Bristol and West Building Society with the City Art Gallery, 1975.

Crisp, Henry. "Art as Applied to Furniture." *Building News and Engineering Journal* 12 (6 January 1865): 7–8.

"Criticising a Critic." Letter to the *Western Daily Press* (24 February 1863): 4.

Crook, J. Mordaunt. *William Burges and the High Victorian Dream.* London: John Murray, 1981; Chicago: University of Chicago Press, 1981.

———., ed. *The Strange Genius of William Burges 'Art-Architect,' 1827–1881: A Catalogue to a Centenary Exhibition Organised Jointly by the National Museum of Wales, Cardiff, and the Victoria and Albert Museum, London in 1981.* Exh. cat. Cardiff: National Museum of Wales, 1981.

Cruickshank, Dan. "Good Godwin." *Architectural Review* 194 [193] (August 1993): 74–79.

Cunningham, Colin. *Victorian and Edwardian Town Halls.* London: Routledge and Kegan Paul, 1981.

Cunningham, Colin, and Prudence Waterhouse. *Alfred Waterhouse, 1830–1905: Biography of a Practice.* Oxford: Clarendon Press, 1992.

Curl, James Stevens. *Victorian Architecture.* Newton Abbot: David and Charles, 1990.

———. *Book of Victorian Churches.* London: B. T. Batsford and English Heritage, 1995.

———. *Egyptomania: The Egyptian Revival, a Recurring Theme in the History of Taste.* Manchester: Manchester University Press, 1994.

Curry, David Park. *James McNeill Whistler at the Freer Gallery of Art.* Exh. cat. New York: W. W. Norton for the Freer Gallery of Art, Smithsonian Institution, 1984.

———. "Whistler and Decoration." *Magazine Antiques* 126 (November 1984): 1186–99.

"Curtain Fabrics." *Building News and Engineering Journal* 30 (31 March 1876): 318 and [320–21].

"Damnatory Art-Criticism." *Building News and Engineering Journal* 22 (5 January 1872): 1.

Darr, Alan. "European Sculpture and Decorative Arts Acquired by the Detroit Institute of Arts, 1978–87." *Burlington Magazine* 130, no. 1023 (June 1988): 500, fig. 115.

Davis, Frank. "Talking About Salerooms: Europe's Favourite Porcelain." *Country Life* 154 (15 November 1973): 1542–43.

Day, Lewis F. "Notes on English Decorative Art in Paris." Part 3. *British Architect and Northern* Engineer 10 (12 July 1878): 15–16.

———. "Munich Glass." *British Architect and Northern Engineer* 17 (24 February 1882): 93.

———. "Victorian Progress in Applied Design." *Art Journal* (June 1887): 185–202.

de Breffny, Brian, and Rosemary Ffolliott. *The Houses of Ireland: Domestic Architecture from the Medieval Castle to the Edwardian Villa.* London: Thames and Hudson, 1975.

"Decorations of Dromore Castle." *Building News and Engineering Journal* 24 (4 April 1873): 390 and [402].

"The Decorative Art Exhibition." *Cabinet Maker and Art Furnisher* 2 (1 August 1881): 23.

"Decorative Fine-Art Work at Philadelphia: Furniture in the British Section." *American Architect and Building News* 1 (18 November 1876): 372–73.

De Courcy, Louis. *Dromore Castle, Pallaskenry, Co. Limerick: Catalogue of Furniture and Effects . . . .* Sale cat. Dromore Castle, Co. Limerick, 19–21 October [1949].

De Falbe, Sophia J. "James Shoolbred and Co.: Late Victorian Department Store Furniture." Master's thesis, Victoria & Albert/ Royal College of Art Masters Program in Design History, 1985.

Descriptive Guide to the New Town Hall, Northampton. Northampton: Taylor and Son, 1881.

"Design for a Piano Case." Letter to the *Building News and Engineering Journal* 26 (9 January 1874): 54.

"Design for a Piano-Case"; "Mr. E. W. Godwin's Design for Piano-Case." Letters to the *Building News and Engineering Journal* 26 (16 January 1874): 81.

"Design for a Pianoforte." Letter to the *Building News and Engineering Journal* 26 (23 January 1874): 105.

"Design for a Proposed People's Palace by the Late . . . ." *Builder* 52 (12 February 1887): 250 and illus.

"Design for Bedroom Furniture by E. W. Godwin, F.S.A." *Furniture Gazette,* n.s., 6 (23 September 1876): 186.

"Design for Leicester Town Hall by E. W. Godwin." *Building News and Engineering Journal* 24 (25 April 1873): 476 and [478–79].

"Design for Proposed Houses of Parliament, Berlin: by Edward W. Godwin, F.S.A., and Robert W. Edis, F.S.A. and F.R.I.B.A." *Architect* (London) 8 (13 July 1872): 24 and illus.

"Design for Proposed Lunatic Asylum." *Building News and Engineering Journal* 23 (23 August 1872): 142 and [144–45].

"Design for Winchester Town Hall." *Building News and Engineering Journal* 21 (25 August 1871): 140 and [42–43].

"Designs for Curtain Materials." *Furniture Gazette* 5 (15 April 1876): following 242.

"The Designs for the Rev. Mr. Spurgeon's Chapel." *Builder* 17 (12 February 1859): 105–7.

"Detached Conservatory." *Architect* (London)

23 (8 May 1880): 323 and illus.

Detroit Institute of Arts. "The Annual Report, 1985." *Bulletin of the Detroit Institute of Arts* 62, no. 2 (1985).

Dictionary of National Biography, Founded in 1882 by George Smith: The Concise Dictionary from the Beginnings to 1930. London: Oxford University Press, H. Milford, 1939.

"A Dining-Room Sideboard." *Building News and Engineering Journal* 39 (15 October 1880): 442 and [453].

Dixon, Roger, and Stefan Muthesius. *Victorian Architecture*. London: Thames and Hudson, 1978.

"Domestic Electric Lighting: Furniture and Decoration." *Furniture Gazette*, n.s., 17 (1 April 1882): 201–3.

"The Drama." *Lady's Pictorial* (15 December 1883): 377.

"The Drama: Between the Acts." *Queen* (22 May 1886): 563.

"Drama: The Greek Plays." *Athenaeum* (22 May 1886): 689–90.

"Drama. The Week, Princess's: *Hamlet*." *Athenaeum* (18 October 1884): 505.

"Dramatic and Musical Gossip. Mr. Wilson Barrett's adaptation . . . advance booking is excellent." *Referee* (19 October 1884): 2.

"Dramatic and Musical Gossip: Hengler's Circus." *Referee* (23 May 1886): 2.

"Dramatic Criticism." *Western Daily Press* (10 October 1864): 2.

"Dramatic Notes." *England* (22 May 1886): 2.

"Drawing Room Furniture Manufactured by D. Blythe Adamson and Co." In *The Cabinet-Makers' Pattern Book: Being Examples of Modern Furniture of the Character Mostly in Demand*. . . . London: Wyman and Sons, 1877–79. Originally issued as a supplement with *Furniture Gazette*, n.s., 9 (13 April 1878): pl. 67.

"*Dress and Its Relation to Health and Climate* by Edward William Godwin." Review in the *Building News and Engineering Journal* 47 (25 July 1884): 119–21.

Dresser, Christopher. "Japanese Ornamentation." *Builder* 21 (2 May 1863): 308–309, 364–65, 423–24.

———. *Japan: Its Architecture, Art, and Art Manufacturers*. London: Longmans, Green, and Co., 1882.

"Dromore Castle." *Building News and Engineering Journal* 24 (21 March 1873): 330 and [339].

"Dromore Castle, County Limerick." *Architect* (London) 4 (20 August 1870): 104 and illus.

Dry, Graham. "Ein Meisterwerk des anglo-japanischen Stils." *Kunst und Antiquitäten*, no. 12 (December 1994): 20–22.

"Dublin Science and Art Buildings Competition." *Builder* (14 January 1882): 57.

"The Dublin Science and Art Museum Competition." *Builder* (1 October 1881): 434.

Dungavell, Ian. "A Lost House Rediscovered: Godwin's Grey Towers." Unpublished manuscript, 1992.

Dunn, Henry Treffry. *Recollections of Dante Gabriel Rossetti and His Circle*. London: Matthews, 1904.

"Durban Town Hall, Natal." *Builder* (26 August 1882): 283.

Dyer, T. F. Thiselton. "Foresters at Home." *Art Journal* (October 1885): 301–4.

———. "Tongues in Trees." *Belgravia: An Illustrated London Magazine* 57 (July–December 1885): 45–51.

"Eagle Eyed." *Traditional Interior Decoration* (May 1989): 46.

Eames, Penelope. *Furniture in England, France and the Netherlands from the Twelfth to the Fifteenth Century*. London: Furniture History Society, 1977.

Eastlake, Charles Lock. *A History of the Gothic Revival: An Attempt to Show How the Taste for Mediaeval Architecture, Which Lingered in England during the Two Last Centuries, Has since Been Encouraged and Developed*. London: Longmans, Green, 1872.

———. *Hints on Household Taste in Furniture, Upholstery, and Other Details*. 1868. Reprint, with an introduction by John Gloag, New York: Dover Books, 1969.

Eddy, Arthur Jerome. *Recollections and Impressions of James A. McNeill Whistler*. Philadelphia: J. B. Lippincott, 1903.

Edis, Robert William. *Decoration and Furniture of Town Houses: A Series of Canto Lectures Delivered before the Society of Arts, 1880*. London: C. Kegan Paul, 1881.

———. *Healthy Furniture and Decoration*. London: William Clowes and Sons for the Executive Council of the International Health Exhibition and the Council of the Society of Arts, 1884.

Edwards, Arthur M. *The Design of Suburbia: A Critical Study in Environmental History*. London: Pembridge Press, 1981.

Edwards, Clive D. *Victorian Furniture: Technology and Design*. Manchester: Manchester University Press, 1993.

Edwards, Ralph. *The Shorter Dictionary of English Furniture: From the Middle Ages to the Late Georgian Period*. London: Country Life, 1964.

Ellmann, Richard. *Oscar Wilde*. New York: Knopf, 1988.

Ellsworth, Robert Hatfield. *Chinese Hardwood Furniture in Hawaiian Collections*. Exh. cat. Honolulu: Honolulu Academy of Arts, 1982.

"English Art Furniture at the Vienna Exhibition." *Globe and Traveller* (London) (22 May 1873): 1–2.

The English Guide to the Paris Exhibition, 1878. London: Mason, 1878.

Entwisle, Eric Arthur. *Wallpapers of the Victorian Era*. Leigh-on-Sea, England: F. Lewis, 1964.

Escott, T. H. S. *Society in London by a Foreign Resident, with a New Chapter on Society Among the Middle and Professional Classes*. 3d ed., London: Chatto & Windus, 1885.

Esher, Lionel. *The Glory of the English House*. London: Barrie and Jenkins, 1991.

"An Exhibition of Historical Costumes." *Pall Mall Gazette* (2 May 1884): 4.

"Exhibits for the Paris Exhibition." *Building News and Engineering Journal* 34 (22 March 1878): 287–88.

"Fair Rosamund." *Era* (24 July 1886): 12.

"*The Faithfull Shepherdesse*." *Society* (4 July 1885): 20–22; *Illustrated London News* (4 July 1885); *Whitehall Review* (2 July 1885): 17–18.

Farr, Dennis. *English Art, 1870–1940*. Oxford: Clarendon, 1978.

Fastnedge, Ralph. *Sheraton Furniture*. Woodbridge, England: Antique Collectors' Club, 1983.

Fergusson, James. "The New Law Courts." *MacMillan's Magazine* 25 (January 1872): 250–56.

Ferriday, Peter, ed. *Victorian Architecture*. Philadelphia: J. B. Lippincott, 1964.

Fiell, Charlotte, and Peter Fiell. *1,000 Chairs*. Cologne: Taschen Verlag, 1997.

"Figure by C. W. Morgan"; "Monument to Bishop Coke." *British Architect and Northern Engineer* 11 (10 January 1879): 16 and illus.

"Figures Designed for Wall Paintings at Dromore Castle." *Architect* (London) 7 (8 June 1872): 300 and illus.

Fine Art Society. *The Aesthetic Movement and the Cult of Japan*. Exh. cat. London: Fine Art Society, 1972.

———. *Architect-Designers: Pugin to Mackintosh*. Exh. cat. London: Fine Art Society and Haslam and Whiteway, 1981.

———. *Spring 1984*. Exh. cat. London: Fine Art Society, 1984.

———. *Spring 1986*. Exh. cat. London: Fine Art Society, 1986.

———. *Spring 1989*. Exh. cat. London: Fine Art Society, 1989.

———. *Spring 1992*. Exh. cat. London: Fine Art Society, 1992.

———. *Spring 1994*. Exh. cat. London: Fine Art Society, 1994.

———. *Spring 1998*. Exh. cat. London: Fine Art Society, 1998.

Fischer Fine Art. *Aspects of Victorian and Edwardian Decorative Arts*. Exh. cat. London: Fischer Fine Art in association with Dan Klein Ltd., 1982.

Fitz-Gerald, Desmond John Villiers (the Knight of Glin), David J. Griffin, and Nicholas K. Robinson. *Vanishing Country Houses of Ireland*. Dublin: Irish Architectural Archive and Irish Georgian Society, 1988.

Fitzgerald, Percy. "On Scenic Illusion and Stage Appliances." *Journal of the Society of Arts* (18 March 1887): 457–58.

———. "*Junius* or The Household Gods." *Dra-*

matic Review (22 February 1885): 72.

Fleming, James. "Historic Irish Mansions, no. 225." Weekly Irish Times (24 August 1940).

Fleming, John, and Hugh Honour. Dictionary of the Decorative Arts. New York: Harper and Row, 1977.

Floud, Peter. "Victorian Furniture." In The Concise Encyclopaedia of Antiques, Compiled by the Connoisseur, edited by Leonard Gerald Gwynn Ramsey. Vol. 3. New York: Hawthorn Books, 1957.

[The Fool's Revenge.] Reviews in the Illustrated Sporting and Dramatic News (10 July 1886): 495; Era (10 July 1886): 14.

Forbes-Robertson, Johnston. A Player under Three Reigns. New York: Benjamin Blom, 1971.

"14th Century Bronze Found in the Seine Hotel Carnavalet"; "Hotel Carnavalet inside Windows." British Architect and Northern Engineer 16 (29 July 1881): [377–78].

Fox, Grace Estelle. Britain and Japan, 1858–1883. Oxford: Clarendon Press, 1969.

Franklin, Jill. The Gentleman's Country House and Its Plan, 1835–1914. London: Routledge and Kegan Paul, 1981.

Freeman, A. B. Bristol Worthies and Notable Residents Past and Present. 1st series, Bristol: Burleigh Ltd., 1907; 2d series, 1909.

"The Friends' School, Bristol." Builder 8 (23 February 1850): 91.

"From the Vienna Exhibition." Builder 31 (5 July 1873): 518–19.

"From the Vienna International Exhibition." Builder 31 (28 June 1873): 500–501.

Fry, Roger. "The Ottoman and the Whatnot." Athenaeum (June 1919): 529.

Fuller, J. F. Omniana: The Autobiography of an Irish Octogenarian. London: Smith, Elder and Company, 1916.

"Furniture at the School of Art Needlework, Exhibition Road, South Kensington." Decoration (April 1884): 22.

"Furniture at the Centennial." Furniture Gazette, n.s., 5 (27 May 1876): 331–32.

"Furniture at the Paris Exhibition." Furniture Gazette, n.s., 10 (7 September 1878): 153–65.

"Furniture by E. W. Godwin, F.S.A." Building News and Engineering Journal 39 (5 November 1880): 528 and [534].

"The Furniture Exhibition at Islington." Furniture Gazette, n.s., 16 (6 August 1881): 72–73.

"The Furniture Gazette Directory." Furniture Gazette, n.s., 8 (7 July 1877): 9.

"Furniture in the Anglo-Japanese Taste." Building News and Engineering Journal 48 (1 May 1885).

"The Furniture Trades Exhibition." Parts 1 and 2. British Architect and Northern Engineer 19 (27 April 1883): 205–8 and illustration; (11 May 1883): 236.

Galeries nationales du Grand Palais and Musée national d'art occidental. Le Japonisme. Exh. cat. Paris: Editions de la Réunion des musées nationaux and Ministère de la Culture et de la Communication, 1988.

"Garden Theatricals at Coombe House." Observer (31 May 1885): 3.

Garrett, Rhoda, and Agnes Garrett. Suggestions for House Decoration in Painting, Woodwork, and Furniture. Art at Home, vol. 2. London: Macmillan, 1876.

"Gateway to the South Avenue at Castle Ashby." Architect (London) 6 (21 October 1871): 202 and illus.

Gaunt, William. Victorian Olympus. London: Sphere Bros., 1952.

———. Chelsea. London: B. T. Batsford, 1954.

Gere, Charlotte. Nineteenth-Century Decoration: The Art of the Interior. New York: Harry N. Abrams, 1989.

Gere, Charlotte, and Michael Whiteway. Nineteenth-Century Design from Pugin to Mackintosh. London: Weidenfeld and Nicolson, 1993.

Girouard, Mark. "Chelsea's Bohemian Studio Houses: The Victorian Artist at Home." Part 2. Country Life 152 (23 November 1972): 1370–74.

———. Sweetness and Light: The "Queen Anne" Movement, 1860–1900. Oxford: Clarendon Press, 1977.

———. The Victorian Country House. Rev. ed. New Haven and London: Yale University Press, 1979.

"Glass Medallions." Architect (London) 7 (29 June 1872): 340 and illus.

Glasstone, Victor. Victorian and Edwardian Theatres: An Architectural and Social Survey. Cambridge: Harvard University Press, 1975.

Glazebrook, Christopher John. The History of Northampton's Town Halls. Northampton: J. Glazebrook and Sons, 1970.

"Glenbegh Towers." Architect (London) 5 (13 May 1871): 248–49 and illus.

"Globe." Stage (20 January 1882): 9.

Godden, Geoffrey A. British Pottery: An Illustrated Guide. London: Barrie and Jenkins, 1971.

"Godwin and Crisp's Designs for the Bristol Assize Courts." Building News and Engineering Journal 20 (21 April 1871) 297 and illus.

"Godwin and Crisp's Premiated Design for the Bristol Assize Courts." Building News and Engineering Journal 20 (9 June 1871): 450 and illus.

"Godwin on Chaucer." Letter to the Architect (London) 6 (2 December 1871): 282.

Gomme, Andor Harvey, Michael Jenner, and Bryan Little. Bristol, an Architectural History. London: Lund Humphries in association with Bristol and West Building Society, 1979.

Goodale, Ernest. Weaving and the Warners. Leigh-on-Sea, England: F. Lewis, 1971.

"Gothic Cottages near Oxford: William E. Godwin [sic], Architect." Building News and Engineering Journal 12 (21 July 1865): [517].

Graham, Clare. "Seats of Learning." Country Life 184 (30 August 1990): 108–9.

———. Ceremonial and Commemorative Chairs in Great Britain. London: The Victoria and Albert Museum, 1994.

Graves, Algernon. The Royal Academy of Arts: A Complete Dictionary of Contributors and Their Work from Its Foundation in 1769 to 1904. Vol 2. London: H. Graves, 1905.

"Greek Armchair, by E. W. Godwin, F.S.A." Building News and Engineering Journal 48 (29 May 1885): 850 and [862].

"The Greek Play at Hengler's Circus." Standard (18 May 1886): 3.

"The Greek Plays: Helena in Troas." Stage (21 May 1886): 15.

"The Greek Performances." Academy (22 May 1886): 370.

"The Greek Theatre and Helena in Troas." Truth (13 May 1886): 725–26.

"A Greek Theatre in London." Daily Chronicle (18 May 1886): 5.

"A Greek Theatre in London." Building News and Engineering Journal 50 (21 May 1886): 818.

Greenhalgh, Paul. Ephemeral Vistas: The Expositions Universelles, Great Exhibitions and World's Fairs, 1851–1939. Manchester: Manchester University Press, 1988.

Greeves, T. Affleck. "London's First Garden Suburb: Bedford Park, Chiswick." Part 1. Country Life 142 (7 December 1967): 1524–29.

———. Bedford Park: The First Garden Suburb. London: Anne Bingley, 1975.

"Grey Towers, Nunthorpe." Builder 25 (21 December 1867): 923–25.

Greysmith, Brenda. Wallpaper. New York: Macmillan, 1976.

Grier, Katherine C. Culture and Comfort: People, Parlors, and Upholstery, 1850–1930. Rochester: The Strong Museum, 1988.

"Ground Plan of Town Hall, Northampton"; "View of the Town Hall, Northampton: Mr. Edward W. Godwin, Architect." Building News and Architectural Review 7 (8 November 1861): 892–93, 901, ills.

Gruber, Alain, ed. L'Art décoratif en Europe: du neoclassicisme à l'art nouveau. Vol. 3. Paris: Citadelles and Mazenod, 1994.

Grubert, Halina. "The Passionate Pursuit of Charles and Lavinia Handley-Read." Antique Collector 56 (April 1985): 64–69.

Guide to the New Town Hall, Northampton. Northampton: Jas. Butterfield, Herald Office, 1864.

Halén, Widar. Christopher Dresser: A Pioneer of Modern Design. Oxford: Phaidon, 1990.

Hall, James. Dictionary of Subjects and Symbols in Art. Rev. ed. New York: Harper and Row, 1979.

Hall, Michael. "Chinese Puzzle." Country Life 185 (25 July 1991): 78–81.

———. "Modern Gothic: Restoration of

Northampton Guildhall." *Country Life* 187 (4 February 1993): 48–51.

"Hall and County Buildings for Chicago, Illinois." *Builder* 31 (27 December 1873): 1029.

Hamilton, Jean. *An Introduction to Wallpaper.* London: Her Majesty's Stationery Office, 1983.

Hamilton, Walter. *The Aesthetic Movement in England.* London: Reeves and Turner, 1882.

Hamilton, Sir William. *Collection of engravings from ancient Vases…in the possession of Sir Wm. Hamilton.* Naples: Wm. Tischbein, 1791–95.

"*Hamlet* at the Princess's." *Times* (London) (17 October 1884): 5; *Era* (18 October 1884): 8; *Illustrated Sporting and Dramatic News* (25 October 1884): 128.

"*Hamlet* at the Princess's: An Interview with Mr. E. W. Godwin, F.S.A." *Life* (16 October 1884): 312.

"*Hamlet* at the Princess's Theatre." *Illustrated London News* (1 November 1884): [428].

"*Hamlet* at the Princess's Theatre Last Night." *Daily Chronicle* (17 October 1884): 6.

Handley-Read, Charles. "England, 1830–1901." In *World Furniture: An Illustrated History,* edited by Helena Hayward. London: Hamlyn, 1965.

Hapgood, Marilyn Oliver. *Wallpaper and the Artist: From Dürer to Warhol.* New York: Abbeville Press, 1992.

Harbron, Dudley. "Queen Anne Taste and Aestheticism." *Architectural Review* 94 (July 1943): 15–18.

———. "Edward Godwin." *Architectural Review* 98 (August 1945): 48–52.

———. *The Conscious Stone: The Life of Edward William Godwin.* London: Latimer House, 1949.

Harper, Maureen. "Here's to the Ingle where True Hearts Mingle: The Revival of the Settle and Inglenook by Nineteenth-Century English Architects." *Journal of the Decorative Arts Society, 1850 to the Present,* no. 12 (1987–88): 10–17.

Harper, Roger H. *Victorian Architectural Competitions: An Index to British and Irish Architectural Competitions in* The Builder, *1843–1900.* London: Mansell, 1983.

Harper Smith, T., and A. Harper Smith. *A Middle Class Townlet: The Building of Bedford Park.* London: T. Harper Smith, 1992.

Harris, Jonathan. "Pieces of the Past." In *Grosvenor House Antique Fair Catalogue.* London, 1983.

Hartmann, Sadakichi. *The Whistler Book.* Boston: L. C. Page, 1910.

Haslam, Malcolm. "Some Furniture from Dromore Castle Designed by E. W. Godwin." *Christie's International Magazine* 10 (May/June 1993): 26–27.

Hawthorne, Mrs. Julian. "Mr. Whistler's New Portraits." *Harper's Bazaar* 14 (15 October 1881): 658–59.

"Haymarket." *Stage* (4 November 1881): 7.

Hayward, John Forrest. *English Cabinets.* London: Her Majesty's Stationery Office, 1972.

Hayward, R. W. G. "Unjust Competitions." Letter to the *Architect* (London) 16 (16 December 1876): 360.

Hefner-Alteneck, Jakob Heinrich von. *Trachten des christlichen Mittelalters.* 3 vols. Frankfurt am Main: H. Keller, 1840–54.

"*Helena in Troas.*" *Morning Post* (18 May 1886): 5; *Telegraph* (18 May 1886): 5; *Era* (22 May 1886): 14.

"*Helena in Troas* at Henglers." *Pall Mall Gazette* (18 May 1886): 4.

"*Helena in Troas* at the Greek Theatre." *Sunday Times* (London) (23 May 1886): 7.

"*Helena in Troas*: Sketches Taken at the Greek Theatre Hengler's Circus." *Queen: The Lady's Newspaper* (5 June 1886): 624–26.

Henderson, Philip. *William Morris: His Life, Work and Friends.* London: Thames and Hudson, 1967.

"Hengler's Circus." *Graphic* (5 June 1886).

"*Henry V* at the Queens." *Pall Mall Gazette* (18 September 1876): 10.

Heskett, John. *German Design, 1870–1918.* New York: Taplinger, 1986.

Hiatt, Charles. *Ellen Terry and Her Impersonations: An Appreciation.* London: George Bell and Sons, 1898.

Hiller, J. *Hokusai.* Oxford: Phaidon Press, 1978.

Hinz, Sigrid. *Innenraum und Möbel: Von der Antike bis zur Gegenwart.* 3d ed. Berlin: Henschelverlag Kunst und Gesellschaft, 1989.

Hitchcock, Henry-Russell. "G. E. Street in the 1850s." *Journal of the Society of Architectural Historians* 19 (December 1960): 145–71.

———. *Richardson as a Victorian Architect.* Katharine Asher Engel Lectures. Baltimore: Barton-Gillet Company for Smith College, 1966.

———. *Architecture: Nineteenth and Twentieth Centuries.* 4th ed. Harmondsworth, England: Penguin Books, 1977. Reprint, New Haven and London: Yale University Press, 1977.

Hoare, Peter. "Lost and Found." *Interiors* 142 (July 1983): 31.

Holding, M. "The Late E. W. Godwin, F.S.A." *British Architect and Northern Engineer* 51 (22 October 1886): 371.

Honour, Hugh. *Cabinet Makers and Furniture Designers.* London: Weidenfeld and Nicolson, 1969.

Hoskins, Lesley, ed. *The Papered Wall: The History, Patterns and Techniques of Wallpaper.* London: Thames and Hudson Ltd., 1994.

Hosley, William. *The Japan Idea: Art and Life in Victorian America.* Exh. cat. Hartford, Conn.: Wadsworth Athenaeum, 1990.

"House and Studio for A. Stuart Wortley, Esq., at Chelsea." *British Architect and Northern Engineer* 10 (29 November 1878): 210 and illus.

"House and Studio for F. Miles, Esq." *British Architect and Northern Engineer* 13 (11 June

1880): 282 and illus.

"House at Northampton." *Architect* (London) 5 (7 January 1871): 10 and illus.

"A House at Northampton, by E. W. Godwin, F.S.A., Architect." *British Architect and Northern Engineer* 24 (2 October 1885): 145 and illus.

"The House of Liberty and Its Founder." *Daily Chronicle* (21 February 1913): 7.

"Houses at Manchester and Northampton." *Building News and Engineering Journal* 36 (18 April 1879): 412 and [418].

"Houses on the Thames Embankment at Chelsea." *British Architect and Northern Engineer* 9 (15 February 1878): [76, 86]; (15 March 1878): [122]; (12 April 1878): [170].

How, Harry. "Illustrated Interviews: No. XV, Mr. Henry Irving." *Strand Magazine* 4 (1892): 280–91.

———. "Illustrated Interviews: No. XVII, Miss Ellen Terry." *Strand Magazine* 4 (1892): 489–503.

Howe, Katherine S., et al. *Herter Brothers: Furniture and Interiors for a Gilded Age.* Exh. cat. Museum of Fine Arts, Houston; Metropolitan Museum of Art, New York; and High Museum of Art, Atlanta. New York: Harry N. Abrams in association with the Museum of Fine Arts, Houston, 1994.

Howell, Peter, and Ian Sutton, eds. *Victorian Churches.* London: Faber and Faber, 1989.

"H.R.H. The Princess Louise's New Studio at Kensington." *British Architect and Northern Engineer* 14 (3 December 1880): 240 and illus.

Hufnagl, Florian. *Tatigkeitsbericht der Ernst von Siemens-Stiftung, 1983–1993.* Munich, 1993.

———, ed. *A Century of Design: Insights and Outlook on a Museum of Tomorrow.* Translated from German by Claudia Lupri. Stuttgart and New York: Arnoldsche, ca. 1996.

Humbert, Aimé. *Le Japon illustré.* 2 vols. Paris: Librairie de L. Hachette, 1870.

Hunt, Thomas F. *Exemplars of Tudor Architecture, Adapted to Modern Habitations.* London: Longman, Rees, Orme, Brown, Green, and Longman, 1836.

Hyde, H. Montgomery. "Oscar Wilde and His Architect." *Architectural Review* 109 (March 1951): 175–76.

———. *Oscar Wilde: A Biography.* New York: Farrar, Straus and Giroux, 1975.

Illustrated Catalogue of the Paris International Exhibition, 1878. London: George Virtue, 1878.

Illustrated Guide to the Second Annual Furniture Exhibition. Supplement to the *Furniture Gazette,* n.s., 17 (1 May 1882).

"Illustrations of Anglo-Saxon Art–II." *British Architect and Northern Engineer* 9 (15 March 1878): [after 122].

"Illustrations of Competitions: No. 1." *Building News and Engineering Journal* 14 (11 October 1867): 702 and [704].

Impey, Oliver. *Chinoiserie: The Impact of Oriental Styles on Western Art and Decoration.* New York: Charles Scribner's Sons, 1977.

"The International Exhibition." *Furniture Gazette,* n.s, 1 (10 May 1873): 75.

" . . . is only to be commended to . . . ." *The World* (11 May 1881): 11.

"J. on 'Jottings'"; "Criticism Critically Criticised." Letters to the *Western Daily Press,* 26 February 1863.

"Jacobean Oak Sideboard, by E. W. Godwin, F.S.A." *Building News and Engineering Journal* 48 (15 May 1885): 766 and [785].

"Jacobean Suite of Furniture." *Building News and Engineering Journal* 46 (14 March 1884): 406 and [418].

Jacobson, Dawn. *Chinoiserie.* London: Phaidon Press, 1993.

Jackson-Stops, Gervase. "Castle Ashby, Northamptonshire: A Seat of the Marquess of Northampton." Part 2. *Country Life* 179 (6 February 1986): 310–15.

Jacquemart, Albert. *History of the Ceramic Art.* London: S. Low, Marston, Low and Searle, 1873.

Jenkyns, Richard. *Dignity and Decadence: Victorian Art and the Classical Inheritance.* Cambridge: Harvard University Press, 1992.

Jervis, Simon. *Victorian Furniture.* London: Ward Lock, 1968.

———. "Victorian Decorative Art at the Royal Academy: Charles Handley-Read's Collecting Achievements." *Connoisseur* 179 (February 1972): 89–98.

———. *High Victorian Design / Le style de la grande époque victorienne.* Exh. cat. Ottawa: National Gallery of Canada, 1974.

———. "'Sussex' Chairs in 1820." *Furniture History* 10 (1974): 99.

———. *The Penguin Dictionary of Design and Designers.* Harmondsworth, England: Penguin Books, 1984.

Johnson, Peter. *The Phillips Guide to Chairs.* London: Merehurst Press, 1989.

Jones, Owen. *The Grammar of Ornament.* London: Day and Sons, 1856.

Jopling, Louise. *Twenty Years of My Life: 1867 to 1887.* London: John Lane, 1925.

Jordan, Robert Furneaux. *Victorian Architecture.* Harmondsworth, England: Penguin Books, 1966.

Joy, Edward T. "The Overseas Trade in Furniture in the Nineteenth Century." *Furniture History* 6 (1970): 62–72.

———. Introduction to *Pictorial Dictionary of British Nineteenth Century Furniture Design.* Woodbridge, England: Antique Collectors' Club, 1977.

J. P. S. "Comments on the Conference: Professional Unanimity." *Building News and Engineering Journal* 22 (28 June 1872): 529.

"*Juana* at the Court Theatre." *Standard* (9 May 1881): 3.

"*Junius,* or The Household Gods." *Era* (28 February 1885): 8.

Kaplan, Wendy, ed. *Designing Modernity: The Arts of Reform and Persuasion, 1885–1945. Selections from the Wolfsonian.* Exh. cat. New York: Thames and Hudson with the Wolfsonian, 1995.

Kauffmann, Edgar, Jr. "Edward Godwin and Christopher Dresser: The 'Esthetic' Designers, Pioneers of the Eighteen-Seventies." *Interiors* 118 (October 1958): 162–65.

Kelly's Directories Ltd. *The Post Office Directory of Birmingham, Staffordshire, Warwickshire and Worcestershire.* London: Kelly and Co., 1860–1880.

———. *The Post Office Directory of London.* London: Kelly and Co., 1860–1880.

Kikuchi, Sadao. *A Treasury of Japanese Woodblock Prints (Ukiyo-e).* Translated by Don Kenny. New York: Crown, 1969.

Kinchin, Juliet. "Collinson and Lock: Manufacturers of Artistic Furniture, 1870–97." Master's thesis, Victoria and Albert Museum, 1978.

———. "Collinson and Lock." *Connoisseur* 201 (May 1979): 47–53.

King, Donald, ed. *British Textile Design in the Victoria and Albert Museum.* Vol. 3, *Victorian to Modern (1850–1940).* Tokyo: Gakken, 1980.

King, E. M. "Co-operative Housekeeping." *Building News and Engineering Journal* 26 (24 April 1874): 459–60.

Kirkham, Pat. "Furniture-Making in London c. 1700–1870: Craft, Design, Business and Labour." Ph.D. diss., Westfield College, University of London, 1981.

Kugler, Franz Theodor. *Handbook of Painting: The German, Flemish, and Dutch Schools.* Enl. and rev. by Gustav Friedrich Waagen. London: J. Murray, 1860.

Kunstgewerbemuseum, Berlin. *Architekten Als Designer: Beispiele in Berlin.* Exh. cat. Berlin: Kunstgewerbemuseum, Staatliche Museen zu Berlin, 1999.

"Lady Archibald Campbell." *Pall Mall Gazette* (8 May 1884).

"Lady Jane Seymour: Historic Dress at Liberty's Dress Studios by E. W. Godwin, F.S.A." *British Architect and Northern Engineer* 21 (13 June 1884): [after 290].

"A Lady on 'G.'s' Jottings." Letter to the *Western Daily Press* (7 October 1864): 4.

Lambert, Susan, ed. *Pattern and Design: Designs for the Decorative Arts, 1480–1980.* Exh. cat. London: Victoria and Albert Museum, 1983.

Lambourne, Lionel. "Pyrrhic Success: E. W. Godwin and the Theatre." *Country Life* 80 (2 October 1986): 1024–25.

———. *The Aesthetic Movement.* London: Phaidon Press, 1996.

Lancaster, Clay. "Oriental Contributions to Art Nouveau." *Art Bulletin* 34 (December 1952): 297–310.

Lasdun, Susan. *Victorians at Home.* New York: Viking Press, 1981.

"A Last Breakfast in Cheyne Walk." *World* (19 June 1878).

Latimer, Clare. "Frieze, Filling and Dado: A Fashion in English Wallpapers, 1860–1900." Museum Studies diploma thesis, University of Manchester, 1985.

———. "The Division of the Wall: The Use of Wallpapers in Decorative Schemes, 1870–1910." *Journal of the Decorative Arts Society, 1850 to the Present,* no. 12 (1987–88): 18–25.

Laver, James. *Victoriana.* Princeton: Pyne Press, 1975.

"The Law Courts and the Commons." *Architect* (London) 7 (30 March 1872): 153.

Ledoux-Lebard, Denise. *Les ebénistes du XIXe siècle, 1795–1889: leurs oeuvres et leurs marques.* Paris: Editions de l'Amateur, 1984. Revised as *Le mobilier français de XIXe siècle, 1795–1889: Dictionnaire des ébénistes et des menuisiers.* Paris: Editions de l'Amateur, 1989.

"Leicester." *Building News and Engineering Journal* 23 (13 September 1872): 210–11.

"The Leicester Competition." *Architect* (London) 6 (12 August 1871): 82.

"Leicester Municipal Buildings." *Architect* (London) 7 (6 January 1872): 10 and illus.; (13 January 1872): 24 and illus.

van Lemmen, Hans. *Tiled Furniture.* Princes Risborough: Shire, 1989.

"Letter to Atlas from E. W. Godwin." *World* (11 May 1881): 13.

"Letters from Paris." *Illustrated Paris Universal Exhibition (London),* no. 3 (21 May 1878): 27.

Lever, Jill, ed. *Catalogue of the Drawings Collection of the Royal Institute of British Architects.* Vol. 5, *G–K.* Sir Banister Fletcher Library. London: Gregg International, 1973.

———. *Architects' Designs for Furniture.* London: Trefoil Books, 1982.

Liberty and Co. *"Liberty" Art (Dress) Fabrics and Personal Specialties, 1887.* London: Liberty, 1887. Copy in the Liberty and Co. Archives, Westminster Library, London.

———. *The "Liberty" Collection of Costume Design.* London, 1893.

———. *Fancy Dress: A Short Chronological Series of Costumes.* London: Ballantyne Press, n.d.

"Liberty's New Shop." *Morning Post* (27 May 1924): 11.

"A List of Articles Exhibited in the Temporary Museum at the New Town Hall, Chippenham, September 11th, 1855." *Wiltshire Archaeological and Natural History Magazine* 3 (1857): 14.

List of the Objects Obtained during the Paris Exhibition of 1867, by Gift, Loan, or Purchase, and Now Exhibited in the South Kensington Museum. London: G.E. Eyre and W. Spottiswoode, 1868.

"Lisieux Cathedral." Letter to *Building News*

and Engineering Journal 38 (18 June 1880): 731–32.

Lloyd-Jones, David. Review of *E. W. Godwin: Furniture and Interior Decoration*, by Elizabeth Aslin. *Charles Rennie Mackintosh Society Newsletter* 15 (Spring 1987): 8.

"Lodge at Castle Ashby." *Building News and Engineering Journal* 24 (7 March 1873): 272 and [279].

"Logement du concierge Château de Ashby, M. Godwin, Architecte." *Moniteur des architectes* (1872): pl. 28.

"London Architectural Association." *British Architect and Northern Engineer* 11 (7 March 1879): 106–7; (19 March 1880): 143.

London Gossip. "Every week seems to bring . . . ." *Birmingham Daily Post* (21 May 1886): 7.

London International Exhibition, 1862. *Official Catalogue of the Industrial Department.* London: Her Majesty's Commissioners, 1862.

"The London International and Universal Exhibition, 1884." *British Architect and Northern Engineer* 21 (2 May 1884): 223–24.

"The London Theatres. The Adelphi: *Storm Beaten.*" *Era* (17 March 1883): 6.

"The London Theatres: The Globe, *The Cynic.*" *Era* (21 January 1882): 6.

Loshak, David. "G. F. Watts and Ellen Terry." *Burlington Magazine* 105 (November 1963): 476–85.

"The love of old things . . . ." *Cabinet Maker and Art Furnisher* 2 (1 December 1881): 103.

"The Lovers of novelty . . . ." *World* (30 July 1884): 13.

"Love's Labours Lost." Letter to the *Architect* (London) 13 (15 May 1875): 295.

Lowry, John. "The Rise of the Japanese Vogue." *Country Life* 123 (10 April 1958): 752–53.

Lubbell, Cecil, ed. *Textile Collections of the World.* London: Studio Vista, 1976.

Lubbock, Jules. "Victorian Revival." *Architectural Review* 163 (March 1978): 161–67.

Lucas, Edward Verrall. *Edwin Austin Abbey, Royal Academician: The Record of His Life and Work.* 2 vols. New York: Charles Scribner's Sons; London: Methuen, 1921.

Luckhurst, Kenneth W. *The Story of Exhibitions.* London: Studio Publications, 1951.

Lumley, John. "The Pickford Wallers." In *Christie's Review of the Season, 1974,* edited by John Herbert. London: Hutchinson, 1975.

Lynn, Catherine. *Wallpaper in America from the Seventeenth Century to World War I.* New York: W. W. Norton, 1980.

"Lys, Archaeology or Art?" *Dramatic Review* (7 August 1886): 13–14.

MacCarthy, Fiona. *All Things Bright and Beautiful: Design in Britain, 1830 to Today.* London: George Allen and Unwin, 1972.

MacDonald, Margaret F. *Beatrice Whistler: Artist and Designer.* Exh. cat. Glasgow: Hunterian Art Gallery, 1997.

Macquoid, Percy, and Ralph Edwards. *The Dictionary of English Furniture from the Middle Ages to the Late Georgian Period.* Rev. and enl. ed. 3 vols. Woodbridge, England: Antique Collectors' Club, 1986.

Madsen, Stephan Tschudi. *Sources of Art Nouveau.* Oslo: H. Aschehoug and Co., 1956. Reprint, New York: Da Capo Press, 1975.

Malcolm, John. *The Godwin Sideboard: The Second Tim Simpson Adventure.* London: Collins, 1984.

Mallalieu, Huon. "Around the Salerooms." *Country Life* 189 (6 July 1995): 82–83.

"Manchester Baths and Washhouses Competition." *British Architect and Northern Engineer* 8 (16 November 1877): 239–41.

Mandelgren, Nils Mansson. *Monuments scandinaves du Moyen Âge: avec les peintures et autres ornements qui les décorent.* Paris: n.p., 1862.

Manvell, Roger O. *Ellen Terry.* London: Heinemann, 1968.

McCabe, James D. *The Illustrated History of the Centennial Exhibition, Held in Commemoration of the One Hundredth Anniversary of American Independence.* 1876. Reprint, Philadelphia: The National Publishing Company, 1975.

Measham, Terence. *Treasures of the Powerhouse Museum.* Sydney: Powerhouse Publishing and Beagle Press, 1994.

"Measured Drawings by E. W. Godwin, F.S.A.." *Building News and Engineering Journal* 26 (27 February 1874): 228.

"Measuring Distances on Ordnance Plans." Letter to the *Architect* (London) 7 (27 April 1872): 218–219.

"Mediaeval Bristol." *Western Daily Press* (9 September 1864): 4; (10 September 1864): 4.

Melville, Joy. *Ellen and Edy: A Biography of Ellen Terry and Her Daughter, Edith Craig, 1847–1947.* London: Pandora, 1987.

———. *Ellen Terry and Smallhythe Place.* Kent: National Trust, 1997.

Menpes, Mortimer. *Whistler As I Knew Him.* London: Adam and Charles Black. 1904.

Mercer, Eric. *Furniture, 700–1700.* London: Weidenfeld and Nicolson, 1969.

"Messrs. Walford and Donkin's Art Furniture." *Building News and Engineering Journal* 15 (25 December 1868): 869–70.

Metropolitan Museum of Art. "Recent Acquisitions: A Selection, 1990–1991." *The Metropolitan Museum of Art Bulletin* 49 (Fall 1991).

———. *The Metropolitan Museum of Art Guide.* 2d ed. New York: The Metropolitan Museum of Art, 1994.

"Metropolitan Residences." *British Architect and Northern Engineer* 13 (2 January 1880): 8 and illus.

"Miss Ellen Terry." *Illustrations from Dramatic Notes 1881–1882* (11 March 1882): 234.

Miyajima, Hisao, ed. *British Design at Home: The Victoria and Albert Museum.* Exh. cat. Osaka: NHK Kinki Media Plan and Victoria and Albert Museum, 1994.

Moderne Gallery. *Rethinking English Arts and Crafts: The Modernist Tradition in Turn-of-the-Century British Design.* Sale cat. Philadelphia: Moderne Gallery, 1995.

Molesworth, Hender Delves, and John Kenworthy-Browne. *Three Centuries of Furniture in Color.* New York: Viking Press, 1972.

Monkhouse, Christopher. "Department of Decorative Arts: Recent Activities and Acquisitions." *Rhode Island School of Design Museum Notes* 78 (October 1991): 18–19.

"Mortuary Chapel." *British Architect and Northern Engineer* 12 (19 December 1879): 242 and illus.

"Mr. A. Stuart Wortley . . . ." *British Architect and Northern Engineer* 12 (29 August 1879): 80.

"Mr. E. W. Godwin's Progress through Manchester and Liverpool." Letter to the *Building News and Engineering Journal* 27 (17 July 1874): 96.

"Mr. Godwin." *Northampton Mercury* (23 October 1886).

"Mr. Godwin's Furniture Designs." Letter to *Furniture Gazette,* n.s., 11 (22 March 1879): 199.

"Mr. Hermann Vezin made his appearance. . . ." *British Architect and Northern Engineer* 15 (4 March 1881): 115.

"Mr. Hermann Vezin will appear . . . ." *British Architect and Northern Engineer* 15 (4 February 1881): 64.

"Mr. Holloway's Competition"; "Professional Custom and Clients' Law." Letters to the *Building News and Engineering Journal* 23 (18 October 1872): 313.

"Mr. Todhunter's *Helena in Troas* . . . ." *World* (26 May 1886): 15.

"Mr. Wills' powerful play or rather tragedy of *Juana* . . . ." *British Architect and Northern Engineer* 15 (13 May 1881): 245.

Munby, A. N. L., ed. *Poets and Men of Letters.* Vol. 1 of Sale Catalogues of Libraries of Eminent Persons. London: Mansell with Sotheby Parke-Bernet, 1971.

Mundt, Barbara. *Historismus: Kunstgewerbe zwischen Biedermeier und Jugendstil.* Munich: Keyser, 1981.

Musée d'Orsay, Paris. *Catalogue sommaire illustré des arts décoratifs.* Paris: Ministère de la Culture et la Communication and Editions de la Réunion des musées nationaux, 1988.

———. *De Manet à Matisse.* Exh. cat. Paris: Editions de la Réunion des musées nationaux, 1990.

———. *De l'Impressionisme à l'art nouveau: acquisitions du Musée d'Orsay, 1990–1996.* Paris: Editions de la Réunion des musées nationaux, 1996.

Museum of Fine Arts, Boston. *The Furniture of H. H. Richardson.* Exh. cat. Boston: Museum of Fine Arts, 1962.

Muthesius, Hermann. *The English House.* Edited

by Dennis Sharp; translated by Janet Seligman. London: Crosby Lockwood Staples, 1979. Originally published in German, Berlin, 1904–5.

Muthesius, Stefan. *The High Victorian Movement in Architecture, 1850–1870.* London: Routledge and Kegan Paul, 1972.

Nala. "Bachelors' Chambers." Letter to the *British Architect and Northern Engineer* 15 (11 February 1881): 82.

Nardo, Antonio di. *Farm Houses, Small Chateaux and Country Churches in France.* Cleveland: O. J. H. Jansen, 1924.

National Art-Collections Fund. *National Art-Collections Fund Review.* London: The Fund, 1994.

National Trust. *Ellen Terry's House: Smallhythe, Tenterden, Kent.* London: The National Trust, 1995.

Nesfield, W. Eden. *Specimens of Medieval Architecture Chiefly Selected from Examples of the Twelfth and Thirteenth Centuries in France and Italy and Drawn by W. Eden Nesfield, Architect.* London: Day and Son, 1862.

Neve, Christopher. "The Cult of Japan." *Country Life* 152 (5 October 1972): 804–5.

"New Greek Church in London, E. W. Godwin, F.S.A., Architect." *British Architect and Northern Engineer* 11 (17 January 1879).

"The New Guildhall, Plymouth." *Building News and Engineering Journal* 27 (24 July 1874): 108; (31 July 1874): 135.

"New Houses at Chelsea on the Thames Embankment." *Building News and Engineering Journal* 34 (15 March 1878): 264 and [266–67].

"The New Midland Hotel, St. Pancras Station." *Architect* (London) 5 (7 January 1871): 10 and illus.

"New Sadler's Wells: *Othello.*" *Daily News* (14 September 1880): 4.

"The New Theatre at Bath." *Western Daily Press* (23 February 1863): 3.

"The New Town Hall." Letter to the *Northampton Herald* (13 April 1861): 8.

"New Town Hall, Leicester." *Architect* (London) 6 (22 July 1871): 40.

"The New Town-Hall Movement." *Leicester Chronicle* (25 May 1861): 5.

Norman, Geraldine. "Price in the Clouds for Whistler's Butterflies." *Times* (London) (5 October 1973): 21.

"North Lodge at Castle Ashby"; "Stables at the Rectory, Little Gaddesden"; "Stables at Treherne House." *Architect* (London) 5 (10 June 1871): 302 and illus.

Northampton Remembers the Guildhall. Northampton Remembers Series. Northampton: Northampton Borough Council, 1989.

"Northampton Town Council: The New Town Hall." *Northampton Herald* (20 April 1861): 6.

"Northampton Town-Hall." Letters to the *Northampton Herald* (11 May 1861): 3.

"Northampton Town Hall"; "The New Town Hall." Letters to the *Northampton Mercury* (27 April 1861): 7.

"The Northampton Town-Hall Competition." *Builder* 19 (27 April 1861): 282.

"Northampton Town Hall Competition"; "The New Town Hall." Letters to the *Northampton Mercury* (4 May 1861): 5.

"Not far from Antwerp . . . ." *British Architect and Northern Engineer* 15 (18 February 1881): 89 and illus.

"Notes on *Claudian.*" *Theatre* 3 (1 April 1884): 218–20.

Notes on Current Events. "The Southport Markets Competition . . . ." *British Architect and Northern Engineer* 8 (16 November 1877): 242–43.

———. "A house and studio for Mr. James Whistler . . . ." *British Architect and Northern Engineer* 8 (23 November 1877): 250.

———. "Mr. Whistler has accepted a commission . . . ." *British Architect and Northern Engineer* 8 (7 December 1877): 276.

———. "It will be noticed . . . ." *British Architect and Northern Engineer* 9 (4 January 1878): 8.

———. "We noticed some time since . . . ." *British Architect and Northern Engineer* 9 (11 January 1878): 20.

———. "As a handbook to conservatory building . . . ." *British Architect and Northern Engineer* 13 (9 April 1880): 170.

———. "Three Irish Crosses"; "We illustrate this week . . . ." *British Architect and Northern Engineer* 14 (26 November 1880): 227–28.

———. "Mr. W. G. Wills' tragedy of *Juana.* . . ." *British Architect and Northern Engineer* 15 (22 April 1881): 203.

———. "A new exhibition is about to be started . . . ." *British Architect and Northern Engineer* 15 (29 April 1881): 216.

———. "Messrs. Gregory and Co. . . ." *British Architect and Northern Engineer* 15 (27 May 1881): 269.

———. "Today we announce . . . ." *British Architect and Northern Engineer* 16 (29 July 1881): 376.

———. "Mr. Wilson Barrett, in endeavouring . . . ." *British Architect and Northern Engineer* 20 (7 December 1883): 264.

———. *British Architect and Northern Engineer* 21 (22 February 1884): 86.

"Nottingham Church Cemetery Competition." *British Architect and Northern Engineer* 8 (24 August 1877): 99.

"Nottingham Church Cemetery Competition: First Premiated Design, E. W. Godwin, F.S.A., Architect." *British Architect and Northern Engineer* 8 (23 November 1877): [after 254].

Obituary [Henry Crisp]. *Western Daily Press* (9 June 1896).

Obituary [E. W. Godwin]. "Edward W. Godwin." *British Architect* 26 (15 October 1886): 347–48.

———. "The Late E. W. Godwin, F.S.A." *Building News and Engineering Journal* 51 (15 October 1886): 589.

———. "The Week." *Architect* (London) 36 (15 October 1886): 217.

———. *Builder* 51 (16 October 1886): 572, 660.

———. *Nottinghamshire Guardian* (22 October 1886).

———. *American Architect and Building News* 20 (30 October 1886): 202.

———. "It is with sincere regret . . . ." *Art Journal* (November 1886): 352.

———. "E. W. Godwin." *Artist* (1 November 1886): 367.

———. "The Late E. W. Godwin, F.S.A." *Pictorial World* (4 November 1886): 461.

———. "The Late Mr. E. W. Godwin." *Cabinet Maker and Art Furnisher* 7 (1 December 1886): 147.

———. *Building* 5 (July–December 1886): 257.

Obituary [James Hine]. *Builder* 106 (1914): 277.

O'Callaghan, John. "The Fine Art Society and E. W. Godwin." In *Fine Art Society: Centenary Exhibition, 1876–1976.* Exh. cat. London: Fine Art Society, 1976.

———. "Godwin, Edward William." In *Macmillan Encyclopedia of Architects,* edited by Adolf K. Placzek. Vol. 2. New York: The Free Press, 1982.

"Old English Furniture." *Furniture Gazette,* n.s., 6 (19 August 1876): 112 and illus.

Oliphant, Laurence. *Narrative of the Earl of Elgin's Mission to China and Japan in the Years 1857, '58, '59.* Edinburgh: William Blackwood and Sons, 1859.

Oman, Charles C., and Jean Hamilton. *Wallpapers: An International History and Illustrated Survey from the Victoria and Albert Museum.* New York: Harry N. Abrams in association with the Victoria and Albert Museum, London, 1982.

"On Professional Practice: Lecture III." *Building News and Engineering Journal* 23 (20 December 1872): 485.

"On Thursday night the long-looked for production . . . ." *Topical Times* (18 October 1884): 6–7.

"Opening of the Theatre Royal, Bath." *Western Daily Press* (5 March 1863): 3.

"Opera Comique." *Stage* (9 July 1886): 16.

"The Oratory Church, Brompton." *British Architect and Northern Engineer* 12 (4 July 1879): 6 and illus.

Ormond, Richard. "Holman Hunt's Egyptian Chairs." *Apollo,* n.s., 82 (July 1965): 55–58.

Our Captious Critic. "Helena in Troas." *Illustrated Sporting and Dramatic News* (29 May 1886): [327].

"Our London Letter." *Cork Constitution* (18 May 1886): 2.

"Our Museum." *Cabinet Maker and Art Furnisher* 2 (1 April 1882): 187–88.

Our Office Table. "Many people know . . . ."

Building News and Engineering Journal 29 (8 October 1875): 409.

"Our Omnibus-Box." *Theatre* (1 September 1884).

"Our Playbill." *Naval and Military Gazette* (22 July 1885): 90.

"Paintings from the Armoire in Bayeux Cathedral." *British Architect and Northern Engineer* 9 (4 January 1878): 8 and [after 8].

"Paisley Town-Hall Competition." *Builder* 33 (12 June 1875): 528.

Paolini, Claudio, Alessandra Ponte, and Ornella Selvafolta. *Il bello "ritrovato": Gusto, ambienti, mobili dell'Ottocento.* Novara, Italy: Istituto Geografico de Agostini, 1990.

Paris Exposition Universelle, 1867. *Complete Official Catalogue, English Version Translated from the Proof Sheets of the French Catalogue Published by the Imperial Commission.* 2d ed. London: J. M. Johnson, 1867.

"The Paris Universal Exhibition" Parts 5 and 7. *Magazine of Art* 1 (1878): 113; (1878): 187–91.

Parker, John Henry. *A Glossary of Terms used in Grecian, Roman, Italian, and Gothic Architecture.* London: C. Tilt, 1836.

Parker, John Henry, and Thomas Hudson Turner. *Some Account of Domestic Architecture in England . . .* 3 vols. Oxford: J. H. Parker, 1851–59.

"Parlour Furniture." *Building News and Engineering Journal* 37 (31 October 1879): 522 and [531].

Parry, Linda. *The Victoria and Albert Museum's Textile Collection: British Textiles from 1850 to 1900.* London: Victoria and Albert Museum, 1993.

———, ed. *William Morris.* Exh. cat. London: Philip Wilson in association with the Victoria and Albert Museum, 1996.

"A Parsonage for £550." *Building News and Engineering Journal* 26 (6 March 1874): 256 and [263, 266–67].

"A Pastoral Performance: *As You Like It.*" *Era* (31 July 1886): 12.

"The Pastoral Play *Fair Rosamund.*" *Illustrated London News* (31 July 1886): 124.

"The Pastoral Players." *Society* (6 June 1885): 12–13; *Era* (6 June 1885): 9; *Daily Telegraph* (29 June 1885): 3; *Evening Post* (29 June 1885); *Stage* (3 July 1885): 17; *Stage* (23 July 1886): 15.

"The Pastoral Players at Coombe House." *Graphic* (4 July 1885): [3] and frontis.

"Pastoral Plays." *Music and Drama* (August 1885): n.p

Payne, Christopher, ed. *Sotheby's Concise Encyclopedia of Furniture.* London: Conran Octopus, 1989.

Peake, Tim H. *William Brownfield and Son(s) 1873–1900.* Taunton, Somerset: T.H. Peake, 1995.

Pearson, Hesketh. *Beerbohm Tree: His Life and Laughter.* London: Methuen, 1956.

"The peculiar characteristic in the . . . ." *British Architect and Northern Engineer* 20 (14 December 1883): 277.

Pemsel, Jutta. *Die Wiener Weltausstellung von 1873: Das gründerzeitliche Wien am Wendepunkt.* Vienna: Böhlau Verlag, 1989.

Pen and Ink Notes. *Cabinet Maker and Art Furnisher* 2 (1 April 1882): 181–84.

———. "At Kensington." *Cabinet Maker and Art Furnisher* 5 (1 April 1885): 181–83.

———. "The Three Historic Music Rooms in the Albert Hall." *Cabinet Maker and Art Furnisher* 6 (1 December 1885): 141–45.

Pendleton, Mary Belle Lawson. "Bedford Park: An Introduction to Further Study." Ph.D. diss., Northwestern University, 1981.

Pennell, Elizabeth Robins, and Joseph Pennell. *The Life of James McNeill Whistler.* 2 vols. London: William Heinemann; Philadelphia: J. B. Lippincott, 1908.

———. *The Whistler Journal.* Philadelphia: J. B Lippincott, 1921.

"The Performance in the Greek Theatre." *Daily News* (18 May 1886): 5.

"Performance of *The Cenci.*" *Era* (8 May 1886): 13; *Stage* (15 May 1886): 352.

"Perry & Co., Carriage Manufacturers." In *Progress/1893/Commerce: The Ports of the Bristol Channel.* London: J. S. Virtue & Co. 1893.

"Persons of taste have long been annoyed . . . ." *Standard* (28 September 1882): 5.

Pevsner, Nikolaus. *Pioneers of Modern Design.* 1936. Rev. and enl. as *Pioneers of Modern Design: From William Morris to Walter Gropius.* 3d ed. Harmondsworth, England: Penguin, 1960.

———. "Christopher Dresser: Industrial Designer." *Architectural Review* 81 (April 1937): 183–86.

———. "Design and Industry through the Ages." *Journal of the Royal Society of Arts* 42 (1948): 99.

———. *Nottinghamshire.* The Buildings of England. Harmondsworth, England: Penguin Books, 1951.

———. "Art Furniture of the Eighteen-Seventies." *Architectural Review* 111 (January 1952): 43–50. Reprinted in Nikolaus Pevsner, *Victorian and After,* vol. 2 of *Studies in Art, Architecture and Design* (London: Thames and Hudson, 1968; Princeton: Princeton University Press, 1968).

———. "Furniture: A Godwin Sideboard." *Architectural Review* 111 (April 1952): 273.

———. "Victorian and Edwardian Design." *Architectural Review* 112 (December 1952): 402.

———. *Victorian and After.* Vol. 2 of *Studies in Art, Architecture and Design.* London: Thames and Hudson, 1968; Princeton: Princeton University Press, 1968.

———. *Cornwall.* 2d ed. Rev. by Enid Redcliff. The Buildings of England. Harmondsworth, England: Penguin Books, 1970.

———. *Some Architectural Writers of the Nineteenth Century.* Oxford: Clarendon Press. 1972.

Pevsner, Nikolaus, and Edward Hubbard. *Cheshire.* The Buildings of England. Harmondsworth, England: Penguin Books, 1971.

Phillips. *Art Nouveau, Decorative Arts and Studio Ceramics.* Sale cat. London, 5 July 1984.

———. *The Fine Art Society.* Sale cat. Edinburgh, Scotland, 26 May 1992.

———. *British Continental and American Decorative Arts.* Sale cat. London, 13 October 1992.

Physick, John, and Michael Darby. *Marble Halls: Drawings and Models for Victorian Secular Buildings.* Exh. cat. London: Victoria and Albert Museum, 1973.

"Piano Case." *Building News and Engineering Journal* 26 (2 January 1874): [10].

Planché, J.R. *A Cyclopaedia of costume or dictionary of dress, . . . from the commencement of the Christian era to the accession of George the Third.* 2 vols. London: Chatto & Windus, 1875, 1879.

———. *History of British Costume from the Earliest Period to the Close of the Eighteenth Century.* 1834. Revised ed. London: Cox, 1847.

———. *The Recollections and Reflections of J. R. Planché.* London: Tinsley Brothers, 1872.

"Plans of St. Philips Schools, Bristol." *Architect* (London) 7 (1 June 1872): 284 and illus.

"The Playhouses." *Illustrated London News* (14 May 1881): 471; (21 May 1881): 495.

"The Playhouse's *Hamlet* at the Princess's." *Illustrated London News* (25 October 1884): 391.

"Plays and Players." *Society* (10 July 1886): 18.

"The Plymouth New Town Hall." *Building News and Engineering Journal* 27 (21 August 1874): 239.

"Plymouth Town Hall." *Architect* (London) 3 (18 June 1870): 305 and illus.

Pocock, Tom. *Chelsea Reach: The Brutal Friendship of Whistler and Walter Greaves.* London: Hodder and Stoughton, 1970.

Poel, William. "Acting Editions of Shakespeare's Plays: *Hamlet.*" *Era* (2 July 1881): 7.

"Pompeii in London." *Art Journal* (1870): 278.

Post, Robert C., ed. *A Treatise upon Selected Aspects of the Great International Exhibition Held in Philadelphia on the Occasion of Our Nation's One-Hundredth Birthday, with some Reference to Another Exhibition in Washington Commemorating That Epic Event, and Called 1876, A Centennial Exhibition.* Washington, D.C.: National Museum of History and Technology, Smithsonian Institution, 1976.

Powerhouse Museum. *Decorative Arts and Design from the Powerhouse Museum.* Sydney: Powerhouse Publishing, 1991.

"The preparation of Mr. Wills' new play . . . ." *World* (4 May 1881): 14.

Prideaux, Tom. *Love or Nothing: The Life and*

Times of Ellen Terry. New York: Scribner, 1975.

"Prince of Wales's Theatre." *Hour* (19 April 1875): 6.

"The Prince of Wales' Theatre." *Morning Post* (19 April 1875): 3.

"Princess's." *Stage* (14 December 1883): 14; (24 October 1884): 14–15.

"Princess's Theatre." *Daily News* (7 December 1883): 3; *Times* (London) (7 December 1883): 6.

"The Principal Competitive Designs for the Proposed New Edinburgh Cathedral." *Building News and Engineering Journal* 24 (17 January 1873): 64.

"Proceedings at the Meetings at the Archaeological Institute." *Archaeological Journal* 7 (1850):315; 8 (1851): 322–40; 10 (March 1853): 77–86; 12 (March 1855): 89–98; (June 1855): 193–96; 18 (March 1861): 84–92; 23 (June 1866): 149–52.

"Professor Willis." *Architect* (London) 13 (6 March 1875): 134–35.

"Proposed East End: Little Gaddesden Church"; "Design for Cork Cathedral." *Building News and Engineering Journal* 21 (7 July 1871): [8, 9].

"The Proposed Monument to Byron." *Builder* 33 (24 July 1875): 655–56.

"Proposed Mortuary Chapel, Nottingham." *Building News and Engineering Journal* 33 (3 August 1877): 100 and [107].

Pugin, Augustus Charles. *Specimens of gothic architecture; selected from various antient [sic] edifices in England . . . to exemplify the various styles and the practical construction . . . Accompanied by historical and descriptive accounts.* 3 vols. London: J. Taylor, 1821–23.

Purslow, Martin. "Middlesborough's Grey Towers." *Victorian Society Northeastern Newsletter* (28 January 1994).

———. "A Seminal Discovery." *Wallpaper History Review* (1995): 3–5.

Quicherat, Jules Étienne Joseph. *Histoire du costume en France depuis les temps les plus reculés jusqu'à la fin du XVIIIe siècle.* Paris: Hachette, 1875.

"Radcliffe Church." *Building News and Engineering Journal* 38 (2 April 1880): 396 and [404].

"Rambling Sketches." Part 1. *British Architect and Northern Engineer* 15 (25 February 1881): 105 and illus.

———. Part 8, "A Visit to Burmantofts." *British Architect and Northern Engineer* 16 (8 July 1881): 345.

———. Part 14. *British Architect and Northern Engineer* 16 (2 September 1881): 444–45 and illus.

"The recently formed Costume Society . . . ." *British Architect and Northern Engineer* 18 (1 December 1882): 570.

Reeves, Paul. "The Anglo-Japanese Buffet by E. W. Godwin: Variations on and Develop-

ments of a Design." *(Journal of the) Decorative Arts Society, 1850 to the Present,* no. 18 (1994): 36–40.

Reid, Aileen. "Dromore Castle, County Limerick: Archaeology and the Sister Arts of E. W. Godwin." *Architectural History* 30 (1987): 113–42.

———. "Homes Fit for Hera." *Country Life* 186 (10 December 1992): 36–39.

———. "Godwin, E(dward) W(illiam)." In *The Dictionary of Art,* edited by Jane Turner. Vol. 12. New York: Grove, 1996.

"The report has reached us . . . ." *British Architect and Northern Engineer* 9 (17 May 1878): 229.

"The Restoration of Westminster Hall." Letter to the *Times* (London) (6 December 1884): 6.

"Retford Town Hall Competition." *Builder* 22 (1 October 1864): 726.

"She Would and She Would Not." Reviews in *Referee* (8 July 1884); *Stage* (13 June 1884): 14.

Reynolds, Ernest. *Northampton Town Hall.* Northampton: Belmont Press, 1956, 1974.

R. F. H. "Suburban Bristol." *Building News and Engineering Journal* 35 (20 September 1878): 285–87.

Richards, Kenneth, and Peter Thomson, eds. *Essays on Nineteenth Century British Theatre: The Proceedings of a Symposium Sponsored by the Manchester University Department of Drama.* London: Methuen, 1971.

Richardson, D. S. *Gothic Revival Architecture in Ireland.* New York and London: Garland Publishing, 1983.

Rickman, Thomas. *An attempt to discriminate the styles of architecture in England from the Conquest to the Reformation.* Liverpool, 1817; reprint, London and Oxford: John Henry Parker, 1848.

Riley, Noël. *Victorian Design Source Book.* Oxford: Phaidon, 1989.

———. , ed. *World Furniture.* London: Octopus Books, Ltd., 1980.

Robins, E. C. "Our Own Affairs." *British Architect and Northern Engineer* 17 (6 January 1882): 2.

Robinson, Duncan. "Burne-Jones, Fairfax Murray and Siena." *Apollo,* n.s., 102 (November 1975): 348–51.

"Rosalind in the Wood." *Truth* (31 July 1884): 174–75.

Rose, Enid. *First Studies in Dramatic Art.* London: W. B. Clive, 1926.

———. *Gordon Craig and the Theatre: A Record and an Interpretation.* London: Sampson Low Marston, [1931].

Rosen, George. "Disease, Debility, and Death." In *The Victorian City: Images and Realities,* edited by Harold James Dyos and Michael Wolff. Vol. 2. London: Routledge and Kegan Paul, 1973.

Ross, Alexander. "Edinburgh Cathedral Competition." Letter to *Building News and Engineering Journal* 24 (17 January 1873): 91.

Rowan, Alistair John. *North West Ulster.* Harmondsworth, England: Penguin Books, 1979.

Royal Academy of Arts. *Victorian and Edwardian Decorative Art: The Handley-Read Collection.* Exh. cat. London: The Royal Academy of Arts, 1972.

Royal Commission for the Paris Exhibition, 1878. *Official Catalogue of the British Section.* 2 vols. London: G. E. Eyre and W. Spottiswoode for Her Majesty's Stationery Office, 1878.

Royal Commission for the Vienna Universal Exhibition of 1873. *Reports on the Vienna Universal Exhibition of 1873.* 4 vols. London: G. E. Eyre and W. Spottiswoode for Her Majesty's Stationery Office, 1874.

Royal Institute of British Architects. *(Paris Exhibition, 1867) Catalogue of Architectural Designs and Models, Photographic Illustrations, and Art Manufactures.* London: J. Davy and Sons, 1867.

Royal Institute of British Architects/Sir Banister Fletcher Library. *Catalogue of the Drawings Collection of the Royal Institute of British Architects.* Vol. 5. Edited by Jill Lever. London: Gregg International, 1973.

Royal Society of Arts. *The Society of Arts Artisan Reports on the Paris Universal Exhibition of 1878.* London: Sampson Low, Marston, Searle and Rivington, 1879.

Rudoe, Judy. *Decorative Arts, 1850–1950: A Catalogue of the British Museum Collection.* London: British Museum Press, 1991.

Ruskin, John. *The Stones of Venice.* 3 vols. London: Smith, Elder, 1851–53. Reprint, London: George Allen, 1907.

———. *The Seven Lamps of Architecture.* 2d ed. London: Smith, Elder, 1855.

Saint, Andrew. *Richard Norman Shaw.* New Haven: Yale University Press for the Paul Mellon Centre for Studies in British Art, 1976.

———. *The Image of the Architect.* New Haven and London: Yale University Press, 1983.

"A Satinwood and Ebony Cabinet." *Building News and Engineering Journal* 48 (1 May 1885): 686 and [702].

Sato, Tomoko, and Toshio Watanabe, eds. *Japan and Britain: An Aesthetic Dialogue, 1850–1930.* Exh. cat. London: Lund Humphries in association with the Barbican Art Gallery and the Setagaya Art Museum, 1991.

Saumarez-Smith, Charles. *Eighteenth-Century Decoration: Design and the Domestic Interior in England.* London: Weidenfeld and Nicolson, 1993.

"Saxon Architecture." *Examiner* (4 September 1875): 996–97.

"Scenes from *Claudian.*" Parts 1–4. *Illustrated Sporting and Dramatic News* (22 December 1883): [384]; (29 December 1883): [396]; (5 January 1884): [420]; (12 January 1884): [444].

"Scenes from *Clito* at the Princess's Theatre."

Illustrated Sporting and Dramatic News (15 May 1886): 262–63.

"School Board for London." *Building News and Engineering Journal* 25 (19 December 1873): 689 and [674].

Schreiber, Lady Charlotte. *Lady Charlotte Schreiber: Extracts from Her Journal, 1853–1891.* Edited by the Earl of Bessborough. London: John Murray, 1952.

Scott, Clement. "*Claudian.*" *Illustrated London News* (15 December 1883): 574; *Theatre* 3 (1 January 1884): 43–49.

———. "The New *Hamlet.*" *Theatre* 4 (1 November 1884): 243–54.

———. "The *Eumenides* at Cambridge." *Illustrated London News* (12 December 1885): 595 and 597.

———. "The Playhouses." *Illustrated London News* (8 May 1886): 476.

———. "Greek Plays." *London Illustrated News* 88 (22 May 1886): 524.

Scott, George Gilbert. *Gleanings from Westminster Abbey.* 2d enl. ed. Oxford: J. Henry and J. Parker, 1863.

"Sculpture, New Town-Hall, Northampton." *Building News and Engineering Journal* 12 (10 November 1865): 788, [795].

Scrutator [pseud.]. "*Juana.*" *Truth* (19 May 1881): 676.

———. "The Coombe Shepherdesses." *Truth* (2 July 1885): 13–14.

———. "Clito Barrett and Nana Eastlake." *Truth* (13 May 1886): 724–25.

———. "*Helena in Troas.*" *Truth* (20 May 1886): 765.

"Secret Deliberations." *Building News and Engineering Journal* 22 (28 June 1872): 531.

Seddon, John P. Letter to *Building News and Engineering Journal* 24 (21 February 1873): 231.

———. "Friends in Council: The Late Mr. E. W. Godwin." *British Architect* 26 (15 October 1886): 348.

Sedille, Paul. "L'architecture moderne en Angleterre." *Gazette des Beaux Arts,* 2d ser., 34 (1886): 89–106.

Service, Alastair. "James MacLaren and the Godwin Legacy." *Architectural Review* 154 (August 1973): 111–18.

———. *Edwardian Architecture and Its Origins.* London: The Architectural Press, 1975.

Sezon Museum of Art. *Birth of Modern Design.* Exh. cat. Tokyo: Sezon Bijutsukan, 1990.

"The Shakespeare Dining-Room Set." *Building News and Engineering Journal* 41 (11 November 1881): 626 and [634].

"Shakespeare under the Greenwood Tree." *Era* (26 July 1884): 8.

"Shakespeare Relics." *Graphic* (1 April 1893): 342.

"Shakespeare's Chair." *Furniture Gazette,* n.s., 7 (10 March 1877): 146.

"A Shakespearian Furniture Relic." *Furniture Gazette,* n.s., 7 (3 March 1877): 137.

"The Shelley Society and *The Cenci.*" *Times* (London) (8 May 1886) 14.

Sheraton, Thomas. *The Cabinet Dictionary . . . .* London: W. Smith, 1803.

James Shoolbred and Co. *Designs of Furniture Illustrative of Cabinet Furniture and Interior Decoration . . . .* London, 1874, 1876, 1889.

"Sitting at a Play: Globe Theatre." *Play* (19 January 1882): 101.

"Sitting at a Play: Haymarket." *Play* (3 November 1881): 13.

"Sitting at a Play: The Princess." *Play* (13 December 1883): 69–70.

"Sketch Design for Toilet Set." *British Architect and Northern Engineer* 11 (14 February 1879): 72 and illus.

"Sketches from *Claudian,* the New Piece at the Princess's Theatre." *Illustrated London News* (15 December 1883): 573.

Small, Ian, ed. *The Aesthetes: A Sourcebook.* London: Routledge and Kegan Paul, 1979.

"Small House on the Estate of Lord Ferrers, Derbyshire." *British Architect and Northern Engineer* 15 (4 February 1881).

Smalley, George W. "A Harmony in Yellow and Gold." *New York Tribune* (6 July 1878) 2. Reprinted in *American Architect and Building News* 4 (27 July 1878): 36.

Smith, John Moyr. *Ornamental Interiors, Ancient and Modern.* London: Crosby Lockwood, 1887.

Snodin, Michael, and Maurice Howard. *Ornament: A Social History since 1450.* New Haven and London: Yale University Press in association with the Victoria and Albert Museum, 1996.

"Some New Competitions." *British Architect and Northern Engineer* 8 (31 August 1877): 109–10.

"Some Scenes from *Clito.*" *Pall Mall Gazette* (4 May 1886): 11.

Somerville-Large, Peter. *The Irish Country House: A Social History.* London: Sinclair-Stevenson, 1995.

Soros, Susan Weber. "Whistler as Collector, Interior Colorist and Decorator," by Susan Weber. Master's thesis, Cooper-Hewitt Museum, 1987.

———. "E. W. Godwin: Secular Furniture and Interior Design." Ph.D. dissertation, Royal College of Art, London, 1998.

———. *The Secular Furniture of E. W. Godwin.* London and New Haven: Yale University Press, 1999.

Sotheby's. *Decorative Arts 1870–1939.* Sale cat. Belgravia, 11 November 1967.

———. *Art Nouveau and Art Deco, Arts and Crafts, Furniture, Works of Art and Studio Ceramics.* Sale cat. London, 31 March 1977.

———. *Decorative Arts including Arts and Crafts, Art Nouveau, Art Deco, Art Pottery and Studio Ceramics.* Sale cat. London, December 1985.

———. *Applied Arts from 1880.* Sale cat. London, 4 March 1988.

———. *Applied Arts from 1880.* Sale cat. London, 21 October 1988.

———. *Applied Arts from 1880.* Sale cat. London, 3 March 1989.

Souder, Alvin. "E. W. Godwin and the Visual Theatre of the Victorians." Master's thesis, Reading University, 1976.

Sparke, Penny. *Furniture.* Twentieth-Century Design Series. New York: E. P. Dutton, 1986.

Sparrow, Wilbur Daniel. "A Survey of the Life and Work of Edward William Godwin and Its Relationship to Ellen Terry and Edward Gordon Craig." Master's thesis, University of Washington, 1938.

"A special performance of *Twins . . . .*" *Morning Post* (4 August 1884): 5.

Spielmann, Heinz, ed. *Die Jugendstil-Sammlung.* Hamburg: Museum für Kunst und Gewerbe, 1996.

Spencer, Charles, ed. *The Aesthetic Movement, 1869–1890.* Exh. cat. Camden Arts Centre. London: Academy Editions; New York: St. Martin's Press, 1973.

———. "Anglo-Japanese Furniture." *Arts and Antiques Weekly* 36 (5 May 1979): 22–23.

Spencer, Robin. *The Aesthetic Movement: Theory and Practice.* London: Studio Vista, Dutton Pictureback, 1972.

———., ed. *Whistler: A Retrospective.* New York: H. L. Levin Associates, 1989.

Squire, Geoffrey. "Orienteering." *Art Quarterly of the National Art-Collections Fund,* no. 7 (Autumn 1991): 34–37.

"St. Gilles near St. Lô." *Building News and Engineering Journal* 27 (14 August 1874): [194].

"St. Johnston, County Donegal, Ireland." *Builder* 15 (9 May 1857): 258–59.

"St. Philip's Church, Stepney." *Architect* (London) 6 (23 December 1871): [314].

"Stained Glass, Fairford and Bledington." *Building News and Engineering Journal* 32 (9 February 1877): 144 and [155].

"Staircase of Northampton Town Hall." *Building News and Engineering Journal* 12 (3 February 1865): 86 and illustration [83].

Stamp, Gavin, and Colin Amery. *Victorian Buildings of London, 1837–1887: An Illustrated Guide.* London: Architectural Press, 1980.

Stamp, Gavin, and André Goulancourt. *The English House, 1860–1914: The Flowering of English Domestic Architecture.* Chicago: The University of Chicago Press, 1986.

Steen, Marguerite. *A Pride of Terrys: Family Saga.* London: Longmans, 1962.

Stephens, W. B., ed. *History of Congleton.* Manchester: Manchester University Press for the Congleton History Society, 1970.

Stokes, John. "Resistible Theatres." In *An Aesthetic Theatre: The Career of E. W. Godwin* by John Stokes. London: Elek Books, 1972.

"*Storm-Beaten* at the Adelphi." *Illustrated London News* (5 May 1883): 442 and [441].

"The Story of Orestes and the Tale of Troy at Prince's Hall." *Queen* (22 May 1886): 550.

Street, Arthur E. "George Price Boyce, R.W.S." *The Old Water-Colour Society's Club (Annual Volume)* 19 (1941): 1–71. Reprinted and rev. as *The Diaries of George Price Boyce,* edited by Virginia Surtees. Norwich: Real World Publications, 1980.

Street, George Edmund. *Brick and Marble in the Middle Ages: Notes of a Tour in the North of Italy.* London: J. Murray, 1855.

———. "The Edinburgh Cathedral Competition." Letter to *Building News and Engineering Journal* 24 (10 January 1873): 57.

Strickland, Margot. "Ellen Terry's six years 'exile' in Hertfordshire." *Hertfordshire Countryside* 25 (July 1970): 28–30.

"Studio at Kensington for H.R.H. the Princess Louise." *British Architect and Northern Engineer* 14 (3 December 1880): [238].

Sudjic, Deyan. *Cult Objects.* London: Paladin, 1985.

Sugden, Alan Victor, and John Ludlam Edmondson. *A History of English Wallpaper, 1509–1914.* London: B. T. Batsford, 1925.

"Suggestive Furniture." *Builder* 36 (30 March 1878): 325, 327.

Sutherland, William George. *Modern Wall Decoration.* Manchester, England: Decorative Art Journal Co., ca. 1893.

Symonds, Robert Wemyss, and Bruce Blundell Whineray. *Victorian Furniture.* London: Country Life, 1962.

Tanaka, Kikuo. *Irohabiki Moncho* [Book of Crests and Designs]. Tokyo: Kyukoko, [1881].

"Tennyson's New Play." *Era* (3 January 1881): 5.

Terry, Dame Ellen. *The Story of My Life.* London: Hutchinson, 1908.

———. *Ellen Terry and Bernard Shaw: A Correspondence.* Edited by Christopher St. John. New York: G. P. Putnam's Sons, 1931.

———. *Ellen Terry's Memoirs.* Rev. ed. with a preface, notes and additional biographical chapters by Edith Craig and Christopher St. John. London: Victor Gollancz; New York: G. P. Putnam's Sons, 1932.

Teynac, Françoise, Pierre Nolot, and Jean-Denis Vivien. *Wallpaper: A History.* New York: Rizzoli, 1982.

"The Theatre." *St. James's Gazette* (12 December 1883): 6.

"The Theatres." *Times* (London) (9 May 1881): 10; *Graphic* (14 May 1881): 470–71; (4 July 1885): 11; (8 May 1886): 495–96; *Saturday Review* (15 December 1883): 765–66.

"The Theatres: Court Theatre." *Observer* (8 April 1881): 4.

"The Theatres: Prince of Wales." *Times* (London) (19 April 1875): 8.

"The Theatres: Princess's." *Times* (London) (2 March 1885): 10.

"Theatres – Their History and Requirements."

Bristol Mirror and General Advertiser (18 April 1865): 6.

"Theatrical Jottings." Letters to the *Western Daily Press* (9 December 1862): 4; (27 February 1863): 4; (8 October 1864): 2; (6 October 1864): 4.

Theatrical Notes. "Mr. E. W. Godwin, F.S.A has been retained . . . ." *British Architect and Northern Engineer* 16 (21 October 1881): 522.

Theatrical Topics. "There is a grove of lime-trees round . . ."; "Coombe House . . ."; "The whole scenic arrangements . . ."; "Now a word on the acting . . ."; "Go and see Arden . . . ." *Topical Times* (26 July 1884): 5.

———. "The Saturday Performance of *As You Like It* in Coombe Wood . . . ." *Topical Times* (2 August 1884): 5.

"Theatrical Trades: Boots and Shoes." *Stage* (16 November 1883): 8–9.

"Theatricals in the Open Air: *As You Like It,* at Coombe House, Kingston-on-Thames." *Illustrated London News* (9 August 1884): [132].

Thiselton, T. H. "*Fair Rosamund.*" *Theatre* (1 September 1886): 170–72.

Thomas, E. Lloyd. *Victorian Art Pottery.* London: Guildart, 1974.

Thornton, Peter. *Authentic Decor: The Domestic Interior, 1620–1920.* New York: Viking Press, 1984.

Tian Jiaqing. *Classic Chinese Furniture of the Qing Dynasty.* Translated by Lark E. Mason Jr. and Juliet Yung-Yi Chao. London: Philip Wilson, 1996.

Tilbrook, Adrian J. *Truth, Beauty and Design: Victorian, Edwardian and Later Decorative Art.* Exh. cat. London: Adrian J. Tilbrook and Fischer Fine Art, 1986.

Timms, W. "Economic Art Furniture in the Prevailing Styles." *Cabinet Maker and Art Furnisher* 7 (1 April 1887): 258–60.

"To Correspondents: G. A. W. (Accrington)." Letter to the *Furniture Gazette,* n.s., 9 (23 February 1878): 120.

"To E. W. Godwin, F.S.A." Letter to the *Building News and Engineering Journal* 27 (14 August 1874): 212.

Tokyo Metropolitan Art Museum. *La Modernité: Collection du Musée d'Orsay.* Exh. cat. Tokyo Metropolitan Art Museum. Tokyo and Kobe: Nihon Keizai Shimbun, 1996.

Tomlin, Maurice. *English Furniture: An Illustrated Handbook.* London: Faber and Faber, 1972.

"A Town Church by E. W. Godwin, F.S.A." *Building News and Engineering Journal* 48 (13 March 1885): 408 and illustration [418].

Tree, Herbert Beerbohm. *Thoughts and Afterthoughts.* New York: Funk and Wagnalls, 1913.

"Two Interiors at the House of Miss Ellen Terry at Chelsea." *Femina* (October 1920): 52.

"Under the Greenwood Tree." *Topical Times* (26 July 1884): 4–5.

"A Unique Comparison." *Powerline* (Spring 1994): 12.

"A Unique Style of Dining-Room Decoration." *Furniture Gazette,* n.s., 7 (14 April 1877): 237.

Vallance, Aymer. "The Furnishing and Decoration of the House." Part 4, "Furniture." *Art Journal* (April 1892): 112–18.

———. *William Morris, His Art, His Writings, and His Public Life: A Record.* London: Bell, 1897. Facsimile ed., London: Studio Editions, 1986.

Veblen, Thorstein. *The Theory of the Leisure Class.* New York, Macmillan, 1899. Reprint, New Brunswick, N.J.: Transaction Publishers, 1991.

Vecellio, Cesare. *Degli Habiti antichi et moderni di diverse parti del mondo . . .* London: John Murray, 1855.

Verdier, Aymar, and F. Cattois. *Architecture civile et domestique au moyen âge et á la renaissance.* Paris: Bance, 1855–57.

Victoria and Albert Museum. *Exhibition of Victorian and Edwardian Decorative Arts.* Exh. cat. London: Her Majesty's Stationery Office, 1952.

———. *Victorian and Edwardian Decorative Arts.* Small Picture Book No. 34. London: Her Majesty's Stationery Office, 1952.

———. *English Chairs.* 3d ed. London: Her Majesty's Stationery Office, 1970.

"The Vienna Exhibition." *Builder* 31 (30 August 1873): 678–80.

"Vienna International Exhibition." *Builder* 31 (16 August 1873): 640.

"Villas, Bedford Park Estate, Turnham Green, by E. W. Godwin, F.S.A." Letter to *Building News and Engineering Journal* 31 (29 December 1876): 679.

"The Villas on the Bedford-Park Estate." *Building News and Engineering Journal* 32 (9 March 1877): 253.

Viollet-le-Duc, Eugène-Emmanuel. *Dictionnaire raisonné du mobilier français de l'époque carlovingienne à la Renaissance.* 6 vols. Paris: Gründ et Maguet, 1854–75. Reprinted 1926.

"The Virginia Water Lunatic Asylum Competition." *Architect* (London) 8 (27 July 1872): 48.

Voysey, C. F. A. "Report of Dinner Given by President and Council to Mark the Jubilee Year of His Practice." *Royal Institute of British Architects Journal* 35 (November 1927): 53.

———. "1874 and After." *Architectural Review* 70 (October 1931): 94.

Wainwright, Clive. "The Dark Ages of Art Revived, or Edwards and Roberts and the Regency Revival." *Connoisseur* 198 (June 1978): 95–117.

———. "The Garden Indoors." In *The Garden:*

A Celebration of 1,000 Years of British Gardening, edited by John Harris. Exh. cat. Victoria and Albert Museum. London: Mitchell Beazley in association with New Perspectives, 1979.

———. "Only the True Black Blood." *Furniture History Society* 21 (1985): 250–57.

———. "Rustic Adornments: Plants in Victorian Interiors." *Country Life* 179 (10 April 1986): 936–38.

———. *The Romantic Interior: The British Collector at Home, 1750–1850.* New Haven and London: Yale University Press for the Paul Mellon Centre for Studies in British Art, 1989.

Wake, Jehanne. *Princess Louise: Queen Victoria's Unconventional Daughter.* London: Collins, 1988.

"The Wakefield Town Hall Competition." *Building News and Engineering Journal* 32 (11 May 1877): 463.

Walker, Annabel, and Peter Jackson. *Kensington and Chelsea: A Social and Architectural History.* London: John Murray, 1987.

Walker Art Gallery. *The Walker Art Gallery, Liverpool.* London: Scala Books in association with the National Museums and Galleries of Merseyside, ca. 1994.

Walkley, Giles. *Artists' Houses in London, 1764–1914.* Aldershot, England: Scolar Press, 1994.

Walkling, Gillian. *Antique Bamboo Furniture.* London: Bell and Hyman, 1979.

"Wall Decorations." *Building News and Engineering Journal* 26 (8 May 1874): 492–93 and [504–5].

"Wall-Papers." *Building News and Engineering Journal* 23 (11 October 1872): 291 and [286–87].

"Wall-Papers and Their Manufacture." *Building News and Engineering Journal* 48 (20 February 1885): 277–80.

Wang Shixiang. *Classic Chinese Furniture: Ming and Early Qing Dynasties.* 2d ed. Chicago: Art Media Resources, 1991.

Wang Shixiang and Curtis Evarts. *Masterpieces from the Museum of Classical Chinese Furniture.* Exh. cat. Chicago and San Francisco: Chinese Art Foundation, 1995.

"Warehouse, Bristol. Street Architecture." *Builder* 16 (30 October 1858): 719.

Watanabe, Toshio. *High Victorian Japonisme.* Swiss Asian Studies, Research Studies, vol. 10. Bern: Peter Lang, 1991.

Watson, Anne. *The Godwin Variations: Designs on a Single Theme.* Brochure Series, Powerhouse Museum. Sydney: Powerhouse Museum, 1994.

———. "Not Just a Sideboard: E. W. Godwin's Celebrated Design of 1867." *Studies in the Decorative Arts* 4 (Spring–Summer 1997): 63–84.

Watt, William. *Art Furniture, from Designs by E. W. Godwin, F.S.A., and Others, with Hints and Suggestions on Domestic Furniture and Decoration.* London: B. T. Batsford, 1877. Reprinted 1878. Reprinted with Messenger and Company's *Artistic Conservatories*, by E. W. Godwin. New York: Garland, 1978.

Way, Thomas R. *Memories of James McNeill Whistler, the Artist.* London: J. Lane, 1912.

"We said the other day . . . ." *British Architect and Northern Engineer* 11 (17 January 1879): 24.

Wedmore, Frederick. Review of *The Cenci* by Shelley. *Academy,* no. 732 (15 May 1886): 352.

Weisberg, Gabriel P., and Yvonne M. L. Weisberg. *Japonisme: An Annotated Bibliography.* New York: Garland, 1990.

"What a pity it is . . . ." *British Architect and Northern Engineer* 11 (18 April 1879): 162.

"The White House." *Vogue* (1 August 1915): 40.

Whitworth Art Gallery. *A Decorative Art: 19th Century Wallpapers in the Whitworth Art Gallery.* Exh. cat. Manchester: Whitworth Art Gallery, 1985.

W.H.L. "Vicarious Act." Letter to *Building News and Engineering Journal* 24 (14 February 1873): 201.

W.H.W. [W. H. White]. "The Prince of Wales's Theatre." *Building News and Engineering Journal* 28 (23 April 1875): 471–72.

Wichmann, Siegfried. *Japonisme: The Japanese Influence on Western Art in the 19th and 20th Centuries.* New York: Harmony Books, 1981.

Wilde, Oscar. "*As You Like It* at Coombe House." *Dramatic Review* (6 June 1885): 296–97.

———[Ignotus, pseud.]. "Pastoral Players: *The Faithful Shepherdesse.*" *Dramatic Review* (1 August 1885): 4.

———. "*Helena in Troas.*" *Dramatic Review* (22 May 1886): 161–62.

———. "The Truth of Masks." 1891. Reprinted in *Intentions.* New York: Albert and Charles Boni, 1930. Reprinted in *The Complete Works of Oscar Wilde: Stories, Plays, Poems, Essays,* with an introduction by Vyvyan Holland. London and Glasgow: Collins, 1990. Reprinted in Richard Ellmann, ed., *The Artist as Critic: Critical Writings of Oscar Wilde.* Chicago: University of Chicago Press, 1982, p. 418.

———. *The Letters of Oscar Wilde.* Edited by Rupert Hart-Davis. London: Rupert Hart-Davis, 1962.

Wilde, W. C. K. "*Helena in Troas.*" *Lady* (20 May 1886): 389.

———. "*Helena in Troas.*" *Theatre* (1 June 1886): 331–35.

Wilk, Christopher, ed. *Western Furniture: 1350 to the Present Day in the Victoria and Albert Museum, London.* London: Philip Wilson in association with the Victoria and Albert Museum, 1996.

Wilkinson, Nancy Burch. "Edward William Godwin and Japonisme in England." Ph.D. diss., University of California, Los Angeles, 1987.

Willemin, Nicolas Xavier. *Monuments français inédits pour servir a l'histoire des arts depuis le VIe siècle jusqu'au commencement du XVIIe.* 2 vols. Paris: Chez Mlle. Willemin, 1839. Engraved frontis., dated 1806, in vol. 1, preceding the plates.

Williamson, George C. *Murray Marks and his Friends: A Tribute of Regard by Dr. G. C. Williamson.* London: John Lane, Bodley Head, 1919.

Wills, Freeman. *W. G. Wills, Dramatist and Painter.* London: Longmans, Green, 1898.

Wills, W. G. *Juana: A Tragedy in Four Acts.* London: Ballantyne Press, 1881.

Wilson, H. Schütz. "The Architecture and Costume of Shakespere's [sic] Plays." Letter to the *Architect* (London) 12 (21 November 1874): 278.

Wilson, Michael I. "The Case of the Victorian Piano." *Victoria and Albert Museum Yearbook,* no. 3 (1972): 133–53.

"Winchester Guildhall, &c." *Building News and Engineering Journal* 20 (19 May 1871): 386 and illus.

"The Winchester Guildhall Competition." *Builder* 29 (28 January 1871): 58–59.

Winstone, John, ed. *Bristol As It Was, 1963–1975.* Bristol: Reece Winstone Archive and Publishing, 1990.

Winwar, Frances. *Oscar Wilde and the Yellow Nineties.* Garden City, N.Y.: Blue Ribbon Books, 1941.

"Wm. Watt, Artistic Furniture Warehouse." Advertisements in *British Architect and Northern Engineer* 9 (25 January 1878): 11; 10 (19 July 1878): xii; 11 (3 January 1879): xiv.

Wohl, Anthony S. *Endangered Lives: Public Health in Victorian Britain.* Cambridge: Harvard University Press, 1983.

Woodville, R. Caton. *Random Recollections.* London: Eveleigh Nash, 1914.

Woodward, William. "Villas, Bedford Park Estate, Turnham Green, by E. W. Godwin, F.S.A." Letter to *Building News and Engineering Journal* 32 (5 January 1877): 26–27.

Woolfe, Vivienne. "Smallhythe Place, Kent: A Property of the National Trust." *Country Life* 184 (30 August 1990): 78–81.

"Working Drawings of Inexpensive Furniture by E. W. Godwin, F.S.A." *Building News and Engineering Journal* 49 (18 December 1885): 1011 and [1008–9].

Worthy, Charles. *Devonshire Parishes, or the Antiquities, Heraldry and Family History of Twenty-Eight Parishes in the Archdeaconry of Totnes.* Vol 2. London: George Redway, 1889.

Wright, Lance. "An Account of the Bristol Society of Architects, 1850–1950." *Journal of Bristol Society of Architects* 1, no. 8 (1950): 6–18.

Ydema, Onno. *Carpets and Their Datings in Netherlandish Paintings, 1540–1700.* Woodbridge, England: Antique Collectors' Club, 1991.

Yorke, James. *English Furniture.* New York: Gallery Books, 1990.

Young, Andrew McLaren, Margaret MacDonald, and Robin Spencer. *The Paintings of James McNeill Whistler.* 2 vols. New Haven and London: Yale University Press for the Paul Mellon Centre for Studies in British Art, 1980.

Zygulski, Zdzislaw Jr. "Shakespeare's Chair and the Romantic Journey of Isabel Czartoryska." *Apollo,* n.s, 82 (November 1965): 392–97.

•INDEX•

Illustrations in chapters 1 through 13 are indexed by page and figure numbers (i.e. "275 fig.9-22"); objects in the exhibition are indexed by catalogue number (i.e. cat.19) and can be found in the checklist beginning on page 375. Footnotes are indexed by page and note numbers (i.e. 261n173). Life dates are given for many of the people mentioned in the text. Entries in the chronology are not indexed.

PHOTOGRAPH CREDITS

The photographs in this book were taken or provided by the individual institutions or collectors credited in the captions, with the following exceptions. Photographs of objects in the collections of The Victoria and Albert Museum, London, the major lender to the exhibition, were provided by The Victoria and Albert Picture Library.

David Allison: figs. 1-2, 1-3, 2-6, 2-8, 6-1, 6-3, 6-5 to 6-7, 6-9, 6-13, 6-14, 6-17, 6-25, 6-39, 6-42, 6-45 to 6-47, 8-3 to 8-5, 8-7, 8-12, 8-13, 8-22, 8-27, 8-36, 8-39, 8-41, 8-46, 11-6, 11-12, 13-2; Chronology, figs. C3 to C5, C7.

David Allison / Bristol Museums and Art Gallery, Bristol: fig. 8-19.

David Allison / The Fine Arts Society, Plc. London: fig. 3-9.

David Allison / Gary Kemp: figs. 8-27, 8-32.

David Allison / Paul Reeves: figs. 8-43, 11-18, 11-19.

Catherine Arbuthnott: figs. 2-16, 8-20.

Art Resource, New York: fig. 1-17.

Dirk Bakker, The Detroit Institute of Arts: fig. 8-33.

By permission of The British Library: figs. 2-11, 2-17, 3-19, 3-22, 4-10, 5-2, 6-26, 6-33, 6-41, 6-48, 6-50, 6-66, 7-28, 7-33, 8-35, 8-42, 12-14, 12-15, 12-22, 12-25, 12-31, 12-32, 12-36, 12-43, 12-45, 12-47, 12-49; Chronology, fig. C6.

Christie's, London: figs. 8-14, 8-16.

Avery Architectural and Fine Arts Library, Columbia University in the City of New York: figs. i, 2-7, 4-11, 5-1, 5-3, 5-4, 6-28, 6-43, 9-21, 11-4, 11-20; Chronology, figs. C2, C9, C10, C13, C15.

Country Life Picture Library: figs. 6-65, 7-36, 7-37.

Crown Publishing, from Isoda Koryu-sai, *A Treasury of Japanese Wood Block Prints* (New York: Crown Publishing, 1969): fig. 7-8.

Margaret and Richard Davies Associates: figs. 7-29, 7-30.

The Detroit Institute of Arts: fig. 4-1.

F. W. Dodge Corporation: figs. 3-25, 3-27.

The Fine Art Society, Plc., London: fig. 6-61.

Haslam and Whiteway Ltd., London: Fig. 9-4.

Hulton Getty Archive, London / Liaison Agency, New York: figs. 6-57, 6-58, 7-44.

Jolyon Hudson: fig. 4-6.

Juliet Kinchin: figs. 4-7, 4-8.

Latimer House, London: fig. 4-2.

Thomas J. Watson Library, The Metropolitan Museum of Art, New York: figs. 3-4, 3-20, 8-9, 10-2, 10-8.

Courtesy of Barbara Morris: fig. 3-3.

Art and Architecture Collection, Miriam and Ira D. Wallach Division of Art, Prints and Photographs, The New York Public Library, Astor, Lenox and Tilden Foundations: figs. 7-3, 8-40, 9-11.

Northamptonshire Libraries and Information Service: fig. 6-15.

George Rouse: figs. iii Crown Copyright. MNR, 4-12.

Victorian Society—LIN12239 Linley Sambourne House, London: The drawing room (photo) (see also 84993) Victorian Society, Linley Sambourne House, London, UK/Bridgeman Art Library, London / New York: fig. 7-4.

Danika Volkert, from Tian Jiaqing, *Classic Chinese Furniture of the Qing Dynasty* (London: Philip Wilson / Hong Kong: Joint Publishing, 1996): fig. 3-8.

Cyril Winskell: figs. 7-23 to 7-25.